D1617426

The Bride of Christ Goes to Hell

THE MIDDLE AGES SERIES

Ruth Mazo Karras, Series Editor
Edward Peters, Founding Editor

A complete list of books in the series
is available from the publisher.

The Bride of Christ Goes to Hell

Metaphor and Embodiment
in the Lives of Pious Women,
200–1500

Dyan Elliott

PENN

UNIVERSITY OF PENNSYLVANIA PRESS

PHILADELPHIA

Published by
University of Pennsylvania Press
Philadelphia, Pennsylvania 19104-4112
www.upenn.edu/pennpress

Printed in the United States of America on acid-free paper

10 9 8 7 6 5 4 3 2 1

Library of Congress Cataloging-in-Publication Data
Elliott, Dyan, 1954–
    The bride of Christ goes to hell : metaphor and embodiment in the lives of pious women, 200–1500 / Dyan Elliott. — 1st ed.
        p. cm. — (The Middle Ages series)
    Includes bibliographical references and index.
    ISBN 978-0-8122-4358-1 (hardcover : alk. paper)
    1. Virginity—Religious aspects—Christianity—History of doctrines—Early church, ca. 30–600. 2. Virginity—Religious aspects—Christianity—History of doctrines—Middle Ages, 600–1500. 3. Marriage—Religious aspects—Christianity—History of doctrines—Early church, ca. 30–600. 4. Marriage—Religious aspects—Christianity—History of doctrines—Middle Ages, 600–1500. 5. Women in Christianity—History—Early church, ca. 30–600 6. Women in Christianity—History—Middle Ages, 600–1500. I. Title. II. Series: Middle Ages series
BV4647.C5E45 2012
241'.660820940902—dc23
                                    2011023302

For my dear friend, Susan Gubar
An inspiration

Late medieval thought . . . frequently moves living thought from the abstract in the direction of the pictorial as if the whole of intellectual life sought concrete expression, as if the notion of gold was immediately minted into coin. There is an unlimited desire to bestow form on everything that is sacred, to give any religious idea a material shape so that it exists like a crisply printed picture. This tendency towards pictorial expression is constantly in jeopardy of becoming petrified. . . . [I]n this supernaturalized atmosphere, the religious tension of true transcendence, the stepping away from the material, cannot always occur.

—Johan Huizinga, *The Autumn of the Middle Ages*

CONTENTS

Introduction

Virginity is a spiritual kind of marrying.

—Optatus[1]

A young woman eschews all mortal ties to unite herself irrevocably with a man who has been dead for centuries, yet has nevertheless managed to lure countless women into this suspect arrangement: a polygamist on a grand scale. Although it may sound like a plot worthy of Bram Stoker, I am, of course, alluding to the traditional understanding of the consecrated virgin as bride of Christ—a concept so intrinsic to female spirituality and so familiar to medievalists that it is difficult to imagine when it was otherwise. But there was a time when the bride was just a metaphor unattached to any particular body—before she tumbled from the symbolic order, became entangled in text, and then finally came to land with a thump upon the body of the virgin who has dedicated her life to God. It is this story of embodiment that is at the heart of the present study.

It is important to remember, however, that although the consecrated virgin is preeminent as the human face of the bride, the image was and would remain a veritable calliope of overlapping metaphors. At its root was the mystical marriage between God and the human soul that, from the perspective of ancient and medieval commentators, found its most eloquent and provocative expression in the Song of Songs. Like the enterprising bride of the Canticles, all true believers should pursue the celestial bridegroom in anticipation of an ecstatic consummation in the afterlife. The mystical marriage was also possessed of an incorporated dimension as evident in Christ's marriage with the church of all believers. In addition, it had important institutional applications. By the eleventh century the bishop, standing in loco Christi, was customarily understood to be married to his see. During the papal schism, John Gerson (d. 1429) would raise the fraught question of what to do if the pope, the church's most immediate proxy for the celestial bridegroom, was bewitched and incapable of providing children for the virginal Ecclesia.[2]

A mystical marriage with Christ simultaneously invested mundane reality with and divested it of meaning. It enhanced carnal marriage through the association with a higher mystery. Yet the representation of the mystical marriage as the purer and more authentic union simultaneously drained its carnal host of vitality. This book is in many ways a testimony to the mystical marriage's predatory symbolism. It was supposed to be a study about medieval matrimony, in theory and practice. A portion was dedicated to the way in which marriage served as a template, structuring many nonmatrimonial relations, and it is was there that I ran into trouble. As soon as I turned my attention to the *sponsa Christi*, to my mind the most vivid example of the matrimonial template at work, the subject developed a momentum all its own, ultimately derailing the entire project. So the tendency to bypass real marriage in favor of its imaginary counterpart is not just a medieval predilection; there are certain modern scholars inclined to follow suit.

The mystical marriage's preemptive claims vividly testify to Christianity's tendency to privilege the spiritual over the carnal. In this world upside down, the despised and derivative institution of marriage is recast as the equivalent of an embodied exemplum or carnal symbol for the higher union. Moreover, mystical marriage was a restless image that seemingly refused to be restricted to the Christian equivalent of the platonic realm of ideas, instead constantly seeking embodiment. The fact that the bride of Christ had a claim on both the abstract and the concrete meant that it could at any moment erupt into people's lives, with tangible consequences. A quodlibet by Peter John Olivi (d. 1298) demonstrates this potential. Olivi asks why someone who had been married to a widow could not be ordained a priest when a widower who had lost his virginity before his marriage could be ordained, provided he had married a virgin. The answer is that marriage is a triple sacrament: the first component, which is the marriage between God and the soul, is designated by the union of souls between flesh-and-blood husband and wife, which occurs when spouses exchange vows in the present; the second is union with human nature, when the word became flesh in the womb of a virgin, and is signified by the sex act that would consummate the union; the third is the union of Christ and the virginal church. For this application to work, it is inconsequential if the man is a virgin; Christ, after all, had been married to Synagoga before he married Ecclesia. In fact, Christ can be joined to concubines "without any corruption of his deity, or his humanity and love." Besides, the priest represents the church militant, which contains both good and evil, so he need not be pure. But if a priest were at one time married, his wife had to be a virgin, otherwise his union could not signify Christ's union with the church triumphant, upon which there can be no spot.[3] These different levels of meaning demonstrate just how encompassing this metaphor could be. But they also point to a basic implacability at the heart of the image. Only a man was fit to stand in loco Christi, and hence only men could be cast as groom in the different orthodox variants of the mystical marriage. While all Christian souls, women and men, were brides of Christ in a mystical sense, consecrated virgins were brides par excellence.[4] And because the bride herself was ever-virgin, and virginity was a fragile asset, throughout the Middle Ages the consecrated virgin would most often pursue her vocation in a cloister.

It would nevertheless be misleading to imply that female religious alone were actively encouraged to identify with the image of the *sponsa Christi*. The ongoing proliferation of monastic commentaries on the Song of Songs attest to a profound degree of attraction to this imagery among male religious as well.[5] In the high Middle Ages, Bernard of Clairvaux (d. 1153) attempted to invoke a still more affective response among his monastic brethren.[6] Yet, as Sarah McNamer has recently argued, the bride was but a "provisional persona" for the monk; in contrast, "female religious—precisely because they were female—could participate in another signifying system, this one historical and cultural."[7] Nor would virginity remain an absolute for the bride. One of the great sea changes in medieval spirituality, and one especially portentous for this study, was when women who were not virgins began to lay claim to this title. Despite these competing claims, however, the female virgin would always take pride of place as Christ's bride. She remained for the Christian community something of a living allegory, inhabiting two realms simultaneously, and was socially construed as such. The bride in Olivi's quodlibet, on the verge of carnal marriage, inhabited this symbolic zone very briefly; for the consecrated virgin, however, it was home.

In spite of this undeniably lofty place in the symbolic order, Christianity's deployment of the bride is at one with other religious systems, where the dominant images associated with women originate in their reproductive/sexual status.[8] From this perspective, it is not surprising to learn that the identification of virgins as brides of Christ probably began as a kind of compromise formation. It was first used by Tertullian (d. ca. 220) in an effort to impose some kind of discipline on the independent virgins of Carthage, who perceived themselves as living the genderless angelic life. Tertullian's response was to insist that these virgins were not only women but matrons of a sort, who must wear veils as a sign of their submission to their celestial bridegroom, Christ. Despite constant reiterations that virginity was primarily a state of mind among church authorities, Tertullian's embodied literalism was the wave of the future. As the female religious vocation developed, Christ's bride became ever more embodied, physical integrity jockeying with mental integrity for the prize.

If we were to stop here, the tale of the *sponsa Christi* might seem to resemble the tragedy at the heart of the gnostic understanding of the fall. For as with the spirits who were wrestled down from heaven and stuffed into bodies, women's gradual assumption of the bridal identity could also be construed as an ungentle story of angelic creatures subjected to enforced embodiment. But this perception necessarily changes in the mystical climate of the high and later Middle Ages, when women clearly embraced the bridal persona, making it very much their own. In particular, the increasing number of nonvirgins who appropriated the title of bride frequently sustained these claims through an extremely embodied spirituality, introducing a more exacting, albeit different, kind of literalism than was ever imagined by the church fathers. Many of these women experienced visions of the celestial bridegroom; some even claimed he appeared in corporeal form. Eventually women such as Bridget of Sweden (d. 1373) and Dorothea of Montau (d. 1394), mothers many times over, were represented by their hagiographers as extremely exacting in their representation of marriage with Christ, including mystical pregnancies that were replete with fetal movement, labor pains, and dilations.[9]

In short, although women may initially have had the bridal persona thrust upon them, it would seem that they ultimately came to relish this point of identification, adding many surprising and unprecedented embellishments, often inspired by very literal readings (whether theirs or their confessors') of the Song of Songs. Even so, the latter part of this book is about the dangers implicit in this level of literalism: how a land where dreams (or visions) literally come true is also an environment that can foster nightmares. In the later Middle Ages, there was a growing suspicion of female mysticism, especially because of flamboyantly embodied marvels. Stories began to circulate in clerical circles of instances in which a female mystic mistook Lucifer, the angel of light, for Christ—misbegotten unions that were essentially mystical marriages gone wrong. The somatic spirituality of female mystics, in conjunction with their aspirations to a kind of supernatural union, played an important role in the rise of witchcraft charges and the solidification of the witch's identity around a female persona.

Chapter 1 begins with an overview of some of the deployments of the bride of Christ in the early church, focusing mainly on Tertullian and his use of the metaphor as an instrument of control over consecrated virgins. The situation, as I see it, is extremely poignant because Tertullian, who was wont to extol virginity and disparage marriage, was reluctant to use this strategy: he was led to it by a literal reading of Genesis 6 and a fear of angelic miscegenation.

The second chapter examines the evolution of the consecrated virgin at the hands of the church fathers: her association with a very reclusive Virgin Mary (conflated with the bride of the Song of Songs), the different disciplines devised for the virgin, and the increasing focus on intact virginity. Patristic adulation of the sealed body not only justified legal restrictions on the woman's freedoms as protection of Christ's bride but, at least for some, validated suicide in the event that her virginity was imperiled.

Chapter 3 focuses on the successor states established in the wake of the Roman Empire's collapse and the conundrum of what to do with a would-be bride of Christ who is not a virgin. The English Aldhelm's initiatives to decenter female virginity include representing virginity primarily as a male virtue, in addition to extending its boundaries with instances of married chastity. By the same token, clerical authorities in the Frankish Empire struggle with polite ways of withholding the title *sponsa Christi* from Queen Radegund, who, although a member of a religious community and an important monastic foundress, was not a virgin. The chapter concludes with the examination of the life of the matron Rictrude and the hagiographer's projection of a rivalry between virginal and nonvirginal nuns.

Both Chapters 4 and 5 contend with the immense changes afoot in the twelfth century in both secular marriage and religion. The fourth chapter points to the new emphasis on intentionality and consensuality and the ways in which they bring carnal and mystical marriage closer together. The proximate nature of the two types of marriage is epitomized in the relationship of Abelard and Heloise—particularly Abelard's desperate attempts to loosen Heloise's determined grip on their failed carnal marriage and reattach her to the celestial groom. Chapter 5 examines the emergence of pious heterosexual couples: men and women whose spiritual and emotional bonds simulate the intimacy of an actual marriage. This phenomenon, which I refer to heteroasceticism, is construed as a form of repressed conjugality. The chapter concludes with a discussion of Bernard of Clairvaux's sermons on the Song of Songs.

"The Eroticized Bride in Hagiography" (Chapter 6) examines how the impact of Bernardine spirituality among the early Beguine mystics provides the impetus for a sensual, embodied, and ultimately eroticized bride of Christ. The tendency to express this spirituality somatically perhaps culminates in the matrimonial embellishments of later pious widows such as Bridget of Sweden and Dorothea of Montau who (as will be seen in Chapter 7) would soon attract the critical eye of prominent clerics such as John Gerson. Yet one of the contentions of this chapter is that the widespread hostility that religious authorities expressed against the Beguine movement from its inception was not only present but cultivated by one of their earliest supporters—Thomas of Cantimpré. It is but an ominous sign of things to come.

The final chapter begins by looking at the predatory incubus, and its progressive tendency to target religious women, before turning to two extremely influential figures in late medieval spirituality, John Gerson and John Nider. Their mutual suspicion of female spirituality spills over into their imagery, with each providing inverted versions of the mystical marriage with Christ. The rise of witchcraft charges accentuates this distorted picture, substituting union with the devil for the mystical union with Christ. Thus we have a grim return of Tertullian's anxiety of miscegenation between fallen angels and human women.

Although this book ends with a discussion of the phenomenon of witchcraft, it is not primarily a book about witchcraft. It does, however, aspire to make sense of witchcraft in the context of female spirituality. Since at least the time of H. C. Lea, scholars have posited some kind of a link between female mysticism and the rise of witchcraft. Most only gesture toward this potentiality fleetingly, and the few works that do engage this question tend to be more descriptive than analytical.[10] This study attempts to discern at least one link in the chain that unites the mystic to the witch: by analyzing the trajectory of the bride of Christ, perhaps the most important vehicle of female spirituality in the entire Christian tradition, I hope to demonstrate how this image ultimately contributed to the concept of the witch.

This is not the first time I have attempted to come to grips with the emergence of witchcraft as an antiwoman phenomenon, and it probably won't be the last. Elsewhere I have identified other factors feeding into the rise of a specific brand of religious antifeminism that found its most extreme expression in works like the inquisitorial manual, *The Hammer of Witches*. My book *Fallen Bodies* in particular alerted me to the manner in which antifeminist rhetoric was destined to become reified centuries later. *Proving Woman* would identify subsequently the inquisitional procedure as a contributing factor in the gradual demonization of female spirituality. The present study is meant to complement and extend these earlier endeavors, approaching some of the same questions as well as key authors from a different angle.

The scope of this topic was sufficiently daunting that I was forced to impose my own version of "virgin sacrifices" throughout. For instance, one could have dedicated an entire study to the way the image of the bride was applied to the Virgin Mary—who was not just Christ's mother but also his supreme bride. And yet there is no extended discussion of Mary as bride. Instead, she is invoked largely in the capacity as role model and advisor to Christ's lesser brides. Then there is the geographical bias. Although this study necessarily begins in the Mediterranean world of the church fathers, the regional vector moves northward and by and large remains there. For the earlier period, I can only say that this is where I thought the materials seemed most prolix and most intriguing. But this orientation also made more sense in the high Middle Ages, where the earliest flourishing of bridal mysticism was a northern phenomenon, arising within the Beguine movement.

The consecrated virgins, mystical matrons, and alleged witches that animate this book come to us through the pages of a religious discourse that is often heavily mediated by authorial efforts to enlist certain images and conform with traditional models. Though this may be true of the majority of the writings remaining from the Middle Ages, it is especially important in this context. For although I am concerned with the experiences and attitudes toward historical women, the bride of Christ remains first and foremost a metaphor that is imposed upon the lives of these women. So on a number of levels, this is a book about language. It examines the process by which something as ephemeral as a metaphor evolves, but ultimately devolves, into matter. Huizinga had famously associated this trend with the later Middle Ages, when, admittedly, such a pattern may have reached a crescendo. But it is important to remember that the process of devolution was present throughout the history of Christianity and was not simply a matter of late medieval decadence. Indeed, in a religion that holds the incarnation as its central mystery, the implicit pull in favor of embodiment was not only integral but often irresistible. Nor should it be a surprise that Christianity's nascent beliefs and devotions likewise teleologically tend toward physical realization. This is as apparent in the theological doctrines of the resurrection of the body or transubstantiation as it is in the more devotional points of emphases such as Mary as Ever Virgin, the cult of relics, or the somatic nature of female mysticism. By focusing on the bride of Christ, this book attempts to engage some of the challenges that invariably faced an incarnational religion that aimed at transcendence but frequently had to settle for so much less.

CHAPTER I

A Match Made in Heaven

The Bride in the Early Church

The association between women and consecrated virginity is an ancient one. Moreover, the evidence suggests that women were already drawn to the condition of lifelong virginity, perhaps in part for some of the practical advantages it conferred, without the kind of patriarchal prodding we will witness in the fourth century. But there is little in scripture to foster the exaltation of the virginal state. Paul, who is usually singled out as the original advocate for celibacy, presents the unmarried as better positioned for serving God (1 Cor. 7.32). His reasons are practical: the time was short and people should be preparing for the heavenly kingdom, not raising families. From this perspective, Paul's counsel on chastity, his tendency to associate marriage with cares for the wife and "tribulation of the flesh" (1 Cor. 7.28), should be considered a branch of what is commonly referred to as the *molestiae nuptiarum*—a discourse disparaging marriage and women alike. This was standard fare in the philosophical tradition and hence intended for a male audience.[1] By the same token, Paul's comments commending chastity were addressed to the male heads of households. But the men in his audience were not only concerned with their own spiritual integrity: they also held the matrimonial destinies of female dependents in their hands, and some of Paul's provirginal remarks addressed men in the capacity of guardians of female virgins. In 1 Corinthians 7 it is unclear whether he is addressing a father who has not yet arranged a marriage for his daughter or a newly made husband who has yet to celebrate his nuptials—the occasion for the consummation of a marriage. In either case, he commends the man for preserving the woman's virginity (1 Cor. 7.36–38). The chill promise of the later pastoral epistles that women "shall be saved through childbearing" (1Tim. 2.15), however, does suggest that there were at least some parties who either consciously or unconsciously excluded women from the privileges of chastity altogether.[2]

In the mid-first century when Justin Martyr was called upon to defend Christianity against pagan accusations of immorality, he pointed to the many Christians who had voluntarily embraced chastity to counter these charges. But he did this without intonating any particular bias favoring one sex.[3] And yet by the time of the apocryphal *Acts of Paul and Thecla*, which was already in circulation by the end of the second century, a presumed female proclivity for the virgin state is apparent. Paul is portrayed as the consummate apostle for chastity, and his target audience is represented as almost exclusively female. Paul's dramatic entry into the city of Iconium is staged around his delivery of a set of beatitudes on the peculiar blessedness of virginity.[4] Watching from her window, the virgin Thecla is portrayed as being mesmerized, imprisoned by a vagabond—at least according to her hostile mother's report to Thecla's fiancé.[5] By the end of the century, the North African virgins with whom Tertullian contends are female.

There are no female-authored writings to tell us what these women sought in a life of virginity, only the testimony of the church fathers. Fortunately, these men were not coy about the presumed motives of their female audience: in their view, the female vocation to virginity was inseparable from a pronounced aversion to marriage, and patristic authors made the most of this projection. Thus patristic treatises on virginity set a precedent in patterning a version of the *molestiae nuptiarum* that was specifically tailored to women, dwelling on the wife's mandatory subjection to her husband and the very real dangers of childbirth.[6] These strategies are represented as so effective that many women suddenly seemed to see the matrimonial goblet as half empty and did, in fact, seek to avoid what had hitherto been the manifest destiny of every freeborn woman in the ancient world. These women, like Thecla, were of marriageable age and probably anticipated a battle similar to the one Thecla was forced to wage against her relatives and their matrimonial ambitions.

But as irresistible as virginity's allure may have been, we only have contemporary patristic speculation about decisions that were individualistic and deeply personal. The very fact that so much of the earliest literature on virginity is rooted in contestation over gender roles suggests that women in particular expected more from the virginal lifestyle than simple freedom from the chains of marriage: there is every reason to believe that they sought to transform the unequal relationship that supported the institution. As Wayne Meeks has argued, Paul was probably responding to this expectation when he insisted that women wear the veil, which emerges as much more than just a symbol of female subjection, but as a marker of gender differentiation.[7] As we shall see, Tertullian's tumultuous relations with the virginal communities in Carthage, who attempted to refuse the veil, suggest as much.

Supposing these women were, in fact, attempting to blur or even destroy gender divisions. How did they imagine their transformed selves? Patristic testimony describes the anticipated change in two basic ways. First, there is the familiar trope of "becoming male": the women who renounced their sexuality are described as being spiritually transformed into men, a clear promotion in a patriarchal world.[8] This metamorphosis is especially widespread in the different sects that are clumped together under the rubric of Gnosticism, whose members were alleged to hold views that their critics describe as immensely attractive to women.[9] These groups, all of which subscribed to varying degrees of dualism, understood humanity's fall from grace in terms of the devolution of spiritual beings, angels according to some accounts, into material bodies. The division into the sexes was regarded as a postlapsarian phenomenon, and the female sex in particular was the most prominent symbol of this division. The Gnostic Gospel of Thomas both articulates the problem and shows the way to the solution: "Simon Peter said to them, 'Let Mary [Magdalene] leave us, for women are not worthy of Life.' Jesus said, 'I myself shall lead her in order to make her male, so that she too may become a living spirit resembling you males. For every woman who will make herself male will enter the kingdom of Heaven.' "[10] Similar claims were occasionally advanced by Eastern theologians. Origen, Methodius, and Gregory of Nyssa (at least in his early writings) all interpreted the prelapsarian Adam as a spiritual androgyne and associated the division into two sexes with the introduction of sin.[11]

Eventually, the orthodox church distanced itself from these dualist-inflected readings, yet the image of "becoming male" persisted in an attenuated form as the "virile woman"—the kind of women that Jerome boasts of in his circle, whose ardent asceticism allowed them to reconstitute themselves as honorary men.[12] But such spiritual transformations also find expression on a less abstract level. The few female ascetics that make an appearance in the lives of the desert fathers are often depicted as either dressing in such a manner or undergoing a physical transformation, whether through asceticism or illness, that their bodies are barely recognizable as female.[13] This is echoed in the hagiographical tradition in the titillating instances of the female transvestite saints who actually manage to pass as men in monasteries, at least until their bodies are prepared for death by the other monks.[14] The extent to which women internalized this image is unclear. *The Passion of Perpetua*, which is one of the few surviving testimonies of a Christian woman from this period, may be instructive in this regard. Perpetua was a Roman matron of patrician lineage. Her conversion to Christianity entailed much more than the simple renunciation of sexual relations: she chose martyrdom over married life, even though she was still nursing an infant child. In the course of her imprisonment, she dreamed that she was transformed into a male gladiator in order to do battle with the devil, who was dressed as a fierce Egyptian.[15]

A second way of formulating the transformation of gender associated with a life of chastity was in terms of the angelic life, or the *vita angelica*. The inspiration for this concept came from Christ himself in his description of the afterlife: "The children of this world marry, and are given in marriage: But they which shall be accounted worthy to obtain that world, and the resurrection from the dead, neither marry, nor are given in marriage: Neither can they die any more: for they are equal unto the angels; and are the children of God, being the children of the resurrection" (Luke 20.34–36). In this future state when "marriage and giving in marriage" would cease altogether, certain adherents seemed to believe that gender itself would be abolished. Yet there was a still more optimistic belief that a life of virginity ushered in a "realized eschatology" here on earth, in which the power of gravity exerted by gender roles was finally suspended and humans lived in angelic androgyny.[16]

Paul's dramatic series of negations in Galatians—simultaneously setting the distinctions associated with race, class, and sex at naught—speaks to the appeal of a church in which there was "no male or female, but all one in Christ" (Gal. 3.28). The fact that Paul is now believed to have been citing an ancient baptismal formula, moreover, makes the anticipated abolition of the sexes still more salient.[17] Even so, androgyny proved to be a challenging and austere concept that could all too easily dissolve into maleness. Biblical references tended to support this devolution: the angels that appeared to humans invariably assumed male form. The prejudice favoring the masculine angel is further corroborated by Christ's ephemeral description of the chaste as "eunuchs for God" (Matt. 19.10–12). In our own era, where eunuchs are relatively thin on the ground, these words may seem something of an abstraction perhaps capable of fostering concepts of androgyny. But the classical world was no stranger to eunuchs. It is quite possible that these sexually nonfunctional beings may have shared physical characteristics that came to be associated with angels: distinct voices, a preternatural elongation of the body that will eventually become a norm in early Christian and Romanesque art, and a reputation as ideal servants. Still there was no getting around the fact that eunuchs "whether born so or made so by men" were still male.[18] By the same token, the virgins following the lamb in the Revelation of St. John, who "have not defiled their clothes with women," are also presumably male (Rev. 3.4, 14.4). The implicit eschatological tendency to regard the female sex as something of an aberration was corroborated by classical medical theory, further tipping the scales of angelic androgyny in favor of men.[19] Hence a Gnostic text cited by Clement of Alexandria describes the consummation of the world as when "the females, becoming male, [are] united with angels. . . . Thus the woman is said to be changed into a man, and the church on earth into angels."[20]

We can only speculate as to how the women in question chose to understand the transformation that virginity seemed to promise. Did they see themselves as equaling men? Surpassing men? As male angels? Androgynous angels? Or just angels, who by their very nature were as aloof from concerns of sex and gender as were the stars in the firmament. Whatever may be the correct answer to these questions, one thing remains clear: the allure of virginity was much more complex than a simple rejection of marriage.

If the assimilation of the bride of Christ with the consecrated virgin was antithetical to the life sought by the women themselves, the personification and ultimate embodiment of the bride was also out of alignment with the original image. God's union with Israel had traditionally been described in terms of a marriage.[21] Christ employs the image as well, lending an eschatological twist to his parable about the ten virgins and their state of preparedness when the bridegroom appears for the last judgment (Matt. 10.25). Paul's later invocation of the metaphor is bifurcated, representing both Christ's mystical union with the soul and Christ's more corporate union with the church—different aspects that will each become important in the development of church hierarchy. For instance with the soul's marriage, Paul appropriates the role of nervous father of the bride: "For I am jealous over you with godly jealousy: for I have espoused you to one husband, that I may present you as a chaste virgin to Christ" (2 Cor. 11.2). Paul's fatherly solicitude in many ways anticipates the rise of a paternalistic clergy from amid a brood of erstwhile egalitarian siblings in Christ.[22] And yet certain hierarchies remain suspended in Paul. In the spirit of Galatians 5.28, the marriage between God and the soul was gender blind: Christ's brides could be either male or female.[23] But this androgynous potential is not sustained in the macrocosmic manifestation of this image in Christ's marriage with the church. Paul, and later his disciples, aligned Christ's rule of the church with the husband's rule of the wife, thereby superimposing this image on the temporal institution of marriage (Eph. 5.23).[24] This application to domestic life could not but fail to strengthen traditional gender roles. Eventually the emergence of the corporate metaphor, which marries the bishop, standing *in loco Christi*, to his see, will be used to confirm clerical authority.[25]

Paul's understanding of the mystical marriage bends gender one way and one way only: there are male brides, but no female grooms. This is the reading that would ultimately prevail in emerging orthodox circles, but it was by no means the only one. For the Gnostic Christians, everyone began as a bride, which designated the carnal nature and literal mindedness of the psychic masses, but everyone had an equal shot at becoming a groom, that is joining the pneumatic elite. This egalitarian view was supported by an allegorical reading of the same texts that orthodoxy used to the opposite purpose. Where Paul saw the opportunity to subordinate wives, the Gnostics preferred to encourage the due submission of fledgling psychics to their pneumatic superiors, to whom they were urged to join themselves as carnal wives would to their husbands. For his part, the pneumatic groom would purify his psychic wife in preparation for the ultimate ritual of the bridal chamber, in which all differences in gender and status would be obliterated and humanity united with the divine. In Gnostic exegesis, scriptural references to marriage and sexual union do not correspond with their carnal counterpart, which anyone even remotely interested in being saved would have abandoned long ago. The human institution was but a bad copy of the celestial reality. So while the bride's spiritual profile may be extremely bleak in the Gnostic cosmos, as was anything female, in practical terms the same interpretative trajectory placed the woman, who bore all the inferiority of her physicality, on an equal footing with the man. It was, after all, the manifest destiny of any woman aspiring to the pneumatic elite to become a groom.[26]

Tertullian: Father of the Bride

So among the Gnostics, no one wanted to be a bride, unless en route to becoming a groom. The situation was probably not much different in orthodox circles. Apart from the classic soul marriage that was the spiritual heritage of every believer, it would indeed be surprising if female virgins felt any special affinity for bridal imagery, not only because it gestured toward the institution they spurned but also because of the way Paul had used this figure to subject carnal wives.[27] It was the fiery Carthaginian theologian Tertullian (b. ca. 160, d. after 220), the first great theological voice in the West, who initially invested the consecrated virgin with the persona of the bride of Christ.[28]

There are many aspects of Tertullian's antifeminist rhetoric that might render him a likely suspect for a spiritual swindle of this magnitude. On the surface he seems unabashed in his attempts to place women under patriarchal control—an impulse abundantly supported by his prolific outpourings on female dress. The preoccupation with dress adheres to the Pauline tradition, which had already drawn a parallel between female modesty in dress and submission to masculine authority, citing Eve's seduction as a rationale (1 Tim. 9–14). Tertullian's treatise *On the Apparel of Women* cranks this association up a notch with its famous condemnation of women as the "devil's gateway" by virtue of their association with Eve.[29] His later treatise *The Veiling of Virgins*, moreover, is an extended indictment of virgins who resist the veil, apparel that we have seen does double service as a symbol of both gender and submission.[30] Nor is Tertullian's concern with female subjection limited to these treatises. He countered the women who looked to Thecla as a precedent for the right to baptize and preach by dismissing *The Acts of Paul and Thecla* as the work of a North African presbyter who wished to enhance Paul's reputation.[31] He also used female prominence, especially in Gnostic circles, as a measure of heretical debasement.[32]

Yet despite such celebrated rhetorical sallies, Tertullian's initiative in wedding the virgin to her metaphoric destiny is distinctly at odds with his pronounced views on marriage and virginity. His opinion of marriage was frequently despairing, while his most cherished hopes for humanity were peculiarly linked with the adulation of consecrated virginity.[33] The extent of Tertullian's matrimonial pessimism might logically coincide with a reluctance to associate the consecrated virgin with the marital state, even metaphorically. It would also be irresponsible to permit Tertullian's potentially misogynist words to trump the way he lived his life: even the most provocative rhetoric aimed at uppity women does not eclipse his attraction to the Montanist movement, or as they called themselves, the New Prophecy. As the latter name implies, this sect believed in the continued access to divine revelation through prophecy, a gift peculiarly associated with virginity, and one through which women assumed leadership roles as select vessels of the Spirit. The virgin prophetesses Priscilla and Maximilla were clear leaders of the movement and, as recent scholarship suggests, on a par with Montanus.[34]

So the conferral of the title *sponsa Christi* seems to be a drastic and uncharacteristic move for Tertullian. The fact that he took this step, however, suggests that there was, to his mind, much more at stake than questions of female discipline or even than the preservation of gender hierarchy. The virgin as *sponsa Christi* was the logical terminus to his long, deliberative process over humanity's singular position in the created order and in which the efficacy and longevity of marriage, virginity, and the human body were of crucial importance.

Tertullian lived under a heightened awareness that the divinely ordained boundaries between humankind and the rest of creation had been breached in antediluvian times by the so-called Watcher Angels—those sons of God who intermarried with the daughters of men (Gen. 6.2). It was, as we will see, an instance of the *vita angelica* gone desperately wrong. Ultimately, Tertullian would become apprehensive of any effort to assimilate humankind and angels—whether sexual, eschatological, or metaphoric. It is in this context that the sexed body emerged as the benchmark of difference in his writings, a difference he projected into the afterlife and that would sharply curtail earlier visions of the *vita angelica*.

Marriage and Remarriage

Tertullian's prejudice against marriage rendered him an unlikely defender of the institution. He basically partook of the aversion shared by the Gnostics and his coreligionists alike, who tended to regard marriage through the unforgiving lens of postlapsarian pessimism. Adam and Eve "had committed murder on themselves," hence "falling from immortality."[35] Their crime eventuated in a hereditary ailment whereby "given over to death on account of [Adam's] sin, the entire human race, infected by his seed [*de suo semine infectae*], were made a transmitter of their own damnation [*damnationis traducem fecit*]."[36] Marriage was nothing more than a makeshift remedy to offset Adam's congenital sin. The gloomy cycle of marriage, birth, and death would relentlessly perpetuate itself until the resurrection, at which point marriage, the carnal vestibule that produced victims for the grim reaper, would be destroyed.[37] Although himself a married man, Tertullian had determined never to marry again were he at liberty to do so, nor did he believe anyone else should. The orthodox church's refusal to follow him in this resolve was a major factor in his attraction to the church of the New Prophecy movement, which likewise condemned second marriages.[38]

Remarriage was Tertullian's psychic "trigger issue," and he devoted three treatises that pressed for its abolition.[39] Yet this adamance seems somewhat misplaced in the context of the views expressed in the first treatise dedicated to what must surely have proven to be Tertullian's toughest audience—his wife. "No restoration of marriage is promised in the day of resurrection, translated as [we] will be into the condition and sanctity of angels. . . . There will at that day be no resumption of voluptuous disgrace between us."[40] Moreover, marriage is not an absolute good in itself, as it is only conceded by "necessity."[41]

Subsequent treatises become progressively strident in tone. *An Exhortation to Chastity*, written to a recently bereaved friend, presents the widower's loss as a cause for celebration—a strategy later made famous by Tertullian's spiritual heir, Jerome. Here marriage itself is characterized as "not so much a 'good' as a species of inferior evil," while second marriages are dismissed as a "species of fornication [*stuprum*]."[42] The third treatise, *On Monogamy*, pushes the basic immorality of marriage still further. Hence Tertullian interprets Paul's recommendation "it is good not to touch a woman" with sophistical cunning: "It follows it is evil to have contact with her; for nothing is contrary to good except evil."[43]

Since marriage was considered as a pro tem institution, one can empathize with Tertullian's contempt for anyone who would waste his or her time in a second marriage. But this does not explain the vigor with which he attacked such unions or why they arguably became the defining issue of his faith. As we will see, the question of whether the institution of marriage endures in the afterlife is beside the point in resolving this problem. Rather it is Tertullian's understanding of the body that renders his obsessive insistence on monogamy intellectually and theologically respectable. For Tertullian, every aspect of humanity was embodied.[44] Even the soul had a body all its own.[45] There was no resurrection without a body, just as there was no human marriage without sexual congress. In the classical world, marital relations were believed literally to mix the bodies of husband and wife. From Tertullian's perspective, this entailed a change (to his mind, a coarsening) of not just the body but also the soul, "dulling" the spiritual senses and "avert[ing] the Holy Spirit."[46] His increased awareness of this taint ultimately is projected into the afterlife, continuing to unite a couple who were once joined in marriage. Paul had shown a similar apprehension of the permanent bond created by sexual intercourse when he extends the unity of husband and wife affirmed by Genesis to casual sexual encounters: "know you not, that he who is joined to a harlot, is made one body? *For they shall be,* saith he, *two in one flesh*" (1 Cor. 6.16, citing Gen. 2.24).[47] This view could potentially find intellectual warrant in the medical tradition. Sperm was, after all, heated blood.[48] From this perspective, sex became more than the mere exchange of fluids: it was a kind of blood transfusion that rendered the woman irrevocably changed. Thus Tertullian's aversion to remarriage is rooted in the physical transformation that an individual has already undergone as a result of marriage.

And so this most transient, dispensable, and hence most despicable of unions effected a permanent commingling of the flesh possessed of enduring spiritual consequences. Thus, while concurring with the gospel's verdict that there would be no marriage or giving in marriage in heaven (Matt. 22.30; Mark 12.25; Luke 20:35, 36), Tertullian nevertheless perceived the bond instituted by marital relations as inescapable in both this world and the next. He uses a fictive dialogue with a widow to make this point: " 'Is not the fact that there will be no restitution of the conjugal relation a reason why we shall *not* be bound to our departed consorts?' [she asks]. Nay, but the more we shall be bound (to them), because we are destined to rise to a better estate destined (as we are) to rise to a spiritual consortship. . . . Since this is so, how will a woman have room for another husband, who is, even to futurity, in the possession of her own? . . . A more honourable husband is he, in proportion as he is become more pure."[49] Ironically, it is only in paradise when body and soul are free from the indignities of the reproductive imperative that the full force of the conjugal bond is felt. But even if marriage did generate a spiritualized bond that was destined to outlast the institution, this bond was but the imprint of a fundamental compromise.[50]

Tertullian's association of marriage with marital relations was, therefore, absolute. He would have been at a loss to comprehend the chastity debates of the fourth century, when orthodoxy's insistence on the perpetual virginity of Mary ultimately triumphed, as did the didactic value of her unconsummated union with Joseph.[51] Giving birth to Christ opened her womb, changing her from virgin to wife.[52] Tertullian assumes as a matter of course that Mary and Joseph would proceed to beget children in the ordinary way after Christ's birth, and he uses Christ's references to his brethren as evidence of his full humanity to counter dualist arguments against Christ's true incarnation.[53]

Although clearly believing that the ground lost through marriage could never be regained, Tertullian still maintained that sexual renunciation was commendable at whatever stage in life it was undertaken. To this end, *An Exhortation to Chastity* distinguishes three types of virginity: physical virginity from birth; the kind embarked upon at the "second birth," when married couples agree to renounce sex upon baptism; and instances in which a once-married widow or widower refuses remarriage.[54] Yet the only true escape from the taint of marriage was to circumvent it altogether. Christ is an exemplar in this context, having been born from "[flesh] not even unsealed by marriage" and inhabiting a body consisting of "[flesh] never to be unsealed by marriage."[55] Thus lifelong virginity alone constitutes "the principal sanctity, because it is free from the affinity with fornication."[56] The virgin drew the happiest lot, enjoying a blessed condition by which her "perfect integrity and entire sanctity shall have the nearest vision of the face of God."[57] Sanctity was a key term for Tertullian because it best expressed God's will for humanity.[58]

The terms *virginity* and *sanctity* are synonyms in Tertullian's lexicon, perhaps gesturing toward a gradual democratization of the virginal vocation as humanity advances toward the eschaton. The fact that humanity's full potential can only be realized in the virginal state works to the detriment of marriage, while at the same time providing an alibi for the very institution it hobbles. Thus, to the Gnostic detractors of marriage, Tertullian will affirm, "If there is to be no marriage, there is no sanctity. All proof of abstinence is lost when excess is impossible."[59]

Virgins and Angels: A Walk in the Dark

Tertullian may have been adamantly opposed to second marriages, but he was nonetheless aware that the person who was at one time sexually active and later embraces chastity requires considerable virtue and moderation, in contrast to the virgin's "total ignorance of that from which you will afterwards wish to be freed."[60] And yet Tertullian values virginity over the virtuous struggle of the sexually seasoned.[61] This predisposition reflects his commitment to virginity as an anticipation of the future kingdom where ignorance was, indeed, bliss and in which any exercise of the virtues would therefore be otiose. His exhortation to his wife sweetens the abolition of marriage with a promise of the "condition and sanctity of angels,"[62] describing those who choose voluntary chastity as "already counted as belonging to the angelic family."[63]

This is a rare moment for Tertullian. Apart from this rather glib promise to his wife that chastity already secures her place in an illustrious angelic lineage, the sanctity Tertullian attributes to virginity is usually rhetorically aloof from the angelic life, which he reserves for the resurrected body. Thus in his treatise on female dress when he asserts that "the same angelic nature is promised to you, women, the selfsame sex is promised to you as to men," he is gesturing toward a future condition that provides temporary shelter from his otherwise steady rain of chastising vitriol.[64]

But we have already seen that the promise of an "angelic nature" is hardly a transparent one, even as not all androgynies are equal. When Tertullian assures women that they are to receive "the selfsame sex" as men, the school of androgyny that he seems to be aligning himself with is at one with the Gnostic predisposition to regard prelapsarian humanity as male.[65] But Tertullian ultimately recoiled from this vision of male-inflected androgyny, which threatened to collapse the angelic and human race, favoring instead a resurrected body that was ineradicably sexed. Intrinsic to this position was his preoccupation with the antediluvian history of the Watcher Angels, whose intermarriage with the daughters of men was perceived as an offense so heinous that it precipitated God's decision to flood the earth (Gen. 6.8). These angels were distinctly male.

This alternative, and perhaps original, story of the fall was mentioned fleetingly by Paul when he was likewise seeking to impose veils on wives, utilizing "because of the angels" (1 Cor. 11.3ff) as possible justification.[66] Dale Martin argues convincingly that Paul did see angels as a threat to the body's fragile boundaries, which explains this allusion.[67] Paul, however, tended to favor the story of Adam and Eve as the origin of humanity's fall. Whether he believed that defilement by angels was a possibility or not, the oblique reference operates as a trump card for enforcing female submission. It is easy to imagine that Tertullian did likewise, seizing upon the tale as a pretext for subduing uppity women. Nevertheless, Tertullian's obsession with this calamity and the significance it assumed in his understanding of salvation history suggest that the incident resonated far beyond its undeniable utility as a disciplinary strategy. The apocryphal Book of Enoch offered an extended account of the baleful history of the Watcher Angels, and Tertullian brooded over its contents, urging in favor of the authenticity of the work at some length.[68] His work *On Idolatry* catalogues practically every evil known to humanity, associating them with the intervention of the rebel angels. Evidence of the calamitous unions seemed to be present to Tertullian at every turn through bizarre vestiges. Thus when arguing for the durability of the flesh, he points to the recent discovery of some ancient bones still covered with flesh and hair, construing these as the remains of giants—the cursed progeny of these blighted unions.[69]

The Watcher Angels were the motor behind Tertullian's frequent return to the question of female dress and modesty. Although this evil legacy overshadowed all women to some extent, the virgins were positioned in its penumbra. By refusing to wear veils these women were, to Tertullian's mind, attempting to deny their sexuality and gender—an effort that he compares with attempts to establish "a third generic class, some monstrosity with a head of its own."[70] He responded to their adamance by arguing that it was virgins and virgins alone who were the special object of angelic lust, thereby proving that virgins were women and that even the chaste human body was inevitably sexual. Tertullian's credulity regarding humankind's prehistorical disaster would determine his efforts to secure a unique destiny for humanity, one that was eternally separate from the angelic host. This would ultimately lead him to maintain that the sexed body was eternal.

Already in his earliest treatment of the subject, Tertullian maintained that the daughters of men, who were not specifically designated as "wives," must, by process of elimination, be virgins. This rationale was not simply based on biblical nomenclature or lack thereof: Tertullian's own aversion to sexual activity made it impossible for him to conceive that angels could possibly settle for matrons.[71] In *The Veiling of Virgins*, Tertullian's expressions of disgust over the taint of sex are allowed to flow unchecked. "Who can presume that it was bodies already defiled, and relics of human lust, which such angels yearned after, so as not rather to have been inflamed for virgins, whose bloom pleads an excuse for human lust as well." Tertullian also attempts to have it both ways: even if the women targeted by the angels were already "contaminated [*contaminatas*]," and hence not virgins, this would only go to show that the temptation afforded by virgins would prove more potent still: "so much more 'on account of the angels' would it have been the duty of virgins to be veiled."[72]

The implications of the unholy union between the angels and erstwhile human virgins were cataclysmic. Not only were the fallen angels themselves transformed into demons, but their offspring became a "still more wicked demon brood,"[73] bent on securing humanity's damnation. Their exemplary malevolence was sharpened by the thirst for revenge. The rebel angels "who certainly thought sometimes of the place whence they had fallen and longed for heaven after the heated impulses of lust had quickly passed," wreaked vengeance upon their hapless wives by showering them with every imaginable luxury: tinted cloth, jewels and makeup, seeking to entrap them by their own vanity.[74] Privy to the secrets of the earth, the erstwhile angels introduced metallurgy, a craft that brought weapons and war in its wake. To make matters worse, the former denizens of heaven exercised immense powers over their mortal victims by virtue of their residual angelic nature. They were thus responsible for plaguing the body with diseases and assailing the spirit with "violent assaults . . . hurry[ing] the soul into sudden and extraordinary excesses."[75] On a more metaphysical level, the fallen angels prompted humans to turn away from God through the introduction of idolatry and occult arts such as astrology.[76]

Ultimately, humanity degenerated so completely that God was compelled to reject it altogether, signaling his disaffection with the comment "My Spirit shall not permanently abide in these men eternally, for that they are flesh" (Gen. 6.3). This was a troubling passage for Tertullian, but he was forced to contend with it because his dualist opponents perceived it as evidence that the creation of humanity was a calamity and as further proof that the good god had never intended to mix flesh and spirit.[77] While eschewing this interpretation, Tertullian clearly regarded the text as indicative of a portentous shift, which, in a later work, he interprets as marking the beginning of the ongoing disjunction between flesh and spirit alluded to by Paul (Gal. 5.17).[78]

The virgins' role in the angelic fall loomed sufficiently large in Tertullian's psychic landscape that it threatened to supplant Eve's transgression in Eden. Yet the two stories were in many ways complementary, constituting formidable proof of woman's ineradicable sexuality, evidenced by her unerring capacity to seduce her superiors—be they men or angels. The opening of *The Apparel of Women* exploits this cumulative case for female perfidy, whether active or passive, by placing the two accounts side by side. The first chapter upbraids all women as daughters of Eve who, while seeking finery, are in reality deserving of penitential garb,[79] while the second reveals the identity of the evil agents responsible for the dyes and metallurgical skill necessary for female fashion: "those angels . . . who rushed from heaven on the daughters of men; so that this ignominy also attaches to woman."[80]

Tertullian took pains at a number of junctures to stress the prelapsarian Eve's status as both woman and virgin since "she has the appellation *woman* before she was *wedded*, and never *virgin* while she *was* a *virgin*."[81] Not only does this emphasis confound arguments in favor of the special androgyny inherent in the virginal state, but it further sets the stage for the remedial intervention of that exemplary virgin (and woman) par excellence, Mary. The Virgin Mary is an antidote to the evil instituted by the primordial virgin, Eve: "it was while Eve was yet a virgin, that the ensnaring word had crept into her ear which was to build the edifice of death. Into a virgin's soul, in like manner, must be introduced that Word of God which was to raise the fabric of life; so that what had been reduced to ruin by this sex, might by the selfsame sex be recovered to salvation. As Eve believed the serpent, so Mary believed the angel."[82]

But while the history of the virginal daughters of men compounds the guilt of Eve, it is a tacit inference achieved by an adroit juxtaposition of references rather than overt articulation. An invisible barrier seems to be erected between this instance of supernatural miscegenation and the incarnation, even as the daughters of men are excluded from the antiphonal rapport between Eve and Mary. There are good reasons for Tertullian's textual restraint. Schooled by the Book of Enoch, Tertullian interprets the antediluvian denizens of heaven as being members of the angelic host. Yet so disturbing an appellation as "sons of God" would caution against any close juxtaposition of the Old Testament text with the incarnation of Christ, the true "son of God." For one might argue with good reason that the Christian faith was born as a result of a woman conversing with an angel. Thus if placed alongside Gabriel's annunciation to the Virgin Mary, the angelic dalliance with the daughters of men reads too much like a misbegotten or even aborted incarnation, a blunder that would necessarily impugn God's infallibility. Although the incarnation of Christ represents a fresh start for humanity, even as Mary provides the antidote to Eve, there was no remedy for the ongoing destruction wrought by the demonic progeny of the fallen sons of God, who would continue to plague humankind until the end of time.

Separate but Equal: The *Vita Angelica* and Its Afterlife

Tertullian's understanding of the Watcher Angels was a dark tribute to the liminal capacity of virginity. By elevating human nature, virginity created a zone wherein angels and humans were permitted to mingle—a propinquity that Tertullian clearly deemed deleterious to both. Although virginity could not raise women to angelic heights, the virgins themselves clearly had the capacity to draw angels down to subhuman depths. And the falling angels would, in turn, do all in their power to drag humanity along with them. It was through the indiscretion of virgins that the sacrosanct boundaries between the human and the angelic races had once been breached. In order to prevent any recurrence of this abomination, Tertullian attempted to squelch the virgins' misguided pretensions of androgyny by asserting their ineradicable womanhood, a case symbolically advanced by the imposition of the veil.

This preoccupation helps explain Tertullian's resistance to Gnosticism. For not only did Gnostic mythology seem to reinvoke parallel instances of crossbreeding between the species, but it also celebrated them. According to Tertullian's rendition of the Gnostics' ultimate ritual of the marriage chamber that would occur at the end of time, worthy human males would be united to angels as brides—a situation he found both obscene and ludicrous. In the final consummation, "I am despoiled of my sex, I am classed with angels—not a male angel, nor a female one. . . . [Nor] will they then find any male energy in me."[83] Furthermore, both holy scripture and the human race alike were compromised further by the irresponsible exegesis of contemporary Gnostic virgins. A certain Philumene taught that Christ was an angel and that his body was not formed from flesh, but extracted from the stars.[84] Paul had allegedly provided the biblical support for this conviction by juxtaposing "the first man is of the earth, earthy; the second man is the Lord from heaven."[85] From Tertullian's perspective, however, an angelic Christ not only denigrated the human body and, by extension, its creator but effectively eliminated any salubrious distance between humans and angels. His horror was duly expressed when he disparaged Philumene with the racial impurity he so dreaded, characterizing her as "an angel of deceit, 'transformed into an angel of light' (2 Cor. 11.14)."[86] His rebuttal was embedded in a theological anthropology that would eventually immortalize the human body in all its particulars, differentiating humans from angels once and for all.

The treatise *The Flesh of Christ* vigorously rejects an angelic Christ, arguing that Christ was fully human and, hence, possessed of the same flesh as humanity. While granting that there were incidents in the Old Testament where angels appeared as humans, even to the point of assuming human flesh, "it is plain that the angels bore a flesh which was not naturally their own; their nature being of a spiritual substance, although in some sense peculiar to themselves, corporeal; and yet they could be transfigured into human shape." Apparently angels did have the capacity to present themselves in human form. But no angel, whether encased in borrowed flesh or no, was born to die, as was Christ, and it was only the death of a human Christ that could redeem humankind.[87]

Tertullian was nevertheless aware that his argument for the flesh could not do away with its essential inferiority and that dualist expressions of incredulity over an incarnate Christ were formulated "lest the Lord should be regarded as inferior to the angels who are not formed of earthly flesh."[88] Initially, Tertullian attempted to quell this objection by insisting on the extraordinary purity of Christ's flesh.[89] But ultimately this problem was tackled more effectively, albeit more obliquely, through his description of humanity as a coherent and inextricable coalition of flesh and spirit. Not only did such a formulation make it impossible to separate the soul from what the Gnostics considered to be its carnal husk, but it had important implications for gender as well. Tertullian adhered to the stoical concept of the corporeal soul, one possessed of its own special kind of body. Both types of bodies, carnal and spiritual, were interdependent, having been created by the same act of insemination in which gender was also integral.[90] "The soul, being sown in the womb at the same time as the body, receives likewise along with it its sex; and this indeed so simultaneously, that neither of the two substances can be alone regarded as the cause of the sex. . . . The insemination of the two substances are inseparable in point of time, and their effusion is also one and the same, in consequence of which a community of gender is secured to them."[91]

The profound unity of humanity in its different dimensions is developed in the treatise *The Resurrection of the Dead*, a prolonged meditation on the role of the human body in salvation history. Humankind, the pinnacle of the

created world, was created body and soul in the image of God: "and so intimate is the union, that it may be deemed to be uncertain whether the flesh
bears about the soul, or the soul the flesh."[92] In opposition to the Gnostic tendency to regard the body as a transitory prison of the soul, Tertullian advances
the eternal codependence of body and soul, arguing that "the flesh is the very
condition on which salvation hinges." Virginity and all other modes of sexual
restraint are thus "but fragrant offerings to God paid out of the good services
of the flesh."[93] Body and soul constituted an integral unit. The inner body of
the soul was naked without the protective covering of the external body of
flesh.[94] Death would transform the outer body even as " 'this corruptible must
put on incorruption, and this mortal must put on immortality' (1 Cor. 15.51–
53)." But even after mortality is "swallowed up," the outer body remains.[95]

   Tertullian's perception of humanity as a seamless and integral union of
spirit and flesh would naturally augment his awareness of the deleterious impact of sexual relations and heighten his appreciation for virginity. When his
provirginal stance is considered independently of his vision of humanity, this
emphasis seems unreasoned, even fetishistic. Hence Tertullian has frequently
been identified as the turning point after which anatomical virginity begins to
eclipse the perception of virginity as a state of mind.[96] Indeed, his tendency to
rank the virgin's effortless attainment above the widow's virtuous perseverance
only compounds this impression.

   The ineradicable view of marriage as carnal conditioned Tertullian's own
idiosyncratic evocation of the mystical marriage—a masterful recasting of
Gnostic nuptial imagery, one that turned the mystery of the bridal chamber
on its head by making the human body the ne plus ultra of consummation.
The body's fragile coalition of flesh and spirit is consummated and sanctified
by the incarnation: "Both natures has He [Christ] already united in His own
self: He has fitted them together as bride and bridegroom in the reciprocal
bond of wedded life. Now, if any should insist on making the soul the bride,
then the flesh will follow the soul as her dowry. The soul shall never be an out-
cast, to be had home by the bridegroom bare and naked. . . . But suppose the
flesh to be the bride, then in Christ she has in the contract of blood received
His spirit as her spouse."[97]

   In his zeal to discern between the angelic and human race, Tertullian
found himself defending the body in all its particulars and projecting it into
the afterlife. Humanity's retention of both sexes was perhaps his coup de grace.
For although angelic androgyny could, arguably, accommodate one sex, it
could not accommodate two—the female sex least of all. Tertullian nevertheless had to acknowledge that he was up against an inexplicable mystery

regarding what possible purpose any body, let alone a gendered body, would serve when death, and hence marriage and procreation, had ceased to exist. And this is where virginity, a condition valued by the proto-orthodox church, the Gnostics, or the New Prophecy alike, came to his aid. While virginity did not solve the conundrum of the body's continued existence, it nevertheless re-posed the question in striking terms by offering a compelling *figura* for how incomprehensible anomalies are nevertheless consistent with God's plan for humanity. Virginity was a condition in the body, but not of the body. To many early Christians, the virgin's sexual abstinence might have anticipated a blissful abolition of gender. But for Tertullian, to whom gender had become inextricable to body and soul, the virgin's sexed body was now possessed of a different potential altogether: her untapped fecundity became the most compelling exemplum for the impenetrable mystery of the body's endurance. In *The Resurrection of the Dead*, Tertullian raises the question of "what purpose can be served by loins, conscious of seminal secretions, and all other organs of generation in the two sexes, and the laboratories of embryos, and the fountains of the breast, when concubinage, and pregnancy, and infant nurture shall cease,"[98] all the time aware that the answer must be postponed until the future kingdom. Until that time, we must be content to contemplate a parallel set of anomalies that are accommodated within the mundane order of things, prefiguring things to be. "Even in the present life there may be cessations of their office for our stomachs and our generative organs. For forty days Moses and Elias fasted, and lived upon God alone. . . . See here faint outlines of our future strength! We even, as we may be able, excuse our mouths from food, and withdraw our sexes from union. How many voluntary eunuchs are there. How many virgins espoused to Christ! How many, both men and women, whom nature has made sterile, with a structure which cannot procreate!"[99]

The sexed body of the consecrated virgin is but an exemplum framed within a series of seeming anachronisms that prefigure humanity's ultimate destiny. The designation of "bride of Christ" serves to distinguish her from her male counterpart, the voluntary eunuch. Their bodies, sexually inactive but gendered, are projected into the afterlife, scuttling all hopes for an androgynous *vita angelica*. Thus Tertullian succeeded in bringing what he perceived as hubristic claims for virginity down to earth in order to secure humanity's due place in heaven.

Equality with angels did not mean assimilation. What Tertullian sought to establish for the human race was its separate but equal status, in both this world and the next. Angels had often appeared on earth, dwelt among humans, even eaten and drunk with them, without abandoning their spiritual natures. In a similar manner, "we shall not therefore cease to continue in the flesh, because we cease to be importuned by the usual wants of the flesh; just as the angels ceased not therefore to remain in their spiritual substance, because of the suspension of their spiritual incidents. . . . When [Christ] ascribed an angelic likeness to the flesh, He took not from it its proper substance."[100] In Tertullian's later works, humanity's much awaited angelic life simply becomes shorthand for eternity and the transformation that the body must undergo when the flesh "is remade and 'angelified' [angelificatum] in the kingdom of God."[101] Humans will become " 'equal unto the angels,' (5 John 6.39) inasmuch as they are not to marry, because they are not to die, but are destined to pass into the angelic state by putting on the raiment of incorruption, although with a change in the substance which is restored to life."[102] Even so, humanity was securely separated from angels by its body of flesh, but its basic equality was nevertheless maintained.

If the Gnostics had won out, the body might have been deemed less consequential, and women may have continued to advance toward the male-inflected androgyny associated with the angelic life. Instead, the full weight of gender and the body reasserted itself, rendering women more fully human than ever before and thwarting attempts to colonize the angelic life on earth.

Hesitations En Route to the Altar

Tertullian's emphasis on intact virginity and the omnipresence of gender clearly set the stage for the virgin's identification with the bride of Christ. But it is not clear how exactly he arrived at this expedient. Jo Ann McNamara depicts Tertullian as searching in frustration for a disciplinary tactic for subduing virgins, irked by the fact that they were theoretically subject to no one. According to her account, he found his answer in the New Testament concept of the eschatological family. "Christians habitually called God their father. . . . It was not, therefore, a giant step for Tertullian to add conjugal imagery to the scheme."[103] Certainly, this string of associations would have helped justify his ultimate decision to change autonomous virgins into dependent brides. But, as seen earlier, Tertullian had already availed himself of the nuptial imagery omnipresent in Gnostic exegesis, inverting it so that the human body becomes both bride and dowry for the celestial bridegroom. What could be more natural than to apply this contract to specific individuals?

As practical as such a solution might seem, however, Tertullian nevertheless hesitates, introducing the motif with uncharacteristic reticence. A measure of his trepidation is reflected in efforts to try versions of the bridal motif out on other categories of Christians before finally affixing it to virgins. An early attempt at binding individual women through a variant of the mystical marriage occurs in *The Apparel of Women* (ca. 198–202), where his audience was matrons and the celestial suitor was constituted as God rather than Christ. "Bow your heads to your husbands—and that will be ornament enough for you. Keep your hands busy with spinning and stay at home—and you will be more pleasing than if you were adorned in gold. Dress yourselves in the silk of probity, the fine linen of holiness, and the purple of chastity. Decked out in this manner, you will have God Himself for your lover."[104] It may have been Tertullian's apprehension of the impact of carnal marriage that led him to depict God as an adulterous lover as opposed to a husband. But by the time Tertullian wrote *To His Wife* (ca. 200), his most fulsome treatment of this particular application of the mystical marriage, God's amorous intentions were now honorably resolved in marriage. Widows who forgo opportunities to remarry are characterized as "prefer[ring] to be wedded to God. To God their beauty, to God their youth (is dedicated). With Him they live; with Him they converse; Him they 'handle' by day and night; to the Lord they assign their prayers as dowries; from Him, as oft they desire it, they receive His approbation as dotal gifts."[105] In an *Exhortation to Chastity* (between 204 and 212), the Father retains the role of bridegroom. Yet Tertullian is emboldened to extend the metaphor in two ways, addressing not only those who had perhaps not yet experienced marriage but also members of both sexes. Hence he commends both men and women in ecclesiastical orders who have preferred to be "wedded to God."[106]

When it comes to consecrated virgins, Tertullian's application of the image is much more halting. And this should come as no surprise: an irreducible contempt for marriage, an ongoing association of virginity and sanctity, and perhaps even a vestigial sentimentality for the very claims of androgyny that he so disparaged must necessarily have given him pause. It was much simpler to attach women to a celestial bridegroom if they already had experience with an earthly prototype because the second union would be deemed a promotion. And among these individuals the title is distributed as if it were an honor. But when it came to virgins, the title "bride" is invoked in a disciplinary fashion that they would probably have found offensive. In an early work, *On Prayer* (ca. 198–200), Tertullian's tone is defensive and his initial efforts to associate the virgin with the matron are fumbling and unlovely, with no heavenly bridegroom in sight: "No one is a 'virgin' from the time when she is capable of marriage; seeing that, in her, age has by that time been wedded to its own husband, that is, to time."[107] Later when the bridegroom finally shows up, the contract is undercut by Tertullian's intonation that Christ is uniting himself to a kind of pseudobride: "You do well in falsely assuming the married character . . . nay you do not *falsely* for you *are* wedded to Christ."[108] Even in his more mature treatment in *The Veiling of Virgins* (written before 207) he exhorts his audience to "Recognize the *woman*, ay, recognize the *wedded woman*, by the testimonies both of body and of spirit, which she experiences both in conscience and in flesh. There are the earlier tablets of *natural* espousals and nuptials."[109] When he attempts to segue into the mystical marriage, however, his tone is hesitant and apologetic. "Wear a full garb of woman, to preserve your standing of virgin. Belie somewhat of your inward consciousness, in order to exhibit the truth to God alone. And yet you do not belie yourself in appearing as a bride. For wedded you are to Christ."[110]

In both *On Prayer* and *The Veiling of Virgins*, the virgin's marriage to her sexed body significantly takes precedence, both sequentially and symbolically, over marriage with Christ. It is only when Tertullian has successfully articulated a nuptial theology that unites body and soul—a union consummated by the incarnation—that the virgin's marriage emerges as a true occasion for celebration. As seen earlier, it is not until *The Resurrection of the Dead* (between 210 and 212) that Tertullian can at last exclaim joyfully over the number of "virgins espoused to Christ"—reveling in the sexed bodies, inactive but still fecund, that united them irrevocably to the only truly human son of God.[111]

It was a match. The virgins must be veiled because their celestial bridegroom would wish it so, as would any groom. At the hands of subsequent theologians, moreover, the celestial bridegroom will become ever more exacting, until he manifests the very same appetite for intact virginity common to erstwhile angelic husbands, and Roman ones as well.

But there was more than discipline and gender hierarchy at stake. An investment in Genesis 6 raised the possibility of an inverted, and very literal, soul marriage. It implicitly explored aspects of the Pauline tradition that were perhaps better let alone. The admonition that young widows remarry had been emphasized by the fact that "some are already turned aside after Satan" (1 Tim. 15.5). This dour alternative would be felt with new urgency. By the same token, Paul's desire of presenting each Christian's soul as a pure virgin resonated ominously with his insistence on women veiling themselves "because of the angels"—raising the specters of debauchery and defilement.

CHAPTER 2

The Church Fathers and the Embodied Bride

If Tertullian had humbled virgins by marrying them to Christ, the subsequent tradition would attempt to transform *sponsa Christi* into a title of supreme honor, concealing the defeat at the heart of this persona. Occasionally we catch a glimpse of the process of metamorphosis. The anonymous continuator of Perpetua's journal describes her entrance into the amphitheatre: "Perpetua followed behind, with a clear gait as a matron of Christ, beloved of God."[1] As Thomas Heffernan points out, this is the first occurrence of Christ as the celestial bridegroom to appear in Christian hagiography.[2] Its application to Perpetua is nevertheless tinged with a kind of irony. The woman whose love of Christ transformed her from a matron into a gladiator ended her days in the ring as would a gladiator, but remained a wife after all. On the basis of shared Montanist beliefs, a number of scholars have advanced that Tertullian was the editor of the passion, hence determining its final form.[3] Even if this is a mistake, the tone of the anonymous continuator may suggest a wry truth buried in the error.

Cyprian: Of Makeup and Adultery

Three decades after Tertullian, Cyprian, bishop of Carthage (d. 258), also had occasion to take up his pen against the city's virgins over the issue of dress. At first glance, his writings suggest that the virginal stock had risen considerably since Tertullian's time. In any event, Cyprian deviates from the belittling strategies of Tertullian, his main source, in order to emphasize the consecrated virgin's distinction. His treatise *On the Dress of Virgins* is addressed to his female subjects "whose glory, as it is more eminent, excites the greater interest. This is the flower of the ecclesiastical seed, the grace and ornament of spiritual endowment, a joyous disposition, the wholesome and uncorrupted work of praise and honour, God's image answering to the holiness of the Lord, the more illustrious portion of Christ's flock."[4] Cyprian is also quick to assign extra merit to virgins in the afterlife, though this privilege was, as we shall see, only definitively secured in the fourth century.[5] Virgins alone among women have escaped Eve's curse of subjection. Only they will be permitted to follow the lamb.[6] The singular glory of the virgin state is only surpassed by martyrdom.[7]

Despite the pronounced debt to Tertullian, however, Cyprian is much more concerned with the possibility of sexual transgressions with men than miscegenation with angels. Thus while the rhetoric of the *vita angelica* is prominent, even including a fleeting profession of equality with men, this elevated state is stripped of all of the heady freedoms.[8] Whether out of genuine deference for the virgin state or for reasons of his own, Cyprian clearly believes that the less said about the prehistoric unions between virgins and angels the better. Thus while concurring with Tertullian's allegation that the apostate angels were the evil geniuses behind cosmetics, Cyprian evades the question of how the wicked peddlers arrived on earth in the first place, simply relating that "lowered to the contagions of earth, they forsook their heavenly vigour."[9] But whether as husbands or as purveyors of satanic beauty aids, the result of their interference is everywhere apparent in the false colors women apply to change their appearance, destroying God's image in them. In so doing, women align themselves with the forces backing these suspect products because "everything which comes into being is God's work, everything which is changed is the devil's." It is an unforgivable breach of virginal modesty: "For although you may not be immodest among men, and are not unchaste with your seducing dyes, yet when those things which belong to God are corrupted and violated, you are engaged in a worse adultery."[10]

Cyprian is invoking a presumptive celestial marriage through the language of sexual transgression. So while the sordid couplings between angels and antediluvian virgins are expunged, the present-day virgins are nevertheless depicted as uniting themselves with the devil in more subtle ways through cosmetic adulteration. This adultery is clearly damnable in Cyprian's eyes, who anticipates God's response as, " 'This is not my work, nor is this our image. You have polluted your skin with a false medicament, you have changed your hair with an adulterous colour, your face is violently taken possession of by a lie, your figure is corrupted, your countenance is another's. . . . As you are adorned in the fashion of your enemy, with him also you shall burn by and by.'"[11]Again the matrimonial strains tend to be tacit and inflected: Cyprian's semantic games circle around transgressions against an implied shadow of marriage that is not initially treated in its own right. But the eventual appearance of the groom soon casts the crime, and hence the marriage, into sharper relief: women who paint their faces "cease to be virgins, corrupted by a furtive dishonour; widows before they are married, adulterous, not to their husband but to Christ."[12] By equating dabbling in cosmetics with dalliance with the devil, Cyprian establishes the virgin's marriage with Christ in the breach. And the tacit implication of physical lapses is inescapable: the makeup was applied through the ministry of fallen angels, but it was applied for the benefit of men and it was through men that their virginity was in danger of being compromised.

A progression can be delineated since the time of Tertullian. The latter resorted to the concept of the bride of Christ tentatively and out of expedience. The virgins "falsely assume[ed] the married character," placing them distinctly at odds with the classical ideal, which aligned outer garb with inner realities. It was a masquerade he deemed as somewhat belittling, even as marriage itself was degrading. But while acknowledging to the virgins that their status as matron was something of a social fib, he also presented it as a necessary disciplinary measure. In contrast, Cyprian energetically embraces the virgin's marriage with Christ, unambiguously presenting it as an honor. And yet the union is most clearly articulated by probing the dark side of the marital contract. His employment of the term *adultery*, in particular, evokes conventional secular discipline. Adultery through cosmetics may be but a metaphor, yet it is a punitive one that immediately conjures up practical and concrete consequences. The use of such terms seems to beg the question of what Cyprian would do were he to find himself at the crossroads where the image of marriage to Christ intersected with the reality of a consecrated virgin who had fallen. Would he turn away, retreating down the ephemeral path of imagery from whence he came? Or would he follow the well-traveled thoroughfare in pursuit of an offense that is not only a sin but also a crime, allowing adultery's penal consequences to drag the image down to the material world of due process?

When such a case did arise, Cyprian chose the latter road, bringing the full weight of the church's fledgling judicial system to bear on Christ's errant spouse. The case involved the unconventional lifestyle of a deacon who cohabited with a handful of consecrated virgins, even sharing their beds, though allegedly in chastity. Risky as this behavior may seem, the individuals in question were doubtless in their own way reaping the benefits of the intimacy that a life of chastity seemed to afford them—experiencing the realized eschatology that dissipated gender, and the incumbent passions, altogether. This lifestyle could be placed on a continuum with the unveiled pride of Tertullian's virgins.

In contrast, Cyprian construed such domestic relations as adulterous and attempted to treat them as such: "If a husband should come and see his wife lying with another man, is he not indignant and maddened, and doth he not in the violence of his jealousy perhaps even seize a sword? How indignant and angered then must Christ our Lord and Judge be."[13] Not only should the guilty parties separate and do penance, but Cyprian also insisted that the women undergo gynecological examinations to ensure that their virginity was still intact. "If any of them shall prove to have been corrupted, let her undergo full penance, because she who has been guilty of this crime is an adulteress, not against a husband, but Christ."[14] Furthermore, the diaconal ménage at Carthage was hardly an isolated case. With the rise of clerical celibacy and the lack of religious options for devout females in the West, the cohabitation of clerics with consecrated virgins, a practice known to modern scholars as syneisaktism, was a practical solution that proved difficult to eradicate even after its eventual condemnation at the Council of Nicaea (325), which clearly forbade the presence of extraneous women in clerical households.[15]

The testimonies of Tertullian and Cyprian both demonstrate the mounting impetus among Western religious authorities, particularly in North Africa, to clip the wings of would-be female angels. Tertullian's strategy was to insist that virgins were not angels, but women. His primary method was to humble them, first by asserting their commonality with all other daughters of Eve and second by blaming them for their inadvertent role in the metamorphosis of celestial angels into demonic husbands. While the virgins' sordid marital careers may be things of the past, Tertullian did his best to ensure that in this instance history would not repeat itself. Cyprian's tactics were different. His fulsome tones of praise and encouragement, couched in the familiar language of realized eschatology, advanced his main purpose: the imposition of marriage, the ultimate restraint, on consecrated virgins. This resulted in a seeming rise in the virgin's status remarked upon earlier. Her spiritual currency was ostensibly ratchetted up to be worthy of such a groom. The union would, in turn, confirm this elevation, inflating her spiritual currency still more. But having been raised to his level, she would have much further to fall: infidelity to the celestial bridegroom would be infinitely more culpable than infidelity to a terrestrial counterpart.

Once this projection of Christ as the jealous husband was in place, the priesthood, standing *in loco Christi*, would be justified in redoubling their vigilance over the said virgins. In contrast to Tertullian, who, for all his heightened awareness of women's seductive powers, advises a male addressee to take a Christian "sister" as housekeeper so as to avoid remarriage, Cyprian's heated response to the perceived crisis would exacerbate the growing division between male and female ascetics.[16] Moreover, Tertullian's preoccupation with intact virginity as a source of sanctification is no match for the gynecological precision that Cyprian enjoins for redressing any potential infidelity against Christ.

So the bride of Christ that was emerging out of Carthage cut an extremely shabby figure. For Tertullian, she was a compromise formation at best—a virgin who posed as a wife to avoid becoming something much worse. For Cyprian, it was the fact that the virgin could commit adultery that seemed to secure her position as bride. Meanwhile the inflated heights of her marriage bed fostered a salubrious restriction of liberty to avert the peril of falling. As we shall see, both Western and Eastern authorities were prepared to follow this lead.[17]

Origen and the Bride Unveiled

Around the same time that the West was attempting to unite flesh-and-blood virgins with a celestial bridegroom who showed every sign of taking after his father, the jealous God, the great Alexandrian exegete Origen (d. ca. 254) was passionately elaborating the allegorical bride of the Song of Songs and her struggle to unite herself mystically with the bridegroom, Christ.[18] Parallels with the Gnostics and the greater mystery of the wedding chamber resonate. Moreover, Origen's view of creation and redemption also had, as we shall see, much in common with Gnostic exegesis—so much so that his later work was deemed heretical.[19] As a result, many of his writings are lost or exist only as fragments. What does remain is largely transmitted through the Latin translations of Rufinus and Jerome, as is the case with his commentary on the Song of Songs. But the obscurity surrounding his work in no way diminishes its originality and eventual impact. For although Origen was not the first to comment on the Song, his interpretative genius provided new wine for old bottles—strong enough to inebriate Western spirituality forever.[20] From the perspective of this study, his significance is twofold. Origen is the ultimate font for the bridal mysticism that will resurface dramatically in the twelfth century. On a more immediate level, Origen will also be tacitly influential for pastoral purposes. For because his bride was a metaphor, she was destined to become a strong component of the medium in which the female religious vocation was subsequently constructed.

Origen interpreted scripture in terms of an ascending hierarchy of complexity in meaning: from literal to moral to allegorical. The ultimate goal was to attain the "anagogic" reading that would raise the soul to a spiritual understanding.[21] As a result, Origen tends not to linger over the literal. Thus he describes the Song as a "simple story. . . . We see a bride appearing on the stage, having received for her betrothal and by way of dowry most fitting gifts from a most noble bridegroom; but, because the bridegroom delays his coming for so long, she, grieved with longing for his love, is pining at home and doing all she can to bring herself to see her spouse, and to enjoy his kisses."[22] Then Origen quickly turns his attention to the two time-honored themes that were at the heart of his allegorical reading. "Let us see if the inner meaning also can be fittingly supplied along these lines. Let it be the Church who longs for union with Christ; but the Church, you must observe, is the whole assembly of the saints. So it must be the Church as a corporate personality who speaks."[23] The second level of allegory, accordingly, treats "the soul whose only desire is to be united to the Word of God and to be in fellowship with Him, and to enter into the mysteries of His wisdom and knowledge as into the chambers of her heavenly Bridegroom."[24]

The bride of the Canticles has little in common with the classical world's ideal of the modest, retiring bride. She is sexually aggressive and proactive in her quest for the bridegroom. Origen does full justice to both her passion and her initiative by emphasizing her unveiled status. This becomes apparent at the juncture when the bride pleads with the bridegroom to reveal "where Thou hast Thy couch in the midday, lest perchance I be made as one that is veiled above the flocks of Thy companions" (Sg 1.6). According to Origen, her apprehension is of appearing "as one that is veiled." For her part, "having no care for modesty, she should fear not to run hither and thither and to be seen of many."[25]

The identity and status of both the companions and their brides are central to understanding the bride's outré behavior. Initially, Origen attempts to conflate the two groups, asking whether the fact that the bride seems to have assumed a veil "may not show that one or more of the companions are as brides wearing the bridal dress and being veiled having a veil upon their head, as the Apostle says."[26] But—soon abandoning the admittedly fraught possibility of the companions doing triple duty as groomsmen, brides, and shepherds—he resolves the companions as angels who shepherd "all those nations divided up like herds."[27] The auxiliary brides, who are veiled, represent "the flocks of the Bridegroom's companions."[28]

Origen momentarily takes the bride's apprehension in a more sinister direction by asking "whether these companions who are said to possess some flocks, do so as servants of the bridegroom, acting under Him as the Chief of shepherds, since they are called His companions; or whether, since the bride flees and is afraid, lest perchance she meet the companions' flocks while she is looking for her spouse, these companions desire to possess something as their own exclusive property in a manner not accordant with the Bridegroom's mind."[29] The passage is ambiguous: the possibility of the companions seeking to possess something "in a manner not accordant with the Bridegroom's mind" could suggest their wrongful appropriation of the flocks. But, considering her apprehension, this menace could just as easily apply to the bride. With the threat of sexual impropriety in the air, compounded by the fact that the potentially wayward companions are angels, it seems as if Origen were about to traverse some of the same terrain that Tertullian traveled in pursuit of the Watcher Angels and the daughters of men. If so, perhaps Origen would consider revising his approbation of his bride's unveiled status.

In fact, the threat of slippage between humankind and the angelic host was omnipresent to Origen.[30] His views on the fall are clearly articulated in his most important theological work, *On the Principles* (*De principiis*), in which God creates all rational beings as incorporeal, "equal and alike, because there was no reason for producing variety and diversity." Diversity, including different kinds of corporeality, resulted from a given creature's initiative in undertaking a volitional movement toward or away from God.[31] Thus "like every rational creature . . . [an angel] is capable of earning praise and blame."[32] Whatever level in the heavenly (or infernal) hierarchy an individual entity might attain was solely on the basis of its own "works and movements."[33] Rational beings, angelic or human, shared the same basic nature.[34] Human souls "according to the deserts and moral progress of each individual" could advance to the order of angels.[35] By the same token, no angel was impervious to change or eternally consolidated in its goodness in the way that later theologians would determine to be the case. A lapse from blessedness could occur at any stage in a rational being's career with disastrous results. Since Origen believed in the preexistence of souls and their reincarnation, such transformations were generally the work of eons as opposed to years. But at the furthest extreme, "Angels may become men or demons."[36]

Origen is, however, determined to give unsullied angelic nature its due. While granting that humankind is, at the end of time, destined to judge certain (i.e., evil) angels, he objects to the tendency to elevate human over angelic nature: "It does not follow, as some suppose, that the men who are saved in Christ are superior even to the holy angels; for how can those who are cast by the holy angels into vessels [i.e., the body] be compared with those who cast them into vessels, seeing that they have been put under the authority of the angels?"[37] Nevertheless, we have already seen that Origen recognizes that the angelic nature of the bridegroom's companions is no guarantee against impropriety. Although his allegorical reading spares the bride the kind of molestation associated with the Watcher Angels, the possibility of angelic devolution is nevertheless present in the commentary. Thus when discussing how the bridegroom "as an apple tree stands out among trees of the wood," he does not hesitate to associate the companions with the lesser trees, which represent "those angels who have been the authors and promoters of every heresy."[38]

When Origen alludes to the Book of Enoch ("if anyone cares to accept that book as sacred") and the Watcher Angels elsewhere, his interpretative bent is characteristically allegorical and reflective of Gnostic sympathies—the very opposite of Tertullian's literal and historical understanding. Thus he introduces the possibility that the fall of the sons of God intimates "the descent of souls to bodies taking the phrase 'daughters of men' as a tropical expression for this earthly tabernacle."[39] This grim vision of embodiment is especially manifest in Origen's ominous interpretation of God's words, "My Spirit shall not remain in these men, because they are flesh" (Gen. 6.3), which advances a version of the very reading that kept Tertullian up at nights.[40] In the world of Origenist allegory, each entity assumes individual responsibility for having alienated God. The flesh may be condemned, but the daughters of men, and even Eve, only warrant personal blame versus blame for the plight of the entire human race.

The biblical dictum that "The letter killeth, but the spirit giveth life" resonated with Origen on multiple levels. To him, the "letter" represented an attachment to bodily things, in contrast to the intellectual pursuits of the spirit that led to God.[41] Origen manifests an undisguised contempt for readers who were incapable of going beyond the literal meaning, thus "refusing the labour of thinking, and adopting a superficial view of the letter . . . yielding rather in some measure to the indulgence of their own desires and lusts, being disciples of the letter alone."[42] Clearly, Origen valued the Song of Songs almost exclusively for its spiritual portent, stressing the purely allegorical nature of his own exegesis in the prologue to his commentary.[43] Yet he anticipated some of the potential pitfalls that the poem and commentary alike might present to the perverse reader who "not knowing how to hear love's language in purity and with chaste ears, will twist the whole manner of his hearing of it away from the inner spiritual man and on to the outward and carnal."[44] But Origen tended to associate such aberrant readings with those who were either spiritually inept or already corrupted by heresy.

If Origen's allegorical understanding of scripture seems to have had the potential to dissipate the blame that women frequently incurred through the literal, this possibility exists more in theory than in fact. In keeping with his Gnostic sympathies, Origen saw the division into the sexes as strictly post-lapsarian: the unfallen Adam and Eve lived in ethereal virginal bodies.[45] The female sex was clearly on the wrong side of the divide because Origen regarded ordinary women as representing a heightened embodiment. Carnal marriage, the lot of most women, left a taint on both body and soul, with none of the redeeming features that Tertullian had tentatively articulated to his wife.[46] Understandably Origen clearly wished to spare Christ's mother this degradation and may even have considered investing Mary with perpetual virginity.[47] When the downward mobility of rational beings was reversed, and each spiritual entity eventually found its own way back to God, the impurity of the body would be shed en route as a matter of course. The return could only be achieved through contemplation, however: an area in which women were believed to be handicapped by virtue of their bodies. Although it may take women longer, however, they too would eventually arrive at this universal destiny. In the meantime, virginity was considered a spiritual circumcision of the flesh that prefigured the angelic life, which was a realization of humanity's past and future state.[48]

The kind of literalism that would eventually fetter the persona of the bride of the Canticles to the intact virgin was very far from Origen's mind. And yet Origen was said to have performed an astonishingly literal enactment of "eunuchs for God" by castrating himself in his youth.[49] If true, the incident is a striking manifestation of Origen's conviction of the spirit's propensity—whether a celestial soul or an abstract metaphor—to devolve into the carnal. It also demonstrates how the letter can trump the spirit, even among the greatest of exegetes.

Athanasius, the Bride, and Her Mother-in-Law

The many commentaries on the Song of Songs attest to the power of an allegorical reading of the soul's marriage to Christ—one that would endure throughout the Middle Ages and beyond.[50] But it was not destined to exist solely on its allegorical plateau. Under subsequent commentators, the bride would be transformed into something of a hybrid between the spirit and the

letter—an applied allegory that provided flesh for spiritual bones. Athanasius (c. 296–373) played a crucial role in her incarnation. Though indebted
to Origen's theological vision in a number of ways, Athanasius nevertheless
perceived humankind's reconciliation with God in terms of an ascetical tam-
ing of the body as opposed to a contemplative ascent.[51] And so it is hardly
surprising that when Athanasius looked to the Song of Songs, he apprehended
a very different kind of bride—one destined to promote his own political
agenda. As David Brakke has so brilliantly demonstrated, Athanasius was
bishop of Alexandria during a time of intense ideological contestation. The
cultivation of women committed to virginity was an integral part of his ecclesiastical politics. His goal was to shape consecrated virgins into supporters of
his episcopacy, thereby separating them from teachers he deemed heterodox
and neutralizing potential resistance. But the virgins of Alexandria were an
active lot, attending the schools and participating in the latest theological debates. Thus for Athanasius, as for the North African theologians before him,
the *sponsa Christi* offered possibilities as a vessel of containment. To this end,
he attempted to place marriage to Christ on the same legal footing as secular
marriage. This alignment enabled his presentation of ascetic seclusion as the
normative condition for consecrated virginity.[52]

To institute the metamorphosis that would transform the feisty virgin
into a stay-at-home wife, Athanasius emphasized the wide-ranging prerogatives of husbands in the secular realm and appropriated them for Christ.
"With women of the world, all their hope is in their husband, and without
him they do nothing. How much more the virgin is completely obligated to
her husband and lord!"[53] Like many husbands, Christ had an irascible side
that was quick to jealousy. The attentive bride must therefore be careful never
to trigger a jealous response in her husband, which basically meant shunning
conversation with all men.[54] Because Athanasius sought to separate the virgins
from a corrosive theological milieu, the threat presented by male religious figures naturally loomed largest in his mind. Potentially like-minded ascetics are
thus warned to keep their distance with admonitions like "You will not dare to
approach a man's wife because of her husband's jealousy, lest you fall into his
hands. But you do not fear to approach a bride of Christ although you know
his fearful jealousy: 'It is a fearful thing to fall into the hands of a living God'
(Heb. 10.31)."[55] The practice of syneisaktism is presented as tantamount to
spiritual suicide, especially considering "how jealous a bridegroom he is, both
avenging sins swiftly and establishing tortures for a great variety of crimes."[56]

Athanasius's deployment of the Song of Songs supports this rigid disciplinary regime. In contrast to Origen's restless and self-motivated allegorical

bride who runs around unveiled, Athanasius's ideal for the flesh-and-blood virgin is "An enclosed garden . . . a sealed fountain" (Sg 4.12–13). She must accordingly be "enshrouded, separated, set apart, and withdrawn in every way, with a steadfast will, and to be sealed up, just as you were sealed by the Lord at the beginning as a servant." The "seal" in this context seems to be doing double duty, evoking the virgin's vow of chastity and tacitly signifying the seal of the hymen. Only the spiritual gardener (presumably Christ) may tread the cloister of her virginity, lest "ferocious foxes from some place or other destroy the beautiful clusters of grapes" (Sg 2.15).[57] The bride's face is ever veiled and revealed to the bridegroom alone.[58] "Cover your toes; let your veil fall down to your eyebrows; let your modesty conceal your fingers to your companions," Athanasius exhorts.[59] The virgin's speech should be reserved for praising God, so she seldom addresses anyone, except for her parents and guardians. On the rare occasion when she does speak, her voice is quiet and dovelike. Even when slandered, she maintains her silence, addressing herself to God alone, so that her "eyes are doves in addition to [her] silence" (Sg 4.1). The virgin rarely goes anywhere, except the house of God; her gait is sober and she does not greet people along the way. Her perfunctory attitude to food and clothing extends to bathing—which is deemed a necessity, not a pleasure. Again taking her cue from the dove, which is an adept at bathing in a basin, the virgin shuns public baths altogether.[60]

When, like the bride of the Canticles, the virgin preserves "all the trees, new and old" (Sg 7.14) for her husband, her loyalty will be rewarded by his warmest commendation: "Behold, you are beautiful, my beloved! Behold you are beautiful; your eyes are the eyes of doves" (Sg 1.5).[61] If she can but deport herself with the due modesty and decorum befitting Christ's bride, she will merit his assurance that "there is no defect in you" (Sg 4.7).[62] The regimen may be exacting, even as the solitude is unnerving, yet the virgin is not without powerful support. The very angels, "the image of whose purity you have," assist in her struggle against temptation, securing the safety of the bridal chamber like "the bed of Solomon, with sixty mighty men from the mighty men of Israel surrounding it, each one holding his sword and trained for war" (Sg 3.7–8).[63]

In the above passage, and elsewhere, the virgin is described as bearing the image of angelic purity—a condition "surpass[ing] human nature and imitating the angels."[64] But ultimately, Athanasius was more comfortable with the angels as guardians of virginity than as exemplars of a condition to which the virgins should aspire, let alone as the ultimate terminus for the virginal life. His evocations of the *vita angelica* are few, formulaic, and eschatological in nature.[65]

In fact, Athanasius's discourse on virginity tends to be even more prejudicial to angelic claims than was the case with Cyprian. This becomes especially apparent with the introduction of a new paradigm for virginity in Christ's mother, Mary, who is invested with a purity so enduring that it rivals the very angels. Although the concept of her perpetual virginity was already advanced in the Alexandrian school by Origen, Athanasius presents the first theological argument supporting this claim. Before such a project could be undertaken, however, it was a matter of first importance that the troublesome references to "Christ's brethren" be resolved, refuting the implications of Mary's post-incarnational fecundity that their unwelcome presence sustained. Athanasius thus adduces Christ's injunctions "Behold, your son" and "Behold, your mother" to Mary and John respectively, as definitive evidence that she had no other children, apart from Christ. "If she had had other children, the Saviour would not have abandoned them and given her to other people."[66] She may be a virgin, but she was also a caring mother.

With her enduring virginity intact, Mary's life of impeccable purity becomes a momentous precedent for humanity, which Athanasius trumpets forth. "You will remember what we said about virginity being beyond human nature, because in Mary its image appeared." Thus Paul's advocacy is based not on the law "but rather through the way of life of Mary."[67] Mary's important historical precedent retrospectively colors how the assertion that virginity is "beyond human nature" should be interpreted. One thing is immediately clear, however: with Mary's advent, angels are no longer the sole exemplars of virginal purity. It was through Mary that humanity managed to progress beyond its former limits, not only challenging the angelic monopoly over purity, but even partaking in a new kind of realized eschatology. When Athanasius declares that "the way of life of Mary [is] as pattern and image of the heavenly life," he is providing humanity with a fully human exemplar that is in no way derivative of angelic purity.[68]

Athanasius also implicates Mary in the skein of the Song of Songs, initiating the theological current that would progressively concede to Christ's mother the privileged, albeit sexually bewildering, position as her son's first and most blessed bride. Mary's multiple personae first begin to assert themselves when the consecrated virgin enters the bridal chamber to claim the "'kisses of [the bridegroom's] mouth' (Sg 1.2). Never relinquishing her grasp on the bridegroom, she proudly proclaims, 'I brought him to my father's house and to the chamber of her who bore me'" (Sg 3.4).[69]

As it turns out, the mother who "bore" her is also her new mother-in-law, the Virgin Mary. It is "she [Mary] with whom you [the consecrated virgin]

have (your) heritage," Athanasius intones. As this assimilation between virginal personae continues apace, it becomes progressively clear that Mary is
not only both mother and mother-in-law to the consecrated virgin but also a
potential rival for the affections of her son, the bridegroom—something that
seems never to have occurred to Origen.[70] So Athanasius's depiction of Mary's
virginal heritage is singular, indeed.

In paradise, Mary will meet the virgins, embrace them, and lead them
to the Lord. He, in turn, presents them to the Father, who pronounces, "'All
these have become and are like Mary, who is mine!'"[71] Finally the moment
arrives when the consecrated virgin is at last admitted to the wedding chamber
of the king (Sg 1.4)—the threshold to the permanent lap of spiritual luxury.
"Then she will live, being served by angels, judging those angels who have
sinned." The prerogative of judging angels has a scriptural basis (1 Cor. 6.3)
and had already been evoked by Tertullian and Cyprian. But the ancillary
capacity in which Athanasius presents the other angels (presumably the good
ones) is innovative, suggesting the extent to which the earthly purity that
Mary had pioneered has triumphed over the angelic.[72]

Being waited on by angels may be a tantalizing prospect, but the virgin
can only participate in Mary's exalted destiny in heaven if she first imitates her
exemplary behavior below on earth. To this end, Athanasius advises the virgin,
"it is best for you to recognize yourselves in her as in a mirror and so govern
yourselves."[73] And the dour model Mary offers is, not surprisingly, mirrored
in the regime Athanasius advocates for Christ's reclusive brides. Stripped of
all frivolity, Mary seldom went out, "remain[ing] in her house being calm,
imitating a fly in honey." Her emotions were perfectly regulated. No one was
permitted to approach her unless she was entirely veiled.[74] Mary was not accustomed to the presence of men of any kind, even male slaves, as the annunciation by the angel Gabriel is used to demonstrate: "it was as a man that
he came to her because he assumed human form. . . . And the girl, when she
heard that she was being addressed by a male voice, immediately became very
disturbed because she was not familiar with the male voice."[75] (In addition to
indicating Mary's commendable aloofness, Athanasius's decision to associate
the archangel with a potentially sexualized male slave is certainly salient, but
hardly complimentary to angelic virtue and dignity.) Mary was abstemious in
food and drink since "instead of wine, she had the teachings of the Saviour . . .
so that she too received the profitable teachings and said, 'Your breasts, my
brother, are better than wine'" (Sg 1.2).[76]

Under Athanasius's careful tutelage, the virginal ascetic's marriage to
Christ evolved into the ultimate disciplinary tool. His approach was destined

to become extremely popular. A series of pseudonymous treatises on virginity, bearing Athanasius's name, would develop in the East.[77] Of still greater importance for the present purposes, however, is the fact that Ambrose, one of the last Western writers still fluent in Greek, became the zealous standard bearer for Athanasius's message.

Though the Athanasian antidote to troublesome virgins was seemingly developed independently of the North African scene, it nevertheless complemented the Carthaginian impulses we have witnessed. A quick glance aside to a theological road not taken suggests that not every application of bride of Christ to women (real or imagined) need be freighted with the secular institution of marriage. Methodius of Olympus (d. ca. 311) is instructive in this context.[78] In his *Symposium*, a treatise on virginity modeled on Plato's dialogue, independent luminaries such as Thecla engage in an active life of ministry: "espoused and wedded to Him that by receiving from Him the pure and fertile seed of doctrine they might collaborate with him in the preaching of the gospel."[79] These "helpmates" to the heavenly groom are represented as engaging in the type of ministry that the Pauline tradition reserved for men, constituting a wistful evocation of prelapsarian gender roles that was fast disappearing.

Ambrose: The Minister at the Altar

Both Origen and Athanasius made deep inroads into the mindset of Ambrose, bishop of Milan—virginity's most important ideologue in the West. Between 377 and 393, Ambrose wrote four treatises on virginity, which were heavily imbued with nuptial imagery and reflective of the pivotal role he would play in both defining and stabilizing the consecrated virgin's identity as *sponsa Christi* in the Latin church.[80] *Concerning Virgins*, the longest and most influential of these treatises, is not merely inspired by but, arguably, ghostwritten by Athanasius, as Ambrose unabashedly (and silently) lifted entire portions from the Eastern father.[81] Of particular importance is Ambrose's adoption of the Virgin Mary as an ideal type of virgin and a model for all who came after. Once again she is presented as the lodestar of virginal deportment. "Consider how Mary was never found anywhere else except in her bedroom when she was sought (Luke 1.28). She will teach you what you should follow. She saw the angel in the shape of a man and feared in her heart, he was alien in aspect. . . . She teaches the modesty of solitude: and retirement is the training school for modesty."[82]

The rare occasion upon which Ambrose does deviate from Athanasius ironically seems to arise from too much deference to the Eastern doctor: an overinvestment in Athanasian doctrine that lent itself to exaggeration. The question of Mary's virginity is a case in point. Virginity as a female vocation had emerged as a hot-button issue in the fourth century. During this time a plethora of treatises on virginity appeared,[83] while active efforts to recruit virgins, not least of all by Ambrose and his circle, became more aggressive.

The proselytizers for virginity encountered considerable resistance. It is not that consecrated virginity was an entirely foreign concept to the Romans. They were familiar with the Vestal virgins, an institution that persisted well after the conversion of Rome until it was eventually disbanded in 394. The Vestal virgins were appointed to attend to the hearth of Rome, and their good behavior was essential for securing the nation's safety.[84] But the singularity of their position did not render them particularly helpful models for patrician daughters. Not only were their numbers strictly limited (they had reached their maximum count of seven during Ambrose's lifetime), but their position was anomalous on many other fronts. Although a virgin, the Vestal no longer partook of the subject role of the nubile daughter, but had advanced to a matron's status. Hence she dressed like a matron, but enjoyed certain important privileges that the average matron did not, such as freedom from guardianship, the right to own property, and the ability to make a will. At the age of thirty, her period of mandatory chastity was at an end and she was free to marry. But since the Vestals enjoyed a life of considerable luxury, and doubtless did not relish the prospect of subjection to a husband, few did marry. Yet despite the prestige associated with this important symbolic role, the Roman emphasis on progeny necessarily rendered the honor inherent in the Vestal's status something of a mixed blessing. For instance, Livy presented the vocation of Rhea Silvia, Rome's founding mother, as the malign scheme of a usurping uncle who convinced her to become a Vestal virgin.[85] In fact, by the late empire, patrician parents had become so reluctant to dedicate a daughter to such a life that the Vestals were forced to recruit plebeian women, or even the daughters of former slaves.[86]

Given this context, the antiascetical backlash that ensued was predictable as was its form: that marriage was the religious equal of virginity. But it would seem that efforts to stem the tide of sexual abstinence were as doomed as the near contemporary efforts of Julian the Apostate to revive paganism.[87] Thus when a monk named Jovinian heroically attempted to use the Song of Songs to dignify carnal marriage, Jerome was ready with an elaborate exegesis of the Song of Songs that corresponded to the mysteries of virginity.[88] Nor was the antiascetical camp insensible to the value of reclaiming Mary for the married, focusing on "the brethren of Christ" as evidence of an expanding holy family. Origen had subscribed to the popular view that "Christ's brethren" referred to the children of Joseph by a previous marriage.[89] Jerome took a different path. In 383 he wrote a treatise against a certain Helvidius, defending Mary's virginal status. Even though Jerome regarded Joseph as the guardian of Mary, and only a putative husband, he nevertheless closes off any suspicion that might arise from the long-term cohabitation of the holy couple by arguing that Joseph was committed to preserving his virginity, along with Mary.[90] Christ's brethren were the offspring of Mary, the wife of Cleopas.

Ambrose entered the fray of the chastity debates in 392 in response to the vocal skepticism expressed over Mary's perpetual virginity by Boninus, bishop of Sardica. Although siding with Jerome, Ambrose in no way shared in the latter's contempt of the married state. As Marcia Colish has recently demonstrated, Ambrose was deeply respectful of the conjugal unit and was a proponent of a reasoned marital chastity, based on mutual fidelity and restraint—a view that had much in common with the views of contemporary pagan moralists. Indeed, in the course of his efforts to dignify (and subtly Christianize) the marriages of the Old Testament patriarchs, Ambrose distinguished himself as one of the very few theologians who were prepared to apply the Song of Songs to carnal marriage.[91]

But Ambrose's deference to marriage did not displace the ascendancy of virginity in his mind, and he shared Jerome's conviction that Mary never lapsed from this higher path. Unlike his cantankerous contemporary, however, Ambrose was not prepared to lob rhetorical missiles at the married state. His theological strategy differed as well: rather than engaging in an exercise in genealogy, the theological alibi framing Jerome's rebuttal, Ambrose again chose to hug the contours of Athanasius's argument, focusing on the incident in which Christ entrusts Mary to John.[92]

Yet where Athanasius had stressed the absence of any natural offspring to whom Mary might have been entrusted at the time of the Crucifixion, Ambrose isolates the absence of her presumptive husband, Joseph, as proof of her virginity: "How could [Christ] take away a wife from her husband if Mary was joined in marriage, or knew the use of the marriage bed?" Parallel to Jerome's designation of Joseph as Mary's guardian rather than husband, Ambrose was likewise implying that their union was not a full-fledged marriage because it went unconsummated. The emphasis on consummation and its consequences is reflective of his legal background, which, as we shall see, is apparent in many of his initiatives on behalf of consecrated virginity. But this focus is also a harbinger of more grandiose claims. For while Athanasius and Jerome are content to establish Mary's virginity in terms of lifelong abstinence from all sexual relations, Ambrose is prepared to make the much bolder and more technical argument for Mary's intact virginity even after having given birth to Christ. Lighting on the passage in Ezekiel that alludes to "a closed door that will not be opened" (Ezek. 44.1), Ambrose then proceeds to apply the prophetic text to Mary. "What is this door, if not Mary, through whom Christ entered into this world when he was brought forth in the virgin birth, and did not unlock the generative cloister of her virginity. It remained a pure enclosure of chastity and an inviolate sign of enduring integrity."[93] Concrete as this claim may be, it was nevertheless constructed with the abstract tools of an exegete.

One of Ambrose's most striking contributions to the cult of virginity was the manner in which he mobilized the concept of *sponsa Christi*, doing full justice to its disciplinary potential. As one might glean from his commendation of Mary's reclusive ways, Ambrose found the Athanasian emphasis on seclusion particularly appealing, advancing it as the only lifestyle appropriate to Christ's bride. The "sealed garden" of the Canticles would become one of his favorite metaphors for virginity.[94] But once again, Ambrose was inclined to push the Eastern father's alignment of marriage to Christ with secular marriage still further. For it was Ambrose who brought the consecration of the virgin in line with secular marriage—affording it an official status of which Athanasius had only dreamed.[95]

A Roman wedding usually entailed two separate events: the formal betrothal, at which time consent was exchanged and the dowry conferred, and then the *deductio* when the bride is led to the husband's home wearing a red veil known as the *flammeum*, after which the union was sexually consummated.[96] Ecclesiastical involvement was generally limited to the betrothal: the *deductio* was frequently a bawdy affair and church personnel were warned to keep their distance. And so it is not surprising that the evidence for active church involvement is sparse and there is nothing approaching a liturgy of marriage before the seventh century.[97] In fact, Ambrose is among the earliest witnesses to an evolving Christianized ceremony when he refers to "sanctifying a marriage with a sacerdotal veiling and blessing."[98] Pope Siricius's contemporaneous letter to the archbishop of Tarragona (385) likewise refers to the veiling of the couple with a single veil and a nuptial blessing by a priest.[99]

Uniting the two-part ceremony associated with Roman marriage, Christ's bride pledged her troth and received her veil—a conflation suggestive of the *sponsa Christi's* peculiar position of remaining always a bride (since consummation was deferred to the afterlife), who had somehow acceded to the status of a wife. Furthermore, she received the *flammeum* not simply from her parents, as in a traditional Roman wedding, but at the hands of the bishop before the altar of the basilica on Easter day. This meant that a number of women would be veiled simultaneously, representing, as Ambrose would have it, a sterile fecundity: the day on which the church gave birth to many children without the pain of labor.[100]

It was none other than Ambrose who hijacked the symbols of carnal marriage and appropriated them for its spiritual counterpart. For although there is evidence of a public consecration of virgins from the mid-fourth century, it was distinguished by neither a veiling nor an episcopal blessing—the two features that, as Raymond d'Izarny notes, were to become the hallmark of virginal consecration under Ambrose.[101] In 377, only three years into his pontificate, Ambrose relates the story of a young noblewoman who confounded her kinsfolk's efforts to arrange a marriage by shoving her head under the altar of the church: " 'Can any better veil,' she said, 'cover me better than the altar which consecrates the veils themselves?' "[102] A contemporary description of the rite shows that by the end of the fourth century, episcopal veiling had become the norm: "The bishop has with words of prayer covered her holy head with the virgin's bridal veil, reciting the while the solemn sentence of the apostle 'I wish to present you all as a chaste virgin to Christ' (2 Cor. 11.2)."[103]

The profound synchronicity between the Christianization of secular marriage and the nuptialization of virginal consecration begs the question of what came first: What was the innovation versus the imitation? If the consecrated virgin beat her secular counterpart in the race for the altar, it is entirely possible that the privilege of a church wedding was first experienced by Christ's brides, a strange confirmation of the Gnostic position that carnal marriage is but a distant image of the true marriage with Christ. But no matter which type of wedding first emerged, there is little doubt that a single ceremony that simultaneously joined not one but many virgins with their spiritual bridegroom constituted the more gratifying spectacle.

Perhaps it is because Ambrose is sufficiently sanguine over his consolidation of the individual virgin's status as *sponsa Christi*, with its implied subjection, that he can afford to conflate virgins and angels so exuberantly, with not a trace of Athanasian reserve: "Chastity has made even angels. Whoever has preserved it is an angel; whoever has lost it a devil. . . . What shall I say of the resurrection of which you already hold the rewards: 'For in the resurrection they will neither be given in marriage, nor marry, but shall be . . . as the angels in heaven' that which is promised to you is already present with you."[104] Indeed, Ambrose is even prepared to throw in the Watcher Angels for good measure, unable to resist the counterpoint they provide for the virgins' glorious

ascent: "What a great thing it is that angels because of incontinence fell from
heaven into this world, that virgins because of chastity passed from the world
into heaven."[105] Such panegyrics read like a robust conceptualization of realized eschatology, indeed—a condition that the Carthaginian virgins had once
believed to be within their reach. And yet Ambrose's glib introduction of this
ideal is predicated on the fact that it is already drained of its vitality.

The impact of Athanasius's thought on Ambrose was immense and unmistakable. But the more subtle exegesis of Origen also had its effect. Athanasius had tended to use the Song of Songs to punctuate the rewards that
awaited the prospective bride, who managed to navigate his disciplinary regime successfully. While Ambrose did not eschew this pragmatic application,
he also wished to annex the contemplative dimension that was the hallmark of
Origen's reading and introduce it to the virginal lifestyle.[106] We have seen how,
as an advocate for virginity, Ambrose had a penchant for making the abstract
concrete through ritual. Yet Ambrose was not a crude literalist. No lesser a
reader than Augustine had acknowledged his debt to Ambrose's mystical reading of scripture.[107] Aspects of Ambrose's exegesis of the Canticles remain true
to the traditional reading of the soul's marriage with Christ. Hence his explanation of the episode when the watchmen (identified as angels) discover the
bride, wound her, and tear off her cloak: "that is, they removed the coverings
of bodily behaviour, so that in utter simplicity the mind could seek Christ.
For no one can see Christ who has assumed the garment of philosophy or,
specifically, the dress of secular wisdom."[108] But such allegorical readings did
not preclude the imposition of the bride of the Canticles on the consecrated
virgin. In *Concerning Virgins*, the virgin is described as "ever a bride, ever
unmarried, so that neither does love suffer an ending, nor [is] modesty lost,"
while the bridegroom's words "Thou art all fair, My love, and no blemish is in
thee [etc.]" is read as "the perfect and irreproachable beauty of a virgin soul,
consecrated to the altars of God."[109]

The occasional uneasy jockeying between the real virgin and the surreal
bride is tacitly acknowledged by Ambrose through disclaimer. For example,
his exhortation for the virgin to seek the bridegroom as ardently as the bride
of the Song of Songs is balanced by the reflection, "Of course the soul has no
gender in itself, but perhaps it is a feminine noun [*anima*] because when the
turbulence of the body acts violently upon it, the soul softens these bodily
assaults by its gentle love and a certain persuasive rationality."[110] This is an
interesting passage because, while decrying a gendered soul, it deploys the
traditional persona of the soul as female yet also as the rational placator to
a bumptious male body, reversing the classic Pauline association of man as

spirit, woman as flesh—however tacitly. Ultimately, however, the allegorical bride cannot elude her virginal double who shadows her every move.

However successful Ambrose's multileveled advocacy for virginity might have been, there was one group that seemed impervious to its allure: that was the parents of the patrician virgins in question, to whom Ambrose must have represented something of a Christian minotaur. His efforts at recruiting virgins were, by his own admission, met with vigorous resistance on his home turf.

Up until this point, the evidence has suggested that the identity of *sponsa Christi* may have been unilaterally and even coercively imposed on female virgins. But by Ambrose's day, the excitement surrounding the virgin's nuptials provides powerful testimony that many women were now clamoring for a quasi-marital status that an earlier age seem to have scorned. Furthermore, even if the patriarchs of Milan refused to be swept away by the virginal tsunami, removing their daughters from its relentless progress, Ambrose's fellow bishops saw to it that a steady stream of virgins continued to arrive from other Italian cities—young women eager to inaugurate their new life with the novel rite.[111] From a propagandistic perspective, it would be difficult to top the spectacle of virgins arriving from far and wide to espouse Christ publicly.

In the dual capacity of apologist and propagandist of the virginal vocation, Ambrose experimented with new methods for capturing the heady excitement for his readership. Discourses on virginity tended to be prolonged exhortations by dominant male voices to a necessarily mute and invisible female audience. Occasionally the writer might vary this pattern by a rhetorical trompe l'oeil. For instance, Athanasius attempts to interrupt the monotony of his own authorial voice with the introduction of yet another, usually more authoritative, male voice. Thus Athanasius attributed the Christological part of his exhortation to the venerable Bishop Alexander, presenting his own treatise as a reprise of Alexander's earlier address to the same group of virgins.[112] Ambrose follows suit when he attributes a parallel discussion on the merits of the bridegroom to an address made by Liberius, bishop of Rome, on the occasion of his sister's consecration as a virgin.[113]

But simulations of the female voice were much rarer. Methodius's *Symposium* was something of an exception here, though the pseudoplatonic form undercuts its realism. Jerome frequently enlivened his works by simulating the voices of "straw women" who required refutation. His letter to a mother and daughter in Gaul, each of whom were living ascetic lives with the cleric of their choice in preference to braving cohabitation with one another, is typical. Punctuated by expostulations like, " 'What then!' you will say, 'is it a crime to have a man of religion in the house with me?'" the fictive female is repeatedly trounced and presumably retreats somewhat abashed, only to rally with yet another fallible retort.[114]

In contrast, the treatise *Concerning Virgins* is a tribute to Ambrose's skill at camouflaging the drone of the male monotone: the strategic deployment of holy case studies provides credible simulations of the voice of female desire.[115] The fact that the work is dedicated to his sister, Marcellina, herself a consecrated virgin, represents mute, but potent, advocacy for sensitivity to the female vocation and the efficacy of his endeavor. Written on the feast of St. Agnes, the treatise fittingly opens with an account of her passion, embossed with a nuptial stamp that the heroine herself impresses. Thus Agnes premises her spirited rejection of carnal marriage on a precontract with Christ: "'It would be an injury to my spouse to look on any one as likely to please me. He who chose me first for Himself shall receive me. Why are you delaying, executioner?'"[116]

Parallel instances of female heroism are placed at pivotal junctures throughout the text, though not all of these case studies end in martyrdom. Ambrose concludes book one with the drama of the noble girl "within my memory," mentioned earlier, who was forced to veil herself. Contextually, this tale becomes martyrdom by association. Strategically, however, the situation was much more germane to the contemporary torments that a resistant family might visit on a determined virginal daughter. To the objections of her indignant relatives, the virgin in question responds, "'Do you offer me a bridegroom? I have found a better.'"[117] Her case is miraculously bolstered when the resistant family patriarch meets with a speedy death.

Such pastoral aggressions against obstreperous relatives culminate in the account of the pious suicide of St. Pelagia of Antioch, along with her entire family, bringing the third and final book to a close. The pious mother is depicted as leading Pelagia's sisters to the river to drown themselves in order to preserve their chastity: "'These victims, O Christ . . . do I offer as leaders of chastity, guides on my journey, and companions of my suffering.'"[118] Pelagia was not present at her family's ultimate sacrifice for some undisclosed reason. But when her chastity becomes likewise imperiled, Pelagia prepares to take her own life, rationalizing, "'God is not offended by a remedy against evil, and faith permits the act.'" Her last act was to don a bridal gown, "knowing she was going to a bridegroom, not to death."[119]

This final grisly *passio* is related in explicit response to the question of whether virgins should take their own lives to escape defilement—a problem allegedly raised by Marcellina. It was a vexed problem to which there was no clear answer. On the one hand, the tradition of the early church forbade believers from voluntarily seeking martyrdom.[120] On the other hand, the premium placed upon virginity seemed to justify such extreme measures. Ambrose is clearly inclined to the latter position. In the event that the story of Pelagia and her family left any room for doubt, Ambrose briefly alludes to the martyrdom of their own ancestress, Sotheris, who died defending her chastity and to whom Marcellina is described as being indebted for her vocation.[121] And with this moving instance of ancestral piety, the treatise comes to a close.

Again Ambrose as reader and exegete was no crude literalist. Yet *Concerning Virgins*, whether through its evocation of the female vocation via family history or imaginative declamations of quasi-legendary martyrs, makes a powerful argument for the importance of intact virginity in ratifying the legalistic bond between bride and bridegroom. One possible terminus for this degree of literalism might be the kind of gynecological examinations undertaken in Cyprian's time. Yet in 383, when the episcopal court in Verona attempted to address parallel charges of unchastity in a similar manner, Ambrose recoiled in horror and insisted on retrying the case himself.[122] The accused was a consecrated virgin named Indicia, who was living with her newlywed sister and her husband, Maximus.[123] The original source of friction between Indicia and her brother-in-law is unclear. Perhaps Maximus attempted to assert the traditional head of household's control over his unmarried sister-in-law and Indicia resisted. But whatever the trouble may have been, Maximus responded vindictively with the trumped-up charge that Indicia had secretly given birth to a child in a monastery and subsequently murdered it—a capital offense.[124] He even assembled a cluster of raffish individuals to support the charge: two lowborn women who claimed to be present at the monastery at the time and their confederates, Renatus and Leontius, "two men of iniquity," who were pivotal in spreading the rumor.[125]

Unfortunately, Indicia was peculiarly susceptible to even such far-fetched and spurious attacks. And it was the very seclusion intrinsic to the modus vivendi advanced by Ambrose that was the source of this vulnerability. Indicia's adherence to the virginal regimen was exemplary. Not only were some of her visitors "put out of doors and thrown out of her home," but she adamantly refused to make customary social visits to her female neighbors.[126] Through her studied lack of social graces, Indicia managed successfully to alienate the entire community, and no one came to her defense. When Maximus erected a wall to separate his wife's chambers from those of her sister, Indicia's isolation was complete.[127]

According to secular law, the punishment for calumny was exile. Thus the women who had apparently falsified their testimony by alleging their presence at the monastery, the sole witnesses to Indicia's alleged infamy,[128] took fright and then flight.[129] (But not before Renatus debauched one of them, at least according to the testimony of an anonymous female slave, whom he had seduced the night before.)[130] Maximus, clearly vulnerable to the same charges, flouted procedure by refusing to register his name as accuser.[131] This technicality did not stop him from circulating letters denouncing his sister-in-law, however.[132] The smear campaign was clearly successful because Syagrius was eventually pressured into demanding a gynecological examination either to affirm or dispel the charges against the maligned virgin. It is certainly one of life's bitter ironies that the defendant's unusual name, Indicia, literally means "evidence" or "proof."

It was at this point that Ambrose intervened. After he conducted separate interviews with Leontius and Renatus (the hapless Rosencrantz and Guildenstern of the tale), who hadn't even bothered to get their stories straight, the case fell apart.[133] Ambrose overturned the verdict, excommunicating Maximus along with his accomplices (who were, in fact, already excommunicated).[134] There is little doubt that this interference was resented by Bishop Syagrius. Yet Ambrose was deeply invested in this case on a number of levels and could not have mutely stood by.[135] A later edict by Emperor Honorius in 412 would require ecclesiastical courts to use the same procedure as Roman law.[136] In light of his own legal background, it is hardly surprising that Ambrose would anticipate a task that was very much in the spirit of his efforts to align virginal consecration with secular marriage. The many flagrant procedural transgressions of the Veronese court were therefore extremely irksome to Ambrose. Both secular and ecclesiastical law theoretically required two or three unbiased witnesses in order to bring an accusation.[137] In addition, the bishop of Verona clearly attempted to conceal the illicit specter of Maximus as accuser, "[who] avoided [using his] name because he lacked the proof,"[138] thereby countenancing what amounted to anonymous accusations. Syagrius's very insistence on a physical examination was, in the judgment of Ambrose, an indication that legal evidentiary criteria had been flouted: "for if you had proof, your sentence would never have required the inspection."[139] Nor did Ambrose concur with Syagrius's professed view that without a physical exam, Indicia's chastity must remain in doubt, objecting that the same logic would thus require that brides submit to parallel exams before marrying and virgins likewise be proved before consecration.[140]

There was also a personal dimension to this case. Indicia had stayed with his beloved sister, Marcellina, in Rome and was therefore something of a family friend. Perhaps hoping to assuage some of the indignities of the physical exam, Syagrius had apparently suggested that Marcellina be in attendance when it occurred. But when Ambrose relayed this request to Marcellina, "she piously objected to the inspection, but did not decline to give testimony that she apprehended nothing in Indicia but virginal modesty and holiness . . . and she hoped that the Lord Jesus Christ was reserving a part of the kingdom of God for herself along with [Indicia]."[141]

Perhaps the greatest cause of alarm for Ambrose, however, was the possibility that consecrated virgins should be subjected to such exams and that "the secrets of their genitalia" be so exposed.[142] Virginity is much more than a state of physical intactness, he argues. "Is there anything more holy in a virgin than her modesty? . . . The virgin of God aspires to the proof of [Christ's] bed, nor does she need any extraneous bridal gifts [*alienibus dotibus*] as [Christ] himself proves the virgin."[143] But despite a marked eagerness to move the discussion away from so graphic a discourse, many of the arguments that Ambrose garnered against the gynecological solution actually validated that kind of proof. Thus he objects that even the opinion of the most venerable experts leave considerable room for doubt. Furthermore, someone capable of conducting a gynecological exam would be just as adept at effecting an abortion. Or the expert could be bribed: Ambrose cites a contemporary instance, over which he is quick to clarify that he did not preside, where the chastity of a female slave was in doubt. A well-trained and well-to-do expert was hired precisely so there would be no suspicion of bribery, and yet the question still remained.[144]

The above line of argument runs counter to the author's main purpose by implying that these exams would be valuable if only they were definitive. And, admittedly, if one were to concede that the exams proffered conclusive legal proof of immorality, they might be said to serve some purpose. But Ambrose's case against physical exams wobbles into the fetishistic when he begins to obsess about the risks presented to the intact hymen. "There will be some woman . . . whether malicious or unskilled, [whose knowledge] the barriers of chastity surpasses, who through flagrant incompetence may annex a spotless chastity. You see in what danger you may lead the entire virginal profession when you decide to use an obstetrician: now not only is it endangered by a loss of modesty, but also by the uncertainty of the midwife [*obstetrix*]."[145] Ambrose further argues that the margin for error is widened by the fact that midwives were trained for assisting women giving birth, not for testing the chastity of virgins.[146] Thus Ambrose challenges the wisdom of placing trust in such uncertain evidence, especially when the defendants themselves so often furnished incontestable proof: "How can she conceal her [swelling] womb; how can she escape the look of a [pregnant] woman in the eyes of the healthy? How can she repress her cries when giving birth?"[147]

Eventually Ambrose shifts his emphasis on technical and manifest proofs to an argument regarding legal precedence. Initially, this is directed toward discrediting the use of midwives for so unprecedented a purpose. To this end, he adduces innumerable instances from scripture in which midwives preside over births and only births. "Why therefore are we opposed to virgins being inspected? What I have never read, I will not apply in the interim; nor in my judgment is it true." With a visit from a midwife "parturition is suspected . . . not an examination of chastity." Thus when Ambrose exclaims, "far be it that a virgin should know [*noscere*] a midwife," the verb carries with it every bit of the double entendre characteristic of biblical usage.[148]

This response seems disingenuousness on a number of levels. In the first place, Ambrose, for all his legal expertise, scrupulously ignores the precedent set in the treatment of the suspect virgins in Cyprian's time, except perhaps in the inflected and rather contradictory comment, "We will leave [physical examinations] to those women, if they are pursued by grievous calumny, oppressed by witnesses, strangled by legal problems; to it they can fly to offer themselves up for inspection as testimony. . . . Nevertheless she is in a bad way when the prerogative of the flesh is preferable to that of the mind. It is a sign of bad morals when virginity is expressed by the hymen [*corporis claustro*]."[149] Moreover, Ambrose presents the possibility of such an exam as a potential advantage when he was writing on the subject of widows dedicated to God: "For a virgin, though in her also character rather than the body has the first claim, puts away calumny by the integrity of her body, a widow who has lost the assistance of being able to prove her virginity undergoes the inquiry as to her chastity not according to the word of a midwife, but according to her own manner of life."[150] And if Ambrose's contemporary, John Chrysostom, is to be taken at his word, midwives were all too often summoned to perform precisely the sorry office of ascertaining intact virginity, at least in the Eastern Church. Thus in his condemnation of syneisaktism he complains, "There is a daily running of midwives to the virgins' houses, as if they were rushing to women in the throes of labor, not to deliver one giving birth (although even this has occurred on some occasions), but in order to discern who is violated and who is untouched, just as people do with slaves they purchase. One virgin readily consents to the examination but another resists it and by her very refusal goes out disgraced even if she has not been deflowered."[151] According to this grim standard, Indicia's case was already lost.

Ambrose's argument against legal precedents becomes still more strained retrospectively in light of his later emphasis on Mary's postpartum virginity, a position he will urge less than ten years after the Indicia judgment. For the suppressed subtext to any discussion of Mary's perpetual virginity is the tale of the two midwives, which first appears in the apocryphal, but immensely popular, *Protoevangelium of James*, which most scholars date to the mid-second century, long predating any more formal theological claims. According to this account, the midwife who assisted in Christ's birth expresses wonder to her colleague, Salome, over the miracle of Mary's postpartum virginity: "Salome, Salome, I have a strange sight to relate to thee: a virgin has brought forth—a thing which her nature admits not of." In a tasteless analogue to doubting Thomas, Salome responds, "As the Lord my God liveth, unless I thrust in my finger, and search the parts, I will not believe that a virgin has brought forth. And the midwife went in, and said unto Mary: Show thyself; for no small controversy has arisen about thee."[152] The similarities in the approaches of Salome and Syagrius are striking. Unlike Indicia, however, Mary was seemingly prepared to comply, for when Salome, good to her word, attempts to insert her finger into Mary's vagina, the investigative hand is immediately blasted by miraculous fire. It continues to burn until she testifies to Mary's virginity and recognizes Christ.[153]

Whether acknowledged or not, any argument for the doctrine of Mary's perpetual virginity is ultimately rooted in the claims of the *Protoevangelium*. It was on the basis of its testimony that the brethren of Jesus were, in fact, sons of Joseph by an earlier marriage that Origen had first been inspired to argue her perpetual virginity.[154] Moreover, the question of her postpartum integrity, which Athanasius did not raise but Ambrose argues with zest, is indebted to precisely the kind of painfully explicit gynecological examinations to which Ambrose objects and to an application of midwifery that he not only scorns but claims to be unprecedented.

Sponsa Christi and the Incarnational Logic of Tarnished Goods

During the years that separated Tertullian from Ambrose, the boundaries securing the virgin state were completely redrawn. The danger of angelic miscegenation had largely receded because few patristic authors were prepared to accept Genesis 6 literally. There were still a handful, however. Tertullian would have been gratified to know that Sulpicius Severus (d. 430) was not only prepared to credit the angelic fall but blamed virgins for the debacle resulting in "angels gradually spreading wicked habits, corrupt[ing] the human family, and from their alliance giants are said to have sprung, for the mixture with them of beings of a different nature, as a matter of course, gave birth to monsters."[155] But Sulpicius was out of step with contemporary theology. Over the course of the fourth century, the Book of Enoch was definitively rejected by central figures like Hilary of Poitiers, Jerome, and, most importantly, Augustine.[156] Meanwhile the dangerous allusion in Genesis retreated into allegory. The anonymous antifeminist treatise *On the Celibacy of the Clergy*, which condemned the practice of syneisaktism and hence frequently attributed to Cyprian, is a case in point. Priests inveigled into these perilous unions were compared to angels lured to earth by the seductive daughters of men.[157] Western theologians would continue to assume the exegetical burden of Jacob, wrestling the angelic sons of God down from heaven to their own level. Augustine suggested that the sons of God were simply men who had lapsed into concupiscence.[158] Likewise, John Cassian (d. after 430) argued against the possibility of spiritual entities having intercourse with carnal women, reasoning, "[I]f this could ever have literally happened how is it that it does not now also sometimes take place?" He thus interpreted the sons of God as "the stock of the righteous Seth" and the daughters of men as belonging to the lineage of Cain.[159]

The dismissal of the angelic-human hybrid also coincided with a tacit disinvestment in the anticipated gender transformation originally associated with the *vita angelica*, leaving the *sponsa Christi* as the core identity for the consecrated virgin. This is not to say that other groups of Christians did not lay claim to the title. Mathew Kuefler has argued that the clergy identified themselves as *sponsae* in order to stress their total submission to God. In St. Benedict's famous rule for monks (ca. 529) there were several tacit efforts to align the monk's formal profession with marriage. The fact that the monk gives himself to God, promising that "he will not have even his body at his disposal," seems to allude to the conjugal debt (1 Cor. 7.4).[160] Moreover, the offering of a child oblate could also be construed in a matrimonial mode. Not only does the provision of gifts correspond to the dowry, but the child's hand is wrapped in the altar cloth—a feature present in some of the earliest extant rites for both the secular marriage of a virgin and her consecration.[161] Yet such oblique provisions were no match for the female virgin's hold on this image.

In short, the motive force behind Tertullian's half-hearted and apologetic application of the trope *sponsa Christi* was rejected, and the expedient itself was eagerly embraced, redoubled, and elaborated upon.[162] The virgin's erstwhile freedoms were vanquished and her singularity increasingly measured against a wifely grid. We have seen in the case of the Vestal virgin that the accordance of the matron's position symbolized an advancement in prestige and independence. But this did not pertain to the Christian virgin who was, in the words of Ambrose, "ever a bride, ever unmarried, so that neither does love suffer an ending, nor [is] modesty lost." Always becoming, but never fully acceding to, the status of matron, the Christian virgin never comes of age. But this does not inhibit a full participation in the most restrictive aspects of wifely deportment. Hence Ambrose frames his injunction for virginal silence as, "How can you be surprised about what I say concerning the virgin when a woman is ordered to be silent? (1 Tim. 2.11)," appealing to one of the most restrictive standards of wifely deportment in the entire New Testament.[163]

From a certain perspective, church authorities were justified in prescribing so restrictive a role for the *sponsa Christi* insofar as the honor of the church was hanging in the balance. For once the consecrated virgin assumed the persona of Christ's *sponsa*, she simultaneously became the ultimate type for the church as virgin bride, a privilege premised on her physical perfection. According to the monk Fulgentius (d. 532), "in other faithful members, who believe in God correctly according to the rule of the Catholic faith and observe conjugal and widow's chastity . . . the Church gains a spiritual virginity only; but in these members in whom he guards the correct faith in such a way that they keep the flesh untouched by any sexual intercourse, the more the Church has a fuller virginity, the more fully and perfectly it possesses the name of the same virginity." By the same token, her physical intactness recommends her as a compelling *figura* of the soul's marriage with Christ: "in the union of spiritual matrimony, the soul is joined with Christ the spouse in such a way that the flesh is also preserved intact."[164] For Fulgentius, virginity is imbued with a virtue so powerful that he perceives it as "the principal gift of spiritual charism" to be prized above all the others—be they prophecy, active ministry, teaching, holy exhortations, generosity, diligence, or acts of mercy (Rom. 12.6–8).[165]

Despite such accolades, by the end of the patristic age the consecrated virgin had more in common with a matron than an angel. And as in carnal marriage, the bride's physical intactness was essential in closing the deal. Many authorities shared Tertullian's conviction that sexual congress involved a different kind of transformation—a physical mixing of bodies that struck at the heart of the pristine individual integrity required for Christ's bride. Thus Ambrose asks, "What is so true as inviolate virginity, whose little sign of modesty guards the genital barrier of integrity? But when a young girl is deflowered through conjugal use, when she mixes with an alien body, she loses what is her own. For that which we are born is true; not what we change into; what we have taken from the Creator, not what we assume from sex."[166] The woman who was forcibly violated would participate in the same metamorphosis with her assailant. The primitive meaning of *stuprum*, in fact, designates the indelible taint resulting from just such a violation, marking the woman forever.[167]

To a mindset so markedly predisposed in favor of virginity, and so repelled by the admixture incumbent upon sexual intercourse, it would be difficult to avoid the conclusion that a forcibly violated virgin had suffered a permanent spiritual demotion. The sentence may seem unjust, but Rome was quite literally built upon such instances of injustice. The Vestal Rhea Sylvia gave birth to Romulus and Remus after having been raped by Mars.[168] A parallel violation of the Roman matron Lucretia resulted in the expulsion of the Etruscan kings. Rhea's end was straightforward enough: her uncle threw her in the Tiber. But Lucretia's anguish over her involuntary lapse from the Roman ideal of the *univira* prompted her suicide.

Livy's account of the Lucretia legend encapsulates the divided legal opinions of the period. Lucretia's view of the situation is the more traditional one. While she maintained "my body only has been violated; my heart is guiltless," she nevertheless refused to become a legal precedent: "Though I acquit myself of the sin, I do not absolve myself from punishment; not in time to come shall ever unchaste woman live through the example of Lucretia." And, in fact, the intractable pollution laws that governed the concept of stuprum determined that Lucretia was no longer a fitting mate. She could either become a prostitute or take the high road by ending her own life, as she did. In contrast, her relatives, articulating the more progressive position that nullifies enforced consent, attempt to exonerate her, blaming Tarquin and assuring her "that the mind is what sins, not the body, and where there is no intention there is no guilt."[169]

Lucretia's fatal, but noble, choice captured the patristic imagination. Despite lip service to chastity as a state of mind, the church fathers ultimately validated Lucretia's extreme form of self-critique, intuiting that a violated bride of Christ would lose considerable ground with her spiritual groom. We have already seen that Ambrose had advised his sister and her community that suicide was an acceptable remedy for a virgin whose chastity was imperiled. Jerome, his companion in arms campaigning for virginity, heartily concurred: his notorious *Against Jovinian* argues the superiority of chastity over marriage by demonstrating that even pagans were sensible of this truism. Expanding the more modest list that had concluded Tertullian's *Exhortation to Chastity*, the treatise offers a series of pagan chaste exemplars. This includes a veritable catalogue of women who ended their lives to avoid being married against their will or forcibly violated, vindicating Jerome's puckish inversion of Paul (1 Cor. 7.9) that it was better "to burn rather than to marry."[170]

Augustine initially seemed to shy away from the contentious question of the demands placed upon an individual in the preservation of her chastity. When the priest Victorianus wrote Augustine, describing the various depredations of the Germans, including the lamentable abduction of holy women, Augustine responded by pointing to the many hagiographical instances in which God had intervened on behalf of a given saint. Such examples demonstrate that "the servants of God are not deserted by their lord. Who knows but that the omnipotent and merciful God may wish to perform his marvels through these women in that barbaric land?" Warming to the subject, Augustine cites the recent example of a nun who was led away captive "but restored to her relatives with great honor." Apparently, the three brothers who were her abductors were suddenly stricken ill. Their mother appealed to the captive virgin, who obligingly saved the brothers through her prayers.[171] But Augustine all too soon turns from his subject in favor of a related problem (which to this callow reader hardly seems of parallel concern): How can the abducted women manage to practice their faith in foreign climes without benefit of churches or priests?[172]

Augustine's letter to Victorianus was written in November of 409. The political instability of the empire, however, rendered the conundrum of the violated virgin less hypothetical by the moment. In a matter of months, Rome was sacked—an event that inspired Augustine's magnum opus *City of God* and compelled him to address the problem of the forcibly violated virgin with less equivocation. Apparently there were certain critics of Christianity who saw the rape of consecrated virgins as an indictment of the faith.[173] It was in this context that Augustine invoked the specter of Lucretia, embracing the moderate view voiced by her relatives. Although this stance was much more compassionate than the position articulated by some of his ecclesiastical colleagues, it was also in many ways more problematical. Certainly Augustine was one author who could be relied upon to take seriously the proposition that chastity was primarily a state of mind, one that prevailed over simple physical integrity. Thus he unequivocally condemns suicide in instances of imperiled chastity, denying that a woman's essential integrity can be polluted without the compliance of the will. He presents this premise in striking terms when discussing Lucretia's plight: "Here was a marvel: there were two, and only one committed adultery."[174] Nevertheless, Augustine does concede that even a resisting body must inevitably experience pleasure in the sex act, basing his assumption (one can only assume) on the mechanics of male orgasm and thus setting an unfortunate precedent in Christian letters by implying that a woman invariably enjoys rape. Even so, the woman's mental integrity was nevertheless safe, provided she refused her consent to the pleasure.[175]

In short, there are two basic, but opposing, lines of patristic counsel directed to the woman whose chastity was imperiled. Augustine, who condemned suicide under any circumstances, even daring to challenge Lucretia's choice, argued that a nonconsenting body was incapable of sin.[176] But his letter to Victorianus did offer the threatened virgin the possibility of a miracle; failing that, his *City of God* speculates on the prospect of a transcendent mental purity. Then there was the suicidal solution championed by Ambrose and Jerome, which promised the double palm of virgin and martyr to those who died in defense of their chastity. As is already apparent in the virginal exempla of Ambrose, this dramatic solution was and would remain the darling of hagiographers. As the emphasis on the intact body continued to gain momentum, the consecrated virgin was increasingly expected to avert Lucretia's lot by anticipating her end. Entire communities of nuns were eulogized for allegedly practicing self-mutilation or suicide to avert rape by pagan marauders, a pattern discussed by Jane Schulenburg.[177]

An ancillary feature of this counsel was to make parents and guardians proactive on behalf of the purity of their virginal charges, a trend also anticipated by Ambrose in his commendation of Pelagia's mother who oversaw the death of her daughters with pious satisfaction. That such a solution could also manifest itself in a more passive-aggressive approach is apparent in Hilary of Poitiers's alleged solicitude for his daughter, Abra. According to Venantius Fortunatus, a young and handsome nobleman sought Abra in marriage during Hilary's exile from Poitiers. Hilary, miraculously apprised of the suit, responded with a letter to Abra, promising to provide her with a spouse "whose nobility would ascend to the heavens, whose beauty outstrips comparison with roses and lilies, whose eyes illuminate the lights of gems." He concluded with the warning that she was already bespoken and the bridegroom was on his way.[178] Eventually, however, Hilary decided to leave nothing to chance and prayed for Abra's death, which God granted. When the wife wished to follow her daughter and besought her husband to provide the same service on her behalf, he was happy to oblige.[179]

With regard to forcibly violated virgins, both church and state united in ensuring that the abductor would, in turn, receive the harshest penalties possible.[180] According to the Council of Tours (567), his action rendered him a permanent excommunicate who was denied last rites. Any priest who knowingly gave him communion would be suspended for a year.[181] The Theodosian Code, moreover, treated the rape of a consecrated virgin or chaste widow as a capital offense.[182] But the woman herself, who bore the heavy responsibility of representing the virgin church and, hence, the honor of the Christian community, was likewise profoundly stigmatized for choosing life over in-violate chastity. The anonymous treatise *On the Fall of a Consecrated Virgin*, wrongly attributed alternately to Ambrose or Jerome, laces keening lament with bitter vituperation. The letter was written to a certain Susanna, who had seemingly been raped and abducted. But she definitely put herself in the wrong by remaining with her assailant.[183] Her anonymous critic perceives her spiritual adultery as far worse than its carnal counterpart because the secular bride would only have ten witnesses or so at her nuptials; Susanna married Christ "amid innumerable witnesses of the church, in the presence of angels and the ranks of heaven."[184] By "accept[ing] the holy veil . . . she united herself with an immortal husband."[185] To make matters worse, Susanna was, perhaps, already culpable prior to her abduction. Three years earlier she was the object of a smear campaign similar to what Indicia had endured. In this case, the anonymous cleric, in conjunction with Susanna's father, struggled valiantly for her vindication, as had Ambrose before him. But Susanna's subsequent fall prompted him to condemn her in retrospect, aghast by her purported du-plicity. "With great daring and temerity, untroubled by your conscience, you imagined that you were even able to deceive God."[186] Only lifelong penance could possibly save her from damnation.[187]

The anonymous cleric was not alone in his harsh assessment. Pope Siricius (d. 399), who set an important precedent by issuing the first papal decretals, drew no distinction between voluntary and involuntary lapses in virginity, arguing that "whether she was abducted or willing, she agreed to go to a man in a perverse condition."[188] Like the Old Testament adulteresses who were stoned for their perfidy (Deut. 22.24), Siricius wants to ensure that their vir-ginal counterparts also "are slain spiritually." Dead in spirit, it would take years of penance before the fallen virgin could reenter a church. This punishment applies not only to the consecrated virgin who had broken her vows but also to the woman who was not yet veiled but had the private intention of being veiled, on the grounds that such propositions constitute clandestine marriages (*furtivae nuptiae*).[189]

Among the more forgiving authorities, involuntary lapses from the chaste ideal continued to receive harsh treatment. Leo I maintained, "Those hand-maids of God who have lost their chastity by the violence of barbarians, will be more praiseworthy in their humility and shame-fastnesses, if they do not venture to compare themselves to undefiled virgins. For although every sin springs from desire, and the will may have remained unconquered and unpol-luted by the fall of the flesh, still this will be less to their detriment, if they grieve over losing even in the body what they did not lose in the spirit." These virgins, however, are not in so desperate a way as to be "degraded to the rank of widows," and although "participation in the sacraments is not to be denied them," they should no longer "be reckoned in the holy number of undefiled virgins."[190]

Even Augustine, who championed the idea that there was no sin without consent, couldn't resist speculating that God would only have permitted such a fall if the women were in some way culpable. "It is possible that those Christian women, who are unconscious of any undue pride on account of their virtuous chastity, whereby they sinlessly suffered the violence of their captors, had yet some lurking infirmity which might have betrayed them into a proud and contemptuous bearing, had they not been subjected to the humiliation that befell them in the taking of the city."[191] In such a case, rape was a harsh, but salubrious, lesson—one that would serve her right in every possible sense.

CHAPTER 3

The Barbarian Queen

Although perhaps ironic, and from some perspectives even tragic, the progressively embodied nature of female spirituality is hardly surprising: the cultural laws of gravity favoring virginity were strong, making it virtually impossible for the Latin fathers to set aside their preoccupation with physical intactness. It was part of the classical heritage. The hearth of Rome was presided over by Vestal virgins. Any sexual lapse on the part of a Vestal was considered a capital offense, which from the fifth century BCE meant being buried alive.[1] Plutarch remarks on how "the Romans . . . give their maidens in marriage when they are twelve years or even younger. In this way more than any other it was thought both their beds and their disposition would be pure and undefiled when their husbands took control of them."[2] The *Didascalia apostolorum*, an anonymous pastoral work of the early third century, likewise encourages early marriage, indicating that contemporary Christian communities shared a similar philosophy.[3] The veneration of the univira is on a continuum with this concern:[4] according to Tertullian, only the virgin was granted the bridal *flammeum*.[5] This distinct prejudice against second marriages would only become exacerbated by the conversion to Christianity.[6] The New Testament explicitly stated that the bishop should only have been married once (1 Tim. 3.2). Eventually second marriages (or a single marriage to a nonvirgin) became an impediment to orders.[7]

The Barbarian presence tended to ratify the late antique emphasis on virginity in two basic ways. The first was indirect. The very creation of an environment in which consecrated virginity was at risk tended to heighten fear for its safety. A number of the early Barbarian codes paid scant deference to consecrated virginity, and those that did applied heavy sanctions, hence emphasizing the problem. Until the seventh century, the Frankish kings were inclined to condone the unions resulting between virgins and their captors.[8] Such relations were roundly condemned by the clerical elite as a matter of course. And yet they seem to have persisted well into the Carolingian period, or perhaps recurred with the gradual dissolution of the central authority. Hincmar of Reims (d. 882) attests that men were still abducting (*raptus*) unmarried women, widows, and nuns with impunity, confident that these unions could be ratified after the fact. From Hincmar's perspective, this practice was never condoned by any law, human or divine, and warranted the death penalty, in keeping with the practice of the ancient Jews and Romans alike. Moreover, any victim who ultimately gave her consent to the illicit union would suffer the same consequences.[9] With respect to the rape of nuns in particular, parents who subsequently furnish consent should be excommunicated for life.[10] Thus the turbulence that appeared in the wake of the Roman Empire's demise, and women's heightened vulnerability, provided new motives for the strict sequestration of religious women. The monastic rule of Caesarius of Arles (d. 540), the earliest written exclusively for women, is a case in point, interpreting claustration in the most literal sense possible.[11]

Second, many of the peoples that overwhelmed the empire also placed a high premium on female virginity, a characteristic noted by Tacitus already in the first century in his *Germania*.[12] The focus on lineage dictated that women who had been violated, whether forcibly or not, should be considered worthless for reasons that resonate with the ancient Romans' concept of stuprum. In the laws of the recently converted Kentish king Æthelbert, the first redaction of Barbarian codes, a rapist had to provide the offended husband with a brand new wife.[13] Sometimes the aggressor himself seemed ready to recognize the heinousness of his crime. Gregory of Tours recounts how the dying Duke Amalo defended the virgin who had dealt him a mortal blow from his avenging servants with his dying words: "Stop, stop, I tell you! It is I who have sinned, for I tried to rape this girl! She only did this to preserve her virginity."[14]

Virginal prestige continued to be reflected liturgically. The earliest extant rite for the consecration of the virgin dates back to the mid-seventh century, but it is not until the tenth century that we are finally provided with more than prayers and are given directions regarding the way the ceremony actually unfolded.[15] In the ordo from the influential *Pontificale romano-germanicum* (ca. 950), the virgin's relatives present her to the bishop, placing her hand on the altar. As with the secular virginal bride, the hand of the future *sponsa Christi* is covered (in her case with the altar cloth). The bishop takes her hand (still in the altar cloth) and leads the others in the triumphal antiphon: "I am married to him whom the angels serve, whose beauty the sun and moon admire."[16] The virgin's veil and religious habit are placed on the altar and blessed with a series of prayers.[17] She retires to change her clothes, returning with a burning candle in each hand—suggesting that she is one of the virgins who was prepared for the bridegroom while simultaneously paralleling the practice of secular marriage rites.[18] A cleric intones the introit for Mass. After the reading of the gospel, the virgin prostrates herself before the altar.[19] The bishop then invokes God, presenting virginity as the antidote to the "diabolical fraud" that vitiated our bodies. He beseeches God for help, lest the palm of continence be seized (*rapiat*) from the virgin's proposed way of life, that God's handmaiden may run to join the choir of angels and be counted among the wise, not the foolish, virgins.[20] The bishop then questions the postulant about her virginal resolve, anticipating the reception of the veil.[21] She also receives two other tangible symbols of the union: a wedding ring and a wreath. The crowning with a wreath coincides with the ancient marriage rites of the Eastern Church.[22] The bishop then levels a solemn ban against anyone who interferes with the virgin's vocation.[23]

These rites continue to display some of the earlier rhetoric that associated virginity with the *vita angelica* and as a remedy to the fall. The virgin is depicted as repairing "the innocence of our first origin." Her purity, "drawing us to the similitude of angels," transcends the "law of nature." But such imagistic feints are contained by the larger matrimonial strategy at play. While scorning carnal marriage, the virgin nevertheless aspires to the mystery (*sacramentum*) of marriage: "they do not imitate what is done in marriage, but love what marriage signifies."[24] She partakes of the peerless status of the originary virgin, Mary. Already in the most ancient extant rite of consecration, the virgin is described as binding herself to a husband who is both "spouse of perpetual virginity, just as he is the son of perpetual virginity"—an inflected reference to Mary.[25] As the ritual evolved, the veil is assumed "out of love of your blessed parent, namely Mary ever-virgin." Thus Mary could be seen as a kind of proxy for the parents' traditional bestowal of the *flammeum* according to Roman custom.[26] For the consecration of a virgin who lives out her private vow of chastity in her home, it is Mary's vestment that will keep her from stain, ensuring that she will eventually be numbered among the wise virgins who keep their inextinguishable lamp burning for the bridegroom.[27]

Through what now might seem like a bizarre liturgical swindle, the drama of the virgin's celestial marriage to Christ entirely overshadowed the institution of marriage in this period. Paul had contended that marriage symbolized Christ's union with the church. But in an interpretive move anticipated by the Gnostics, theologians understood this figuratively, hence presenting carnal marriage as a bad copy of the celestial mystery—a bad copy necessary for

illuminating the full measure of virginity's glory. And, indeed, this position
was arguably sustained from the perspective of liturgical development: the
earliest rituals redacted for either type of wedding only emerged in Carolingian times. And, as suggested earlier, which came first is as inscrutable as the
paradigmatic chicken and egg.[28]

But amid such confusion, one thing was certain: the two rites were mutually exclusive. With the exception of unconsummated unions, any woman
who had participated in the terrestrial ceremony was barred from the celestial.
In the context of a monastic institution, this placed matrons and widows at
a distinct disadvantage. Ineligible for the consecration that distinguished the
true virgin bride of Christ, the erstwhile secular bride was seen as a lesser bride,
or perhaps even a concubine, and was eventually subsumed under categories
of deaconess or consecrated widow. Although the history of these two offices
in the early church is fragmentary and contested, they were clearly once perceived as positions of honor and authority.[29] But by the time of the Germanic
kingdoms, the two were gradually collapsed into a frequently undifferentiated
grey zone that accommodated the formerly married woman.[30] Most of the
remaining ceremonies that inducted women into these categories share in an
apologetic, penitential tone.[31] From the time of the very earliest liturgies of
marriage, the nuptial blessing was withheld from second marriages.[32] Indeed,
in the early penitentials, couples were assigned penance for remarrying.[33] The
ordo for the would-be deaconess asks that God lead the woman "to pardon
that she should merit to be cleansed from all filth of trespasses and reconciled
to you."[34] The supplication on behalf of the widow beseeches God to "concede
to her the fruit of chastity, that she not be mindful of past desires [antiquarum
voluptatum]. May she be ignorant of the inflamed desires of the vices."[35] Both
the deaconess and the widow are compared with the prophetess Anna (Luke
2.36–37), whose alleged seven years in marriage was balanced by almost eighty
years of chaste widowhood "mixing days and nights with prayers and fasts"
until she received the gift of prophecy on the occasion of Christ's presentation
in the temple. The primacy of virginity, and its hundredfold reward, is tacitly
acknowledged when God is besought to "give to this your servant [who has
received] the thirty fruit among the married, the sixty fruit of the widowed."[36]

But the liturgical stigmatization of these women was above all signified
by the manner in which the deaconess and widow were veiled, which reflected
their inferior standing in both this life and the next. The virgin's consecration
occurred on auspicious days: preferably Easter or Ephipany or, failing that, a
feast of one of the apostles or, at the very least, a Sunday. The deaconess was

ordained in Lent.[37] Virgins were sometimes veiled before the reading of the gospel, paralleling the ordination of the clergy, while widows were invariably veiled after.[38] According to some authorities, the virgin's *flammeum* should be distinct from the veils of her lesser sisters, adorned with a cross that, tradition had it, dated back to the time of Pope Soter (d. ca. 174).[39]

Perhaps of greatest importance, however, was that the episcopal imposition of the veil was reserved for virgins alone. An oft-cited canon of Pope Gelasius (d. 496) states explicitly that no bishop should dare attempt to veil a widow, that such a practice is authorized by neither divine nor canon law.[40] Nonvirgins were generally required to veil themselves with a veil that had been previously blessed by the bishop. Thus in the consecration of the deaconess the woman takes the veil from the altar and, in the presence of all, imposes it on her own head with the simple declaration, "I am married to him."[41] Alternatively, the widow could also be veiled by a simple priest, even though this method of consecration was controversial.[42] In 567, the Council of Tours argued vociferously against the veiling of widows. "Everybody knows that a blessing of the widow is never to be read in any canon law books, because her proposition [of chastity] alone ought to suffice for her." The council goes on to cite Avitus, bishop of Vienne: "the consecration of widows, who are called deaconesses, we totally abrogate from all our religious practices."[43]

This is not to deny the occasional advantage afforded widows by the expectation that they veil themselves. When threatened with remarriage, the widowed Frankish noble Rictrude (d. 688) was said to have surprised her suitor-cum-dinner guest by covering her head with a previously blessed veil that she happened to have secreted in her bosom.[44] But this refreshing anomaly aside, the loss of virginity did not simply represent a spiritual demotion but also was laden with important practical consequences in religious life. An overwhelming consensus maintained that the abbess of a religious community should be an intact virgin. Indeed, this expectation was reflected in the ceremony for the consecration of the abbess, which became closely aligned with the spousal imagery that was particularly reserved for virgins.[45]

Aldhelm and Socialized Chastity

While the impact of the invaders may have helped to secure the preeminence of virginity, there were nevertheless some heroic attempts to adapt the discourse to changing times. The work of Aldhelm (d. 709), a monk who advanced to the position of abbot of Malmesbury and ultimately bishop of Sherbourne, is a case in point. Inspired by the treatise *Concerning Virgins* that Ambrose wrote for his sister and her community, Aldhelm dedicated a treatise on virginity to Hildelith, abbess at Barking.[46] In contrast to the Roman Marcellina who had presided over a community of women, however, the Anglo-Saxon superior governed a double monastery, which consisted of monks and nuns.[47] So while Aldhelm's preface only mentions individual nuns by name, and the community itself is referred to as female, Aldhelm clearly wished to embrace a wider audience of men and women.

Aldhelm responded to the type of audience associated with a double monastery with a revisionary paradigm of virginity that not only included men along with women but actually foregrounded virginity as a male virtue.[48] This was a decided innovation. In the Eastern Church, there had been a series of treatises on virginity that were addressed to an exclusively male audience.[49] But in the West, the specter of the male virgin was conjured up by patristic authorities with a view to tamping down the claims of female virgins. Hence Tertullian would argue that, since the maintenance of virginity was more difficult for men, the male virgin was deserving of greater merit. Even in secular unions, Augustine had maintained that virginity was more glorious in the groom because the bride's was controlled by fear of her parents or the law.[50]

Aldhelm's prologue sets the stage for his masculine recasting of virginity. For having just addressed the nuns as "catholic maidservants of Christ—or rather adoptive daughters of regenerative grace," Aldhelm goes on to compare their spiritual toil with "talented athletes under some instructor training in the gymnasium through wrestling routines and gymnastic exercises. . . . [O]ne athlete, smeared with the ointment of (some) slippery liquid, strives dexterously with his partner to work out the strenuous routines of wrestlers, sweating with the sinuous writhings of their flanks in the burning centre of the wrestling pit." The athletes' variegated activities include javelin-throwing, archery, running, and horseback riding, until Aldhelm winds up with a set of naval exercises right out of *Ben Hur:* "the naval companies of sailors . . . [are] encircled by dense throngs of rowers . . . with the streersman urgently inciting [them] and the master-rower beating time with his truncheon."[51]

Aldhelm is in essence offering a male prototype as a point of identification to both male and female members of the community. This is not merely intended as an extension of the patristic predilection to apply male imagery to ascetic women but also augurs other salient changes. What follows are two columns of exemplary virgins divided according to gender, in which men not only precede women but actually outnumber them twenty-nine to twenty.

The men are depicted as pursuing vigorous ministries that were grounded in their virginal strength. Virginity was intrinsic to the prophetic vocation of Elijah, Elisha, Jeremiah, and Daniel.[52] Salubrious clean living, coupled with virginity, permitted the three Hebrew youths to withstand incineration.[53] It was the "torrid ardour of chastity" that prompted John the Baptist to "reprove the forbidden nuptials of the king's [i.e., Herod's] marriage . . . , putting a check on the polluted cohabitation of a reeking union."[54] John the Evangelist's purity made him a favorite with Christ, a receptacle for revelation, and a miracle worker capable of raising the dead. Indeed, John's spectacular purity even seemed to ward off death, inducing a kind of suspended animation: "Certain people contend indeed that he did not depart according to the usual death, but that he lies alive in the tomb, put to sleep in a special trance."[55] (This claim renders the miracles that we will see generally associated with a virginal corpse tepid by comparison.) Paul's chastity paved the way for his conversion and mighty works. "The privilege of his pure integrity" even enabled him to "traverse the third heaven contemplating the secrets of heavenly citizens with chaste vision."[56] Such scriptural exemplars are followed by a succession of church fathers, distinguished bishops, and monastic founders. This triumphant choir of purity is rounded off by a series of charismatic ascetics, who became great miracle workers, as well as a string of martyrs.

Interestingly, these last two categories include four potential husband-and-wife teams: Amos of Nitria and his wife, Chrysanthus and Daria, Julian and Basilissa, and Malchus and his spouse. All four couples were allegedly forced into marriage. Only the captive Malchus is presented as acting unilaterally, abandoning one wife only to have his pagan master attempt to thrust another upon him. He chose martyrdom over marriage.[57] But in the other instances, the couple mutually vowed chastity on their wedding night, thereafter keeping their irregular relations concealed under the cloak of spiritual marriage.[58] Even though both husband and wife ultimately win glory, it is male chastity that is at the center of each of these dramas, even as the husband is the one who acts as catalyst for the vow of chastity.

When it is finally the female virgins' turn, Aldhelm seemingly adopts a more passive line. For the most part, the women tend to distinguish themselves with a martyr's death. Thus, in contrast to the male virgins' burgeoning activity, their female counterparts focus on fending off threats to their faith that, more often than not, are intrinsically linked with threats to their virginity. In certain instances, their achievements seem deliberately diminished. Cecilia, who is the first in the column of virgins, is a case in point. Not only was the Cecilia legend one of the most popular accounts of spiritual marriage for the entire Middle Ages, but Cecilia's alleged initiative in converting her husband, Valerian, to chastity is much more typical of this tradition than Adhelm's male emphasis would imply.[59] According to her anonymous *passio*, Cecilia warned her husband on her wedding night that her guardian angel would destroy him if he so much as dared to lay a finger on her. When Valerian asks astutely why he cannot see the angel, Cecilia responds that he must first be baptized. Once Valerian is baptized, not only does he see the angel, but the couple is angelically crowned with roses and lilies. Beginning with Valerian's brother, Cecilia goes on to convert a multitude of others until she is finally martyred.[60]

But Aldhelm's account of Cecilia is much shorter than the other instances of spiritual marriage, receiving less than half of the space given to Amos of Nitria and about one-sixth of the entries concerning Chrysanthus and Daria and Julian and Basilissa, respectively. (Even the churlish Malchus warrants slightly more attention.) The resulting account of Cecilia's legend is therefore somewhat garbled. The husband is not mentioned by name and the pivotal conversion scene in the bedroom is omitted. Indeed, both the marriage and the vow of chastity must be inferred by the conversion of "her own suitor and her future brother-in-law—if her condition of virginity were to allow it" and the angelic crowning.[61] Not only is Cecilia's conversion campaign excised, but even her martyrdom is omitted.[62] Eventually, as if he was dissatisfied with his own performance, Aldhelm mysteriously abandons the column of virgins to revert to his male starting point, offering a string of Old Testament figures.[63]

One might almost suppose that Aldhelm was conspiring to deemphasize female virginity, which is, in effect, what I believe to be the case. But this seeming de-emphasis should not be construed as simply an uncalculated side effect of the focus on men; it was rather an important strategy for developing a spirituality better suited to a community of women of such disparate marital backgrounds. This was a period when marriage was extremely unstable, at least in practice, and would remain so until the twelfth century. Kings freely repudiated their wives—sometimes divorcing them outright, sometimes forcing them into religious institutions.[64] Indeed, as the famous example of the Frankish queen Theutberga indicates, the very lives of the women who refused to accept their repudiation were often at risk.[65]

It is more than likely that a number of the female members of Hildelith's community would not fit into the traditional categories of virgin or widow, whether because they had been repudiated or left their marriages unilaterally. Aldhelm's treatment of virginity presents a more inclusive model that accommodates the anomaly of the Barbarian quasi-wife within the trifold hierarchy of the chaste.[66]

There are other elements that speak to this impetus toward inclusion. First, there is the fact that Aldhelm treats the worthiness of the married state so extensively before even broaching the subject of virginity.[67] This initiative softens the inevitable conclusion that "the sublimity of praiseworthy virginity, like a lofty lighthouse placed on the uprearing promontory of a cliff, does not shine so resplendently that the strict moderation of chastity, which is the second grade, is scorned as completely inferior and grows vile; or so that the legitimate fertility of marriage, undertaken for the issue of children, becomes perceptibly foul."[68] Thus virginity's admitted superiority in no way depreciates the lower, but still estimable, two other degrees of chastity. Despite Aldhelm's supposed model, the approach is in many ways more Augustinian than Ambrosian. For while Ambrose claims he does not intend to speak against marriage, he proceeds to articulate his own detailed version of the *molestiae nuptiae*. In contrast, Augustine wrote his treatise *On the Good of Marriage* before *On Holy Virginity* precisely to contradict the assumption, most famously expressed in Jerome's *Against Jovinian*, that praise of virginity necessarily entails a vilification of marriage.[69]

Furthermore, Aldhelm's articulation of the three degrees of chastity is more than a simple reiteration of the patristic model, having been subtly shaped to meet the demands of a disparate community. For while the second degree of chastity had traditionally been "chaste widowhood," Aldhelm introduces the more flexible category of "chastity," which could accommodate members of the community dedicated to a life of chastity whose former spouses were deceased or even still living.[70] In a potentially antihierarchical move at a later point in the poem, Aldhelm even attempts to collapse the three degrees of chastity into two. Thus true virgins in both mind and body transcend "all the lofty greatness of (merely) temperate persons, all the sublime loftiness of wedded folk, takes second place."[71]

As the above passage indicates, Aldhelm is prepared to give virginity its due. Yet he simultaneously attempts to undercut any sense of superiority that the virginal members of the community might justifiably feel. Thus he makes the bold and possibly unprecedented statement that marriage has a sublimity all its own. He further admonishes the fortunate few who have maintained the hundredfold reward of virginity not to despise others (presumably members of the community) who only merit the sixtyfold reward of chastity.[72] And herein lies the deeper meaning of the several accounts of spiritual marriages that rounded off the column of male virgins: they serve as forceful reminders of some of the unexpected ways in which marriage could be understood as a mystery. Only God knows whether a given couple secretly merits the virgin's

hundredfold reward. All three of the unconsummated unions proved to be
sources of immense spiritual fecundity. Amos of Nitria and his nameless wife
"lived together—with God alone as witness—in chastity for a lengthy period
of time . . . in their strict observance of the holy way of life. Under their instruction a numerous crowd of either sex streamed to the faith of Christ and
to contempt of this world."[73] "A great multitude of either sex would flock in
crowds" to hear the instruction of Chrysanthus and Daria. Likewise, Julian
and Basilissa converted "a crowd of believers of either sex."[74] These last two
couples died as martyrs. In the instance of Chrysanthus and Daria, moreover,
the sanctity of their union receives particular ratification through a common
grave "ready to receive together the rewards of their merits, just as they had
shared together in their union."[75] In addition, each of these married partner-
ships demonstrates the united strength of chaste men and women. And it is
this united spirituality of its different members, male and female, that the
community must celebrate: not just the singular glories of individual solitaries.

But equally important is the way Aldhelm follows his assurances of virginity's superiority with the rueful reflection that these different degrees of
chastity are by no means stable.

> And yet—unfortunately—it usually occurs the other way around
> with the hierarchical positions reversed, so that the station of the
> inferior life, advancing on all fronts little by little, takes the place
> of the superior grade as it languishes tepidly; and urged on by the
> goad of most bitter remorse obtains its wish and overtakes the once
> superior victor; and he who was counted last through the negligence
> of his past life, henceforth, kindled by the flame of divine love, is in
> first place, reminding (us) of the maxim in the Gospels, "Many sins
> are forgiven her because she hath loved much" (Luke 7.47).[76]

In other words, someone who has been married in the past not only can but
all too often does, supplant the chaste virgin in holiness. Aldhelm proceeds
to berate at length virgins "of either sex who, inflated with the puffed-up arrogance of pride, exult in the integrity of the flesh alone."[77] But the tacit evocation of the nameless female penitent who anointed Christ's feet in the Gospel
of Luke, who had become assimilated with Mary Magdalene by Gregory the
Great, renders this message especially hopeful to the women in the community who might otherwise seem blighted by a sexual past.[78]

The message is clear: the three degrees of chastity are extremely volatile.
Nonvirgins can rise; pure virgins can fall. And this emphasis on spiritual

motility is key to apprehending the rather anomalous lot of Old Testament figures that immediately follow the list of female virgins. First there was Joseph: "for as long as he was a companion of pure virginity and a despiser of the enticing bawdy-house, divine protection guarded him from the menacing danger of multifarious calamities . . . the conspiracy of his envious brothers, who did not shrink at all from fratricide . . . [and] the depraved advances of his master's treacherous wife. . . . Divine protection (also) inspired Joseph with a certain prophetic vaticination."[79] Then David "the most illustrious of kings, endowed with a stainless virginity in the boyhood of his youth before he was tied by the bond of matrimony and the shackle of marriage." Samson "who from the very tender age of the cradle was sacred to the Lord . . . before he was caught in the fraudulent embraces of Dalila [sic] and, weakly deceived by the debauchery of this treacherous concubinage." Aldhelm's point is that "each of these patriarchs was most pleasing to the heavenly majesty for as long as he consumed the air of the atmosphere and the breath of life, nonetheless, after their joining in carnal union, the glory of their virtues slackened and became less."[80]

The emphasis on male chastity is, again, unmistakable. And it is certainly not encouraging that by choosing these male exemplars, Aldhelm simultaneously conjures up female undesirables like Potiphar's wife, Bathsheba, and Delilah. But there is also a sunny side: it is rather refreshing to see men held up as exemplars of failed chastity rather than women. Moreover, Aldhelm's examples demonstrate that, even though these singular men all lapsed into bad marriage or worse, they *were still pleasing to God*. This point achieves even greater acuity in Aldhelm's final biblical exemplar, ostensibly introduced as a cap to a diatribe against sumptuous dress.[81] "Judith . . . scorned the flattering allurements of suitors after the death of Manasses, taking up weeds of widowhood and rejecting a wedding dress—and (this at a time) when the clarion-calls of the apostolic trumpet had not yet put out the call: 'But I say to the unmarried and to the widows; it is good for them if they so continue' (1 Cor. 7.8). Flowering like a bright lily in her devout chastity and hiding from public gaze she lived a pure life in an upstairs solar." In order to bring about the downfall of the leader of the Assyrian army, Holefernes, Judith bedizened herself. Unable to resist an ill-timed, albeit on-message jibe against female finery, Aldhelm uses Judith's example to demonstrate: that "the adornment of women is called the depredation of men!" Yet Aldhelm recovers himself with a justification of her position. "But, because she is known to have done this during the siege of Bethulia, grieving for her kinsfolk with the affection of compassion and not through any disaffection from chastity, for that reason, having kept the honour of her modesty in tact, she brought back a renowned trophy . . . in the form of the tyrant's head [cf. Jth. 13.19]."[82]

Aldhelm's mobilization of Judith as quasi-ambassadress for chastity is, in its own way, as idiosyncratic as his parallel deployment of men like David or Samson, although her sexual profile is more complex. For she enters history, not as a virgin, but as a chaste widow, epitomizing the life of prayer and seclusion recommended by the church fathers for virgins and widows alike.[83] In contrast to the dire passions of a David or a Samson, moreover, her movement away from this kind of chaste seclusion is reasoned and informed—dictated by duty rather than choice. As such, her example dignifies the lot of the non-virginal women in the community in two ways. First and foremost, it upholds chaste widowhood as an honorable estate. Second, the rational deployment of her sexuality *for her kinsfolk with the affection of compassion* vindicates the women in the community who perhaps would have preferred to remain virgins, but married out of duty.

But one of Aldhelm's most potent strategies for de-centering female virginity is, arguably, dependent more on what he suppresses than what he stresses. For the virgin as *sponsa Christi* has all but disappeared from the treatise. The few exceptions are muted: John the Baptist is referred to as the bridegroom's assistant; Constantina and the patrician women she converted to chastity rejected marriage "for the embraces of a heavenly bridegroom, and were hastening, with shining lamps and frequently uttered sighs, among the wise virgins"; and Aldhelm cites what was allegedly Jerome's letter to Demetrias regarding the end of the world, when she would "fly to meet [her] bridegroom."[84] But that is the extent of it.

If the suppression of the bride represents a profound deviation from patristic tradition, it may have seemed both pragmatic and necessary. The ceremony that made the virgin a bride of Christ, and the ensuing spiritual prestige, probably rendered this title one of the most divisive aspects in any community of religious women. In this context it is significant that the bride is not only rarely evoked but never upheld as a point of identification for either the women or the men of the community. As a result, the *vita angelica* is once again free to emerge as a vital image in itself, and not simply an appendix to marriage with Christ.

> The future eminence of the angelic life is now in a certain sense
> seized by violence beforehand by the male and female followers of
> intact virginity. . . . For it is assuredly clear—because the violence
> is of the strictest and the way of life most difficult—that the man,

whom maternal fecundity brought forth into the world from the natural womb of nativity, if he spurns the laws of nature, is bound to exist as an inseparable fellow of angelic chastity, and, before the dominion of horrendous death is driven into black hell by the supreme glory of the resurrection "this corruptible [body] puts on incorruptibility" (1 Cor. 15.53), earthly are compelled in a wonderful way to become heavenly citizens. Whence our Lord dismisses the factious slander of Pharisaical temptation. . . . "In the resurrection they shall neither marry nor be married, but shall be as angels of God in heaven" (Matt. 22.30).[85]

Aldhelm closes his lengthy panegyric by comparing the virgin to an athlete struggling for the prize. But he also feels free to mix genders in the same sentence. Hence elsewhere the transcendent virgin is compared to "'*a queen* on the right hand' of divine majesty' (Psalm 44.10) . . . accompanied by heavenly cohorts, blessedly found worthy to be perpetually present at and have the joy of indivisible *fraternity* of angelic companionship!"[86] Imagery and language such as this suggest that, in the context of a double monastery, the androgynous implications of the *vita angelica* were making a comeback.

This democratic vision of chastity simultaneously hearkened back to a pristine standard, while also speaking to modern concerns. It was a bold attempt to intervene in the discourse, albeit an ephemeral one, that did not prosper—even with the author himself. For when Aldhelm undertook the poetic rendering of the same subject, as he had promised Hildelith at the close of his original treatise, the earlier enterprise was altered in some crucial ways. Although the aggressive foregrounding of male virginity persists, there is no mention of Hildelith and her community.[87] With the double monastery as intended audience disappearing from view, the complex motives underwriting the foregrounding of male virginity are also lost. What remains no longer resembles an exercise in democracy so much as a hostile takeover.

Once the double monastery recedes, the attitude to marriage changes as well. Gone is the conciliatory outreach to individuals pledged to chastity but formerly married. The long preface is drastically condensed: although the accommodating category of "chastity" remains in the place of chaste widowhood, there is no rueful discussion of the frequency with which an individual with a sexual past, by dint of penitential prowess, outstrips the proud virgin in merit. This retrenchment is also apparent in the way the ending of the original treatise has been transformed. The anomalous catalogue of Old Testament men who had failed to fulfill their chaste promise, along with the eminently adaptable, but ultimately chaste, Judith were all confirmation of the fluidity between degrees of chastity, for good and for ill. The conclusion has been excised in favor of an allegorical battle between the Vices and the Virtues. This alteration is in many ways predictive of the new tenor of the poem. Virginity becomes an ever more aggressive virtue, constantly stomping on vice. This combative note will, in turn, enhance the dualistic nature inherent to the discourse: fervor for virginity is more consistently fueled with a revulsion for the flesh.[88] And carnal marriage cannot withstand all this stomping. The extended apology for marriage has almost completely vanished. The "sublime loftiness of wedded folk" gives way to sober assurances that "the eternal gift of Christ is not withheld from those who maintain the sanctioned marriage of lawfully wedded life."[89] Indeed, Aldhelm's deference to the marriage bond itself wanes. Hence the second degree of chastity is associated with those "who now break the yoked union of marriage," not simply condoning but even encouraging the unilateral repudiation of marriage.[90]

Aldhelm's reinvestment in the virgin as *sponsa Christi* consolidates the polarization between virginal purity and the flesh, casting carnal marriage as a dark mirror to the spiritual union. Cecilia is now described as "scorning the sweet sports of carnal excess, since she loved instead the sweet kisses of Christ." The violent persistence of Lucia's rejected suitor is described as "attempting to take from Christ this beautiful bride." Agnes, perceiving an offer of marriage as a "trap" and a "deadly risk"—and scorning gifts from her suitor, "foul words," and "shameful kisses" alike—vowed that "preserving her body at all times in a virginal contract, she would be a spouse of Christ, Who duly pledged her with a dowry of faith and Whose ring consecrated the maiden's body." "Throngs of wealthy suitors" sought the virgin Demetrias in marriage, drawn by her beauty and immense dowry. But she "wished to abandon all this inherited ostentation and instead of it to cling to the kisses of the divine Spouse, offering sweet kisses, cheek to cheek." The twin sisters Rufina and Secunda "rejected their betrothal rights and spurned all the patrimony of the deceitful world, in order that they might be joined perpetually in marriage to the Spouse who reigns in heaven." Similarly after rejecting many noble suitors, the sisters Anatolia and Victoria were assured by an angel that "a nuptial couch is prepared for you in the seat of Paradise, in which the company of the eternal Spouse is never lacking and where there is long-lasting bliss, if virginity, an unwear[i]ed companion, should protect you."[91]

In these accounts, the women in question explicitly reject carnal marriage in favor of a spiritual union with Christ. Aldhelm's entry on Jerome's virginal correspondent Eustochium reifies these options by articulating the very different spiritual destinies accorded to virgins and nonvirgins. The prose version mentions in passing Eustochium's sister Blesella [*sic*], an erstwhile matron, characterizing her as "the blessed Blesella."[92] But in its rhymed counterpart Blaesilla, blessed no longer, is introduced as a tragic foil for Eustochium's ecstatic union with Christ.

> The fortune of the world bound . . . Blesella to a union of the marriage couch and the nuptial torches, to endure the seductive bonds of a luxurious marriage. Nevertheless, the bride greatly lamented the loss of her virginity when her husband had concluded his earthly time, just as a matron is accustomed to lament the loss of her husband when, in grief, she bewails his death by sobbing. . . . Eustochium, a virgin, did not feel with bitter tears, for she despised the honied contagion of worldly pleasure. She spurned kisses on her cheeks as the bite of an asp, but rather pressed the sweet kisses of Christ to her lips and gave in return pure kisses to her supreme Spouse.[93]

In fact, Blaesilla's extreme penance is a vivid example of the principle Aldhelm advanced in the earlier treatise: that the zealous penance of those who were at one time married often outstrips virginal merit. In the rhymed version, however, the example of Blaesilla only functions to condemn carnal marriage.

The resurfacing of the *sponsa Christi* also signifies a tendency to retreat into discrete and conventional gender roles. Not surprisingly, the androgynous aspects of the treatise are greatly diminished as well. The long analogy between the nun and different kinds of athletes falls by the wayside. The foreshortened prologue also excludes the lengthy meditation on the *vita angelica*. And with no mention of a female readership, moreover, the stock reference to "chaste soldiers" that opens the treatise loses much of its gender-bending potential.[94]

A Grim Grid: The Dilemma of the Monastic Matron

We have no way of knowing what factors, or possibly pressures, led Aldhelm to back away from his more democratic vision of chastity: reproof from Hildelith for perceived snubs of female virginity (for which Aldhelm retaliated by writing her out of his work)? Or perhaps with Aldhelm's accession to the bishopric, his disciplinary struggles over clerical celibacy both caused him to second-guess the wisdom of a common life for professional virgins of both sexes and undermined his tolerance for individuals with a sexual past.

It is also important to remember that Aldhelm at no time disinvested in virginity: he merely attempted to share the wealth (and perhaps warn stock-holders of the volatility of the market). Even in the more experimental prose version, Aldhelm never challenged the caliber of the coin, nor its superiority to all other currencies. "So that virginity is gold, chastity silver, conjugality bronze; that virginity is freedom, chastity ransom, conjugality captivity; that virginity is sun, chastity a lamp, conjugality darkness; that virginity is a queen, chastity a lady, conjugality a servant; that virginity is the homeland, chastity the harbour, conjugality the sea; that virginity is the living man, chastity a man half-alive, conjugality, the lifeless body; that virginity is the royal purple, chastity the re-dyed fabric, conjugality the (undyed wool)."[95] In short, since the gold standard was always in place, it is not surprising if the pristine impression of the mint reasserted itself.

Where did this leave the high-ranking women of royal and noble birth? Whether as venerable dowagers or discarded wives, many of these women, recovering from forced and humiliating retirements from court, aspired to founding monasteries on their own lands in the hopes of ending their lives with a modicum of honor. But if we were to adopt the unyielding standard articulated by Aldhelm, these women were (metaphorically) but dead slaves, fettered in bronze, dressed in undyed wool, and set adrift in a dark sea. This grim measure is obliquely reflected in the fact that women who had at one time been married, and subsequently went on to establish monasteries, very often did not become abbess.[96] A small percentage of these women beat the odds through the anomaly of an alleged spiritual marriage—the claim that the marriage was, in fact, not consummated. This would secure their position as virgin-abbess. Perhaps the most celebrated instance of this trajectory is the Anglo-Saxon Queen Æthelthryth (d. 679), who allegedly preserved her virginity through two marriages before withdrawing to her monastic foundation at Ely, which she ruled as abbess.[97]

The example of Æthelthryth also emphasizes the way in which the fragility of the marriage bond finds expression in hagiography, with its characteristic obfuscation of causality. Hence childless queens, like Æthelthryth, who may have been repudiated, are depicted as heroically resisting consummation and then unilaterally entering religious life. Interestingly, this behavior was exculpated by the gradual shift that had occurred in matrimonial theory. According to the late patristic standards of Roman law, the marriage bond was a consensual contract that did not require consummation.[98] But consummation was the all-important factor in most Barbarian codes, which, as we have seen, recognized the legality of marriage by capture, provided that the predatory suitor compensated the woman's guardian.[99] Even in Carolingian times when Archbishop Hincmar of Reims was attempting to articulate a more stable definition of marriage, it adhered to a complex model that consisted of betrothal, exchange of dowry, a public wedding and blessing of the union, and consummation—the latter still a requirement for the validity of a marriage.[100] Hence in the early Middle Ages any marriage that remained unconsummated could easily be dismissed as nonbinding.

But this alibi for dissolving a marriage clearly would not work for the Thuringian-born princess Radegund (ca. 520–87), founder of the auspicious female community of the Holy Cross at Poitiers. Her brutal marriage-by-capture at the hands of the not-so-heavenly king Clothar I was too well known. Thereafter, she fled her husband and converted to religious life, going against biblical and patristic counsel, which required that both parties convert to religion.[101] In other words, the same rules that would have exonerated Ætheltryth's escape from marriage and secured her reputation for chastity would have the effect of shackling the unfortunate Radegund. For although one might argue that her initial consent was certainly defective according to Roman matrimonial theory, it would hardly help her reputation to claim that the marriage was invalid. Not one of her admirers were brazen enough to claim that the marriage was unconsummated—in spite of the fact that there were no offspring. Certainly by Frankish standards, Radegund was married and continued to be married after she was consecrated by the bishop of Noyon. From a hagiographical standpoint, her position was legally and spiritually anomalous. The patristic measure—which accorded the virgin a metaphoric crop of a hundredfold yield, the consecrated widow sixtyfold, and the faithful married a mere thirtyfold—had long been and would remain the instrument for assessing the meritorious "harvest" of different degrees of chastity.[102] Radegund did not fit into any of these categories.

The sources for Radegund's life are excellent and provide a prime opportunity to observe how Radegund and her admirers contended with her murky status. Considering the feeble remains of female-authored texts, it is remarkable that there are some writings attributed to the saint herself: a letter of foundation for her community at Poitiers, cited in its entirety by Gregory of Tours, as well as *The Thuringian Wars*, a lengthy poem written either by Radegund or by the poet Venantius Fortunatus with Radegund's help.[103] In addition, there are three detailed accounts of Radegund's life by contemporaries who knew her well: the historian Gregory, bishop of Tours, who was well acquainted with Radegund and, as we shall see, became a kind of default bishop for her community; Fortunatus, Radegund's possible coauthor who wrote poetic eulogies for the queen during her lifetime and a hagiography after her death; and finally, the nun Baudonivia, a member of Radegund's community at Poitiers who grew up knowing the saint and would subsequently write a sequel to Fortunatus's life.[104] Each provides a different perspective on the queen and, more generally, insight into the challenges that a conversion to monasticism posed for the matronly foundress of a monastic community.[105]

Ostensibly Gregory of Tours would seem to be among the queen's admirers, even including her among his collection of confessor saints.[106] And yet, there were certain irregularities in Radegund's premonastic career that Gregory, as chronicler of the Merovingians, could hardly overlook. Not only did Clothar, Radegund's captor and later husband, maximize upon what may have been a Frankish royal prerogative of multiple wives, but he did not balk at forming relationships that the church would have deemed incestuous.[107] Thus after committing incest by marrying Gunthuec, widow of his brother Chlodomer, Clothar went on to even greater acts of incest by marrying two sisters, Ingund and Aregund, in quick succession. He subsequently married a certain Chunsina.[108] Gregory carefully chronicles Clothar's various alliances, not forgetting to mention the occasional seduction.[109] Furthermore, as none of these wives seems to have been repudiated, it is probable that Clothar already had at least three wives, and possibly four, at the time of his marriage to Radegund.[110]

It was Jerome's harsh judgment that "just as not every congregation of heretics is able to be called the church of Christ, so not every marriage in which the wife is not united to the man according to Christ's precepts, is able to be called marriage, but rather adultery."[111] Many clerics from a patrician background may have shared this rigid assessment, and Gregory might have been among them. In any event, when it came to discussing Radegund's married life, Gregory seemed convinced that discretion was the better part of valor and that the less said about the queen's premonastic career the better. Her marriage and entrance into the religious life receive short shrift. "When the time came to return home Clothar took with him as his share of the booty Radegund, the daughter of King Berthar. Later he married her. This did not stop him afterwards from arranging for her brother to be murdered by assassins. Radegund turned to God, took the habit of a religious and built a nunnery for herself in Poitiers."[112] Gregory goes on to add that Radegund soon became famous for her prayers, fasting, and charity. As we learn from her letter of foundation, she never assumed the role of abbess, a renunciation widely perceived as a gesture of humility over her nonvirginal state, but appointed the virginal Agnes in her stead. Radegund describes Agnes as "like sister to me, and whom I have loved and brought up as if she were my daughter from childhood onwards."[113]

But whatever case might be made for Radegund's piety or merit as a monastic founder, there are two interrelated issues that seem in danger of eclipsing her reputation throughout Gregory's history: the attitude of Maroveus (d. 590), bishop of Poitiers, to Radegund's community, and particularly his antipathy to the saint herself, and the community's scandalous revolt following the death of its founder.

As Gregory makes abundantly clear, Maroveus's ungracious attitude to the community was apparent with his accession to office. Radegund had acquired some important relics for her community from the Holy Land, as well as a piece of the true cross from the Byzantine emperor, and requested that Maroveus conduct a ceremony for the formal deposition of these relics. "He refused point blank: instead, he climbed on his horse and went off to visit one of his country estates." When another bishop's assistance was secured for the service, "Maroveus deliberately stayed away." Thereafter Maroveus was nothing if not consistent. Radegund had "frequent occasion to seek the help of the Bishop, but received none, and she and the Mother Superior whom she had appointed were forced to turn instead to Arles," accepting the rule of the recently deceased Bishop Caesarius. They also relied on the protection of the queen's estranged husband, Clothar, who after resigning himself to Radegund's loss, became a great supporter of her monastic endeavors. But the reason given for her recourse to royal patronage was that "they aroused no interest or support in the man who should have been their pastor." Only after Radegund's death did Maroveus reluctantly agree to attend to the community. But Gregory interjects, "All the same, or so it seems to me, Maroveus still harboured some resentment against the nuns, and, indeed, they declared this was one of the causes of their revolt."[114]

Maroveus's attitude probably caught the queen off guard since, as Michel Rouche points out, Radegund tended to get her own way with bishops.[115] But the bishop's resentment was not unprovoked. Radegund's eager acquisition of high-profile relics presented a distinct threat to the cult of St. Hilary, on which the prestige of the bishopric of Poitiers hung.[116] This is, perhaps, clearest in Baudonivia's brief account of the trouble, in which the bishop remains discreetly unnamed: "The bishop of that place should have wished to welcome it [the true cross] devoutly with all the other people but the Enemy of humankind, to subject the blessed Radegund to trials and tribulations, worked through his satellites to make the people reject the world's ransom and refuse to receive it in the city."[117] It is probable that this turf war was, in turn, responsible for the tone of Radegund's so-called letter of foundation and its scrupulous efforts to secure her community against any overweening interference from external authorities, secular or ecclesiastical, but clearly aimed at the bishop of Poitiers, the natural guardian of the monastery. The letter is replete with ominous conjurations by the Trinity and the Day of Judgment against "any person whatsoever, either the bishop of this city, or some representative of the kind, or any individual" to disturb the community or appoint another superior; or if "any person, possibly even the bishop of the diocese, shall wish to claim, by some newfangled privilege, jurisdiction of any sort over the nunnery," or "if any prince, or bishop, or person in power . . . shall attempt with sacrilegious intent to diminish" its holdings.[118] We have seen that the altercation with Maroveus also determined Radegund's decision to look to the nearby bishopric of Arles for guidance and ultimately adopt the rule of St. Caesarius. The rule had the advantage of being adamant about the community's independence from a region's suffragan bishop; the downside was its insistence on strict claustration.[119]

It is doubtless true that Maroveus's attitude to Radegund was premised on the threat she presented to his see. As Raymond Van Dam has observed, Gregory is careful not to take sides in the dispute. Sensitive to anything that might diminish a fellow bishop's prestige, and aware of his symbolic relationship with the patron saint of the region, Gregory is hesitant in acknowledging the power associated with the true cross.[120] But Gregory's relation of events is sufficiently diffuse as to render Maroveus's behavior rather opaque. At one point, Gregory even refers to Maroveus as "a deservedly praiseworthy disciple of the most blessed Hilary."[121] This is unfortunate as it leaves the reader free to adduce other reasons why a professional celibate like Maroveus might feel rancor toward the former queen. The clerical case against Radegund's integrity (on many levels) is all too easily made. First there is the question of how Radegund achieved her royal stature in the first place—the ease with which she made the transition from a mere casualty of plunder to queen. But did she really merit the title of queen? On the one hand, there was postclassical matrimonial law with an increased emphasis on the exchange of dowry (*dos*) as a constitutive element separating a wife from a concubine. We know that the village of Saix, where she initially resided after her separation from Clothar, was part of her marriage settlement.[122] On the other hand, Ruth Karras has made the compelling argument that property was not the deciding factor in Christian marriage: church recognition was.[123] The clerics memorializing

Radegund all wrote after her monastic conversion and probably would have been hard-pressed to say anything positive about marriage generally, let alone this marriage. The clash between the laissez-faire attitude toward marriage that characterized the Frankish aristocracy and clerical strictures are epitomized in the episode when Queen Brunhild attempted to present King Theuderic's children, and her grandchildren, to St. Columbanus: " 'These are the king's sons: pray strengthen them with your blessing.' 'Know,' rejoined Columbanus, 'that they shall never hold the royal scepter, for they were born in adultery.' "[124]

Theuderic had allegedly been guilty of preferring multiple concubines over a single wife. His situation was not unlike the polygamous Clothar, whose multiple wives may well have been deemed concubines by the clerical establishment. Radegund's position was not helped by the fact that she had lived in the Frankish court, possibly for as many as ten years before Clothar actually married her—a lengthy interval under any circumstances that could cast doubt on her virginal status at the time of marriage. The wicked Fredegund (d. 597), whom we know from her daughter Rigunth's taunt, began her career at the Frankish court as a slave, made the tricky transition from the concubine of Clothar's son, Chilperic, to wife—at least in the eyes of the Frankish aristocracy.[125] And so when Radegund embarked on her religious life, she may have been regarded as a quasi-married woman at best: one flesh with a celebrated libertine who was already one flesh with a plurality of other wives. Gregory—who never warmed to Fredegund, mentioning only her evil deeds—may well have been skeptical about Radegund's marriage.[126] It probably did not help that Radegund fled, rather than making the best of a bad situation by converting the scoundrel Clothar to a better life, in keeping with the Pauline expectation that the unbelieving spouse shall be saved by the believing (1 Cor. 7.14). Thereafter, the feckless "wife," seemingly concerned with only her own salvation, wrangled an illicit veiling out of the doddering bishop of Noyon—an incident described in full by Fortunatus, and discussed later. And then, in Gregory's words, Radegund "built a nunnery for herself in Poitiers." At least she did not have the audacity to assume the position of abbess, but, as Gregory's description of the concerted appeal of Agnes and Radegund to Arles implies, she clearly presided through her puppet abbess. Dependent on the patronage of her royal husband, she seemed to have relinquished none of her queenly prerogatives. For all her vaunted humility, Radegund continued to occupy a throne at Poitiers—just like any queen, or bishop for that matter.[127] Maroveus was significantly absent from the funeral for the former queen. He was, however, persuaded to attend to the community after Radegund's death.

But Maroveus was not writing this history, Gregory was. And Gregory took it upon himself to relate very faithfully a bishop's graceless behavior to a holy woman, all the time maintaining a dangerous impartiality. Was Gregory sufficiently naïve that he didn't see how these tensions might reflect badly on the erstwhile queen? While not participating in Maroveus's active hostility, Gregory may well have shared the prejudice that any celibate male would have to a religious woman who, through no fault of her own, slipped so far from the virginal ideal by a union with so revolting a husband. In fact, Gregory's own rendition of the chaste hierarchy of merit suggests a theological conservatism even more disparaging of marriage than was the norm. In his *Glory of the Confessors*, Gregory describes the huge flock of doves in attendance at the funeral of the nun Georgia, demonstrating how "she busied her mind with a spiritual cultivation in such a way that she harvested the produce of her virginity, the sixty-fold fruit."[128] A mere sixtyfold fruit. In other words, Gregory continued to subscribe to the pristine and more austere assessment of the pre-Constantinian church in which only martyrdom is deserving of the full hundredfold reward, while virginity receives sixtyfold, and widowed chastity a meager thirtyfold. The married faithful receive nothing.[129]

According to this exacting measure, Radegund could accrue no spiritual merit in her married state and, at best, could end her life deserving only the thirtyfold reward of chaste widowhood. When Gregory mentions Radegund respectfully for her zeal in gathering relics in the Holy Land, he compares her to St. Helena, Constantine's mother, who allegedly went to the Holy Land in search of the true cross. It is doubtless to sharpen the comparison with Helena that he repeatedly refers to Radegund as "the queen" throughout this account. But it simultaneously speaks to the impossibility of a woman with such a past leaving the secular world behind.[130]

This view might help to explain certain idiosyncrasies in Gregory's treatment of Radegund in his *Glory of the Confessors*. It should be reiterated that Gregory gives ample evidence in his *History* that he did, in fact, honor Radegund's piety. His attempts to resolve the community's difficulties after the death of its foundress were prefaced with the reflection, " 'What Saint Radegund built up by her fasts and never-ending prayers and constant acts of charity must not now be dispersed in this wanton way."[131] And yet when Gregory comes to place her alongside the other confessor saints, he makes no mention of her life, or the nature of her claims to sanctity, but focuses entirely on her death or, more precisely, her funeral. Given this orientation and the fact that Gregory is writing in a hagiographical genre, one might expect to find the face of the deceased "so bright that it surpassed the beauty of lilies and roses," and is not disappointed.[132] But the rest of the entry is far from conforming with conventional expectations. For one thing, the name of Bishop Maroveus makes an ominous appearance. Fortunately, Gregory does not allude to the bishop's ongoing feud with the deceased in his conversation with the grieving nuns, instead focusing on practical matters. "Behold, our brother Maroveus, the bishop of Poitiers, is not present because the task of visiting his parishes has detained him. Now, however, form a plan so that the holy body is not injured and so that the grace that God has bestowed on these holy limbs is not removed while the time of burial is delayed. Speed up the funeral that is due her, so that she might be placed in the tomb with honor."[133] Gregory gracefully covers for Maroveus, using his absence, whether legitimate or feigned, as a pretext for rushing up the burial and officiating—"reserving for the local bishop [Maroveus the honor of] celebrating mass and covering the tomb with a lid."[134]

But Gregory's care to display due deference to the rights of a fellow bishop has distinctly ungallant repercussions for the woman whom Gregory is ostensibly putting forward as a confessor saint: he is suggesting that the "beauty of lily and roses" might collapse into inglorious corruption. This danger is further reinforced by the comment that "the foresight of the abbess had prepared a wooden casket in which she placed Radegund's body, packed in spices."[135] According to Gregory's *History*, Radegund died on August 13, so his concern for the preservation of the body was hardly trifling.[136] Furthermore, Baudonivia relates that Radegund remained unburied for three days as they waited for the nameless bishop's return.[137]

This distinctly antihagiographical allusion to a putative saint's bodily corruption runs counter to the many stories of miraculous preservation that are given lively play throughout Gregory's hagiographical corpus. For instance, the bodies of the martyr Mallosus of Birten, Abbot Branchio of Clermont, and Bishop Valerius of Saint-Lizier all allegedly remained uncorrupted for years, while Mallosus and Valerius exuded the odor of sanctity.[138] Nor were such marvels restricted to celibates. St. Gregory, bishop of Langres, who once had a wife with whom he fathered a number of sons, remained perfectly intact, as did his vestments, several years after the burial. "It was not without reason that he was seen to be glorious after his death, since his living flesh had not been corrupted by the passions. That integrity of body and heart is truly great which shows grace in this present life and which, in the future, is rewarded with eternal life."[139] Even the matron Pelagia of Limoges was deserving of a modest miracle because she was the mother of a famous abbot. After four days "such a sweet fragrance flowed from her body that everyone was surprised," not to mention the comet that seemed to hang suspended over the church where she was laid out.[140]

In fact, the presumption of holiness associated with the intact body was so strong that the process could work in reverse and the marvel of bodily preservation alone reveal "that a friend of God was buried there."[141] Thus a young girl, whose body was in a state of perfect preservation after many years, but whose identity remained obscure, was deemed responsible for healing a woman from blindness. As Gregory explains, "There is hence no doubt that this girl who could offer such benefits to an ill woman possessed outstanding merit."[142]

So Gregory's anxiety over the possible corruption of Radegund's body sounds a jarring note. Perhaps Gregory, attempting to apologize for his presiding role at Radegund's funeral, felt compelled to recount the attenuating events with heightened precision. Yet this very exactitude seems to have led to something akin to a confusion of genres, almost as if he momentarily forgot that he was supposed to be writing hagiography, not an entry in a bishop's register. A less guarded eulogist might have overlooked such practical considerations in favor of the saint's many merits. Instead, Gregory prefers to focus on the profound sorrow of the grieving community of virgins that its foundress left behind. He cites at length their moving dirge for their mother whose "words shone for us like the sun; like the moon they were a clear lamp of truth."[143] He also inadvertently reveals the darker side of their rule: "As we passed by beneath the wall, a crowd of virgins began to cry and weep from the towers and from the tops of the fortifications of the wall."[144] The rule of Caesarius may have freed the nuns from the interference of Maroveus, but at the cost of a claustration so strict as to prohibit the nuns from attending the funeral of their foundress. Upon his return to the monastery, Gregory would have succumbed to this emotional outpouring "if I did not realize that the blessed Radegund had departed from her convent in body but not power, and that she had been taken from the world and placed in heaven."[145] Thus Gregory, reminded of his ostensible purpose in writing, refrains from weeping and concludes by pointing to Radegund's place in heaven.

Finally, the famous revolt of the community at Poitiers against the abbess Leubovera, which arose after Radegund's death, is probably the longest sustained narrative in Gregory's entire history. This cannot help but reflect badly on the legacy of its foundress. But what is equally suggestive is that Gregory does little to occlude the role Radegund inadvertently played in nurturing the seeds of rebellion during her own lifetime. She did this by abetting and defending the vocation of a nun who was destined to become one of two ringleaders of the revolt, Basina—daughter of Clothar's son Chilperic and hence stepson of a sort to Radegund—and Chilperic's former wife, Audovera.

Basina's family had been decimated by the concerted machinations of her own father, Chilperic, and his wife, Fredegund—the erstwhile concubine. Considering that both Basina's mother and her brother, Clovis, were slain, the girl's sentence was comparatively light: "[Clovis's] sister was tricked by Fredegund's servants and persuaded into entering a nunnery, where she has become a religious and remains to this day."[146] Despite its terseness, this account suggests that Basina's entrance into monasticism was no less violent than Radegund's induction into married life.

Even when Basina was sequestered in a monastery, however, she was not altogether forgotten by Chilperic. Some four years later, he entertained the possibility of reclaiming Basina for a marriage with King Recared of Spain. "For a time he [Chilperic] considered the idea of sending another daughter to Spain instead [of Rigunth], Basina, whom he had shut away in the nunnery in Poitiers. . . . She was unwilling, and the blessed Radegund backed her up. 'It is not seemly,' she said, 'for a girl [*puella*] dedicated to Christ to turn back once more to the sensuous pleasures of this world.' "[147]

Thus we hear for the first time that it was Radegund's community of Poitiers that served as Basina's monastic jail, information that one assumes was withheld from the reader until it ostensibly ceased to be a jail. And yet Gregory reiterates the bleak history of Basina's forced vocation in the same breath that he describes her seeming unwillingness to leave the cloister. Yet an unwillingness to go to Spain does not necessarily imply that Basina altogether rejected marriage as a possibility, let alone had developed a sincere vocation. Any apprehension about the potential rigors of the journey were certainly justified by the ordeal undergone by Rigunth—Chilperic's daughter who was slotted for the Spanish marriage, but was pillaged for her dowry en route, abandoned by her retinue, and even temporarily imprisoned.[148]

Alternatively, it is not difficult to imagine how a young woman in Basina's circumstances could momentarily believe herself to be committed to the monastic life. What had begun as forced enclosure may have led to some medieval correlative to the Stockholm syndrome, temporarily encouraging Basina to identify with her monastic guardians. Gregory could have dispelled some of these doubts by developing Basina's reasons for refusing the marriage, possibly transforming them into some kind of tribute to the monastic life, but he chooses not to. Perhaps Gregory is mindful of Basina's eventual role in the revolt, which could not but cast doubt on the authenticity of her vocation. Instead, Gregory leaves it to Radegund to play the role of the abbess (Agnes is not mentioned in this incident) and articulate the most obvious motive for Basina's refusal—that once dedicated to Christ it is "unseemly" to return to the world. Yet what may pass as a noble position in the context of book 6 clearly has disastrous ramifications three books later. In short, Basina remains silent, the queen steps up, and Gregory is content to step back.

Radegund's role in the Basina debacle could be dismissed as an unfortunate twist of fate. And yet Gregory's account is sufficiently scrupulous that when the reader begins to connect the dots, the onus of Basina's vocation lands squarely on Radegund's shoulders, calling into question the queen's judgment and perhaps even the nature of her intervention. Radegund could hardly remain indifferent to the predicament of her young kinswoman, especially considering the similarities in their pasts. She too had lost a beloved brother at the hands of her own husband, who happened to be the father of the murderous Chilperic. We know from *The Thuringian Wars* that Radegund would continue to grieve this loss her entire life. In fact, it was her brother's murder that had prompted her entrance into religion. But these very parallels may have rendered the queen an unreliable advocate for the young woman's happiness, encouraging a projection of her own experience, and hence her choices, onto Basina. Such a reading finds tacit support in Baudonivia's account of the manner in which Radegund herself responded when her husband, Clothar, had attempted to reclaim her from religious life many years earlier: "she [Radegund] said that if the king truly did want to take her back, she was determined to end her life before she, who had been joined to the embrace of the heavenly King, would be united again to an earthly king."[149] Even through Baudonivia's elaboration of spousal rhetoric, both the sentiment and the manner in which it is expressed closely parallel Radegund's reported intervention on behalf of Basina.

A similarity in circumstances may have blinded Radegund to certain essential differences. But there was one difference that no medieval woman, let alone one with a religious vocation, could overlook: one presumes that Basina was still fortunate enough to have remained a virgin, while Radegund had not. The privilege of Basina's physical integrity may have increased Radegund's tendency to project a monastic vocation on her relative.

Was Radegund helping her kinswoman to the life that the latter desired, restoring the choice which had been so violently wrested from both women? Or was Radegund determined to hold Basina to a forced monastic vow, consciously or not? The predicament of the hapless widow Theudechild, "one of [Charibert's] queens," is suggestive in this context. Theudechild had approached her brother-in-law Guntram to offer herself in the capacity of wife—a marriage that would clearly be incestuous by Christian standards. Guntram pretended to agree, but used the opportunity to seize Theudechild's goods and consign her to a monastery at Arles, home to St. Caesarius's rule, where strict enclosure was enforced, perhaps even more rigidly than its daughter foundation of Poitiers. Theudechild, who "bore ill the fasts and vigils to which she was subjected," covertly attempted to form a union with a Goth general, promising him whatever remained of her wealth. "As she was about to make her escape from the nunnery, she was surprised by the vigilant abbess. The abbess, who had caught her red-handed, had her beaten mercilessly and locked her up in her cell. There she remained until her dying day, suffering awful anguish."[150] Theudechild's plight serves as an eloquent warning against women who presume to direct their own matrimonial destiny. Radegund was singularly fortunate in this regard.

If in the harsh world of Merovingian politics monasteries frequently functioned as prisons for discredited royals, Radegund did not seem to object to her foundation serving that punitive function. Even some bishops had shown no compunction about forcing disobedient female relatives to take the veil.[151] While considering her own experience, Radegund might well regard earthly marriage as frangible and disposable, just as the celestial bond with Christ was as impermeable as it was indissoluble. By upholding a constrained vocation, she was but an exponent of the dominant clerical ideology.

And yet, while Radegund's view of marriage to Christ may have been as absolute as the letter of canon, it was not, strictly speaking, canonical. Or rather, it was a canonical vision filtered through a Merovingian lens—one that focused on vocation as opposed to volition and consent. Such a mentality is often pushed to extremes in the lives of other saints from the period. Amator (d. 418), eventual bishop of Auxerre, and his bride, Martha, were allegedly compelled to separate and enter religion because a priest had mistakenly read the wrong prayer over their heads—binding the couple to God rather than to one another.[152] Although Wandrille was martyred by the kinsmen of his wife, Scariberge, for refusing to consummate his marriage, the dying saint stole the final march on the angry relatives by extending his hand to impose a consecrated veil on Scariberge.[153] Consent probably played a negligible role in Radegund's marriage to Clothar. And so Basina, like Radegund before her, was destined to become the booty bride to a powerful king. Indeed, the fate of the younger woman was even more completely determined since she was bound to a celestial king from whom there was no escape. Radegund supported this union, the community would eventually pay a high price for this intervention, and Gregory—whether as impartial redactor or censorious cleric—saved the story for posterity.

The apparent fissures in Gregory's portrayal of Radegund could be explained by the exigencies that his interlocking personae as historian, bishop, and hagiographer imposed—that the bishop and historian felt compelled to relay information that the hagiographer would have deemed better to withhold. From this perspective, Fortunatus, poet and hagiographer, might feel less constrained and provide a more favorable account of Radegund's past.[154] A possible hurdle, however, was the importance Fortunatus attached to a woman's physical integrity: we have already had a taste of this conviction in the context of his vita of Hilary of Poitiers and the remarkable death of the virgin, Abra. Moreover, the poetry of Fortunatus testifies to a vivid emphasis on the most technical understanding of virginity and the ensuing prerogatives it bestows on the *sponsa Christi*.

The turn that Fortunatus's adulation of virginity takes is not particularly exceptional. Virgins are the "offspring of men joined to the angelic throngs." But this gesture toward the angelic life is muted by an extremely gendered Virgin Mary, who leads the virginal flock in the procession that follows the lamb.[155] Moreover, under Fortunatus's pen, the assimilation of the consecrated virgin with the Virgin Mary is complete. God chose to be born from this exemplar of purity, and it is this same impetus that draws him to the consecrated virgin.

> Look who wished himself to be born in the womb [*ventre*] of a
>   virgin,
> and of the highest lord, by whose flesh he comes into the flesh:
> the venerable spirit touches the intact womb,
> desiring to inhabit a virginal home,
> this God enters one who does not know the use of men. . . .
> The chaste limbs of a virgin are the temple of the creator
> and God lives very properly in such a bedroom. . . .
> Therefore here the holy one now chooses in the womb [*viscera*] of
>   the spouse
> what he earlier chose in his mother.[156]

At the wedding feast that awaits the virgin in heaven, she will be "caressed, cherished, venerated, honored and overshadowed / and he [the bridegroom] places her chaste members in the marriage bed."[157] The matriarchs of the Old Testament—Sarah, Rebecca, Rachel, Esther, Judith, Naomi—are the unfortunate foil to the virgin state. For although they may rise to the height of the stars in merit, not one merits to give birth to the Lord, as did Mary.[158]

Such comparisons are relatively benign. But Fortunatus's often grotesque portrayal of some of the tragedies associated with carnal marriage renders the virgin's bridal bower all the more enviable. A pregnancy, perceived as a condition distasteful and dangerous enough in its own right, could generate still greater unanticipated horrors:

> [The pregnant woman] cannot hide a torpid womb with its
>   enclosed fetus,
> saddened, she lays down, burdened by the proof.
> The heaving of body and soul between gasps, her health suspended
>   in doubt, its stamina depleted
> when, with its javelins, the wound of the uterus swells
> and the woman, sick because of lust, gives birth to a monster.
>   Unruly skin alone swelled out, beyond all human appearance
> so that it shames the mother that she bore it with love.
> Fleeing from her own relatives, ashamed, she carries it away
> until she destroys the burden, deposited in a sack.[159]

The unfortunate mother is thus stripped of any desirable, or even recognizable, status: "she merits neither to be called mother, by virtue of offspring, nor virgin."[160] And the life of a young bride can be wrenchingly altered by sudden death:

> from wedding bed to tomb [de thalamo ad tumultum], now in
>   white, then suddenly black
> she holds frigid limbs with which she once burned together. . . .
> Often she seeks the marital tomb,
> scorning home; the once loved woman worships the dead.
> She lies on the tomb, seeking empty solaces; once it was his living
>   limbs which she pressed, now only his bones. . . .
> It is hardly any better for a queen who remains a widow.[161]

In short, Fortunatus spares his reader none of the carnality of marriage, including painful labor and the tragedy of the deformed stillborn child. Although Radegund had no surviving offspring, she might well have had pregnancies—maybe terminating in just the kind of lifeless lumps to which Fortunatus alludes. Perhaps the queen was even the source of this horrific imagery. Either way, Radegund belongs to the despised category that Fortunatus descries above: neither virgin nor mother. Moreover, Fortunatus makes it clear that such diminished prospects pertain to queen and commoner alike.

It is not surprising that the poet's effusions on virginity were addressed to Agnes.

If Fortunatus did nothing to mitigate the distance between virgins and matrons, he did what he could to redeem the ontological profile of his old friend by depicting her as part of a quasi-maternal infrastructure that made possible the virginal life of the nuns. In this capacity, Radegund, in turn, becomes as essential as the rule itself: "by the love of Radegund, conceiving by the faith of Christ, / the rule of Caesarius bathes whatever it holds."[162] Above all else, it is their "pious mother, the very dear one urging you, who gathers you to join the celestial choir."[163] In poems invoking Abbess Agnes, Radegund's fecund spirituality is even more pronounced. Hence on Agnes's birthday, Fortunatus congratulates Radegund on the birth of her daughter "born not by your uterus, but by grace."[164] Elsewhere, Agnes is described as the product of a dual pregnancy between her birth mother and Radegund. "You fed on one milk flowing from two."[165]

The case for this kind of spiritual prowess is best made after Radegund had separated herself from Clothar. So it may come as a surprise that Fortunatus renders the most detailed account of Radegund's life prior to her conversion to monasticism—secular detritus that Gregory refused to touch. In contrast, Fortunatus's ingenious strategy was to address the different roles that Radegund had been forced to assume head-on.[166] The result is three distinct, but overlapping personae, corresponding to the different stages of Radegund's life. Thus she is represented as the outer wife of a secular king, but inner partner (or quasi-spouse) of the celestial king; outer queen, inner *monacha* or religious woman; and finally outer confessor saint, inner martyr. This double aspect of the successive personae was rooted in the interplay between external appearance versus internal reality.

The life proper begins with the Frankish invasion of Thuringia, an event that left deep and enduring scars on Radegund. But because Fortunatus was committed to dignifying Radegund's life at every stage, this meant de-emphasizing the savagery of the lineage with which she was forced to unite herself, and hence the extent of Radegund's emotional trauma. He merely introduces Radegund, who must have been about eleven at the time, as the object of a Homeric-inflected dispute: "the royal girl became part of the plunder of these conquerors, who began to quarrel over their captive. . . . Falling to the lot of the illustrious King Clothar, she was taken to Athies in Vermandois, a royal villa, and her upbringing was entrusted to guardians." Radegund was given just time enough to manifest her childhood piety—a propensity to lead other children in religious observances and a professed desire to be martyred—before Clothar attempted to reap the rewards of his booty. "She escaped by night from Athies through Beralcha with a few companions. When [Clothar] settled with her that she should be made his queen at Soissons, she avoided the trappings of royalty, so she would not be great in the world but in Him to Whom she was devoted and remained unchanged by earthly glory."[167]

This foreshortened account, in which flight and marriage are awkwardly, if seamlessly, united, reflects a shrewd calculation. Although Fortunatus presents the queen as precociously pious, the predictable hagiographical expression of a childhood desire to preserve her virginity is lacking. This is in spite of the fact that her nocturnal flight could easily have been bent to support this pious trope. But what might seem an unfortunate omission is, in fact, a measure of Fortunatus's canonical savvy. The official position articulated by Leo I and his successors aligned a private resolve of chastity with a clandestine marriage. If Radegund had determined to preserve her chastity for God, the only honorable recourse available was suicide or—failing that—suffer rape, effect a subsequent escape, and pay the penitential price for her lost integrity. Rather than a mechanism for preserving inviolate virginity, the flight from Authies is thus presented as an astute response—a maneuver safeguarding her honor and ensuring her destiny as queen as opposed to concubine.

As we can see from Gregory's fulsome chronicle of Clothar's marriages, this was no negligible point. Clothar was a bigamist several times over. Thus Radegund could not be considered wife, let alone queen, by any Christian standard. Naturally, Fortunatus suppressed all mention of possible rivals, eager to establish Radegund as uncontested queen and thereby secure the highest degree of merit available to her—the honorable, albeit pedestrian, thirtyfold measure of marital chastity. But, even if he carried this point and established her as sole and uncontested wife, what was good solid coin in the promiscuous realm of Merovingian politics, where every king was a lothario and royal wives and concubines abound, was cheap in hagiographical currency.

Fortunatus's solution was to create a kind of double persona for the duration of Radegund's married life: externally, she was united to Clothar, but internally to Christ. It was a pious bigamy that covertly countered Clothar's profligate polygamy. Yet, because Radegund was not a virgin, Fortunatus only hints at the marriage to Christ, always implying, never asserting, that she was a kind of virgin manqué. Furthermore, the distance between inner and outer realities, the real and the ideal, is bridged by a penance that was, more often than not, covert. This complex identity is established immediately after marriage. For the very statement that proclaimed Radegund as queen "unchanged by earthly glory" is followed with the assertion that "though married to a terrestrial prince, she was not separated from the celestial one."[168] This claim is sustained by the queen's propensity to alms and holy works but, most of all, by her penitential disposition. Her humility was time and again demonstrated by an extreme deference to the priesthood, tacitly proclaiming to all that "she was more Christ's partner than her husband's companion." Thus if a member of the clergy approached by night, Radegund felt impelled to rush out "through snow, mud, dust, [so that] she herself would wash the feet of the venerable man with water she had heated beforehand and offer the servant of God something to drink." The painstaking acts of mercy, the pious subterfuge that masked her abstemiousness at table, the concealed hair shirt, the selfless distribution of rich clothes all worked to the same end.[169] But Radegund's penitential disposition was especially in evidence when it came to her circumspect behavior in the bedroom:

> when she lay with her prince she would ask leave to rise and leave the chamber to relieve nature. Then she would prostrate herself in prayer under a hair cloak by the privy so long that the cold pierced her through and through and only her spirit was warm. Her whole flesh prematurely dead, indifferent to her body's torment, she kept her mind intent on Paradise and counted her suffering trivial, if only she might avoid becoming cheap in Christ's eyes. Reentering the chamber thereafter, she could scarcely get warm either by the hearth or in her bed. Because of this, people said that the King had yoked himself to a *monacha* rather than a queen.[170]

The term *monacha* has an interesting resonance. Jerome first used it in a letter of consolation to his beloved friend Paula, the occasion being the death of her daughter, Blaesilla. "If I identify you as a parent, I do not reproach you for weeping; if as a Christian and *monacha*, however, the name of mother is excluded by those names."[171] *Monacha* was, of course, the female counterpart to *monachus*, a word derived from *solitary* that will become the common term for monk. And Paula did, in fact, end her days in a religious community that she founded in Bethlehem. In the West, however, monasticism was still in its infancy, and its vocabulary yet to be determined. The term *monacha* seems to have dropped out of usage in favor of *sanctimonialis*—a term closely associated with *sanctimonia*, which could be used as a euphemism for chastity and virginity.[172] In other words, *sanctimonialis* tacitly implied a consecrated virgin. *Monacha*, conversely, was invaluable for its flexibility: while decidedly signifying someone who dedicates her life to God, it could just as easily accommodate the cloistered *sponsa Christi* as the widowed recluse. This was the word that Gregory of Tours chooses to describe the group of women that Monegonde gathered around her—an anchoress who began her life of seclusion first as a matron (albeit with her husband's consent) and later as a widow.[173] It was a term generous enough to both capture the fraught spirituality of Radegund's married life and anticipate her eventual life in religion. Moreover, it is significant that Fortunatus also applies this term to the other members of her community at Poitiers, whether or not they were virgins. In fact, the *virgo*, who looms so large in Fortunatus's other writings, never makes an appearance in Radegund's vita, effacing the boundaries between the erstwhile royal matron and her virginal sisters.

By capitalizing on the tension between inner and outer person—between inner disposition and outer expectations; between the inner marriage of the spirit and the outer marriage of the flesh—Fortunatus crafted a paradigm for the holy matron that was durable enough to last throughout the Middle Ages.[174] One has only to look at the life of Elisabeth of Hungary, a latter-day Thuringian princess, to recognize the extent to which these contours would remain virtually unchanged through the centuries.[175]

Fortunatus's muted identification of Radegund as a would-be bride of Christ remained a compromise formation at best: an inner condition that depended on the tension created by the outer reality of her marriage to Clothar and was sustained by the contrast between inner vocation and outer obligation. Thus the status was never absolute, but always a product of comparison: "she was more Christ's partner than her husband's companion." A more positive declaration of Radegund as Christ's *sponsa* is never attempted. Furthermore, this relative and introspective disposition for a union with Christ would be no match for the public recognition accorded to Christ's paradigmatic bride, the consecrated virgin—a position that Radegund, even after her conversion to religion, could never hope to attain. Thus Fortunatus's invention of Radegund as quasi–*sponsa Christi* was dependent on what we have seen the clerical world might regard as her quasi-marriage to Clothar. It was a persona created for the world that must be abandoned with her conversion. And, in fact, all traces of an implied spousal rhetoric that had associated Radegund with the heavenly bridegroom vanishes at the point at which she separates herself from Clothar.

The next phase of Radegund's life, that of outer queen–inner *monacha*, is introduced abruptly with her flight from her husband's court—an event occurring sometime between 550 and 555. According to Fortunatus, Radegund's departure was prompted by the murder of her brother. She went directly to Médard, the bishop of Noyon, and "earnestly begged that she might change her garments and be consecrated to God." But the holy Médard hesitated to veil the queen, allegedly out of the deference to the principle of indissolubility upheld by Paul (1 Cor. 7.22). It certainly did not help that Clothar's men had pursued Radegund into the basilica, vociferously opposing the consecration and attempting to drag the bishop from the altar, "lest the priest imagine he could take away the king's official queen as though she were only a pros- titute."[176] Radegund, who had in the meantime dressed herself in monastic garb, attributed the bishop's hesitation to cowardice: "'If you shrink from con- secrating me, and fear man more than God, Pastor, He will require His sheep's soul from your hand.'" It is not exactly clear what Radegund is threatening on God's behalf. But it is a threat, one that could even be read as a tacit threat of suicide. We have seen that in Baudonivia's account Radegund did threaten sui- cide if she was forced to return to Clothar. Fortunatus's rendition suggests that Radegund was taking refuge in the unyielding canonical position wherein a woman is bound to God from the moment she has determined upon a chaste resolve. And Médard would be called to account if it came to this.

Doubtless Radegund was correct in her assumption that the bishop was afraid—afraid to take an awful step that would place the queen beyond the reach of her carnal husband. And yet the terms in which Clothar's henchmen framed their objections provide yet another motive for his reluctance. At issue for them was Radegund's freedom to enter religion. But rather than juxtapos- ing the married woman to a virgin or even a single woman—more propi- tious candidates for the monastic life and hence providing a clearer contrast to Radegund's encumbered status—they compared the queen with someone that was technically free but totally unworthy of consecration: a whore. The articulation of this objection served Fortunatus's purposes insofar as it un- derlined the fact Radegund was, indeed, the publicly recognized queen, not a mere concubine. Fortunatus even managed to get his message across with a clever play on words: "reginam non publicanam sed publicam." Ironically, however, Fortunatus's witticism acts as a covert marker of how perilously close the two categories were in the queen's case. For technically, Radegund's union to the polygynous Clothar was a fictive marriage in the eyes of the church. Legally, she was not a wife, just a very *publica publicana*. And this stark reality provides a window into Médard's confusion: whether true queen, polygynous quasi-queen, or mere concubine, all of these categories were unworthy of the particular consecration that transformed the virgin into a bride of Christ. So Médard, "laying his hand on her . . . consecrated her as a deaconess," a seem- ingly slick answer to a sticky dilemma.[177]

But Médard's solution was far from perfect, considering that this vexed rank had been under attack for more than a century—most recently at the second Synod of Orleans (533).[178] And while the bishop does ordain the deaconess to her office, he does not veil her. Significantly, Fortunatus tells us that Radegund dressed herself in monastic garb in order to force the bishop to act, without mentioning the veil, begging the question of whose hand was responsible for its imposition. A subsequent reference to "the time she was veiled, consecrated by Saint Médard" is more ambiguous still.[179] This equivocation is exacerbated by the fact Radegund's eventual enclosure at Poitiers occurred on Easter day, a fact that makes the day doubly joyous for Fortunatus. But Easter is, of course, the day most associated with virginal consecration.[180]

Radegund's consecration by Médard marks the end of her old life without exactly inaugurating a new one, epitomizing her anomalous spiritual condition. It is but a bridge leading to yet another bridge—the latter consisting of a prolonged and peripatetic grey zone, spanning from her consecration as deaconess to her enclosure at Poitiers. Radegund had won her point and received consecration but was still to some extent considered married. We learn from Baudonivia that Radegund spent a number of years at her villa in Saix, which was part of her marriage settlement, and that it was only after St. Germain intervened with Clothar that the king finally agreed to let Radegund enter the monastery.[181] In fact, her actual entrance into the cloister may not have occurred until after Clothar's death in 561.[182] But Fortunatus masterfully shapes this potentially awkward hiatus in the saint's life into a liminal story of physical and spiritual pilgrimage to the monastery. Thus, despite Radegund's consecration, the transformation from queen to nun is portrayed as a gradual process that speeds up the nearer she approaches her monastic destiny.

Radegund's metamorphosis is both symbolized and effected by a ritual undressing, reenacted many times en route to Poitiers. It commences immediately upon her consecration as deaconess, when she "divested herself of the noble costume which she was wont to wear as queen when she walked in a procession on the day of a festival with her train of attendants. She laid it on the altar and piled the table of Divine Glory with purple, gems, ornaments and like gifts to honor Him." Radegund reenacts this sacrifice as she makes the rounds of a series of celebrated local hermits. One day, "ornamented . . . in queenly splendor" she arrived at the cell of Jumerus to divest herself there. Similar stops were made at the cells of Dato and Gundulf on separate occasions.[183] Soon the spectacle moved south to be repeated at Tours.[184]

Radegund's repetitive divestment functions in two ways: one looking back to the past, the other to the future. Her queenly garb reinforces the efficacy of her past marriage and subsequent queenship, even as its disinvestment anticipates her future role of cloistered *monacha*. Indeed, the world looks on as the outer persona of queen is painstakingly stripped away again and again, until at last the inner *monacha* is exposed. One can sense the process nearing completion when, after many repeat performances, the mode of Radegund's queenly divestment becomes less literal, assuming the form of charity and miracles.[185] By the time she reaches Poitiers, she is ready. With the queen annihilated, the nun emerges for that moment of enclosure that is every bit as public as the many disrobings: "Weren't there such great gatherings of people on the day that the saint determined to seclude herself that those who could not be contained on the streets climbed to fill the roofs?"[186]

As with Radegund's two previous identities, Fortunatus loses no time in announcing her new and final persona. Directly following her enclosure, he affirms, "Anyone who spoke of all the most holy woman had fervently accomplished in fasting, services, humility, charity, suffering and torment, proclaimed her both confessor and martyr."[187] It was the role of martyr as opposed to virgin that Fortunatus had claimed to be anticipated by her childhood yearning. Furthermore martyrdom was actually positioned above virginity on the scale of grace—a fact that, as we have seen, was not infrequently used to humble proud virgins. But because Radegund had failed to avail herself of martyrdom in defense of her virginity, nor, despite her threats—overt and veiled—was she ever called upon to make this supreme sacrifice in defense of her new vocation, she was only eligible for what patristic authors had come to describe as white martyrdom: one based on asceticism rather than bloodshed.[188]

Despite Fortunatus's best efforts, however, the final persona was fraught with a tacit, but irresolvable, conflict. He was not prepared to belabor the obvious: that the former queen was no virgin. We have seen that the word *monacha* was chosen precisely for its capacity to close the yawning gap that separated the brides of Christ from the less fortunate members of their cohort. By the same token, Fortunatus, unlike Gregory, never makes mention of the fact that Radegund did not assume the role of abbess out of humility, stepping aside in favor of the virginal Agnes.[189] Indeed, Fortunatus's attempts to distract the reader from the stigma of a virginity lost prompt him to banish not only all bridal imagery but even mention of virgins from the community at Poitiers. With this essential hierarchy suspended, Radegund would be on a par with the other sisters.

And yet, en route to becoming a martyr, Radegund engages in a series of penances sufficiently punishing as to bespeak a profound sense of inferiority to the other nuns. Radegund's humility is so extreme, her self-abasement so complete that she might as well have been engaging in the kind of penitential abjection that canonical authorities prescribe for the fallen virgin. This is especially apparent in her exaggerated deference to the other, presumably purer, nuns, and the types of tasks she assumes. She would secretly collect and clean their shoes by night, scour suspect corners "never too disgusted to carry off what others shuddered to look upon," and clean the toilets.[190]

Radegund is also depicted as manifesting a degree of physical self-punishment that is unique in the lives of the holy women of the early Middle Ages, anticipating the extremely embodied asceticism of a later age. In addition to donning hair shirts ever the more hirsute and redoubling her punishing fasts,[191] she also contrived ingenious instruments of self-torture in secret. On one occasion, she chained three circles of iron to her body as a Lenten observance. "When she wished to remove the chains locked under her skin, she could not for the flesh was cut by the circlet through her back and breast over the iron chains, so that the blood nearly drained her little body to the last drop."[192] Another time, she ordered that a brass plate in the shape of a cross be made. "She heated it up in her cell and pressed it upon her body most deeply in two spots so that her flesh was roasted through." Perhaps her most vehement extremity was to hold a basin of burning coals against her body "so that she might be a martyr though it was not an age of persecution. . . . She imposed the burning brass and her burning limbs hissed. Her skin was consumed and a deep furrow remained where the brand had touched her. Silently she concealed the holes, but the blood betrayed the pain that her voice did not reveal."[193] This statement both reiterates and sustains her claims to martyrdom. Indeed, so drastic are the austerities described that the walls between the red martyrdom of bloodshed and the white martyrdom of asceticism begin to buckle.

While Fortunatus made a valiant effort to suppress the bride in favor of the martyr, he arguably lacked the conviction to back it up. Radegund's sexual past casts a long shadow over his narrative. Her self-inflicted torments are more convincing as penance than as martyrdom. Ultimately Radegund with her several personae parallel the tragic predicament of the matron who gave birth to a sack of flesh: neither virgin nor mother. It is only in the nun Baudonivia's account that we finally find a picture of Radegund that is integral and perfect in every way. From a certain perspective, her task was certainly easier. Baudonivia's account was intended as a sequel to Fortunatus's work, so she did not feel compelled to renarrate Radegund's early life, instead focusing on her life in religion.[194] But it is precisely in this area that Baudonivia succeeds where the more seasoned hagiographer failed. In Fortunatus's account, Radegund's past was never quite behind her, as the degree of her penance would suggest. The queen's asceticism is not expunged from Baudonivia's account. Yet her penitential exercises are relaxed and rationalized, removing the personal culpability implicit in Fortunatus's vita.

When discussing the queen's austerities, Baudonivia does, of course, allude to Fortunatus's account: "As the first book related, she occupied herself wholly in these efforts until she was totally and unreservedly in God's service."[195] Yet there is no mention of chains or heated disks. The onset of Radegund's more severe vigils and fasts are depicted as preparation for her entrance into the cloister, prompted by her release by Clothar. "[Radegund] rejoic[ed] that she had been snatched from the jaws of the temporal world. Then she prepared herself for God's service, hurrying to follow Christ wherever He might lead, speeding with devoted soul to Him she had always loved. Thus intent, she guarded her body through the night with an additional round of vigils as though she were its jailor."[196] Furthermore, the disciplines that Radegund embraces after her entrance into the cloister are not only toned down but tacitly engineered to emphasize aspects of the rule of St. Caesarius—"the ceaseless prayers and vigils," her "devotion to reading," her "small bed . . . which was painfully uncomfortable"—banishing any inferred burden of guilt.[197] Baudonivia even manages to portray some of Radegund's physical disciplines in a pragmatic light: supplicatory offerings to God that would thwart Clothar's efforts to reclaim her, support her campaign for auspicious relics, or mediate on behalf of peace.[198] These latter two causes are not exclusive to Radegund: she both exhorts her nuns to join her and guides them in their disciplines. Likewise, the decision not to assume the role of abbess is cast in terms of Radegund's desire for liberty "to follow the footsteps of Christ more swiftly and heap up more for herself in Heaven the more she freed herself from the world"—dispelling any hint of a humility based on physical imperfection.[199]

In Baudonivia's vita, however, the final proof of Radegund's perfection was that Radegund is deemed worthy of becoming Christ's bride in the eyes of God. We have seen that Fortunatus's *sub voce* use of bridal imagery was limited to the married queen's covert identity as a quasi-bride of Christ, a persona that disappears with her entrance into religion. Baudonivia is both more traditional and more radical than her senior colleague. She is more traditional in that her bridal imagery is reserved for when Radegund embarks upon a religious life, but more radical because the application of this imagery reflects an inclusive as opposed to exclusive vision of the *sponsa Christi*. This is not immediately apparent because Baudonivia's brief treatment of Radegund's life at court seems to follow the lead of Fortunatus. For instance, we are told that "united with an earthly prince, the noble queen proved herself more celestial than earthly."[200] Yet this dichotomy of celestial and earthly simply evokes, rather than invokes, Radegund's deferred union with Christ. It is but a promise to be fulfilled when Radegund embarks on the religious life where "she would seek to gather ornaments of perfection, a great congregation of maidens for the deathless bridegroom, Christ."[201]

There is no doubt that Radegund is included among these "ornaments of perfection," bespeaking a happy nonchalance to the prerogatives of intact virginity on behalf of the author. In this context, it is worth revisiting Baudonivia's account of how the queen reacted to rumors that Clothar wished to reclaim her: "that if the king truly did want to take her back, she was determined to end her life before she, who had been joined to the embrace of the heavenly King, would be united again to an earthly king."[202] It is significant that Radegund was alleged to have made this remark while she was still living at her villa at Saix—after she had been consecrated deaconess but before she entered the cloister. By the same token, a year after her conversion, she had a dream that she was in a man-shaped ship "with people sitting on every limb and she was sitting on the knee. Christ said to her: 'Now, you are sitting on my knee, but in time you will find a place in my bosom.' Thus was she shown the grace she would come to enjoy some day."[203] As Radegund draws nearer to the fulfillment of this promise toward the end of her life, she receives divine ratification that not only does she merit consideration as one of Christ's brides, but that her spiritual merit has earned her a singular place in his love.

> Before the year of her transition, she saw the place prepared for her in a vision. A very rich youth came to her. He was most beautiful and had, as the young do, a tender touch and a charming way with words as he spoke to her. But she jealously protected herself and repelled his blandishments. So he said to her: "Why then have you sought me, with burning desire, with so many tears? Why do you plead, groaning, and call out with copious prayer, afflicting such agony upon yourself for my sake who am always by your side? Oh, my precious gem, you must know that you are the first jewel in the crown on my head." Who can doubt that this visitor was He who had her whole devotion while she lived in the flesh and that He was showing her what she was to enjoy in her glory. She confided this vision most securely to two of her faithful ones and made them swear to tell no one while she lived.[204]

It would seem that Radegund's sexual past, compounded by the cloud surrounding her marriage to Clothar, and her idiosyncratic entrance into religion was more clearly reflected in the narratives of her male admirers. Gregory neither mentions nor attempts to compensate for the queen's nonvirginal status. Yet his narrative is riddled with strange absences and inappropriate presences. Fortunatus attempts to level the playing field by banishing all allusions to virgins, reserving a semblance of bridal imagery for Radegund alone—but only so long as she lived in the world. Baudonivia, however, is the only author who dares to take the church fathers at their word by treating virginity as a state of mind. As a result, her vita is blessedly oblivious to virginal privilege and free to claim the mystical marriage with Christ for all female religious of merit. With the disappearance of the standard of technical virginity, moreover, the taint of Radegund's sexual past is simultaneously expunged. This is helped by the fact that Baudonivia in no way disparages marriage. On the contrary, she is prompted to describe Radegund as rejecting the "sweetness of a spouse." Regardless of how fitting this epithet might be, it is still a refreshing contrast to the morbid ruminations of Fortunatus on married life.[205] So Baudonivia is capable of both embracing and extending Gregory's analogy between Radegund and Helena without any danger of compromising her subject.[206]

Finally, Baudonivia shows particular daring when she reiterates and amplifies Gregory's reflection when gazing upon Radegund's corpse. "For, as he [Gregory] said tearfully afterwards, on his oath, as he came to the place where the holy body lay, he saw an angel's face in human form, a face refulgent of roses and lilies and he was stricken with fear and trembling, a devout man filled with God as though he were standing in the presence of the Lord's holy mother herself."[207] The "angel's face in human form" and the analogy with Mary, both unmistakable allusions to virginal purity, are Baudonivia's embellishments. Furthermore, there are no potential rivals introduced to compete for these accolades: the tender homage is the singular prerogative of Radegund, the erstwhile matron.

We do not know if Baudonivia's optimistic vision of Radegund as *sponsa Christi* carried the day with the Merovingian clergy. But it was clearly persuasive to some readers. Hence a fleeting reference to Radegund in the life of Queen Balthild (d. ca. 680) is followed up with the comment "we may read in her acts all the good she did for Christ her spouse."[208] Moreover, Baudonivia's life proved precedential in many ways. Her rendition of Radegund's visions of Christ, particularly as wooing bridegroom, anticipates the very explicit mystical marriages that would mark the spirituality of female mystics centuries later.[209] Such a parallel is especially reinforced by the visionary Christ, who explicitly associates penitential suffering with the favor of increased intimacy. Because these traits anticipate a pattern of spirituality that will become especially identified with women, it is all the more significant that they first appear in a female-authored text. As such, it provides some of the earliest, if not the earliest, evidence that the persona of *sponsa Christi* had evolved beyond patristic disciplinary tactics to become a point of identification that women had themselves come to embrace. But it is especially important to note that, for Baudonivia at least, this coveted role was not restricted to virgins. Nor need it be enacted in the cloister.

Monastic Mothers and Virginal Daughters

Baudonivia's accommodating and more inclusive perception of *sponsa Christi* was the wave of the future: it was not to be resurrected until the twelfth century with its renewed interest in intentionality. In the meantime, the elevation of virginity and consequent disparagement of the married state and widowhood is more the rule than the exception, operating as a hidden source of tension in the vitae of holy matrons. This could have been a factor determining Radegund's treatment of her kinswoman Basina. But the life of the feisty self-veiling Rictrude, alluded to earlier, suggests ways in which such tacit rivalries could erupt into violence.

Although the Gascon-born Rictrude lived in the seventh century, her life was only redacted by the monk Hucbald of Saint-Amand in the early tenth century in response to an appeal from the community at Marchiennes in modern-day Belgium.[210] Their community had been devastated by Viking invasions and required a new vita of their foundress. The result is a fascinating study of suppressed rivalries between monastic mothers and their virginal offspring, writ large through monkish projection.

Rictrude married the Neustrian noble Adalbald and eventually gave birth to four children—a boy and three girls—all of whom were destined for the religious life.[211] Because the entire family would eventually be honored as saints, the life necessarily presents the marriage in a positive light: "[Adalbald] took a wife, not for incontinence, but for love of progeny. In both of them, those things which people customarily expect in choosing husband or wife were combined. The man had strength, good birth, good looks and wisdom, which made him most worthy of affection. And the wife had good looks, good birth, wealth and decorum which should be sought above all else. So let us remember the words of the Apostle on honorable marriage and an unsullied marriage bed."[212] Hucbald goes on to cite a series of Paul's statements authorizing marriage.

The blessed and fecund union between Rictrude and Adalbald provides an interesting foil to the plight of Dagobert, king of Neustria, who is described in the same life as "excessively given over to the love of women" and doomed to a series of sterile unions and illicit repudiations.[213] Adalbald, who fell victim to Merovingian factional politics, could even be described as something of a martyr to marriage insofar as he died as a result of an ambush "by certain wicked people, obviously [her relatives] who had been displeased by their holy matrimony."[214] Moreover, Rictrude distinguishes herself from most holy matrons by deeply mourning his loss.

After Rictrude had confounded the king's efforts to remarry her, she went on to enter a monastery.[215] And it is at this point that a derogatory monastic sensibility toward marriage, temporarily suspended but nevertheless discernible in the elaborate efforts to defend the institution, begins to assert itself. In fact, Hucbald rather tactlessly takes every opportunity to note the spiritual disparity between Rictrude and her three virginal daughters. "She offered the first fruits of earth, that is her womb, holy and excellent, to the undivided Trinity: that is, her three daughters, white as doves, as most gracious offerings that with immaculate body and soul, preserving perpetual virginity they might follow the Lamb . . . that they might be always without stain before the throne of God singing to Him a new song, that is, rejoicing perpetually with Him about the uncorrupted flesh. For though they can hear the song, none of the saints can sing it but the white-robed throngs of the uncontaminated."[216] But lest the reader not grasp the full import of the comparison, the hagiographer is determined to be even more explicit: "Therefore, the faithful woman of God . . . espoused her three daughters at one time, while they were still young, to Christ as husband. So they might always follow in the footsteps of the Lamb and that song which she could never make her own could be made to sound for her on her daughters' cithars."[217]

These, of course, were the expressions of Hucbald—a tenth-century hagiographer, working from fragmentary sources presented to him by the nuns, but since lost.[218] Even so, the subsequent tensions described between Rictrude and her daughter Eusebia suggest that these differences may have been acutely felt in monastic circles. Apparently Eusebia had been brought up in a religious community at Hamay, which was founded by her paternal great-grandmother, Gertrude. When Gertrude died, moreover, she bequeathed the position of abbess to her great-granddaughter.[219] But Eusebia was only twelve at the time of Gertrude's passing, and presumably too youthful for this responsibility. So Rictrude used her influence with the king, who forthwith ordered Eusebia to join her mother at Marchiennes. Eusebia reluctantly obeyed, bringing with her not only the community's relics, which included the body of Gertrude, but her entire flock. Every night, however, she rose and went to the site of the other community, where she celebrated the vigils and the hours. The mother caught wind of this "truthful deception" and consulted with her son, the priest Maurontus. "He ordered the servants to hold her [Eusebia] tightly by the arms and she was subjected to the decreed correction. One of the boys who held her was girdled with a sword and while the virgin twisted this way and that under the pain of the whips the hilt struck her tender ribs. This so wounded her that, through the rest of her life, pus and blood sometimes mixed with the saliva which she spat from her mouth."[220] Eusebia, however, was undeterred by such harsh treatment, and, in response to the combined counsel of various bishops and abbots, Rictrude succumbed and let Eusebia return to Hamay. But Eusebia was not to enjoy her victory for long: "Living there the life of an angel on earth, she was carried off to the chamber of her heavenly spouse in the middle of her adolescence."[221]

Hucbald, who realizes that this acrimonious episode of Eusebia's "correction" must redound on the reputation of the entire family, attempts to anticipate the objections of the presumed antagonists: "Look who they are calling saints: a mother who attacked her innocent daughter for wanting to serve God; a daughter who detested her own mother and fled her as an enemy; a son who, with his mother's consent, branded his sister like a fugitive taken away in secret, or like a condemned thief whipped her so viciously that she nearly died. And even though she did not perish on the spot, she wasted away in slow agony. Is this how they make saints pleasing to God? What sanctity is here? What peace? What charity?"[222] This leads to a prolonged defense of the mother's right, nay duty, to discipline a disobedient child.

Whether this harsh instance of maternal discipline devolving into child abuse is an actual reflection of Rictrude's behavior or a mere projection, it points to a real problem: a mother's frustration at having a daughter who effortlessly outranks her in every way—spiritually through the automatic accession to the privileged position of Christ's bride, but also temporally as abbess. For although Rictrude may have been founder of Marchiennes, Hucbald makes it clear that she never ruled as abbess: "Subjecting herself to the rule of others she appeared most obedient to their orders serving others as a servant."[223]

Jerome had cheerily posited that the whole point of marriage was to furnish virgins. Rictrude's life suggests how thankless a task this could be. The conflict with Eusebia provides a baleful projection of some of the tensions that the rhetoric of virginity might instill in a community of women. It suggests that even devoted mothers such as Rictrude could become fatigued by listening to the sound of cithars that they could never hope to play.

CHAPTER 4

An Age of Affect, 1050–1200 (1)

Consensuality and Vocation

The Cult of Virginity: A *Longue Durée?*

> I will say it boldly, though God can do all things He can-
> not raise up a virgin when once she has fallen. He may
> indeed relieve one who is defiled from the penalty of her
> sin, but He will not give her a crown.
>
> —Jerome[1]

The twelfth century was a time of immense social and cultural change—a period of turmoil during which society took comfort in the belief in a substratum of unchanging values.

Virginity was certainly one of these values, and its allure was augmented by a redoubling effect: it was not only deemed a timeless value in its own right but was further imbued with the power to make time stand still. Nowhere is the dual capacity clearer than in the hagiographies of Goscelin of St. Bertin—a Norman monk who arrived in England as part of an episcopal entourage toward the end of the eleventh century.[2] Around 1106, Goscelin was to be found acquainting himself with his adoptive country by examining its claims to sanctity, composing and revising the pivotal lives of the saints associated with the various monastic houses he visited.[3] In his compositions for the royal saints of Ely, the foundation of the remarkable Æthelthryth, the cult of virginity loomed understandably large. Much of Goscelin's rhetoric is familiar, expanding upon patristic polemic concerning the special privilege extended to the virgin, including the joys of the bridal chamber that await them. But a key to the difference between Goscelin's time and the time of the church fathers is the extent to which the rewards for virginity were realized through the miraculous preservation of the virginal corpse. It is difficult to imagine a more graphic rendering of time standing still. Æthelthryth remained wholly undecayed when her tomb was opened some sixteen years after her death, a marvel that Goscelin notes was first revealed by Bede. But a lot had happened post-Bede. This feisty saint, who, as we have seen, was said to have preserved her virginity through two marriages, would remain equally vigilant after her demise. When an "impudent priest" attempted to procure a piece of her garment by shoving a forked stick through a hole in her tomb, the saint's dead hand indignantly pulled the garment around her. The priest persisted in his folly, this time using the stick to insert a lighted candle into the hole. When the candle predictably fell and a conflagration ensued, the holy body remained undamaged, but the perpetrator ultimately perished along with his entire household.[4]

As if the prurient priest thrusting his stick in a hole was not disturbing enough, Goscelin could be even more overt in his sexualization of the saintly cadaver. When Wihtburh, Æthelthryth's sister, was translated to Ely, a senior cleric came forward and "with the wondrous audacity of faith, touched the virgin limbs all over, by their tips reverently lifting the supple joints of her hands and arms. . . . However, no irreverent eye lit upon her beautiful body, shielded by its snowy-white coverings. Her face glowed for the Lord with rosy cheeks, animated with the breath of life; her breasts are firm and upright in their incorruption, her unwedded limbs blossom with the loveliness of paradise."[5] Seemingly prompted by saintly sibling rivalry, Wihtburh's miraculous preservation persisted miraculously 353 years, right up until the time that Goscelin was writing.[6] Predictably, no such marvels are wasted on Æthelthryth's married sister or niece—Seaxburgh and her daughter, Eormenhild—worthy women that they were. Their posthumous reward was burial at either side of the virginal Æthelthryth.[7]

Clerical authors also continue to address treatises extolling the beauty of virginity to women, foregrounding many traditional themes.[8] Around the same time that Goscelin was touring England, an anonymous cleric was penning a dialogue titled *Speculum virginum* for the benefit of two consecrated virgins. In this context, Mary is presented as the ultimate mirror of virginity and the perfect model for any *sponsa Christi* in training. Moreover the possible tension between Mary's roles as Christ's mother and as his bride is ingeniously resolved in favor of maternity when the Virgin, suckling the infant Christ, is inspired to say, "Let him kiss me with the kiss of his mouth. A bundle of myrrh is my beloved to me, he shall abide between my breasts" (Cant. 1.1, 1.12).[9] The work appropriately ends with an epithalamium.

One of virginity's most vocal spokesmen was the Cistercian writer Ælred of Rievaulx, who wrote a rule for recluses (ca. 1160) addressed to the now proverbial virgin sister:

> Think always how precious a treasure you carry in a fragile vessel, and what a reward, what glory, what a crown virginity garners when preserved; moreover what punishment, what confusion, what damnation its loss occasions. Is there a treasure more precious—through which heaven is purchased, the angel delighted—of which Christ is [so] desirous, by which he is seduced. . . . The virgin thinking constantly about the most precious treasure of virginity, as profitably possessed as it is irreparably lost, should be guarded with the greatest care and the greatest fear. She should think without intermission for whose bed she is adorned, for whose embrace she is prepared.[10]

This apprehension translates into a regimen requiring a degree of silence and reclusion worthy of Athanasius or Ambrose.

The tyranny of the intact body continues to prevail in canon law and theology into the twelfth century. Ivo of Chartres (d. 1116) had assembled a number of texts stressing virginity as a state of mind. But then he included powerful patristic testimonies to the contrary, such as the section from Cyprian's letter to Pomponius that authorized the gynecological examination of consecrated virgins.[11] Ultimately the case for the virginal nun's physical perfection carried the day, a position canonized in Gratian's *Decretum*.[12] Gratian cites innumerable patristic authorities who acknowledge with Augustine that "the violent lust of another cannot remove that sanctity of body." Yet Gratian himself asserts "that although women who are violently overcome would not lose their modesty (*pudicitiam*), having been contaminated they nevertheless should not dare to follow the virgins."[13] This position is justified by Leo I's ominous view maintaining that a woman who has been raped should not dare to compare herself to a true virgin, but nevertheless commending the sullied woman for her superior "humility and shame."[14] Liturgical practice continues to reflect this perspective: the formal consecration that rendered a virgin *sponsa Christi* will still be withheld from a victim of rape. Liberal theologians such as Thomas Aquinas (d. 1274) will eventually concur,[15] judging virginity to be so fragile and complex a condition that even God is incapable of restoring the woman to her pristine state.[16]

Nor was the cult of virginity just a matter of theoretical panegyric: the religious odyssey of Christina of Markyate (d. 1155) was inseparable from her efforts to retain her virginity against terrible odds.[17] The anonymous vita implicitly draws parallels between the many obstacles Christina was forced to overcome and the ordeals that the ancient virgin martyr underwent to preserve virginity and faith alike. Christina's path was strewn with lecherous and corrupt clerics who were a match for the wicked pagan rulers of old.[18] As in the case of Thecla and her cohort, Christina's parents were the scourges that raised sanctimonious welts in their pious offspring, first forcing Christina into a marriage and then goading her putative husband, Burthred, into consummating the marriage by force.[19] Like the thwarted suitor who condemns his object of desire to the brothel, the frustrated mother "swore that she would not care who deflowered her daughter, provided that some way of deflowering her could be found."[20] On her wedding night, Christina attempted to convert her husband to a spiritual marriage, like Cecilia, whose legend she invoked. But Burthred's noncompliance forced her to flee the marriage bed, following the example of St. Alexis, whose cult was becoming increasingly popular in this period. The fact that a picture from the life of St. Alexis was included in the still extant St. Albans psalter that was made particularly for Christina further suggests her conscious identification with Alexis's filial recalcitrance.[21]

And as with virgin martyrs such as Catherine of Alexandria, Christina demonstrated a flair for debate with her various judges.[22] Hence she rebuts Prior Fredebert's well-meaning defense of marriage with the theological truism "If many mothers of families are saved . . . certainly virgins can be saved more easily." When Fredebert asks how he can be sure that she is not rejecting Burthred for a wealthier husband as a follow-up question, Christina gives a spirited, but conventional, response: " 'A more wealthy one, certainly. . . . For who is richer than Christ?' "[23] Likewise, when Christina asked Burthred what he would do if another man claimed her for himself, he fell into the Cyprian-inflected rhetorical trap. " 'I would never allow it, as long as I lived. Indeed I would slay him with my own hands, if there was no other way of keeping you.' At this, she retorted: 'Beware then of taking to yourself the spouse of Christ, lest in His anger He will slay you.' "[24] In other words, Christina justified her marriage to Christ in terms that resonated with both Cyprian and Radegund.[25]

Monasticism's virgocentric orientation persisted in the burgeoning new religious foundations. The monk Herriman's parents took a vow of chastity in order to enter monastic houses. His mother, Maisend, aspired to being admitted to the new female branch of the monastic community of St. Martin's, established in the familial home that Maisend had donated. Yet far from being honored as a foundress of sorts, she was first humiliated by the abbot, who insisted on testing her devotion by requiring that she spend time in town weaving wool and begging for the most meager of alms. (She was told to accept only crusts of bread, never entire loaves.)[26] Maisend was subsequently humiliated by the abbot's sister, a nun (*sanctimonialis*) named Eremburg, whom he summoned to preside over the portion of the community whose members were probably consecrated virgins, housed in Maisend's former home; the others, designated *conversae*, resided in town.[27]

Maisend was admitted into Eremburg's community, presumably as a sign of favor. But whatever deference was initially shown to the prior owner of the house dissolved into antipathy.[28] Eremburg excommunicated the bedridden Maisend, placing the bed out of doors under a step where the water from the kitchen was dumped. "Lying there for three days, although gravely ill, she exulted in her soul because in the house where she was formerly the mistress, she now sustained tribulation for God."[29]

The community at St. Martin's was a Benedictine foundation. Nevertheless, its traditional appreciation for virginity was emulated by the new orders. The wandering preacher Robert of Arbrissel (d. 1116) manifested a Christlike indifference to essential social boundaries. Lepers, prostitutes, and sinners of all description were allegedly included in his following. Moreover, when Robert founded the double monastery of Fontevrault, he appointed Petronilla, herself a *conversa laica*, as the first abbess—a liturgical oddity.[30] And yet, there were two distinct cloisters for women at Fontevrault: one was dedicated to the Magdalene and contained women who were no longer virgins. The second, more conventionally dedicated to the Virgin Mary, was inhabited by virgins.[31]

Finally, an instance from a fledgling order in England, founded by Gilbert of Sempringham (d. 1189) as a double monastery, suggests that certain women internalized the virginal standard to an alarming degree. The nuns seized a laybrother who had impregnated a member of the community and, turning the violence that nuns had traditionally been represented as visiting on themselves outward, they forced the unfortunate nun to castrate her lover. As the famous case of Peter Abelard would suggest, castration was in keeping with the secular code of honor, indicating the extent to which the claims of the earthly and heavenly bridegrooms had become assimilated.[32]

Consensual Marriage: Celestial and Terrestrial

The above examples are striking testimonials to medieval society's uninterrupted adulation of virginity. And parallel instances could doubtless be found for the duration of the Middle Ages. Even so, the cult of virginity, and the persona of the *sponsa Christi* in particular, were destined to become swept up into larger ideational fronts that brought considerable change in their wake. The net result was that virginity began to lose its spiritual edge, even as the virginal nun's monopoly over the title *sponsa Christi* came to be challenged.

One such challenge was a function of subtle liturgical changes instituted by the post-Gregorian papacy. According to René Metz, the matrimonial flourishes of the old Romano-Germanic pontifical were much more representative of Northern European tastes and ill-suited to Italian climes.[33] The more autonomous Roman pontifical that emerged in the twelfth century was more sparing in accolades for the consecrated virgin. Rather than the traditional dates of Easter or Epiphany, her liturgy was relegated to Sundays or other feast days—such as the feasts of the Virgin or the apostles. The ring was presented as optional, ring and wreath alike were deracinated from any association with marriage, and the matrimonial imagery was much more niggardly. Thirteenth-century liturgists, moreover, would exaggerate this minimalist approach.[34]

Yet another motor of change was a radical reconsideration of marriage, an initiative that can be construed as rehabilitating and even dignifying the institution. And this help was certainly timely. Over the course of the eleventh and twelfth centuries, the conjugal unit endured a series of low blows from which it was still reeling. Everyone had long grown used to humble expectations for the married in the hierarchy of merit, recognizing that any couple lucky enough to be admitted to heaven would still be observing God and his saints from the bleachers. But suddenly in the eleventh century there were new forces threatening to strip the married of even this comparatively pedestrian satisfaction.

The threats to marriage were threefold. Along with the revival of towns, commerce, government, literacy—and just about everything else—came the revival of heresy. Certain isolated sects that emerged in the first half of the eleventh century were united by their condemnation of marriage as a source of corruption.[35] In the twelfth and thirteenth centuries the more unified threat of the dualist Cathars would second this gloomy prognosis. They argued that Satan was the creator of the material world as evidenced by the diabolical injunction to "be fruitful and multiply."[36] Bernard of Clairvaux (d. 1153), the first orthodox respondent to the Cathars, immediately perceived the danger of such disparagement for Christendom, arguing, "Take from the Church the honourable estate of marriage and the purity of the marriage-bed, and you will surely fill it with concubinage, incest, masturbation, effeminacy, homosexuality—in short, with every kind of filthiness." Count Raymond VI of Toulouse (d. 1222), a Cathar sympathizer, would emerge as a vivid confirmation of Bernard's apprehension.[37] Indeed, the count's disdain for marriage and its incumbent sanctions were construed as among the most powerful proofs of heretical perfidy. According to the chronicler Peter of Vaux-de-Cernay, Raymond had four wives in all: three were repudiated, two were within the forbidden degrees of relation. This penchant for incest was also demonstrated in more flamboyant ways as well: Raymond not only relished sleeping with his father's concubines but even abused his own sister.[38]

But the other factors menacing marriage could boast of distinctly orthodox pedigrees. The Gregorian reformers' campaign against clerical marriage had the inevitable effect of tarnishing the institution from which they wished to extricate themselves. In fact, the contemporaneous rise of popular piety was in large part owing to the reformers' stance, resulting in the laity's growing conviction that it was difficult for the married to be saved. There is also a link between the emphasis on sacerdotal purity and the rise of the cult of the Virgin Mary, the mystery of whose motherhood did little to dignify the average marriage. Mary was destined to emerge even more triumphantly as a pillar of popular piety and the ultimate *sponsa Christi*.[39] Furthermore, the rise of the schools led to a refurbishing of the antimatrimonial strains associated with antique philosophical circles and appropriated by the church fathers.[40] Such scholarly disparagement of marriage was seconded in the vernacular by certain literary conventions that scholars lump together under the rubric of courtly love.[41]

Apologists for marriage doubtless recognized that an effective strategy for defending the institution was by its spiritualization and ultimate sacramentalization—a process of purification that could be most expeditiously achieved by divorcing marriage from the marital act.[42] This impetus eventuated in a reversion to Augustine's view that marriage was entered into by consent alone (following the lead of late Roman matrimonial law) and that the ensuing bond was essentially spiritual. Augustine had used the unconsummated marriage of Mary and Joseph, as fecund as it was inimitable, as the model of the perfect marriage.[43] This revised Augustinianism was advanced first by the monastic theologian Hugh of St. Victor (d. 1142) and soon adopted by Peter Lombard (d. 1160).[44] The Lombard's authoritative *Sentences*, moreover, would ensure that marriage was included in the list of seven definitive sacraments.[45]

Thus the consensual definition of marriage did not merely champion consent as a key element in marriage, but the sufficiency of consent in the creation of the bond, arguing for the validity of a union independent of ritual, witnesses, or consummation. Consent must be freely given, however; it could not be constrained. It was also determined that not all types of consent were equal; in order for consent to be binding, it must be heartfelt. A person who merely consented to marriage on the outside, all the time resisting inwardly, was not married.[46] The unprecedented emphasis on the sufficiency of consent certainly raised the bar for what constituted a valid marriage from the perspective of individual volition, even as it lowered the bar from the perspective of legal requirements. In short, consent and intention must be united before the union of a man and woman would be valid in the eyes of God.

For all intents and purposes, the emphasis on consensuality probably seemed like an innovation. For in the wake of the Roman Empire's collapse, the new settlers brought with them different matrimonial standards that, as we have seen, tended to set consent at naught in the face of a fait accompli. A woman's entrance into religion was often tarred by the same brush. As Basina's baleful example implies, Christ was perceived as no more concerned about his bride's consent than was Clothar when he married Radegund. The two types of marriage differed, however, in degree of dissolubility, which was a reflection of the extent of church involvement in the earthly union. The Frankish clergy had neither the capacity nor perhaps even the inclination to police the carnal institution's all too fluid boundaries. On the basis of what they witnessed, members of the clergy might well be forgiven if they perceived marriage to be as despicable as it was frangible. But they more than compensated for this laxity by a rigorous enforcement of the prerogatives of the celestial bridegroom. Hence the bishop of Noyon was ultimately moved to consecrate the desperate Radegund as deaconess, valuing her firm proposition over her childless marriage to Clothar. By the same token, Radegund was inclined to accept the resisting Basina into her community and to make sure she stayed there.[47]

With the disappearance of sexual intercourse as an essential component for the marriage contract, however, secular marriage and marriage to Christ were suddenly drawing closer to one another, while the presumption in favor of the heavenly bridegroom began to lose its pride of place. We can see this change refracted through the hagiographical career of St. Osyth, who, if she existed, had lived during the seventh century. In late eleventh-century lives, Osyth, who had been forced to marry and nobly resisted consummation, fled her husband and convinced two bishops to veil her. In later versions, they refuse, and Osyth is forced to veil herself—in spite of the fact that she is a virgin and presumably deserved better.[48]

These shifting ideologies also had practical consequences. In 1106 Ermengard of Brittany attempted to flee her unhappy marriage with Alan Fergent, count of Brittany, by escaping to Robert of Arbrissel's new foundation of Fontevrault.[49] But far from emulating the bishop of Noyon's accommodation of the matron Radegund, Robert deferred to the claims of secular marriage and insisted she return to the world. There were, however, those who still allowed the claims of the celestial bridegroom to best the terrestrial. After she left Fontevrault, Ermengard received a letter from Abbot Geoffrey of Vendôme, reprimanding her for returning to the world "in which you will find nothing besides that which is pernicious. A false blessedness attends the present world, and hence a true misery, so that whosoever embraces it seldom or never is able to possess God."[50] To his mind, even Ermengard's intention to enter religion (and that is as far as it probably went since Robert seemed determined not to receive her into Fontevrault) was binding.

Geoffrey's admonition was distinctly old school and would come to seem increasingly out of step with the times. For the same emphasis on intention that had formerly made a woman's pious resolve to preserve her chastity iron-clad would permit the quintessentially secular institution of marriage to push back against centuries of bias favoring chastity, even *after* the woman had seemingly entered religion. This new resistance is apparent in the correspondence of Anselm (d. 1109), archbishop of Canterbury, and his interactions with two princesses: Mathilda, daughter of King Malcolm III of Scotland, and Gunhilda, daughter and last descendant to the unfortunate Anglo-Saxon king Harold.

Both women were inhabitants of the monastery at Wilton. Mathilda had allegedly been placed with the sisters for the sake of her education; Gunhilda, for her safety from Norman marauders. But neither woman had made her final vows or received the consecration that formally bound her in marriage to Christ. Not only did both decamp from Wilton in order to marry, but the two princesses were interconnected in another strange way.[51] Mathilda's father had originally intended that she marry the puissant Count Alan Rufus, lord of Richmond. But when Rufus covertly visited Wilton in the hopes of catching a glimpse of his intended, he observed that Mathilda was already veiled and hence, to his mind, no longer marriageable. Rufus ended up eloping with (or possibly abducting) Gunhilda. It is, of course, possible that he had already become interested in the other princess before he saw Mathilda. But whether an elopement or an abduction, Anselm stated in no uncertain terms that Gunhilda's salvation was at stake if she did not return. In a letter circa 1093 he wrote,

> For it is impossible for you to be saved in any way unless you return to the habit and the vowed life which you rejected. Even though you were not consecrated by the bishop and did not read your vows in his presence, nevertheless these vows were evident and cannot be denied since you wore the habit of your holy intention in public and in private and through this you affirmed to everyone who saw you that you were dedicated to God no less than if you had read your vows. . . . You are without excuse if you desert the holy intention which you long professed by your habit and way of life, even though you did not read the customary vows nor were you consecrated by the bishop. . . . The King who desired your beauty in order to become your lawful spouse is still waiting for you and calling you back so that you may be his lawful bride, and if not a virgin at least chaste. For we know of many holy women who, having lost their virginity, were more pleasing to God and were closer to him through their penitence in their chastity than many others, even through their holy virginity.[52]

He thus advises her, "Throw off and trample on the secular dress you have assumed" forthwith.[53]

This letter yielded no immediate returns. When Rufus died before the marriage, moreover, Gunhilda did not return to the community but instead formed an alliance with Count Alan Niger, brother and heir to her late fiancé. In a subsequent letter the following year, Anselm rebukes the unfortunate princess for her folly in backing the wrong kind of bridegroom, mocking her choice with grisly rhetorical contrasts: "Your loved one who loved you, Count Alan Rufus. Where is he now? Where has that beloved lover of yours gone? Go now, sister, lie down with him on the bed in which he now lies; gather his worms to your bosom; embrace his corpse; press your lips to his naked teeth, for his lips have already been consumed by putrefaction."[54] It is possible that Gunhilda returned to Wilton eventually. But if this was, in fact, the case, her return was more likely prompted by the untimely death of Niger than Anselm's letter.[55]

Anselm construed the donning of the monastic garb alone as equivalent to a public profession of chastity. The fact that Gunhilda neither wore a veil nor was consecrated was beside the point. Both Anselm and his contemporary

Ivo of Chartres agreed that a monastic vocation was binding without being professed publicly, arguing that there was no ceremony of profession in monasticism's earliest days.[56] The possibility of a binding entrance into religion in which the individual's explicit consent was not a factor was defended in other ways as well. Anselm's predecessor, Archbishop Lanfranc (d. 1089), did acknowledge the importance of profession to the indissolubility of a religious vocation, yet still considered oblates (i.e., children offered by their parents) as permanently bound.[57] And there were plenty of ancient sources that likewise dispensed with the need for a formal profession. We have seen that Leo I construed a pious resolve to pledge perpetual chastity as binding. A number of early church councils advanced that widows and girls living in their own homes who assumed a religious habit, but subsequently married, would be permanently excommunicated—regardless of whether their pious modus vivendi was their own or their parents' decision.[58] Furthermore, a number of these sources found their way into Gratian. According to this standard, looking like a nun was tantamount to being a nun—a position that placed dependent women at a distinct disadvantage. Thus when Mathilda, our second princess, left the cloister, Anselm referred to her as "the fallen daughter" of the king of Scotland in a letter to the bishop of Salisbury.[59]

But the increased emphasis on intentionality provided (some) women with the ammunition they needed to fight for greater autonomy, Mathilda being a case in point. According to Eadmer, Anselm's secretary and biographer, Mathilda was aware of the many rumors generated by her sojourn at Wilton. Thus in 1100, when she was on the verge of her wedding to England's Henry I, she approached Anselm to seek his advice. Anselm (who, as we have seen, had contributed to the rumor mill that was currently grinding up Mathilda's good name) "declared that he was not to be induced by any pleading to take from God his bride and join her in marriage to an earthly husband." Mathilda, however, stood her ground. She acknowledged to wearing the veil, but maintained that she only did so out of constraint. " 'That hood I did wear in her [my aunt's] presence, chafing at it and fearful; but, as soon I was able to escape out of her sight, I tore it off and threw it on the ground and trampled on it." (Anselm may have been taken aback by this bizarre inversion of his earlier advice to Gunhilda that she "throw off and trample on the secular dress" that she had precipitously assumed.) According to Mathilda, it was never her father's intention that she become a nun, that in fact "when by chance he saw me veiled [he] snatched the veil off and tearing it in pieces invoked the hatred of God upon the person who had put it on me."[60]

Anselm, who had only recently been made archbishop of Canterbury and clearly felt the full awkwardness of his position, convoked an assembly of clerics to adjudicate this delicate matter. (It is interesting that Anselm himself left the room while they were deliberating, whether because he had already made up his own mind, or out of ambivalence, or because he did not want to influence the deliberations.)[61] The assembly resolved that Mathilda was free to marry on the basis of an analogy in the time of Lanfranc when a number of women entered religious communities to preserve their virtue from marauders. A council convoked by Lanfranc determined that the women were free to leave their communities if they so wished—a condition that would have exonerated Gunhilda's flight. Mathilda's situation was deemed similar: " 'Though we realize that her case is less serious than theirs, seeing that, while all wore the veil for a like cause, they did so of their own accord, she under compulsion.' "[62] The royal couple was duly married, with Anselm presiding.[63]

Eadmer implies that Anselm became the target of considerable criticism for countenancing Mathilda's marriage to Henry. And, indeed, his eventual support of the marriage was a reversal of his original position that a religious habit spoke for itself: whoever wore one was either married to Christ or all but married to Christ. This begs the question as to whether it was adultery for such an individual subsequently to contract carnal marriage, and, if so, were these subsequent unions invalid? Augustine had sidestepped the adultery issue, arguing that whether such behavior merited this label, it was worse than mere carnal adultery from the perspective of the sin committed. Even so, he upheld the validity of these unions, pragmatically deferring to the rights of the spouse who had not vowed chastity.[64] But any woman who had broken her vow was automatically a lifelong excommunicate, one who could not even be admitted to penance until the death of her husband.[65] In the meantime, the prevailing pastoral recommendation was that the offending party should render, but not exact, the conjugal debt.[66]

It is unlikely that Anselm would agree to preside over the marriage of an excommunicate. Even so, Mathilda seems to have required a modicum of reassurance on that score. Soon after the marriage, Mathilda sends Anselm a concerned letter, entreating him to desist from excessive fasting. Amid the myriad of accolades underlining Anselm's importance to the kingdom, Mathilda does not neglect to mention "by whose blessing I was sanctified in legitimate matrimony, by whose consecration I was raised to the dignity of earthly royalty and by whose prayers I shall be crowned, God granting, in heavenly glory."[67] Anselm's response is polite but restrained: "through me Your highness was espoused in legitimate marriage, crowned and raised to the eminence of royalty with my blessing."[68] Still, consecration is reserved for her coronation, not her marriage. And there is no mention of the afterlife.

It was the renewed emphasis on consent that ultimately gave Mathilda the boost that helped her over the cloister wall. She went on to become a good queen, whose mediation was fundamental in bridging the chasm that had opened up between her husband and Anselm over the issue of lay investiture.[69] But Mathilda's option was probably never offered to the Frankish Basina, to her own discredit and the detriment of the community at Poiters. And this is a tragedy. For while Basina may well have made a good queen, whether in Spain or elsewhere, she would almost certainly have made a terrible nun just about anywhere.

In Mathilda's case, secular marriage won out because she had never consented to a mystical marriage with Christ. With Christina of Markyate, however, the new emphasis on the consent in secular marriage (or at least the appearance of consent) undercuts marriage to Christ in a different way. As the example of Æthelthryth implies, an unconsummated marriage had at one time been easily dispensed with for the purpose of entering religion. But around the time that Christina was bullied into her unfortunate union with the still more unfortunate Burthred, the clergy were attempting to juggle the implications of both intentionality and consensual marriage. It is only to be expected that they would drop a few balls.

In Christina's case, this meant that the clergy seemed to err through extreme deference to secular marriage, and the sufficiency of consent. Although one would think that the combination of constraint, nonconsummation, and a preexisting vow were sufficient to nullify any marriage, a number of the clerics that Christina encounters persist in regarding her as married. At the beginning of the interview with Fredebert, Christina's father readily admits that she was forced into marriage. Nevertheless the prior attempts to make Christina accept Burthred—even after Christina declares that she vowed chastity in the presence of witnesses long before the marriage.[70] When Canon Sueno and an anonymous chaplain meet with Burthred and temporarily convince him to release Christina, Burthred assumes the responsibility of paying for the entrance of his spouse (*sponsa*) into religion, and the two clerics praise him for " 'his wise and religious sentiments.' "[71] Even Roger, an anchorite schooled in the tradition of the misogamic desert fathers, becomes irate when approached by the well-meaning Eadwine on behalf of the hapless Christina: " 'Have you come here to show me how to dissolve marriages? Get out of here quickly and think yourself lucky if you get away safe and sound: you deserve a whipping.' "[72]

Christina's difficulties suggest the ways in which the spiritualization of secular marriage occasionally allowed the human husband to edge out the divine. This trend is again exemplified in the life of the confessor saint Alexis. Like Malchus, Aldhelm's example of defiant male chastity, Alexis left his marriage unconsummated and fled. Unlike Malchus, however, Alexis did not leave without the knowledge of his wife. Instead, he preached to her in their wedding chamber and gave her three gifts before he left: a gold ring, a richly wrought belt, and a veil. The first two gifts were symbolic indications of Alexis's full recognition of the marriage and its indissoluble nature. But the veil was multivalent. It could be read as the head-covering of a matron, underlining the validity of the union and binding his virgin wife to marital chastity for the duration of his life.[73] But the veil could also mark his pious intentions for his wife as *sponsa Christi*, in which case she was bound to virginity for her entire life. From this perspective, Christina's attraction to the cult of Alexis is laced with irony. For although Christina fled her marriage bed as did Alexis, her fate also resonates with the woman that Alexis abandoned—a virgin, pawn to her parents' matrimonial strategies, and hence bound for life to a virtual stranger after a mere exchange of promises. Fortunately, Christina did not have to await her putative husband's death in order to regain her freedom. Subdued by two nights of terrifying visions (sent expressly by the Virgin Mary), Burthred was finally prepared to release Christina from her wedding vows after somewhere between four to eight years had elapsed. He did so by "placing his right hand in the right hand of Roger and promising and confirming her release" in the presence of three priests and five hermits.[74]

Concurrent with these striking testimonials to the binding force of consent in secular marriage, there is a dissonant awareness of the consequences of Christina's pious proposition that runs like a steady stream throughout the narrative. Christina makes a private vow of virginity in her youth, which she regards as binding.[75] She shares her secret with her mentor, Sueno, who subsequently gives her up for lost when he hears of her marriage.[76] In Christina's spirited defense of her position before Fredebert, she maintains, "'from my infancy I have chosen chastity and have vowed to Christ that I would remain a virgin: this I did before witnesses, but even if they were not present God would be my witness to my conscience continuously.'"[77] When Fredebert referred the matter to Bishop Robert of Lincoln, his response (at least before he was bribed) was that "'no bishop under heaven . . . could force her into marriage, if according to her vow she wishes to keep herself for God.'"[78] Even the prickly Roger shows he is of two minds, eventually regretting his stern response to Christina's plight: "'I know, O Lord almighty and most rigorous judge, that Thou wilt claim her soul at my hands. For I knew that she had a good will, but I was unwilling to give her my help when she asked for it.' "[79]

Christina's union with Burthred was dissolved sometime between 1118 and 1122. Over the course of the twelfth century, however, some of the tension between the consensual marriage, nonconsummation, and entrance into religion would be resolved. Two decades later, in his account of the evolution of woman's religious vocation, Abelard remarks, "Betrothed virgins also, if before they have mingled carnally with their husbands they have decided to choose the monastic life, and rejecting man to make God their Husband, have the freedom of action in this matter which we nowhere read granted to men."[80] Eventually, Gregory IX's *Decretals* will extend this privilege of unilaterally entering a religious institution to both husband and wife, but this option is only available for the first two months of marriage. It hearkened back to the good old days when virginity trumped marriage and was very much at odds with the newly spiritualized definition of carnal marriage. But while undercutting the sufficiency of consent as a principle, it had the advantage of validating the behavior of both Christina and Æthelthryth alike.[81]

Virtual Virginity / Virtual Vocation / Virtual Heloise

Clarissa Atkinson has argued that over the course of the high and late Middle Ages, virginity would be progressively valued as a state of mind in religious discourse, a phenomenon that she associates with the rise of female lay piety in the thirteenth century.[82] But we can already perceive this process at work in the twelfth century as the new emphasis on intentionality and consent begins to seep into the virginal ideal. While intact virginity would remain the gold standard for religious women, there is a renewed emphasis on the possibility of a woman losing her integrity, or the merit that her virginity might accrue, while still technically remaining a virgin.[83] This was a familiar enough patristic trope. Yet women were by and large spared the disturbing discussions generated by sexual thoughts that gave rise to the prolix and explicit discourse surrounding nocturnal emissions and the problem they presented for the ascetic male.[84] The virgin had only herself to blame for succumbing to spiritual vices like overweening pride. But when it came to the more fundamental, carnal sins, she was generally understood to have a partner in crime, and hence pastoral authorities severely restricted contact with men. This gendered difference is somewhat surprising considering that classical tradition perceived women as more lascivious than men. In the twelfth century, however, treatises on virginity begin to make up for lost time, generating a discourse that was both cerebral and clinical. Hence Ælred, who as we have seen cautioned about the extreme fragility of virginity, raised the ante in his discussion of the virgins who follow the lamb in the Apocalypse: "But virginity is more often corrupted, and chastity violated, without the mixing with another's body, but a heat striking the flesh with great force would subdue the will, and rape the members." "[H]er virginal limbs [could] be stained by a simple motion."[85] The virgin's imagination was her own worst enemy.

There is evidence that women took the implications of these dark warnings to heart. On the eve of her consecration as a virgin, Christina of Markyate was "mindful of the thoughts and stings of the flesh with which she had been troubled, and even though she was not conscious of having fallen either in deed or in desire [*voluntate*], she was chary of asserting that she had escaped unscathed." Christina's confusion was such that she was not sure how she should answer the bishop when he questioned her about her virginity. She was reassured by a vision in which she was hailed as a virgin of Christ by three youths of extraordinary beauty and crowned amid a throng of angels.[86]

But while the emphasis on the will and intention may have presented possible minefields for Christina of Markyate's virginal introspection, it also opened up an arena of rich possibilities for the woman who was no longer a virgin. Augustine could again be said to lead the way with his assertion of Lucretia's essential integrity: "Here was a marvel: there were two, and only one committed adultery."[87] This conclusion need not apply to acts of violence alone. Marital sex could be parsed with similar results: the one who exacted the marriage debt might be guilty of a venial sin (excused by the good of marriage), while the one who obediently rendered, though mentally resisting the inevitable pleasure that Augustine believed to be inherent in the act, was sinless.[88] In the twelfth-century climate of intentionality, it was believed that a virgin could be undone by wayward thoughts. But could this principle be applied inversely? Was it possible for a matron to somehow retain her claims to virginity through outward compliance in the sex act, but an inward aloofness, even a resistance?

It seems that at least one matron believed this kind of virtual virginity was within her reach.[89] The woman in question was the unusually pious mother of Guibert of Nogent (d. 1124). If an aversion to the marital act was one of the criteria for virtual virginity, she gave every indication of being fully credentialed. What Guibert tells us about his parents' relationship bespeaks his mother's resistance at every turn. The marriage remained unconsummated for either three or seven years.[90] Although the alleged reason was enchantment, it is more than likely that his mother's exemplary trepidation contributed to the couple's problems. Guibert describes his mother as "terrified of sin, not from experience but from dread of some sort of blow from on high, and—as she often told me herself—this dread had so possessed her mind with the terror of sudden death that in later years she grieved because she no longer felt in her maturity the same stings of righteous fear."[91] Throughout the Middle Ages, the payment of the conjugal debt presented a huge psychic obstacle for most religiously in-clined women, perhaps inducing different degrees of what medieval authorities recognized as frigidity.[92] And such conditions are psychologically contagious, which could explain the husband's inability to consummate the marriage. The husband had, in the meantime, begotten an illegitimate child, proving that he could function sexually with other women.[93] Eventually the enchantment was broken, however, and Guibert reports that his mother "submitted to the office of the marriage bed as faithfully as she had kept her virginity."[94]

Guibert tells us little of his mother's married life. But apparently she "cherished her widowhood as if . . . she had always loathed a wife's bedtime duties"—a disclosure that prefaces a vision of her husband in purgatory. There was one incident that allegedly occurred prior to Guibert's birth that is also suggestive. Guibert's father was taken prisoner by an opponent reputed to en-slave his captives rather than accept ransom. Lying awake in anxiety, Guibert's mother was visited by a demon in the dead of night: "the Enemy himself lay upon her and by the burden of his weight almost crushed the life out of her."[95] The demon in question was most certainly an incubus, but not of the seducing variety. The ancients were familiar with creatures who sat upon the chest of its sleeping victims in an effort to smother them, and these were also known as incubi.[96] The distance between these two kinds of harassment may not be so great, however. For Guibert's mother, the sense of being smothered under a heavy burden could be construed as an ugly approximation of the sex act.[97] Guibert was aware of the lascivious version of the incubus, elsewhere making explicit reference to "stories about demons who covet the love of women and even intercourse with them."[98] The fact that Guibert refrains from the proper demonic nomenclature in both instances probably suggests his awareness of a possible slippage between different facets of the nocturnal creature and his fear of associating his ultrachaste mother with an attack that could impugn her chastity. Still, his choice of verbs to describe the demon's assault on his mother—*incubuit* (lit. "he laid upon")—gives the game away.

There is no suggestion of pleasure in the above visitation. One might more easily imagine her acute discomfort as a representation of her feelings when her husband's body lay upon her in the dead of night "crush[ing] the life out of her." If so, the anxiety that kept Guibert's mother awake might represent her ambivalence over her husband's plight rather than simple concern for his well-being. She knew that she should pray for his safe return, but nevertheless found his sexual demands insupportable. This could also explain why her horror of sin lifted when she was a mature woman, who also happened to be widowed. Once free of the marital debt, she was also free of all of the guilt and revulsion associated with the act.

The incubus was eventually routed when a good spirit attending Guibert's mother (presumably her guardian angel) invoked Mary. The spirit's parting words were, " 'Take care to be a good woman.' " And she certainly seems to have taken this warning to heart, at least according to her own lights.[99] Some twelve years after her husband's death, when Guibert's mother was privately contemplating a withdrawal from the world, a "devil-possessed dependant of hers" shouted out that " 'the priests have put a cross in her loins.' "[100] But it had clearly been there all along.

Guibert's mother would later retreat to an anchor-hold that she had built near the monastery of Fly. There she modeled her devotional practices upon the observances of an old woman who lived there in "the habit of a nun" (*sanctimoniali habitu*).[101] But imitating was not enough, and three years before her death, she "conceive[d] a strong desire to take the sacred veil." Interestingly, she met with considerable resistance from every quarter, including her devoted son, Guibert: "I tried to dissuade her, putting forward as authority the passage where it is written, 'Let no prelate [*nullus pontificum*] attempt to veil widows,' saying that her most chaste life would be sufficient without external robes and Anselm, abbot of Bec and afterward archbishop of Canterbury in England . . . had also forbidden this to her in the past."[102] Such strong objections at first seem rather opaque. Certainly there was nothing illicit about a widow being veiled, provided she veiled herself. And it is hard to imagine that Anselm would discourage a devout woman's public profession when she was so near to death—that is, unless he were asked to impose the veil. And this is, in fact, what Anselm seems to have denied her. The Gelasian decretal that Guibert cites does not imply that there is anything wrong with a widow assuming the veil. What is at issue is whether the bishop imposes it. Anneke Mulder-Bakker suggests that Guibert's mother wished to be veiled as a deaconess, which she describes as an "upgraded widow's blessing."[103] Mulder-Bakker is correct in asserting that this ritual does require the bishop's presence. But the bishop only blesses the deaconess when he imposes her stole (*orarium*). He does not impose the veil. As in the consecration of a widow, the prospective deaconess puts the veil on herself.[104]

An episcopal veiling is reserved for a virgin. And it is this type of veiling that I believe is what Guibert's mother sought for the spiritual capital it afforded.[105] The measure of her religious aspirations is most clearly revealed in her dreams, which serve as a perfect vindication of Freud's premise that a dream is a wish.[106] The first occurred when she was contemplating a possible retreat from the world. Her resolve was strengthened when "she saw the following vision in a dream: she seemed to be marrying a man and celebrating her nuptials, much to the amazement and stupefaction of her children, friends, and kinfolk." When she shared this revelation with her clerical confidant, "One look at [his] face and without speech from him she knew the vision pointed . . . to the love of God, to Whom she longed to be united."[107]

As we have seen, her relatives were just as incredulous and resistant in mundane reality as they were in her dream. Yet sometimes dreams come true: in all probability, Guibert's mother received the episcopal consecration as bride of Christ. Paralleling the interrogation by the bishop that Christina of Markyate had anticipated with trepidation, Guibert tells us that his mother was also questioned about her worthiness in the course of the ritual. Christina had been fearful lest her virginity had been mentally compromised. The situation of Guibert's mother may have been more delicate still. She could not possibly argue that she was literally a virgin; she could, however, have argued that, while submitting to marital sex dutifully, she had never initiated sex. In fact, she had always inwardly resisted sex, permitting her to qualify as a virtual virgin. Whatever explicit claim she intended to advance on her own behalf, however, was both reiterated and supported by a vision. A beautiful and richly dressed woman loaned Guibert's mother a veil, with the understanding that she would return it at the proper time.[108] In the ordo for the consecration of virgins, the blessing of the veil is a prayer addressed to Christ that represents the supplicant virgin as receiving the veil "on account of your love of your blessed mother, namely the ever-virgin Mary."[109] The dream was thus compelling "proof" that Guibert's mother had already been vetted as a bride by Mary, ultimate bride and future mother-in-law. Everyone agreed that the veiling was preordained by God.

If, in fact, Guibert's mother received the episcopal veiling, one might ask why his account seems so obscure. The interrogation alluded to earlier seems to have been conducted by John, the abbot of Fly. Why is there no mention of the bishop? This question may not have occurred to a knowing medieval reader. The fact that Guibert refers to the veil consistently as the *velamen sacrum*—a term reserved for the virgin's veil alone, and never applied to the widow or deaconess—speaks volumes. There are other encoded pieces of evidence as well. In the ritual for the consecration of a virgin, the presiding bishop says, "accept the sacred veil and wear it without stain until [you appear] before the judgment seat of our Lord Jesus Christ."[110] Guibert's final words on his mother's veiling are a variation on this theme, reconstituted through the medium of his mother's Marian vision: "She faithfully guarded this holy veil [*sacrum velamen*] to the best of her powers for almost three whole years, and on that day she carried it back to the Lady who had entrusted it to her."[111] There was no need to mention the bishop. Of course he was there.

Guibert's mother died sometime after 1104. About three decades later, Peter Abelard would be hard at work developing a more flexible set of criteria for the bride of Christ—one sufficiently accommodating to include his estranged wife, Heloise.[112] As we shall see, his focus on individual intention as the sole determinant for assessing sin and merit would have enormous implications for human sexuality, going a long way to redress the plight of the "virginally challenged." The individual's self-referential focus was supplemented by a positive view of nature, complementing the period's parallel fascination and anticipating the liberalizing influence of Aristotle. But Abelard did not attempt to reunite the individual's fissured sexual persona(e) in one fell swoop; it was a process, and he took his time.

In a remarkably short period, Abelard and Heloise were forced to assume a series of different roles, each of which irrevocably changed the footing upon which they were expected to interact with one another: they went from lovers to prospective parents to husband and wife to, finally, a spiritual kinship in Christ. Heloise attempts to capture these different personae in the rueful salutation that initiates her correspondence with Abelard. "To her lord, or rather father; to her husband, or rather brother; from his handmaid, or rather daughter; from his wife, or rather sister."[113] Such convolutions read like a medieval correlative to Polanski's *Chinatown*, with Faye Dunaway's climactic revelation of incestuously overlapping relations.

These fluctuating personae of Abelard and Heloise showcase various degrees of volition and constraint, raising the play of inward resistance and outward compliance (and perhaps vice versa) to new heights of complexity according to philosophical, ethical, and practical standards. Abelard and Heloise's cognizance of these tensions is especially articulated in the focus on the primacy of intention over action alluded to earlier, commonly referred to as the "ethic of pure intention"—a measure invoked by Heloise in particular. Thus she could defend herself against charges of fornication with a clear conscience: "Wholly guilty though I am, I am also, as you know, wholly innocent. It is not the deed but the intention of the doer that makes the crime, and justice should weigh not what was done but the spirit in which it is done."[114] Heloise's remarks demonstrate how the ethic of pure intention was a generous and forgiving standard when applied to something as heartfelt as her love for Abelard. But when applied to more conflicted issues, such as the couple's contentious marriage and entrance into religion, this same criterion could seem a harsh and impossibly exacting standard, calling into question the efficacy of the marriage and religious profession alike.

Heloise is probably the most famous spokesperson for a sincere aversion to marriage common to many, if not most, twelfth-century intellectuals.[115] And her revulsion was well-publicized. In his autobiography, Abelard details Heloise's objections to marriage at length, which, according to his self-serving recollection, mostly turn on the institution's negative impact on his intellectual career.[116] Heloise will later expand upon her reasons "for preferring love to wedlock and freedom to chains,"[117] emphasizing her resistance to constraint and institutionalization.

And yet this adamant critic of matrimony nevertheless married Abelard at his behest and soon after, against her inclination but again at Abelard's insistence, entered religion. From the perspective of the ethic of pure intention, the grave misgivings she expressed on the brink of these two life-changing commitments could be construed as raising impediments to each. When Abelard proposed marriage, "She was strongly opposed to this proposal"; and again, "She absolutely rejected this marriage" (*Detestabatur vehementer hoc matrimonium*). Her eventual acquiescence was characterized as an admission of defeat, only wrested from her when she "at last saw that her attempts to persuade or dissuade me [Abelard] were making no impression on my foolish obstinacy."[118] Furthermore, when Fulbert and his allies began to spread the word that Abelard had made reparation for his assault on the honor of the canon's household by marrying his niece, she "cursed them and swore that there was no truth in this."[119] Heloise allegedly denied the marriage to protect Abelard's career. Even so, the strange complicity between her inner hostility to marriage and her outer oaths that there was no marriage is striking. She opposes the institution, generally, but this marriage in particular; marries anyways; yet persists in maintaining publicly that she was not married. Such tortured permutations beg the question of whether she was actually married—at least according to the tribunal of intentionality.

Heloise's entrance into religion is even more problematical. The terms in which Abelard describes Heloise's veiling are telling: she was "veiled willingly at my command" (*ad imperium nostrum sponte velata*). This sounds like a parting act of submission from a dutiful wife.[120] Heloise will later liken this compliance to suicide: "I found strength at your command to destroy myself. . . . I did more, strange to say—my love rose to such heights of madness that it robbed itself of what it most desired beyond hope of recovery, when immediately at your bidding I changed my clothing along with my mind, in order to prove you the sole possessor of my body and my will alike."[121] It is with a desperate clarity that she reasons, "I can expect no reward for this from God, for it is certain that I have done nothing for love of him."[122] Her next letter bears vivid testimony to this sad admission, recounting how she continues to be preyed upon by sexual fantasies that she cannot bring herself to repent. "I can win praise in the eyes of men but deserve none before God, who searches our hearts and loins and sees in our darkness (Ps. 7.10)."[123]

It seems to have been Heloise who first deploys this memorable image of God as both solitary reader and ultimate judge of the intentions. The image and philosophy that went with it would eventually be at the center of Abelard's *Ethics*—the philosophical treatise that would present the ethic of pure intention to the world, pressed to its logical conclusions. Yet Heloise uses it here and again in a subsequent letter well before the appearance of *Ethics*.[124] It is therefore possible, perhaps even likely, that not only the use of this image but the ethical emphasis on the import of intention originated with Heloise and that Abelard's later thesis was built upon her core beliefs.[125]

But whether the emphasis on intentionality originated with Heloise is immaterial to her spiritual dilemma. It was clearly the standard by which she judged herself. And so, if Heloise had indeed privately withheld her consent to religion, as she implies, she was not a true nun—at least according to the code she subscribed to herself and ascribed to God. But we know that this was hardly the majority view. If we were to apply the standard advanced by Anselm in his letter to Gunhilda, Heloise's entrance into religion was not only preordained but even overdue. Anselm had insisted that Gunhilda was already a nun, even without a veil or public profession, precisely because her vows "were evident and cannot be denied since you wore the habit of your holy intention in public and in private and through this you affirmed to everyone who saw you that you were dedicated to God no less than if you had read your vows." Heloise had signaled a similar intent. Abelard reveals that he had made Heloise don a religious habit, though he is careful to stipulate without the veil, when he spirited her away from Fulbert and placed her among the nuns at Argenteuil.[126]

Yet despite these outer appearances, Heloise's position is as consistent as it was eloquent: it was Abelard, not Christ, that was her true love, and hence at the center of whatever vocation she assumed. So although her outer dress and deportment might have sustained the illusion that she was on her way to becoming a nun, her inner commitment gainsaid this impression. The private sentiments of Abelard, however, who was the motive force behind most of Heloise's ambiguous behavior, were much less certain. As will be seen below, Abelard's writings on the religious life demonstrate an excellent grasp of canon law and liturgy alike. He was doubtless aware of the symbolic importance attached to monastic garb, with or without the veil. So rather than arguing that Abelard made a mistake in this instance, it is much easier to make the psychoanalytic case that there are no mistakes. Heloise had been correct in her assessment that marriage would be detrimental to Abelard's career. The Gregorian reform had succeeded in making marriage the ultimate barrier between the clergy and laity. In 1139, the second Lateran Council outlawed marriage for anyone in major orders.[127] Thus in dressing his wife as a nun, Abelard, a man with a talent that was matched only by his ambition, was expressing a wish. And this wish was to be free of Heloise in the only licit way possible, which was for her to become a nun.[128] This is, of course, what Fulbert assumed were Abelard's motives in dressing Heloise in such a garb. Moreover, if we assess Abelard's deception in light of Heloise's eventual fate, his wish was granted, Fulbert's interpretation of Abelard's intent fully vindicated, and the castration deserved. Abelard's later recollections of his monastic ruse express evident satisfaction over the ultimate outcome, although he strategically imputes Heloise's entrance into religion to God's will: "You know too how when you were pregnant and I took you to my country you disguised yourself in the sacred habit of a nun, a pretence which was an irreverent mockery of the religion you now profess. Consider, then, how fittingly divine justice, or rather, divine grace brought you *against your will* to the religion which you did not hesitate to mock, so that you should willingly expiate our profanation in the same habit, and the truth of reality should remedy the lie of your pretence and correct your falsity."[129] Interestingly, in this instance Abelard permits the fait accompli to trump intention. In fact, God and Abelard alike seem indifferent to the fact that Heloise's entrance into religion was constrained.

This is the background against which Abelard began framing complicated questions about how an individual's sexual identity impinged upon his or her future salvation, questions that would continue to preoccupy him throughout his career. This line of inquiry first appears in *Sic et non*, written around 1120—soon after the couple's joint entrance into religion. The whole point of the work was to emphasize the conflict among various authorities over a wide range of theological and moral questions as preparatory to a scholarly resolution. All of the 158 questions are thus provided with a series of dueling authorities proving or disproving a given contention. Since *Sic et non* was intended as a kind of student exercise book, however, there is no attempt to reconcile the sources, and the questions remain unresolved. Yet this very equivocation could also be reflective of the author's own mental turmoil during this period. The series of questions regarding marriage, virginity, and consent are especially suggestive. One can almost hear the wheels of that finely tuned mind turning over possible solutions to the many perplexing issues surrounding his marriage.

Question 129: *That a person should be permitted to marry many times, or not* reviewed the church's toleration of and repugnance for remarriage. Could remarriage have been an option for Heloise? Probably not. Even so, Abelard made sure that it wasn't, as he himself admits to Heloise: "At the time I desired to keep you whom I loved beyond measure for myself alone for ever. . . . Had you not been previously joined to me in wedlock, you might easily have clung to the world when I withdrew from it."[130]

Question 130: *That no sexual intercourse is possible without sin, and the contrary* borrowed largely from Augustine's *On Marriage and Concupiscence*. Augustine's sexual pessimism draws a dark curtain over the sex act, through which only occasional glimmers of optimism from the opposing Pelagian camp peep.[131] Heloise's "perpetual complaint" was that God punished them once their relations were licit—licit, perhaps, but, from the perspective of fallen humanity, never pure. There was no purity for the married.[132]

Question 131: *That a fornicator is not permitted to marry the woman with whom he fornicated.* The sources seem pretty evenly divided on this one.[133] Abelard's marriage to Heloise was valid; but, considering their prehistory as exuberant fornicators, was it really licit? Food for thought.

Question 132: *That a sterile woman is not fit to marry and the contrary* primarily addresses under what circumstances you can unilaterally dismiss a wife,[134] which, from Fulbert's perspective, is what Abelard was attempting when he disguised Heloise as a nun. Perhaps Abelard was prepared to acknowledge that Fulbert had a point.

Question 133: *That virginity is now enjoined, or not* emphasizes that a life of chastity should not be forced on anyone.[135] Poor Heloise!

Question 134: *That nuptials are also enjoined and not.* The Apostolic injunction to marry and avoid burning is balanced against

Chrysostom's prediction of the perdition in store for the religious who falls from his chaste resolve by a forced marriage (not to mention the punishment visited upon whoever forced them to marry).[136] Abelard had once been committed to chastity. But no one forced him to marry, as he had Heloise. And now she was the one in danger of falling from a commitment to a chastity to which he had bound her! The only positive side is that he still had time to do penance for his multiple offenses in this area.

   Question 135: That nuptials are good and the contrary. The enduring goodness of marriage is placed cheek by jowl against reminders of how it is good not to touch a woman, marriage diminishes time for God, the insistent obligation of the marriage debt, and the bad time in store for those who give suck in the last days. (To make things worse, most of this was construed through the lens of Jerome's *Against Jovinian*—a work that was not only merciless on the subject of marriage but also happened to be a particular favorite in the good old days when Abelard and Heloise were free-wheeling lovers.)[137]

It makes for gloomy reading. The cumulative impression is that human sexuality was either always in need of restraint or in constant danger of being wrongfully constrained. Whatever the extent of his guilt over his treatment of Heloise, Abelard doubtless felt some relief that he was well out of it.

But there was one question that does open up the possibility of liberty from the darker aspects of embodiment. *Question 143* addresses the tangled contention *that sin is an act, not a thing, and the contrary.* The authorities are heavily freighted with Augustine's writings against Pelagius, the bulk of which associate sin with an external act. At one point Augustine poses the question of whether sin is "some substance, or wholly a name without substance, whereby is expressed, not a thing, not an existence, not some sort of a body, but merely the doing of a wrongful deed." This determination is confirmed by a proverb ascribed to Seneca: "Every sin is an action; moreover every action is voluntary, the good and the bad, therefore every sin is voluntary."[138] But this tentative consensus is soon undermined by a remark ascribed to Jerome: "There are two kinds of sin: one from intent, the other from neglect."[139] Far from equating sin with an action, sin is presented as the actual antithesis to action.

The tipping point that severs sin and action altogether occurs with Augustine's treatment of sinful acts being perpetrated on or by an innocent body—a female body. This point is first made by the exoneration of a virgin who unwittingly consummated her marriage with a man who was not her husband. But it is soon followed by the familiar evocation of Lucretia: "Marvelous to say: there were two and only one committed adultery." For the most penetrating view would assess "not the union of bodies . . . but the disparity of spirits."[140] Abelard then follows up with instances that consolidate the spirit of Lucretia's example: Augustine's statement that continence is not primarily a virtue of the body, but one of the soul—significantly taken from *The Good of Marriage* and assorted patristic authorities on virginity as a state of mind. The isolation of both sin and chastity as mental attributes had the potential to free the individual from the bondage of physical accidents.[141]

This separation of body and soul in the assessment of sin provides the scaffolding for what will eventually become Abelard's iconic work *Ethics*, which was written sometime in 1139. With the possible exception of his pastoral writings for the Paraclete, which cannot be dated with any precision, *Ethics* was Abelard's final work.[142] It is in this treatise that the ethic of pure intention is finely honed, permitting Abelard a vantage point from which he could provide not just questions but also answers to some of life's most troubling moral dilemmas. It is significant that Abelard referred to the treatise as "Know Yourself" after the famed inscription of the Delphic oracle. And indeed the treatise could be read as an exercise in self-scrutiny and introspection in which the interior self is elevated over the outer acts of the public self.

At the center of the work is Abelard's conception of sin as "consent to what is not fitting"—to something that is scornful of, and hence condemned by, God.[143] This definition rendered sin intensely personal. It was completely divorced from any outer act: even an act that was considered culpable by both secular and religious authorities could be sinless, potentially pitting human and divine law against one another. For while human justice necessarily assesses good and evil on the basis of outer actions and expressions, God "who reads our hearts and loins" (Ps. 7.10; Prov. 24.12; Jer. 11.20) judges on the basis of intentions alone.[144] In the same spirit of Christ's unnerving allegation that a man with lascivious thoughts commits adultery, the standard advanced in *Ethics* had the potential for expanding the ambit for sin considerably. Yet, from the standpoint of salvation, it also negates the significance of what might be regarded as life's accidents: countless incidents over which one has no control, including the body's many mortifying treacheries.

In *Ethics* Abelard gives the appearance of having worked through the morass of pain and guilt from his own carnal past to what is in many ways an upbeat view of human sexuality. Intrinsic to this newfound optimism is the conviction that what is natural cannot be sinful, anticipating the more liberal stream of Aristotelian-inflected theology associated with the Dominican order by a century. Thus armed, he ridicules the widespread view that the pleasure inherent in certain acts renders the act sinful:

> If they really admit this, it is definitely not lawful for anyone to have fleshly pleasure. Therefore, spouses are not immune from sin when they unite in this carnal pleasure allowed to them, nor is he who enjoys the pleasurable consumption of his own fruit. Also, all invalids would be at fault who relish sweeter foods to refresh themselves and to recover from illness. . . . And lastly the Lord, the creator of food as well as bodies, would not be beyond fault if he put into them such flavours as would compel to sin those who eat them with pleasure. For how would he produce such things for our eating or allow their eating if it were impossible for us to eat them without sin? And how can sin be said to be committed in that which is allowed?[145]

Abelard derides the possibility that marital intercourse or eating are permitted but that pleasure is not, arguing that "no natural pleasure of the flesh should be imputed to sin nor should it be considered a fault for us to have pleasure in something in which when it has happened the feeling of pleasure was unavoidable." As the quintessential philosopher drama king, Abelard did not fail to punctuate his points with provocative exempla: "If someone compels a religious who is bound in chains to lie between women and if he is brought to pleasure, not to consent, by the softness of the bed and through contact of women beside him, who may presume to call this pleasure, made necessary by nature, a fault?"[146] This proposition is reinforced by the sharp distinction between body and spirit—a distinction that, at least in this context, seems salubrious. "As if an exterior and corporeal act could contaminate the soul," the master scoffs. "[Nothing] pollutes the soul except what is of the soul."[147]

A number of the principles advanced in the *Ethics* were vetted in Abelard's teaching as well. A set of his *quaestiones* that can probably be dated to 1140, toward the end of Abelard's teaching career, have been preserved in one of his student's marginalia. The focus is on the limits and meaning of religious chastity. For instance, Abelard declares it impossible to pronounce upon whether or not a monk or a layperson sins more by committing adultery because it is impossible to know who is displaying greater contempt for God. For what if the contempt in the layperson was such that, were he to have become a monk, he would still have committed adultery in spite of his obligation to God? In this latter scenario, to which only God could be privy, the degree of culpability for both the monk and the layman would be identical. By the same token, Abelard argues that it is impossible to assess whether it is worse for a man to sleep with a single woman or a married woman because we have no way of knowing if the individual in question would have slept with the woman regardless of whether she was married or not. Abelard also visited his casuistic speculations on biblical figures with considerable aplomb.[148] John the Baptist was probably just as prepared for martyrdom as Peter and was, hence, deserving of equal merit. Had the business of peopling the world been completed, Abraham would doubtless have been as ready and able to preserve his virginity as was John the Evangelist and should therefore be rewarded as such. Likewise, if a woman vowed chastity and never wavered in her resolve, nothing could remove her right to follow the lamb—even if she were not a virgin. This is borne out by Augustine's comment on Lucretia's rape: "there were two in the bed, but only one committed adultery while the other remained whole."[149]

In other words, God could judge a layperson according to the proverbial road not taken: a monastic career never embarked upon, a martyrdom never endured. The above *quaestio* also breaks down the barriers between various degrees of chastity by interrogating motive. This was no idle pastime. We have seen that Heloise's consent to both marriage and entrance into religion was less than perfect. Heloise also saw to it that Abelard was fully aware that she construed not just her commitment to chastity but her entire vocation, as an elaborate sham. She was sufficiently convincing on this score that Abelard feared for her salvation. This is clear when he responds to her "perpetual complaint":

> I had thought that this bitterness of heart at what was so clear an
> act of divine mercy had long since disappeared. The more danger-
> ous such bitterness is to you in wearing out body and soul alike, the
> more pitiful it is and distressing to me. If you are anxious to please
> me in everything, as you claim, and in this at least would end my
> torment, or even give me the greatest pleasure, you must rid your-
> self of it. If it persists you can neither please me nor attain bliss with
> me.[150]

But although Abelard may have been tormented by the possibility of Heloise in hell, his penchant for hypothetical and counterfactual speculation may also have afforded him glimpses of more optimistic vistas. For if he could imagine an Abraham who was every bit as virginal as John the Evangelist, he was also doubtless capable of imagining another Heloise: a virtual Heloise whom Abelard had never pursued, who had never been seduced, and who thus remained both emotionally and physically intact. The flesh-and-blood Heloise whom he had married claimed that her performance as the perfect nun was merely a posturing, sufficiently at odds with her inner self as to render her behavior hypocritical in her own and, she believed, God's eyes. But this Heloise still had qualities that could bridge the chasm between inner and outer selves. In Barbara Newman's words, Heloise "fulfilled to perfection the classical ideal of the *univira*."[151] Like Lucretia, Heloise had tenacity and courage in abundance, which she demonstrated in her love for Abelard. In the virtual world, however, Heloise's exemplary devotion would have a worthier object: a tenacious commitment to chastity resulting from love of Christ—a possibility that Abelard had personally thwarted. The flesh-and-blood Heloise would have died for Abelard; the virtual Heloise would have died for Christ, earning her the double crown of virginity and martyrdom.

Although Abelard might be able to conceive of such a Heloise, only God could clearly apprehend her and, when the time came, reward her. But Abelard doubtless longed to gaze upon this Heloise as well. To accomplish this, he had to make the virtual real, which required nothing less than suturing the terrible wound that had opened up between Heloise's public persona and her private self—the source of all her confusion and pain. As spiritual director, Abelard would naturally work for such an outcome, as he would for any spiritual daughter troubled in her vocation. But Abelard also needed this resolution for himself, as Heloise's husband: the man whose callous seduction had literally ruined her life. For, supposing he had been misled in his casuistic speculation and there was no virtual Abraham who had remained a virgin, no virtual layperson whose commitment to chastity was as portentous as if he were a monk, and no virtual Heloise. If this were the case, and Heloise remained unrepentant, she would be damned. And in God's eyes, and probably his own, he would be held responsible. And thus Abelard had to restore his estranged wife to her true bridegroom, the celestial one, from whom she was doubly estranged. As monumental as this task might be, there was still more required of him: he had to secure an honorable place in the celestial hierarchy for women such as Heloise so that they too could partake of the honor due to a bride of Christ.

Abelard's efforts to reconcile Heloise to her vocation are in evidence throughout their correspondence. In fact, Heloise's very first letter suggests that she was well ahead of the game, already anticipating Abelard's efforts to unite her with Christ and, dedicated *univira* that she was, prepared to resist wholeheartedly. In addition to her painful laments, Heloise registers her resistance through a powerful symbol. Her famous appeal to God as witness that she would choose to be Abelard's whore over honorable marriage to Augustus, "Emperor of the whole world," was not really hypothetical: it was but a thinly veiled protest to her coerced marriage with Christ, lord of the universe, infinitely preferring a dishonorable union with Abelard.[152]

Abelard's response to this letter is warm without being personal—even when addressing the question of marriage. For instance, he extols the salvific prayers of women, especially of wives for their husbands, and begs for the prayers of Heloise and her community.[153] He also requests to be buried at the Paraclete, perhaps alluding to the husband's prerogative to be buried at his wife's side. But if this were the motive behind his request, it was likewise buried.[154] For he takes the opportunity of his own projected burial, the burial of Heloise's terrestrial bridegroom, to segue into a discussion of holy women at the tomb of the celestial bridegroom:

> Wherever my body may lie, buried or unburied, I beg you to have
> it brought to your burial-ground, where our daughters, or rather
> our sisters in Christ may see my tomb more often and thereby be
> encouraged to pour out their prayers on my behalf. . . . Nor do
> I believe that there is any place more fitting for Christian burial
> among the faithful than one amongst women dedicated to Christ.
> Women were concerned for the tomb of our Lord Jesus Christ,
> they came ahead and followed after, bringing precious ointments,
> keeping close watch around this tomb, weeping for the death of the
> Bridegroom.[155]

Through associating terrestrial and celestial bridegrooms, an elision potentially as therapeutic to Heloise as it was flattering to its author, Abelard attempted to channel his own version of the perfect spiritual director.

But it was when the exasperated Heloise responded with still more graphic descriptions of longing that Abelard's pandering on behalf of the celestial bridegroom began in earnest. Heloise had objected in her second letter to Abelard putting her own name before his own. He responds, "you must realize that you became my superior from the day when you began to be my lady on becoming the bride of my Lord; witness Jerome, who writes Eustochium 'This is my reason for writing "my lady Eustochium." Surely I justly address as "my lady" her who is the bride of my Lord.' It was a fortunate trading of your married state: as you were previously the wife of a poor mortal and now you are raised to the bed of the high king." Although Jerome had been deferring to the virgin Eustochium, this does not stop Abelard from appropriating the honor for his wife and forthrightly plunking her "in the bed of the high king." Such a move constitutes a tacit response to Heloise's earlier statement of choosing Abelard over the "Emperor of the world": whatever her preferences might be, she is already the king's property. "By the privilege of this honour you are set not only over your *former* husband but over every servant of that king."[156]

Jerome had begun his letter to Eustochium with the reflection that the bridegroom was not "haughty or disdainful" since he had chosen an Ethiopian bride (Num. 12.1, Sg 1.4–5). Even so, her color was destined to be transformed once she was led to the royal chambers. Abelard will, in his turn, generate a lengthy meditation on the color of the bride, not so much as a means of commending the groom's accommodating largesse, but rather as a vehicle for proving Heloise's worthiness to be considered one of his brides. Abelard begins by likening the bride's color to the nun's dark habit: "the mourning worn by good widows who weep for the dead husbands they had loved." This is yet another allusion to the end of earthly marriage, only in this case the death of the earthly spouse acts as a springboard for a religious vocation. He proceeds to align the earthly widow with widows of the early church who lived on church stipends (1 Tim. 5.16) and then, once again, with the women at the tomb of Christ, described as "widows [grieving] for their spouse who was slain."[157]

In a final coup de grace, Abelard deploys the bride's color to forestall any objection that Heloise's mottled past could render her ineligible as Christ's bride, first in the articulation of what she holds in common with other (i.e., virginal) women: "The Ethiopian woman is black in the outer part of her flesh and as regards exterior appearance less lovely than other women; yet she is not unlike them within, but in several respects she is whiter and lovelier, in her bones, for instance, or her teeth." But any defect incumbent upon her color is ultimately rendered an advantage: blackness is a sign of "bodily affliction through the repeated tribulations of adversity," like Christian martyrs. In time, Christ will change the bride's color, "that is, he makes her different from other women who thirst for earthly things and seek worldly glory, so that she may truly become through her humility a lily of the valley, and not a lily of the heights like those foolish virgins who pride themselves on purity of the flesh or an outward show of self-denial, and then whither with the fire of temptation."[158] Unlike Jerome, Abelard does not propound that the bride's color would change with her induction into the royal chambers. Instead, he argues that the bride's black loveliness is the reason she was selected for the king's bed in the first place: "to that secret peace and contemplation. . . . Indeed the disfigurement of her blackness makes her love what is hidden rather than open, what is secret rather than public. Such a wife desires private, not public delights with her husband, and would rather be experienced in bed than seen at table."[159] Intimacy like this must ultimately supplant her physical relationship with Abelard.

This image of celestial fulfillment, framed within the sensual embrace of a surreal carnal love, is a prelude to Abelard's denigration of the very excesses of physical love to which Heloise clung, recasting his physical castration as a spiritual liberation.[160] In his stead, he offers her the unmutilated love of Christ, whose love is a match for her own. Heloise had professed to Abelard, "God knows I never sought anything in you except yourself; I simply wanted you, nothing of yours." She further maintains that the name of friend (*amicae vocabulum*) would always be sweeter to her than wife.[161] Abelard echoes this profession in his description of Christ's selfless love. "What . . . does he seek in you except yourself? He is the true friend [*amicus*] who desires yourself and nothing that is yours."[162] Hence "it was [Christ] who truly loved you, not I. My love, which brought us both to sin, should be called lust, not love."[163] The letter opens and closes with an invocation of Heloise as Christ's bride.

This second letter to Heloise closed the door on any explicit discussion of their past intimacy, and he warned Heloise against attempting to reopen it. Demonstrating commendable wifely submission, Heloise puts aside her physical and emotional longing in her third letter, now addressing her husband in the only role in which he is prepared to offer himself: that of spiritual director. Furthermore, Heloise presents him with specific tasks that are fully consonant with his new role, requiring him to compose a treatise elucidating the history of nuns and a rule better suited to women's needs.[164]

Heloise's requests are complicit with the vocational soundings that we have already seen Abelard undertake on her behalf. Attention to the origin of nuns begs the question of where a woman of Heloise's background could possibly fit into the lofty sweep of female religious history. The desire for a rule is more pragmatic: now that she has obediently entered religion at his behest, it was up to him to make her tolerably comfortable. But although seemingly complicit with the agenda that Abelard had voluntarily assumed, Heloise is nonetheless pressuring Abelard to justify the life choices he essentially made on her behalf. Thus, while it would seem that the barbed reproaches that Abelard found so torturous may have disappeared, the way in which her requests are framed still bristle with tacit resistance. We have seen that Abelard's epithalamium on marriage with Christ contains sensual rhapsodies on the skin of the black but comely bride. Heloise's argument favoring the need for a female rule is couched in a graphic and unlovely description of the female body. Consider her quotations from Macrobius Theodosius:

> Woman has an extremely humid body, as can be known from her smooth and glossy skin, and especially from her regular purgations which rid the body of superfluous moisture.
>
> A woman's body which is destined for frequent purgations is pierced with several holes, so that it opens into channels and provides outlets for the moisture draining away to be dispersed. Through these holes the fumes of wine are quickly released.[165]

The fragile foibles of the female form counteract the idealized intact sealed body that is at the center of the female monastic vocation.[166] And Heloise's unnervingly porous body is evinced in the service of a physical indulgence that is difficult to spiritualize: that nuns be permitted to drink more wine than St. Benedict had allotted for monks.

Whatever the implicit degree of recalcitrance, Abelard was clearly relieved by Heloise's change in tone and responded to her request for a history of nuns with alacrity. The most straightforward approach would have been to focus on virginity, or more expansively, the three degrees of chastity, presenting the development of the female vocation in terms of the triumphant institutionalization of chastity. Abelard could have taken a page from Aldhelm's treatise on virginity, turning to biblical figures as prefigurations of the virginal vocation. But this would clearly work against Abelard's (and probably Heloise's) best interests. Instead, Abelard's organizing principle was at one with his larger task of reconciling Heloise with her (un)chosen profession.

Abelard, moreover, did share at least one goal with Aldhelm: the decentering of female virginity and the redistribution of some share of virginal privilege. Aldhelm had achieved this by foregrounding male virgins and, at least in his earlier efforts, introducing the hybridity of virginal marriages. Abelard enjoins a more subtle rhetoric, sustained by means of significant elisions, omissions, and some ingenious preemptive strikes. The result is an idiosyncratic polemic that goes a long way toward explaining why many have often found this treatise convoluted and verbose.

Scholars have tended to accept a tacit division between the "personal letters" and "the letters of direction" that Betty Radice employed in her translation of the letters. But this is extremely misleading.[167] The groundwork for this treatise had already been laid in his first letter to Heloise, which culminated by identifying women like herself as true brides of Christ: their dark hue securing their progressive humility until such a time that Christ chose to imbue them with a new color. Abelard's discourse on the origin of nuns adopts a similar strategy at the outset with the treatment of the New Testament women. Despite the fact that the Old Testament mandate to "be fruitful and multiply" had been preempted in the new age, the first woman he mentions is Anna, the widowed prophetess who was present at Christ's presentation in the temple: "assiduous in the Temple and in divine worship . . . filled with the spirit of prophecy."[168] This choice sets the tone for the entire piece insofar as any mention of virginity is considerably deferred. It is only after we are a quarter of the way into the treatise that we come upon Philo's description of the Christian men, accompanied by "several virgins already great of age, who have preserved the chastity and integrity of the body not from any necessity but from devotion."[169] Abelard summarizes the goals of the early Christians as "devot[ing] themselves to prayers and psalms, to learning, and also to continence [*continentiae*]"—in that order. Compared to virginity or even chastity, *continence* is an expansive term because it includes, but is not limited to, sexual discipline.[170] Finally, the first mention of the bride of Christ is used with respect to the widow's church stipend in the early church: "just as if it was from the property of their spouse Christ."[171]

The treatment of the Virgin Mary is just as circumspect, even as references to her are (with one significant exception) fleeting. There is "an assembly of holy women with [Christ's] Mother" discussed in relation to the apostles;[172] an acknowledgment of Mary as a corrective to Eve; a reference to the earlier discussion of "Anna and Mary [and] the form of their holy profession as shown to widows and virgins" (the example of Mary as an early model for virgins must be implicit to the "assembly of holy women," however, as no mention was made of her virginity); and a discussion of Mary's role in the incarnation. It is only at the very end of the treatise that there is any reference to "innumerable virgins [who] follow the Mother of the Lord . . . able to follow the lamb Himself."[173]

The only substantive treatment of Mary is the one that addresses her role in the incarnation—an experience that is construed as dignifying the entire female sex as a whole by virtue of their reproductive organs. "[Christ] far more highly consecrated [women's] genitals by His Birth than He had done those of the male by circumcision."[174] This bold statement stands in clear opposition to Heloise's implicit critique of the female body. It is also a vindication of the maternity of all women, including Heloise. There is no mention of Mary's virginity, however.

In fact, the Virgin Mary seems to have been routed by her antithetical rivals: the fallen Marys and their equally besmirched associates, presented as living instances of the "last shall be first" order of salvation. Mary Magdalene, "the apostle of the apostles," receives the bulk of the notice, further attesting to the twelfth-century rise of her cult.[175] But the Magdalene is not the only representative of her reputedly fallen profession: Mary of Egypt is also included as yet another instance of "divine mercy to the very abjectness of common harlots."[176] Also folded into the mix is the Samaritan woman at the well, whom Christ rebuked for a plethora of husbands and who later prophesied about Christ.[177] This pivotal encounter is interpreted as the beginning of Christ's ministry to the Gentiles.

It is a treatise on holy women in which the Mary Magdalenes of the world crowd out the virgins. Indeed, the Magdalene's only serious rival is the widow, Anna. After her initial introduction, she returns in the capacity of a projected Nazarite, who consecrates her chastity to God. "She was of great age, and had lived with an husband seven years from her virginity. And she was widow of about fourscore and four years, which departed not from the temple, but served God with fastings and prayers night and day."[178] She is subsequently compared with Elisabeth, the mother of John the Baptist, whose fetus leapt in his mother's womb at the news of Christ's impending birth, suggesting that they share the title "Prophet of Prophets."[179]

Abelard's emphasis on Anna is a key to his efforts to reconcile Heloise with her vocation. For Anna was the prototype used in the consecration of the deaconess (and to a lesser degree, the consecration of the widow), and Abelard was intent on claiming the title of deaconess for Heloise. The twelfth-century prayer in the ordination of the deaconess, which Abelard cites, begins as follows:

> God, just remunerator, who led Anna, the daughter of Phanuel, who lived for seven years allotted to the conjugal yoke, so that at eighty-four in years she served you in holy and chaste widowhood and mixing prayers and fasts night and day, to the gift of prophecy at the circumcision of Christ and who then through apostolic institution with the application of holy chrism ordered the adolescents and younger members of her sex to be instructed at the hands of holy women of this order; omnipotent God of all things most piously deem to accept the hard and laborious proposition of this your servant; nor does it fail to harmonize with a proposition of holy widowhood.[180]

A mere widow could become one with the prophets, if she would but asceti-cally apply herself.

Abelard did his best to publicize Heloise's alleged status. He dedicates the *Problemata Heloissae*—his answers to a series of theological questions that Heloise had posed—to "Heloissa diaconissa"[181] and refers to the position of abbess as deaconess throughout the rule he was to write. But what exactly did the title deaconess mean at this point? We have already seen that the office of deaconess had become a catch-all office for formerly married women that had been officially under fire since the sixth century. And yet people kept ordain-ing deaconesses. The bishop of Noyon resorted to this rite when Radegund asked to be veiled. There are also instances in which the wife of a priest would assume the office of deaconess, often after they had mutually agreed to a vow of chastity.[182]

But the title had also at times been applied to virgins. It is significant that, while the twelfth-century rite of ordination equated the deaconess's com-mitment with that of a pious widow, the rite in the tenth-century *Pontificale romano-germanicum* drew an analogy between the deaconess and the virgin.[183] Moreover, there were at least some nuns who aligned themselves with this tradition. In 1145, just after Abelard's death, the hitherto all-male Carthusian order accepted the nuns of Prébayon, who claimed to have been consecrated simultaneously as virgins and deaconesses from the community's inception— allegedly in the seventh century. As anomalous as this might have seemed, the nuns were permitted to adhere to their rite. Therefore, in addition to the crown and ring, Carthusian nuns also received the stole and maniple. That the women in question were necessarily virgins is underlined by the fact that Carthusians did not accept widows.[184]

In short, the position of deaconess may have been invaluable precisely because of its nebulous status. It was remarkably inclusive. The prayer of con-secration intones: "Give, therefore lord, at our petition to your servant the thirty-fruit among the married, [or] the sixty fruit with widows."[185] This may explain why the office persisted as a liturgical possibility. Its survival among the twelfth-century rites disseminated by the papacy is remarkable, given the antifemale spirit of Gregorian reform, and a testimony to the antiquity of the office. It even persists into the thirteenth century, when William Durandus will pointedly refer to the title as a thing of the past. And yet the rite was still included in his authoritative pontifical.[186]

Yet Gary Macy has argued that the office of deaconess represented much more than a one-size-fits-all status. For she was not simply blessed by the bishop, as was the consecrated virgin, but ordained to an office that arguably gave her a clerical status. Macy perceives Abelard's emphasis on the deaconess as "the last defense" to an ancient tradition that was fast succumbing to the new post-Gregorian regime.[187] This position corresponds to the image of Abelard as a vehement partisan for women's dignity.[188] Abelard's reforming instincts did not always favor female initiative, however. In his rule for the Paraclete, for example, Abelard placed particular emphasis on the evils of female speech and the apostle's injunction to silence.[189] Likewise, he opposed the widespread custom of abbesses imposing the veil on novices.[190] He even restricted the community's autonomy by the imposition of a male superior.

Therefore, even if Abelard's theological mission to preserve the title deaconess is construed as a protofeminist gesture, it was probably also infused with a personal brief that corresponded to his agenda for Heloise. Like Radegund before her, Heloise entered the cloister while her husband was still living, thus defying the rubric of either virgin or widow. Still, there were important differences. Radegund was fleeing her husband, Clothar, and may well have wished herself a widow; Heloise, however, the once proud misogamist, now clung to the name of wife, reminding Abelard on a number of occasions of her status.[191] We do not know what words of consecration, if any, were spoken, or by whom they were spoken, when Heloise "hurried to the altar, quickly took up the veil blessed by the bishop and publicly bound herself to the religious life."[192] But clearly in her heart of hearts, she would never consider herself a widow.

The office of deaconess, however, was "marriage friendly," which meant that the title could be much more than the mere compromise formation it might have represented for Radegund. Abelard would have been aware that priests' wives were often ordained deaconesses. Indeed, in his rule for the Paraclete, Abelard projects this later usage backward onto the deaconess of the apostolic past, citing the guidelines for the demeanor of the deacon's wife as if they were associated with (and hence corroboration of) the office of the deaconess.[193] We know nothing of Abelard's clerical standing at the time of his marriage. But the fact that he did eventually take orders would make Heloise by the mere fact of being his wife an eminent candidate for deaconess according to the pre-Gregorian model. And from the perspective of Heloise, the designation of deaconess may have appealed to her precisely because it tacitly acknowledged her marriage to Abelard. And unlike *sponsa Christi*, it was clearly one that she embraced. The office of deaconess figured in another of Heloise's clever riffs on their varied and interlocking subject positions in the context of her reproach to Abelard for inscribing her name ahead of his. This inversion was the equivalent of placing "woman before man, wife before husband, handmaid before lord, nun before monk, deaconess before priest, and abbess before abbot."[194] Heloise again mentions the deaconess in the course of her request for a female rule: "canon law has taken our weakness into account, and laid down that deaconesses must not be ordained before the age of forty."[195]

There may also have been liturgical reasons that further prompted Abelard to secure the position of deaconess for his wife. For in addition to the accommodating nature of the office, the deaconess is accorded the title of "bride of Christ"; the widow is not. In the twelfth-century consecration, she is given a ring *before* the reading of the gospel, as would a member of clergy, with the words, "Take this ring of faith, the sign of the holy spirit, so that you will be called bride of Christ and serve him faithfully." Then she is given a marriage wreath with the words, "Accept the sign of Christ on your head, so that you will be made his wife [*uxor*]. If you remain with him, you will be crowned in perpetuity."[196]

Despite such bridal attributes, however, the prayer of ordination still contained the kind of penitential language common to deaconess and widow alike. The fact that these words seem peculiarly suited to Heloise's temperament and predicament was probably not lost on Abelard: "Creator of all creatures, you prove to us that we cannot avoid worldly temptations [*illecebras*], but since she [the candidate] is come to you through you, let neither the blandishments of pleasure nor terrible passions solicit souls once brought to life; for by what senses you deign it to be infused, there is nothing more desirable than your kingdom, nothing more terrible than your judgment."[197] Fear of damnation must ultimately efface all memory of passion and pleasure.

And yet, having once identified the office of deaconess as a position of honor suitable for Heloise, Abelard does not manifest his usual due diligence in differentiation when it comes to identifying the deaconess's actual status and her responsibilities. Instead he collaborates in the historical confusion already afoot, proceeding to throw the term into the pot with every other formal manifestation of the female vocation. As we have seen, the deaconess had historically conflated other more transparent identities of widow, abbess, and, occasionally, virgin. Hence the "true widows" of the pastoral letters (1 Tim. 5.3) were declared to be of the same "profession and proposition of Anna"— although she was never a Christian per se. By the same token, the honor in which *widows* were held can be adduced from the financial support they received as *Christ's brides*.[198] The requirements for a widow's admission into the *diaconate* is articulated by Paul's insistence that widows be three score years, married only once, and reputed for charity (1 Tim. 5.9–11). Abelard claims that Jerome urges deaconesses to set a good example by citing the church father's exhortation to *male deacons*; this exhortation is further associated with Paul's apprehension about the behavior of *younger widows* (1 Tim. 5.11–15). Gregory the Great is brought in to second the apostle's guidelines in selecting deaconesses, writing, "Youthful *abbesses* [*iuvenculas abbatissas*] we most vehemently forbid."[199] Abelard provides the following gloss to clarify this last set of conflations. "And what we now call *abbesses* [*abbatissas*] *anciently we named deaconesses* [*diaconissas*], that is ministers rather than mothers."[200] In short, the deaconess and the abbess are basically the same.

If, in fact, Abelard was advancing a theological argument defending the ordination of women, why did the master of distinctions deliberately plant the deaconess on such a slippery slope? Is it because he realized that the office of deaconess was ephemeral and the only way to save it was to hide it amid widows and abbesses—positions that were there to stay? Or was it that he wished to blunt the deaconess's claims to be a part of the clergy? The final conflation of widow/deaconess/abbess would seem to undermine any bid for a truly clerical status. But it is nevertheless significant that this bewildering elision implicitly challenges the privilege of the normative virginal abbess. The elevation to abbess had become progressively aligned with the *ordo* for consecrating virgins, associating the candidate with the virginal choir of wise virgins who were always on the lookout for their bridegroom.[201] In this context, the very hybridity of widow/deaconess/abbess could be construed as a deliberate intervention.

The same strategic slippage is apparent when Abelard approaches the subject of virginity halfway through the letter. The apostolic admonitions to "Honour widows that are widows indeed (1 Tim. 5.3)" is followed up with the comment that it was generally believed that the woman whom Paul hailed as another mother was a widow (Rom. 16.13), as was the woman that John the Evangelist hailed as "lady."[202] The honorific address was due to the nobility of "your profession" (i.e., Heloise's profession), hearkening back to Jerome's commendation of Eustochium as "lady" in her capacity of *sponsa Christi*.[203]

Although de-centering virginity, Abelard never challenged its position of superiority and the extra merit accrued by virgins. Indeed, at several junctures he draws attention to its ascendancy. Thus in contrast to the more modest plight of the monk, who was blessed by the abbot, the bishop alone could consecrate the virgin and only on the highest feast days. The very title *sanctimoniales* attests to their sanctity.[204] Toward the end of the treatise, Abelard alludes to the virgins who "offered themselves as a holocaust in martyrdom" as well as those who "did not hesitate to lay hands on themselves, lest they forfeit the incorruption which they had vowed to God. . . . This also not a little commends the dignity of holy women, that they consecrated themselves by their own words, saying: 'With His Ring He hath espoused me: I am betrothed to him.' For these are the words of Saint Agnes, whereby the virgins who make their profession are betrothed to Christ."[205] Moreover, his subsequent rule gives virginity even more distinction:

> We would have two sorts of veil, one for the virgins already consecrated by the bishop, the other for those not to be consecrated. The veils of the former should have the sign of the Cross marked on them, so that their wearers shall be shown by this to belong particularly to Christ in the integrity of their virginity, and as they are set apart from the others by their consecration, they should also be distinguished by this marking on their habit which shall act as a deterrent to any of the faithful against burning with desire for them. This sign of virginal purity the nun shall wear on the top of her head, marked in white thread, and she shall not presume to wear it before she is consecrated by the bishop. No other veils shall bear this mark.[206]

The virgin's singularity must be apparent to all.

Yet despite these panegyrics, there is an important change compared to when Abelard had made a similar case for virginity's special privilege over a decade before. Formerly he maintained that "only virgins consecrated to God are veiled by the hand of the highest priest and they obtain the preeminence of deaconesses."[207] The deaconess that emerges in the course of his letter on the origin of nuns, however, is explicitly not an untried virgin but an experienced woman with knowledge of the world.

Abelard's tacit preemption becomes a reality in the rule that he subsequently writes for the Paraclete. Here again he will invoke "the deaconess, who is now called abbess," and stubbornly continue to designate the abbess as deaconess throughout the rule.[208] Moreover, he will denounce the "pernicious practice [that] has arisen in the Church of appointing virgins to this office [i.e., abbess/deaconess] rather than women who have known men, and often of putting younger over older women."[209] As with Fontevrault, both age and degree of experience were important criteria in the selection of an abbess. This is not surprising, considering that Abelard was an admirer and defender of his fellow Breton, Robert of Arbrissel.[210]

That Abelard's history of nuns was written at Heloise's request and spoke so poignantly to her situation lends it a personal, even intimate quality. This sense is heightened by the many allusions that hearken back to their earlier correspondence intended especially for Heloise. For instance, Abelard's second mention of *sponsa Christi* occurs in a citation of Jerome's letter to Eustochium, who is called "a virgin of your profession" (*ad vestrae professionis*).[211] It was from this letter that Abelard borrowed his justification for deferring to Heloise in the way he addressed a letter, which he again repeats: "For I must call her my lady who is the Bride of Our Lord."[212] The reemergence of this passage must have evoked feelings that were bittersweet: It was sweet (saccharine sweet, perhaps) when Abelard first applied it to Heloise because it attempted to raise her in stature by conflating her condition with the superior virgin state. It was bitter, however, in that Abelard intended it as a reproof to Heloise's assumption that the terrestrial hierarchy of husband and wife still pertained, only to learn that she had a new lord. It was also bittersweet because this would be the last time that Abelard would take up the discussion of their marriage directly.

In case Heloise missed the point, however, Abelard's history of nuns again borrows from Jerome definitively to "set this profession above every boast of earthly happiness."[213] Abelard further cites Jerome's caution to Eustochium, "I will not that thou consort with matrons, I will not that thou approach the houses of nobles, I will not that thou frequently look upon that which despising thou hast willed to be a consecrated virgin. If the ambition of courtiers gather around the wife of the Emperor, wherefore dost thou an injury to thine husband? To the wife of man wherefore dost thou, the Bride of God, hasten? Learn in this matter holy pride. Know that thou art better than they."[214] What for Eustochium was doubtless an abstract admonition for Heloise would be saturated with meanings more bitter than sweet. For while the quotation again associates the destiny of Heloise with that of the virginal brides of Christ, it is yet another, and still more pointed, reprimand for Heloise's taunt that she would choose to be Abelard's whore rather than the wife of the emperor of the world: as bride of Christ, she is indeed the wife of the emperor of the whole world; she has no business dallying with her former husband, who is merely one of the great monarch's courtiers.[215]

Heloise had once reproached Abelard for requiring her to be veiled before he entered religion, interpreting this as a lack of trust: "perhaps you were thinking how Lot's wife turned back."[216] Despite his best efforts to reconcile Heloise with her vocation, it is doubtful that Abelard ever got over the fear that she may still turn back, rejecting the celestial bridegroom altogether. It is surely no accident that the rule emphasizes that the lapse of the abbess/deaconess went far beyond her own spiritual suicide. "Whoever is seen to have authority in the Church must think carefully what his own fall will bring about when he takes his subjects along with him to the precipice." "It is sufficient for each of the subject souls to provide for itself against its own misdeed, but death hangs over those who also have responsibility for the sins of others for, when gifts are increased, the reasons for gifts are also multiplied, and more is expected of him to whom more is committed."[217] If, in fact, Heloise was prepared to go "to the flames of Hell" for love of Abelard, his rule was there to remind her of the many others that she would likewise bring down if she failed in her responsibilities as abbess.[218]

There are also a number of contexts in which Abelard's pointed references to married sexuality serve a similar admonitory function, as if he were fearful of any residual hold that their carnal past might still exert over Heloise. In his *Ethics*, Abelard had used the biblical dictum that only spiritual things can pollute the soul in order to exonerate marital intercourse from any whiff of sin, likening it to the natural pleasure derived from eating. In the Paraclete's rule, Abelard again applies the same verse to the question of food.[219] Yet later in the discussion he takes an unexpected turn, maintaining that "the use of meat and wine, like marriage, is considered to lie between good and evil, that is, it is indifferent, *although the marriage tie is not wholly free from sin*, and wine brings more hazards than other food."[220] Again, in the course of *Problemata Heloissae*, Heloise raises a neutral question on the Beatitudes—neutral insofar as it has nothing to do with sex. But Abelard rather strangely construes the blessing for the pure in heart as especially directed to the married: "When he [Christ] says 'in heart' rather than 'in body,' he insinuates that the conjugal life especially indulges the pleasure of the flesh and gives way to the concupiscence of desire. For even if the union of spouses has an indulgence . . . nevertheless the flesh draws some contagion and uncleanness of lust or stench of stain from the fall."[221] Not surprisingly, Abelard will elsewhere state explicitly that marriage, unlike the other sacraments, does not confer grace.[222] At such times, Abelard seems to draw back from his bold vindication of what was natural.

In the above instances, the subject of married sexuality was introduced by Abelard, not Heloise, and somewhat gratuitously at that—almost as if he were attempting to add some theological ballast to his deprecation of their sexual past. Heloise had, after all, had her say about the pleasures of the sex, after which, at Abelard's request, she held her peace. But in the very last question of *Problemata Heloissae* she takes the lead in reopening the subject of marital sex, almost as if she were goaded into responding to the mixed messages that Abelard had sent her way. She asks "Whether anyone is able to sin in that which was conceded to him by God, or even ordered."[223] True, the conjugal debt is not mentioned explicitly. But the reference to a thing as both ordered (as in God's "Be fruitful and multiply") and conceded (as in Paul's "He who marries does not sin" and "I pardon you") makes the implication unmistakable.

Rather than hiding behind discussions of food, Abelard does Heloise the honor of going immediately to the place to which he was summoned. He acknowledges the gravity of the question, recognizing that if answered in the affirmative it would have calamitous ramifications for marriage, both ancient and modern.[224] Abelard's voice is clearest in his discussion of the mandate to reproduce in the Old Testament, glossing many of the biblical citations with his own comments.[225] But when it comes to the altered terms of the Christian era, where sexual continence trumps the reproductive imperative, Abelard relies very heavily on Augustine, adding virtually none of his own comments. Thus the basic good of the institution is affirmed, provided the institution is put to good use (primarily offspring).[226] The shadow cast by shame is unmistakable, however: even spouses who use sex in a temperate manner feel a sense of shame and seek privacy. And anything that is truly an unmitigated good should not be the source of shame. The fact that both honest spouses and profligates blush over their sexual activities suggests that the sex act has more in common with evil than good. In short, sex is much like human nature, which can arise just as easily from sinful unions as from ones that are licit and approved. "If it were evil, it would not be fit to be endured; if it did not have evil, it would not need to be regenerated."[227]

Heloise was asking essentially the same question that we already saw addressed in Abelard's *Ethics*. But in the context of the *Ethics*, the question, "How can sin be said to committed in that which is allowed?" is rhetorically staged to express contempt for the blighted mindset that associated any action permitted by God with sin. Earlier I raised the possibility that Abelard's treatment of married sex in the *Ethics* suggests that he had ultimately laid to rest the ghosts haunting his sexual past, allowing a liberal and optimistic view of married love to emerge. It would certainly be a comfort to believe this. In the pastoral writings to the Paraclete, however, Abelard's valiant efforts at decentering virginity coexist with a more somber view of human sexuality. Moreover, the difficulty in dating his later works makes it impossible to know Abelard's final word on the subject. It could be that Abelard, back in Paris brooding over the virtual Abelard that might have been had he never heard of Heloise, was rethinking the optimism in *Ethics*, which was, after all, a work in progress never to be completed.

Of course Abelard may have been genuinely conflicted. But it is also possible that he chose to be divided. In the context of a virtual sex act in a philosophical treatise, he could afford to be positive. But when it came to pastoral writings for the Paraclete, and his special project of transforming Heloise into the perfect bride of Christ, he would take every opportunity that came his way to disparage carnal love, even in the context of marriage. In this strategically bifurcated view of sex, the master no longer anticipates the influence Aristotle, a figure that he not only identified with but to whom he was frequently compared by contemporaries.[228] Rather he anticipates the thirteenth-century commentators, the so-called Latin Averroists (named for an Arabic commentator on Aristotle). Buckling under the weight of irreconcilable conflicts between Aristotelian and Christian doctrine, these scholars resorted to maintaining that there were, in fact, two truths—one philosophical and one theological. Abelard's double truth, however, was less the product of philosophical expedience than of pastoral pragmatism, animated perhaps by a somewhat less selfless desire for peace.

An Age of Affect, 1050–1200 (2)

The Conjugal Reflex

Alternative Intimacies

The saga of Abelard and Heloise is every bit as extraordinary as the lovers themselves. Nevertheless, their relationship can in many ways be taken as representative—expressive of a new emphasis on interpersonal relations and the life of the emotions that characterized this period. In a religious context, this new relational affect could manifest itself in a number of ways. For instance, John Boswell identified the triumphant flowering of a gay subculture among the clergy, while Brian McGuire and others have pointed to the emphasis on spiritual friendship that was awakening in monastic communities. The devotion to Christ's passion and the cult of the Virgin Mary were on a continuum with these developments, premised on a two-way intimacy between the venerated and the venerator.[1] And it is precisely this devotion that laid the groundwork for the affective meditation that Sarah McNamer links with the rise of compassion.[2]

Amid this spectrum of emotional attachments is the rise of what could be referred to as heteroasceticism: a man and a woman, each committed to the celibate life, manifest an intense attachment to one another, the likes of which have rarely been seen since patristic times. The relationship between Jerome and his spiritual companion and confidante, the matron Paula, could be regarded as the forebearer of these later unions and was even identified as such by the couple themselves. The bond between Jerome and Paula was remarkable not simply for the intensity of their mutual devotion, but also for the way in which this union was at the center of their spiritual lives. This bond would ultimately inspire the pious couple to abandon Rome and carve out a unique destiny in the Holy Land where they founded separate religious communities.[3]

Of course, there had always been close relations between the·clergy and holy women, the rapport of Fortunatus and Radegund being a case in point. From the mid-fifth century, however, there were few, if any, relationships that exhibit the same degree of spiritual interdependence, perhaps even codependence, as had once subsisted between Jerome and Paula. When this possibility begins to emerge in the later eleventh century, it is once again Peter Damian, the reformer who adopted such a hard line against clerical wives, who is on the cusp of this change. Damian's personal piety was an uncanny predictor of approaching trends. On a devotional level, Peter was an early promoter of the eucharistic piety that emphasized the humanity of Christ and the cult of the Virgin Mary, key zones for the burgeoning religious feeling of the age, while from the perspective of introspection and the burden of personal guilt he was fully the equal of Augustine.[4] Peter's correspondence with religiously inclined women, particularly the Empress Agnes, demonstrates his role in the inauguration of what I am calling the age of affect.[5] Thus he writes, "Dejected, I mourn daily while you are absent; indeed I sigh with a singular grief that my heart is far away from me. It is certain that where my heart is, there lies my treasure (Matt. 6.21). For my treasure is beyond doubt Christ. Because I am not unaware that he is hidden in the treasury of your breast, I appoint you as the parlor of the celestial treasure and on that account, though I may turn from you to whatever place, I do not in fact go away."[6] This was not mere rhetoric. After Agnes departed from Rome, Peter was in constant anxiety lest she would be drawn back into the worldly ambit of the court.[7] He wrote to his nephew, Damianus, praising the empress's piety and her recent conversion. Peter welcomes the opportunity to relive some of their cherished moments together. He recounts with relish the tale of two captive princesses, one of whom ingeniously preserved her virginity by concealing rotten meat in her bosom, confident that the smell would avert any sexual overtures. Agnes shared that story with him the night before she left.[8]

But Peter's expressions of sorrow pale in comparison with his slightly later contemporary, the hagiographer Goscelin, and the grief sustained by the sudden departure of his spiritual daughter, Eve, a nun at Wilton. Goscelin was about twenty years Eve's senior and befriended Eve in her youth. Sometime around 1079, Eve had suddenly departed England to live as a recluse, eventually settling down in Angers with Hervey, a monk-turned-anchorite.[9] We do not know the reasons behind Eve's departure. When the poet Hilarius of Orleans, a student of Abelard's, would later write a poem commemorating

Eve, he suggests that the community at Wilton was lax.[10] In any event, Eve left England without a word to Goscelin, a show of independence that occasioned a long treatise titled *Liber confortatorius*. It is a book laced with bitter reproaches, rendering the title purposefully ambiguous, as the author himself is quick to acknowledge: "How, I ask, will I console your solitude by exhortation, being myself more in need of consolation, or even inconsolable?"[11]

Eve abandoned her community for the only admissible pretext from a vocational perspective: to embrace the more rigorous life of an anchoress. The fact that her companion in this undertaking was Hervey did not seem to elicit censure, despite the Council of Nicaea's explicit condemnation of similar relations.[12] Far from being disgraced, moreover, Hervey continued to be a mainstay of his community and was still relied upon to train novices after Eve's death. Around 1102, the couple was warmly commended in a letter by Geoffrey of Vendôme, abbot of La Trinité, who encouraged them to seek salvation through persisting in their holy way of life.[13] Yet Hilarius intonates that this relationship may not have eluded criticism altogether:

> Eve lived a long time with her companion Hervey
> As to you who hears these things, I feel that I disturb you with this
>   utterance
> Brother drive off [the impulse] to suspect, nor should you be
>   suspicious in this case,
> For this love was not of this world, but in Christ.[14]

Hilarius fondly lingers over the strength of their bond: "a wonderful love of such a man and such a woman, / which is found proven without any crime." Their attachment to each other was absolute: Hervey was left desolate by Eve's death.[15]

Heteroascetics are usually given to forming devotional pairs. Guibert's mother enjoyed considerable intimacy with her chaplain, who also happened to be her son's tutor. By the same token, Christina of Markyate had at one point been on intimate footing with a succession of holy (and not so holy) men.[16] But occasionally we find instances in which one man had spiritual custody over a group of women. A person of no lesser consequence than Anselm in his capacity as archbishop of Canterbury writes to a certain Robert with considerable warmth,

> and his sisters and daughters the most beloved Seit, Edit, Thydit,
> Lwerun, Dirgit, Godit. . . . I rejoice and give thanks to God for

your holy proposition and holy way of life, which you have together in love of God and a life of sanctity. . . . I seek your dear love, dearest daughters, as I write some admonitions which should teach and elevate you to living well, although you have our beloved son Robert with you, whom God inspired to have care of you, and teach you daily how you ought to live by word and example, according to God.[17]

The spiritual direction that Anselm himself proffers in this context has nothing to do with the potential dangers of heterosexual cohabitation, as one might expect. Rather he addresses the kinds of issues that had traditionally preoccupied desert solitaries: the human will versus God's will, what to do when afflicted by a "depraved will," and how to address unbecoming movements of body or soul.[18] His concluding message to Robert speaks in glowing anticipation of the divine reward Robert will receive for undertaking the care of these women.[19]

In contrast, the example of a very different kind of heteroasceticism will test the limits of episcopal tolerance. Robert of Arbrissel was repeatedly accused of sleeping alongside his female followers. This scandalous behavior first breaks in a censorious letter from Marbod, bishop of Rennes, written sometime between 1098 and 1100. Echoing the bewilderment of patristic writers over the issue of syneisaktism, Marbod is suspicious of a man who, having already spurned the opportunity for a wife, continues to have any contact with women at all.[20] Even if by some miracle Robert could have maintained his physical purity, Marbod considered one who refused to take a wife yet continued to indulge in the sight and speech of a woman as a covert proof of lust.[21] Predictably, such an attitude draws upon misogynist polemic, which compares women to hissing serpents and the like, warning Robert of the impossibility of handling snakes safely.[22] But Marbod is also concerned by the undisciplined nature of Robert's following. The letter ends with a graphic description of the wretched little women unprepared for the life of perfection. They constitute new wine in old wineskins (Matt. 9.16–17): "Their wombs are burst from the spilling of childbirth and they have lost their wineskins by scorning commandments."[23]

When Marbod wrote, Robert's transgressive ways were, if not excusable, at least understandable: Fontevrault was only established in 1100. Robert was engaging in an itinerant lifestyle with a mixed following, whose sleeping arrangements were probably haphazard. But the accusation resurfaces around 1106, this time in a letter by Abbot Geoffrey of Vendôme. The tone is more respectful than in Marbod's case; Geoffrey is even prepared to believe that Robert's motives are pure. Yet Geoffrey shows none of the sympathy apparent in his letter to Hervey and Eve. He regards Robert's sleeping arrangements as foolhardy in the extreme, but women again bear the brunt of his displeasure.[24]

In short, few, if any, of Robert's contemporaries seemed to have understood what he was attempting, and Robert's daredevil antics were passed over in silence by his biographers. But Robert may eventually have found a sympathetic reader in Abelard, some thirty years later. Not only was Abelard a fellow Breton, but he was also the erstwhile abbot of St. Gildas in Brittany, who, as mentioned earlier, was one of Robert's admirers. Both were charismatic figures: Abelard drew students wherever he went; Robert drew everyone. Both men were sexually active before their conversions: Abelard's past is one of history's open books, of course. But when Marbod berates Robert for his own brand of syneisaktism, he introduces it in the following manner: "You are said to love greatly cohabitation with women—in which matter you once sinned."[25] Perhaps it is this intimate knowledge of women that led both men to prefer the more worldly, experienced woman over the cloistered virgin as abbess.

Robert's ascetic feats of derring-do may also have appealed to Abelard's flair for sexual casuistry, perhaps inspiring the vivid example in his *Ethics* of the religious man who, lying on a soft bed between women, inadvertently experiences an orgasm. Abelard's point here is that the man in question was innocent so long as he withheld his consent to the pleasure. It is true that he depicted the religious man in question as chained to the bed—more in line with the famous Augustinian example of the defiled Lucretia's transcendent chastity. For without this modification, such an experiment would seem more brash than holy to everyone except Robert—and possibly Abelard, who would be accused of excessive familiarity with women throughout his life.[26]

Repressed Conjugality

Some scholars have interpreted the reawakening of various forms of heteroasceticism in terms of the spirit of experimentation, a condition under which normative gender roles were suspended.[27] Certainly these individualistically calibrated living arrangements suggest that considerable experimentation was at play. But a change in a modus vivendi does not necessarily lead to a change in gender roles. Marbod and Geoffrey's censure of Robert of Arbrissel's sleeping arrangements are telling in this context. Although certainly reminiscent of the misogynistic invectives against syneisaktism, both authors seem complacent about the stability of gender roles in a way patristic authors were not. John Chrysostom had believed that syneisaktism's apparent threat to chastity concealed a deeper peril: that shared accommodation, free from the restraints of marriage and family and unimpeded by physical relations, was uncharted territory with the capacity to disrupt patriarchal rule. He expressed concern that clerics would become womanly, too comfortable with gossip and distaffs, while the virgins would, in turn, become masculine and overbearing.[28] Chrysostom's fears may be an inflected acknowledgment that the pristine understanding of the *vita angelica* had not yet been entirely stifled by clerical strictures. In line with Tertullian's unveiled virgins, moreover, it is possible that in Chrysostom's time some clerical households still perceived the dissolution of gender roles as a desirable end.

But if the androgynous ideal was very far from the disciplinary mindset of Marbod and Geoffrey alike, it also seemed to be at a remove from the practitioners of alternative lifestyles. Instead the gender roles of our heteroascetics were secured and safeguarded by what might be described as a suppressed conjugal model. This supposition may seem implausible in light of phenomena such as same-sex bonding or spiritual friendship, which could have functioned as emotional alternatives to marriage. The concurrent cultural trend of *fin amor*, moreover, has often been portrayed as violently opposed to marriage.[29] While the exact relationship between courtly love and the affective discourse in religious letters remains unclear, there is little doubt that the two were destined to become intertwined.[30]

Despite these possible countervailing factors, there are good reasons why the heteroascetical relations in question should be construed as quasi-conjugal in nature. For even though the church was lamentably slow to develop a positive model of spiritual collaboration between husband and wife, marriage was nevertheless the only paradigm on offer. There simply was no orthodox model for shared ascetical practices between a man and a woman outside of marriage. Syneisaktism had been soundly defeated in patristic times, if not in practice at least in theory. Indeed, Jerome himself had added his voice to condemning the danger implicit in such relations.[31] Despite having gone on record denouncing such unconventional intimacies, however, his rapport with Paula was a source of intense scandal, as Jerome himself laments: "Of all the ladies in Rome but one had the power to subdue me, and that one was Paula. She mourned and fasted, she was squalid with dirt, her eyes dim from weeping. . . . The only woman who took my fancy was one whom I had not so much as seen at table. But when I began to revere, respect, and venerate her as her conspicuous chastity deserved, all my former virtues forsook me on the spot [i.e., in the eyes of Rome]."[32] The result was that when Jerome and Paula were invoked in the context of male-female ascetical couples it was rarely a model for religious practice, but for transhistorical commiseration over unwarranted slander. Thus when Abelard's relationship with Heloise continued to generate prurient speculation, even after his castration, he looked to the maligned Jerome for comfort: "I often repeated to myself the lament of St. Jerome . . . 'The only fault found in me is my sex, and that only when Paula came to Jerusalem.'" And again: "Before I knew the house of saintly Paula, my praises were sung throughout the city."[33] When the anonymous hagiographer of Christina of Markyate invokes the patristic twosome, it was to dignify, if not to quell, the gossip surrounding his heroine's relations with Abbot Geoffrey.[34]

If the disparagement of syneisaktism meant that the only heterosexual model available was matrimonial, the age-old mistrust of sex still ensured that but a handful of marriages were extolled, and these tended to be sexually abstinent or even unconsummated unions. As Aldhelm's work suggests, holy couples such as Cecilia and Valerian, or Daria and Chrysanthus, were and would remain icons of ascetical collaboration, reaping many conversions before suffering a mutual martyrdom. Saintly bishops who had at one time been married almost invariably resolved their conflicting obligations in the context of a spiritual marriage. Yet despite this long line of married celebrities, the model of spiritual marriage was never actively promoted for fear that any couple, however resolute, still lived in constant danger of lapsing from their chaste resolve.[35] This made the successful pairs even greater objects of wonder, perpetuating their cults—hence the model persisted. We should also factor in the development of a matrimonial doctrine in the high Middle Ages that downplayed, even disparaged, the role of sex in a union, making a completely unconsummated marriage not just a possible option but a highly esteemed one at that. And so while a given pair of heteroascetics may not technically be married, the contours of their relationship arguably bore much in common with the twelfth century's rarefied vision of marriage.

There are also certain gender-specific factors that favored a tacit matrimonial model. The men in these pious couplings were all clerics of some description, and the Gregorian reform had been remarkably successful at extricating the clergy from the conjugal unit. If we were to adopt the vantage point of writers such as the Norman Anonymous, perhaps the most passionate defender of clerical marriage, the triumph of sacerdotal celibacy would mean the creation of a caste of professionally bereaved clergy—a cadre of psychic widowers who longed for the company of their wives.[36] This very triumph of church reform may have contributed to a devotional sublimation: the proliferation of nuptial metaphor evident in the heightened interest in the Song of Songs.[37] Its impact on monastic letters would be epitomized in the sermons of Bernard of Clairvaux.

Not surprisingly, female spirituality was especially inclined to follow the contours of a quasi-conjugal relationship. This is in spite of the fact that the women in question constituted a more diverse group than the men, in terms of both matrimonial history and official standing in the church. We have clearly come a long way since the proud virgins of Tertullian's day who eschewed marriage and all its symbolic trappings. On the contrary, nuptiality was gaining momentum in women's spiritual lives. Baudonivia's life of Radegund provides the earliest evidence that at least some women personally identified with the *sponsa Christi* persona. In the twelfth century, religious women's implication in this model transcends mere metaphor and is frequently superimposed on flesh-and-blood relations that were nonmarital.

Ermengard of Brittany's fraught matrimonial history presents a compelling tableau vivant of the theoretical and practical imprint of marriage on her life. On the occasion of her first marriage to William of Aquitaine, her graces were celebrated in an epithalamium by none other than Marbod of Rennes.[38] The marriage was dissolved as consanguineous, and she remarried Alan Fergent, count of Brittany, in 1092. Around 1105, however, she fled the notorious violence of Brittany and sought refuge in Fontevrault, again under the pretext of a consanguineous marriage.[39] When Ermengard's petition for annulment was denied, Robert of Arbrissel's letter of 1109 defended marriage in its sternest guise, presumably to instill resignation. Far from sympathetic, the letter opens with a warning against simulated piety and false inspiration, tacitly challenging the ostensibly pious impulse that prompted Ermengard's flight. Robert is then at pains to justify some of the harsher mechanisms of justice such as corporal punishment, the confiscation of goods, and even the death penalty.[40] It may be that Robert was attempting to reconcile Ermengard with the implacable and often brutal ramifications of secular law, which she doubtless had witnessed firsthand. But in so doing, he simultaneously affirms the efficacy of the law and the gravity of transgressing against its strictures.

And it is by way of this stony legal path that Robert segues into the subject of Ermengard's marriage. Even if her husband was in his own way an infidel, Robert asserts, Ermengard was nevertheless required to take Queen Esther as a model who remained married to a pagan ruler. "You are married [*coniunga*]: you cannot be unbound [*disiungi*] by law."[41] To have the marriage dissolved, she must furnish legitimate witnesses who can testify to its illegality.

Robert's insistence on marriage as a binding contract, and the emphasis on legal forms, hearkens back to his disquisition on the legality of secular punishments. Thus his defense of the marriage bond is premised upon its subtle alignment with the most punitive aspect of law. The implication seems to be that if Ermengard's marriage is a punishment to her, this punishment is not simply licit but also just—this is in spite of the fact that Robert acknowledges at the end of the letter that Ermengard's marriage (as well as that of her daughter) was truly incestuous.[42] The letter concludes on a gentler note with the rule of life alluded to above.

So Ermengard was stuck. Considering the tenor of Robert's letter, it would hardly be surprising if her aversion to her husband and secular marriage spread to her spiritual director and the institutional alternative that she believed was within his power to offer her. But this was not the case. With her husband's eventual monastic conversion, Ermengard was at last permitted to enter Fontevrault licitly. In a perfect world, this would be Ermengard's well-deserved happy ending after a career of marital strife. Yet the monastic vocation that ensued was every bit as troubled as her speckled matrimonial past. This vocational unease may correspond with the virilocal disposition that Ermengard developed in relation to her spiritual directors, in keeping with the usual expectations of aristocratic marriage that required the wife to move to the husband's estate. For example, Ermengard never permanently settled at Fontevrault, leaving and reentering as many as three or four times.[43] On the basis of her subsequent behavior, it seems probable that these comings and goings were prompted by Robert's movements. Fontevrault had never been his permanent residence. Robert's death in 1118, however, seems to have left Ermengard shaken, suggesting that her religious vocation was contingent upon her personal relations with masculine figures of authority. The following year marked the death of her husband, the former count of Brittany (who, somewhat ironically, had managed to remain true to his monastic vows). Ermengard then proceeded to launch a complaint against her first husband, William of Aquitaine, for having abandoned her.[44] When this pathetic attempt failed, she left Fontevrault.

Some years later, Ermengard heard Bernard of Clairvaux preaching only to fall under the spell of the mellifluous doctor. The great Cistercian foundation of Buzay that she built might be construed as the dowry she brought to their projected union.[45] Mercifully, Bernard's letters to his avid disciple were of a different ilk than Robert's grim gospel of fortitude—in fact their febrile tenor, which even leaves Peter Damian's admiration for Agnes in the dust, has troubled a number of scholars.[46]

I wish I could find words to express what I feel towards you! If you could but read in my heart how great an affection for you the finger of God has inscribed there, then you would surely see how no tongue could express and no pen describe what the spirit of God has been able to inscribe there. Absent from you in body, I am always present to you in spirit and, although neither of us can come to the other, yet you have it within your power, not yet indeed to know me, but at any rate to guess something of what I feel. Do not ever suppose your affection for me is greater than mine for you, and so believe yourself superior to me inasmuch as you think your love surpasses mine. Search your heart and you will find mine there too. . . . But your modesty is so great that you are more likely to believe that he who has moved you to esteem me and choose me as your spiritual counselor has also moved me with a like feeling of affectionate concern for you. It is for you to see that you have me always by you; for my part, I confess, I am never without you and never leave you.[47]

As Bernard's great series of sermons on the Song of Songs indicates, nuptial metaphor, with its languorous language of love, was his spiritual mother tongue. Here at last was a spiritual director who could respond in full to the conjugal reflex that had dominated Ermengard's life. She thereupon followed Bernard to Dijon and became a Cistercian nun, though apparently not at the encouragement of Bernard but of Geoffrey, abbot of Vendôme, Robert of Arbrissel's old critic.[48] Bernard nevertheless wrote enthusiastically, congratulating Ermengard on her conversion and newfound peace. "After having long since conceived of the fear of God you have at last given birth to the spirit of salvation, and love has cast out fear. How much sooner would I converse with you in your presence than to you in your absence! Believe me, I become angry with the affairs by which I always seem to be hindered from seeing you, and I greet with joy the opportunities of seeing you which I seem to get so seldom. . . . I offer you a foretaste of joy which will soon be satisfied for I hope to come to you quite soon."[49]

We do not know if Bernard's "taste of joy" was ever followed up by a visit. But even if never present to her in the flesh, Bernard made his excuses for their prolonged separations like the adept spiritual lover that he was. And the prospect of a visit from Bernard may have had a temporary stabilizing effect. When Bernard departed for Italy, however, Ermengard, probably close to sixty years of age, once again left the religious life in order to follow her half-brother to the Holy Land, where he had been made king of Jerusalem. It was as if she finally construed herself as a bereaved widow who must now look to her natal family for shelter.[50]

Thus Ermengard was barred from ever becoming a true bride of Christ, remaining very much the married woman. Her two marriages, happy or not, left a considerable imprint, reflected in her seemingly relentless quest for a surrogate husband. While perhaps an extreme case, Ermengard's male/ matrimonial-centric vocation was not unusual. Heloise clearly revered Abelard as the intellectual, spiritual, and emotional center of her universe—the husband who forced her into the religious life and then (if we are to believe her complaints) attempted to forget her. And despite Heloise's antipathy to the institution, she was, in one way or another, forced to submit to its yoke for most of her adult life. As mentioned earlier, there is a sad irony to the fact that while Abelard was extolling Heloise's mystical marriage with Christ, replete with all the sublimated sensuality of the Song of Songs, Heloise clung to her bittersweet status as Abelard's wife.

Goscelin's Eve, although a cloistered bride of Christ, may also be tacitly indebted to a matrimonial understanding of her relations with her spiritual directors. Although Eve had left her community at Wilton and her spiritual director, this spirited show of independence could also be perceived as merely exchanging Goscelin for Hervey. And this is probably the way Goscelin construed the situation. Thus when exclaiming over the transience of worldly friendship, he inserts the telling analogy:

> Whoever ceases to be seen, ceases to be loved, while the one who is present more often starts to be preferred. The interloper has strangled the husband: by this achievement he takes his place with the widow as husband. The murdered man is covered over with earth and trodden underfoot; the murderer is loved more and is taken up in embraces. . . . A young man who is fortunate, handsome and charming is loved, as long as one who is younger, more fortunate, more handsome, more charming is not met with. . . . What she had cherished earlier is a fable, what she had loved more than all is a dream.[51]

Though his avowed point is that only the love of Christ is true, the path en route is littered with bitter innuendo. All the same, Goscelin may be articulating a truth that Eve would understandably resist: that he was once as dear to Eve as he could hope and her defection to Hervey was essentially a unilateral divorce.

One might think that the feisty Christina of Markyate's prolonged struggle to be free of Burthred would be sufficient to extinguish any impulse to
act out the conjugal reflex beyond her union with Christ. And initially this
seems to be the case, even though her circumstances were hardly propitious
for independence. Living in opposition to and later hiding from her parents
and would-be husband for years, Christina was forced into a state of utter
dependency on her several spiritual directors, all of whom were male. Even
so, the anonymous hagiographer goes out of his way to align Christina with
other nonmatrimonial models of holiness. Initially Christina is presented as a
modern Thecla, with her first mentor, the canon Sueno, standing in for Paul
as prophet of virginity.[52] Her first taste of the religious life occurred in Flam-
stead, where she spent two years in a female community under the protection
of the anchoress, Alfwen.[53] Her four years with Roger, which were spent in
hiding under intolerable conditions including extremes in temperature, were
appropriately modeled on the lives of the desert fathers.[54] After Roger's death,
Christina even had a brush with syneisaktism during a brief sojourn with
an anonymous cleric, barely avoiding the disastrous results that the church
fathers had predicted.[55]

Christina escaped with her chastity intact through the help of the Virgin
Mary, who freed her of all future fleshly temptation.[56] This corresponds with
Christina's accession to Roger's cell: a movement from discipleship to mastery,
a perspective that is supported by the fact that a community of women sprang
up around her hermitage. These developments also correspond to her meeting with Abbot Geoffrey of St. Albans, to whom she is said to play the role of
spiritual director, reversing the expected gender dynamics of such relations.
And yet if Christina's potential as a director of others seems to imply a degree
of spiritual independence, this is clearly a scenario in which the whole is less
than the sum of its parts. As Stephen Jaeger points out, the passion between
Christina and Geoffrey is presented as a kind of climax to a love story.[57] Her
feelings for her spiritual subordinate were expressed in quasi-romantic endear-
ments: Christina referred to Geoffrey as "her beloved" (*dilectum suum*), or
her "most familiar one" (*sibi familiarissimum*).[58] Moreover, her feelings were
fully requited: "Their affection was mutual, but different according to their
standards of holiness. He supported her in worldly matters: she commended
him to God more earnestly in her prayers. If anything, she was more zealous
for him than for herself and watched over his salvation with such care that,
surprising to say, the abbot, whether near or far, could not offend God, either
in word or deed, without her knowing it instantly in spirit."[59] Christina's relationship with Geoffrey becomes the entire focus for her spirituality. The text is

relentlessly and (somewhat monotonously) laced with proof of her preoccupation. Aware of any errors he might commit during his absence, "she was more
zealous for him than for herself."[60] "She was so zealous on his account that she
prayed for him tearfully almost all the time and in God's presence considered
him more than herself. . . . There was none of those who were dear to her for
whom she could plead to God with such devotion and instant prayer."[61] An
inner voice asked if she would like to be able to see Geoffrey miraculously
during an absence—an offer she gratefully accepted, "as she was in some ways
more anxious for him than herself."[62] The life itself breaks off with an account
of various measures Christina took to ensure that she could intercede more
effectively on Geoffrey's behalf.[63]

The subordination of Christina's presumably more potent spirituality
to Geoffrey's well-being parallels the traditional understanding of the wife's
role as ancillary to the male. The clergy had always expected wives to focus
their spiritual energy on their husbands. During the conversion of Europe
this was frequently enacted by a Christian princess converting her pagan
husband—a living testimonial to Paul's expectation that the unbelieving
spouse would be sanctified by the believing (1 Cor. 7.14).[64] The message
of wife's spiritual subordination was clearly imbibed by the Carolingian
Dhuoda (fl. ca. 843) who, despite the neglect and mistreatment she received
at her husband's hands, consistently placed his concerns—his soul, his de-
scendants, his ancestors—before all else.[65] We have seen that Heloise will
continue to pursue this thankless strategy. This discourse was prolonged in
the emerging pastoral literature that designates the husband's salvation as
the wife's primary concern.[66]

Geoffrey's appropriation of Christina's spiritual gifts is epitomized in a
dream he relates: "One night . . . he saw himself holding a flowering herb in
his hands, the juice of which was very efficacious for driving away maladies.
If he squeezed it strongly, little juice came out, but if gently and quietly he
would get what he wanted."[67] A hermit friend tells him that the herb represents Christina, the flower her virginity, and that she should be approached
carefully and treated gently. But whatever meaning the hagiographer may attach to this dream, the perception that Christina has been commodified to
meet Geoffrey's needs is inescapable—a spiritualized herbal remedy. And so
Christina too was sucked into the conjugal vortex. Her preoccupation with
Geoffrey accords with some of the larger structural determinants of her life.
It evokes her earlier rejection of Alfwen's community in favor of a virilocal
move to Roger's cell. And it anticipates her eventual acquiescence to Geoffrey's
insistence that her community be amalgamated with his own.[68] Moreover, the

anonymous hagiographer presents this quasi-conjugal model, with its heteronormative gender roles, as the apex of Christina's spiritual development, surpassing all of the discarded roles or experimentations in gender that Christina
inadvertently encountered or willfully assumed in the course of her spiritual
quest.

In all fairness to Christina, it should be noted that she sought neither the
desert nor the anchor-hold. The various ascetical topoi that Christina assumed
in hiding were all thrust upon her. The relationship with Geoffrey was the only
one she ever seemed to have chosen for herself. From childhood, her chief ambition was to join a religious community and be consecrated as a virgin—an
official *sponsa Christi*. In short, Christina had in a certain sense always been
a bride in training, although the realization of her dream was long deferred.
When the momentous consecration did occur, however, it was largely through
pressure from Geoffrey. Christina, "persuaded by the frequent pleadings and
humble sweetness of the abbot . . . gave her consent."[69] Hence the terrestrial
surrogate groom prepared the way for his master.

Historians such as Judith Bennett have analyzed the ways in which a
woman's independent identity was quite literally subsumed by marriage: the
wife's world continues to contract until she entirely disappears from public
life, while the man's world expands, benefiting from the personal relations and
material assets that his wife has brought to the union.[70] Similarly in heteroa-
scetic relations, women's greater identification with the spousal role imparts
a parallel dependence on men, while the men in question were not nearly as
emotionally or spiritually preoccupied with their female charges. Much of
this imbalance undoubtedly springs from implacable external factors, such
as women's inability to perform the sacraments, which impinged upon their
religious autonomy in the pursuit of a vocation. In this context, it is worth
emphasizing that a number of the celebrated founders of various female communities often stumbled upon their destinies by accident, without any apparent desire to benefit women. The foundation of Fontevrault resulted from
expediency: the women of Robert's following needed somewhere to go. And,
if Jacques Dalarun is correct, women may have been purely instrumental in
Robert's unusual sexual discipline.[71] Gilbert of Sempringham initially looked
for a community of men to patronize without success.[72] He soon discovered
that the women of the area were both more pious and in greater need of his
attention. Abelard's role as founder was accidental. Heloise and her nuns had
been expelled from Argenteuil and needed somewhere to go; Abelard himself
was anxious that someone attend to his oratory.[73] The letters of direction and
the rule were all at Heloise's specific behest. In short, women seemed to have

a greater investment in these relationships and generally seemed to be the motive force behind them.

The exception to this rule is Goscelin, whose matrimonial attachment to
Eve is intense, unwavering, and ultimately disturbing. Goscelin is something
of a literary shapeshifter, however, frequently assuming female personae. For
in addition to the more conventional paternal identification, Goscelin often
describes himself as Eve's mother.[74] At other times, he associates his suffering with that of the Virgin Mary at the cross.[75] These different shapes do
not disguise that his core identification is as Eve's husband, a persona that is
expressed on multiple levels. Initially, Goscelin had functioned as Eve's spiritual director with the normative hierarchy prevailing (or so his reminiscences
would suggest). With her accession to the anchor-hold, however, Goscelin's
recognition of her spiritual ascendancy is expressed through expectations that
she will manifest a wifely solicitude for his salvation, parallel to Christina's
attitude to Geoffrey. Goscelin even anticipates Eve's future power as a saintly
intermediary: "I have a patron in place of a daughter, of whose prior claim I
am unworthy as I am unequal to her in life."[76] Despite his alleged unworthiness, Goscelin believes his union with Eve to be as intimate as it is enduring.
Eve is described as "O soul, dearer than light," whom he assures, "your Goscelin is with you in inseparable presence of soul . . . one with you from which
no distance may separate you." The book concludes with the request that Eve,
"the sweet offspring of my soul," show compassion and "have pity for the
bereavement of Goscelin, whom you have loved as the home of your soul in
Christ."[77] Moreover, this union of souls anticipates a still fuller reunion in the
afterlife—an expectation that Goscelin often evokes for his own comfort.[78]

Lest his assimilation with Eve be construed as but another instance of
gender-bending being perpetrated by our monkish changeling, one should be
mindful of how similar terms of spiritual intimacy are often applied to those
who had once lived in the world as husband and wife. This was the promise
that Abelard extended to Heloise in the prayer, "Now, Lord, what thou hast
mercifully begun, most mercifully end, and those whom thou hast parted for
a time on earth, unite forever to thyself in heaven."[79] Peter the Venerable's
anticipation of unity is even more complete when he reassures Heloise, "him
[Abelard], I say, in your place, or as another you, God cherishes in his bosom
and keeps him there to be restored to you through his grace at the coming of
the Lord."[80] Significantly, such expressions resonate with the words employed
by Peter Damian to convey his feelings for Agnes: love created a domicile for
the soul—a shared domicile erected in Christ.

Is there something inherently conjugal in this expectation? I believe there is. It is one of the only, perhaps the only, positive vestiges of a physical union in the spiritual realm. We have seen how the conviction that some physical bond endures led the misogamic Tertullian to project the marriage bond into the afterlife, despite Christ's intonations to the contrary (Matt. 22.30). Tertullian clearly perceived this as a liability. But the many miraculous instances of funerals in which the tomb is opened and the cadaver of a deceased husband or wife makes way for, or even raises its arms to embrace, the long-awaited body of his or her recently deceased spouse suggests that the belief in a reunion in the afterlife may have been a comfort to many.[81] In the next century, Christ will promise the Beguine mystic Mary of Oignies (d. 1213) that her husband, John. "would be returned to her in heaven with the marriage restored, as it were, who out of love of chastity withdrew himself from carnal commerce on earth."[82] Later Damian's intimate image will be attributed to Christ himself, who will assure his various brides that he has prepared a habitation for them in his heart.[83]

Even if the wish for reunion beyond the grave is in itself matrimonially neutral, there is no mistaking the conjugal strains in Goscelin's rendition of this theme: "we will pant and hasten to be united in that homeland where we can never ever be separated."[84] The verb Goscelin uses to describe their union is *coniungere*—a term difficult to separable from the ambiance of marriage. Still, there may be nothing shocking in this portrayal: Goscelin's investment in nuptial metaphor could be an innocent (albeit potentially volatile) way of describing the affective, but chaste, relations between a spiritual director and his female disciple. Goscelin's much earlier life of Edward the Confessor, completed by 1067, had, after all, described the spiritual marriage that existed between the king and his much younger wife, Edith, who would sit in filial piety at the feet of her older and wiser husband.[85] Perhaps Goscelin had come to regard his relationship with Eve in a similar light.

But one exemplum, intermixed with various spiritual directives to Eve, may suggest that Goscelin was very far from sublimating whatever conjugal impulses he had repressed. The story, ostensibly demonstrating the devil's relentless attacks on the holy and God's mercy on the truly penitent, concerns a certain Alexander, an anchorite in the forest who was so great "now with his virtues he could reach heaven."[86] The infant daughter of a neighboring king was stolen and entrusted to the hermit by a demonic monk. Alexander raised her, only to seduce her and ultimately impregnate her. Fearing exposure, the panic-stricken hermit confessed his sin to his demonic friend, who, in turn, convinced him to murder the hapless girl, arguing that a single murder was far preferable to the scandal ensuing from the fall of someone reputed so holy.

Then Alexander's friend, "that excellent teacher of perdition," helped to bury the girl.

Eventually this pastiche of lust, sin, and crime is put to rights: Alexander's hands become miraculously stuck in a tree for some fifteen years to facilitate his penance. He confesses his offense to the girl's father, who got waylaid on a hunting expedition. Realizing that the murdered girl must be his daughter, the king exhumes her only to discover "a great supernal grace: for after so many years she shone forth all whole, as she had been when living." Alexander besought the king to obtain his daughter's forgiveness, and the king in turn touched the fallen hermit with the girl's undecayed finger. Alexander was immediately freed from his tree and forgiven by the king, and they proceeded to build a monastery in the place.[87]

The story ends well, but the errant hermit continues to hover in this reader's mind as an ominous instance of projection. Moreover, any exculpatory vision of marriage that might have been inspired by Edward the Confessor's chaste union with Edith is undermined by the fact that the poor murdered girl is referred to as the hermit's "dead wife" (*extinctamque coniugem*). The incorruption of her defiled corpse is even more miraculous than wonders wrought on the virginal cadavers in Goscelin's hagiographies: it suggests that the violated girl herself had been saved, with virginity restored and hence free to follow the lamb, while at the same time exculpating Alexander. This impression is seconded by the fact that "Blessed Alexander rejoiced that, from the crime of a corrupter and murderer, he [God] had made the fruit of a martyr, and that she would triumph in heaven for him, in the inseparable bond of love."[88] Indeed rape, murder, and subterfuge have still not dampened Alexander's expectation that his victim will petition for his entry into heaven (just as Goscelin expected of Eve) and that he will even be united in heaven with the girl he had abused. The presence of this tale is hardly nugatory, moreover: it is probably the longest exemplum in the entire work. Soon after, when Goscelin admonishes Eve that "in loving uniquely one so worthy of love [Christ] you conceive him, carry him, give birth to him, feed him," the wall between metaphorical and physical birth has been rendered uncomfortably thin.[89]

In the above passage, tacit identification with Christ allows Goscelin to explore sexual intimacy with Eve. However unseemly an assimilation with Christ might appear in this context, it is doctrinally sound. Paul had, after all, compared Christ's love for the church with the love between the husband and wife (Eph. 5.23–29). We have already witnessed Abelard deploying this conflation between the husband and Christ to great effect. When anticipating his own death, Abelard associates Heloise's widowed state with the women who wept at Christ's tomb. Occasionally, Abelard has to counter Heloise's recalci-trance, however, by reversing the supernatural order of things. For instance, while Paul's assimilation of the husband's will with Christ's was intended to legitimize the husband's rule, Abelard is continuously eliciting Heloise's obe-dience to Christ on the basis of what she owes to Abelard as husband. But regardless of which of her two lords Heloise is attending in her heart of hearts, their wills are ultimately presented as united. Abelard acknowledges this shadow collaboration in the declaration, "divine grace brought . . . the truth of reality,"[90] suggesting a tacit and ultimately sanctified motive for dressing his pregnant wife in a religious habit.

Of course, Abelard and Heloise had, in fact, been married, so their con-jugality, repressed in very different ways, first by concealment and later by separation, was nevertheless a reality. And so Abelard was justified in laying claim to the redoubled authority as husband and Christ. As a result of the progressive assimilation between Christ and members of the clergy, however, a female ascetic's clerical affiliate was gradually being authorized to assume a quasi-spousal role. The Benedictine rule stated explicitly that every abbot (the capacity in which Abelard regarded himself in relation to the Paraclete's community) held the place of Christ.[91] The symbolism that cast the bishop as Christological groom married to his see, dating from the ninth century and revived during the Gregorian reform, was gradually extended downward to ac-commodate the entire priesthood. The priest's association with Christ during Mass was soon to be symbolically reinforced by the Fourth Lateran Council of 1215 when the priest's words of consecration, echoing Christ's words at the Last Supper, were understood to "transubstantiate" the bread and wine into the real presence of Christ. This doctrine was publicized through every me-dium available—local councils, preaching, graphic exempla, catechisms, and antiheretical discourse—until it reverberated throughout Christendom. We can see this message register in the life of Francis of Assisi, who knelt in the mud to kiss the hand of a concubinous priest with the comment, " 'These hands touch my God.' "[92] By the same token, annual confession was first made mandatory at Lateran IV. Over the course of the thirteenth century, the seal of confession was safeguarded by the theological insistence that the confessor saw as God saw.[93]

The increased emphasis on the priest as a type of Christ may have encour-aged women to engage in something akin to the psychoanalytic phenomenon of transference[94]—when the feelings of the analysand for a parent or lover are unconsciously redirected to the analyst. In psychoanalysis, transference is not only expected but even encouraged as an essential part of the therapy.

But there is also a risk that this therapeutic redirection of affect could elicit an all too human response in the analyst so that he actually begins to return the patient's feelings. This reaction, known as countertransference, was considered both unprofessional and dangerous. There are a number of striking parallels between the therapy-driven phenomena of transference and countertransference and the ways in which the delicately calibrated relations between heteroascetics could go awry. For instance, one might consider that Geoffrey became a kind of proxy for Christina of Markyate's deep feelings for Christ—an affective substitution that would become more and more common in the relations between holy women and their spiritual directors as the Middle Ages progress. But it is also arguable that Geoffrey himself was unprepared for this flood of affect, as he began to respond to Christina's transferred feelings for Christ as if they were intended for him. One particular instance stands out. When Geoffrey was embarking on a journey, he requested a favor from Christina—to make him some underwear. Christina, who had experienced all too many inappropriate overtures from a wide assortment of clerics, may have been alarmed by the request: when God canceled the trip, he ordered her to get rid of the underwear.[95] In short, the roles assumed by heteroascetics could nurture something similar to both transference and countertransference of emotional affect, and these feelings would be vindicated by the priest's assimilation with Christ. With the thirteenth century's increased emphasis on auricular confession, moreover, the rapport between the questioning/listening confessor and the confessing/speaking penitent creates even more striking parallels with psychoanalytic dynamics.[96]

An understanding of transference and countertransference could help us fathom the meaning behind Robert of Arbrissel's bizarre sleeping arrangements with the women in his following. Geoffrey had rebuked Robert for his preferential treatment of some of the women—behaving with excessive familiarity, indulging in private conversations, and even sharing their beds. "But with the others, if ever you speak to them, you always appear too harsh in address, too severe in correction; you actually torture them with hunger and thirst and nakedness, all compassion forsaken."[97] The two groups of women are understood to be the inhabitants of the two distinct houses—the one dedicated to the Virgin, the other to the Magdalene, at Fontevrault. Yet there is no indication of which group of women was favored or slighted. Did Robert for once acquiesce to the traditional ranking, honoring virgins over nonvirgins, or did he persist in his commitment to inversion?

I believe that in this instance Robert upheld the conventional ranking, but with unconventional results. Robert's biographer, Baldric, alleged that

Robert's following included "prostitutes." This could be interpreted as women who actually sell their bodies for money (unlikely), the abandoned wives of priests, or women like Petronilla who had experienced multiple marriages, or a combination of these categories.[98] As so many patristic sources demonstrate, however, how these women came to lose their virginity is a matter of indifference—at least from the perspective of lost virginal entitlement. The very existence of two separate houses suggests that Robert was hardly indifferent to the question of who was and who was not a virgin. Like the contemporaneous foundation of St. Martin, which divided the virginal choir nuns from the worldly conversae, women possessed of any sexual backstory were probably destined for the Magdalene house.[99] Whatever treatment they might have received at Robert's hands, however, the nonvirginal women of Robert's following clearly venerated him as they would a saint. And their very adulation may have been pivotal in the hagiographically inflected form that Robert's countertransference took—the assumption of a saintly persona appropriate to the situation of these fallen women. From the perspective of nonvirgins, the hagiographical tradition that had evolved around Mary Magdalene was little help, as she undertook penance for her many sins entirely on her own, engaging upon a harsh ascetical regime in a cave in southern France.[100] But there were traditions associated with other female saints, perhaps less august than the Magdalene but with equally problematical pasts, who were indebted to extremely exacting spiritual directors for supervising their penance. The Egyptian courtesan Thais, for example, was salvaged from her vice-ridden life by the desert father Paphnutius. His strategy was simple but effective: he enclosed Thais in a shack in a desert, where she suffered from hunger and thirst in addition to all the environmental rigors of the Egyptian desert.[101] Her legend, moreover, was becoming extremely popular in this period: Marbod of Rennes, the first to question Robert's sleeping arrangements, actually wrote a metric life in her honor.[102] What would be more natural than for Robert to collaborate in the salvation of his sexually savvy followers by assuming the role of Paphnutius? This was why Robert deliberately tormented the Thais-like courtesans (i.e., the nonvirginal members of his following) with the "hunger and thirst and nakedness" that constituted their penance.

But Robert's treatment of the virginal part of his following was familiar and intimate, even to the point of sharing their beds. Although Robert left no writing to clarify his motives, Geoffrey of Vendôme pretends to firsthand knowledge: "in this way, so you claim, you seem to bear worthily the cross of the Holy Savior when you attempt to extinguish fleshly ardor wickedly aroused. If you do this now, or ever did, you have discovered a new and unheard of but fruitless kind of martyrdom."[103] From Geoffrey's perspective, the women in question are objects of temptation to be transcended, an interpretation that is yet another reminder of how far we have come from any vision of virginal androgyny.

But I believe that the women in question meant more to Robert than just indifferent instruments of penance, subordinated to his own salvation, and that his exacting *imitatio Christi* was directed to a different end than Geoffrey's allegations imply. Perhaps what we are witnessing is yet another pattern of transference and countertransference enacted on an allegorical plane through embodied metaphor. In this case, the virgins were encouraged to regard Robert not only *in loco Christi* but, more specifically, in Christ's spousal persona. The response that their regard stimulated in Robert would serve to deepen his already profound identification with Christ—in this instance, in the persona of the celestial bridegroom. Thus his unconventional sleeping arrangements could be construed as a kind of realized eschatology, rewarding the purity of his virginal following with a premature taste of the mysteries of the wedding chamber. Robert would hardly be alone in such enactments: Hildegard provided elaborate ornamentation for her nuns, in anticipation of the glories of heaven, and was likewise criticized for her efforts.[104] In Robert's case, he was both prefiguring and eliciting the experience of the ultimate conjugal vision, which is by its very nature otherworldly.

From a certain perspective, this reading indicts everyone involved: Robert's arrogance in appropriating Christ's persona and the perversity of his female followers that allowed them to subordinate themselves to this holy make-believe. It would be tempting to dismiss women's slavish gravitation to the nuptial model as an instance of false consciousness, yet another example of the victims of oppression working against their own best interests. And indeed, the cumulative experiences of women such as Ermengard of Brittany, the mother of Guibert of Nogent, Christina of Markyate, or Heloise render it difficult to envisage marriage as an edifying paradigm. Yet, before dismissing what is destined to become the prevailing paradigm for female spiritual expression as retrograde, it is important to emphasize that women's participation in this form of nuptiality was hardly passive. Much like Origen's bride, these women were prepared to take to the streets unveiled in search of their respective grooms. In so doing, they were exercising their prerogative of consent, which, as we suggested in the previous chapter, was not only the essence of marriage but also the spirit of the age. The freedom to choose a spiritual mate was at least partial compensation for the disappointment and injustices endured by these women in secular marriage. Moreover, female transference/

devotion actively "groomed" select members of the clergy, transforming them from mere mortals into plausible surrogates for the celestial bridegroom. It was women who performed this rarefied transubstantiation.

The Ultimate Intimacy:
Bernard, the Canticles, and the Mystical Marriage

An important index to the newly felt power of the emotions and the gravitation toward nuptiality alike is the renewed interest in the Song of Songs. Even as the fourth century represented the zenith in the production of treatises on virginity, the same can be said for the twelfth century and commentaries on the Song of Songs.[105] Among these were the first commentaries on the Canticles that were devoted to the Virgin Mary in the role of bride—an ancient possibility that had flickered briefly through many treatises on virginity and commentaries on the Canticles alike, but was never fully realized until the twelfth century.

In addition to providing an index to the flourishing of Mariology, the renewed interest in the Song of Songs was also a vehicle for the dramatic resurfacing of the mystical marriage between Christ and the soul. We have already seen this imagery evoked by Peter Abelard in his efforts to reconcile Heloise to her vocation. It occupies a pivotal place at the beginning of his rule for the Paraclete: "I too, then, in wishing to depict the beauty of the soul and describe the perfection of the bride of Christ, in which you may discover your own beauty or blemish as in the mirror of one spiritual virgin always held before your eyes, propose to instruct your way of life through the many documents of the holy Fathers."[106] This avowed emphasis on the soul's marriage to Christ again deflects the habitual identification of this image with the consecrated virgin—further evidence of his desire to make room for Heloise as one of Christ's brides.

In 1135, around the time that Abelard was still engaged in or perhaps even finishing his writings for the Paraclete, Bernard of Clairvaux was just beginning his eighty-six sermons on the Song of Songs.[107] Bernard too was attempting a return to a pristine bride and her spiritual meanings before she was pressed into service on behalf of the consecrated virgin. He thus pays tribute to the ancient metaphor of the church as bride of Christ.[108] His main focus, and the one that will leave the greatest impression on medieval spirituality, however, was the identification of the bride with the individual soul—a parallel that, as time would tell, had great potential for the democratization of the mystical marriage. Abelard's similar efforts at democratization would remain, by comparison, much more limited and local. In spite of his innovative spirit, moreover, Abelard's invocation of the bride still adhered to conventional stereotypes. For whether or not the union between his wife and the celestial bridegroom was uppermost in his mind, Abelard was writing for a female community, precisely the personnel who had been encouraged to identify with the bride. Bernard too was writing for a monastic community, his immediate audience being the monks of Clairvaux.[109] But the fact that it was a male community made all the difference. Commentaries on the Song of Songs had long been a mainstay of monastic letters. Bernard, however, was writing in a more immediate form of address—the sermon. Nor can Bernard's sermons be considered traditional insofar as he was requiring his monastic brethren to embark on an unprecedented spiritual enterprise. The terms of passage were personal identification with the figure of the bride because "No sweeter names can be found to embody that sweet interflow of affections between the Word and the soul, than bridegroom and bride."[110] In other words, along with the intensity of the identification required, Bernard also expected his male audience to switch genders in order to identify with a female persona.

Bernard's reading of the Canticles both reflects and fosters the development of a mystical sensibility: a facet of the contemplative life in which the individual seeks a direct experience of God, insofar as it is possible while still in the body. Throughout, he stresses certain extraordinary experiences as markers of the mystical journey. Of particular import are the visions consisting of images produced by angelic powers,[111] and the state of ecstasy—in which the bodily senses are suspended and mental images are dispelled.[112] Ecstasy represents union with God, the ultimate goal of the contemplative.[113] Such a union is perceived as the consummation of the mystical marriage: it takes place in the king's bedchamber and lends itself to endless sensual elaboration.[114]

What adds to the persuasiveness of Bernard's reading of the Canticles is that he draws on his own experience.

> [W]hen the Bridegroom, the Word, came to me, he never made known his coming by any signs, not by sight, nor by sound, not by touch. . . . It was not by any of my senses that I perceived he had penetrated to the depths of my being. Only by the movement of my heart did I perceive his presence. . . . But when the Word has left me, all these spiritual powers become weak and faint and begin to grow cold. . . . When I have had such experience of the Word, is it any wonder that I take to myself the words of the Bride, calling him back when he has withdrawn.[115]

This personal investment provides both the drama and the immediacy of claims of similar out-of-body experiences once made by Paul. Bernard encourages the listener to believe that this intimate experience of God is not only possible but can be courted and provides tools to this end. Lingering over the events of the life of Christ, which include fanciful projections of Joseph playing with the baby Jesus,[116] Bernard actively enlists the imaginative faculties. While vividly depicting Christ's passion and meditating upon his wounds, Bernard simultaneously invites his audience to do likewise.[117]

Bernard did much more than simply retrieve the Canticles for a male audience: his reading of the Song of Songs would quite literally set the spiritual agenda for the rest of the Middle Ages. The emphasis on the humanity of Christ; the reliance on the imagination; the mistrust of the intellect in favor of affect; and the outpouring of love without restraint, contiguous with the implicit and explicit eroticism of the bridal imagery, are mainstays to the spirituality of subsequent centuries.[118] Bernard was also rumored to have been graced with being nursed by the Virgin herself—anticipating the rise of the somatic spirituality that would be so characteristic of female mysticism.[119] And even though Bernard will occasionally cavil about the unworthiness of the average person to identify with the bride, he also maintained that the king was not limited to just one bedroom: "for he has more than one queen; his concubines are many, his maids beyond counting."[120] It was a world in which anyone could be a bride.[121] With the spread of Cistercian spirituality in the thirteenth century, just about anyone was.

CHAPTER 6

The Eroticized Bride of Hagiography

Nowadays not only do the sons of God copulate with the
daughters of men, but with the daughters of God, which is
worse. Namely, religious men are copulating with religious
women. Alas we see, and see frequently, that what certain
men began in the spirit is consummated in the flesh.
—Thomas of Cantimpré[1]

Few people question the ubiquity of sex in our own culture, whether this term
is understood implicitly or explicitly. Sex is as invasive as kudzu: its imagery
dominates every medium and art form. It is used to sell just about anything.
Distaste over the omnipresence of sex in advertising unites religious conserva-
tives and feminists alike.

A person situated in Latin Christendom in the high Middle Ages might
well have considered their own society in a similar light. For instance, the literary discourse of courtly love, however refined, was ultimately concerned with
either gaining or losing the sexual favors of the beloved. This refinement of
seduction was soon followed by the trash-talking fabliaux, which embellished
their unabashedly sexual telos with a cheerful commercialism. Nor were the
quasi-clerical groups of students attending the cathedral schools or the later
universities left behind in these developments. Students snickered over the
racy bits in Ovid, a regular part of the curriculum for study of the trivium.[2]
And these same students may either have laughed or shifted uncomfortably
while listening to Alan of Lille's *Plaint of Nature* (1170) in which Dame Nature
ingeniously describes same-sex coupling in terms of bad grammar.[3] Meanwhile, lapsed students took to the roads as goliards, singing of wine, women,
and song. Works such as Andrew the Chaplain's *Concerning Love* (between

1186 and 1190) both extolled and satirized courtly traditions through mock-serious dialogues between members of the secular elite, nevertheless insinuating that priests made the best lovers anyway.[4] These fraught discourses on sex were seconded by the emergence of a new set of professionals: university-trained physicians who argued about whether women ejaculated seed, female theoreticians on birth and gynecology suddenly emerged, and the practitioners of the oldest profession once again reared their saffron-covered heads.[5]

The Eroticization of Religious Discourse

The development of erotic discourses in religion is on a continuum with these other phenomena. The reappearance of prostitution is reflected in the increasing popularity of the prostitute saints. Abelard enlists flamboyant sexual scenarios en route to scoring ethical points, while an increasingly technical interest/concern about the physiological effects of autoeroticism grace Ælred's treatment of virginity.[6] The twelfth-century's celebration of nature's fecundity will be corroborated by the rediscovery of Aristotle and wide-ranging interest in reproduction across the various species. Theologians such as Albert the Great (d. 1280) discussed the sex act in detail, alleging that because human beings are worthier by nature, and nobler in complexion, their pleasure in coitus is proportionately greater than in the case of any other animal.[7] His student Thomas Aquinas (d. 1274) anticipated Freud by arguing that the concupiscible power of love was at the root of all appetites, including the rational/intellectual one, and hence ultimately responsible for most creative endeavors.[8] Thirteenth-century scholastics, Aquinas included, will carry on a very lively discussion about the sex lives of demons.[9] It is hard to imagine what sexual taboos remained to be breached discursively.

But the preoccupation with sex in canon law and pastoral theology arguably had the most direct impact on society. In the twelfth century, the church waived the taboo against sex during the lengthy penitential periods, designating the former strictures as counsels rather than precepts.[10] This new aura of tolerance represented a total reversal of centuries of teaching. Indeed, some historians have perceived this canonistic reprieve as momentous in a manner extending far beyond the ideological. Jean-Louis Flandrin, for example, links this new dispensation with the population surge of the twelfth century.[11] Whether or not this was, in fact, the case, it is no exaggeration to say that the emphasis on sexual abstinence during marriage was succeeded by an increasing concern that both husband and wife render the marriage debt when required.[12] The inclusion of marriage among the list of seven sacraments placed the clergy in the awkward position of policing both sexual infractions and failures in ecclesiastical courts. Inability to pay the conjugal debt was one of the very few licit reasons for the dissolution of a marriage.[13] Likewise, a plea for the restitution of conjugal rights was the surest way of attempting to retrieve an errant spouse.[14] A prelate could even, in theory, dispense with either party's sexual reticence by ordering the payment of the debt.[15] The church's novel deference to married sex was the ultimate deathblow to a unilateral entrance into religion.[16]

The clergy's new role in monitoring sexual relations is especially reflected in the genre of confessors' manuals.[17] These works were intended to educate the clergy in the penitential process in the wake of Lateran IV's universal mandate for annual confession. This new clerical responsibility could be extremely taxing. Ideally, penitents were supposed to prepare for confession ahead of time, so they could "vomit up" their sins with little prompting.[18] But if the penitent proved shy or recalcitrant, the confessor was required to apply an inquisitorial manner of interrogation to elicit possible infractions. The confessor was not merely expected to concern himself with obvious sins, such as fornication or adultery, but also to probe admittedly less grievous but potentially more embarrassing matters such as nocturnal emissions.[19] If the manuals themselves are any indication, the finely calibrated degrees of culpability were worthy of the desert fathers. These confessional forays into the penitent's sex life were reinforced by an increased emphasis on preaching. The collections of exempla in circulation to assist preachers were chock-full of a surprising number of titillating anecdotes of the tragedies that could befall a couple who abused the conjugal debt.[20]

So suddenly the post-Gregorian priesthood was required to enter into the most intimate areas of their parishioners' lives, eliciting salacious details about a basic drive that they themselves had turned their backs upon and, ideally, had little experience with satisfying. Should the priest be heterosexual, the temptation would doubtless be all the greater if the penitent were a woman, especially one he found attractive. This possibility was recognized as a genuine area of concern: a number of manuals would eventually offer the confessor some tactics for minimizing temptation.[21] But the risks went both ways: the priesthood's potential sexual fallibility also left the penitent vulnerable to abuse—a problem so rife that heavy sanctions were eventually imposed by the Council of Trent against sacerdotal "soliciting," but to no avail.[22] Clerical indiscretion could also present serious problems. The Franciscans and the Dominicans had been created specifically for ministering to the laity in the wake of Lateran IV, and the mendicants were also associated with some of the earliest infractions against the seal of confession.[23]

At the eye of this erotic storm were the Beguines—a burgeoning group of Christ's brides intent on enjoying the pleasures of his marriage bed.

The Early Beguines and Bridal Mysticism

The Beguines were a pious group of laywomen that emerged in the Low Countries toward the end of the twelfth century. Although these women frequently lived in communities known as beguinages, they were not an official religious order and took no formal vows.[24] Their devotional practices grew out of many of the religious points of emphases that developed over the course of the twelfth century. The dedication to the humanity of Christ and his passion, which had been receiving increasing emphasis since Anselm's time, was especially stressed. In the wake of Lateran IV, attention to Christ's body was often translated into a focus on the Eucharist, sometimes to the point of obsession.[25]

This section primarily focuses on the early Beguines in the diocese of Liège and surrounding areas where the movement first arose.[26] The materials on these women are largely hagiographic. With the important exception of Beatrice of Nazareth (d. 1268), none of these women wrote down their revelations. Yet if we momentarily extend our purview beyond these geographical confines, we discover Beguines whose writings provide striking evidence that the figure of the bride and the attendant language of love were not simply male projections, but important vehicles for expressing female spirituality. The rhetoric of love also became a venue for considerable innovation: a number of Beguine authors were versed in the conventions of secular love literature, deftly uniting them with the tradition associated with the Song of Songs.[27] The poet Hadewijch of Antwerp (d. 1240) aligns herself with the courtly wooer in pursuit of God, the sometimes elusive, but much beloved mistress. This gender inversion suggests that the idiom of courtly love may have been more flexible than the seemingly intractable personae of human bride and divine groom at the heart of the Song of Songs.[28] In a similar vein, Mechtild of Magdeburg (d. between 1282 and 1294) creates an interactive relationship between the soul and God, so that it is not invariably the female soul languishing in love, but God himself suffers lovesickness over the female soul.[29]

Eventually Mechtild would retire to the monastery of Helfta, a Benedictine community that was strongly influenced by Cistercian spirituality.[30] There she would go on to inspire the remarkable sisters Mechtild of Hackeborn (d.

1299) and Gertrude the Great (d. 1301 or 1302). That both sisters grew up in the convent is suggested by the profound influence of the liturgical calendar on their respective spiritualities. Their writings were also informed by a strong sense of virginal privilege, as one might expect of two lifelong *sanctimoniales*. Gertrude's *Spiritual Exercises* embellishes the mystical contours of the consecration of the virgin with a heightened sensuality.[31] Much of this work tracks the actual words of the rite of consecration quite closely. But Gertrude's improvisations add an active and insistent edge to the virgin's role. When the bishop initially summons the virgins, Gertrude includes a passionate appeal to Christ: "Behold, I am approaching you, O consuming fire, my God. Ah! Devour me, a speck of dust, in the fiery vigor of your love, consume me utterly and absorb me into yourself. . . . Behold, I am approaching you, O most blessed union. Ah! Make me one with you by the glue of living love [*amoris glutino*]."[32] Christ in his "fiery divinity" is depicted as leading a circular dance, "followed by thousands upon thousands of the very brightest virgins. . . . in snow-white robes, jubilantly singing the dulcet songs of everlasting marriage."[33]

Mechtild of Hackeborn is especially articulate about the prestige of the virginal bride. Her visionary Christ alleges that his father so loves individual virgins that when each arrives in heaven his joy equals that of any king over the arrival of his one and only wife—the legitimate one with whom he was destined to produce heirs.[34] For his own part, Christ prizes virgins over all the saints in heaven.[35] A number of Mechtild's visions occur at the deathbeds of various nuns in which onlookers either saw or sensed "the spouse of virgins" approach to claim his bride.[36] And yet in Mechtild's spiritual landscape, it is the Virgin Mary who remains the ultimate bride.[37] It is she who prepares the virgins for their nuptials, doling out the wedding *arrhae*—the very rings that signify their vows of chastity.[38]

Mechtild also enlisted nuptial imagery as a medium for expressing spiritual satisfaction and discontent equally, both of which sentiments would be bent to pedagogic ends. Certainly one of the spiritual high points of her revelations is when Mechtild herself is depicted as experiencing a mystical marriage with Christ. Dressed like a royal spouse in glorious white, Christ will proceed to invest Mechtild in white and red robes. The white signifies her innocence; the red stands for both his passion and the various trials he has prepared for her. The couple stands in front of Love, who has assumed the form of a beautiful virgin. She binds Mechtild and the Lord together in her mantle, and their souls, in turn, become as one.[39]

At other times, however, Mechtild uses nuptial imagery to convey dissatisfaction with her own spiritual progress. For instance, Mechtild complains that on the day of her wedding (presumably her actual consecration as a virgin) she was insufficiently devout in her celebration and she did not harbor the kind of faithfulness that would befit the intimacy expected of husband and wife. She is placated when Christ crowns her with a diadem of perfect virtues and embraces her with his bare arm.[40] On another occasion, when Mechtild sees the Virgin Mary placing a ring on her son's hand, she bursts out, "Oh if he could give me such a ring as a sign of marriage!" Christ forthwith gave her a ring with seven stones, each representing one of the seven phases of his life on earth, which, in turn, correspond to the preparatory stages leading up to a wedding. The seventh was the wedding itself, signified by the Crucifixion.[41] By the same token, when Mechtild complains that they have no children, as do other couples, Christ reminds her that he gives her children daily in the form of the seven canonical hours.[42] Christ imparted one of his greatest consolations when Mechtild was suffering from a certain "bitterness of the soul," and he showed her how to renew her marriage vow at his feet.[43]

All of the Beguine mystics describe their union with Christ in frankly erotic terms. Mechtild of Magdeburg depicts the soul performing a passionate dance in which she leaps for love. The soul is subsequently summoned to the bed of love, where she strips before her celestial lover so that nothing can come between them.

> Then a blessed stillness
> that both desire comes over them.
> He surrenders himself to her,
> And she surrenders herself to him.[44]

Mechtild of Hackeborn envisions Christ lying by her side in bed, holding her with his left arm so that "the wound of his heart was joined so sweetly to her heart."[45] Yet despite this heightened degree of sensuality, there is little doubt that these revelations were limited to the spiritual versus the corporeal senses. In other words, none of these women ever crossed the boundaries of the imagination by suggesting that their revelations had any experiential claims in the outer world.[46] Readers sometimes fail to make this distinction, however. For instance, Hadewijch's restless imagery often engages taste and touch in its approach to God.[47] But, as Gordon Rudy has argued, the senses enlisted are spiritual, not corporeal, and cannot be translated into the type of physical craving for the Eucharist that characterizes many other female mystics.[48] By the same token, when Mechtild of Magdeburg describes how Queen Soul embarks on the sevenfold path of love, it is explicitly "beyond the influences of the flesh." In preparation for the bridegroom, the soul dresses herself in the slip of humility, the white dress of chastity, and the cloak of good name (adorned with all the virtues). Yet her chamberlains, the five senses, are significantly left behind.[49] Mechtild of Hackeborn scrupulously distinguishes between the inner senses (which God augments in the course of a vision) and outer senses, against which she offers certain safeguards.[50] Even more to the point is that Mechtild's mystical union is represented as the kind of annihilation that necessarily transcends the body and its senses alike. Christ tells Mechtild that he seeks a union in which "your soul adheres to my soul by the glue of love [*glutino amoris*]," in which "the soul is entirely liquefied in the beloved so that it seemed as if she was one spirit with him."[51] This kind of unity is anticipated in Mechtild's raptures, in which "just as a drop of water when it is poured into wine is totally changed to wine, so, when this blessed soul went over to God, she was made one spirit with him. In this union the soul is annihilated."[52]

Occasionally the voluptuousness of this imagery seems to be pressing the visionary envelope beyond the mere metaphoric.[53] This is especially true of Gertrude the Great. For instance, her *Herald of Divine Love* relates how Christ first approached her as a handsome youth, about sixteen years of age and "entirely pleasing to the outer eye." After that, she was often favored with his "visible presence" (*visibili praesentia tua me dignareris*) at communion. In this latter case, however, she only saw him "as if in the dim light of dawn"— perhaps a subtle indicator that it was the spiritual, not the corporeal, vision that was being engaged.[54] With respect to her reception of the stigmata, however, Gertrude is very explicit that these wounds were wrought "interiorly in my heart."[55] Likewise, her experience of the beatific vision is couched in analogy. When the light from Christ's eyes entered her own, "it was as though my bones were being emptied of all the marrow, then even the bones with the flesh were dissolved so that nothing was felt to exist in my substance."[56]

Although Gertrude herself included the above safeguards, the perspicacious nuns who were responsible for recording and assembling the majority of Gertrude's visions found it propitious to insert a comment by Hugh of St. Victor as a further amulet against such literalism: "In order to refer things familiar to this lower world and to come down to the level of human weakness, Holy Scripture describes things by means of visible forms, and thus impresses on our imagination spiritual ideas by means of beautiful images which excite our desires. . . . Read the Apocalypse of St. John and you will find Jerusalem ornamented with gold and silver pearls. . . . Now we know that there is nothing of this sort in heaven. . . . But if none of these things is to be found materially, all are there spiritually."[57] These literal images are but crude approximations of spiritual realities.

If the above female writers were generally careful not to cross the line between the spiritual and material realms, the hagiographers of the Low Countries were not always so scrupulous, frequently providing a very literal translation of mystical imagery. Such literalism was at least partially driven by a kind of pragmatism: as will soon become apparent, the case for sanctity required concrete proofs, which meant that the apprehension of the divine presence by the spiritual senses was often registered on their corporeal counterparts, even as spiritual graces were enacted directly on the body.[58] Thus in addition to voluntary feats of self-mortification or painstaking efforts to reenact the passion of Christ, much of Beguine spirituality is represented as passive symptoms of devotion as opposed to active expressions.[59] For instance, a number of the Beguine saints were seemingly afflicted with extreme ill health, which the sufferers generally bore cheerfully, considering illness and disease as heaven-sent means for testing the elect.[60] The Beguines were also recipients of celestial visions and revelations, which inspired mystical ecstasies or raptures: during these times, the body was rendered insensible to outside stimuli.[61] God's favor could also induce spontaneous wounds. The Cistercian nun Ida of Louvain (d. ca. 1261) not only was a recipient of the stigmata but would also experience copious bleeding from her nose and mouth during Mass.[62] Other women were graced with divine lactations.[63] These characteristics would identify the Beguines as forerunners of the kind of somatic spirituality that the work of Caroline Bynum has demonstrated to be particularly associated with women.[64]

Despite its more flamboyant manifestations, the spirituality of the Beguines was nevertheless shaped under Cistercian auspices. Not only were many of their confessors drawn from the Cistercian order, but there were a number of Cistercian nuns who began their lives as Beguines or whose piety marked them as honorary Beguines, in spite of the cloister.[65] Mary of Oignies, the first Beguine to warrant a vita and hence frequently construed as a founding mother, is presented as acknowledging this indebtedness when she has a vision of a winged Bernard of Clairvaux while praying in church. When she inquired about the meaning of his wings, the visionary Bernard replied that "like an eagle, he attained the high and subtle things of divine Scripture through high flying and that the Lord had opened to him many of the heavenly secrets."[66]

Bernard's reading of the bride in the Song of Songs was, however, the vehicle in which the Beguines are presented as doing their high flying. This attention to the heavenly bridegroom would complement the increasing focus on the humanity of Christ, both of which emphases had been present in Bernard's writings.[67] Through the Bernardine vision of the Song of Songs, these women came to construe a Christ that was both embodied and eroticized. It was with him they sought the ultimate union that Bernard upheld as the most elevated of spiritual goals. And it was the ardent, questing love of the bride that made this union possible.[68] For the expression of this union, mystical hagiographers often looked to an image drawn from Bernard's other great mystical work, *On Loving God*: "As a drop of water seems to disappear completely in a big quantity of wine, even assuming the wine's taste and colour . . . so it is necessary for the saints that all human feelings melt in a mysterious way and flow into the will of God. Otherwise, how will God be all in all if something human survives in man?"[69] We have already met with a version of this image in the writings of Mechtild of Hackeborn. The image also appears explicitly in the lives of thirteenth-century Beguines such as Lutgard of Aywières (d. 1246) and Ida of Gorsleeuw (d. ca. 1270).[70] It was destined to become increasingly controversial as the Middle Ages progressed.[71]

Under the pressure of twelfth-century intentionality, the bridal persona was gradually becoming less exclusive to virgins, accommodating all women regardless of sexual past. Although this level of democratization is perhaps not surprising, there is certainly some irony at play: whether intended or not, Bernard had staged a powerful intervention through his sermons on the Song of Songs. He had retrieved the pristine meaning of the soul marriage from centuries of treatises on virginity directed to the consecrated virgin and promoted it as a point of identification for men rather than women. Yet whatever Bernard's intentions, this gesture of democratization made the persona of the bride much more widely available for appropriation. Cistercian hagiographers attempted to perpetuate the monk's identification with the bride, jealously guarding this motif from the order's lay brethren.[72] Ultimately, however, biology determined the destiny of this image, which would continue to be overwhelmingly connected with women. The many contemporaneous commentaries on the Song of Songs associated the bride with the Virgin Mary, the model for virgins and mothers alike, which would tend to reinforce normative gender identification. Furthermore, the somatic nature of female spirituality would not only perpetuate but strengthen the ancient link between the bridal persona and the female body. As a result, the bride was rendered less virgocentric, yet more embodied than ever before—a factor that would contribute immensely to the contemporaneous eroticization of religious discourse.

The Beguines seemed to live under conditions that permitted considerable familiarity with the select priests who catered to their religious needs. In a sacramental sense, these women could be described as dependent on these men—a dependency that would be deepened by the emphasis on frequent confession and communion. From a spiritual perspective, however, the clerics in question acknowledged their indebtedness to the charismatic grace they found in these women, depicting themselves as clients or even suppliants.[73] A number of these clerics would eventually honor their spiritual patronesses through hagiography and related pastoral media, and it is to these sources that we are largely indebted for information about the early Beguines. The corpus as a whole paints a fascinating picture of an erotically charged climate through which women's spiritual intimacy with the heavenly bridegroom would overflow into their relations with the priesthood.[74]

The inclusive nature of bridal mysticism and its sensual pleasures are already apparent in the works of the Beguines' earliest admirers. James of Vitry (d. 1240 or 1244) was a theologian who became bishop of Acre and ultimately cardinal bishop of Tusculum. He was drawn to Liège by the reputation of the holy matron, Mary of Oignies (d. 1213), whom he would afterward honor as his "spiritual mother."[75] His ensuing life of Mary would provide a blueprint for all the mystical biographies to come. Of particular salience is his famous prologue to her life, in which the Beguines, regardless of individual sexual histories, are designated brides of Christ.

> You saw many bands of holy virgins in different places of the lily
> gardens (cf. Sg 6.1) . . . [who] clung to the heavenly Bridegroom in
> poverty and humility. . . . You saw holy women [*matronas*] serving
> God. . . . With what zeal did they preserve their youthful chastity,
> arming themselves in their honourable resolve by salutary warnings,
> so that their only desire was the heavenly Bridegroom. Widows
> served the Lord in fasts and prayers, in vigils and manual labour,
> in tears and entreaties. Just as they had previously tried to please
> their husbands in the flesh, so now the more did they attempt to
> please their heavenly Bridegroom . . . and promised to bear fruit
> sixty-fold.[76]

All three degrees of chastity are carefully presented, and each one warrants the title bride. But even the spirit of democratization has its limits: James did not accord anyone who was still sexually active the title. The matrons alluded to in the above passage we later learn were the "many [who] abstained from licit embraces with the assent of their husbands . . . leading a celibate—indeed, an angelic—life." Mary of Oignies had made a vow of chastity with her husband,

John. It was probably out of recognition of the extra merit incurred by one who abstains from what was sanctioned, as well as homage to Mary, that prompted James to break with the usual order and list this select set of matrons ahead of the chaste widows.[77] Moreover, the fact that the widow is still represented as receiving sixtyfold reward suggests that the sexually abstemious matrons rank still higher, hovering somewhere just beneath the virgins' laudatory hundredfold.

The life weaves ascetic feats, bodily illness, mystical raptures, and eucharistic devotion together into a single skein, which is gracefully intertwined with the sensuality of the Canticles.

> [W]omen were wasting away with such an intimate and wondrous state of love in God that they were faint with desire and who for many years could only rarely rise from their beds. There was no other cause for their sickness except him, since their souls melted with desire (cf. Sg 5.6) for him. . . . They cried aloud in their heart[s] . . . "Stay me with flowers, compass me about with apples, for I languish with love" (Sg 2.5).

> Others were so rapt outside themselves with such a spirit of inebriation, that they rested in that holy silence throughout almost an entire day, "while the King was on his couch" (Sg 1.12); they neither spoke nor were sensible of anything external to them.

> I saw another who, for almost thirty years, was kept with such zeal by the Bridegroom . . . no one could entice her out of her cloister.

> Some of them ran with such desire after the fragrance (Cf. Sg 1.3) of such a great sacrament [the Eucharist] that in no way could they endure to be deprived of it; and unless their souls were frequently invigorated by the delights of this meal, they obtained no consolation or rest but utterly wasted away in languor.[78]

Each in her own way was languishing with love.

When it comes to the vita proper, Mary's rich inner life is likewise represented as saturated with bridal imagery. When praising her humility, James rhetorically addresses her: "Why do you not show your Christ to the world? . . . When 'the King led you into the wine cellar' (Sg 1.3), is it not possible that you sometimes cried out in inebriation, 'O Lord why are you hiding yourself? . . .

For if the world knew you, it would sin no more but would immediately *run after the fragrance of your ointment*' (Sg 1.3)."[79] Her prayers lead her to "the bridal bed of divine counsel."[80] She is decorated as "the supreme King adorned his daughter with the seven gifts of the Spirit and beautified her most excellently" with the spirit of wisdom. "With the savour of this wisdom" she "'lean[s] upon her Beloved (Sg 8.5)' . . . [eating] milk and honey from the lips of the Bridegroom (cf. Sg 4.11)."[81] Toward the end of her life, Mary will move away from her relatives to be "more sweetly 'under the shadow of him whom she desired' (Sg 2.3)." She was divinely accorded prophetic knowledge of the time of her death, and as that day drew nearer "[she] now could not contain herself . . . impatient that there be any delay before she was able to embrace the Lord." "While she was being tortured with such violent desire and rapt outside herself, her entire body almost seemed to burst from the fullness of her heart." "[S]he was inebriated and could not be silent." When marveling over the intensity of that rapture, God revealed to her, "'There is not much time left to you,' and she heard the voice of the Lord calling her, 'Come my friend, my turtle dove! You shall be crowned.'"[82] The day of her death is presented as her wedding day. In anticipation of this great event "the voice of the turtle was heard in our land (Sg 2.12)," as Mary sang her version of the Canticles: a song of exultation that lasted for two days and three nights.[83]

The voluptuous language of the Song of Songs continued to be deployed by those who followed in James's footsteps, sometimes with more energy than skill. For instance, the Dominican Thomas of Cantimpré (d. between 1265 and 1270), a fervent admirer of James and another important advocate for the Beguines, would eventually write a biography for his own spiritual mother, the Cistercian nun Lutgard of Aywières (d. 1246).[84] His deployment of the imagery of the Canticles is an enthusiastic, if slightly flat-footed, effort to shape an exegesis of the Song around Lutgard's spirituality. "Lutgard's feelings were like those of the bride in the Song of Songs whose soul melts, is wounded, languishes, pants, arises, and searches among the districts of the new grace (the saints) and the streets of the Old Testament." Thomas then directs us to "the triple mode of her search," which turns out to be three different references to bed in the Canticles. Each corresponded with a state of her soul: penitential, spiritually combative, and contemplative.[85]

Of course, the overt eroticism of the Canticles was always in danger of descending into what might appear prurient. For instance, once when Ida of Gorsleeuw was attending matins, the celestial bridegroom "sending forth his heavenly hand through the key hole, visited his spouse as secretly as it was sweetly."[86] These words must needs resonate with the suppressed continuation

of that verse in the Song of Songs, which is even more suggestive: "My beloved put his hand through the key hole [*foramen*], and my womb [*venter*] was
moved at his touch (Sg 5.4)."

Anyone who attempts to draw a direct line between metaphor and external realities generally ends up looking foolish. It is not to the credit of
the community of Juliana of Mont-Cornillon (d. 1258) that when she told
her fellow nuns that she was "sick with love," they actually believed she was
physically ill and tried to shoo away any visitors.[87] By the same token, a direct
translation of erotic imagery into feelings or actions would not only lack nu-
ance but also be totally out of sympathy with our medieval subjects, who were
clearly aware of important differences.[88] Even so, biblical exegesis was becoming more literal,[89] and this trend was seemingly exaggerated in hagiography.

Metaphors progressively materialized, rendering bridal imagery ever more
concrete. When Ida of Louvain invited another Beguine to dinner, one whose
vocation was in jeopardy, she had no wine. She went on to serve the beer,
joking, "How seemly and fair it would be if the Heavenly Groom were to
entertain his assembled brides to a draught of wine—nuptial wine!" Nor was
her palate disappointed: whatever they ended up drinking tasted exactly like
wine. By the same token, she had but to read that "*the Word was made flesh
and dwelt among us* . . . behold the very word, which her tongue formed and
her mouth brought forth, was transformed into the substance of meat at the
same moment."[90] Literalism such as this gradually began to draw the celestial
marriage from the heavens until it was more tangible than ever before. Sometimes this was effected simply through timely specificity. Ida of Nivelles (d.
1231) would languish with such love for the Eucharist that she was incapable
of following the other sisters to work. Because her indisposition is rendered in
situ, it becomes much more vivid than the anonymous hoards of languishing
women in James of Vitry's prologue. Ida was also visited by a man (presumably Christ) who appeared with his lips literally oozing white liquid that he
dripped into her mouth, wishing to instill "bountifully into [her] this tasti-
est of honeycombs." This hearkened back to "Thy lips, my spouse, are as a
dropping honeycomb (Sg 4.11)."[91] Ida of Louvain drank from honey-flavored
liquid that streamed from Christ's breast, which granted her access to the wine
cellar of the king.[92] While Thomas of Cantimpré's metaphoric interpolation
of the Song of Songs into Lutgard's spirituality occasionally left something
to be desired, he was a virtuoso at representing more tangible effects. When
Lutgard pressed her mouth to the visionary Christ's side and drank, her saliva
remained sweet like honey for a long time (Sg 4.11), as "those to whom she
revealed this event have reported and could certify."[93] (One can only wonder

about the manner of certification.) An elderly Beguine from Cantimpré was literally annihilated in her union with God when listening to a sermon describing how the soul mixes with God as water with wine. Her feelings of devotion, likened to new wine deprived of a vent for fermentation, caused her heart to burst (Job 32.10).[94]

In Thomas's vitae of Lutgard and of the recluse Margaret of Ypres (d. 1237), the sublimation of erotic feelings from terrestrial to celestial groom is not just suggested but realized. In other words, bridal imagery literally drives the action.[95] Lutgard was sitting in conversation with her suitor when Christ appeared in human form and besought her not to marry: "Here I pledge that you shall attain the delights of total purity."[96] But the same scenario could be enacted on a more mundane level, with the priest acting as Christ's proxy. Margaret of Ypres was already in love with a young man when Friar Zeger picked her out from a group of other young female penitents as a "vessel of election," chiding her to reject worldly things. For Margaret, the process of sublimation seems to have stalled at an interim point with Friar Zeger, "lov[ing] her spiritual father more than anybody or anything she had in the world."[97] As we shall see, this attachment rivaled even the most fervent of twelfth-century heteroascetics.

In other Beguine hagiographies, the priesthood's identification with the celestial bridegroom could be represented even more seamlessly. In her anonymous life, Beatrice of Nazareth's consecration as a bride of Christ is described as follows: "When the bishop came in the usual course to do what was to be done to the Lord's chosen [Beatrice], she was wonderfully seized from within and enlightened with heavenly brightness. She saw with the eyes of her mind that everything the venerable pontiff was doing in a visible bodily way—reading, blessing, placing a crown on her head and a mystical ring on her finger and other actions pertaining to this office—our Lord Jesus Christ, the true and eternal bridegroom was doing sensibly [*sensibiliter*] in her soul."[98]

Some of the more intriguing associations between the priest and Christ occur in the life of Ida of Nivelles. Upon the reception of the host, for instance, Ida would experience an "inner sweetness that she felt her own spirit being bonded to the divine spirit, bonded through the glue of love, a glue so potent that she became *one spirit*, as it were, with God (1 Cor. 6.17)."[99] But Ida also had the capacity to enjoy parallel experiences with select members of the clergy. A certain priest, who had doubted the many marvelous things he had heard about Ida's spirituality, was presented with a vision of Ida's face during Mass by Christ himself, with the words, "'Such is my beloved' (Sg 5.16)." The next time the priest saw Ida, who "seemed to be glorified in soul and in body," he responded by entering into a rapture himself. "Ida, on seeing this, likewise perceived him as if glorified in soul and body; and she too was instantly . . . raptured into heaven, where both now mutually beheld one another and celebrated *festivity together* (Ps. 75.11)."[100]

Some clerics are represented as entering into these spiritual friendships with explicit expectations. Another priest with whom Ida of Nivelles was friendly apparently lived in hopes that their relationship would intensify his spirituality. He was not disappointed. While he was in the midst of a conversation with the local abbess, he was swept away in rapture. Upon returning to consciousness, the priest remarked to the astonished nun, " 'Had I bow and arrow at hand, I'd shoot her back for shooting me.' " The abbess became even more confused, until he explained that while Ida was experiencing her usual ecstasy at Mass she had taken the opportunity to make a special appeal to Christ on the priest's behalf. The explanation itself induced another rapture, however, in which he encountered "his beloved Ida" already in Christ's presence. Christ was requesting that Ida share some of her graces with her friend. Ida willingly obliged by kissing the priest. "At that moment it seemed to the man of God that his own spirit became so inseparably joined to Ida's spirit as to become through *an unfeigned charity, one single spirit in the Lord* (1 Cor. 7.17; 2 Cor. 6.6)."[101]

A regular canon of the Premonstratensian order experienced a unity with Ida of Louvain that was even more complete. He first encountered Ida during an ecstasy in which she was presented before his mind's eye as equal in merit before God. He returned to himself covered with rose stains—as if he had been weeping tears of blood. When he eventually sought Ida out, each immediately could penetrate the other's spiritual state with the power of the inner eye: "Seeing themselves mutually, not differently, as if they had lived together the entire time of their lives. They recognized scarcely any dissimilarities in themselves, knowing that both were of equal merit before the highest Judge. . . . Therefore from this point they existed as one heart in God, but the petulance of carnal affection did not bind them, but the connecting glue of the Holy Spirit [*glutinosa connexio*]."[102]

Good Love, Bad Love: James of Vitry and Thomas of Cantimpré

The mantle of nuptial metaphor that descended upon the priesthood also corresponded with a rising note of concern over the age-old problem of confusing carnal and spiritual love. This is already apparent in the vita of Mary of

Oignies. James of Vitry presents Mary as possessed of an exuberant and joyful spirituality, but occasionally her exhilaration manifested itself in movements or expressions that suggested "perhaps a tiny bit of excess." This surplus of affect could also spill over into her relations with the clergy. "Sometimes she would even receive some of her friends who had come to her with a small shamefaced embrace or, from the intensity of her devotion would kiss the hands and feet of certain priests." Eventually she would "return to herself after this mental inebriation" and sift through her past actions for any trace of wrongdoing.[103]

The subtext is that Mary was examining herself for any vestige of carnal love. The one time this slippage does occur, however, she is not the one at fault. A close friend "clasped [Mary's] hand from an excess of spiritual affection," and he felt "the first stirrings of masculine lust." The saint was blessedly oblivious to any problem. Even though Mary had once been married, it had been years since she felt the stirrings of lust, which rendered her somewhat naïve sexually. Nevertheless, she did hear a voice saying, "Do not touch me" (John 20.1). Confused, she told her friend what she had heard, still uncomprehending. Her friend understood, however, and went away, mortified, but grateful that his lapse had remained a secret.[104]

If the hapless cleric was indeed James of Vitry himself, which seems likely, this would not be the only time that he inadvertently crossed the boundary between carnal and spiritual love, as shall be seen below. Aware of his own susceptibilities, James also warns others against the thin divide between the two loves in his sermons. To an audience of Cistercian nuns, he rails against men who insinuate themselves into women's affections "imped[ing] the spirit, taking away their freedom of heart." Even if these men do not sin mortally in cultivating such relations, the attachments would inevitably impede their prayer lives. "And if they were not to see those persons once a day or many times, they would not be able to have peace."[105] Such affections had the potential for quickly morphing into carnal feelings—a concern that was reinforced by spicy exempla.[106]

Thomas of Cantimpré, whose hagiographic career spans several decades, provides an interesting gage for registering at least one man's growing apprehension of the perils of love.[107] Although his initial awareness of the problem is negligible, it will eventually rise to a near obsession. His first effort at a saint's life was the vita for Abbot John of Cantimpré (d. between 1205 and 1209), the beloved founder of Thomas's first religious community of Augustinian canons at Cantimpré. It was written between 1223 and 1228, begun when he was still a young man of twenty-three.[108] John's community was founded for both men

and women, who initially resided together in the same building.[109] Not surprisingly, the abbot is depicted as being on an easy footing with any number
of women, but was particularly intimate with a widow named Ivetta, one of
the many who "followed the venerable John so ardently that they could not
bear his absence for even a short time."[110] Eventually, John became concerned
about potential criticism for accommodating men and women under the same
roof (even though they were decorously separated from one another), so he
built the nuns their own habitation, and Ivetta became the prioress of the
female branch of the community. The two remained sufficiently close, however, that "nothing to do with the holy man could escape the prioress's shrewd
observation, and with her blandishments [*calliditates*] she extorted [any] secret . . . from his heart."[111] Thus, when she was watching over him during an
illness, he had a revelation of the Virgin Mary and Christ, which he would
have concealed out of modesty, but which she compelled him to share.[112]

Later in life, John became especially familiar with the countess of Champagne, who was deeply reliant on his counsel. Not only would she send her
carriage to fetch the aging John, wearing down his ascetical resistance, but she
would even insist that he take her own bedroom when he stayed at the palace,
a kindness that many a holy man would have rejected outright. But John's
services went far beyond mere counsel: he is presented as pivotal in sparing
the countess from near certain death in childbirth. After nine days of the
most painful labor, the countess summoned John and tearfully begged him to
intercede with God. John, himself weeping, did as she asked, and a girl baby
was soon born.[113]

John was reputed to have frequently intervened for other women as well.
For instance, he absolved a female murderess in confession, who subsequently
managed to pass the ordeal of hot iron and was released as innocent. (The
brother, her partner in crime, was not so lucky, presumably not having availed
himself of confession.) John also convinced a woman "goaded by the Enemy
and burning with fires of lust" to repent. Unfortunately, he was unable to
free a usurer's widow from the affliction of a demonic lapdog, only visible to
herself. But the saintly exorcist can hardly be blamed as the woman in question apparently continued to benefit from ill-gotten goods. John was forced to
send her home, pet in lap, with the recommendation that she repent.[114]

Thomas's next hagiographic work was the supplement to the life of Mary
of Oignies, written sometime between 1229 and 1232. He had already prepared
the groundwork for this venture by including, rather tangentially in the life
of John, some miracles associated with Mary of Oignies that James had omitted "lest he tire his readers with excess."[115] The supplement was allegedly on

a continuum with this initiative. His introductory letter to Giles, prior of Oignies, presents the supplement as a reluctant concession (due to his own unworthiness and the glory of James of Vitry) to the multiple requests for an account of the many wonders associated with Mary of Oignies that had yet to be recorded.[116] But whatever the surface incentive, the real aim of this work was to recall James from his glittering ecclesiastical career to what Thomas deemed to be his true ministry: the holy women of Liège. It is to this end that Thomas reveals many of the intimate details of the relationship between Mary and James, a number that James had apparently chosen to withhold.

The work proper opens with a series of powerful disclosures intended to demonstrate the devotion that James had once possessed for Mary. James is first pictured as abandoning his theological studies in Paris and moving to Oignies so as to be near Mary, whom he knew by reputation alone. Two revelations underlining his spiritual indebtedness to Mary follow: that James himself was the anonymous preacher mentioned in the original vita who received his vocation (and ability) in answer to Mary's appeal to God for a surrogate preacher, as she could not herself preach, and that the many deathbed prayers "for her preacher" attributed to Mary were for James. Thomas further contextualizes at least one occasion on which Mary's devotion got the better of her while she was kissing the hands of priests. Apparently James had just arrived from his ordination in Paris. Mary and a number of priests ran out to meet him "and, as is customary in such circumstances, they kissed his hands that had been anointed with sacred chrism." But if such behavior represented conventional piety, what followed did not. Mary walked behind James, kissing his footprints. A devout noble chided her, " 'Mistress, what are you doing? If those ahead of us see this, what will they say? I beg you, stop, don't do it.' She replied, 'No, no I can't. I am forcefully impelled by the spirit who now reveals to me inwardly that God has chosen him from among mortals to exalt him gloriously.' "[117] Thomas follows this disclosure with Mary's prediction that James would be made bishop in the Holy Land.[118]

Cumulatively, these anecdotes impart considerable insight into the spiritual interdependence of Mary and "her preacher" during the holy woman's lifetime. Their continued intimacy after Mary's death is even more revealing. After addressing some miracles that Mary performed on behalf others, Thomas circles back to James and Mary, particularly the powerful postmortem interventions that she effected on his behalf. Thus in the course of his many crossings between Rome and the Holy Land, James was caught in a storm and invoked Mary: " 'O venerable mother and lady, while you were on earth you loved me with a special love. I loved you in return, not as much as I should

have, but as much as I could according to the measure of my imperfection.' "
He then appealed for her aid. An apparitional Mary responded, " 'Behold, I,
your protector, am here because you called me. I did really love you in life and
since my life ended, I have been ceaselessly praying for your salvation.' "[119]

These moving professions of, quite literally, undying love between (spiritual) lovers is followed by Mary's assurance that James would not die, but
would return to Oignies where, she correctly predicted, he would consecrate a
church with five altars, the last of which would be dedicated to the Holy Trinity. (Such a church was, as it happens, still in construction when James arrived,
making the prophecy all the more portentous.) But she added, " 'If you wish,
before this altar Christ will give you the peace you have sought. . . . But you
are a man with a will of your own, and you have never wanted to accede to my
counsels and the counsels of those who loved you spiritually.' "[120] Thomas proceeds to uphold Mary's infallible prophetic people sense: after the predicted
consecration, James left for Rome with assurances of his return despite the
lamentations of the spiritual community at Oignies and the intense opposition of the visionary Mary. Upon arriving at Rome, James was promptly made
a cardinal and bishop by his good friend Gregory IX.[121] (Thomas's chagrin
over the promotion of James could explain why he included the embarrassing
revelation that Gregory IX was once afflicted by the spirit of blasphemy and
indebted to a relic of Mary's for his cure.)[122] Thomas closes with an extended
appeal for James to return.[123]

Thomas's supplement to the life of Mary of Oignies probably reveals as
much about his own love for James and his desire for a closer relationship with
his beloved mentor as it does about the spiritual rapport between James and
his *mater spiritualis*. The departure of James seems to have been devastating to
the younger man. This becomes especially apparent through a touching personal revelation that concludes the work: "When I was not yet fifteen years old
and you were not a bishop, I heard you preaching in Lotharingia. I loved you
with such veneration that I was happy just at the sound of your name. From
then on a special love for you stayed with me. It is no wonder; the things we
learn as children take firm root in us."[124]

The supplement to Mary's life was Thomas's first effort at capturing Beguine spirituality. He manages to depict the intimacy between James and his
spiritual mother—an intimacy that continues beyond the grave—without
ever sounding an alarm or even raising a literary eyebrow. The same holds true
for his next hagiographic venture, the vita of Christina of St. Trond, better
known as Christina Mirabilis (d. 1224). From the moment Christina awak-
ened at her own funeral and flew up into the rafters until her third (and

last) death, it is clear that her life does not conform to any recognized hagio-graphical paradigm.[125] In contrast to the Beguine spirituality described above, there is virtually no nuptial imagery, and whatever heteroasceticism Christina can muster is spent on a layperson, Count Louis II of Loon. Christina repri-manded Louis, wept for his many faults, correctly prophesied the treason of an alleged friend, remained at Louis's deathbed at his request; and even heard his confession. (Thomas is careful to inform the reader that Louis did not construe this so much as a sacrament as a way to ensure Christina's prayers. It is nevertheless clear that Louis had reason to believe her prayers more ef-ficacious than any sacrament.) Christina was also loyally prepared to share his various punishments in purgatory.[126] Yet, however close Christina might seem to Louis, theirs was a one-way and hierarchical relationship of spiritual patron to client. Besides, as one who "crept into fiery ovens"; who would also "remain for a long time under the waters of the Meuse"; whose "body was so subtle and light that she walked on dizzy heights and, like a sparrow, hung suspended from the most slender branches of trees"; who rolled around like a hedgehog when she prayed; whom chains could not hold, and was, by necessity, "bound fast by a heavy wooden yoke," Christina seemed far too weird to inspire sala-cious thoughts.[127]

Thomas left the Augustinian house of canons at Cantimpré to join the Dominicans in Louvain in 1232, probably around the same time he was writ-ing the life of Christina. One might also speculate that Thomas only left Cantimpré for faraway Louvain when he realized that James was not coming back. A number of years would pass before he had the leisure to indulge his fascination with the holy women of the region again. In the intervening time, he was sent to study at the Dominican *studium generale* in Paris (ca. 1237–40). Probably as a result of these studies, Thomas began to experience the ubiquitous fascination with the natural world that was rife in the scholarly community. The twelfth-century's learned absorption was not only unabated but even sharpened by the gradual reintroduction of Aristotle, whose work exerted a particular influence over the Dominican order. All this is reflected in Thomas's next work titled *On the Nature of Things*, a thoroughgoing study of the many created life-forms, including the human species, which represented a true departure from his hitherto exclusively hagiographical interests.[128]

When Thomas did at length return to hagiography, it was to write the life of Margaret of Ypres (d. 1237)—a vita that was, in its own way, as strange as his life of Christina. The work's idiosyncrasies do not so much reside in the exceptionality of the material, however, as one's sense that Thomas lacked any real conviction that the subject of his hagiography was, indeed, a saint. And,

in fact, Thomas had not known his subject, either personally or by reputation. He first learned of Margaret through the account of her confessor, the
Dominican friar Zeger. We know from the vita's prologue, dedicated to Zeger
along with a copy of the life, that Thomas had gone out of his way to make
his acquaintance, visiting Ypres during his return journey from Paris. Thomas
acknowledges to Zeger that his interest "was aroused by your fame" and that
he had been anxious to meet for some time.[129] It may be that Thomas desired
his confrère's acquaintance by way of garnering possible allies in the order; he
had, after all, only been with the Dominicans a scant eight years, and several
of these had been spent away from his house at Louvain.[130]

It is also significant that 1240, the year Thomas sought Zeger out, also
marked the death of James of Vitry. This event could hardly have left the
younger man unmoved. James had not heeded the impassioned plea of Thomas's supplement to the life of Mary and, as far as we know, never returned
to Oignies. But to reiterate Thomas's sentiment that "the things we learn as
children take firm root in us," James doubtless continued to occupy a central
symbolic role in the younger man's psychic life. Thomas had initially been
drawn to James by his reputation for preaching, and it is likely that this was
the source of Zeger's celebrity. Zeger, for his part, may well have known of
Thomas by reputation as a hagiographer, or perhaps the two men fell to talk-
ing about the absorbing subject of female spirituality. In any event, Zeger
saw his opportunity and told Thomas about Margaret. As Thomas says in his
prologue, "I was amazed, struck by such wonderful news, and though I say so
myself, aroused to better things." If "better things" is interpreted as willing-
ness to embrace what progressively appears to be the relatively thankless task
of writing Margaret's life, one can only imagine that this generous impulse
was set in motion almost immediately, as Thomas goes on to say, "Thus, early
one morning at your request, I filled two small sheets of parchment with some
memorable facts about her life as you recounted them."[131]

And so Thomas was prepared to assume the job of commemorating Friar
Zeger's holy penitent, just as he had once shouldered the responsibility of
further promoting Mary's cult after her confessor had defected to Italy. But
Margaret of Ypres was no Mary of Oignies. Indeed, it is unfair to compare
the spirituality of someone who died when she was just over twenty with that
of a mature woman who had struck out on her own to found a leper colony.
In contrast, Margaret lived at home all her life, treating her family to such a
petulant, even hostile, display of ascetic manners that modern scholars have
justifiably likened her general attitude to teenage rebellion.[132] Thomas manages to sculpt a few pretty phrases in praise of Margaret: that when he and his

companion were hastening away from Ypres, their prayers to Margaret seemed to have dispelled some ominous clouds, and that "the first fruits of goodness of Christ's bride" was that he found himself with unprecedented leisure in which to undertake the vita, "which I attribute wholly to her merits." But one could easily interpret the speed with which he fulfilled his promise to Zeger as a symptom that Thomas wished to be done with the task as soon as possible. For it is difficult to discern much investment or pride in a work when its preface contains remarks such as "[I]f the work has to be corrected anywhere, then correct it yourself, or if you do not have the time, send it back to me for corrections. For it is more fitting for me to be soiled by my own dirt and wash it myself than to let another be stained by my dirt. Go and, as you have promised, pray for me."[133]

All this talk of personal dirt is slightly unsettling. In fact, it could suggest the reverse: that Thomas was at some level implying that Margaret was Zeger's "dirt" and not his own. This would certainly be a rather churlish reading, but perhaps not entirely unwarranted. For if Thomas spent any time at all revising the work, he probably would have noticed that this image was infelicitous to say the least. But the holy women that Thomas had experienced were all, in their own way, possessed of an independent spirituality that could accommodate close relations with men without compromising the integrity or the basic independence of the women in question. Margaret manifested none of this self-possession and no real stability of vocation. We saw that Friar Zeger selected Margaret from among a group of young women. Allegedly after heeding Friar Zeger's call, "she was as changed from her former state as heaven is distant from earth." Her mother, however, predicted, "'If you embark on a religious life today, tomorrow you will return to the world,'" disparagement at which Margaret scoffed. Yet initially the mother's skepticism seemed justified. In the next day or so, Margaret saw the young man with whom she had been so enamored "and felt faint stirrings of that affection she had so recently withdrawn from him creeping seductively back into her mind." Margaret recouped any potential loss by running to the church, begging for Christ's help, and pledging chastity. "[F]or the rest of her life, never would she feel even the first stirrings of temptation in her flesh."[134]

As if to consolidate this change, Christ appeared to Margaret in the following chapter with three crowns, one for herself and two others for each of her sisters, the latter two bequests contingent upon the sisters following the example of Margaret in the preservation of their virginity.[135] The vision of the three crowns was timely, to say the least, for the very next chapter reports that "about the same time" there were rumors afoot that each of Margaret's sisters had borne a child out of wedlock, "although they were utterly unsullied in every respect and very well known for their good character."[136] The close juxtaposition of the vision of the three crowns with the slander against Margaret's siblings would seem to imply that the former was intended to redress the latter—or so one might suppose. Yet the vision clearly fails in this regard because the crowns are conditional on the good behavior of the sisters. The presence of the condition could even be construed as confirming the rumors: that is, the sisters had lost the crowns because they did not behave. The fact that Margaret will later receive a visionary assurance from the Virgin Mary that her sister would not die in childbirth seems to corroborate this reading, confirming that at least one sister had forfeited her crown.[137]

One way to account for this implied slight on the virtue of Margaret's sisters is to assume that in Margaret's original vision the crowns were conferred without condition, and perhaps the vision was timed in such a way as to offset gossip. But when at least one sister did, in fact, prove to be pregnant, expedience would dictate that either the visionary appearance of Christ with the crowns or the Virgin Mary's intervention in childbirth be dropped or, failing that, amended in some way. Thomas, who seems to have been writing quickly, did neither—whether unaware of the extent of the problem or simply heedless of it.

At the same time the chastity of the sisters was being impugned, Margaret's vow of chastity was again tested—this time by a serious illness that the doctor pronounced could only be cured if she took a husband. Margaret stoically resisted, responding, "'Truly I am the more fully espoused to Christ because of this.'"[138] Even so, such stalwart words were undercut by her actions because right after her recovery she contacted her former admirer (who happened to be a carpenter—the same profession as Christ in his terrestrial days) on the pretext of mending a wooden goblet that she had dropped. Christ himself seemed to perceive Margaret's initiative as a kind of relapse, as he chose to absent himself from her temporarily.[139] But soon after, Margaret's attitude toward men was resolved as follows:

> Because this blessed woman was unable to bear the sight of men, she frequently passed through town in such a way that she saw neither man nor woman. There was a boy in her mother's house, perhaps twelve years old, who used to wash the dishes. She begged her mother that he be removed from the house because he was male, for her spirit shrank from the presence of men so much that she quivered with alarm whenever she saw one. And where did this come

from? Certainly her jealous Spouse, Jesus, who in former times had spoken through the prophet Isaiah: "The bed is so narrow that the other must fall out: and a short blanket cannot cover both" (Isaiah 28.29).[140]

Although rather extreme, this position would necessarily help to shore up a commitment to chastity.

Apart from Christ, there was room for only one man in Margaret's metaphorically narrow bed, and that, of course, was Friar Zeger. Her dependence on him is depicted as absolute: when he was not physically present, Margaret was often able to sense his support as if he were present. On one occasion, however, she awoke to an unwonted feeling of spiritual emptiness. Even her confessor seemed to have absented himself, both internally and externally. When she ran to an unnamed cleric for help, "he lacked discernment in such matters and, laughing, he looked down on her and drove her off." Eventually, Margaret, in a frenzy of anxiety, entered a church and was comforted by Christ with a mystical host. One of the effects of the special grace she received as a result of this experience was that she could "not bear to see or hear anything trivial or secular." When forced into mundane situations, Margaret would either block them out entirely or fall asleep.[141]

Margaret's obedience to Friar Zeger was sufficiently intense as to arouse her own apprehensions. "From the simplicity of her heart, however, she began to fear this was against the Lord in some way . . . and she said to him in prayer: . . . [S]ince mutual love and frequent conversation between a man and a woman seem suspicious to our superiors, I ask . . . that you mercifully show me, your handmaid, whether I will incur any loss of your love by loving and conversing with your servant [Friar Zeger]." As with Christina of Markyate a century earlier, Christ reassured Margaret that she had nothing to fear.[142] Indeed, on one occasion, Margaret was even permitted to see Friar Zeger when he was five leagues away in Lille.

The argument in favor of Margaret's sanctity is not strong. But perhaps anyone who had been asked to make the case would have run into difficulties. She was not the venerated founder of a religious order (like John of Cantimpré); a well-to-do matron who gave it all up for beguinal service to others and intimacy with Christ (like Mary of Oignies); or a feral virgin who could live in fiery ovens and icy riverbeds (like Christine of St. Trond). Furthermore, Margaret's life was tragically cut short. Even so, there are a number of ways in which Thomas seems to have further sabotaged the unpromising material he had at his disposal. First, and most important, the sequence of events he presents, and Margaret's own doubts, impugns her all-important commitment to chastity. There is a lingering impression that Margaret's carnal love may have been resolved in her attachment for Friar Zeger. In a telling passage, Thomas describes the Dominican as *the man in whose absence she could have no peace in her heart*—a situation close to the kind of spiritual love against which James cautions in his sermon to Cistercian nuns. Ultimately, Margaret's confessor is presented as so essential to her vocation that her devotion to him threatens to overshadow her love of Christ.

Finally we come to Thomas's treatment of Margaret's vision of Zeger in Lille. After having established the impossibility of this phenomenon for the human eye, Thomas goes on to ask,

> What therefore shall I say? Would it be right to believe that so perfect a bride of Christ lied? By no means. For I do not believe that, even if her life were at stake, she would have deliberately and knowingly told a lie, especially not about this.
>
> What then shall I say? If, as *The Book of the Nature of Things* says, nature has given the lynx the ability to penetrate solid and opaque bodies with the light of its eyes (contrary to the normal condition of animals, yet without any miracle), why then couldn't Christ, who is said to be wonderful in his saints, have been willing and able to let Margaret see for awhile, to comfort her, the man in whose absence she could have no peace in her heart—and to see him even from a great distance? But you will perhaps respond, "I do not believe that such a miracle occurred in this girl, nor do I believe that the lynx's vision can penetrate solid and opaque bodies." To this I reply: "It is not necessary to prove that a divine miracle occurred in the girl because Christ, who wished to do this, was able to do it; and that is reason enough." But I do wish to prove that nature is operating in the lynx according to its own law.[143]

He goes on to apply Aristotle's discussion of the operation of the eye to vindicate his theory. Doubtless Thomas could not resist showing off for his new friend. But in so doing, he also managed tacitly to undermine the miraculous nature of the event by providing so clear an analogy with the lynx. Although Thomas declares it a miracle, his work *On the Nature of Things* suggests that he was more cognizant than most of just how many uncanny abilities humans generally, but women in particular, were believed to share with the animal kingdom. A celebrated example of this commonality is the widespread belief that it was possible for one human to harm another by a mere look, an ability that postmenopausal women in particular shared with the basilisk. This lethal glance was a side effect of the retention of corrupt seed, which these women were no longer able to expel on account of the cessation of their menses.[144] Many eminent intellectuals, the likes of Aristotle and Aquinas who shared this view, would concur that such a phenomenon was certainly not a miracle; simply science as usual.[145]

Ostensibly, Thomas was satisfied with examining only one incident from Margaret's life through a scientific lens and stopping there. Even so, Thomas's scientific learning may have provided him with a possible key to understanding the riddle of Margaret's puzzling physiology and the reason behind her early demise. Margaret died horribly of internal hemorrhaging at the age of twenty-one.[146] This was clearly linked to the various "women's problems" treated by *On the Nature of Things*. For instance, Thomas discusses the suffocation of the uterus—a malady resulting from the uterus pressing against the heart, causing a loss of heat in the subject, which in turn provokes a collapse. The condition was caused by sexual abstinence, resulting in the retention of menstrual blood. This in turn causes the uterus to swell up, primed for a collision with the heart. Eventually the retained "seed" becomes poisonous—a situation that could even eventuate in the lethal glances alluded to above. Although most commonly associated with widows, the specter of this condition loomed behind the doctor's diagnosis the first time Margaret fell ill at eighteen, prompting his recommendation that Margaret marry or suffer the consequences. But Margaret seemingly recovered: "Behold a worthy miracle; for, contrary to nature and the doctor's judgment, God soon cured her."[147] Thomas's learning would argue otherwise, however: what passed for a cure may have been only a reprieve. Her hemorrhaging was consistent with the retention of poisonous seed.[148] If Thomas privately wondered whether or not Margaret's condition was linked to her sexual abstinence, he never lets on. For such a disease would almost certainly call the validity of Margaret's revelations into question, which, as Thomas's *On the Nature of Things* makes perfectly clear, could be stimulated by illness, excessive abstinence—in fact, by any kind of humoral imbalance.[149]

But a scientific reading of Margaret's condition might argue for her sanctity in a different way. If it were true that Margaret had indeed died from the illness that was diagnosed when she was eighteen, it would follow that had she heeded the doctor's advice and married, she would have lived. In other words, Margaret had very literally given her life for her virginity, which rendered her a martyr of sorts. And it is significant that Thomas's very sympathetic treatment

of Margaret's immense sufferings before her death is the most compelling
aspect of any case he attempts to make for sanctity. Furthermore, after her
death, Margaret appeared in "a transparent crystalline body and a rosy colour
in her breast," speaking the words of the virgin martyr, Agnes: " 'Behold, what
I have desired, I now see; what I hoped for, I now possess. I am united in
heaven with him whom I loved with total devotion on earth.' " These words,
which appear prominently in the liturgy for the consecration of a virgin, are
taken directly from the *passio* of St. Agnes, who, as we saw earlier, is depicted
as recasting her martyrdom in terms of a marriage to Christ.[150] Thomas goes
on to explain what the red and white of Margaret's visionary form represent:
"the diaphanous red of roses is pleasantly mixed with the translucent whiteness of lilies, virginity is signified by the whiteness and her charity denoted by
the red." No one would have to remind the medieval reader, however, that the
red roses stood first and foremost for martyrdom.[151]

At the time that Thomas was writing the life of Margaret there was a scandal hovering over his order. One of his Dominican brethren, Robert le Bougre, a convert from heresy and, as mentioned above, the first papal inquisitor,
was active in the Low Countries between 1234 and 1239. Robert was a brutal
fanatic. He is alluded to by Hadewijch in the context of another Beguine
"killed by Master Robert because of her true love."[152] Despite the vigorous
opposition to his reign of terror by local secular and ecclesiastical authorities
alike, Robert's downfall may well have resulted from a botched seduction.
According to one chronicler, Robert spotted a beautiful woman when he was
preaching a sermon. He detained the woman afterward: she assumed his purpose was to hear her confession, which is generally what occurred after these
public sermons, when, in fact, he was bent on seduction. When she resisted,
he countered by charging her with heresy. Robert was finally apprehended and
imprisoned in 1239, perhaps for this very offense.[153]

The circumstances surrounding Margaret's meeting with her confessor in
1234, the year that Robert was just beginning his ferocious career as inquisitor,
contains a number of eerie parallels with the above episode. "Friar Zeger of the
Order of Preachers in Lille had come to Ypres and, after his sermon, he was
sitting in the church to hear the confessions of repentant people. By chance
he cast his eyes on Margaret, who was dressed in secular clothing among other
women, and saw with a kind of divine instinct . . . that she would be apt to
receive God's grace and become a chosen vessel, as Christ revealed to him." So
Zeger also attempted seduction under the pretext of confession, only he was
acting on behalf of the celestial bridegroom.[154]

Thomas could not help but be aware of Robert's career. (Neither could

Friar Zeger, for that matter, as in 1234 Robert had undertaken an intensive purge in Lille, where Zeger's community was located.) In Thomas's final work, *Concerning Bees*, intended as a history of the Dominican Order, he claims that he knows "almost all those of the holy order who fell into scandal."[155] There is an allusion to an inquisition in Cambrai that would have been conducted under Robert's auspices, but with the inquisitor's name significantly suppressed.[156] When Thomas visited Ypres in 1240, the final scandal that brought about the inquisitor's downfall had just broken and would have been fresh in his mind. So if Thomas's description of the meeting between Zeger and Margaret accurately reflects the confessor's account, it is difficult to imagine that the circumstances did not conjure up Robert's final abuse, the aborted act of seduction attempted over confession.

The two meetings between confessor and penitent function like positive and negative images of a picture, which was perhaps deliberate. Thomas may have framed the circumstances surrounding Friar Zeger's meeting with Margaret to echo and, ultimately counteract, the infamous Dominican inquisitor Robert's meeting with the nameless penitent. By the same token, Robert's shameless attacks on a nameless woman's chastity would be neutralized by Zeger's encouragement that Margaret consecrate her virginity to God. This motive might even help us to further understand why Thomas was prepared to assume so challenging a hagiographical burden: perhaps he regarded the life of Margaret as an opportunity to expunge Robert's blight on the Dominican order. If this was the case, Thomas's salubrious juxtaposition may also point to an emerging, but perhaps unacknowledged, consciousness. Whatever Thomas's intentions may have been, by foregrounding the parallels between the two cases, all close relations between holy women and their confessors are rendered suspect.

Simone Roisin has identified the life of Margaret as a turning point in Thomas's hagiographical works, heralding a more mature understanding of female spirituality.[157] It is impossible to doubt this. Even so, it is difficult to ignore the ways in which an expanding comprehension of female spirituality was tracked by increasing apprehension of contact between the sexes. Some six years after the completion of Margaret's life, Thomas will write his life of Lutgard of Aywières—a woman he both knew and admired. This was by far Thomas's most eloquent and mature hagiographical venture. Retrospectively, the life of Margaret could even be construed as a dry run for this later life insofar as some of the imagery that is first introduced in Margaret's life is developed in the life of Lutgard.[158] But the similarities end there. Lutgard lived a long life and is depicted as developing a mature spirituality with Christ, not her confessor, at its center. For although Lutgard had a circle of male admirers, they are presented as being more her dependants than she theirs, a position secured by the depth of her spiritual life and scope of her intercessory power.

Lutgard's power as intercessor was manifest at many levels—shortening the purgatorial sentences for some, exorcising demons from others, helping fellow religious in the day-to-day hardships of following a rule. As John Coakley has argued, moreover, the life of Lutgard represents the culmination of Thomas's progressive emphasis on the correspondence between the charismatic powers of his female subjects and the powers of the priesthood throughout his hagiographical corpus.[159] This is evident in the spiritual services Lutgard performed for Thomas himself as well as for James of Vitry—holy interventions that bore directly on the difficulties and temptations the two men incurred as confessors and spiritual directors of women. When Thomas was a young man, he was appointed as a confessor in the bishop's curia, authorized to hear reserved sins—sins considered too heinous for a parish priest that only the bishop could absolve.[160] Thomas found the job extremely difficult: "I became agitated inwardly with the stirrings of temptation." He appealed to Lutgard for help, who, upon praying, assured him that he would no longer be tempted. And it was true. Thomas never again experienced temptation in the confessional.[161]

James's debt to Lutgard was perhaps even greater. Just prior to his appointment as bishop of Acre (ca. 1216), James had apparently become attached "to a certain religious woman, languishing in bed, not lustfully but with an all too human love," to the extent that he was neglecting his preaching. "Lutgard, sensing in her spirit the fetters of his heart and the deceit of the devil, approached the Lord with many tears to intercede for him." At first her prayers proved ineffectual because, as the Lord told her, "'The man for whom you entreat is striving against your prayers.'" At length she had to issue a holy threat to God: "'Either separate me from yourself or liberate that man for whom I pray, even if he is not willing.'" This did the trick. Lutgard was later raptured into heaven precisely at the time that the soul of the deceased bishop was ushered in. She then learned that James was only required to spend two days and three nights in purgatory, which suggested that he never suffered any significant recidivism.[162]

Thomas's own lapse into autobiography was, as he acknowledges, embarrassing, but necessary "for the praise of Christ and his handmaid." Whatever the sacrifice, he clearly understood the impact of the personal exemplum in getting his message across. From this perspective, the episode concerning James of Vitry is especially compelling: here is a man who spent much of his life fostering the spirituality of the holy women of Liège who is nevertheless unwittingly preyed upon by an unruly attachment.

These two incidents represent vignettes of the kinds of obstacles a priest necessarily incurs in the course of his ministry. An incident from Lutgard's past gives the alternative perspective: the danger a carnal-minded pastor might present to his flock. The circumstances surrounding the instance seem innocuous. The abbot who was patron to Lutgard's first monastic community was returning from a journey and wanted to greet the individual nuns with a kiss. Lutgard refused, but was nevertheless pushed forward by the other nuns—part in jest, part in earnest. Fortunately, Jesus interposed his hand between the abbot's lips and Lutgard's cheek "so that she did not feel the taint of even the first carnal stirrings of a man's kiss." On surface, this might pass for an interesting variation on the miracle from the life of Mary of Oignies, when a man went to clasp her and she heard a voice saying, "Don't touch me." What distinguishes this anecdote is what follows: an intense denunciation of "contemporary devotion, more disgraceful than blind . . . whereby men 'who have the outward appearance of piety' (2. Tim. 3.5) think they can kiss women and virgins with impunity, without offending divine grace." He proceeds at length to argue against the view that Paul's injunction to "Greet one another with a holy kiss" (2 Cor. 13.12) should be interpreted as including members of the opposite sex. Those committed to chastity, who would scorn to commit adultery or fornication "fall into something even graver through kisses and illicit touching." Such individuals are worse than fornicators, sinning against the Holy Spirit by pretending to love chastity.

> Do you then, virgin, whether you are a bride of Christ or any
> woman who loves chastity, flee such things as Lutgard did. . . . If
> anyone wishes to solicit from you as it were a holy kiss, if anyone
> tries to put his hand on your breast, your bosom, or any other part
> of your body, give him spittle instead of a kiss and let your fist meet
> his groping hand. . . . Nor should you defer to any cleric or person
> of rank in such matters. . . . Look upon such a one not as a servant
> of Christ, but as Satan.[163]

It is definitely something of a rant—a passage very much out of keeping with the general tenor of Lutgard's life.

A number of years will pass before Thomas again returns to writing, during which time he clearly reconsidered what were appropriate relations between religious men and women. In his final work, *Concerning Bees*, written between

1256 and 1263, his growing apprehension concerning relations between the sexes no long remains suppressed. Instead, the spirit of mistrust and the spirit of collaboration openly vie with one another, lending the text a fractured and uneven quality. Part of this is undoubtedly owing to the structure of the work. *Concerning Bees* is a miscellany that brings together all of the different kinds of learning that Thomas has accrued over the course of his career. The result is a work that defies all genres: where the miraculous, the marvelous, the scientific, the holy, and the unholy all jostle each other for attention. His interest in all things holy is still paramount. But the saintly people who populate his text are not the subject of sustained narratives. Rather they are treated anecdotally in a manner that evokes Gregory the Great's *Dialogues* or the work of Thomas's contemporary, the Cistercian Caesarius of Heisterbach, whose *Dialogue on Miracles* was self-consciously modeled on Gregory's work.[164] In many ways, *Concerning Bees* resembles these texts. Though Thomas has abandoned the familiar dialogue form, he too relies on pious hearsay for many of his anecdotes. Hence we learn about a nun from Brabant who would elevate when they sang *Veni creator* every Pentecost; the virgin from Germany who could not be confined by cloisters, locks, or chains when she was moved by the spirit; the nun whose face became incandescent, while a marvelous harmony emerged from between her throat and breast whenever she heard anything about heaven.[165] But Thomas also included information that is explicitly associated with Mary of Oignies and Lutgard, which he doubtless learned firsthand.[166]

The work draws widely on other facets of Thomas's studies and experiences. For instance, he makes considerable use of his practice as both a confessor and a preacher. Furthermore, as the title of the work would suggest, Thomas's interest in natural phenomena is unabated, as is his appetite for analogies between the animal kingdom and humankind. Bees were very much admired by ancient and medieval cultures alike for their community, industry, and alleged chastity, providing a living exemplum for well-regulated Christian communities, especially monasteries.[167] His prowess as a naturalist and reader of Aristotle would doubtless be enhanced by his period of study in Cologne (1250–51) under no lesser a teacher than Albert the Great.[168]

Thomas's Dominican affiliation becomes progressively prominent in his work. This is apparent not just in terms of the interest in nature but also in a progressively censorious position regarding clerical interaction with women—an attitude frequently expressed by members of both mendicant orders, often in association with their pastoral responsibilities for women.[169] *Concerning Bees* was dedicated to the master general of the Dominican order, Humbert of Romans (d. 1277), probably intended as a complimentary emulation of some of

Humbert's own writings. Humbert had, for example, written a history of the Dominican order that *Concerning Bees* could be understood to supplement. But Thomas also seems to have been influenced by Humbert's pastoral writings, particularly a treatise titled *Letter on the Three Substantial Vows of Religion* (before 1254), which speaks to the question of relations between the sexes very directly. Humbert presents chastity as the nuptial garment without which the religious is forever expelled from eternal marriage with Christ and must therefore be preserved at all costs.[170] To this end, Humbert offers "five circumstances of lust" in order for a given friar to recognize when he is on the slippery slope.[171] Ultimately the path of chastity requires that not only lascivious women be shunned but holy women as well: "for earth is good, and so is rain, but mix them together and you get mud."[172] The mud is much harder to avoid than one would suppose because, as Humbert is at pains to point out, holiness tends to act as a kind of aphrodisiac. Women find it especially difficult to resist good men, which in Humbert's lexicon means male religious, and he provides numerous instances of importunate women and virtuous men.[173] Sadly, the worst offenders are continent women, especially young ones, whose limited contact with laymen means that their misdirected libido is expended on holy men. "You ought not to be less cautious if women are proved to be of a good disposition or pious life: the better their fame, the more they allure because under the affect of piety the bowels [*viscus*] of impious lust lurks, projecting the pernicious poison of death, which is uniquely theirs."[174] Fortunately there are visual clues that reveal the worst offenders: chaste women have deeply set eyes, but the eyes of lascivious women are prominent.[175]

Compared to Humbert, Thomas's engagement of the subject is not only augmented in length but amplified in tone by vehement rhetoric and anecdote. He begins with an exhortation to chastity: how the faithful working bees and the cloistered bees are careful to avoid sexual contact. His caution is conditioned by a sobering historical parallel. The flood in the time of Noah was brought about because the sons of God engaged in sexual relations with the daughters of men. But conditions have since deteriorated:

> Nowadays not only do the sons of God copulate with the daughters of men, but with the daughters of God, which is worse. Namely, religious men are copulating with religious women. Alas we see, and see frequently, that what certain men began in the spirit is consummated in the flesh. The men wished to make spiritual daughters in a good way; but they turned them into concubines. And conversely, some women who wished to make spiritual sons out of select men,

instead become carnal mothers, giving birth to carnal sons from
their spiritual sons.[176]

The allusion to Genesis is as familiar as it is ominous. Thomas adapts the Augustinian solution of transforming the sons of God into clerics and milks it
for all it is worth. Like Tertullian, Thomas projects the fate of the daughters of
men onto the religious women of his day—Thomas's daughters of God. The
result is one of the most fully imagined and carnal readings of this passage to
date. Predatory spiritual parents incestuously coupling with their children;
spiritual sons begetting carnal sons on spiritual mothers. Such debauched in-
carnations are presented as worse than a generation of giants. This riff on
Genesis is followed up with the sobering story of a priest and a nun who were
found dead, and literally inseparable, in one bed, and were necessarily buried together.[177] To ensure that those struggling for purity avert similar fates,
Thomas develops a series of signposts writ large on which he designates the six
paths to fornication. This list is seemingly modeled on Humbert's "Five Circumstances of Lust," which had consisted of sight, touch, kisses and embraces,
frequent speech, and laughter. Thomas's version is more sexually explicit: unclean thoughts, inordinate looking, speech via a go-between, lustful words and
speech, the lascivious kiss, and actual contact with illicit members.[178]

Thomas's six paths entirely overturn the gender dynamics developed in
his earlier writings. In his hagiography, Thomas had been inclined to represent men as sexual predators. After their conversions, both Margaret of Ypres
and Lutgard were the victims of masculine sexual aggression, while Lutgard
herself only narrowly escaped being raped.[179] But any tendency to see female
chastity as imperiled by masculine aggression now is overturned. Although
Thomas could not go so far as to present women as rapists, they are often
presented as instigators and, more often than not, the more blameworthy
for sexual misconduct. The first exemplum presented under the category of
unclean thoughts (number one in his series of six paths) involves people of
whom Thomas claims firsthand knowledge. A wanton girl in Brabant sought
the love of a handsome, upright young man. "The impious act led the youth
to deflower [*deflorare*] the virgin. He rejected the lustful behavior, fled, and in
the sight of his family's home returned safe from the girl. But she was more
shameless, following him to his residence. Then falling on her knee with up-
turned eyes, she gave a great sigh and breathed out her wretched soul." The
young man was deeply sorrowful "as if he were guilty for the sudden death in
the girl. I comforted him as well as I could, I applauded his constancy and the
righteous judgment of God upon the dead woman, just as I ought."[180]

The above story is representative of the realignment of Thomas's gender loyalties and the perceptible encroachment of a progressive antifeminism. His bias is especially in evidence when it comes to his discussion of the pastoral care of religious women. Augustine warns in his rule that the concupiscence of women not only seeks but is sought: hence, women are almost invariably more attracted to religious men, and vice versa.[181] A sterling instance of this kind of perversity is depicted in a celebrated case from Spain. A beautiful prostitute made a wager with the king that she could seduce a famed Dominican with a reputation for holiness. She thus feigned conversion in the course of the Dominican's sermon, prostrating herself on the ground and distraughtly weeping for her sins. The preacher, in turn, exhilarated by his triumph, was especially gratified when she changed her worldly dress. Indeed, failing to discern the reason behind her continual stream of penitential tears, he became determined to dedicate himself entirely to her salvation. At last she whispered to him the reason for her grief: that her salvation depended on sleeping with him. The preacher, who immediately understood "the treachery of her viper's mind," ostensibly agreed, and the prostitute informed the king of her triumph with glee. But when the appointed time came for the tryst, the preacher lay down on a bed of hot coals and beckoned her to join him. The preacher was coaxed out of the fire, and the prostitute would have been compelled to take his place had the holy man not intervened.[182]

In case we missed the moral of the story, Thomas spells it out. This vile woman, who could have had any fornicator in Spain, was specifically drawn to a holy man, proving Solomon's words that a woman is more bitter than death, a snare of hunters, an arrow to his heart, or a chain to his hands (Eccles. 7.27). "Who pleases God should flee her; and whoever is a sinner is seized by her."[183] Be mindful that the disciples themselves marveled that Christ spoke to a woman. What hope has the average person "who wears infirm flesh and infected nature" of withstanding such temptation? To anyone who claims that pious zeal for the salvation of his neighbor's soul compels him to minister to women, Thomas responds, "'Don't men have souls? Why don't you have assiduous conversations with them?'" He goes on to recommend that conversations with women be strictly limited time-wise and occur only in the presence of a witness, "and then go about your business, even if the women are not content. . . . Good character and honest life are no guarantees of safety because the more religious they seem, they more enticing they are."[184]

No woman is seemingly exempt, moreover, as the threat of "conflagration" pertains to both "green wood" and "dry" (i.e., young women and old women)—a point demonstrated by a recent and lamentable episode in

Cambrai. A cleric, chaste from youth, was a canon in a conventual church. Out of dedication to pastoral work, he relinquished his prebend for a parish, in which he piously toiled for seven years. But then, on a fateful day, the sixty-year-old virgin who was accustomed to washing the priest's hair shirt entered his bedroom unattended. "Before the woman and the priest separated, they were both deprived of their long preserved lily of virginity and chastity." The woman soon died of sorrow; the man, reveling in his vice, went from bad to worse.[185]

The kiss (the fifth and penultimate path to fornication) is necessarily lustful, as it involves the joining of two animal spirits.[186] We have already witnessed Thomas's residual resistance to an exchange of kisses between two religious of the opposite sex in his life of Lutgard. In *Concerning Bees*, his indignation knows no bounds. "I don't like to reveal how great the enormity of the filth comes from kisses to those who don't know lest they try something forbidden and are tempted most grievously by the devil. Perhaps you say: I am moved by no lust in kisses, but I venerate God in the virgin and I am affected by the presence of him who dwells within her. Whoever claims this is lying most wickedly."[187] Even if one were to suppose that such a person was telling the truth and had somehow become impervious to the kiss, he still must consider the safety of the "fragile vessel" upon whom the kiss is bestowed. It is precisely women who are inexperienced sexually, devout women who have never known coitus, who are most likely to be affected because the sexual pleasure elicited increases proportionally with the lack of sexual contact. Thomas thus categorizes such osculatory overtures as mortal sins and authorizes virgins of Christ to punch any clerics attempting to solicit a kiss.[188]

The sixth and final path to fornication is the illicit touching of breasts and genitals. "Humanity alone, the head of rationality, is defiled with such noxious matters of irrationality. No other irrational animal is stained by its feces in this way." Men and women lie together naked, assuming that they can do whatever they please provided that the hymen remains intact. That it is women dedicated to God that Thomas has in mind is indicated by his exclamation, "Far be it from the son of the most clean virgin that he should repute this most wickedly sullied woman a spouse."[189]

Throughout this work, Thomas consistently reinforces his arguments with allusions to the animal kingdom, and this is especially true with discussions that touch on female sexuality. Women should follow the example of the Virgin Mary's chastity (emphasized by her time-honored suspicion of the annunciating Gabriel) by keeping their ears rigid rather than letting their ears lie flat like sows—which, as Aristotle claims, indicates a desire for coitus. The many women who are more attracted to holy men than any others are likened to sows who, as Pliny would have it, would rush at anything in white when agitated by the furies of lust. (The Dominican habit was white and black; the Cistercian habit was all white.)[190] Aristotle also claims that horses begin to breathe heavily and pant before coitus. Confessors know how true a representation this is from experience with some of their female penitents.[191]

Even when men are the temporary objects of derision, this tends to redound on women. For example, while acknowledging that taste and touch are common to both humans and beasts, Thomas introduces an exemplum demonstrating how certain men veer toward the bestial in other ways as well. A certain uncouth man stated his preference for the company of women over philosophers in the hearing of Pythagoras. The latter responded that he was then inclined to be occupied with the dirt rather than the flowers.[192]

It would seem that Thomas's anxiety about relations between men and women dedicated to religion had reached a high water mark toward the end of his career. Very possibly his apprehension was heightened by his year of study with Albert the Great. In 1249, the year before Thomas arrived in Cologne, Albert was hypothesizing about a heresy whose adherents posited that fornication was sinless. Perhaps Albert had already caught wind of a Swabian group exhibiting some serious antinomian tendencies which he would go on to denounce some years later.[193] But elsewhere Albert tends to backpedal, claiming that sectarians only attempted to vindicate less extreme sexual overtures, such as kissing and illicit touch. Could some of Thomas's increased mistrust of interaction between men and women committed to religion be based on rumors he heard of such convictions?[194]

Whether or not this was the case, Thomas was hardly alone in his growing awareness of the dangers of spiritual intimacy. When it was rumored that Ida of Louvain's friendship with a certain Dominican had left her pregnant, the suspicion was taken seriously enough for the Dominican chapter to adopt the very anti-Ambrosian measure of sending a medical expert to ascertain if Christ's bride were still a virgin. (Fortunately, the test was very Ambrosian insofar as the medical expert seemed to believe that a pregnant woman would be betrayed by her eyes alone, requiring no additional examination.)[195] In the case of Odilia of Liège (d. 1220), not one but two amorous priest-cum-sorcerers used magic to achieve their lascivious ends.[196] The life of the widowed recluse Yvette of Huy (d. 1228) is especially riddled with such instances of inappropriate behavior between the clergy and their female dependents.[197] One priest attempted to ingratiate himself with Yvette "under pretence of false religion" because he was sexually interested in one of her servants.[198] A priest "under the pretense of his religion and . . . conversation on the salvation of [the girl's] soul" ran off with Yvette's adopted daughter.[199] Yvette also learned through a vision about a certain matron who, "warmed through her religious fervour and devotion," was thus rendered easy pickings for the parish priest.[200]

But unlike these other sources, in which the men were the sexual predators, Thomas was now blaming women for these lapses, as a result advocating the kind of avoidance tactics that would have rendered Beguine spirituality unsustainable.

Considering Thomas's reputation as a stalwart advocate of the Beguines, his presentation of gender in *Concerning Bees* is perhaps surprising. Retrospectively, however, one can see that there had always been a slender but steady stream of misogyny running throughout Thomas's works.[201] As noted above, John of Cantimpré is described as sharing a vision with Prioress Ivetta because "with her blandishments she extorted this secret, like so many others, from his heart." When John was brought back from the edge of death by a vision of the Virgin, he again confided in Ivetta, who "true to the proverb about women—could not remain silent.[202] Margaret of Ypres, in contrast, is commended for her reserve, sharing her revelations with her confessor alone—which presents a refreshing contrast with the "many religious women in our day [who] follow the pernicious conduct of the hen: as soon as they produce an egg, they begin to cackle," Thomas quips. His validation of the vision witnessed by Margaret, in which she and another woman saw an angel hovering over a Dominican delivering a sermon, comes with the wry observation that "according to ecclesiastical and divine law, even women must be heeded when two speak."[203] Lutgard experienced early menopause at the age of twenty-eight, a phenomenon that Thomas characterizes as "the termination of the nuisance with which God tamed pride in the sex of Eve."[204] At one point, when Thomas was fiercely negotiating with the abbess of Lutgard's community in order to secure the saint's right hand after her death, his gripe about female loquacity resurfaces: "But since it is women's nature to be unable to keep secrets (as the vernacular proverb says, 'be quiet woman—if you can'), the nuns told Lutgard how I ordered her hand to be cut off."[205] (This extra virulence could be because Lutgard seemed far from pleased when she learned of Thomas's wish.)

Of course the kinds of swipes that Thomas takes at women in the course of his hagiographies are, perhaps, rather routine in clerically authored texts, so readers tend to overlook them. In Thomas's case, such foibles cannot be dismissed so easily because they seem to point to an escalating pattern, providing a context for the degree of backlash in *Concerning Bees*. There are also other subtle indicators, further suggesting that Thomas's view of women had, in fact, deteriorated in the few years that intervened between the completion of Lutgard's vita and the composition of *Concerning Bees*. Particularly noteworthy is a mysterious retelling of what we can only assume to be the story of Lutgard's conversion. In Lutgard's vita, she is represented as being wooed by a young man of breeding and wealth. "Thus in wondrous ways, the devil zealously urged that she bend her mind to girlish consent—but in vain, for the Almighty did not permit it." The young man made sufficient headway into her affections that he began to watch for a convenient night when he could visit. Upon approaching the house where Lutgard was sleeping, however, "he was gripped by sudden fear and ran away." Later when the girl was conversing with the young man "Christ appeared to her in that human form in which he had lived among mortals; drew back his garment to reveal his bleeding side and then said 'Do not seek any longer the caresses of unseemly love. Here you may perpetually contemplate what you should love and why you should love it. Here I pledge that you shall attain the delights of total purity.' "[206]

Concerning Bees has a strikingly similar story about a nameless girl under the rubric "Concerning the girl violently tempted to whom Christ appeared and cured of all temptation." In this instance, a girl from a well-to-do family in Brabant was prey to "the many assaults of demons for many years," all for the love of a young man. Frequently in confession she would divulge the diabolical plots in tears, and Thomas urged her to proceed with the utmost caution, lest she consent to her longings or by some word furnish an occasion of temptation to the youth. The woman became more and more distraught, not able to sleep or eat, until "One night she was agitated by such a great demonic impulse that she rose at dawn secretly to go to the youth. Nor was there any delay: upon rising she opened her eyes and saw Christ with wounds as if recently crucified, saying in sweet words in her native tongue: 'You should love me, I am so handsome/Good and sweet, noble and loyal.' "[207]

In other words, it was now the enamored woman stalking the man as opposed to the parallel incident from Lutgard's life. This would certainly be in keeping with Thomas's naturalist views that assign women a higher degree of lust generally, but religiously inclined women in particular. Could this be the same incident? If so, Thomas was careful to cover his tracks and cushion Lutgard from the possible aspersions that might derive from his retelling. The words Christ spoke were in French. Lutgard, in contrast, was famously Flemish-speaking. In fact, she only entered a French community to avoid being promoted to abbess. The Virgin Mary was on her side, moreover, since Lutgard was somehow miraculously secured against the threat of ever learning French.[208] Besides, Thomas only met Lutgard around 1228, some eighteen years after her community was officially received by the Cistercian General Chapter, and more than twenty years since she had been formally consecrated a virgin, and he was never, as far as we know, her confessor.[209]

Still, it seems unlikely that Thomas knew two women who were converted by a vision of the bleeding Christ. So if the story of *Concerning Bees* is the "true" story of Lutgard's conversion that Thomas determined to suppress, why bother to reveal it now? If it was a fabrication inspired by Lutgard's life, why invert it and cast the female character as the one who is out of control, demonically inspired to visit the young man's house? Either way, the manifest ambivalence about women accords with the uneasy tenor that permeates *Concerning Bees*, rendering Thomas something of a fifth column in his promotion of the Beguines. By characterizing most of the clergy's interactions with women as suspect, he was not simply following, but in many ways leading, the charge in mendicant efforts to separate themselves from pastoral care of women by providing them with enough evidence of sexual scandal to corroborate the orders' self-protective skittishness.

Thus we are confronted with the irony that Thomas of Cantimpré, one of the earliest and most important sponsors of the Beguines, was also a major force in the growing mistrust of female spirituality. Nor would his warnings regarding women's instability, especially the instability of affection, fall on deaf ears. Some thirty years after Thomas's death, the Council of Vienne (1311) provided a showcase for this anxiety, identifying a mystical heresy afoot among the Beguines that went by the name of the "Free Spirit," the very hallmark of which was the slippage between carnal and spiritual love. This was probably the same movement originally targeted by Albert the Great. Only now the cancer had progressed, and the group was believed to have devolved into still greater spiritual depravity.[210]

Granted, it would be the rare man who had not internalized at least some of the misogyny that was rife in clerical circles. James of Vitry was hardly exempt in this respect. His exempla are famous for their excoriation of women. But at least he had the wisdom to keep his discourses straight, saving most of his antifeminism for secular women or clerical concubines, not daring to use hagiography for this purpose.[211] For we know from James of Vitry's prologue, and from Thomas himself, that the Beguines were troubled by detractors from their very inception.[212]

In all fairness to Thomas, however, *Concerning Bees* was not a work of hagiography. It was a mixed genre: part chronicle, part exempla, part confessors' manual, part hagiographical, part naturalist. Herein lies the work's greatest danger. It provided much too many and too graphic demonstrations of how far a bride of Christ could fall: of how spiritual daughters became carnal mothers. In a couple of centuries, moreover, *Concerning Bees* would provide a model for another work by a pastorally oriented Dominican theologian with a penchant for analogies with the animal kingdom: *The Anthill* by John Nider, a book famous for its misogyny and severe line on religious women. It was also the first work to discuss the emerging witch's cult extensively and to associate it with women.[213]

The Somatic Bride

> A nun asked the virgin how it is possible that the body
> rejoices with the soul when it is the soul that is the one
> transfused with spiritual joy.
> —*The Life of Blessed Ida of Gorsleeuw*[214]

Like their northern sisters, the female mystics who proliferated in thirteenth-century Italy were also penitential zealots possessed of a profound devotion to both the Eucharist and Christ's passion.[215] And yet their hagiographers made little or no effort to claim the title of *sponsa Christi* for their holy subjects.[216] There is nothing in the lives of Gerardesca of Pisa (d. 1269) or Humility of Faenza (d. 1310) to set them apart as Christ's brides.[217] Margaret of Cortona (d. 1297) was frequently raptured in the course of communion and told by the visionary Christ that he loved her more than any living woman. And yet he routinely addressed her as daughter, not spouse.[218] Especially telling in this respect is the series of sermons that Humility herself dictated in the vernacular, potentially suggesting her own spiritual point of identification.[219] All in all, there are nineteen allusions to the mystical marriage, but none of them are especially personal: there is a single reference to the privileged position of nuns as brides of Christ, several references to the wedding chamber that awaits the soul, and a solitary reference to John the Evangelist's wisdom in choosing marriage to ecclesia over a human bride. (John was commonly believed to be the groom at Cana who was called away by Christ.)[220] The other thirteen references were to the Virgin Mary and her singular position as mother, daughter, and bride.[221]

The contemporary life of Humiliana of Cerchi (d. 1246) is somewhat more forthcoming in its use of bridal imagery. But, as in Humility's sermons, the evocations of Christ as bridegroom tend to be either formulaic or generic, by which I mean true for every Christian. Humiliana was only twenty-two when she was widowed and hence was pressured to remarry. When she prayed for confirmation of her chaste resolve, she was reassured by "the true Spouse."[222] The most extensive invocation of bridal imagery, however, occurs in a lengthy citation of Gregory the Great describing the behavior of the soul during ecstasy. But even though the discussion functions as a gloss on Humiliana's raptures, its import is generic rather than specific to the mystic herself: "Through a high mountain we ascend the mountains of contemplation. The holy soul, the spouse of Christ, seeks rest from the annoyances of the world; and in the breast of the Spouse, with earthly desires asleep, she desires to sleep in holy leisure."[223] By the same token, her affection for a Camaldolese monk is explained with the comment that "the amiable lover of the Spouse faithfully loved all true lovers"—placing the monk's relationship with Christ on a par with her own.[224] Although this sentiment may suggest that the affective bonds indicated between the Beguine mystics and their clerical cohort are just as prevalent in the Italian peninsula, both the monk and Humiliana warrant the name spouse. Humiliana is not singled out as a particular favorite.

Certainly the question of virginity is a salient factor in this context. The only time that Humiliana of Cerchi is explicitly called "sponsa" is in a vision occurring after her death. The ghostly voices of a choir of virgins were heard, inviting Humiliana to accept the crown of virginity and join their ranks. The apparitional Humiliana explained that her grieving over her lost virginity had finally won her this reward.[225] In other words, the boundary between virgin and nonvirgin is evoked so that Humiliana could triumph in the breach. But the very iteration of this divide is a reminder that the bridal persona is still the special preserve of virgins and that only they are permitted to follow the lamb in the afterlife.

Humiliana was fortunate. None of the Italian mystics mentioned above were virgins, and if any of them regained their virginal status, we never hear of it. And yet bridal mysticism was not extensively exploited on behalf of the fortunate women who remained intact. This was true of Benevenuta Bojani (d. 1295), whose commitment to virginity dated from her youth.[226] It was certainly not the idiom allegedly chosen by Clare of Montefalco (d. 1308), abbess of the Hermits of St. Augustine, who had been living a monastic life since the age of six. Instead, she is primarily represented as cosufferer with Christ, as the symbols engraved in her heart will ultimately reveal.[227] The Dominican penitent Vanna of Orvieto (d. 1306) was an intact virgin so pure that men who dared to look upon her lustfully breathed their last; she was one who had "not even been violated by the illusions of dreams," and whose corpse was suffused with the odor of sanctity. And yet her hagiographer takes little effort to associate Vanna with the persona of the bride.[228] The exception is rather formulaic: we are told that she preserved her baptismal vestment of innocence in preparation for the celestial nuptials. Yet when she was formally invested as a penitent, hence solemnizing her chaste resolve, marriage to Christ is eclipsed by her meditation on the significance of the Dominican habit: white for the preservation of virginity, black for mortification of the body.[229]

It is on the cusp of the fourteenth century that nuptial imagery begins to appear south of the Alps. The *Memorial* of Angela of Foligno (d. 1309) dramatizes the mystic's extremely sensual relationship with Christ, depicting her as boldly stripping in front of the cross and offering her body to Christ. Later she is embraced by the crucified Christ and enters his wound.[230] But on her return from a pivotal pilgrimage to Assisi, Angela is actually betrothed to Christ. When Angela expresses anxiety over Christ's potential departure, he reassures Angela as follows: "'You are holding the ring of my love. From now on you are engaged to me and you will never leave me.'"[231]

From this point nuptial imagery develops apace in Italy, at least in part as a result of the dissemination of Beguine literature.[232] As the example of Catherine of Siena (d. 1380) suggests, moreover, the mystical marriage was destined to become more of an actual event that becomes progressively more elaborate and literal. Catherine was the daughter of a wealthy dyer whose resistance to marriage, and concerted efforts to make herself unattractive, were consolidated by a pox that ruined her complexion. Eventually, her family gave up trying to marry her and accepted her vocation, giving her a room in the basement where she lived as a third order Dominican.[233] Catherine's revelations not only fostered her deep inner life but also provided a platform from which she was able to play a vital role in church politics.[234] Her confessor and hagiographer, Raymond of Capua, will use the vehicle of marriage with Christ in order to consolidate both inner and outer aspects of Catherine's spirituality.

According to Raymond's account, Catherine's wedding was in response to her ardent prayers for an increase in faith. Christ responded rather tersely: "I will espouse you in faith." Catherine kept repeating the petition only to receive the same reply. On the last day of the carnival before Lent, however, Christ came to fulfill his promise—accompanied by a heavenly entourage consisting of the Virgin Mary, John the Evangelist, Saints Paul and Dominic, with David on his cithar. Mary took Catherine's hand, spread her fingers apart, and held them toward her son. Christ then espoused Catherine with a ring of gold, surmounted by a magnificent diamond that was flanked by four pearls. As promised, Christ "espoused her in faith," pledging that the faith between them would be kept "untarnished until the day when you celebrate with me the everlasting wedding-feast in heaven." But at this point Christ's avowals began to take a political turn, tacitly serving to validate Catherine's intervention in public affairs. For he additionally enjoined that from "now on you must never falter accepting any task my providence may lay upon your shoulders. Remember, you have been confirmed in faith, and will prevail over your enemies." The vision vanished, "but the ring remained on her finger not seen, indeed, by the eyes of others, but visible to Catherine's eyes." Raymond goes on to expatiate about the symbolism of the diamond.[235]

Raymond presents marriage to Christ as the cornerstone of Catherine's spirituality, emphasizing the experience more than Catherine does herself in the course of her writings.[236] He was, however, reticent about the extent of its physicality. In a letter to Queen Johanna of Naples, Catherine makes it clear that the ring with which Christ espoused her was his foreskin, which she perceived as a symbol of voluntary suffering.[237] This is a strikingly individualistic application of matrimonial metaphor. It is not the only one, however. Catherine seems to have envisaged possible proxies for the celestial bridegroom much more fully than her predecessors. Her mystical mindset was sufficiently flexible to accommodate nonclerical surrogates. She even had the daring to imagine herself as other than the bride. In 1375 Catherine accompanied the Perugian noble Niccolò di Toldo, envoy to Siena and possible spy, to his execution, providing him with spiritual consolation in the face of death. Catherine describes the event in a famous letter to her confessor, Raymond of Capua. Before the execution, Niccolò is pictured as saying to Catherine:

> "Stay with me; don't leave me alone." . . . his head was resting on my breast. I sensed an intense joy, a fragrance of his blood—and it wasn't separate from the fragrance of my own, which I am waiting to shed for my gentle Spouse Jesus.
>   With my soul's desire growing, and sensing his fear, I said "Courage, my dear brother, for soon we shall reach the wedding feast." . . . And he said, "I shall go all joyful and strong, and when I think that you shall be waiting for me there, it will seem a thousand years until I get there!"

The marriage was consummated on the scaffold.

> Then he arrived like a meek lamb, and when he saw me he began to laugh and wanted me to make the sign of the cross over him. "Down for the wedding, my dear brother, for soon you will be in

everlasting life!" He knelt down very meekly; I placed his neck [on the block] and bent down and reminded him of the blood of the Lamb. His mouth said nothing but 'Gesù!' and 'Caterina!' and as he said this, I received his head into my hands, saying 'I will!'"

Catherine saw Christ receive Niccolò's soul through the wound in his side. And Niccolò "made a gesture sweet enough to charm a thousand hearts," turning around as would a bride who had reached her husband's threshold, as if to thank her attendants. Catherine could not bear to wash away the blood that had spattered on her.[238]

Catherine presents this event as a marriage in which both she and Niccolò could, arguably, be seen as acting as proxies of Christ for one another. Initially, Niccolò is undergoing a Christlike martyrdom. He is compared to a lamb and is about to be washed in the blood of the lamb. But, ultimately, Niccolò is presented as the bride about to enter heaven, while Catherine is associated with Christ. This is tacitly suggested when he requests that Catherine sign him with the cross, according her a quasi-sacerdotal status. But it is the transference that Niccolò articulates on the edge of death, his last words being "Gesù!" and "Caterina" that confirm this association. Catherine again acts as a surrogate when she receives Niccolò's head in her hands, even as Christ would receive his soul. In the end, however, Catherine gracefully cedes her place to the celestial bridegroom himself and watches as Niccolò's soul enters heaven, recasting herself as one of the attendants of the bride. Not only does Catherine's dramatic and original reworking of traditional nuptial imagery extend to accommodate the execution of a spy, it also produces a very avant-garde, perhaps even precedential, female groom.[239]

Catherine's union with Niccolò was clearly destined to remain singular. But her mystical marriage with Christ was the source of inspiration for others. For instance, when Lucia Brocadelli of Narni (d. 1544) was married to Christ at seven years of age, she was flanked by the Virgin Mary, St. Dominic, and, of course, Catherine of Siena.[240] As if in anticipation, Catherine was also said to have watched over Lucia's cradle. The mystical marriage would even be celebrated as a public ritual by the notorious Benedetta Carlini (d. 1661), replete with an elaborate set that had been dictated by the visionary Christ. During the ceremony proper, the bride channeled the voice of the celestial bridegroom, praising his bride.[241]

It was in Northern Europe, however, where the Bernardine influence was strongest that we find an unbroken continuum of female spirituality, consistently structured around the bridal persona.[242] Indeed, the mystical lexicon of the noblewoman Bridget of Sweden (d. 1373) emphasizes the geographical reach of nuptial spirituality to the north.[243] Bridget's visions provided her with a platform for political intervention on the world stage that allowed her to travel widely throughout Europe and the Holy Land, exhorting and reviling world leaders in the secular and ecclesiastical realms alike. Late in life, however, Bridget became particularly involved in papal politics, with Rome serving as her most important base. When Bridget died, moreover, the members of Gregory XI's circle scrambled to fill the political gap left by the Swedish prophet's death, selecting Catherine as her successor.[244] As politico-visionaries who had urged the pope's return from Avignon to Rome, both women would be ignominiously lumped together and blamed for precipitating the papal schism. On a spiritual register, however, both would also be celebrated for their respective roles as *sponsae Christi*.

And yet the spiritual profiles of the two women were as much at odds as their circumstances of birth: Catherine's lifelong virginity versus Bridget's almost thirty years of marriage and eight children. That this was, indeed, still a salient difference is suggested by the fact that Bridget had to become a widow before she was distinguished by the appearance of the visionary Christ.[245] And yet neither a carnal past nor a late start in any way inhibited Bridget's new identity as "the Spouse"—the mystical shorthand by which Bridget is designated throughout her revelations. Occasionally there is a visionary allusion to Bridget's lost chastity. But more often than not, Bridget's apparitional allies are there to transform this potential weakness into a position of strength. For instance, at one point Bridget is championed by none other than St. Agnes, who anticipates, and counters, any incredulity over the fact that a "corrupted" woman such as Bridget could find such favor with Christ. To this end, Agnes points an apparitional finger at the many contemptible women who were virgins in name only, and probably would have chosen to marry had the opportunity arisen. Bridget, in contrast, had a pristine resolve to remain chaste—one that, admittedly, God "from his hidden justice" did not permit her to keep, but for which she still derived credit.[246] "Corrupted" or not, the Virgin Mary seems every bit as solicitous in preparing Bridget for her union with Christ as she would have been had her daughter-in-law elect been a nubile virgin.[247]

Bridget's very secure sense of herself as Christ's spouse paved the way for other veterans of the marriage bed. The most celebrated is Margery Kempe (d. after 1438), who was married for approximately thirty-eight years and experienced fourteen pregnancies in all.[248] Margery was constantly measuring her spiritual progress against that of Bridget—to whom she refers by the graphic, but appropriate, abbreviation of "Bride."[249] Despite her apparent adulation, however, Margery still exhibited the kind of behavior that one might expect from a new girl in an established harem, striving to advance her intimacy with the sultan. And Margery did manage to outstrip Bridget in some significant ways. For instance, when Margery saw the consecrated host move as if alive, Christ reassured her that "My dowtyr, Bryde, say me nevyr in this wyse."[250] Many of Margery's advantages were concretely logistical, however. For instance, Bridget had to wait until the death of her husband before Christ addressed her. But Christ first appeared to Margery as a handsome young man when she was still very much a wife and mother, suffering from postpartum depression.[251] Bridget only managed to talk her husband, Ulf, into abstaining from sexual intercourse late in life when he was already ill.[252] Margery, however, convinced John Kempe to vow chastity while he was still young and vigorous.[253] Furthermore, Margery's relationship with Christ had ostensible effects. Even prior to John's conversion, Christ had allegedly commanded Margery to advertise her spiritual advancement by wearing white, outwardly articulating the chastity she so eagerly sought.[254] Christ required Margery to commission an actual ring inscribed with the words *"Jhesus est amor meus."*[255] (The only comparable token that Bridget had was a visionary brooch that the Virgin Mary fastened on her breast when adorning her for the bridegroom: there was no ring as yet.)[256] When instructing Bridget on the duties of the bride, Christ had said that the bride should always be in readiness in case the bridegroom suddenly decides to name the day.[257] Unlike Bridget, however, Margery did not suffer the indignity of a long engagement: she experienced a visionary wedding to God the Father himself at the church of the Holy Apostles in Rome.[258]

Finally, the entire tenor of Margery's relationship with Christ was more intimate than was the case with her Swedish role model and rival. Margery often received tender reassurances that Christ's love for her was equal to what he felt for any virgin.[259] By the same token, he reminded her that it was appropriate for the wife to be "homly wyth hir husband. . . . Be he nevyr so gret a lorde and sche so powr a woman whan he weddyth hir, yet thei must ly togedir in joy and pes. . . . Therfore most I nedys be homly wyth the and lyn in thi bed wyth the. . . . And therfor thu mayst boldly take me in the armys of thi sowle and kyssen my mowth, myn hed, and my fete as swetly as thow wylt."[260] So while Christ kept his relations with his fiancée, Bridget, on a formal footing, he invited Margery to snuggle in bed.

Margery was ridiculed for her spirituality, particularly in her homeland. Yet her visionary life was relatively tame by continental standards, where the

eroticization of religious discourse, compounded by substantial efforts at an
exacting literalism, showed no sign of abating. These trends especially left
their mark on the Prussian mystic Dorothea of Montau (d. 1394). Not only
was Dorothea another of Bridget's spiritual protégés, but she was also a possible influence on Margery Kempe, who had visited Dorothea's hometown of
Danzig.[261] All three of these matrons felt the tensions between terrestrial and
celestial marriage, and each, in their own way, struggled against the former to
pursue the latter. Dorothea's terrestrial marriage left a heavy imprint on her
relationship with Christ, however, suggesting that she was least successful in
her struggle.

The serendipitous chronology of life events was certainly a determining
factor. Both Bridget and Margery had long widowhoods in which they were
free to cultivate their spiritual lives. Dorothea, however, had been married
for practically all of her adult life. Although ostensibly preferring to preserve
her virginity for God, Dorothea was nevertheless married in 1363 at the age
of seventeen to an affluent weaponsmith in Danzig named Adalbert, a much
older man. The marriage lasted until Adalbert's death in 1391, although the last
ten years had been spent in chastity—a situation wherein Adalbert's ill health
finally collaborated with the wife's piety.[262]

Perhaps even more important than the duration of Dorothea's marriage
was its tenor. Dorothea had no appetite for the married life. Her experiences
of sex were especially bleak. Witnesses at her process for canonization would
attest to a difficult and delayed consummation of the marriage. Furthermore,
ostensibly to avoid experiencing physical lust during the marital act, Dorothea
would place nutshells and other sharp objects in the mysterious wounds that
spontaneously erupted all over her entire body and that, as we shall see below,
became so important to her spirituality. Absenting herself from the marital
bed whenever she could, Dorothea wept whenever her husband attempted
to remove her clothing. Her husband, Adalbert, moreover, was generally depicted as obstreperous and brutal. Mistaking Dorothea's frequent raptures for
disobedient inattention, he beat her mercilessly. A similar construal of Dorothea's constant church attendance resulted in her being chained up for several
days. Significantly, these afflictions were often rewarded by celestial consolations in the form of mystical raptures.[263]

The experience of motherhood did nothing to alleviate the pains of married life. During her various pregnancies, Dorothea's wounds would reopen,
while new ones would erupt.[264] One great wound appeared between her
breasts at the time of her first pregnancy that would last for the rest of her life.
Ostensibly put there by Christ to temper Dorothea's love for her children, the

wound made nursing excruciating. With the same motive in mind, Dorothea was accustomed to scorching her nipples after about six months of nursing. The injuries were such that the two sides of the nipple nearly met when the bandages were removed, being almost entirely burned through. One witness at her process for canonization would allege that the lesser pain of the burning would help to ward off the greater pain of the central wound.[265] Only one of Dorothea's nine children survived infancy.

After Adalbert's death, when Dorothea was finally free to seek an appropriate spiritual director, she left Danzig for Marienwerder. It was under the tutelage of John of Marienwerder that Dorothea's spirituality came to fruition. It proved to be a narrow spiritual window, however: Dorothea only survived her husband by three years.[266] In the meantime, John of Marienwerder seemed to have stepped into the vacuum in authority left by Adalbert's death. As in the case of Friar Zeger, who called Margaret of Ypres away from the prospect of marriage, John would receive much of the affect generally reserved for a husband—sentiments that he would soon come to return. Indeed, John adduced his exceptional love for Dorothea, which outstripped his feelings for his other female penitents or even his own brother, as one of the proofs of the authenticity of Dorothea's visions.[267] Both John's authority and affection were mystically and canonically ratified. Already in 1389, when first hearing about John, Dorothea experienced a vision in which her future spiritual father appeared to her.[268] The romantic/prophetic undertones implicit in this vision were brought to fruition at Dorothea's first interview with John, when she confessed and received communion: "Immediately her soul was glued to her own most recent Confessor through so immense a friendship so quickly as she had ever had for any person, loving him with all her heart and trusting him so much that she [opened] the secrets of her heart to him."[269] As seen in the lives of the various Beguine mystics, the idea of one soul being glued to another was frequently used for describing mystical unions.[270] Dorothea's spontaneous outpouring of affection was soon formalized by a twofold vow to John, taken at Christ's behest. In order "to stabilize" (*stabilire*) Dorothea, Christ first required that she vow never to leave John—creating a bond that Dorothea felt (and Christ confirmed) to be a kind of marriage.[271] Four days later, Dorothea vowed obedience to John, whereupon "no longer knowing any will of her own, she did and refrained from doing whatever [John] enjoined and ordered without any exception."[272] Their symbolic marriage was virilocal: Dorothea would spend the duration of her life in an anchor-hold attached to the cathedral of Marienwerder, with which John was already associated as a canon.

In addition to the quasi-matrimonial strains of her relationship with her

confessor, there was Dorothea's relationship with the celestial bridegroom—
one that was fraught with a violence that almost resembled her temporal marriage. Adalbert had attempted to discipline Dorothea by repeated beatings;
Christ also punished Dorothea by the infliction of "wounds of sin."[273] This is
not without precedent: Thomas of Cantimpré provides a possible precedent
for this type of wounding by positing that a truly holy person should perceive
sin as a kind of lesion. He goes on to commend a female recluse in Brabant
who actually experienced her various defects as wounds.[274] More often than
not, however, Dorothea experienced "wounds of love"—an allusion to the
Canticles (Sg 4.9) and a mark of Christ's affection. Again, such wounds of
love were not exactly an innovation. For example, in response to Gertrude of
Helfta's prayers, Christ appeared and inflicted a wound on her heart. It was
another person, more capable than Gertrude of listening "to the soft mur-
mur of [Christ's] love," who taught her how to bathe, anoint, and bandage
such wounds, suggesting that the wounds referred to purely spiritual graces.[275]
This was not true for Dorothea, however. Not only could the wounds of love
manifest themselves either physically or spiritually, but they were at the very
center of her spirituality. The corporeal wounds appeared on the fleshy parts
of her body and were often a couple of inches in depth. Generally, they appeared while she slept, but they could also arise during the day like a boil,
erupting suddenly. Not only were these wounds exceedingly painful, making sleep almost impossible,[276] but they were also exceptionally slow to heal.
When Dorothea was nine years old, she received "a great and cruel wound"
on her spine that kept her bent over like a cripple and did not heal until she
was seventeen.[277] Despite the inevitable oozing and bleeding of such wounds,
Dorothea nevertheless managed to conceal them not only from her family
but, more remarkably still, from Adalbert.[278] Christ only authorized Dorothea
to reveal the existence of these wounds to her confessor toward the end of her
life, after she had become enclosed as an anchoress.[279]

As gifts from the bridegroom, Dorothea's wounds were invested with a
number of symbolic meanings. First and foremost, they were a reminder of
Christ's passion, through which she could experience simultaneously the special
love she was accorded along with the pain she was being permitted to share.[280]
In keeping with the celestial favor she enjoyed, Dorothea's wounds were explicitly assimilated with the stigmata of Christ.[281] The longer Dorothea lived, the
more her suffering increased, in keeping with Christ's own experience.[282]

Avidly complicitous with this divine program, Dorothea did what she
could to exacerbate the divinely administered wounds. As mentioned above,
she was constantly inserting sharp and abrasive objects or substances into her

wounds (ranging anywhere from twigs to scorpions) in an effort to inflame them.[283] Dorothea's predilection to wound herself began at the early age of seven and only abated when she was forbidden by Christ in the last year of her life. His injunction against Dorothea wounding herself is prefaced by the following statement:[284] "I will wound you however many times and whenever I wish. Indeed, I will shoot you through your heart, soul, body, flesh, and blood, and all your inner and outer powers—nor is there anything left in you that is not wounded by me."[285] The visionary Christ's identity as the one who inflicts wounds is key to his self-presentation, ultimately overshadowing his more conventional and empathetic role, as cosufferer.[286]

The wounds of love were inflicted by a bewildering array of weapons: mystical lances, darts, arrows, or spears. When addressing Dorothea on the subject, Christ's analogies were naturally steeped in predatory violence. Christ recounted how he shot through Dorothea, like a deer, until she was eventually brought down by dogs. He also likens Dorothea, injured in so many places in both body and soul, to someone wounded in the line of action.[287] But, as the designation of wounds of love would suggest, they were particularly amenable to the ambit of the nuptial imagery, wherein their associations were rendered explicitly sexual, but no less violent.

Two particularly painful encounters illuminate the character of Dorothea's relationship with Christ. One is especially freighted with phallic prerogative. Dorothea was transfixed with a large spear that penetrated her flesh from the right shoulder to the elbow, piercing her heart. The spear seemed to move of its own volition throughout the day. Each time it moved, Dorothea besought God for help. After vespers, all spiritual consolations receded as the spear continued to thrust itself, ever more strongly. As prayer became impossible, all Dorothea could do was weep and scream. Christ explained this experience as follows:

> When the bridegroom and lover of his bride wishes to go away from her, then he is wont to leave her a memento by which he is retained in her memory and she should pant continuously for him. The carnal bridegroom also sometimes afflicts his wife with labors and weighs her down with pressures so that she sickens and languishes. But he does not abandon her lying in bed, but looks after her solicitously, cherishes her and restores her. And if I did not exercise you with labors and press you down with the swellings of the magnified uterus [*magnificati*], how else would you know that I, your spouse, existed?

John provided an appropriate gloss: "It was as if he were to say: the groom is known through his actions, just as a cause is known through its effect, and as if that comment of John's in the Apocalypse (3.19; cf. Prov. 3.12; Heb. 12.6) were adduced: such as I love, I rebuke and chastise."[288]

During the last weeks of Dorothea's life, her celestial groom came to her, flower bearing and lovesick, and began to separate, distend, and dilate the different sections of her heart with his hand, temporarily putting aside his lances and darts. The process was so excruciating that Dorothea was only aware that she was in the grip of a powerful being, but by no means certain whether this entity was to be identified with the Lord or with death. She accordingly began looking around for a place to curl up and die. But this process stimulated the opening up of her spiritual senses, which enabled her to see two new lances in her heart with long handles ascending to a throne: one of the lances was manipulated by Christ, and the other by the Virgin Mary. When the celestial pair saw Dorothea gazing up at them, each grasped their respective handles, ramming their spears into Dorothea so forcefully that she expected the point of the spears to emerge through her back. The pain of insertion was nothing compared to the withdrawal of the spears.[289]

As Caroline Bynum has shown, the heart and the womb were often interconnected in the mystical lexicon.[290] The visionary Christ makes this association explicit to Dorothea in his explanation of the above encounter. In this instance, Christ purposefully eschewed assuming a furtive or passive role, instead preferring to approach Dorothea as a powerful and violent man, intent on doing violence by distending, dilating, and penetrating her heart.[291] He expatiated upon the phenomenon of the lances on another occasion when, appearing with "serious maturity" (*cum seriosa maturitate*), he compared his own activities to those of the carnal bridegroom, who overpowers his wife sexually. "I also now wish to inflict violence on you [*tibi volo violenciam inferre*], so that you have plenty to report back to your dearest friends."[292] The implicit comparison between Dorothea and a giddy newlywed, who would regale her girlfriends with anecdotes from the bedroom, is especially jarring.

Even when such experiences are described as delectable, which they sometimes are, it is the new thresholds of pain that are invariably in the foreground. Rather than a sublimation of sexual desire, Dorothea's bridal mysticism is better construed as a relocation of her entire experience of marriage. Such a reading may seem at odds with the ostensible rivalry between earthly and celestial husbands represented at various junctures in Dorothea's life. For instance, the great wound over her heart was put there by her celestial bridegroom at the time of her first pregnancy to be as a "bundle of myrrh" between her breasts that would act to deter excessive earthly love (Sg 1.12).[293] Likewise, with her growing intimacy with Christ, she eventually regained the lost innocence of virginity—that most lamented of casualties of carnal marriage. Ultimately, however, material and spiritual planes resonate with shared meaning. Christ would remind Dorothea, "I frequently raptured [*rapui*] you from your husband when . . . he thought he possessed you."[294] The Latin word *raptus* simultaneously signifies rape and mystical rapture: so in essence, Christ is simply exchanging one kind of sexual congress for another kind.[295] But both forms of union are forced. This concurrence points to the greater tautology underlying Dorothea's mystical marriage: that behind the face of the Christ who wounds with serious maturity, violently imposing himself on his bride, looms the face of Adalbert.[296]

Dorothea's nuptial spirituality culminates around the reception of the Eucharist, which is represented as an actual marriage with Christ. John Marienwerder describes one such instance in detail, which allegedly occurred on September 16, 1393. The preparations for this event are described as ritualistic and dignified. First the bride is betrothed and dowered with inexpressibly beautiful gifts. Her body and soul, illuminated and crystalline, seem to run together. The soul is then splendidly adorned, while all the time weeping with tears of joy. The betrothal culminates in the arrival of the bridegroom, an event that is signified in the reception of the host at Mass.[297] Thereafter, bride and groom become a globe of fire, and the bride is promised eternal life.[298] Subsequently raptured into a starry palace, Dorothea is saluted by various groups of saints before being conducted to the wine cellar, where she is inebriated by the bridegroom's desire and knowledge.[299] When the marriage itself is to be solemnized, the bridegroom hastens to his bride with a great entourage, while she, though insufficiently prepared, shamelessly flies to him, calling his name. The union is instantly consummated in an embrace that fills the bride's heart and soul; the more intimately they are united, the more she weeps.[300] The embrace has instantaneous and palpable manifestations. The bride's heart dilates while her uterus simultaneously swells and becomes distended, "just as if there was a large fetus inside waiting to be born." The pressure of the spiritual fetus causes the bride to gasp.[301] Details such as these bear the stamp of the quotidian, dovetailing with Dorothea's extensive experience with pregnancy.

The phenomenon of the mystical pregnancy is not new.[302] It is but another instance of the seeds of an image growing into a tangible form—a pregnancy in its own right. Yet the beginnings of the process are modest and allusive. For instance, in the poem "Allegory of Love's Growth," Hadewijch imagines the kind of humility required for perfect love—the kind that "God brought down

into Mary"—in terms of nine months of joyful suffering.[303] In the revelations
of Mechtild of Hackeborn, the Virgin Mary bestows on St. Agnes the reward
of virginal maternity "that she [Agnes] would be a spiritual mother of God by
grace, just as she [Mary] was by nature." On her deathbed Mechtild herself
would merit a parallel distinction.[304]

The image is realized more concretely elsewhere. When Ida of Louvain lay
in bed on the eve of Ephiphany meditating on the infancy of Christ, her entire
body became painfully swollen from sheer joy. While this may not have been
a mystical pregnancy per se, Ida of Gorsleeuw's experience is more explicit,
albeit less dramatic. Ida's hagiographer aligns her sensitivity to the Eucharist with the circumstances surrounding the Virgin Mary's visit to her cousin,
Elisabeth—future mother to John the Baptist: "It also happened that it was
found to be renewed in the said virgin [Ida] what is reported most miraculously concerning the blessed John the Baptist. For just as in the uterus of his
mother he felt the presence of God coming, so the most sweet virgin [Ida] felt
the coming of the Lord descending on the altar when it was at hand."[305] In a
similar vein, the spiritual pregnancy of the Dominican nun Margaret Ebner
(d. 1351) was inspired by a desire to know Christ intimately through maternity,
as had Mary.[306] Margaret, however, represents herself as experiencing a painful and graphic labor. Her intense spasms provoked screams that could be
heard throughout the monastery. "Swollen like a woman great with child,"
it took three nuns to support Margaret. "They said they had to lean against
one another with full strength and under their hands they felt something living, moving inside me."[307] Her efforts in this direction were validated by her
spiritual director, Henry of Nördlingen, who referred to Margaret as "bearer
of God"—a title associated with the Virgin Mary since the Council of Ephesus
(431).[308]

The spiritual pregnancy of Bridget of Sweden (d. 1373) was an even more
direct outcome of her relationship with Mary, significantly occurring on
Christmas Eve. Bridget suddenly felt movements in her heart that she likened
to the stirrings of a child. The Virgin Mary reassured Bridget that it was not
a diabolical illusion, "but a similitude of the sweetness and mercy that was
wrought in me."[309] But despite Mary's professions, Bridget was still sufficiently
sensitive to the possibility of demonic illusion that she allegedly required that
her confessor place his hand over her heart so he could feel the divine movements.[310] Her caution was understandable. William of Auvergne (d. 1249) had
warned that demon incubi had the ability to make women swell up so that
they believed that they were pregnant by demons. When the time of par-
tum arrived, however, "they de-tumenesced, with only the emission of a great

windiness."[311] In fact, a woman with a version of this affliction actually approached Bridget with her problem. Bridget's diagnosis was that she was being assailed by the demon of lust, brought on by infidelity and incontinence.[312]

What distinguishes Dorothea's pregnancy from her spiritual forebearers is its explicit link with eroticized nuptials. For while Dorothea's pregnancy represented the culmination of her union with the celestial bridegroom, her predecessors' parallel experiences were the result of a profound devotion to the Virgin Mary, which resulted in a very literal *imitatio Mariae*. Moreover, paralleling the experience of Margaret Ebner, Dorothea's pregnancy has a painfully mundane quality—more evocative of Eve's cursed lot, to bring forth children in suffering, than Mary's painless and blessed parturition.[313] Even the visionary Christ shows a certain amount of circumspection when addressing Dorothea about her mystical pregnancy. In particular, he cautions Dorothea against disclosing any unfamiliar religious phenomena that were not expressly present in scripture: she was only free to reveal the pregnancy because Bridget had already made reference to her own experience. At the same time, Christ took the opportunity to assure Dorothea that her experience far surpassed Bridget's, even as her heart and uterus became more dilated.[314] The comparison with Bridget manages to obscure a number of awkward differences, however. Bridget's experience was carefully restricted to the heart alone: the womb was never mentioned, except through the kind of mystical innuendo implicit in references to the heart. Likewise, the impetus behind Bridget's pregnancy was associated with the incarnation and did not involve an erotic encounter with the celestial bridegroom.[315]

However sexually explicit Dorothea's mystical experience might seem, she was still sufficiently within the boundaries of orthodoxy for her confessor to suppose her a worthy candidate for canonization.[316] But there were also more extreme manifestations of what might be termed "spiritual carnal knowledge" that were ultimately censured. According to a later source, certain female adherents to the antinomian heresy decried by Albert the Great claimed that they had known Christ carnally.[317] It is possible that these women were riding the same mystical wave as Dorothea and Bridget, pushing bridal mysticism and the cult of the physical Christ to its natural (if not logical) conclusion. And yet such intensely palpable claims were, in certain contexts, deemed unequivocally heretical.

Bridget, Margery, and Dorothea were all matrons and hence clear beneficiaries of the democratization of bridal imagery that had been under way since the twelfth century. But there were also cases in which women would continue to be stigmatized for their sexual past. This is certainly true for Odilia of Liège, whose vita vacillates between a strong apprehension of the indelible taint of sex and the anonymous hagiographer's herculean efforts at denial. According to this account, Odilia, who was married against her will, never felt "the pricking of lust" in the course of her marriage, instead "remaining like straw in the fire without flame or burning."[318] Indeed, the Holy Spirit extinguished any kindling of sin within her "so that the virgin remained most integral [*integerrima*]." Her eldest son, John, was literally "consecrated in his mother's womb," emerging with the sign of the priest's stole between his shoulders, which signified his sacerdotal destiny.[319] Yet Odilia's virtual virginity proffered little comfort. "Despising the filth of the flesh with her unpolluted mind . . . she washed the marriage debt in tears." The first two years following her husband's death was spent in mourning for her lost chastity: "as if waking from a heavy sleep, she lamented excessively that she had dissipated her substance by living carnally." So as a widow "she hoped to be reinvested with the glory of chastity." It was through meditating on the passion of Christ, "that lover and restorer of innocence," that "her body and soul were dressed with the purity of total chastity, just like the most beautiful gown." Ultimately all the fire of lust was extinguished in her "so that she no longer knew she was a woman, a living woman without the weakness of a woman [*mollitie mulieris*]." "Thus the blessed woman daily exalted in her soul at the marvelous way the crucifixion was a daily help in the recuperation of her chastity."[320]

It took seven years of affliction for Odilia to regain her lost chastity and for her body to be "reformed by such purity and grace." But having just reached that blissful plateau, Odilia was suddenly afflicted by the spirit of blasphemy.[321] If this seemed rather daunting, there was much worse to come. Victimized by the spells of her clerical confidants, covert necromancers whose advances she had scorned, Odilia was dismayed that she "felt a kind of voluptuous sensuality." This was in spite of the fact that "her flesh was dead, and only her spirit was vigorous."[322] One of the clerics "afflicted her with so much magic that . . . he imagined she would run around through the world just like a whore."[323] The fact that Satan himself was the prime demon responsible for Odilia's trials could account for the potency of the magic. Even so, the demons could only take control of her tongue, forcing her to say wicked things: they were still unable to "enter" the saint. After Odilia endured years of this "martyrdom," however, the demons began to make considerably more headway. The wretched woman became so worn down by her afflictions that she begged her son to keep vigil with her lest she be forced down the path where "her spirit became involved in such impurities that, upon returning to herself she would say, lamenting, that if she were to remain inwardly for a long time, she would be able to feel more that pertains to the flesh than was the case during that time when she was bound to render the marriage debt."[324] And so Odilia's chastity was seemingly imperiled by psychic temptations more pernicious to her chastity than married life. Not surprisingly, the anonymous hagiographer never refers to Odilia as Christ's spouse. At the very most we have the saint's frequent iterations in the course of her trials that "the bonds of prayer, the act which joined her to God [*conjunxit*], could not suffer a divorce [*divortium*] by any force, unless she earlier relaxed her prayer."[325]

Ermine of Reims (d. 1396) was yet another female penitent whose holiness was to a large extent measured by resistance to spiritually inflicted sexual overtures.[326] She too was a widow. As in the case of Dorothea, Ermine's husband, Regnault (d. 1393), was considerably her senior—by some twenty-six years, in fact.[327] And as with both Bridget and Dorothea, it was only after her husband's death that Ermine's revelations captured the attention of her confessor, John Le Graveur, the subprior of a Franciscan community in Reims. Ermine and Odilia lived as religious recluses in the world, yet neither was formally enclosed in the manner of Dorothea.

Ermine's religious trajectory could likewise be construed as a kind of hybrid of the patterns pertaining to the widows discussed above. Ermine also left her hometown en route to establishing her religious vocation: Bridget and Margery were peripatetic, Dorothea went from Danzig to Marienwerder, Ermine from Reims to Paris. Ermine's friends from her hometown tried to convince her to return, maintaining that she was too poor and too isolated to remain in Paris. Her confessor argued against her removal, however, urging Ermine to persevere in a semireligious life under his direction—a life that most clearly paralleled Dorothea's with respect to her relationship with John. Ermine, in turn, asked permission to follow the commands of her confessor, another John, as strictly as if he were her religious superior, paralleling Christ's injunction to Dorothea. Living in near seclusion in a single room, Ermine ended her days overlooking the priory where her confessor lived.[328]

Outwardly, the lives of Dorothea and Ermine were in many ways similar: both lived as recluses of sorts—more or less under obedience to a confessor. Their inner lives also correspond in a number of respects: both women were privy to erotically charged revelations, and both were the recipients of supernaturally inflicted wounds. But it is at this point that Ermine parts company with Dorothea. For while Dorothea was the beneficiary of Christ's wounds of love, Ermine was covered with wounds and punctures from the shifting team of demons in different forms who visited her practically every night.[329] Dorothea was permitted to bask in the often painful but spiritually gratifying union

with her bridegroom; Ermine expended much of her visionary energy fending off demons who offered close encounters of the lurid kind that promised
to be pleasurable. This is not entirely unprecedented. For instance, Odilia of
Liège and Margery Kempe also struggled against nebulous but powerful sexual
temptation.[330] Ermine's predicament was much more concrete, however: she
was tormented by numerous demons who attempted to have sex with her
themselves. In other words, she was afflicted by a series of incubi whose guile
was apparent in the different personae they adopted. For instance, on one
occasion a demon appeared as her deceased husband, who got into bed and,
"spooning" with Ermine, proceeded to fall asleep.[331] Another time there was a
demonic simulation of a beautiful couple making love in front of Ermine "in
order to incite her to do the same."[332] Once after a demonically induced erotic
dream, Ermine awoke to find three strapping men dressed in hoods, black
hose, shoes from horse's hide, and short tunics cropped near their buttocks.
The three of them attempted to seduce her, uncovering their genitals in order
to tempt her. (When this did not work, they hung her up by her feet.)[333]

Revelations such as these may have been physically onerous, but they
were nevertheless relatively tolerable because Ermine had no doubts about the
demonic nature of her tormenters. But often she could not tell. St. Paul had
identified spiritual discernment as a gift of the spirit, and Ermine clearly had
no such gift.[334] Sometimes demons assumed the shape of angels, with golden
wings, lighted candles, and accompanied by a beautiful fragrance; sometimes
they appeared as saints.[335] Their voices were often lovely and perfectly suited
to the holy entity in question.[336] It was only when these visitations caused her
hair to stand on end or instilled uncontrollable trembling that Ermine knew
she was in the presence of demons.[337] Other times she was uncertain. So even
when Ermine saw what she believed to be good spirits, she could never enjoy
the experience because she could never really be sure that they were truly
good.[338] Everyday annoyances were likewise fraught with a disturbing uncertainty. For instance, when she was visiting a local church as penance, a man
asked her where she was going and called her a whore. Was he really a man or
a demon in the shape of a man? Ermine had no way of knowing.[339]

This kind of uncertainty was even more troubling when the apparitions
were, on the surface, holy, yet sought to undermine her faith in the church.
For instance, one demon appeared disguised as Paul the Simple—a saint who
frequently had succored Ermine in the midst of her tumultuous spiritual life.
Though not attempting to seduce her himself, the demon instead predicted
that her confessor eventually would, thereby revealing his true colors. Her tormentor further charged that Ermine's many demonic tussles were due to her

misplaced trust. In fact, he insisted that all the marvels she saw at Mass were demonically wrought by magicians and witches.[340]

Demonic probation of female mystics was not uncommon. Italian saints seemed to have been especially afflicted. The demons' tactics varied. Sometimes their main intent was to horrify, as when a demon appeared to Humiliana bearing newly dead bodies, dismembered and bloody.[341] On another occasion, Satan appeared corporeally as a great serpent, threatening to crawl between her legs while she slept.[342] But demons also frequently adopted a more gentle address. A demon appeared to the youthful Benevenuta as a handsome young man, asking her what she was doing and why she wasn't taking advantage of the solaces of youth—something we know from Caesarius of Heisterbach that demons were wont to do.[343] Vanna of Orvieto experienced demons in various shapes: as a serpent, a female religious, an Ethiopian, and, more suggestively, a handsome youth with ornate clothes and a gold belt. If stoically resisted, demons often resorted to brute violence. When Vanna was praying for her city, a demon grabbed her, stuck her on its shoulders, and threw her to the ground, causing multiple fractures. Another time a demon gave her a black eye.[344] Demons threw stones at Benevenuta, dropped her from considerable heights, and pushed her around until she spewed blood.[345] Posing as her deceased husband, one demon beat Gerardesca of Pisa until blood gushed out of her nostrils and mouth. Still unsatisfied, the demon transported Gerardesca to a little boat on the Arno, where he attempted to drown her.[346]

Nor is this level of demonic activity unknown in Northern Europe. The German Beguine Christine of Stommeln (d. 1312) frequently endured physical violence from her demonic foes, who strove to keep her from Mass and meditation alike. More insidious still were demonic efforts to plant doubts in her mind about matters of faith.[347] A number of Christine's travails were more sexually explicit than the proverbial handsome buck or intrusive Freudian snake. For instance, over the course of six weeks, a demon appeared to Christine every night with a mother and child in tow. He repeatedly copulated with the woman, remarking, "There is no joy greater than the joining of a man to a woman and that which a woman has with a child."[348]

It is important to keep in mind, however, that each of these women was also party to divine consolations, which presumably more than compensated for the traumatic side of their spiritual lives. With respect to Benevenuta, we are told explicitly that her diabolical tribulations were followed by saintly or angelic visitations. Sometimes even the Virgin Mary herself would make an appearance.[349] Christine's consolations were frequently cast into a nuptial mold, in keeping with her northern climes.[350]

In Ermine's case, however, it was not divine revelation, but demonic activity that was at the very center of her spirituality, so there was no parallel respite. Ermine's life is devoid of bridal mysticism. In its stead we find an unprecedented degree of demon-ridden eroticism: the possibility of a perverted coupling with demons supplanting the focus on a mystical union with Christ. Ermine's extreme plight points to a progression at work. The twelfth-century Christina of Markyate also endured bouts with lust. But her struggle was with an abstract devil working through a weak, all too human but essentially good, cleric. Eventually, she was rewarded for her struggles by a special intimacy with Christ, her spouse. Odilia's demonically inspired lust was also an internal torment. Even so, Satan's power was no longer so abstract. Odilia's temptations were engineered by demons conjured up by human agents—priestly magi who sought physical consummation.

Some two hundred years after Odilia, demons and magic continue to loom large: indeed one of the demons afflicting Ermine claims that her mystical perception of the Mass was a result of sorcery. Odilia's demons had identified themselves by specific names, but were still internalized; Ermine's demons, who frequently identified themselves as specific saints, were apprehended by her corporeal vision, hence appearing to her as objective reality. Worst of all, in Ermine's life, any possibility of an intimacy with Christ seems to be entirely effaced by the ongoing torment of demons. And as was the case with the progressively somatized and eroticized Christ, these maleficent agents of evil appeared in physical bodies in quest of sexual consummation.

CHAPTER 7

Descent into Hell

We must realize also that, just as an illicit and unlawful
love may happen to the outer man—as that, for instance,
he should love a harlot or adulteress instead of his bride or
wife; so also may the inner man, that it is to say, the soul,
come to attach its love not to its lawful Bridegroom, who
is the Word of God, but to some seducer or adulterer. . . .
And this spiritual love of the soul does flame out, as we
have taught, sometimes to certain spirits of evil.

—Origen, *On the Song of Songs*[1]

The Sons of God and the Daughters of Men: A Redux

Once upon a time there were five widows: Bridget of Sweden, Margery
Kempe, Dorothea of Montau, Odilia of Liège, and Ermine of Reims. Three of
them were lucky. Bridget of Sweden was engaged to Christ—an arrangement
that brought her both personal satisfaction and power. Margery also prospered
in her own way: she was engaged to the son, but married his father. Dorothea
enjoyed parallel prestige: she was not just destined to become the bride, but
the wife of the Son of God. The marriage was consummated, and Dorothea
proved remarkably fecund. But the other two widows did not fare so well.
Odilia's allure had less success with the celestial bridegroom than the local
clergy, who resorted to magical aphrodisiacs to win her. Although she did not
succumb, she was nevertheless subjected to the full range of libidinous urges
that medical experts projected onto women, and then some, to the extent that
she felt physically defiled. But it was Ermine who came up particularly short
in the mystical marketplace. She was never wooed by Christ but rather by a

series of incubi, often credibly disguised in various ways, sometimes seeking physical consummation. Nor was Ermine alone. As we shall see, religiously inclined women seemed to be progressively confronted by an array of ever-more embodied experiences, some of which were distinctly unsavory. We are entering upon a time when mystical marriages with Christ begin to misfire, and the mysteries surrounding Genesis 6 resurface with a vengeance. For both Odilia of Liège and Ermine of Reims ran the risk of uniting themselves with the alternative sons of God, whether this is understood in terms of depraved members of the clergy or, worse still, fallen angels.[2] In short, Tertullian's grim nightmare of sexual commerce between the human and the angelic race was making a comeback.

In many ways, the Cathars had led the way. They believed that the human race resulted from the debacle of angelic entanglement with the material world, the side effect of a cosmic disaster. When Satan revolted against God and was cast out of heaven, he retaliated by creating his own world—a material one in wicked (and somewhat tasteless) imitation of the spiritual homeland. It was populated by angels who had been tricked into material bodies with the promise of wives.[3] Their bodies were synonymous with the "tunics of skin" that the Old Testament God had administered to the newly fallen Adam and Eve.[4] According to Dominican Moneta of Cremona (d. 1241), Satan set the example for what was expected of the fallen angels by first corrupting Eve with his tail; she, in turn, corrupted Adam.[5] The union of Adam and Eve was interpreted as the forbidden fruit with different degrees of literalism: "the tree which was in the midst of Paradise is the womb of woman."[6] The account of the reformed Cathar Bonacursus (fl. 1176–90) further avers that Cain was the devil's progeny by Eve, while Abel was the son of Adam.[7] Such tales effortlessly segue into a dualist version of Genesis 6.2, whereby the miscegenation between Eve's daughters and demons produced a race of giants.[8]

We have seen that orthodoxy tended to choose the dominant Augustinian alternative, interpreting Genesis 6 as describing the fall from grace of certain holy men. This view was ultimately canonized in the *glossa ordinaria*.[9] Between the fourth and the twelfth centuries, however, there were a few holdouts who were not inclined to read the antediluvian disaster metaphorically. The ninth-century Hincmar of Reims (d. 882), for example, claimed that all sorcery "arises from a certain pestiferous union between humans and demons."[10] Hincmar gives special attention to the ongoing threat that demons posed to society in general, but to human sexuality in particular—a threat that could manifest itself in various ways. First, there is the stimulation of perverse desires: How else would one explain David's illicit lust for Bathsheba or Amnon's incestuous love for his sister, Thamar, Hincmar reasons.[11] In a similar vein, Hincmar relates a miracle from the life of St. Basil in which a man uses magic in order to marry a woman who was not only far beyond his reach socially but also destined for the cloister. The lovesick swain paid a necromancer to bewitch his beloved. This proved to be a sound investment because the girl instantly began burning with such love for her aspiring groom that she warned her parents she would die if they refused to allow the marriage.[12] Even in Hincmar's own parish, there was a man so violently in love with a woman that he managed to overcome her parents' reluctance to the match. Once wed, however, the young couple proved incapable of consummating the marriage—the source of such great frustration that the man threatened to kill his wife if Hincmar refused to grant them a divorce. Fortunately, the good bishop intervened with penance and "church medicine" (*medicina ecclesiastica*), vanquishing the spell that held the couple hostage.[13] Hincmar expostulates at length against the horrible ligatures responsible for sterility that were wrought by spiteful women working wool or weaving textiles, presumably because they were adept at tying knots.[14]

Nor did demonic efforts to undermine humankind stop there. Hincmar further attested to a brood of demons, referred to by the inhabitants of Gaul as Dusi, who sought coition with mortal women. Yet it was impossible to eradicate this problem because the tainted women tended to keep such relations secret. Their spiritual and physical health were therefore compromised because freedom from sexual thralldom could only be achieved through confession, in conjunction with strenuous intervention by the appropriate authorities. For instance, a neighboring priest told Hincmar about the plight of a nun who was only saved from demonic molestation by confession and a series of industrial-strength ecclesiastical purifications. Even after the demon had departed, the woman was afflicted by ulcers covering her entire body from where the demon had touched her. After much trial and error by the local clergy, the sores were finally dispelled by a salubrious combination of holy salt and chrism.[15]

Such incidents aside, many religious authorities may have been mistrustful of women's accounts of their contacts with the supernatural. This level of skepticism in the clerical world is famously articulated by the *Canon Episcopi* (ca. 906) and later reiterated by Burchard of Worms (d. 1025), which dismiss the stories of women's night flights with the goddess Diana as products of demonic illusion.[16] Burchard also seems to disparage belief in incubi and succubi. He assigns penance to whoever believes in "Sylvaticae"—women who take a material shape when they wish, and show themselves to their lovers, but can just as quickly vanish into thin air.[17] Be that as it may, the possibility of supernatural miscegenation continued to find expression through other avenues. In the twelfth century, uncanny lovers achieve a new prominence in vernacular literature via the so-called matter of Britain. The magician Merlin was touted as the product of a union between a princess and a mysterious youth. When King Vortigern inquired into Merlin's parentage, his mother related, " 'when I was among my companions in our chambers, a very handsome young man appeared to me and, embracing me tightly in his arms, kissed me over and over again. And though he stayed with me for a little while, he suddenly vanished without a trace. Many times afterward he would come and speak to me secretly, without appearing. He visited me for a long time in this fashion and had sex with me frequently in the shape of a man. Then he went away, leaving me pregnant.' " When a wise man was consulted, he attested to the plausibility of the story, remarking, " 'Between earth and moon, there are certain spirits which we call incubus demons. These beings possess partly human and partly angelic nature, and when they wish they can assume human form and have intercourse with women.' "[18] Marie de France's protagonist in *Yonec* is a shape-shifting faery king who mates with a mortal woman. But in Marie's lai of *Lanval*, the faery lover is a woman—which is more representative of what will become the romance paradigm.[19]

Merlin is something of an exception for this period because his ancestry was explicitly demonic. But, generally, folkloric icons seem to be possessed of a different pedigree than the sons of God and did not readily conform with the categories of either angel or demon. Even so, outside of their romance provenance, they seldom acted as forces for good. Walter Map represents the various supernatural lovers that people his *Courtier's Trifles* (between 1181 and 1193) as either true occurrences or at least current hearsay. The female faeries he presents, moreover, range from morally ambiguous to downright sinister. Several of them appear at midday, which tacitly aligns them with the noonday demon (*daemonio meridiano*) alluded to in Psalm 90.6.[20] Moreover the woman who appears to Gerbert of Auriallac (d. 1003), facilitating his ascent to the papal throne as Sylvester II, is explicitly named Meridiana.[21]

These women's contentious relations with the holy render them particularly suspect. The wife of a certain Henno, who first appeared to him in a forest glade at noon, would leave Mass before the consecration of the host to enter a bath in which she would assume her true form as a dragon.[22] Gerbert's relations with Meridiana seem to have cast a pall over his sacerdotal ministry. "During the whole course of his priesthood, when the sacrament of the Lord's body and blood was celebrated he never tasted it, either in fear or respect, but by the most wary concealment he feigned the act which he could not perform." He was only freed from Meridiana's influence by a public confession.[23]

Furthermore, any children resulting from miscegenation with Map's supernatural creatures suffered from strange infirmities, tacitly suggesting that such unions were cursed by God. Alnoth, the offspring of Eadric Wild and his nameless wife, although a man of great holiness, suffered from a seemingly incurable palsy.[24] This blight upon posterity will later be epitomized by the memorable children of the faery Melusine—a serpent wife who, like Henno's bride, would also absent herself from Mass in order to revert to her true reptilian form.[25]

Whatever their alarming traits, Map still distinguishes these women from incubi and succubi. Thus the account of Eadric and his holy heir, Alnoth, is followed by the comment: "We have heard of demons that are *incubi* and *succubi*, and the dangers of unions with them; but rarely or never do we read in the old stories of heirs or offspring, of them, who ended their days prosperously, as did this Alnoth."[26] But when Meridiana herself attempts to reassure Gerbert that she was not a demon, the distinction between types of supernatural lover begins to dissolve: "You fear, perhaps, an illusion, and are meaning to evade the subtlety of a Succubus in my person. You are mistaken. Those whom you fear are equally shy of the deceits of men, and do not trust themselves to any without a pledge of faith or other security, and only bring sin to those whom they beguile."[27] Yet the fact that Map applies epithets like "daughter of Babylon" to Meridiana, and that the lady herself attempts to swindle Gerbert into dying unconfessed, further suggests that her true nature is, in fact, demonic.[28]

As supernatural lovers become progressively tainted with demonic features, the incubus, the male-seeming demon, gradually gains center stage, at least in clerical discourse.[29] In the twelfth century, it is matrons who are primarily preyed upon. The pious mother of Guibert of Nogent, a young widow who would have been considered seething with stored-up sexual juice, was seemingly primed for just such an encounter.[30] Fortunately, she attracted the kind of incubus that was inclined to smother its victim to death—a figure known since antiquity and more in keeping with her disinclination for sex. But parallel encounters are generally acted out sexually and, from the twelfth century onward, progressively described as mutually gratifying. In a miracle related in the life of St. Bernard of Clairvaux (d. 1153), an incubus seduced a noblewoman. Her consent was followed by an idiosyncratic ritual. "And when he obtained the assent of the woman, with his arms stretched out, he placed one of his hands on her feet, and he covered her head with the other hand and with this sign of the contract he betrothed her to himself."[31] There is a certain irony to the fact that an incubus, who clearly constructed himself as a type of groom, should first appear in the life of the saint who so winningly presented the celestial groom to the world.

Bernard was also at the forefront of the resistance against the Cathars: he was the first authority that Eberwin, abbot of Steinfeld, consulted concerning what is arguably the first Cathar sighting. With supernatural miscegenation so dramatically placed in the foreground by the Cathar heresy, orthodoxy attempted to put an end to any possibility of a human-angelic hybrid. In 1215, Lateran IV declared in its opening statement of faith that God created all creatures—both the material and the purely spiritual beings. The implication was that all angels, whether good or evil, were austerely spiritual creatures without bodies.[32] But in striking demonstration of the perverse principle "less is more," the demonic body was destined to loom even larger in the medieval psyche once it was determined not to exist, corresponding with an inflated interest in angels and demons among orthodox authorities.

This learned fixation is first palpable in the writings of William of Auvergne, writing in the wake of Lateran IV—the first scholastic theologian to devote himself extensively to angelology. In the penultimate chapter of his monumental work *On the Universe*, he entertains the question "Concerning demon incubi and succubi, and whether they are able to generate." It is a conflicted performance. On the one hand, William considers the evidence for miscegenation between angels and humans to be overwhelming. Not only do historical narratives ascribe such mixed parentage to the Cypriot, Hunnish, and Trojan races, but he also finds the marriage of the sons of God with the daughters of men, not to mention their gargantuan progeny, credible. While acknowledging that apocryphal literature is much more forthcoming about this episode, William defers to Paul's insistence that women cover their heads as evidence of incubi: "certain men understand this to be on account of the evil angels, namely the demon incubus, and these men judge that the beauty of women's hair especially provoke and inflame to lust." On the other hand, William cannot deny that there are certain doctors who are inclined to interpret the episode with the sons of God metaphorically, "not wishing to believe lustful concupiscence in spiritual substances." He does concede that this last group has a point and ultimately is forced to corroborate the impossibility for immaterial angels, good or bad, to generate or even feel lust.[33]

Thus keeping faith with Lateran IV, William was obliged to recognize that immaterial entities were incapable of reproduction and that the giants were, in all likelihood, human, as were the Huns. Even so, he is not prepared to let it go at that: "Someone may say, perhaps, that those women, as were mentioned in the aforesaid histories, were female witches [*mulieres maleficae*] who, on account of evil magic [*maleficia magica*] removed themselves from the middle of human habitation, then for this reason fleeing to deserted land and forests, lived there, where they most easily and familiarly adhered to demons, which were their companions [*familiares*]: from which familiarity followed libidinous habits and couplings, from whom the entire generation of a race proceeded." Although William again acknowledges that the demons could not really generate, he nevertheless maintains that they were somehow able to procure generation. He attempts to substantiate this conjecture by exploring some of the more bizarre aspects of female reproductive capabilities. For instance, William ingeniously advances theories of parthenogenesis, pointing to instances of spontaneous pregnancy wrought solely by a breeze.[34]

Even though William does his best to reconcile demonic immateriality with a theory of demonic insemination, it remained for Thomas Aquinas to have the final word. Thomas overcame what had to be the most daunting demonic physical handicap of all, immateriality, by devising a way in which the incubi could still debauch and impregnate by garnering sperm from a man as a succubus, which was subsequently injected into a woman by an incubus.[35]

Pop theology also played an important quasi-evidentiary role in the growing awareness of incubi. In his *Dialogue on Miracles*, Caesarius of Heisterbach (d. 1235) demonstrates an unfeigned fascination with demons of all stripes, especially the masterful self-fashioning of their simulated bodies.[36] In a single chapter chronicling the demonic misadventures of Herman, abbot of Marrienstatt, demons assumed a series of baffling forms: a thick-set peasant with fashionably dressed hair (in the front at least, but an absolute mess at the back), a calf's tail, a woman with a black veil, a dragon the length of a spear, a series of infant-sized mites with faces the color of glowing iron, a huge Ethiopian, a very bright eye the size of a fist, and a misty insubstantial cloud.[37]

But Caesarius's awareness of the potential of demons as lovers seemingly trumps his gratuitous fascination with their shape-shifting virtuosity. Hence we learn that despite their seemingly unpropitious bodies, which were comprised primarily from wasted human seed, demons proved to be prodigious breeders. Caesarius relates how the Goths expelled all their deformed women from their ranks, who, in turn, were beset upon by incubus demons, giving birth to the Hunnish nation; how Merlin was fathered by an incubus; and how the very kings of England descended from a "phantom mother."[38]

Like the demon in Bernard's vita who was intent on some sort of marriage, the demons presented by Caesarius likewise appear surprisingly honorable in their intentions. Equally remarkable is the way in which demons seem to be setting their sights higher, advancing from the allure of the worldly matron to the cloistered brides of Christ. These "honorable" demons seemed to be cut from the same cloth: a "very good looking and well dressed" demon appeared to a nun of Nivelles "and began to woo her with the words of a lover, offering her jewels, praising the fruitfulness of marriage and scoffing at the barrenness of virginity."[39]

Not all of Caesarius's nuns could be chided for their virginity, however. Aleidis was the former concubine of a priest in Bonn who had died by his own hand. Filled with horror, she rushed to enter a convent only to experience a different kind of horror when a handsome devil began to woo her. When she at first rebuffed him, he responded, "'Kind Aleidis, do not speak like that; only consent to me and I will give you a husband who shall be well born, honorable, and upright. Why should you torture yourself with hunger in this miserable place. . . . Go back to the world and enjoy the pleasures which God created for man; you shall want nothing under my protection.'"[40] The demon who approached the novice Euphemia employed similar rhetoric: "'do not be converted [to the religious life], but take instead a young and comely husband.'" (When she said the angelic salutation, however, he jumped out the window in the shape of an enormous dog.)[41] Caesarius also took the trouble to clarify aspects of Merlin's puzzling parentage. In Geoffrey of Monmouth, the wizard's mother had been the daughter of the king of Demetia, who "lived among the nuns" (*inter monachas degebat*) at the time that King Vortigern summoned her.[42] The implication was that she was not necessarily herself a nun. But in Caesarius's rendering, Merlin was born from the liaison between an incubus and a nun.[43] And thus while the afflicted nun in Hincmar seems to have been something of an anomaly for her age, the representations of Caesarius suggest that the demonic seduction of holy women had reached epidemic proportions by the thirteenth century.

Fortunately, not one of Caesarius's religious women took the bait by giving in to diabolical suasions. This is just as well, judging from the sorry fate of the priest's daughter who did succumb and went mad as a result. (The strange symptom of her madness was that she ran around with a little purse full of worms that she would snack on.) But in her case as well, the matrimonial overtones are sustained. When the father attempts to conceal his daughter, his questionable son-in-law shows up shouting, "'Where's my wife?'" and kills the priest with a single blow.[44] We know from other contemporary accounts, however, that not all religious women were as resilient against their demonic suitors as was Caesarius's cohort. Indeed, Thomas of Cantimpré claims to have often heard his female penitents admit to such relations. This dire form of female weakness was seemingly on the rise. By the fourteenth century, religious women's special susceptibility to incubi had become something of a commonplace: thus Bishop Alvar Pelayo (d. 1352) relates that incubi were so firmly ensconced in a certain convent that they were impervious to prayer and penances.[45]

A Mystical Marriage Gone Wrong

And thus, with a new spiritual democracy in the ascendant and female mystics of disparate backgrounds for the first time enjoying the embraces of the celestial bridegroom, demon lovers were not only appearing but gaining momentum—with religiously inclined women seemingly their preferred objects of desire. Indeed, it is no exaggeration to say that the interest in holy women and demon lovers advanced in lockstep, sponsored, as they were, by the same personnel. Caesarius of Heisterbach's literary legacy is a case in point. Not only was Caesarius responsible for the vita of St. Elisabeth of Hungary (d. 1231), the first contemporary matron to receive papal canonization,[46] but he was also a fervent admirer of the various holy women of Liège. This admiration is expressed in a handful of tales in his *Dialogue on Miracles*. For instance, Caesarius tells how his friend, Walter, abbot of the neighboring community of Villers, received the gift of tears (a pious trait made famous by Mary of Oignies) from a Beguine.[47] Caesarius's demonically challenged nun of Nivelles was from the same region and shared in the same Cistercian ambiance as these holy women. More compelling still is the role of Thomas of Cantimpré. Not only was Thomas a figure of unquestionable importance for Beguine hagiography, but he was also the author of that strange medley *Concerning Bees*—a work that is teaming with demons. We have seen how Thomas's medical studies made him privy to the ill effects of sexual abstinence on women. This apprehension would receive compelling corroboration from physician Arnaldus of Villanova (d. ca. 1312), who actually recommended that widows and nuns use dildos to offset the threat of hysteria.[48] Religious authorities' increased medical proficiency could only stoke their fears about the susceptibilities of the female body. Such apprehensions both fostered and corroborated the progressive tendency to link religious women with incubi.

Meanwhile, increased emphasis on consent, whether in the determination of sin or merit or in the formation of the marriage bond, had left its mark on unions with Christ and demons alike. It was the woman's consent that enabled the demon's strange ritual of betrothal described in the life of Bernard of Clairvaux, mysteriously tracking some of the contemporary changes in the theology and canon law of marriage. Likewise, when Caesarius's importunate demon recognizes that his suit is going nowhere and reveals his true identity, the theologically savvy nun asks why a disembodied being would be so intent on intercourse. " 'Only consent, all I want is your consent to marriage,' " is the demon's equally savvy answer.[49] The contractual nature of these bonds is not only shaped by marriage but also anticipates the treatment of the sorcerer's consensual pact with the devil articulated by theologians such as Thomas Aquinas.[50] Furthermore, canonists and theologians alike would determine that verbal consent was not absolutely required in marriage when the intent could be discerned, anticipating a parallel articulation of the tacit pact with the devil.[51]

The emphasis on consensuality in demonic courtship rendered any woman who suffered such demonic infestation automatically culpable. The alterations in another of Thomas of Cantimpré's twice-told tales are extremely revealing in this respect. According to his life of Lutgard, a nun in her community who was afflicted by an incubus was freed by the prayers of the saint. Thomas lingers over the incident, perturbed by the fact that an incubus was permitted to afflict a virginal nun in the first place: "Certainly it is by a wondrous, a most wondrous, permission of the Saviour and Redeemer that Satan should receive power over a pure body, even a virginal body—power that is not only exercised for the pollution of the flesh, but can even proceed to the corruption of the mind and the detriment of the soul. What is cleaner than a bride of Christ? What is cleaner than a virgin who is 'holy in body and spirit'? And yet it was to such a one that we perceived such things happening." Thomas did have the beginnings of a theory, however. He believed that God's judgment was just, albeit hidden, and that the "women are brought to this defilement through an illicit excess of temptation [*per excessum tentationis illicitum*]."[52]

It is by no means clear what an "illicit excess of temptation" means. Illicit insofar as it is beyond what the devil should presume? It is unlikely insofar as Paul had assured his followers that God would not test them beyond their endurance (1 Cor. 10.13). Or was the nun in question in some mysterious way responsible because she did not temper her response? Thomas's position is clarified by the time he revisits the same incident again in *Concerning Bees*, now furnishing details that make the nun's complicity absolutely clear. Apparently when her dilemma was first revealed in confession, the nun claimed that she had never consented to the incubus. Thomas was skeptical in the extreme, doubting that God would permit this to happen to "an unconsenting soul." When he forced the nun to take, as he called them, "horrific oaths" (*horrificis iuramentis*) in support of her position, she broke down and confessed "with tears and blushing" that she was corrupted first mentally and then carnally. Thomas says with evident relief, "Behold how hidden and marvelous is the judgment of equity." The nun for her part almost died of grief and confessed every day, but nothing seemed to help: not the sign of the cross, not holy water, not even the Eucharist. Finally, the incubus was routed by Lutgard's prayers. Thomas concludes, "Indeed we believe and confess (however with the sound judgment of a better opinion) that sex with the demon was the punishment of the fault [*culpa*] rather than the fault itself, because she wept and sorrowed bitterly afterward from her own sin."[53] The recasting of the original story is also indicative of Thomas's progressive rigidity toward religious women.

The omnipresence of the male-seeming incubus contravenes the literary convention of representing faery lovers as female, as well as the tradition of the desert fathers, who tended to be harassed by female-seeming demons.[54] But a creeping cognizance of women's heightened susceptibility seems to have overshadowed any awareness of this change. Later authorities will rationalize women's vulnerability to demonic attacks in terms of the transmission of doctrine, which descended from God, to Christ, to man, and only then to woman—an indirect legacy fully justifying Paul's censure of women's teaching (1 Tim. 2.12). Women, in contrast, received teaching directly from the devil (Gen. 3.1–5) and then, lacking the discernment of spirits, passed it on to man—an argument that would be cited with approval by the later writers on witchcraft.[55] The legacy of women's mutable bodies and even more malleable souls was also believed to impart a heightened susceptibility to sins of the flesh, rendering them easy marks for the incubus.[56] The most extreme expression of this bias appears in the notorious chapter of *The Hammer of Witches* (*Malleus maleficarum* ca. 1486), which traces women's involvement in witchcraft to active lust, especially manifest in their voluntary subjection to incubi.[57]

The intense interest in demons and the rise of mysticism were concurrent phenomena: William of Auvergne and James of Vitry were both students at the University of Paris in the early thirteenth century—their presence there could even have overlapped. Thomas of Cantimpré and Thomas Aquinas both studied with Albert the Great in Cologne at the same time. It is no accident that female susceptibility to demons would increase exponentially in the context of a mystical spirituality, wherein the inspired woman is already regarded as having one foot in the spirit world. Many, if not most, theologians believed that mystical experiences required the mediation of angels. Bernard of Clairvaux had placed considerable emphasis on the role of angels in the spiritual ascent: angels receive specific petitions through our prayers.[58] However antithetical bodies may be to their nature, angels acquire them in service to humanity.[59] The bridegroom's leap upon the mountains is but a metaphor for his appearance through angelic intermediaries (Sg 2.8); his bounding over the barren hills represents his triumph over the fallen angels.[60]

Bernard's message concerning the necessary ubiquity of angels was taken very much to heart in Beguine circles. In the prologue to the life of Mary of Oignies, James of Vitry refers to a woman who was frequently raptured, but "would remain immobile in whatever posture she was placed until she returned to herself, but she never fell, no matter how far she was bent, for her familiar spirit [*familiari spiritu*] was holding her up." Mary herself was "frequently visited with consolations of holy angels," as was Lutgard.[61] Whenever Margaret of Ypres was weak from prayer, two angels would bear her up. An "ever familiar spirit" danced constant attendance upon Ida of Nivelles.[62] Ida of Louvain received communion from an angel.[63] An unnamed woman confessed to Thomas of Cantimpré (perhaps as a penitent) that she was privy to conversations with angels. Not only was she possessed of the remarkable capacity to recognize in the visages of those among her contemporaries who would be saved, she also received visions of the elect who were yet to be born. Thomas believed this kind of prophecy was probably dependent on the mediation of angels—although he was not absolutely certain that the angels in question were necessarily of the unfallen variety.[64]

Perhaps most important, however, is the fact that the religious vocation is grounded in desire for a mystical marriage with Christ: a love story that, as we have seen, increasingly sought erotic expression. Mystical theologians like Bernard of Clairvaux perceived carnal and spiritual love on a continuum, ideally possessed of an evolutionary momentum that encouraged a movement from lower to higher.[65] Nevertheless, Bernard also recognized the possibility for a devolution: "[The soul] strays—as is the nature of a spiritual substance, in its affections, or rather defections."[66] Two exemplary tales apprise us of the volatility of love in this context. The nameless woman invoked by Thomas of Cantimpré who, driven mad by lust for a certain youth, besought his house in the hopes of sexual satisfaction was stopped by a vision of the bleeding Christ. He sang her a love song, and her temptation subsided.[67] But if the quest for human love is sometimes resolved by its divine correlative, the pattern can also work in reverse. Stephen of Bourbon (d. 1256) recounts the lamentable history of a nun who thought that her exceptional piety merited special spiritual "consolations." The demon appeared before her one night as Christ with a glittering retinue of angels and apostles. He returned the next night alone, however, and promptly seduced her.[68] On surface, the very different fates of these two protagonists appear to be more a matter of luck than of merit. A woman seeking a carnal love rises to a union with Christ; a nun seeking a union with Christ descends to carnal love with a demon.

Thomas's heroine was the fortunate one. Yet it is interesting that the anecdote is framed in such a way that might suggest the random nature of her spiritual destiny. For the incident follows fast upon a discussion of demons, introduced with the comfortless rubric *Concerning certain spiritual wickedness in the heavens which never ceases to tempt.* Apparently there are special demons, more powerful than all the others, who "frequently mix themselves with corporeal apparitions." And these super demons delight in the deception and damnation of humans even more than their diabolical colleagues. It is through the work of these astute demons that the most perfect individuals fall. For while lesser kinds of demons eventually give up when thwarted, these demons never do. They will circle and torment their select prey until he or she is absolutely enervated.[69]

In the face of adversaries like this, can there be any real certainty that Thomas's protagonist, wooed by the true Christ, was any better than the debauched nun described by Stephen of Bourbon? How does one differentiate between conjugal consent to Christ and a pact with the devil?

John Gerson and the Evil Queen

The scholastic world could hardly remain indifferent to such matters of religious perplexity. Indeed, in the fourteenth century, a *quaestio* began making the rounds in academic circles that addressed the problem of whether a woman worshipping Satan in the appearance of Christ sinned mortally.[70] It was in response to spiritual conundra such as these that a series of treatises on spiritual discernment appeared—a genre devoted to differentiating between divine and diabolical forces.[71] A number of scholars, including myself, have discussed the prolific contribution of John Gerson, chancellor of the University of Paris, to this genre, and his vigorous efforts at curtailing female mysticism.[72] His tactics were many: he medicalized the discourse surrounding visions, associating female revelations with disease and dementia; impugned the motives of women who revealed their revelations by arguing that women were enjoined by scripture to remain silent and subject; and attacked the clerics who supported female mystics.[73] On the most public level, Gerson addressed *On the Proving of Spirits*, his most celebrated work on spiritual discernment, to the assembled dignitaries at the Council of Constance (1415) to challenge the recent canonization of Bridget of Sweden.[74] Gerson was one of the most prominent intellectuals of his age, and many of his works were widely circulated. *On the Proving of Spirits*, in particular, was a phenomenal success.[75]

But Gerson was much more than the average clerical intellectual: he was a gifted writer with a remarkable range. Comfortable in both the vernacular and Latin, Gerson could reach a large audience of probably unprecedented breadth. He also had the ability to write in many genres: not only scholarly treatises and sermons, but poetry and song as well. Thus equipped, a number of his initiatives for undermining female mysticism were flexible and subtle, manipulating metaphor and images in different registers. In this context, I am particularly concerned with his efforts to dissociate women and bridal mysticism. This might seem like an impossible task—especially since Gerson seemed prepared to grant women's special entitlement in this domain. Indeed, he acknowledged that women possessed a particular susceptibility to certain supernatural experiences that he likened to the melting or liquefying love associated with "the holy soul in the Song of Songs."[76] In addition to recognizing that this capacity was a crucial assist in the ascent toward God, he also noted that all the authorities, from Paul to Bonaventure, saw learning as an impediment, arguing that God could be reached through ecstatic love alone.[77]

And yet Gerson clearly did not consider this an open-and-shut case. An individual was dependent on the senses for receiving information from the external world, and sensual impressions would be stored in the imagination as phantasms. But if someone who was still vice-ridden were to attempt to meditate, he or she could end up wallowing in the filthiest images and thoughts.[78] Proper contemplation entailed the ability to abstract intellectual concepts from the sensually garnered phantasms residing in the imagination, and this required training.[79] Those who were insufficiently trained could fall prey to illusions from the devil. An overreliance on the imagination, with its sensual diet of corporeal phantasms, was dangerous. It could even result in insanity. So it was that a number of people who wish to be reputed holy end up in error. Their reveries on the elevation of the host or the Crucifixion could lead them to believe that they were actually perceiving Christ in his corporeal form, or hearing the voice of Christ or his saints.[80] Those who began their meditations by first focusing on corporeal things were likewise at risk: concentrated focus on any given object could lead to all kinds of mental disorders, as is apparent from those suffering from lovesickness.[81] At heart, Gerson was inclined to favor the kind of contemplation associated with abstractive, intellectual knowledge.[82] But the fact that Gerson often returned to the question of "whether it is better to have knowledge of God through a repentant affectivity rather than through an investigative intellect" suggests that this remained a real question for him.[83]

Gerson's contemplative elitism was more a question of university training versus a person's religious status in the world. He did not in any way hold with the traditional perception of the religious orders as the heirs to the contemplative life—far from it. In fact, Gerson, who was intensely critical of any such monopoly, was sympathetic to movements such as the contemporary Devotio Moderna that had arisen in the Low Countries and defended its adherents' right to pursue a religious vocation in the world at the Council of Constance.[84] Even so, he was apprehensive about lay access to scripture and the increasing number of patristic and other religious texts in translation.[85] This kind of ambivalence carries over into his spiritual direction of his sisters. On the one hand, he encouraged his sisters to embrace a pious regime of chastity and prayer while living at home with their parents, and he wrote vernacular works such as *The Mountain of Contemplation* (1400) explicitly in support of this modus vivendi. On the other hand, *The Mountain* continues to divide contemplation into two parts: learned and affective. The first kind is the particular domain of the cleric, grappling with God and the mysteries of faith through reason, pitting himself against unbelievers and heretics, and occasionally even stumbling upon "new truths" to be revealed in public. This type of contemplation is, arguably, presented by Gerson as the higher path: it is considered "more subtle" and "not for ordinary people." The second kind of contemplation, however, "concentrates principally on loving God and enjoying his goodness without trying to acquire clearer knowledge than that which the faith has inspired and given. To this type of contemplation ordinary people can come."[86]

Despite Gerson's proclivity for university training and his tendency to look askance at some of the traditional religious orders of his own time, Gerson was a fervent admirer of St. Bernard of Clairvaux, particularly his sermons on the Song of Songs. From Gerson's perspective, no other work "handed down the arc of learning contemplation with such order." He repeated with approval a comment from the sermons: "This vision is not of industry but of grace; of revelation, not investigation."[87] And so Gerson was divided: although drawn to Bernard's affectivity, he remained extremely apprehensive about the spousal imagery at the center of Bernard's sermons, at least for private devotional purposes, and this apprehension is apparent in a number of ways. In *The Mountain*, Gerson describes his sisters as unmarried virgins, who, according to Paul, are free to please the Lord as opposed to a husband (1 Cor. 7.34). Yet he does not take the next obvious step taken by Tertullian long ago and marry them to Christ.[88] In fact, it is rather remarkable that in a treatise expressly addressing the subject of contemplation and one dedicated to virgins devoted to God, there are but three references to the soul as Christ's bride.[89] At one with this imagistic solicitude is Gerson's explicit warning to his sisters about the dangers of bridal mysticism. "It is true that this topic is perhaps too lofty and rather dangerous to deal with at the beginning of one's conversion to the mystical life, for when one believes one is thinking about spiritual marriage, one easily can slide into thoughts about carnal marriage."[90]

Gerson was, in fact, equipped with an arsenal of hair-raising stories in which women came to grief precisely over the confusion of the two types of love, though he considerately spared his sisters the details. Elsewhere, however, he alleges that some women out of ignorance "have been affected by a harmful love toward God or toward other holy persons, rather than being moved by true, holy and sincere charity." The Beguines and Beghards were identified as especially culpable "because of their excessive love that was disguised as devotion."[91] At various junctures Gerson also takes the opportunity to invert or satirize the imagery associated with Beguine circles. Hence God's "gluing of souls" was revisited in terms of the mystic and her chosen clerical confidant diabolically glued together by a false affection, hurtling the religious twosome toward ruination.[92] Likewise, with regard to the annihilating love of mystical union, Gerson observed that the women in question were "not so much insane with love as out of their minds [*insanias amantium immo et amentium*]."[93]

Still, this did not mean that the *sponsa Christi* was banished from Gerson's purview. Far from it. Gerson was at work on a treatise on the Song of Songs when he was overtaken by death. Not surprisingly, it was to scholastic methodology that he turned in order to ward off the kind of excesses he deplored. "It behooves us . . . to use the scholastic rules of theology and philosophy, especially when we seek to convey the Song of Songs to a general understanding, so that no one be made to doubt the chastity of the inner senses, which the smoke of the carnal or literal meaning obstructs. Nor should anyone incur the scandal of a disgraceful carnality. It would be shameful to report what I, as an expert [in spiritual matters], have heard; for it would offend chaste ears." And thus affectivity is kept at bay while Gerson sets out to determine "the quiddity of love in its different species."[94]

The imagery of the Canticles also makes frequent appearances in the various typological lists that are one of the hallmarks of his treatises. In the vernacular work *Spiritual Poverty*, for instance, the last in a series detailing different kinds of affection is love for God, which is compared with married love: "the most high and perfect and worthy affection . . . for with the other [types of love] one is kissed on the feet or the hands, but, according to the declaration of St. Bernard, for this affection one is kissed on the mouth; and this affection makes the soul, who has the ability, as near and familiar with God as husband and wife." In his *Tract of the Eye*, the last in a series of metaphoric eyes are the eyes of love, representing affect and intellect. "And thus there are two eyes of the bride and groom in the Canticles, namely of cognition and of love."[95]

Gerson's evocations of the mystical marriage tend to walk the line between tradition and innovation. The sermon *On the Marriage of Christ and the Church*, for example, uses ancient imagery to address the dire straits of the contemporary papal schism. In keeping with the tradition of the bishop's marriage to his see, the pope is presented as the vicar of Christ and hence the church's earthly groom. In this context, however, Gerson manages to pose what is probably an unprecedented question, emphasizing the late medieval preoccupation with magic: What if the papal groom were "frigid or bewitched [*maleficiatus*] and on that account was incapable of the spiritual generation of children?"[96] In a similar vein, *The Removability of the Spouse from the Church* daringly examines the conditions under which an unsuitable pontifical bridegroom could be removed from office.[97]

The Virgin Mary's traditional association with the bride in the Song of Songs might have presented an obstacle to Gerson's efforts at reorientation. But Gerson was by no means backward in according the Virgin her due. And indeed Mary in her spousal capacity was a theme upon which Gerson himself was wont to wax effusively—a predilection he acknowledges elsewhere. In his simulated dialogue on the Magnificat, the disciple interrupts the master to complain that his exegesis on Mary as the bride in the Song of Songs is derailing the explication of Mary's own personal prayer.[98] Even so, the Virgin's preeminence as bride is still recast in a quasi-masculine mode by virtue of Gerson's constant inclusion of her husband, Joseph. For Gerson was tireless in his efforts to promote the cult of St. Joseph—as epitomized in his lengthy poem *Josephina*.[99] The unconsummated union of Mary and Joseph is used to signify Christ's marriage with the church, which, as with the union of his holy parents, was both virginal and fecund.[100] Gerson further emphasized that, by virtue of the sacrament of marriage, Joseph partook of the same flesh as Mary (in spite of the lack of carnal commerce) and participated in all her virtues.[101] Perhaps most important in the present context, however, is Gerson's construal of their marriage as both symbol and realization of Christ's marriage to the soul, explicitly associating their union with the Song of Songs.[102]

Despite this vigorous recasting of the image of *sponsa Christi*, there were certain conventions that could not entirely be circumvented. For example, it would have seemed strange, even churlish, had the pious brother denied his virginal sisters the honorific title of bride altogether. Nor did he. The treatise *Discourse on the Excellence of Virginity*, written the year before *The Mountain of Contemplation*, also expressly for his sisters, opens by invoking Christ, "the true spouse of virginity." True to form, however, Gerson proceeds to treat this union as something potentially perilous, promising to show his sisters "the manner in which to begin, continue, and fulfill this spiritual marriage very slowly, without peril to body or soul."[103] Interestingly, when Gerson would later use the same evocation of Christ as "the true spouse of virginity" in *The Mountain of Contemplation*, he cross-references his usage, but not with the *Discourse* that he had so recently penned for his sisters. Instead he cites a prayer, also written the year before *The Mountain*, which begins with the line, "Jesus, true groom of virginity."[104] It is a salient cross-reference because the poem itself, aptly named *The Pitiful Complaint*, has the effect of styling Gerson himself as bride. In this prolonged mea culpa, written in the first person, Gerson begs Christ's pardon for his unruly and disobedient soul. Not only has the soul broken her marriage vow to Christ, hence losing her ring, but she has even accepted the ring of the enemy.[105] The inherent flexibility of the imagery of the Canticles was certainly in his favor, and Gerson knew it. At one point he describes Christ as being "at the same time husband and wife, father and mother, boyfriend and girlfriend, because spiritual love does not recognize sex."[106] Such attributions even have the potential for expanding the already generous contours of the mystical marriage with Christ by imagining Christ as a wife, not unlike Bernard's earlier projection of Christ as mother.

Gerson's desire to realign bridal mysticism along lines that he could approve eventually prompted him to go right to the source: in 1402, Gerson used the opportunity of a sermon preached on the feast of St. Bernard to manipulate the imagery of the mellifluous doctor himself.[107] With the bride's wistful "Sustain me with flowers, refresh me with apples, for I am languishing with love" (Sg 2.5) as a starting point, Gerson launches immediately into a bold preemptive move: "the church now reads them [these words] in praise of the singular bride of Christ, the glorious Virgin."[108] An exuberant reference to Mary as "the goddess of a love not impure but divine" follows soon after.[109] Although we have seen that the tradition of the Virgin as the bride goes back to patristic times, it is certainly not one that overrode or precluded others, as Gerson seems to be suggesting. Nor, as we have seen, was this the primary direction that Bernard's own interpretative genius had taken.[110]

The nod to the Virgin is followed by Gerson's lamentation over his own inadequacy in apprehending, let alone matching, the fiery love of Bernard, asking, "how can there be hope that from my cold, and in fact frozen, heart any flame of love will produce words on fire"? This sense of inadequacy not only prompts him to enjoin the spirit of Bernard to "touch and purge my lips" but ultimately paves the way for the appropriation of the master's voice. To this end, Gerson ingeniously requires his audience to "let his [Bernard's] person, so good and trustworthy, be introduced as if we were listening to him speaking about his love in this world," and to "turn your attention from me and imagine it is Bernard himself who speaks and not I."[111] In this assumed voice, Gerson then re-creates the spiritual progress of Bernard's soul. The first stage was a turning away from the world. The soul subsequently sought training on the subject of the love of God in the schools, where youths were taught "to inquire about causes, to dispute, to analyze books, and to distinguish with acumen truth from falsity." These exercises were eventually deemed hollow: merely engaging the intellect and not the emotions.[112] Ultimately, the soul learned the requisite lessons of love in three schools of higher education: contrition and penance, meditation, and contemplation.[113]

One can only wonder what Bernard would have made of the chancellor's tribute. As Brian McGuire has argued, Gerson fashioned a Bernard that reflected his own plight: a friendless, isolated academic rather than a parental abbot surrounded by beloved sons.[114] In a similar vein, Gerson totally altered the spirit of Bernard's reading of the Song of Songs. For in spite of Gerson's own critique of the limits of university training, not to mention Bernard's own aversion to the nascent schools of his time, Gerson nevertheless refashions the bridal soul in the image of a scholar. In keeping with the surprising new vocation for the soul, Gerson incorporates details from Bernard's life into the soul's trajectory, effectually recasting the traditional female bride/soul into a male persona. Hence Bernard's soul reminisces, "It is known how unhappy women twice impudently attacked me when I was naked. When I felt the one, I cried out 'Robbers, robbers,' and awoke my comrades. The other time when the sight of a woman aroused more strongly than usual this little old woman of the flesh, I submerged myself to the neck in freezing water until I almost caused my own death."[115] Thus instead of asking a group of monks to identify with a female soul, as had Bernard, Gerson was simply asking a group of clerics to identify with a soul that Gerson clearly thought was pretty close to home: although referring to its flesh disparagingly as a "little old woman," the soul seems to be the spiritual projection of the heterosexual male, periodically tempted by women and lucky enough to enjoy the benefits of a superior education. It was more of a stretch for the metaphor than for the audience.

But despite such ingenious attempts to preempt the female mystic's position as bride of Christ, Gerson did not abandon her to a free fall into a symbolic void. Rather Gerson secured her to another image—a matron at the very top of the symbolic food chain: the evil queen. The image first surfaces in his *Mountain of Contemplation*. The worldly love that alienates us from God is likened to a series of metaphors: a snare, a chain, some mortar, a performing animal held by a leash, a captive bird, "the evil queen who founds the city of confusion for our enemy from hell in the human creature." He follows this image up with sterile earth, carrion that detains Noah's raven (Gen. 8.6), or a madwoman making so much noise she drives the soul from the body.[116]

The same year, Gerson links the image of the queen to an inverted motif of the mystical marriage wherein the soul eschews marriage with Christ in favor of fornication with the devil. In so doing, Gerson was tapping into an ancient tradition. Despite the disinclination of religious authorities to endorse Tertullian's very literal belief in human-demonic miscegenation, the concept nevertheless made for rich metaphorical fodder across the centuries. It was in this spirit that God had berated Israel for her multiple fornications.[117] In a similar vein, the church fathers had referred to pagan practices like idolatry or divination as spiritual fornication or, as Augustine put it, "when the soul prostituted itself to false gods."[118] Jerome applied the term explicitly to heresy.[119] And indeed this type of spiritual fornication would be very much alive in the later Middle Ages, as it remained one of the very few grounds for a legal separation in marriage.[120] But the metaphor could also be put to more quotidian uses: a preacher whose sole concern was self-aggrandizement was sometimes described as committing adultery against the word of God.[121]

Similar imagery was used to depict consent to sin, usually through a female persona. Abelard enlisted Satan's seduction of Eve to demonstrate the three stages of sin: suggestion, the anticipation of pleasure, and consent.[122] In later pastoral literature we find an analogous schematization of sin depicted as a marriage between the (female) soul and the devil: the initiation of sin constitutes betrothal, consent to sin represents the exchange of vows, and the completed sin is the equivalent of consummation.[123]

Occasionally, this imagery was strategically embodied, having been assigned to specific groups or even individuals. Jerome, for instance, had admonished virgins, "But if even real virgins, when they have other failings, are not saved by their physical virginity, what shall become of those who have prostituted the members of Christ and have changed the temple of the Holy Ghost into a brothel?"[124] Peter Damian had decried clerical wives as concubines of the devil.[125] Finally, the mother of the future Antichrist, by virtue of her whorish ways, had, in essence, united herself to the devil. According to

Hildegard of Bingen's version, Antichrist's mother was sent into the desert by the devil disguised as an angel of light. It was there that she was debauched by a series of men and begot Antichrist.[126] Infected by the eschatological fever of the later Middle Ages, many were convinced that the virginal ecclesia was on the verge of corruption or already had been corrupted.[127]

But Gerson's regal projections of the errant soul are probably more directly indebted to a tradition arising from the Song of Songs, with its allusions to the bedchamber of the king of kings, Christ. This is the Christ who graciously woos his beloved in mystical discourse, including anchoritic literature.[128] But there is, as we have seen, a darker side to this tradition. As early as Cyprian, Christ had been invoked as a jealous bridegroom, intolerant of any laxness on behalf of his bride. We have already witnessed Abelard's efforts to chasten Heloise with reminders of how the high king would tolerate no dalliance with inferiors. Stephen Langton's sermon *Concerning Virgins* (also probably written for nuns) puts more imaginative ballast behind the various ways in which the mystical marriage could be derailed.[129] Taking as his starting point Paul's assertion, "For I have espoused you to one husband that I may present you as a chaste virgin to Christ" (2 Cor. 11.2),[130] Langton imagines scenarios in which this expectation comes to naught. For instance, the truculent bride who makes no effort to please her exquisite spouse is told to get out and "follow the steps of the flocks" (Sg 1.7).[131] Her churlish persona is fleshed out with an exegetical exemplum from the book of Esther, in which Queen Vashti defies the command of her husband, King Assuerus, refusing to appear before an assembly of revelers (1.10–19). Langton associates Queen Vashti with the faithful soul of the Song of Songs and King Assuerus with the King of Kings. But the marriage falls apart when the queen is betrayed by her servants, who "made their mistress prostitute herself before the devil. They frequently went across to the infernal regions for the sake of their black lovers who are evil spirits."[132] Langton subsequently envisions the soul as unfaithful queen, dallying heedlessly with her lover (greed or some other vice) while Christ, her royal lord, knocks upon the locked door. Eventually the king breaks in, kills the lover, but spares the wife.[133]

While building on this tradition, Gerson improvises with a personification that has the merit of being abstract and concrete at the same time: he depicts the soul's consent to sin in terms of the queen of France's reception of a messenger from her husband's enemy, the king of England. There are six stages that lead up to her dishonor. In the first stage, the messenger arrives to proposition the queen on behalf of the king of England, but she refuses to give him an audience, hear his words, or receive his gifts. Not only does she assume a stern and uninviting expression, but she attempts to chase him out of her lodging, shouting, " 'Fie on you! Fie on your master!' " She returns to her husband, denouncing the villainy of his enemy and demanding vengeance, so firm and unshakeable is she in her love for her husband. In the second stage, she reluctantly hears what the messenger has to say. He brings but a single gift, which she refuses, preferring that he had never come. In the third stage, the queen willingly sees the messenger, who exhorts her to leave her spouse and come to his master. She remains where she is, but nevertheless takes great pleasure in the messenger's words. In the fourth stage, she consents to the English king's wish, receives his presents, and makes good cheer for his messenger. In the fifth stage, she is not content simply to have consented to the king and received his messenger graciously: she begins to develop so great a hatred for her husband and such a perverse love for his enemy that she would willingly prostitute herself before the latter. In the final stage, the queen is obdurate, unwilling to turn away from her sin. No sweetness from her husband, abuse from the English king, or a general sense of shame can make her relent.[134]

This is a fascinating allusion to France's desperate political straits in the Hundred Years' War, when rumors of Charles VI's madness were rife and his queen, Isabel of Bavaria, was forced to take control of the government. It is also an eerie prefiguration of her negotiations with the English to end the war, eventuating in the Treaty of Troyes (1420). The terms of this treaty passed over the claims of the dauphin, the future Charles VII, to the French throne in favor of the English monarchy. Between 1422 and 1429, moreover, rumors of Isabel's infidelity with her brother-in-law, allegedly generated by the pro-English faction, further undercut the dauphin's claims to the throne.[135] One can only imagine that over the intervening years Gerson's provocative tale of the regal soul's consent to adultery lent itself to an ever more literal and embodied construal.

The image appears under slightly different auspices in a treatise discerning the signs that indicate when a person is headed for spiritual disaster. One ominous portent is if the individual is disappointed in the special spiritual consolations, be they visions or other supernatural gifts, that he or she seeks. Gerson enumerates the many reasons why God might seem to withhold such evidence of favor. For example, a soul may not be rewarded for its good deeds in the present because it is destined to be punished for its bad deeds in the future. There is the possibility that such spiritual graces coincide with sin; indeed, the soul can use these very signs of grace to fornicate, separating itself from God, "just as a queen fornicates with the beautiful messenger of a king."[136] Though the temporal moorings have vanished, the identity of the queen has narrowed.

She no longer represents the generic human soul, but a rarefied kind of sinner: an individual who has become attached to certain spiritual consolations, not realizing that these can coexist with sin. The queen is no longer treacherous, simply deluded. And she is not even given the opportunity to sleep with the foreign king, only his messenger. In other words, she has turned into the female mystic.

The queen is an evil version of the bride of the Song of Songs, destined for a debased union—a parody of what awaits in the celestial chamber of the high king. But the image also taps into society's fears at a more concrete level: unlike the ever virginal bride of the Canticles, Gerson's queen is secularized and normalized, metamorphosed into the sexually savvy bedfellow whose chief responsibility is to produce an heir. A central contradiction of patriarchal ideology, and one to which Gerson subscribed, was that women, despite their fleshly failings, were nevertheless invested with heightened moral responsibility when it came to sex by virtue of their reproductive role. He thus toes the party line in maintaining that adultery is more culpable in a wife than a husband, albeit theoretically worse for the morally stronger male.[137] Corruption of lineage was, to Gerson's mind, the most bestial sin—the kind of heedlessness one associates with dogs, who impose no order on their sexual appetites, or horses which, as Aristotle points out, do not even recognize their own mothers.[138] Hence the conundrum of the spurious heir looms large for Gerson: How does one spare a revealed bastard from the husband's wrath while maintaining the rights of the legitimate heir?[139] Heaven forefend a spurious heir at the head of a kingdom. In short, the adultery of a queen is both more portentous and more despicable than a parallel transgression by a normal matron. This point of emphasis would gain significance over time as the future Charles VII's claims to the throne became progressively impugned by rumors of Isabel's alleged adultery.

The fact that the errant mystic is represented as sexually initiated rather than virginal is significant for other reasons as well. Gerson often argued that virginity was ultimately much easier than the thorny path of married chastity—which presumably would be more difficult still for women, given their susceptibility.[140] But he also shared in the understanding of sexual activity as catalyst to an irreversible change for the worse: once accustomed to sex, it was much harder for anyone, especially women, to do without. Adhering to the Platonic dictum "souls follow bodies," Gerson had argued for the correspondence between physical and spiritual states throughout his works.[141] Thus a sexually experienced woman would certainly be more prone to confuse carnal and spiritual love than would a virgin.[142]

In this context, it is certainly salient that a number of the most high-profile mystics of the high and later Middle Ages were matrons or widows: this was as true for Mary of Oignies—the Beguine mystic—as it was for Bridget of Sweden, Gerson's most public target. Gerson's writings are further punctuated with examples of wayward matronly mystics. There is the nameless woman who underwent a conversion experience and subsequently observed rigorous chastity with her husband, but nevertheless would have fallen had her clerical advisors not been stronger, and Ermine of Reims, whose visions Gerson had at one point endorsed at the behest of her confessor, but was later denounced as a tricky widow who almost "seduced" him (albeit posthumously) into approving her visions.[143] (And the highly sexual content of Ermine's demonic temptations would not have been lost on Gerson.) There was also a nameless matron of Arras, whose dangerous regime of abstinence, undertaken without clerical counsel and against the husband's wishes, convinced Gerson that she was in the grips of a demon.[144] The mystics that Gerson impugns are all married. By the same token, he condemns a mystical text by a woman whom he implies was debauched by her devolution into the wrong kind of love, but endorses a mystical text that he believed was written by a virgin.[145] Ultimately, the only female mystic he not only celebrated but even defended was Joan of Arc, whose contemporary fame for virginity was reflected in her nickname, La Pucelle.[146]

Gerson had warned his virginal sisters away from bridal mysticism as simply too dangerous—especially for beginners in the mystical life. One can imagine his alarm over the effects of female mysticism with its self-styled brides languishing in love. So he routed them by transforming the mystic's bridal soul into a deluded queen copulating with the king's satanic messenger.

John Nider, the Secular Bride, and the Witch

Gerson's treatises were circulated at the great councils of his time, particularly Constance and Basel. Indeed, the Council of Basel acted as a kind of clearing-house for his work, ensuring that his impact on Germany was especially profound.[147] The theologian John Nider, prior of the Dominican community in Nuremberg, was a particularly ardent admirer of Gerson. This is not surprising since the two men shared much more than baptismal names. Both Johns were important reformers whose personal efforts were especially manifest at the Councils of Constance and Basel respectively.[148] Both authors engaged in a pastorally oriented theology, evidenced in the special attention paid to matters such as the sacrament of confession from the perspective of both confessor and penitent.[149] Nider promoted lay spirituality in his own way, as had Gerson before him. Like many of the intellectuals of their day, both were preoccupied with "superstitious" practices, be they different kinds of spells or efforts to see into the future, dreading the implicit reliance on the demon world.[150] Both men also expressed a similar apprehension over the rising mystical tide and were especially concerned that it was women who seemed to be riding this wave. Their mutual antipathy took the form of learned antifeminism, each becoming rather extreme exponents of this tradition. The brands of antifeminism they embraced were equally sophisticated in terms of medical lore—far outstripping Thomas of Cantimpré's feints at interpreting women through their physiology. Finally, Gerson and Nider were each in their own way successful public authorities on religion: not only were their works widely circulated in their own lifetimes, but they often either were called upon personally to assess matters of spirituality or managed to intervene.[151] In short, the voices of the two men were destined to carry far.

If both authors were considered in terms of who had recourse to the most antifeminist slurs in the totality of their writings, the assessment might well end in a draw. If this contest were reframed in terms of who managed to cram the most misogyny into a single work, however, Nider's *The Anthill* would come in first, hands down. But this appraisal should not be taken to imply that Nider's view of women was in any way monolithic or straightforward. Like Gerson, Nider believed that female inferiority was physiologically based. And yet for both authors, this very weakness ensured that women were more susceptible to spiritual impressions—both good and bad—which rendered female frailty something of a mixed blessing.[152] Nider provides many positive examples of women whom he believed to be high in God's grace and pursuing exemplary lives—a feature not so prominent in Gerson's work. The dialogue format of *The Anthill*, which casts "Theologus" as the inspired pundit and "Piger" (lit. slow-witted) as his plodding interlocutor, is peculiarly suited to Nider's conflicted views on women.

Although a religious himself, Nider's unabashed admiration for virginity did not extend to the traditional female religious vocation. In this respect he shared Gerson's disaffection with aspects of monasticism. We have seen that Gerson explicitly discouraged his sisters from entering a monastery, urging them to live out their religious vocations in the world—a preference that, at least in part, was influenced by his disapproval of female religious communities in his day. But while Gerson had been intentionally discreet about his reservations, Nider was not.[153] In fact, Nider was outspokenly critical of what he construed as women's obstreperous role in resisting reform. "In the six years since Constance, there was not one monastery of the fragile sex to be reformed on account of the vicious lives of their inhabitants," at least according to Theologus's embittered estimate.[154] Nider had allegedly witnessed this resistance firsthand when, in the capacity of reforming prior of the Dominican house in Nuremburg, he attempted to assist the master general of the order in the reform of the female community of St. Catherine. According to Nider's account, he was stonewalled by the entire community.[155] In 1428, however, the sisters were finally brought to their knees by two very different kinds of intervention: the civic authorities came to side with the reformers, even as the beleaguered community "bore the weight of a war against the wrath of demons."[156]

Yet there is some inconsistency in Nider's account of the nuns' war on (demonic) terror, as he later represents the disturbance as occurring after "the species [*gens*] of the fragile sex submitted their stubborn necks to the yoke of obedience." In other words, in this subsequent account, reform was the demon's cue for wrecking havoc. At first, the demon limited itself to making noises at night, annoying only select nuns. When the nuns first approached Nider for help, however, he responded with an unflattering mistrust, attributing the disturbance to mice or rodents of some sort "or a delirious weakness of the head that I suspected affected the women." But on a certain night when a sister in the community died, significantly one of the rebellious ones, the sheer extent of demonic antics made it impossible for her to be buried. Indeed, the demons made so much noise that the terrified nuns refused to go anywhere alone and a watch had to be set over the community. "The weak female sex were rendered so stupid that no one knew what to do with them," Nider reminisces. Naturally, some of the recalcitrant sisters took the opportunity to observe that "when we walked under the wide and ancient path [i.e., prereform] this never happened." But in the end of all, the devil was confounded because the stubborn ones who had resisted reform were sufficiently terrified to confess all their offenses and commit to the new life.[157]

It is worth noting that Nider's rather severe assessment of St. Catherine's monastery is at odds with his earlier assertion that the devil was more inclined to afflict religious who were engaged on the more perfect path and that reformed houses were particular targets. From this perspective, the above fracas could have been construed as a sign of merit for having been one of the elite reformed houses. And this is precisely how Nider chooses to interpret the bout of demonic affliction visited upon a recently reformed Dominican house in France. Not content with breaking windows and ringing bells, the demon possessed a twenty-four-year-old novice, tore his clothes and left him lying bloodied in the woods. Another time he appeared before the novice in the form of a black cat, threatening to kill him in three days if he did not leave the order. The novice's lengthy ordeal was eventually terminated by a personal appearance by St. Dominic—albeit in apparitional form. The routed devil ran throughout the monastery screaming.[158]

And so, while demonic disturbance is a seemingly productive response to masculine reforming zeal, the demonic poltergeists of St. Catherine's are indicative of the nuns' malingering sinfulness, a perversity reinforced by delirium and mental illness. It is also very likely that these latter two ailments are Nider's shorthand for various kinds of mystical claims among the nuns. An extant letter by Eberhard Mardach, Nider's predecessor as prior at Nuremberg and spiritual director to the community of St. Catherine between 1425 and 1428, just before its reform, suggests as much. Addressed to his "spiritual daughter," the letter states explicitly that the sisters who have constant ecstasies, continuously envisage the suffering of Christ, or experience bouts of insensibility to the outside world had taken the wrong path. In short, the letter constitutes a full-on critique of bridal mysticism, highlighting the same areas of anxiety emphasized by Gerson.[159] There is every indication that Nider not only shared his predecessor's apprehension about mysticism at St. Catherine's but extended it to female religious at large. Certainly some of Nider's most spectacular examples of spiritual vanity and mystical fraud occur among cloistered women.[160]

In contrast, Nider demonstrates a surprisingly optimistic streak of considerable breadth when it comes to the spirituality of women living in the world.[161] Granted, much of this enthusiasm seems to be predicated on his disenchantment with cloistered women, and this, in turn, prompts him to present virginity as a largely secular virtue, available to every class. Thus the rustic Adelheyd dedicated herself to Christ in the fields at the age of seven, "bending her knees and raising her hands to the spouse, whom she chose." Her manner of living approximated an informal monastic regimen, with taxing manual labor on the farm, self-imposed austerities, and prayer. At the age of twenty-four, Adelheyd moved to town with her three virginal sisters, where she attracted a following: "nearly fifty virgins, in the midst of the world, serving God most devoutly, while thus preserving their [religious] proposition."[162] A number of similar chaste marvels further illuminated Nider's spiritual horizon. The city of Basel had found a "living sanctuary" in yet another woman named Adelheyd—also a poor girl of humble background who pursued a life of faultless virginity.[163] Elsewhere in the diocese of Constance a humble serf, living alone with her sister, not only foils her tyrannical master's machinations against her virginity, but lives to become a "spiritual mother and generator of many virgins."[164]

Nider's enthusiasm for lay religiosity even emboldens him to extend the exquisite boundaries of virginity to accommodate matrimonial chastity. In particular, Theologus describes the diocese of Constance as a land "not great for vine bearing but virgin bearing" (*vinifera sed multum virginifera*). But the example he gives is counterintuitive. A beautiful and modest woman virtuously rejects the salacious overtures of her parish priest. He warns her, however, that she would eventually fall in love with him. As in the case of the unfortunate Odilia of Liège, the priest was something of an enchanter (*incantator*) who worked magic (*maleficium*), so his threat was hardly nugatory. As predicted, the woman began to fantasize about the priest until, turning to the Virgin Mary for help, she made a pilgrimage to one of the Virgin's important shrines. After she judiciously made her confession, just in case some malign spirits lingered around her, she was divinely apprised of her rosy matrimonial future. And when the prophecy came to fruition and this exemplary virgin was a virgin no more, her devout life was such that "she never remembered she was married." She taught her husband to live piously, raised many children with holy habits, and could be seen daily in church, rapt in ecstasy "not less than the most devout woman in a monastery."[165] When Nider returns to this holy woman later in *The Anthill*, her exemplary family has gained in quasi-monastic momentum. One of her many sons became a priest, while the others went on to live laudably in marriage. Her only daughter made a vow of virginity and continued to live at home, following her mother's regimen. In short, the household resembled a monastery, except, Nider adds, that both a husband and a wife lived there.[166]

The oddity of using a virgin destined for the marriage bed to demonstrate the "virgin growing" capacity of the region is not lost on Piger. Although politely enthusing about the exemplum, the disciple nevertheless contests the theologian's characterization of the area as "virgin bearing" because there is no "no monastery of virgins there; nor reformed religious; nor any Beguines."[167] Theologus, however, counters with the observation that seemingly sterile spots can be remarkably fruitful. Galilee was just such a spot, where the "spouse of virgins" was born. By the same token, the area around Nuremberg has such an abundance of virgins, for the most part living piously in their fathers' homes working textiles, that only the past year the aggrieved bachelors of the region complained that the clergy were stealing their brides.[168] And yet this tribute to Nuremberg's remarkable "fruit" is not a prelude to the panegyric on virginity that one might expect. On the contrary, Nider launches into a detailed discussion of different degrees of chastity in marriage, including the perpetual virginity of an unconsummated union, hence effacing the boundaries between the married and the celibate even more completely.[169] Indeed, Nider's most heartfelt accolades seem to be reserved for the widow Margaret of Constance, who made the laudable transition to intramarital chastity with her husband and raised her children to love God. But even more praiseworthy was the extent of her piety amid the distractions of home. Her piety was so impressive that it occasions an interesting disclosure from Nider: "the mind of the holy woman very often had a higher and greater degree of awareness concerning divine things in the contemplation of Christ than I know that I ever experienced in thirty years in the name and profession of religion. Among those visions, as I was often able to learn, she foresaw with the divine spirit things which humanity is not able to know, concerning which revelations she made little, but cared about loving God and especially about observing his precepts and counsels without sin." When Margaret's husband died, she was still of marriageable age but sought no other husband than Christ.[170]

And so a humble matron outstrips a professed religious and theologian, thirty years into his vocation, in the profundity of her contemplation. This principal will be generalized in a later rubric, which maintains that one often sees people living in the world without a vow who have a greater zeal for the salvation of souls than those who perform the Mass.[171] Unlike the desperate female religious straining to find fame through supernatural fakery, moreover, Margaret received visions and held them as naught in comparison to a sinless life in Christ.

The allusion to Margaret in her widowed status as Christ's bride is noteworthy because this honor is accorded a fecund matron, while conspicuously withheld from the denizens of the cloister.[172] And thus cumulatively the possibility of a different kind of bride of Christ emerges: a secular woman of modest background, whose commitment to chastity is as complete as her station allows, who not only transforms the world into a monastery but converts everyone around her and whose intimacy with Christ is based on a regimen of prayer and service, not flamboyant visions. In contrast, women who pursued the mystical path, or were naturally susceptible to visions, ended badly, usually seduced and abandoned by their clerical confidants.[173]

Given Nider's suspicion of the supernatural trappings frequently associated with female spirituality, it is no surprise that bridal mysticism never enters into the formula. The one notable exception is Nider's allusion to the dark antithesis to the mystical marriage, introduced specifically to undermine the kind of spirituality he wished to censure. It appears under the rubric "How venereal delectation ought to be fled; regarding women under a virile shape saying publicly that they are sent from God; and three things which rarely keep to the middle: the tongue, an ecclesiastic, and a woman—who in good works is the best, but in bad is sometimes the worst."[174] Nider opens with the metaphor of how the ant occasionally eats cadavers as a representation of perverse lust—likening the ant's unsavory tastes to men who surrender to their lust for sinful women. Such behavior is anathema to God. Divine censure of the Israelites for adhering to the Moabite cult of Beelphegar, whose practices included eating sacrifices of the dead, is but a metaphor for this lust (Ps. 105). The Israelites' fornication with the daughters of Moab, and the offerings they made to their gods, is an even more overt reference to this kind of perversity. Such infidelity prompted God, in his anger, to command Moses, "Take all the princes of the [Moabite] people and hang them up on gibbets against the sun: that my fury may be turned away from Israel" (Num. 25.4–5). Fornication is a violation of the body, the temple of God, transforming the members of Christ into the members of alien whores.[175]

At this point, Nider segues from carnal to spiritual offenses by remarking that, if physical lust is bad, still worse is the "general fornication," which contains every conceivable kind of sin:

> [N]amely when the soul, made one in company with the word of God, and bound in marriage . . . is corrupted by its enemy. The word of God, Christ, is spouse and husband of the clean soul. I marry you all to one man, Christ, as a chaste virgin, says Paul (2 Cor. 11). When the soul, therefore, adheres to the spouse and is embraced, she hears his word and accepts the semen of his word, and conceives and produces children: chastity, justice, patience and all the virtues. If the soul remains in faith and charity, it is good for the generation of such children (2 Tim. 2). If however the soul prostitutes herself to the devils and demons, she brings forth sons of adultery—namely every sin.[176]

And thus, in a blink of the eye, the soul's marriage with Christ is perverted into prostitution with demons. This inversion accomplishes two things: it not only provides a bridge between carnal and spiritual offenses but points to the way in which the mystical experience could devolve into devil worship. This association is sealed with a fitting exemplum: Piger follows up with the question of whether there are men in this day and age deceived by magicians and witches.[177] Nider, in turn, counters with an account of the most famous female visionary of the day: "a virgin by the name of Joan, shining, as it is reputed, as much with the spirit of prophecy as with the power of miracles."[178] After a brief account of Joan's career, Nider turns to the question that interests him most: whether her mystical revelations were inspired by God or Satan. Although acknowledging support for both sides of the question, Nider eventually seems to settle for the opinion of one of his cronies: "And just as I heard from Nicolaus Amici, licensed in theology who was ambassador of the University of Paris, nevertheless she confessed herself to have a familiar angel of God who, after many conjectures and probations, was judged to be a malign spirit according to the judgment of the most literate of men—through which spirit she was rendered the same as an enchantress [*maga*]."[179] Despite the elaborate pretense of impartiality, by calling Joan an enchantress, Nider made it clear that Joan exemplified "general fornication"—the inverted mystical marriage wherein "the soul prostitutes herself to the devils and demons." The larger context is important here: the account of Joan is included in *The Anthill*'s notorious fifth book, dedicated to "On Witches and Their Deceptions." The pertinent chapter, moreover, is sandwiched between discussions regarding the various capacities of witches and the reality of incubi.[180]

Over the course of book 5, the final one, whatever optimistic edifice of lay spirituality that Nider had begun to build is gradually laid waste. His treatment of Joan of Arc provides a microcosm of this process of decomposition. Joan conformed perfectly to the profile of simple laywoman of humble background. Nider reminds us repeatedly of her virginal status. But because she did not follow the example of the widowed Margaret, who held her revelations at naught, she prostituted herself to the devil and devolved into a type of witch. We subsequently learn through the example of the woman who was impregnated while she slept, thus giving birth as a virgin, that one could potentially enjoy the guilty pleasures of an incubus while still keeping the hymen intact.[181] Thus by the end of *The Anthill*, female claims to chastity have become ephemeral, even as the barriers between virginity and promiscuity come tumbling down.

From Bride of Christ to Devil's Concubine

Chronologically, the rise of witchcraft charges coincides with the gradual debasement of bridal mysticism described above.[182] The ambiguity of Joan's spiritual profile is presented as increasingly common for the religiously inclined women of this period. This is even true for Nider's exemplary Margaret of Constance. Although disinclined toward all things sexual, she rendered the marriage debt, and even exacted for the sake of reciprocity, in compliance with the more liberal clerical views on married sex.[183] Even so, she never desisted in prayers to the Virgin Mary that her husband's sex drive would disappear altogether. Nor were her prayers in vain. For one day he said privately to Margaret, "'I believe . . . (unless I am mistaken), that I am frigid, but I do not know how you managed it.' For he did not suspect his pious wife of witchcraft, whom he knew detested such things with the greatest horror."[184] His wife might make him impotent, but she was no witch!

Nider's discussion of Margaret of Constance, who prayed for her husband's impotence rather than stooping to witchcraft, encapsulates the inverted relationship between holy woman and witch. And, as many scholars have pointed out, the saint and the witch appear to mirror each other in multiple ways: a spiritual union with the humanized Christ versus sex with a (seemingly) incarnate devi; feasts in heaven versus diabolical orgies; eating Christ's body versus devouring children; and the stigmata versus the area of insensibility on the body that came to be referred to as the witch's mark.[185] To be sure, these parallels emerge gradually through a many-layered process. Yet it is certainly significant that the earliest writers on witchcraft, such as Nider, had a heightened interest in both female sanctity and spiritual corruption. This is also true for later witchcraft luminaries like Heinrich Kramer, Dominican inquisitor and author of the profoundly influential witch-hunting guide, *The Hammer of Witches*.[186] But even had this not been the case, we have seen that orthodox polemicists, like Damian, tended to favor the kind of rhetorical inversion that would encourage the crystallization of such polarities.

The pairings of saintly and diabolical phenomena demonstrate the extent to which the witch appropriates, sacrilegiously imitates, and mocks all that is good in Christianity.[187] But it is also important to remember that the spiritual climate that laid the groundwork for witchcraft charges was not based solely, or even primarily, on a sense of opposition or inversion, but on a fear of convergence: a basic recognition that power derived from Satan was indistinguishable from power derived from Christ.[188] The rise of treatises on spiritual discernment vividly testifies to the growing anxiety about deciphering divine from diabolical inspiration. Ultimately despairing of any precise science for discernment, the experts looked on helplessly as the self-styled, mystical brides of Christ, locked in erotic overdrive, veered into the diabolical ditch. Both Gerson and Nider imagine scenarios in which an imagistic proxy for the female mystic ends up dedicating herself to Satan as opposed to Christ, and in each case this dedication is expressed through sexual imagery.

Of course, Gerson and Nider were both describing mystical transgression in terms of metaphor, not as a concretely realized act. We cannot afford to fall into the trap that Gerson believed had ensnared female mystics: the tendency to confuse the imaginary and the real. Even so, it is impossible to ignore the way Gerson's critique transcends the ambit of female spirituality and can be applied to the Christian faith in general. Phenomena as disparate as the theology of transubstantiation and the appearance of the stigmata (both points of doctrine), are vivid reminders that for an incarnational religion, with the word becoming flesh as its central mystery, the distance between an abstract concept and its concrete realization is more imagined than real.[189] The spiritual entities at the center of Origen's cosmos devolved into matter with the passage of time. Similarly, it is the weight of centuries that draws metaphors down to earth; the progressive embodiment of the bride of Christ remains a striking testimonial to this truth. As the figure of the bride becomes increasingly embodied, the dangers of her becoming sordid likewise increase. By the same token, her degree of volition becomes sharper. Gerson's queen is simply deluded; but the perverted soul in Nider's mystical marriage seemingly chose her manner of debauchment. Furthermore, this debasement was enacted amid detailed discussions of the workings of incubi and succubi. Nider was also the first theologian to write extensively on the phenomenon of witchcraft. Although his discussions of demon lovers and witchcraft were handled discretely, the witch who voluntarily has sex with the devil at the witches' sabbath is just around the corner.[190]

Nider was one of five contemporaneous writers who render the earliest descriptions of nocturnal assemblies, from which the classic description of what comes to be known as the witches' synagogue or sabbath begins to emerge.[191] Its central features are the nocturnal flight to an assembly presided over by a demon, induction into the cult through a formal renunciation of God and a pact with the devil, the devouring of infants, and orgiastic feasting.[192] Not all five texts contain each of these elements. Nor is there any consensus about the existential status of nocturnal flights.[193] Yet the parallels between these different accounts are striking.

The earliest relation of a sabbath-like event is provided by Hans Fründ of Lucerne, who chronicles the sorcery trials that took place in Valais between 1428 and 1430. According to his account, aspirant witches dedicate themselves to the service of the devil (referred to as the "evil spirit," usually in the form of a black animal), further deny God and the saints, and renounce their baptism. Those initiated into the sect also agree to pay the devil an annual tribute: for some it is an animal offering, but for others it could be the promise of a limb after death. The devil, in turn, forbids them to attend Mass or listen to a sermon and especially bars participation in the sacrament of confession.[194]

Fründ never specifies where exactly this induction occurs, nor does he provide any account of the sabbath per se.[195] The report of Claude Tholosan (ca. 1436), a lay magistrate of the Dauphiné is more forthcoming. Prospective sectarians make an oath into the hands of the devil (who can appear as either a man or an animal), promising not to betray one another—even if this means dying at the hands of the authorities. The devil, for his part, promises to protect his followers under torture by rendering them insensible to pain, and even appearing to comfort them. The postulants formally deny God (who is demoted in status to "the prophet"), promising to leave the faith of Christ—a pledge that is sealed by turning the hand away (from God?) or by inverting some other object. This is followed by a series of sacrilegious acts: adherents drink from an urn containing the devil's urine, raise their hands and renounce the sacraments and the articles of faith, undress from the waist to "moon" the heavens with their naked buttocks; and trample a crucifix underfoot. The finale comes when they kiss the devil on the mouth, offering themselves body and soul on bended knee, along with one of their children (usually the firstborn).[196]

Later in his same report Tholosan renders a vivid account of what he refers to as the witch's synagogue, even though its professed reality quotient is somewhat in doubt. For instance, we are told that the devil "deludes them [his adherents] in dreams, so that they believe that they go corporeally in the night, especially on Tuesdays and Saturdays, in the company of devils, to suffocate children and impose infirmities. Draining the blood from children, they cook and eat them on the spot; and they go to a certain spot, where they hold synagogue." Somewhere along the line, however, the demonically induced dreams become a reality. Apparently the witches claim to have come from afar, some on sticks anointed with a diabolical concoction, some on brooms, others on animals.[197] The devil presides under a banner bearing his own image, that of "the principle devil"—implying that the devil in question is Lucifer himself. It is to him that the witches report on the evil they have accomplished and that new members of the sect are presented. The sectarians each kiss the devil in reverence and then, upon his order, engage in indiscriminate sex with one another. The demons join in as well.

Although Tholosan separates the ceremony of induction from the nocturnal assembly in his text, the reference to the presentation of new members at these gatherings may imply that they are, in fact, inducted into the sect at the sabbath. In contrast to Fründ's account, Tholosan's induction has also become imbued with feudal imagery: a solemn pledge made into the hands of the devil, the mutual exchange of promises, a formal oath of fealty (symbolized by the inverted hand), the kiss on the mouth.[198] But the chief devil's presence also lends an episcopal quality to the event. Not only is the meeting referred to as a provincial synagogue (*synagoga de provincia*), but the devil is seated on a throne, designated a cathedra.

The induction described by Nider will to some extent sustain these ecclesiastical overtones by moving the ceremony into the church early Sunday mornings, before the holy water is consecrated. The candidate first renounces Christ, his religion, and baptism, then proceeds to do homage to the devil (referred to as "little master" [*magisterulus*]). The pact is sealed when the disciple drinks from a flask of liquid distilled from the limbs of children.[199]

The above three accounts were either written by members of the laity or, in Nider's case, relayed by a lay informant—the secular magistrate, Peter of Bern. They all show signs of what Richard Kieckhefer describes as diabolism— explicit worship of the devil that reflects the imposition of an ecclesiastical frame upon popular beliefs. The remaining two texts are unequivocally clerical in origin, however, and not surprisingly, these diabolical features are even more pronounced.[200] The anonymous cleric responsible for the short treatise *Errors of the Gazari* (ca. 1437) was in all likelihood an inquisitor.[201] In this account, the devil appears at the synagogue as an animal, usually a black cat or, more rarely, a man—but always a man who is in some way deformed. He interrogates the prospective witch as to his intention of remaining in the community, who responds in the affirmative. Then the devil receives the oath of fealty (*iuramentum fidelitatis*) through a series of promises: to be loyal to the devil; to assemble with his fellow witches; to die before revealing the sect's secrets; to kill as many children under the age of three as possible, bringing their cadavers to synagogue; to hasten to synagogue when summoned; to use magic to impede marital sex; and to avenge all injuries to the sect. Then the supplicant kisses the presider on the anus or under the tail (depending on whether the devil has appeared as a man or an animal) as a sign of homage, promising a limb after his death. The fellowship celebrates by feasting upon murdered children. As a finale, the presiding devil demands the lights to be extinguished and shouts "Mestlet, Mestlet." This is a cue for the members of the assembly to throw themselves into acts of sexual abandon.[202]

The fifth and final of these formative texts is also the last chronologically. *The Champion of the Ladies* was written sometime between 1440 and 1442 by Martin Le Franc, secretary to later antipope Felix V. It is a poem staged as a mock dialogue between the Adversary of women, who persistently points to their vices and follies, and Free Will, the Champion, who is women's self-appointed advocate. The Adversary emphasizes women's involvement in witchcraft to the extent that it emerges as a primarily female vice. Not just two or three women, he alleges, but more than three thousand attend assemblies in the wilderness where they meet up with their familiar demons. According to a trial record from an old woman from Valpute, who flew to synagogues on a broomstick, the assemblies consisted of ten thousand women who assumed the shape of cats and goats. They all approached the devil with deference, again literally kissing his ass as a show of obedience, and denied God with impunity. While some received instruction in the working of evil magic, the others amused themselves with dancing and feasting. The devil (now shaped like a cat) walked among his following, praising and rewarding the loyal but beating mercilessly those who threatened to leave the sect. He then sat in judgment like a judge or lawyer, entertaining various requests. The sabbath concluded with an orgy: any woman who was short a partner received a male-seeming devil to oblige.[203]

Le Franc's Adversary also makes reference to infernal activities that take place outside the sabbath, which are possibly even more disturbing. A certain old hag who paid homage to the devil was rewarded with an ointment that allowed her to wreck havoc upon her unsuspecting neighbors.[204] But this claim is ultimately overshadowed by an even greater perversity:

> The devil made himself into a man
> And took her [the witch] with the ardor of lust. Oh God, what a
>   horror!
> Dear God, the couple is worthy of note!
> Oh dear God Jesus Christ, what an error!
> The woman is married to the devil![205]

Le Franc was drawing on much of the same traditional material as his clerical cohort. The devolution of the feudal-inflected kiss between lord and vassal into the obscene kiss on the posterior of an animal was something brooded about in clerical circles since the time of William of Auvergne.[206] The orgy that rounded off the *Errors of Gazari*, commencing with the command of "Meslet," resonates with earlier cases of diabolism, such as Guibert of Nogent's denunciation of a dualist sect in which the code word for the commencement of the orgy was "Chaos."[207] Even so, Le Franc helped move this conglomerate of superstitions in a specific direction in two fundamental ways. First, his dialogue implied that the witches' sect primarily consisted of women—a tacit allegation visualized in a display manuscript executed some ten years after the poem's composition, which depicted women riding on broomsticks.[208] Le Franc's second intervention resides in the nature of the demonic sex he describes. Paralleling Tholosan's account, Le Franc alleges that the sabbath concludes with an orgy in which demons participate when a human partner was lacking.[209] But Le Franc takes this one step further by maintaining that some women retain their own familiar demons. This raises the question of whether these demonic familiars might not also service their mistresses sexually as incubi, bringing to mind the relations between sorceresses and familiars, which, according to William of Auvergne, some credited with the origin of the Huns. If this were the case, these demons were more than makeshift substitutes for human partners at the sabbath. Nor could such women be construed as passive victims in their relations with these incubi.[210] Then there is the alternative ritual of homage in return for a malevolent ointment described as occurring outside the sabbath. The old hag subsequently copulates with the devil in human form. The supernatural entity in question is referred to as the devil himself, while the couple's sexual union is described as a marriage.

The concept of the witch having sex with *the* devil, as opposed to a mere incubus-demon, could likewise be construed as both old and new. It is old insofar as it resonates with the kind of orthodox imagery alluded to above: the spiritual debauchment of the priest's wife, the trajectory of the errant soul, the error of the deluded mystic are all described in the context of sexual congress with the devil. Cathar mythology also offers possible analogies alleging, for example, that Eve had first been corrupted by Satan before she was sexually known by Adam. Unlike their orthodox counterparts, however, Cathars did not insist that their originary tales were necessarily invested with literal truth. As far as I know, the actual allegation that women slept with the devil himself, let alone became his wife, is new to the annals of heresy, or other religious discourses for that matter. Of course, the fact that the accusation first arose in the dialogue format may well suggest that Le Franc was personally skeptical of witchcraft charges. Furthermore, there is every indication that the poem was intended as entertaining satire. But these considerations hardly matter. We do not need Freud to tell us that a joke is generally at someone's expense—in this instance women.[211] Since sex with the devil was a charge that had not only a future but one that helped to consolidate women's alleged overrepresentation in witchcraft, we can only observe that the cost of Le Franc's joke was unreasonably high.

All of these sources deemed seminal in the development of the witches' sabbath refer to a very specific area within and around the Alps.[212] This literature, working symbiotically with regional trials, ultimately gave rise to a series of charges that became widely disseminated by the end of the fifteenth century. But, as Richard Kieckhefer has suggested, different regions have their own mythologies of witchcraft that would affect the reception of this nascent "script" of interrogatories.[213] For instance, fifteenth-century Italy had its own set of witchcraft beliefs—one that was quicker to distinguish the preponderance of female witches than was the case in northern Europe. This was probably because the crimes believed to be perpetrated by Italian witches were framed against domestic, especially maternal, values (Italian witches tended to be bloodsuckers who fed upon children), while their northern counterparts attacked religious norms.

Bearing these considerations in mind, I would like to consider the regional contours of one particular set of witchcraft trials: the so-called Vauderie of Arras, which took place between 1459 and 1461. The Vauderie consisted of an unprecedented wave of witchcraft charges that would eventually engulf much of the citizenry of Arras, and ultimately Tournai, Douai, and Lille. The sources for this crisis are excellent. In addition to the ecclesiastical records of the trials, there are also detailed contemporary accounts—most particularly the memoirs of an educated layman, James du Clercq.[214] The Vauderie was set in motion in Langres with the burning of a hermit named Robinet de Vaulx, who was accused of witchcraft. When compelled to name his supposed confederates in evil who also attended the sabbath, he named Deniselle of Douai and John Lavite of Arras.[215] John was an elderly painter, about sixty or seventy years of age, who, according to du Clercq, was "welcome in many places." The accused had also written many poems and ballads to the Virgin Mary "and by this had brought happiness to many."[216] He was familiarly known as the "Abbot of Little Sense"—a nickname perhaps bestowed by some fun-loving confraternity. Deniselle was a prostitute, a member of a group that the trials at Arras and elsewhere suggest was particularly vulnerable to accusations of witchcraft.[217]

Unfortunately these accusations did not fall on deaf ears. By some strange and calamitous coincidence, Peter Le Broussart, the inquisitor of Arras, was present in Langres for the annual Dominican chapter and felt compelled to follow up on these leads. The bishop of Arras was away in Rome during the trials and hence unlikely to mount much opposition. Le Broussart was assisted by the Dominican inquisitor Nicolas Jacquier, who, by another lucky coincidence, had completed a treatise against "the abominable sect" of witches the year before in which he argued that the debaucheries of the witches' sabbath were real, not dreams.[218] The inquisitors were abetted by the local episcopal vicars and the titular bishop of Beirut. The liberal use of torture, alternating with false promises of freedom, ensured that the inquisitor and his assorted clerical accomplices were very soon provided with an impressive list of suspects.

Despite the incredulity of most of the populace, the trials proved to be something of a spiritual juggernaut that, fueled by avarice and fanaticism, crushed some of the wealthiest citizens of Arras. Anonymous poems, accusing the inquisitors of greed and corruption, began to circulate on little rolls of paper.[219] Eventually when some of the more highly placed defendants appealed to Parlement, the instigators and their allies were summoned to answer for their misdeeds.[220] Only then did the inquiry finally grind to a halt.

One of the driving forces behind the trials was John du Bois, a young canon and dean of the cathedral chapter at Arras, who received his doctorate in theology from Paris. Du Bois valiantly fought off every internal and external pressure that favored clemency for the accused. When the vicars representing the absentee bishop got nervous about the escalation of arrests and wanted to let the prisoners go without punishment, du Bois resisted.[221] The advice of an external team of experts to suspend the death penalty likewise fell on deaf ears.[222] Unfortunately, du Bois himself could not be brought to justice because he went mad before he could answer Parlement's summons. When he regained his sanity, moreover, he had lost the use of his limbs. Public opinion was divided over whether the dean's tribulations were the result of *maleficia* or God's vengeance.[223]

It is quite likely that John du Bois was responsible for the anonymous *Recollection of the Cause, State, and Condition of the Waldensian Idolaters*—a treatise allegedly drawn "from experience and the tracts of many inquisitors and other experts and the confessions and processes of the Waldensians of Arras," and clearly the work of a trained theologian.[224] The treatise begins with an impassioned, but meticulously argued, defense of the reality of night flights, supported by appropriate authorities.[225] The remainder of the article discusses how devious the defendants prove in the course of cross-examination, offering some strategies for torture.[226] So there is every indication that the author of the treatise was not simply an aloof theoretician, but intimately acquainted with the actual inquisitional proceedings. This is proved beyond doubt by the kind of anecdotes he drops: that the devil gave the prostitute Belote Moucharde (simulated) money;[227] that "the Abbot of Little Sense" hated the man who had stolen his wife some twenty-two years ago, yet still refused to denounce him.[228]

The centerpiece of the *Recollection* is a composite account, allegedly drawn from the various confessions, portraying the induction of a witch and culminating in the presentation at the sabbath. It begins with the candidate, who is represented as female, being duly prepared for the ritual ahead of time by either a familiar demon (who seems to be mysteriously in attendance before she is even a member of the sect) or her fellow witches, and it is their responsibility to present her to the presiding demon at a nocturnal assembly. Bearing a black candle, she approaches the demon, who sits upon an elevated seat.[229] After formally renouncing God, Christ, the glorious Virgin, the saints, and the sacraments,[230] the candidate is required to cast some holy water behind her and trample the area, and then spit and trample upon a cross she has drawn on the ground.[231] In contempt of the master of the world, she strips from the waist and exposes her buttocks to the heavens. Subsequently, she kneels before the demon in adoration and does homage, kissing his hand or foot, and offering the black candle of wax and perhaps some money. Once the candle is accepted by the demon, it is extinguished—by either the candidate herself or those standing nearby (presumably her sponsors). Then the demon turns around and the novice kisses his posterior. At this point, the prospective witch dedicates her soul to the devil.[232] As a symbol of this donation, she provides some bodily offering: a finger, some hair, fingernails, or a bit of blood.[233] Finally, the demon gives the candidate a sensible token such as a ring, whether of gold, copper, or silver.[234]

These proceedings are followed by a sermon that the demon preaches to the congregation (*predicacionis formam*), assuring them that humans have no immortal soul and that there is no other paradise apart from these assemblies, where sectarians are free to feast and copulate with whomever they choose.[235] He thereupon leaves his dais and draws the newly made witch aside into the grove, where the two have intercourse. Out of malice (*cui ex malicia dicit*), he insists that she lay her face and two hands and feet on the ground, so he can enter her from behind.[236] The newly made witch hereafter returns to the congregation, which is decorously arranged in rows, before which she dances in joy to musical accompaniment. With a touch of the presiding demon's staff, cloths appear on the ground and a sumptuous feast is served.[237] When the table is cleared, the devil orders that the lights be extinguished and the orgy begin. As a final parting, the demon, speaking in menacing tones, reminds the congregation of his precepts.[238]

The reference to "homage" might suggest that the bond between the would-be witch and demon is best construed as a variety of the diabolical feudalism represented in documents like the *Errors of the Gazari*. And, indeed, scholars continue to see the induction described in the *Recollection* largely in feudal terms.[239] But the feudal trappings tend to obscure what I take to be a more salient resonance between the witch's induction and that female ritual par excellence: the consecration of the virgin as bride of Christ. When one compares the diabolical ritual to the revised and definitive thirteenth-century pontifical of William Durandus, the parallels are indeed striking. In both ceremonies, the postulants are presented to the presiding authority by sponsors of some sort (4–8).[240] In each instance, they carry candles and are presented to a man seated on a raised platform bearing a staff. Like the bishop, who is the vicar of Christ, the demon is a stand-in for Satan (6, 8, 19). The sacrilegious aspersion of holy water parallels the holy water sprinkled to bless the veils (24). The ritual veiling by the bishop is countered by an irreverent unveiling of the woman's buttocks (36). In the virginal rite, the woman offers her candle to the bishop along with "something else" if she wishes (perhaps a discreet reference to the nun's customary dowry). The bishop clasps the virgin's hands between his own (a gesture traditionally associated with homage) and inquires into her intention to preserve her virginity. She, in turn, kisses his hand in reverence (17). By the same token, we are told that the would-be witch kneels before the devil in adoration and does homage. She offers him the black candle and perhaps some money. When she pledges her soul to him, she additionally makes a physical oblation of "her finger, hair, or nails"—an offering that could be likened to the cutting of the postulant's hair, which takes place prior to the ceremony. It is also noteworthy that the word invoked for this diabolical offering is *arrha*. This term is peculiarly associated with symbolic objects attached to marriage, particularly the ring or other personal gifts that are exchanged to ratify the contract. One of Mechtild of Hackeborn's revelations depicts Mary as doling out *arrhae* to consecrated virgins in the form of rings, emphasizing the spiritual currency implicit in the image. Both the virginal and the diabolical contracts are sealed with rings (41).[241]

The ugly scene of ritual intercourse is a concrete rendering of the promised consummation in the wedding chamber of the celestial bridegroom, intoned throughout the consecration of the virgin (34). The triumphal words of St. Agnes, "Behold, what I desired, now I see, what I hoped for, now I possess" (51), articulated by the nun immediately following the consecration, is countered by the newly made witch's jubilant dance. The dance is accompanied by cithars and tambour, instruments heavy with biblical associations.[242] But the resonance with the female mystical tradition is even more noteworthy. Mechtild of Magdeburg represents the bridal soul as performing a very similar dance to the one described in the *Recollection*. The wedding ring that Mechtild of Hackeborn besought from Christ contained two stones which represent Christ himself both as cithar and as handsome youth leading the dance at the nuptials. By the same token, Gertrude the Great's *Spiritual Exercises*, which, as noted above, closely track the virgin's rite of consecration, alternately represents the celestial bridegroom leading his virgins in a circular dance and serenading them dulcetly on the cithar.[243]

The silent witnesses are integral to each rite. Thus in the sermon during which the devil asserts that there is no other paradise apart from his assemblies with their indiscriminate orgies, he is inverting the bishop's traditional anathema against anyone who attempts to defile the virgin (54). The orgiastic feasting that follows parallels the nuptial mass subsequent to the virgin's consecration (57). (Although the witches have their choice of partners, they are still obliged to engage in the sex act as payment of their "debt"—reminiscent of the marriage debt.)[244] In lieu of the bishop's final benediction, the devil concludes by threatening his followers in horrible tones. Throughout the ritual induction and subsequent orgy, the assembly is referred to as a *congregatio*—a word charged with ecclesiastical meaning. The members of the congregation are arranged in rows, moreover, as would be the case in a church.[245]

Nor does the feudal imagery that embellishes the witch's induction contend with the essential contours of the consecration of the virgin; it corroborates them. Over a century earlier, Durandus's rite had introduced the sequence in which the virgin kneels before the bishop with clasped hands while the bishop, in turn, clasps her hands between his own. The virgin then proceeds to make her solemn vow to preserve her virginity, subsequently kissing the bishop's hand. According to René Metz, this was an explicit importation from feudalism.[246] Durandus's feudal emphasis is not his only intervention in the tradition. Twelfth- and thirteenth-century liturgists had developed a more restrained rite in which the marriage to Christ was downplayed, perhaps reflecting the Gregorian reform's efforts to appropriate nuptial imagery for the clergy. The bride's ring was pronounced optional; no longer was the rite to be celebrated on Easter or other high holidays.[247]

In Durandus's version, however, the mystical marriage with Christ returns with a vengeance. The bishop is more explicitly associated with Christ the bridegroom, bestowing the virgin's ring with the words of the *Sponsus* from the Song of Songs (33).[248] With the augmentation of the mystical marriage motif, the level of solemnity rises proportionately. The ritual is once again recommended for Epiphany or Easter (1). Holy water is introduced for the blessing of the nun's habit. There is also a heightened sense of drama. In the twelfth- and thirteenth-century rites, the postulant had approached the bishop bearing candles only after she had changed out of her secular clothes. William's rendition is more compelling: the postulant is already bearing candles when she first approaches the bishop, as was mirrored by her diabolical counterpart

(5). The antiphon "I am married to him," common to most rites, migrates to the virgin's reception of the ring, at which point the nun is directed to demonstratively raise her hand to reveal the ring (42, 44). The alignment with secular marriage is also much more deliberate. Durandus includes new blessings for the ring and wreath, which are imported directly from secular rites (26, 27). And while the twelfth-century liturgists had insisted that the ring (if there was one) should be placed on the nun's third finger, in Durandus's version the ring had migrated to the fourth finger, corresponding to secular custom.

Durandus's conflation of feudal and matrimonial imagery should come as no surprise. Jacques Le Goff has posited that one of the more plausible origins for the rite of homage was, in fact, the exchange of promises in betrothal.[249] But if indeed feudal relations descended from marriage vows, they were clearly modified over time to accommodate the union of equals that was supposed to subsist between lord and vassal. Such a modification does not sit well with the devil's unequivocal mastery of his devotee, however.[250] If the diabolical pact is interpreted through the lens of the liturgical tradition associated with the consecration of the virgin, however, this inconsistency disappears entirely. For in the consecration of the virgin, the prospective bride of Christ is the soul of abjection, filled with supplications and prostrations both before Christ, the bridegroom, and his episcopal surrogate (11, 13, 34).[251]

By the time of the trials at Arras, the primary association of women with witchcraft was coming to the fore. Nider, writing between 1435 and 1438, was the first theologian to argue that women were more inclined toward witchcraft than men.[252] This insight would be corroborated within five years by the near complete assimilation of women with witchcraft by the figure of "the Adversary" in Le Franc's poem, including a prescient description of the witch as the devil's spouse. *The Hammer of Witches* will finish the job, not only by using the Latin feminine form in the title to signify that the witches at issue were female but also by providing an entire theological rationale as to why.[253] Eventually, the alleged female predisposition for witchcraft would be borne out by the number of women accused and sentenced in the actual trials.[254] But at the time that Nider and Le Franc were writing, they were somewhat ahead of the curve. When the anonymous *Errors of the Gazari* makes the point that the description of the induction of a witch pertains to both sexes, he nevertheless utilizes the masculine article throughout. His account is also, as we have seen, heavily feudalized—a ritual generally associated with men.

The anonymous *Recollection* likewise makes the point that the rite of induction recounted applies to both men and women. And, indeed, it is interesting that there were ultimately more men accused in the Arras trials than women. Nevertheless, the *Recollection* uses a female novice through-out, suggesting that the perception of women as witches was becoming more widespread. Not surprisingly the feudal framework is supplemented, and ulti-mately dominated, by marriage, a structure more conducive to women. Since marriage was now firmly ensconced as a sacrament, the witch's induction was, by definition, already sacrilegious. It is the appropriation of the consecrated virgin's marriage to Christ, however, that is the diabolical trump. Moreover, the inversion of the marriage to Christ would have been immediately leg-ible to church authorities outside the small circle of Aragois persecutors. In this context the letter written in 1460 by Giles Carlier, dean of Cambrai and bishop's officialis, describing the confession of the prostitute Deniselle, is espe-cially suggestive, comparing her offense to a breach in the soul's marriage with Christ: "she committed the apostasy of perfidy because she withdrew from the faith, denying it, and even from God, because she withdrew from the bond (*vinculum*) of faith, by which she was united to him, according to that [say-ing] of Osee 2[20]: 'And I will espouse thee to me in faith.' "[255] The fact that Deniselle was, moreover, a prostitute provides a vivid realization of the errant female souls represented by the likes of Gerson and Nider, who prostitute themselves to the devil.

Le Franc had described a scene in which an old woman followed up her homage to the devil with carnal intercourse. But the *Recollection* is the first time that copulation with the devil (or his demonic vicar) is incorporated into a formal rite of induction. The fact that there are no representative instances of ritual copulation with the devil described in the accounts of the Arras tri-als themselves, however, seems to beg the question of whether the anony-mous author was really providing the representative, composite account he alleged or whether he was, perhaps unconsciously, creating a script that corre-sponded to his theological expectations, which were essentially heteronorma-tive. Nor were these preconceptions unique, for while we have seen a number of instances in which women and men were engaged in orgies that included demons, it is always implied that the sexual excesses were perpetrated with members of the opposite sex. For instance, Le Franc tells us explicitly that any female witch who lacked a partner was provided with a male-seeming demon. While Le Franc's witches only resort to demons when a human partner is lacking, the sectarians of the *Recollection* are occasionally required to have sex with demons. And yet the same heteronormativity holds true. Hence we are told, "A man [*vir*] with a female-devil [*dyabola*] or a woman [*mulier*] with the demon [*demone*] never experiences pleasure, but only consents to copulation out of fear and obedience."[256]

The wording is extremely interesting. For the term *dyabola* and its male counterpart *dyabolus* is used here and elsewhere for female- and male-seeming demons. The term *demon*, however, seems to be reserved for the one who presides over the ceremony—either the chief demon or the devil himself. And, as the above passage seems to indicate, this entity is only represented as being sexually partnered with a woman. So while the anonymous author of the *Recollection* may assert that the ritual of induction was essentially unisex, he clearly flinched when it came down to describing a male postulant having sex with the devil, who is invariably described in masculine form. This antipathy is also latent in descriptions of the trials themselves, in which there are no instances of encounters between men and a male-seeming devil. There are sound theological reasons for this aversion. A number of theologians, Nider included, believed that the demon's residual angelic nature imparted an utter revulsion of sodomy, in which case a same-sex consummation was proscribed.[257] An alternative would be for the devil to transform himself into a succubus, simulating a heteronormative act. But such a metamorphosis would clearly be at odds with the devil's symbolic puissance. And thus the prominence of ritual copulation with the devil necessarily removed the rite from the homosocial ambit of feudalism, even as it articulated a liturgy more accommodating to women.

It is not surprising that this debased version of spiritual nuptials should surface when and where it did. The Council of Basel was the common denominator for many of the seminal thinkers on witchcraft. Nider actually wrote *The Anthill* while the council was in session; Le Franc was there in attendance of the count of Savoy when the council elected him Pope Felix V. And Nicolas Jacquier, one of the main inquisitors at Arras, was prominent both as a reformer at Basel and later as one of witchcraft's important theorists.[258]

But of equal importance is that Arras was situated in the Low Countries, which had long been associated with daring expressions of mystical love linked with antinomian heresy. Already in the early thirteenth century, Hadewijch tells of a Beguine who was persecuted for her noble *Minne*. Such violent disciplinary actions would escalate: a century later Marguerite Porete of Hainaut (d. 1310) was executed for writing a book believed to cultivate a depraved form of mystical love, sparking off the so-called heresy of the Free Spirit. This led to the temporary suppression of the Beguines, who were persecuted sporadically throughout the Middle Ages.[259] A clandestine group of heretics arose in Douai in 1420 whom chroniclers referred to as the Turlupins—presumably Beghards (the male counterparts to Beguines) and the women they allegedly corrupted through an antinomian line of seduction.[260] Gerson's deluded mystic, whom he believed to be in the grip of a demon, hailed from Arras. Nor should we be surprised that one of the defendants in the Vauderie was a woman called Mariette de Drue, whose nickname was "the Beguine" ("dit *Baiguine*").[261] In their identification with the bride of the Canticles, who was sick with love, women ended up dying for love.

By the later Middle Ages, bridal mysticism had become simultaneously the spiritual and theological lingua franca par excellence and an anxious area for concern. This is especially true for the Low Countries. Marguerite Porete's *Mirror of Simple Souls* was framed as a dialogue between the Soul and her mentor Lady Love, who prepares the Soul for her union with God. The work outlines seven stages of ascent that lead to total annihilation in God, the seventh reserved for when the soul separates from the body.[262] The Soul's spiritual odyssey contains some provocative twists and turns. Especially noteworthy is the claim that the annihilated soul "neither desires nor despises poverty nor tribulation, neither mass nor sermon, neither fast nor prayer, and gives to Nature all that is necessary without remorse or conscience."[263] To Marguerite's judges this reads as a presumptuous declaration that the heedless individual venturing on this precarious path had not only dispensed with the church but believed that she could commit any act, however depraved, without incurring sin—a clear indication of antinomian leanings.

The judgment against Marguerite would find corroboration in the Low Countries by later proponents of bridal mysticism. Book 2 of John Ruusbroec's mystical classic *The Spiritual Espousals* contains a virulent attack on false mystics, providing as a negative exemplar a summary account of Marguerite Porete's *Mirror*, with its misguided sense of union.[264] By the same token, his treatise *On Twelve Beguines* laments how many women had strayed from the proper path of contemplation, again emphasizing how the contemplative life could go wrong by veering off into fallacious assertions regarding union with God.[265] But Ruusbroec's efforts to separate himself from Marguerite and her ilk did not spare him the critique of Gerson, who believed that Ruusbroec himself had veered off into fallacious assertions regarding union with God.[266]

Some prominent authorities were proficient in many of the different conflicted discourses touched on in this chapter. The learned Flemish monk, Denis the Carthusian (d. 1471), wrote a lengthy exposition on the Song of Songs. For all its passion, however, Denis is careful to cite Gerson's baleful warnings about the dangers of devolving into a "disgraceful carnality" that would "offend chaste ears."[267] His treatise *On the Reform of Nuns* took the form of a dialogue between the *sponsa* and her celestial bridegroom. As the epithet "Doctor Ecstaticus" suggests, Denis was himself a mystic who wrote about contemplation firsthand. He also contributed to the discourse of spiritual discernment.[268] And like many, if not most, clerics invested in the cause for reform in this period, Denis was also deeply concerned about witchcraft. A contemporary of the Vauderie, Denis apparently added his theological ballast in support of the witch trials through a treatise now lost.[269]

The *Recollection* exists on a continuum with this provocative discourse. By utilizing the consecration of the virgin as bride of Christ as a template for the ritual induction into the witch's cult, the anonymous author was aligning Arras's latest religious disturbance with the mottled legacy of the region. Mystics and theologians alike had carefully prepared the marriage bed and were now compelled to lie in it. The groom was not the one they had hoped for; it was the one they had always feared.

Conclusion

Who is there that is not led out of himself in dreams and
nocturnal visions, and sees much when sleeping which he
had never seen waking? Who is so stupid and foolish as
to think that all these things which are only done in spirit
happen in the body?

—*Canon Episcopi*[1]

This study is framed by two alarming instances of credulity. Early in the third
century, Tertullian married the consecrated virgins of Carthage to Christ out of
the conviction that the antediluvian flood of biblical lore was visited by God as
punishment for miscegenation between the angelic and human races. Fearing
that history would repeat itself, he insisted that the virgins remove any possible temptation they might provide for angels by covering their heads in the
manner of matrons, arguing that they were, after all, married to Christ. Yet the
horrible rendezvous between women and angels was not averted—merely postponed. For in the fifteenth century, religious authorities were not only prepared
to believe that it was possible for humans and angels to mix sexually but were
convinced that such abominable acts were taking place in their midst.

Although there is over a millennium separating Tertullian from the rise of
diabolical sabbath-centered witchcraft beliefs, these discrete encounters with
the supernatural are nevertheless united by a shared anxiety over the interplay
between a woman's spirituality and sexuality, and a desire to control these
dynamics. It is not difficult to see the repressive strategies deployed by the
church fathers, with their emphasis on Christ's brides as virginal, submissive,
silent, and, ideally, cloistered. And the monastery, ever the habitat par excellence for Christ's brides, will always retain something of this punitive legacy.
Despite the very different backgrounds of the Frankish Basina and the urbane
Heloise, both were in their own ways held prisoner by the claims monasticism
propounded on behalf of the celestial bridegroom.

But from the time of Ambrose, if not earlier, there were signs that the title of Christ's bride was not simply the marker of an earlier defeat but a coveted accolade that women ardently sought—at least this is one way of understanding the accounts of throngs of virgins publicly consecrated by Ambrose. In Merovingian Gaul, the nun Baudonivia uses spousal imagery to describe the spirituality of the Frankish queen, Radegund, providing the concrete evidence that women themselves identified with the bridal persona. Indeed, the Radegund presented in Baudonivia's vita anticipates the rise of later female mystics both in the intensity of her ascetic practices and in her direct revelations from Christ. Some of the evidence for this identification is darker, however. If there is any truth to ninth-century Rictrude's much later vita, the intact virgin's effortless connection with Christ was also the potential source of rivalry in religious communities, which led to cruel retaliations. In a similar vein, the later Gilbertines were prepared to avenge themselves by castrating the man who had dishonored a member of their community.

Twelfth-century heteroascetics, such as Christina of Markyate and her beloved, Geoffrey, arose in a culture that not only gave an unprecedented degree of validation to the emotions but had even begun to smile upon the institution of marriage. With the rising status of the clergy, moreover, it became increasingly plausible for a religious woman to associate the male object of her desire with Christ—a conflation that advanced the disparate and idiosyncratic causes of both Abelard and Robert of Arbrissel. It was in this climate of affectivity that Bernard of Clairvaux wrote his sermons on the Song of Songs, which acted as tinder to the mystical conflagration of the next century. Only with the rise of the Cistercian-inspired mysticism of the Beguines does the full extent of women's assimilation with the bridal persona come into focus. Although there have been ingenious efforts to widen the perimeters of what it meant to be a *sponsa Christi* since the time of Radegund, it is in the thirteenth century that we find an irresistible groundswell of nonvirgins claiming a place at the celestial groom's side. The virgin's special prerogative is never entirely dissipated: and yet the sheer force of identification by women of mixed status will gradually change the contours of the bride altogether.

Equally important are the many different ways in which the mystical marriage with Christ is deployed: Dorothea of Montau is represented as entering into a mystical union characterized by a startling degree of physical pain. Catherine of Siena anticipated her mystical marriage to Christ on the scaffold with the execution of Niccolò di Toldo. There are as many mystical embellishments as there are mystics. But two factors tend to unite the disparate visions: the identification of bride of Christ is so complete that for Italian virgin and

Prussian widow alike, their confessors used the simple shorthand of *sponsa* when referring to their holy charges. Second, marriage with Christ was associated with the progressive tendency to embody spiritual truths or manifest them concretely in some other fashion.

In the later Middle Ages, bridal mysticism offered select women an unprecedented degree of freedom and privilege in the church—privilege and authority perhaps unparalleled since the time of Tertullian's unveiled virgins. Religious authorities in each period responded with their own strategies of containment. Tertullian had insisted on the veil as marker of gender and submission; Cyprian and others had denounced the relations between the *virgines subintroductae* and their clerical sponsors—relations eventually outlawed at the Council of Nicaea (325); Ambrose would tighten the parallels between mystical and secular marriage. Such efforts augur the eventual claustration of nuns. The clergy of the later Middle Ages would apply a different set of disciplinary tools for controlling religious women's spirituality. By this time, however, the brides of Christ no longer presented a unified group: some of the most visible, and problematical, were neither virgins nor cloistered and hence less easily controlled. Thus the disciplinary measures took various forms. The Beguines were actively persecuted. But other strategies of containment operated on a more subtle rhetorical level. Gerson would attack the intimacy of pious women and their clerical confidants, honing the genre of spiritual discernment for suspect mystics. Whereas Athanasius and Ambrose had introduced Mary as Christ's ultimate bride in order to humble the virgins, Gerson would introduce Joseph to share in Mary's special prerogatives as bride, attempting to supplant the female mystics' hold on the mystical marriage by this new incorporated vision.

There is an additional irony hovering over the female religious vocation that covertly unites antiquity with the later Middle Ages. Tertullian's solution of marrying consecrated virgins to Christ was a response to what he perceived as the dangerous liberties that these women were taking in his day. But in the later period, female mystics' marriage with Christ had actually become part of the problem. The all-important leaven for change was the implacable operation of the laws of gravity: the propensity for powerful metaphors to be realized in the material world. Tertullian argued that the virgins in question should not consider themselves angels, but as submissive spouses of Christ who must dress and behave accordingly; by Ambrose's time the role of spouse had solidified, appropriating not only the legal status but even the ceremony associated with secular marriage. With the rise of bridal mysticism in the high Middle Ages, the mystic's status as *sponsa Christi* was often realized in very concrete and flamboyant terms, replete with marriage ceremonies, painful consummations, and externally perceptible pregnancies.

Gerson and Nider were both responding to what they perceived as the dangerous excess that had crept into female spirituality, largely through the medium of bridal mysticism. Yet the corrective imagery they implemented was no more immune to the laws of gravity than was the bride herself. Gerson attempts to discredit the female mystic by turning her into a faithless queen, fornicating with the messenger of a foreign king. Nider, in turn, will preface his discussion of witches (a discussion interspersed with anecdotes about female mystics) by depicting the soul betraying its union with Christ through prostituting herself to devils. In other words, both invert the mystical marriage to the detriment of female mystics. And in no time at all we see the rise of witchcraft charges in which copulation with the devil assumes center stage, framed by a diabolical version of the virgin's marriage to Christ. In addition, both men tended to disparage the spirituality of women in monastic institutions—undermining the efficacy of even the traditional bride of Christ. This is especially true of Nider.

Yet it is unfair to make individuals such as Gerson or Nider shoulder the responsibility for the antifemale turn that late medieval religion seemed destined to take. To begin with, their imagery was not an instigator of change, merely its register, comparable to a pulse that reveals the spiritual condition of an era. Furthermore, such images were not formed in a vacuum. Clerical culture's antipathy to the female sex was as venerable as it was robust: it often blossomed into full-on antifeminism when women were perceived as a threat to religious men. So it was with Thomas of Cantimpré, best known as a chief proponent and hagiographer of the Beguine movement. But Thomas's legacy is mixed. Despite his overt fascination with holy women, his writings reveal a progressive ambivalence that will render him something of a dangerous ally for the Beguines in particular, but pious women generally. Ultimately, his interest in holy women becomes tempered by fear of contact between the sexes. Some of the images he chooses to decry as dangerous are striking. In particular, Thomas segues from the sons of God corrupting the daughters of men to the much more contemporary religious scene: the sons of God debauching the daughters of God (i.e., religious women); spiritual mothers giving birth to carnal children, fathered by spiritual sons.

But Thomas's tactical reading of Genesis 6 should not be taken to imply that he believed that the original sons of God (i.e., fallen angels) had ceased to be a threat. In fact, Thomas does not just represent, but is on the cutting edge of, both clerical culture's rising interest in the demonic world and the perception that religious women were particular targets. Women such as Mary of Oignies and Lutgard of Aywières did heroic battle against the hoards of demons assailing Christendom; yet religious women were also progressively presented as victimized by the sexually predatory incubus.

Thomas of Cantimpré was a spiritual trendsetter in many ways. Not only are his writings a key source for understanding female religiosity in his own period, but also for anticipating some of the directions it will be represented as taking. On the one hand, there is his support of the Beguine movement, conveyed through the many mystical wonders of the disparate brides of Christ he wrote about; on the other hand, there is the growing preoccupation with women as sexual threats to religious men and incubi as sexual threats to religious women. The most compelling heir to Thomas's different initiatives is his later Dominican confrere, John Nider. As Nider himself mentions in the prologue to *The Anthill*, his work was modeled after *Concerning Bees*. But Thomas's influence extended beyond genre to gender: *The Anthill* reflects many of the preoccupations and biases of the earlier work. In particular Nider inherits Thomas's fatal attraction to both religious women and the demonic world.

In short, there are factors that must necessarily modify the usual historiographical representations of Thomas of Cantimpré as unquestioned friend to holy women and Gerson as their unequivocal foe. Even Thomas's positive representations of women are not without a darker side. Through his astounding accounts of somatic spirituality, Thomas managed to bring earth and heaven, the natural and the supernatural, ever closer together. The more proximate relation of women with the demonic world is but an aspect of this. And as an avid chronicler of the mystical life, Thomas was necessarily an abettor of the dangerous tendency to mix visions with reality. In contrast, Gerson was aware of the danger: that the breakdown between spiritual and corporeal vision, between fantasy and reality, could only lead to disaster. Insofar as he was correct, he could be presented as a defender of religious women.

In the time that elapsed between Thomas of Cantimpré and John Nider, there was an undeniable escalation in the efforts to render spiritual truths in material terms, as is apparent in the progressively embodied nature of the *sponsa Christi*. It is this constant intermingling of the sacred and profane, "this fatuous familiarity with God" in daily life, that Huizinga had regarded as dangerous.[2] The danger he anticipated was a deterioration in the quality of religious life and thought, auguring the need for the Reformation. But the same intermingling presented attendant dangers, particularly for women. Subsumed by her bridal identity, the female mystic was alternately represented as passive object and active subject of voluptuous desire for her supernatural lover. It was the intersection of these desires that drew down the unwelcome attention of the discourse of spiritual discernment; it was the changing perception of these desires that contributed to the eventual profile of the witch. The bride's expressions of ardent longing, existing on a continuum with the perception of women's unbridled lust, eventually took their toll. As a result, women were no longer regarded as the passive objects of supernatural predators, as was the case in Tertullian's day, but as ardently complicit. This expansion of the female appetite is refracted through *The Hammer of Witches* with the observation that while formerly women had been harassed by incubus lovers against their will, they now sought them out.[3]

There was a "blending of spheres" that was even more dangerous than the intermingling of the sacred and profane that Huizinga eschewed, and that was the distinction between external reality and internal states. There is no doubt that mysticism cultivated this kind of convergence. On the most basic level, there were unprecedented visions of, and traffic between, heaven, hell, and purgatory—so that the interpenetration of earth with these supernatural zones was, arguably, experienced as never before. But this intermingling could also happen in more quotidian ways. Ida of Louvain allegedly had but to read that "*the Word was made flesh and dwelt among us*" and meat would materialize in her mouth.[4] Mystics went on to stake even more fantastic claims. For instance, Alfonso of Jaén, one of many confessors to Bridget of Sweden, alleged that Bridget was permitted to see Christ with her corporeal eyes on her deathbed. In other words, on the brink of death divine revelations were no longer confined to her imagination, but had become perceptible to her senses.[5] Christ had actually appeared before her eyes. By the same token, Ermine of Reims would experience the real presence of demons on a regular basis.

As I implied earlier, few saw the danger in this kind of elision as clearly as Gerson. He often derided such mystical follies. "If a miracle lacks any devout purpose or meaning, for that reason it is to be suspected or rejected, as it would have been if Christ had flown through the air, and as with all sacrilegious stunts of magicians. There was in our times a woman who was well known for revelations in such matters. This sign of truth has shown, unless I am mistaken, that she was out of her mind."[6] And, in fact, Gerson said explicitly that those who confuse the realm of the imaginary with the outside world were mentally ill. Yet Gerson was painfully aware that, just as there was no set formula for discerning spirits, neither was there a sure way for differentiating between dreaming and waking, or illusion and reality.[7]

The learned men who were the engines behind the Arras witchcraft trials chose illusion over reality. Much of their intellectual energy was expended on proving that what former generations had perceived as dream or illusion was, in fact, real. The texts they produced in support of the witch trials read like the wrong side of a dream. The main impetus behind Inquisitor Nicolas Jacquier's *Scourge of Heretics* is a case in point. Its purpose was to attack gainsayers who deny the reality of the sabbath. Such people are perceived as obstructive because they would also be inclined to argue that if the sabbath was not real, the people who confess to attending them were deluded, and their testimony against others necessarily worthless. It is to skeptics such as these that Jacquier frames the ingenious retort that it is the demons themselves who inspire the claims that the sabbath is simply a dream or illusion.[8] To sustain his argument, and to remain on the right side of orthodoxy, Jacquier was forced to take on the ninth-century *Canon Episcopi*, with its declaration that night flights and feasting were simply the delusions of old women and that it was heretical to believe otherwise. So he made it his business to prove that the modern-day witches' sect was of an entirely different ilk than the illusions described by the *Canon*.[9]

Secular authorities, however, were less convinced. At one point they pressured the clerics from Arras into seeking the opinion of theologians from Louvain and elsewhere as to the reality of the sabbath. There was no consensus. Some said that it was not real, others said it was an illusion that could become real with divine permission, and still others believed that it was entirely real and that sectarians were transported there body and soul.[10] Undaunted by these countervailing views, however, the clerical prime movers at Arras continued to be united in their conviction that the sabbaths were every bit as real as were the people they continued to execute for their attendance.[11] The first part of the *Recollection* is, as we have seen, devoted to the reality of the sabbath. The theologian John Tinctor also lent his learned support at the critical juncture when the witch hunt was about to descend on his hometown of Douai.[12] The anonymous treatise *Vauderie of the Lyonnais*, written in 1460 and probably influenced by the trials in Arras, skips over the debates and just presents the sabbath as a grim fact.[13] Presumably Denis the Carthusian's lost treatise defending the trials would have maintained the party line.

Bridal mysticism contributed to a culture in which the distance between reality and fantasy was fast disappearing and the impossible was becoming commonplace. Embodied desire was sufficiently compelling to create a space where dreams came true, and it was powerful enough to drag the bride down to hell.

AA SS	*Acta Sanctorum*. Paris: Victor Palmé, 1865–.
ACW	*Ancient Christian Writers*. Westminster, Md.: Newman Press, 1946–.
ANF	*Ante-Nicene Fathers*. 1890. 10 vols. Reprint, Grand Rapids, Mich.: Eerdmans, 1994.
Caesarius	Caesarius of Heisterbach. *Dialogus miraculorum.* Edited by Joseph Strange. 2 vols. Cologne: J. M. Heberle, 1851. Translated by H. Von E. Scott and C. C. Swinton Bland. *The Dialogue on Miracles*. 2 vols. London: Routledge, 1929.
CCCM	*Corpus Christianorum, Continuatio Mediaeualis*. Turnhout: Brepols, 1966–.
CCSL	*Corpus Christianorum Series Latina*. Turnhout: Brepols, 1954–.
CM	*The Life of Christina of Markyate*. Edited and translated by C. H. Talbot. Oxford: Clarendon Press, 1959.
CSEL	*Corpus Scriptorum Ecclesiasticorum Latinorum*. Vienna: F. Tempsky [et al.], 1866–.
Du Clercq	Du Clercq, James. *Mémoires J. Du Clercq sur le règne de Philippe le Bon, Duc de Bourgogne.* Edited by F. de Reiffenberg. 4 vols. Brussels: J. M. Lacrosse, 1835–36.
DVC	Aldhelm. *De virginitate (carmen)*. Edited by Rudolf Ehwald, *MGH, Auct. Ant.* Translated by Michael Lapidge and Michael Herren, *Aldhelm: The Prose Works*. Ipswich: D. S. Brewer, 1985.
DVP	Aldhelm. *De virginitate (prosa)*. Edited by Rudolf Ehwald, *MGH, Auct. Ant.* Translated by Mi-

chael Lapidge and Michael Herren, *Aldhelm: The Prose Works*. Ipswich: D. S. Brewer, 1979.

FC   *Fathers of the Church*. Washington, D.C.: Catholic University of America Press, 1947–.

Fredericq   Fredericq, Paul, ed. *Corpus documentorum inquisitionis haereticae pravitatis Neerlandicae*. 5 vols. Ghent: J. Vuylsteke; The Hague: Martinus Nijhoff, 1889–1903.

GC   Gregory of Tours. *Liber in gloria confessorum*. Edited by Bruno Krusch, *MGH, Scriptores rerum Merovingicarum*, 1:474–820. Translated by Raymond Van Dam, *Glory of the Confessors*. Liverpool: Liverpool University Press, 1989.

GL   Gerson, Jean. *Oeuvres complètes*. Edited by Palémon Glorieux. 10 vols. Paris: Desclée, 1960–73.

GM   Gregory of Tours. *Liber in gloria martyrum*. Edited by Bruno Krusch, *MGH, Scriptores rerum Merovingicarum*, 1, 2: 484–561. Translated by Raymond Van Dam, *The Glory of the Martyrs*. Liverpool: Liverpool University Press, 1988.

Gratian   Gratian. *Decretum Magistri Gratiani*. Edited by A. Friedberg. In *Corpus Iuris Canonici*. 2nd ed. Vol. 1. Leipzig: B. Tauchnitz, 1879. Reprint, Graz: Akademische Druck-U. Verlagsanstalt, 1955.

Imaginaire *L'Imaginaire du sabbat: Edition critique des texts les plus anciens (1430 c.–1440 c.)*. Edited by Martine Ostorero, Agostino P. Bagliani, and Kathrin Utz Tremp. Lausanne: Cahiers lausannois d'histoire médiévale, 1999.

Ld   John of Marienwerder. *Vita Lindana, AA SS*, October, 13:499–560.

LHX   Gregory of Tours. *Libri historiarum X*. Edited by Bruno Krusch and Wilhelm Arndt, *MGH, Script. Rer. Merov.*, 1, 1. Rev. ed., Hannover: Hahn, 1951. Translated by Lewis Thorpe, *History of the Franks*. Harmondsworth, Middlesex: Penguin, 1974.

LNPNFC	*A Select Library of Nicene and Post-Nicene Fathers of the Church.* New York: Christian Literature Co. [et al.], 1887–92. Reprint, Grand Rapids, Mich.: Eerdmans [et al.], 1952–.
LSG	Mechtild of Hackeborn. *Liber specialias gratiae.* In *Revelationes Gertrudianae ac Mechtildianae II: Sanctae Mechtildis virginis ordinis Sancti Benedicti Liber specialis gratiae; Accedit sororis Mechtildis ejusdem ordinis Lux divinitatis.* Edited by Louis Paquelin [et al.]. Vol. 1. Poitiers: Oudin, 1877.
MGH	*Monumenta Germaniae Historica.* Hannover: Impensis Bibliopolii Hahniani et al., 1826–.
MGH, Auct. Ant.	*Monumenta Germaniae Historica, Auctores Antiquissarum.*
MGH, Scrip.	*Monumenta Germaniae Historica, Scriptores.*
MGH, Scrip. Rer. Merov.	*Monumenta Germaniae Historica, Scriptores Rerum Merovingicarum.*
MHW	*Medieval Holy Women in Christian Tradition.* Edited by Alastair Minnis and Rosalynn Voaden. Turnhout: Brepols, 2010.
PG	*Patrologia cursus completus . . . series Graeca.* Edited by J.-P. Migne. 162 vols. Paris: Garnier Fratres and J.-P. Migne, 1857–66.
PL	*Patrologia cursus completes . . . series Latina.* Edited by J.-P. Migne. 221 vols. Paris: Garnier Fratres and J.-P. Migne, 1844–64.
PR	*Le Pontifical Romain au Moyen-Age.* Vol. 1 of *Le Pontifical Romain du XIIe siècle.* Edited by Michel Andrieu. *Studi e Testi* 86. Vatican: Biblioteca Apostolica Vaticana, 1938.
PRC	*Le Pontifical Romain au Moyen-Age.* Vol. 2 of *Le Pontifical Romain de la Curie Romaine au XIIIe siècle.* Edited by Michel Andrieu. Studi e Testi 87. Vatican: Biblioteca Apostolica Vaticana, 1940.
PRG	*Le Pontifical Romano-Germanique du dixième siècle.* Edited by Cyrille Vogel and Reinhard Elze. Studi e Testi, 226. Vatican: Biblioteca Apostolica Vaticana, 1963–71.

SC	*Sources chrétiennes*. Paris: Editions du Cerf, 1940–.
SE	*The Standard Edition of the Complete Psychological Works of Sigmund Freud*. Edited by James Strachey. 24 vols. London: Hogarth Press, 1953–74.
Sept.	*Septililium B. Dorotheae*. Edited by Franz Hipler. *Analecta Bollandiana* 2 (1883), 3 (1884), 4 (1885).
SW	*Sainted Women of the Dark Ages*. Edited by Jo Ann McNamara, John Halborg, and E. Gordon Whatley. Durham, N.C.: Duke University Press, 1992.
VER	John Le Graveur. *Entre Dieu et Satan: Les visions d'Ermine de Reims (+ 1396)*. Edited and translated into modern French by Claude Arnaud-Gillet. Florence: Sismel, Edizioni del Galluzzo, 1997.
VL	John of Marienwerder. *Vita Dorotheae Montoviensis Magistri Johannis Marienwerder*. Edited by Hans Westpfahl. *Forschungen und Quellen zur Kirchen- und Kulturgeschichte Ostdeutschlands*, vol. 1. Cologne: Böhlau, 1964.
VP	Gregory of Tours. *Liber vitae patrum*. Edited by Bruno Krusch. *MGH, Scrip. Rer. Merov.*, 1, 2:661–744. Hanover: Hahn, 1885. Translated by Edward James, *The Life of the Fathers*. Liverpool: Liverpool University Press, 1985.
VRV	Hucbald. *Vita S. Rictrudis viduae*. *AA SS*, May, 3:81–88. Edited and translated by Jo Ann McNamara, John Halborg, and E. Gordon Whatley, *Sainted Women of the Dark Ages*, 195–219. Durham, N.C.: Duke University Press, 1992.
VSRB	*De vita Sanctae Radegundis* by Baudovinia. *De vita Sanctae Radegundis libri duo. MGH, Scrip. Rer. Merov.*, 2:377–95.
VSRF	*De vita Sanctae Radegundis* by Fortunatus. *De vita Sanctae Radegundis libri duo. MGH, Scrip. Rer. Merov.*, 2:364–77.

X   *Decretales Gregorii IX.* In *Decretalium Collectio-nes.* Edited by A. Friedberg. In *Corpus Iuris Canonici.* 2nd ed. Vol. 2, cols. 5–928. Leipzig: B. Tauchnitz, 1879. Reprint, Graz: Akademische Druck-U. Verlagsanstalt, 1955.

NOTES

INTRODUCTION

1. Optatus, *De schismate Donatistarum* 6.4, *PL* 11:1074.

2. For the bishop's wedding, see Chapter 4; for Gerson, see Chapter 7.

3. Peter John Olivi, quodlib. 4, q. 26, in *Quodlibeta quinque*, ed. Stephan Defraia (Grottaferrata, Rome: College of St. Bonaventure at Claras Aquas, 2002), pp. 286–90.

4. For an eloquent devotional treatment of these interlocking meanings, see Dom Marmion, *Sponsa Verbi: La Vierge consacrée au Christ* (Namur: Editions Maredsous, 1948).

5. See Denys Turner, *Eros and Allegory: Medieval Exegesis of the Song of Songs* (Kalamazoo, Mich.: Cistercian Publications, 1995).

6. On Bernard's sermons, see Chapter 5.

7. Sarah McNamer, *Affective Meditation and the Invention of Medieval Compassion* (Philadelphia: University of Pennsylvania Press, 2010), p. 29

8. Judith Hoch-Smith and Anita Spring, eds., *Women in Ritual and Symbolic Roles* (New York: Plenum Press, 1978), editors' introduction, p. 2.

9. See Chapter 6.

10. H. C. Lea, *Materials toward a History of Witchcraft* (New York: Thomas Yoseloff, 1957), ed. Arthur Howland, 1:431–22; Lynn Thorndike, *History of Magic and Experimental Science* (New York: Columbia University, 1934), 4:123. For bibliography on recent work on the relationship between saints, witches, etc., see Chapter 7, n185, below.

CHAPTER I

1. The most famous patristic representation of this tradition is in Jerome's *Adversus Jovinianum* 1.47, *PL* 23:276–78, trans. *LNPNFC*, 6:383–86. For its continuation into the Middle Ages, see Katharina Wilson and Elizabeth Makowski, *Wykked Wyves and the Woes of Marriage: Misogamous Literature from Juvenal to Chaucer* (Albany: State University of New York Press, 1990); and R. Howard Bloch, *Medieval Misogyny and the Invention of Western Romantic Love* (Chicago: University of Chicago Press, 1991). See Alcuin Blamires's edition of some of the key texts in *Woman Defamed, Woman Defended: An Anthology of Medieval Texts* (New York: Oxford University Press, 1992). Biblical quotations are from the Douay-Rheims translation of the Latin Vulgate.

2. On Paul's attitude toward sexual relations, see Peter Brown, *The Body and Society: Men, Women, and Sexual Renunciation in Early Christianity* (New York: Columbia University Press, 1988), pp. 33–64; Dale Martin, *The Corinthian Body* (New Haven, Conn.: Yale University Press, 1996), pp. 163–79.

3. Justin Martyr, 1 *Apologia* 15.6, in *Apologie pour les chrétiens*, ed. and trans. Charles Munier, SC, 507 (Paris: Editions du Cerf, 2006), p. 168, trans. *ANF*, 1:167.

4. *Acts of Paul* c. 2, trans. M. R. James, *The Apocryphal New Testament* (Oxford: Clarendon Press, 1924; reprt., 1966), p. 273. On this text, see Sheila McGinn, "The Acts of Thecla," in *Searching the Scriptures: A Feminist Commentary*, ed. Elisabeth Schüsler Fiorenza (New York: Crossroad, 1994), 2:800–828.

5. *Acts of Paul* c. 3, trans. James, *Apocryphal New Testament*, p. 116.

6. See, for example, John Chrysostom's *La Virginité* 40.1–41.4, 44.1–2, 50.1–58.1, ed. Herbert Musurillo, *SC* 125 (Paris: Editions du Cerf, 1966), pp. 232–37, 250–55, 284–319, trans. Sally Shore, *On Virginity: Against Remarriage* (New York: Edwin Mellen, 1983), pp. 59–63, 81–95; Jerome, *De perpetua virginitate B. Mariae* c. 20, *PL* 23:203–4, trans. *LNPNFC*, 6:344–45; Jerome, Ep. 54, To Furia, c. 4, *PL* 22:551, trans. *LNPNFC*, 6:103.

7. Wayne Meeks, "The Image of the Androgyne: Some Uses of a Symbol in Earliest Christianity," *History of Religions* 13 (1974): 165–208. On veiling in classical culture, see Martin, *Corinthian Body*, pp. 233–37.

8. Jo Ann McNamara, *A New Song: Celibate Women in the First Three Christian Centuries* (Binghamton, N.Y.: Harrington Park Press, 1983), pp. 77–84, 108–9. Also see Ross Kraemer, "The Conversion of Women to Ascetic Forms of Christianity," *Signs* 6 (1980): 298–307; and Elizabeth Clark, "Ascetic Renunciation and Feminine Advancement: A Paradox of Late Ancient Christianity," in *Ascetic Piety and Women's Faith: Essays on Late Ancient Christianity* (Lewiston: Edwin Mellen, 1986), pp. 175–208; Grace Jantzen, *Power, Gender, and Christian Mysticism* (Cambridge: Cambridge University Press, 1995), pp. 50–53; Matthew Kuefler, *The Manly Eunuch: Masculinity, Gender Ambiguity, and Christian Ideology in Late Antiquity* (Chicago: University of Chicago Press, 2001), pp. 221–44.

9. Gnosticism's appeal to women is especially argued by Elaine Pagels, *The Gnostic Gospels* (New York: Random House, 1979). Recently the designation "Gnosticism" has come under attack by scholars who argue that there is no single religious movement associated with the term. David Brakke takes a middle ground, however, arguing for a Gnostic school of thought versus actual religion. See David Brakke, *Gnostics: Myth, Ritual, and Diversity in Early Christianity* (Cambridge, Mass.: Harvard University Press, 2010), esp. pp. 29–51. On the disparate sets of beliefs associated with the term "Gnosticism," see Brakke, "Self-Differentiation among Christian Groups: The Gnostics and Their Opponents," in *The Cambridge History of Christianity*, vol. 1, *Origins to Constantine* (Cambridge: Cambridge University Press, 2006), pp. 245–60.

10. *Gospel of Thomas*, in *The Nag Hammadi Library*, ed. James Robinson, rev. ed. (San Francisco: Harper and Row, 1990), p. 130.

11. John Bugge, *Virginitas: An Essay in the History of a Medieval Idea* (The Hague: Martinus Nijhoff, 1975), pp. 16–19; Norman Powell Williams, *The Ideas of the Fall and of Original Sin* (London: Longman's, Green, and Company, 1927), pp. 271–74.

12. Rosemary Ruether, "Misogynism and Virginal Feminism in the Fathers of the Church," in *Religion and Sexism: Images of Woman in the Jewish and Christian Traditions*, ed. Rosemary Ruether (New York: Simon and Schuster, 1974), pp. 175–77.

13. See David Brakke, *Demons and the Making of the Monk: Spiritual Combat in Early Christianity* (Cambridge, Mass.: Harvard University Press, 2006), pp. 184–99.

14. See Evelyne Patlagean, "L'histoire de la femme déguisée en moine et l'evolution de la sainteté feminine à Byzance," *Studi medievali*, ser. 3, 17, 2 (1976): 597–623.

15. W. H. Shewring, ed. and trans., *The Passion of SS. Perpetua and Felicity* c. 10 (London: Sheed and Ward, 1931), p. 11, trans. p. 31. For an introduction to this text, see Maureen Tilly, "The Passion of Perpetua and Felicity," in *Searching the Scriptures*, ed. Elisabeth Schüssler Fiorenza, 2:829–58; and Thomas Heffernan, *Sacred Biography: Saints and Their Biographers in the Middle Ages* (Oxford: Oxford University Press, 1988), pp. 185–230. Also see Aviad Kleinberg's analysis of how the *passio* was transformed in hagiographical tradition, ironing out all of Perpetua's possible doubts as well as her grief for her natural family (*Flesh Made Word: Saints' Stories and the Western Imagination* [Cambridge, Mass.: Belknap Press of Harvard University Press, 2008], pp. 54–80).

16. See Bugge, *Virginitas*, pp. 330–35. According to Peter Brown, the *vita angelica* had particular currency in Syrian circles (*Body and Society*, pp. 323–38).

17. Meeks, "Image of the Androgyne," p. 166.

18. For the conflicting attitudes toward eunuchs in late antique circles, see Kuefler, *Manly Eunuch*, pp. 245–82. For the conflation of eunuchs and angels in a later period, see Kathryn Ringrose, *The Perfect Servant: Eunuchs and the Social Construction of Gender in Byzantium* (Chicago: University of Chicago Press, 2005), pp. 38, 40–41, 80. For the gender ambiguity of male religious, see Brakke, *Demons and the Making of the Monk*, pp. 182–83.

19. On the sexism implicit in the concept of androgyny, see Martin, *Corinthian Body*, pp. 230–32.

20. *Excerpta ex Theodoto*, in Clement of Alexandria's *Stromata*, as cited by Elaine Pagels, *The Gnostic Paul: Gnostic Exegesis of the Pauline Letters* (Philadelphia: Fortress Press, 1975), p. 127.

21. See Pierre Adnès, "Le mariage spirituel," in *Dictionnaire de la spiritualité*, edited by Marcel Viller, F. Cavallera, and J. de Guibert (Paris: Beauchesne, 1932–95), 10:388–91. For usage of a parallel image in pagan sources, see Bugge, *Virginitas*, p. 59.

22. On the use of familial language and other strategies of equalization, see Rosemary Rader, *Breaking Boundaries: Male/Female Friendship in Early Christian Communities* (New York: Paulist Press, 1983), p. 113.

23. See Elizabeth Clark, "The Celibate Bridegroom and His Virginal Brides: Metaphor and the Marriage of Jesus in Early Christian Ascetic Exegesis," *Church History* 77 (2008): 1–25.

24. For a review of this set of associations, see Dyan Elliott, "Flesh and Spirit: Women and the Body," in *MHW*, pp. 13–46.

25. See Jean Gaudemet, "Note sur le symbolisme médiévale: Le marriage de l'évêque," *L'Année canonique* 22 (1978): 71–80. For the later period, see Megan McLaughlin, "The Bishop as Bridegroom: Marital Imagery and Clerical Celibacy in the Eleventh and Twelfth

Centuries," in *Medieval Purity and Piety: Essays on Medieval Clerical Celibacy and Religious Reform*, edited by Michael Frassetto (New York: Garland, 1998), pp. 210–37; and Gabriella Zarri, *Recinti: Donne, clausura e matrimonio nella prima età moderna* (Bologna: Il Mulino, 2000), pp. 282–84, 316–46.

26. Pagels, *Gnostic Paul*, pp. 68ff., 115, 124–27; cf. Brown, *Body and Society*, pp. 103–21. McNamara, *New Song*, pp. 68–70. On the mystery of the bridal chamber, see especially the Valentinian *Gospel of Philip*, in *The Nag Hammadi Library*, ed. Robinson, cc. 64–65, p. 139; c. 67, p. 140; c. 69, pp. 141, 142; c. 70, p. 142; c. 71, p. 143; c. 72, p. 143; cc. 75–76, p. 145; c. 82, p. 149; cc. 84–85, p. 150; cc. 185–86, p. 151. For the antifemale content in Gnosticism, see Jorunn Jacobsen Buckley, *Female Fault and Fulfillment in Gnosticism* (Chapel Hill: University of Chapel Hill Press, 1986).

27. Cf. the rhetoric of the Ps.-Clementine epistles on virginity and the disparagement of marriage. See Ep. 1, c. 4, in *Patres Apostolici*, ed. F. Diekamp (Tübingen: Henricus Laupp, 1913), 2:6, trans. *ANF*, 8:56.

28. René Metz, *La Consécration des vierges dans l'église romaine* (Paris: Presses universitaires de France, 1954), p. 120; McNamara, *New Song*, p. 121; Bugge, *Virginitas*, pp. 58, 66.

29. Tertullian, *De cultu feminarum* 1.1.2, in *Quinti Septimi Florentis Tertulliani opera*, CCSL, 1 (Turnhout: Brepols, 1954), p. 343, trans. *ANF*, 4:14 (hereafter cited as *Tertulliani opera*). For a more sympathetic reading that attempts to get beyond the "devil's gateway" trope, see F. Forrester Church, "Sex and Salvation in Tertullian," *Harvard Theological Review* 68 (1975): 85–101. McNamara is also aware of this more positive side (*New Song*, pp. 94–95, 110–11).

30. Meeks, "Image of the Androgyne," pp. 200–201.

31. Tertullian, *De baptismo* 17.1, in *Tertulliani opera*, 1:291, trans. *ANF*, 3:677.

32. Tertullian, *De praescriptione haereticorum* 41.5, in *Tertulliani opera*, 1:221, trans. *ANF*, 3:263; cf. his indictment of an anonymous woman's heretical teaching on baptism (*De baptismo* 1.3, in *Tertulliani opera*, 1:277, trans. *ANF*, 3:669). See his discussion of the virgin Philumene, below.

33. See Jérôme Alexandre, *Une Chair pour la gloire: L'anthropologie réaliste et mystique de Tertullien* (Paris: Beauchesne, 2001), pp. 426–54.

34. Tertullian groups the three prophets together in *Adversus Praxean* 1.5, in *Tertulliani opera*, 2:1159, trans. *ANF*, 3:597. For a rather fanciful account of the New Prophecy movement, including Tertullian's defense of it, see William Tabbernee, *Prophets and Gravestones: An Imaginative History of Montanists and Other Early Christians* (Peabody, Mass.: Hendrickson, 2009), esp. pp. 111–17. Tabbernee dates Tertullian's involvement in the New Prophecy movement to 208 (Ibid., p. 8). Also see Eric Osborn, *Tertullian: First Theologian of the West* (Cambridge: Cambridge University Press, 1997), pp. 210–13. Subsequent church fathers presented Tertullian as a schismatic, but it now seems doubtful that he actually left the church (Ibid., pp. 176–77). I am indebted to Maureen Tilly for her helpful comments and references concerning Tertullian's relationship with the New Prophecy.

35. *Adversus Iudaeos* 2.2, in *Tertulliani opera*, 2:1341, trans. *ANF*, 3:152. Cf. Ton H. C. Van Eijk's discussion of formative ancient and early Christian thinkers on this nexus of ideas in "Marriage and Virginity, Death and Immorality," in *Epektasis: Mélanges patristiques*

offerts au Cardinal Jean Daniélou, ed. Jacques Fontaine and Charles Kannengiesser (Paris: Beauchesne, 1972), pp. 209–35.

36. *De testimonia animae* 3.2, in *Tertulliani opera*, 1:178, trans. *ANF*, 3:177. I have altered this translation to make it more literal.

37. *De resurrectione mortuorum* 36.4–6, in *Tertulliani opera*, 2:969, trans. *ANF*, 3:571.

38. In fact, Montanists seemed to have been required to shun bigamists (i.e., those who had remarried). See Cyrille Vogel, "Les rites de la célébration du mariage: Leur signification dans la formation du lien durant le haut moyen âge," in *Il Matrimonio nella società altomedievale*, Settimane di studio del Centro Italiano di studi sull'alto medioevo, 24 (Spoleto: Presso la sede del Centro, 1977), 1:416, esp. n29.

39. Tertullian was hardly alone in his aversion. In the early church, the bishop could only have been married once (1 Tim. 3.2). There was also considerable scorn heaped on second marriages by the church fathers. See, for example, Chrysostom, *De non iterando conjugio*, *PG* 48:609–20, trans. Shore, *On Virginity*, pp. 129–45; and Jerome's infamous *Adversus Jovinianum*, esp. 1.14–15, *PL* 23:243–45, trans. *LNPNFC*, 6:358–59.

40. *Ad uxorem* 1.1.5, in *Tertulliani opera*, 3:374, trans. *ANF*, 4:39.

41. Ibid. 1.3.3, in *Tertulliani opera*, 3:375, trans. *ANF*, 4:40.

42. *De exhortatione castitatis* 3.8, 9.1, in *Tertulliani opera*, 2:1020, 1027, trans. *ANF*, 4:52, 55.

43. *De monogamia* 3.2, in *Tertulliani opera*, 2:1231, trans. *ANF*, 4:60.

44. See Alexandre, *Une Chair pour la gloire*.

45. See the discussion later in this chapter.

46. *De exhortatione castitatis* 11.1, in *Tertulliani opera* 2:1030–31, trans. *ANF*, 4:56.

47. Brown, *Body and Society*, pp. 51–52; Martin, *Corinthian Body*, pp. 168–79.

48. See the review of classical perspectives on the fabrication of sperm in Danielle Jacquart and Claude Thomasset, *Sexuality and Medicine in the Middle Ages*, trans. Matthew Adamson (Princeton, N.J.: Princeton University Press, 1988), pp. 48–55.

49. *De monogamia* 10.5–6, 7, 8, in *Tertulliani opera*, 2:1243–44, trans. *ANF*, 4:67.

50. In the treatise addressed to his wife, however, this same liability is rendered a plus. "What kind of yoke is that of two believers, (partakers) of one hope, one desire, one discipline, and one and the same service? Both (are) brethren, both fellow servants, no difference of spirit or of flesh; nay, (they are) truly 'two in one flesh' (Gen. 2.24). Where the flesh is one, one is the spirit too. . . . Where two (are), there withal is He Himself (Matt. 18.20)," *Ad uxorem* 2.8.6, in *Tertulliani opera*, 3:394, trans. *ANF*, 4:48. Tertullian is one of the first theologians to apply this text to the conjugal unit. He was anticipated by Clement of Alexandria (*Stromata* 3.10).

51. The closest he came to endorsing such an arrangement was, in fact, an argument against marriage to counter his recently widowed friend's hypothetical argument in favor of a wife to answer domestic needs:: "Take to yourself from among the widows one fair in faith, dowered with poverty, sealed with age. You will (thus) make a good marriage. A plurality of *such* wives is pleasing to God" (*De exhortatione castitatis* 12.2, in *Tertulliani opera*, 2:1032, trans. *ANF*, 4:56).

52. *De carne Christi* 23.3–4, in *Tertulliani opera*, 2:914, trans. *ANF*, 3:541. See Willemien

Otten, "Christ's Birth of a Virgin Who Became a Wife: Flesh and Speech in Tertullian's *De carne Christi*," *Vigiliae Christianae* 51 (1997): 247–60.

53. Matt. 12.18; Luke 8.20, 21; *De carne Christi* 7.1–2, in *Tertulliani opera*, 2:886–87, trans. *ANF*, 3:527.

54. *De exhortatione castitatis* 1.5, in *Tertulliani opera*, 2:1015–16, trans. *ANF*, 4:50.

55. *De pudicitia* 6.16, in *Tertulliani opera*, 2:1291, trans. *ANF*, 4:79.

56. *De exhortatione castitatis* 9.4, in *Tertulliani opera*, 2:1028, trans. *ANF*, 4:55.

57. *Ad uxorem* 1.8.2, in *Tertulliani opera*, 3:382, trans. *ANF*, 4:43.

58. *De exhortatione castitatis* 1.3–5, in *Tertulliani opera*, 2:1015–16, trans. *ANF*, 4:50.

59. *Adversus Marcionem* 1.29.5, in *Tertulliani opera*, 1:474, trans. *ANF*, 3:294. This elision occurs throughout this treatise.

60. *De exhortatione castitatis* 1.3, in *Tertulliani opera*, 2:1015, trans. *ANF*, 4:50. Elsewhere he attempts to assign greater merit to male virgins because their greater ardor makes their struggle in maintaining chastity the more praiseworthy (*De virginibus velandis* 10.3, in *Tertulliani opera*, 2:1220, trans. *ANF*, 4:33).

61. *Ad uxorem* 1.8.3, in *Tertulliani opera*, 1:382, trans. *ANF*, 4:43.

62. Ibid. 1.1.5, in *Tertulliani opera*, 1:374, trans. *ANF*, 4:39.

63. Ibid. 1.4.4, in *Tertulliani opera*, 1:377, trans. *ANF*, 4:41.

64. *De cultu feminarum* 1.2.5, in *Tertulliani opera*, 1:346, trans. *ANF*, 4:15.

65. Cf. Tertullian's *De resurrectione mortuorum* 27.1, in *Tertulliani opera*, 2:956, trans. *ANF*, 3:564.

66. See Thomas Schirrmacher, *Paul in Conflict with the Veil* (Nürnberg: Verlag für Theologie und Religionswissenschaft, 2002); also see Lloyd Llewellyn-Jones, *Aphrodite's Tortoise: The Veiled Women of Ancient Greece* (Swansea, Wales: Classical Press of Wales, 2002). On Genesis 6 as the original legend of the fall, see Williams, *Ideas of the Fall*, pp. 20–28.

67. Martin, *Corinthian Body*, pp. 242–46.

68. *De cultu feminarum* 1.2.1, in *Tertulliani opera*, 1:344–45, trans. *ANF*, 4:15. See the *Book of Enoch* 1.6–22, in *The Apocryphal Old Testament* (Oxford: Clarendon Press, 1984), pp. 188–213.

69. *De resurrectione mortuorum* 42.7, in *Tertulliani opera*, 2:977, trans. *ANF*, 3:576.

70. *De virginibus velandis* 7.1, in *Tertulliani opera*, 2:1226, trans. *ANF*, 4:31. See Brown, *Body and Society*, pp. 80–82; McNamara, *New Song*, pp. 109–12.

71. *De oratione* 22.5, in *Tertulliani opera*, 1:270, trans. *ANF*, 3:687.

72. *De virginibus velandis* 7.2, 4, in *Tertulliani opera*, 2:1226–27, trans. *ANF*, 4:32.

73. *Apologeticum* 22.2, in *Tertulliani opera*, 1:128, trans. *ANF*, 3:36.

74. *De cultu feminarum* 1.2.4, in *Tertulliani opera*, 1:345, trans. *ANF*, 4:14–15.

75. *Apologeticum* 22.4, in *Tertulliani opera*, 1:129, trans. *ANF*, 3:36.

76. *De idololatria* 4.2–4, 9.1, in *Tertulliani opera*, 2:1103–4, 1107, trans. *ANF*, 3:62–63, 65.

77. *De resurrectione mortuorum* 10.2, in *Tertulliani opera*, 2:933, trans. *ANF*, 3:552.

78. *De monogamia* 1.3, in *Tertulliani opera*, 2:1229, trans. *ANF*, 4:59.

79. *De cultu feminarum* 1.1–1.2, in *Tertulliani opera*, 1:343–46, trans. *ANF*, 4:117–18.

80. Ibid. 1.2.1, in *Tertulliani opera*, 1:344, trans. *ANF*, 4:14; n.b. that in *Against Marcion* he blames the daughters of men by referring to the "scandalized angels" [*angelorum scandalizatorum*], *Adversus Marcionem* 5.18, in *Tertulliani opera*, 1:720, translated as "angels entrapped into sin by the daughters of men" in *ANF*, 3:470.

81. *De virginibus velandis* 5.2, in *Tertulliani opera*, 2:1214, trans. *ANF*, 4:30.

82. *De carne Christi* 17.5, in *Tertulliani opera*, 2:905, trans. *ANF*, 3:536; cf. his discussion of Mary's womanhood in *De virginibus velandis* 6.1–3, in *Tertulliani opera*, 2:1215–16, trans. *ANF*, 4:31.

83. *Adversus Valentinianos* 32.5, in *Tertulliani opera*, 2:776, trans. *ANL*, 3:519.

84. *De carne Christi* 6.1–3, in *Tertulliani opera*, 2:883–84, trans. *ANF*, 3:526.

85. 1 Cor. 15.47; *De carne Christi* 8.5, in *Tertulliani opera*, 2:890–91, trans. *ANF*, 3:529.

86. *De praescriptione haereticorum* 6.6, in *Tertulliani opera*, 1:191, trans. *ANF*, 3:246. According to Tertullian, Apelles, a one-time follower of Marcion, learned this heresy from Philumene and became its main proponent. The two were said to have become lovers, and afterward Philumene became an "enormous prostitute" (Ibid., 30.6, in *Tertulliani opera*, 1:211, trans. *ANF*, 3:257).

87. *De carne Christi* 6.9, 5; 14.1–3, in *Tertulliani opera*, 2:885, 884, 899, trans. *ANF*, 3:527, 533–34; on angels' assumption of human flesh, also see ibid. 3.6–7, 2:876–7, trans. *ANF*, 3:523; *Adversus Marcionem* 3.9, 5.11, in *Tertulliani opera*, 1:519–21, 695–99, trans. *ANF*, 3:328–29, 329–30. See Alexandre, *Une Chair pour la gloire*, pp. 199–225.

88. *De carne Christi* 15.3, in *Tertulliani opera*, 2:901, trans. *ANF*, 3:534.

89. Ibid. 16.3–4, in *Tertulliani opera*, 2:902–3, trans. *ANF*, 3:535.

90. See *De anima* 5.1–9.8, 27.1–4, in *Tertulliani opera*, 2:786–94, 822–23, trans. *ANF*, 3:184–89, 208–9; cf. *De resurrectione mortuorum* 53.8, in *Tertulliani opera*, 2:999, trans. *ANF*, 3:587. On the negative ramifications of Tertullian's emphasis on seminal identity and its role in establishing original sin, see Williams, *Ideas of the Fall*, pp. 233–38.

91. *De anima* 36.2, in *Tertulliani opera*, 2:838, trans. *ANF*, 3:217.

92. *De resurrectione mortuorum* 7.9, in *Tertulliani opera*, 2:930, trans. *ANF*, 3:550; Caroline Walker Bynum, *The Resurrection of the Body in Western Christianity, 200–1336* (New York: Columbia University Press, 1995), pp. 34–43.

93. *De resurrectione mortuorum* 8.2, in *Tertulliani opera*, 2:931, trans. *ANF*, 3:551.

94. Ibid. 42.12–13, 43.6, in *Tertulliani opera*, 2:978, 979, trans. *ANF*, 3:576, 577.

95. Ibid. 42.3, 5, in *Tertulliani opera*, 2:976, 977, trans. *ANF*, 3:575.

96. See Claude Rambaux, *Tertullien face aux morales des trois premiers siècles* (Paris: Société d'Edition "Les Belles Lettres," 1979), p. 213.

97. *De resurrectione mortuorum* 63.1–3, in *Tertulliani opera*, 2:1011, trans. *ANF*, 3:593–94. A similar sense is present in the Pauline-inflected logic of his antidualist treatise *Against Marcion*: Christ's love for his bride, Ecclesia, is equated with the husband's love for his wife, and hence the flesh, dignifying the created world in general, and the body in particular (*Adversus Marcionem* 5.18.8–10, in *Tertulliani opera*, 1:718–19, trans. *ANF*, 3:468–69). See Alexandre, *Une Chair pour la gloire*, pp. 279–328.

98. *De resurrectione mortuorum* 60.3, in *Tertulliani opera*, 2:1008, trans. *ANF*, 3:592.

99. Ibid. 61.5–6, in *Tertulliani opera*, 2:1010, trans. *ANF*, 3:593.

300   NOTES TO PAGES 27–31

100. Ibid. 62.3–4, in *Tertulliani opera*, 2:1011, trans. *ANF*, 3:593.

101. Ibid. 26.7, in *Tertulliani opera*, 2:954, trans. *ANF*, 3:564 (I have provided a more literal translation); cf. *De anima*, where the reunion of the soul and body is treated as short-hand for human perfection: "We therefore maintain that every soul, whatever be its age on quitting the body, remains unchanged in the same, until the time shall come when the promised perfection shall be realized in a state duly tempered to the measure of the peerless angels" (ibid. 5.76, in *Tertulliani opera*, 2:864, trans. *ANF*, 3:232–33).

102. *De resurrectione mortuorum* 36.5, in *Tertulliani opera*, 2:969, trans. *ANF*, 3:571.

103. McNamara, *New Song*, p. 121.

104. *De cultu feminarum* 2.13.7, in *Tertulliani opera*, 1:370, trans. *ANF*, 4:25.

105. *Ad uxorem* 1.4.4, in *Tertulliani opera*, 1:377, trans. *ANF*, 4:41.

106. *De exhortatione castitatis* 13.4, in *Tertulliani opera*, 2:1035, trans. *ANF*, 4:58.

107. *De oratione* 22.8, in *Tertulliani opera*, 1:270. trans. *ANF*, 3:688.

108. Ibid. 22.9, in *Tertulliani opera*, 1:271, trans. *ANF*, 3:689.

109. *De virginibus velandis* 12.1, in *Tertulliani opera*, 2:1221, trans. *ANF*, 4:34–35.

110. Ibid. 16.4, in *Tertulliani opera*, 2:1225, trans. *ANF*, 4:37.

111. *De resurrectione mortuorum* 61.6, in *Tertulliani opera*, 2:1010, trans. *ANF*, 3:593.

CHAPTER 2

1. Shewring, ed. and trans., *Passion of SS. Perpetua and Felicity* c. 18, p. 17, trans. pp. 37–38. I have altered the translation to make it more literal.

2. Heffernan, *Sacred Biography*, p. 190.

3. For a summary of the evidence regarding the *passio*'s relationship with Montanism, see Rex Butler, *New Prophecy and "New Visions": Evidence of Montanism in the Passion of Perpetua and Felicitas* (Washington, D.C.: Catholic University Press, 2006), pp. 127 ff. William Tabbernee advances that neither Tertullian nor Perpetua broke with orthodoxy, however, both evidencing the same level of commitment to Montanism ("Perpetua, Montanism, and Christian Ministry in Carthage," *Perspectives in Religious Studies* 32 [2005]: 430–31). In addition to there being a number of passages common to some of Tertullian's treatises and the *passio*, Tertullian also explicitly honors Perpetua as a martyr. For a summary of the arguments in favor of Tertullian's editorship, see Butler, *New Prophecy and "New Visions,"* pp. 49–57. Maureen Tilly, however, sees the association of Tertullian with the *passio* as just another instance of learned sexism, literally deauthorizing the woman. She also questions the text's alleged Montanism. See "Passion of Perpetua and Felicity," 2:832–36.

4. Cyprian, *De habitu virginum* c. 3, in *S. Thasci Caecili Cypriani opera omnia*, ed. W. Hartel, *CSEL*, 3, 1 (Vienna: C. Geroldi Filium Bibliopolam Academiae, 1868), p. 189 (hereafter cited as *Cypriani opera*), trans. *ANF*, 5:431.

5. Ibid. c. 21, in *Cypriani opera*, 3, 1:202, trans. *ANF*, 5:436.

6. Ibid. c. 22, in *Cypriani opera*, 3, 1:202–3, trans. *ANF*, 5:436.

7. Ibid. cc. 4, 21, in *Cypriani opera*, 3, 1:190, 202, trans. *ANF*, 5:431, 436.

8. "with that of men, your lot and condition is equal," ibid. c. 22, in *Cypriani opera*, 3, 1:263, trans. *ANF*, 5:436.

9. Ibid. c. 14, in *Cypriani opera*, 3, 1:197, trans. *ANF*, 5:434.

10. Ibid. c. 15, in *Cypriani opera*, 3, 1:198, trans. *ANF*, 5:434.

11. Ibid. c. 17, in *Cypriani opera*, 3, 1:199, trans. *ANF*, 5:434.

12. Ibid. c. 20, in *Cypriani opera*, 3, 1:201, trans. *ANF*, 5:435.

13. Cyprian, Ep. 4, *To Pomponius* c. 3, in *Cypriani opera*, 3, 2:475, trans. *Library of the Fathers* (Oxford: Henry Parker, 1844), p. 9.

14. Ibid. c. 3, in *Cypriani opera*, 3, 2:475–76, trans. *Library of the Fathers*, p. 10.

15. See 1 Nicaea (325) c. 3, in *Decrees of the Ecumenical Councils*, ed. Norman Tanner (London: Sheed and Ward, 1990), 1:7. Susanna Elm notes that legal restrictions to syneisaktism coincide with the rise of the term *virgines Deo dicatae (Virgins of God: The Making of Asceticism in Late Antiquity* [Oxford: Clarendon Press, 1994], pp. 50–51).

16. Tertullian, *De exhortatione castitatis* 12.2, in *Tertulliani opera*, 2:1032, trans. *ANF*, 4:56. See Brown, *Body and Society*, p. 79.

17. See, for example, the Synod of Ancyra (314) c. 19, *ANF*, 14:71. This canon, which treats consecrated virgins who subsequently marry the same as someone who remarries while still married to another, will be repeated in Gratian, C. 27 q. 1 c. 24; Aphrahat, *Les Exposés* 6.7, trans. Marie-Joseph Pierre, *SC* 359 (Paris: Editions du Cerf, 1988), 1:385–86; Gregory of Nazianzus, *Epigrammata* 11, 14, *PG* 38:90, 91; John Chrysostom, *On the Necessity of Guarding Virginity* cc. 2, 3, 6, 9, 10, 12, ed. Jean Dumortier in *Les Cohabitations suspectes: Comment observer la virginité* (Paris: Société Editions "Les Belles Lettres," 1955), pp. 101, 104, 116–17, 125, 129, 136–37, trans. Elizabeth Clark in *Jerome, Chrysostom, and Friends: Essays and Translations* (New York: Edwin Mellen, 1979), pp. 214, 216–17, 228, 235, 239, 246 (this second of the two treatises is specifically addressed to the women). An exception to this general trend is in the third century Pseudo-Cyprian treatise, *De singularitate clericorum*. As its title suggests, it addressed itself to the clergy alone. The author's extreme misogyny would make emphasizing woman's role as *sponsa Christi* extremely difficult, so he does the next best thing, making the offending cleric an adulterer to his union with Christ (*De singularitate clericorum* cc. 11, 30, in *Cypriani opera*, 3, 3:186, 206). He speaks derisively of the great miracle wherein virginal love makes virgins into wives and conjugal love causes spouses to be adjudged virgins (*De singularitate clericorum* c. 32, p. 207).

18. On the erotic overtones of bridal imagery, see Turner, *Eros and Allegory*, esp. pp. 25–70; Bernard McGinn, *Foundations of Mysticism: Origins to the Fifth Century*, vol. 1 in *The Presence of God: A History of Western Christian Mysticism* (New York: Crossroad, 1997), pp. 118–20. Also see Stephen Moore's discussion of the necessary "queering" implicit in monastic commentaries in order for a given monk to adapt the persona of bride ("The Song of Songs in the History of Sexuality," *Church History* 69 [2000]: 328–49).

19. See Elizabeth Clark, *The Origenist Controversy: The Cultural Construction of an Early Christian Debate* (Princeton, N.J.: Princeton University Press, 1992).

20. For his influence on the cult of virginity, see Bugge, *Virginitas*, pp. 61–62.

21. On Origen and reading scripture, see McGinn, *Foundations of Mysticism*, pp. 112–13, 121–23.

22. Origen, *In Canticum canticorum* 1:1.1 (= bk. 1, Song of Songs c. 1, v. 1), *PG* 13:83, trans. *Commentary on the Canticle of Canticles*, in *Origen: The Song of Songs: Commentary and Homilies*, trans. R. P. Lawson, *ACW*, 26 (New York: Newman Press, 1956), pp. 58–59. The commentary was translated into Latin by Rufinus; the homilies by Jerome.

23. Ibid. 1:1.1, *PG* 13:84, trans. p. 59.

24. Ibid. 1:1.1, *PG* 13:85, trans. p. 60.

25. Ibid. 2:1.7, *PG* 13:119, trans. p. 121.

26. Ibid. 2:1.7, *PG* 13:119, trans. pp. 120–21; cf. 1 Cor. 10.15.

27. Deut. 32.8; Origen, *In Canticum* 2:1.7, *PG* 13:119–20, trans. p. 122; cf. *In Canticum* 2:1.11, 12, *PG* 13:133, trans. p. 148, where they are also identified with prophets or patriarchs. Also see ibid. Prol., *PG* 13:77, trans. p. 46.

28. Origen, *In Canticum* 2:1.7, *PG* 13:119, trans. p. 122.

29. Ibid. 2:1.7, *PG* 13:119, trans. p. 120.

30. On the fall into diversity and mystical return, see McGinn, *Foundations of Mysticism*, pp. 112–18.

31. Origen, *De principiis* 2.9.6, *PG* 11:230, trans. *ANF*, 4:292.

32. Ibid. 1.5.2, *PG* 11:157, trans. *ANF*, 4:256; cf. ibid. 1.8.3, *PG* 11:178, trans. *ANF*, 4:265–66.

33. Ibid. 1.8.4, *PG* 11:179, trans. *ANF*, 4:266. Also see 2.9.5–6, *PG* 11:229–31, trans. *ANF*, 4:291–2.

34. Ibid. 1.8.2, *PG* 11:176–77, trans. *ANF*, 4:265.

35. Ibid. 1.8.4, *PG* 11:279, trans. *ANF*, 4:266; cf. his comment on the commonality between the human soul and angels "for it is generally thought that one sort of rationality cannot by any means differ from another" (*In Canticum* 2:1.8, *PL* 13:127, trans. p. 136).

36. Fragment from *De principiis* bk. 1, from Jerome's Epistle to Avitus, as cited in *ANF*, 4:71.

37. Origen, *Commentarium in Matthaeum* 10.13, *PG* 13:863–66, trans. *ANF*, 9:420–21. For instance, Novatian, a schismatic who was martyred between 257 and 258, had argued that through virginity, humankind surpassed the angels (*De bono pudicitiae* c. 7, in Cyprian, *Cypriani opera*, 3, 3:18). Novatian's treatises circulated under Cyprian's name, thereby lending them greater authority.

38. Origen, *In Canticum* 3:2.3, *PG* 13:152, trans. p. 181.

39. Origen, *Commentariorum in Evangelium secundum Joannem c. 25, PG* 14:274, trans. *ANF*, 9:371. On Origen's Gnosticism, see Bugge, *Virginitas*, pp. 60–61, 63.

40. Origen, *Commentariorum in Epistolam B. Pauli ad Romanos* 6.13, *PG* 14:1100, trans. Thomas Scheck, *Commentary on the Epistle to the Romans*, *FC*, 104 (Washington, D.C.: Catholic University Press, 2002), p. 56; ibid. 1.18, *PG* 14:866, trans. Scheck, *FC*, 103, p. 94.

41. Origen, *De principiis* 1.1.2, *PG* 11:122, trans. *ANF*, 4:242.

42. Ibid. 2.11.2, *PG* 11:241, trans. *ANF*, 4:297; cf. ibid. 4.9, *PG* 11:359, trans. *ANF*, 4:358. On Origen's teaching and the encouragement of freedom of thought in Alexandrian theology generally, see David Brakke, *Athanasius and Asceticism* (Oxford: Clarendon, 1995; reprt., Baltimore: Johns Hopkins University Press, 1998), pp. 59–63.

43. See E. Anne Matter, *The Voice of My Beloved: The Song of Songs in Western Medieval Christianity* (Philadelphia: University of Pennsylvania Press, 1990), p. 28.

44. Origen, *In Canticum*, Prol., *PG* 13:63, trans. p. 22; cf. his discussion of corrupted spiritual love (ibid., Prol., *PG* 13:67, trans. p. 30).

45. Henri Crouzel, *Virginité et mariage selon Origène* (Paris: Desclée de Brouwer, 1962), p. 26; note that Crouzel is careful to specify that the body was not exactly a product of the fall, but a free decision of God consecutive with the fall (pp. 44ff.).

46. Ibid., pp. 33–34, 51, 60–62, 82.

47. Crouzel posits that Origen is the first theologian to pronounce upon Mary's perpetual virginity (ibid., p. 84). J. C. Plumpe claims that Origen was anticipated by Irenaeus, but the evidence for this is rather equivocal ("Some Little-Known Witnesses to Mary's *Virginitas in partu*," *Theological Studies* 9 [1948]: 569). Leaving questions of priority aside, Origen's position on Mary's perpetual virginity is rather complicated. He acknowledges that there are those who, basing their arguments on works like the Gospel of Peter and the *Protoevangelium of James*, deny that Mary had children subsequent to Jesus, arguing that Christ's brethren were from Joseph's previous marriage. Although Origen clearly sympathizes with this view, he does not make the argument for Mary's intact virginity postpartum, which the *Protoevangelium* does with vigor (Origen, *Commentarium in Matthaeum* 10.17, *PG* 13:875–79, trans. *ANF*, 9:424–25; cf. Origen, *In Lucam homilia 7*, *PG* 13:1818). The Gospel of Peter, also dating from around the mid-second century, only exists in fragments. See M. R. James, trans., *The Apocryphal New Testament* (Oxford: Clarendon, 1924), pp. 90–94. Nothing pertinent regarding Mary has survived. The *Protoevangelium* is discussed later in this chapter. When writing on Leviticus, Origen also maintained that Mary is immune from the impurity associated with birth not only as a woman but as a virgin (*In Leviticum homilia 8*, *PG* 12:493–94). Origen seems to have been inconsistent on this point, however, because elsewhere he says explicitly that Mary, as a human, was in need of purification (*In Lucam homilia 14*, *PG* 13:1834). For other instances of vacillation, see Ambrose Agius, "The Blessed Virgin in Origen and St. Ambrose," *Downside Review* 50 (1932): 128–29. For an overview of Mary in the early church, see Miri Rubin, *Mother of God: A History of the Virgin Mary* (New Haven, Conn.: Yale University Press, 2009), pp. 3–49.

48. See Crouzel, *Virginité et mariage*, pp. 18, 29; Bugge, *Virginitas*, pp. 36–37.

49. Eusebius, *Historia ecclesiae* 6.8, *PG* 20:535–38, trans. *LNPNFC*, 2nd ser., 1:254. The motive given is so that he could teach his female students without gossip. See Kuefler, *Manly Eunuch*, pp. 261–69.

50. For an analysis of monastic commentaries, including an appendix of translations of some of the major authors, see Turner, *Eros and Allegory*.

51. Brakke, *Athanasius and Asceticism*, p. 198; also see pp. 145–46.

52. Ibid., pp. 21, 52.

53. Athanasius, *On Virginity* c. 1, trans. Brakke, *Athanasius and Asceticism*, app. C, p. 303. Origen's two letters *To Virgins* remain in Coptic and Syriac, respectively, while his treatise *On Virginity* remains in Syriac. I will be relying on the translations in Brakke's appendix.

54. Athanasius, Ep. 2, *To Virgins* c. 19, trans. Brakke, *Athanasius and Asceticism*, app. B, p. 298.

55. Ibid. c. 27, trans. Brakke, *Athanasius and Asceticism*, app. B, p. 300.

56. Ibid. c. 21, trans. Brakke, *Athanasius and Asceticism*, app. B, p. 299.

57. Ibid. c. 30, trans. Brakke, *Athanasius and Asceticism*, app. B, p. 301.

58. Ibid. c. 7, trans. Brakke, *Athanasius and Asceticism*, app. B, p. 294.

59. Athanasius, *On Virginity* c. 15, trans. Brakke, *Athanasius and Asceticism*, app. C, p. 307.

60. Athanasius, Ep. 2, *To Virgins* cc. 13–15, trans. Brakke, *Athanasius and Asceticism*, app. B, pp. 297–98.

61. Athanasius, Ep. 1, *To Virgins* c. 31, trans. Brakke, *Athanasius and Asceticism*, app. A, p. 284.

62. Athanasius, Ep. 2, *To Virgins* c. 4, trans. Brakke, *Athanasius and Asceticism*, app. B, p. 293.

63. Athanasius, Ep. 1, *To Virgins* c. 31, trans. Brakke, *Athanasius and Asceticism*, app. A, pp. 284–85; cf. the image of purity in ibid. cc. 19, 21, p. 280.

64. Ibid. c. 3, trans. Brakke, *Athanasius and Asceticism*, app. A, p. 275.

65. In one telling section concerning the afterlife he assures the virgin, "Then [Christ] will bring you into the bridal chamber not made by hands, the unending marriage feast, the kingdom of heaven, eternal life, the place of the angels. . . . There face to face you will see the [children of the resurrection, the] angels, who do not marry nor are given in marriage (Luke 20.35–36)" in Athanasius, *On Virginity* c. 16, trans. Brakke, *Athanasius and Asceticism*, app. C, p. 308. Athanasius's subtle rearrangement of scripture ensures that virgins and angels keep their distance from one another. The biblical passage in its entirety reads: "they which shall be accounted worthy to obtain that world, and the resurrection from the dead, neither marry nor are given in marriage: Neither can they die any more: for they are equal unto the angels and are the children of God, being the children of the resurrection." In Athanasius's rendering, however, angels seem to be crowding out the virgins as children of the resurrection. Virgins do not equal angels, much less become them: they only meet up with them in the afterlife.

66. Athanasius, Ep. 1, *To Virgins* c. 10, trans. Brakke, *Athanasius and Asceticism*, app. A, p. 277.

67. Ibid. c. 18, trans. Brakke, *Athanasius and Asceticism*, app. A, p. 279.

68. Ibid. c. 45, trans. Brakke, *Athanasius and Asceticism*, app. A, p. 288.

69. Athanasius, *On Virginity* c. 17, trans. Brakke, *Athanasius and Asceticism*, p. 308.

70. Ibid. c. 17, trans. Brakke, *Athanasius and Asceticism*, p. 308. Origen only mentions Mary twice in his discussions of the Song of Songs, and in neither instance is she implicated in the persona of the bride. See *In Canticum* 1.1, *PG* 13:88, trans. p. 66; *Homilia in Cantica canticorum* 2.2, *PG* 13:52, trans. p. 293.

71. Athanasius, Ep. 1, *To Virgins* c. 21, trans. Brakke, *Athanasius and Asceticism*, p. 280.

72. Athanasius, *On Virginity* c. 17, trans. Brakke, *Athanasius and Asceticism*, app. C, p. 308.

73. Athanasius, Ep. 1, *To Virgins* c. 12, trans. Brakke, *Athanasius and Asceticism*, app. A, p. 277; on her perpetual virginity, see ibid. cc. 9–11, pp. 277–78.

74. Ibid. c. 13, trans. Brakke, *Athanasius and Asceticism*, app. A, pp. 277, 278.

75. Ibid. c. 17, trans. Brakke, *Athanasius and Asceticism*, app. A, p. 279.

76. Ibid. c. 14, trans. Brakke, *Athanasius and Asceticism*, app. A, p. 278.

77. See Pseudo-Athanasius, *Discourse on Salvation to a Virgin* cc. 11, 22, 23, trans. Teresa Shaw, in *Religions of Late Antiquity in Practice*, ed. Richard Valantasis (Princeton, N.J.: Princeton University Press, 2000), pp. 90–91, 96–97. Occasionally the message is not entirely in keeping with the teaching of Athanasius, however. See, for example, David Brakke's edition of Pseudo-Athanasius's *On Virginity*, written sometime between the fifth and ninth centuries (*Corpus Scriptorum Christianorum Orientalium*, vol. 592, *Scriptores Syri*, vol. 232 [Louvain: Peeters, 2002], trans. Brakke, *Corpus Scriptorum Christianorum Orientalium*, vol. 593, *Scriptores Syri*, vol. 233). In this instance, the author seems to be addressing virgins who did not live in their homes, as was the case in Athanasius's time (see ibid., introd., vol. 592, p. XI). Although the anonymous author associates the female virgin with Christ's bride, he or she evokes the model of Thecla, whose lifestyle is very out of line with the deportment Athanasius was promoting (ibid. c. 7, p. 3, trans. p. 3). Mary is invoked rather less, and it is her holiness and blessedness that are to be imitated versus her restrictive lifestyle (ibid. cc. 78–81, pp. 30–32, trans. pp. 29–31). Ambrose will be discussed below.

78. Little is known of Methodius's life: Jerome claims that he was bishop of Tyre. Among Methodius's lost works is a commentary on the Song of Songs and a treatise on the Witch of Endor (1 Sam. 28) denouncing Origen.

79. Methodius, *Le Banquet* 3.8, ed. Herbert Musurillo, *SC* 95 (Paris: Editions du Cerf, 1963), pp. 110–11, trans. Herbert Musurillo, *The Symposium: A Treatise on Chastity*, *ACW*, 27 (London: Longman, 1958), p. 67.

80. For Athanasius's influence on Ambrose, see Brakke, *Athanasius and Asceticism*, p. 269; Thomas Camelot, "Les traités 'De virginitate' au IVe siècle," in *Mystique et continence: Travaux scientifiques du VIIe congrès international d'Avon* (Paris: Les Etudes Carmélitaines chez Desclée de Brouwer, 1952), p. 275. Neil McLynn argues that Ambrose wrote on virginity, in many ways a pastoral concern, as an alternative to crossing swords with more adept theologians (*Ambrose of Milan: Church and Court in a Christian Capital* [Berkeley: University of California Press, 1994], p. 60).

81. Cf. Ambrose, *De virginibus (Über die Jungfrauen)* 1.3.12–13, ed. Peter Dückers (Turnhout: Brepols, 2009), pp. 118–22, trans. *LNPNFC*, 2nd ser., 10:365; and Athanasius, *Ep. 1, To Virgins* cc. 7–8, trans. Brakke, *Athanasius and Asceticism*, app. A, pp. 266–67. The discussion of Mary is in many places verbatim: see Ambrose, *De virginibus* 2.2.6, 2.2.9, 2.2.11, 2.2.16, 17, pp. 212–14, 220, 222–24, 228, 230, trans. *LNPNFC*, 2nd ser., 10:374, 375 (bis), 376; (bis) and Athanasius, Ep. 1, *To Virgins* cc. 12, 15, 17, 21, trans. Brakke, *Athanasius and Asceticism*, app. A, pp. 277, 278, 279, 280–81.

82. Ambrose, *Exhortatio virginitatis* 10.71, *PL* 16:374.

83. See Camelot, "Les traités 'De virginitate' au IVe siècle," pp. 273–92.

84. See, for example, Livy's instructive account of how the alleged lapse in chastity of Oppia, a Vestal virgin, was responsible for the internal and external conflict that embroiled Rome (Livy, *Ab urbe condita* 2.42, Loeb Classical Library, trans. B. O. Foster [Cambridge, Mass.: Harvard University Press, 1961], 1:358–59). Also see Jerome's emphasis on the Roman

appreciation for both sacred and profane virginity in *Adversus Jovinianum* 1.41, *PL* 23:282–85, trans. *LNPNFC*, 2nd ser., 6:379–80.

85. Livy, *Ab urbe condita* 1.3, 1:16–17.

86. Robin Lorsch Wildfang, *Rome's Vestal Virgins* (London: Routledge, 2006).

87. On the chastity debates, see Gillian Cloke, *'This Female Man of God': Women and Spiritual Power in the Patristic Age, AD 350–450* (London: Routledge, 1995), pp. 38–56.

88. Jerome, *Adversus Jovinianum* 1.30, *PL* 23:263, trans. *LNPNFC*, 2nd ser., 6:368. See David Hunter's *Marriage, Celibacy, and Heresy in Ancient Christianity: The Jovinianist Controversy* (Oxford: Oxford University Press, 2007).

89. See n47, above.

90. Jerome, *De perpetua virginitate B. Mariae adversus Helvidium* cc. 11–17, 21, *PL* 23:199–201, 204–5, trans. *LNPNFC*, 2nd ser., 6:339–43, 344.

91. Marcia Colish, "Ambrose of Milan on Chastity," in *Chastity: A Study in Perception, Ideals, and Opposition*, ed. Nancy van Deusen (Leiden: Brill, 2008), pp. 42–45. For the parallels between Ambrose's view of marital moderation and late classical thought, see Michel Foucault's *The Care of the Self*, vol. 3 of *The History of Sexuality*, trans. Robert Hurley (New York: Vintage, 1988), pp. 176–85.

92. Ambrose's *De sancta Mariae virginitate perpetua* (which also goes by the title *Liber de institutione virginis*, *PL* 16:319–48) was written in response to Bishop Bonosus of Sardica, who is only referred to tacitly in the text (ibid. 5.36, col. 328).

93. Ambrose, *De sancta Mariae virginitate perpetua* 8.52, *PL* 16, col. 334. See Charles Newman, *The Virgin Mary in the Work of St. Ambrose* (Fribourg: University Press of Fribourg, 1962). While Jerome regarded the marriage of Mary and Joseph as a pious fiction, Ambrose considered the couple bound by a nuptial contract, which was consensual and which did not require consummation in Roman law. On the degree to which Ambrose regarded the Virgin as married, see ibid. pp. 85–102. On his conception of marriage in general, see William Dooley, *Marriage according to St. Ambrose* (Washington, D.C.: Catholic University Press, 1948). For Mary and Joseph, see ibid. pp. 1–2. Ambrose's emphasis on the consensual nature of Mary and Joseph's union anticipated Augustine's treatment, which upheld the holy couple's union as the ideal Christian marriage. Hence Mary was destined to become the ultimate model for matrons as well. The latter's treatises *On the Good of Marriage* and *Of Holy Virginity* were written as a pair to demonstrate that one need not denigrate marriage in order to praise virginity. *Of Holy Virginity* endorses the Athanasian-Ambrosian premise that Mary was the ultimate model for virgins, asserting that all virgins partake in the virgin birth (Augustine, *De sancta virginitate* c. 5, *PL* 40:398–99, trans. *LNPNFC*, ser. 1, 3:418).

94. Ambrose, *De virginibus* 1.8.45, p. 174, trans. *LNPNFC*, 2nd ser., 10:370; Ambrose, *Exhortatio virginitatis* 5.29, *PL* 16:359.

95. Dyan Elliott, *Spiritual Marriage: Sexual Abstinence in Medieval Wedlock* (Princeton, N.J.: Princeton University Press, 1993), pp. 39–40, n94; Hunter, *Marriage, Celibacy, and Heresy in Ancient Christianity*, pp. 288–89. Ambrose's preoccupation with this ceremony occasionally prompts interesting embellishments. Thus Athanasius describes the procession of virgins in the afterlife as a single chorus chanting, "I will go in to the altar of God" (Ps.

42 [43].4). Ambrose, however, adopting the same passage, cannot resist the opportunity of adding, "Nor would I hesitate to admit you to the altars of God, whose souls I would without hesitation call altars" (Athanasius, Ep. 1, *To Virgins* c. 21, trans. Brakke, *Athanasius and Asceticism*, app. A, p. 281; Ambrose, *De virginibus* 2.2.18, pp. 230–32, trans. *LNPNFC*, 2nd ser., 10:376). On what can be pieced together of the actual liturgy in fourth-century Rome, see Metz, *La Consécration des vierges*, pp. 99–138.

96. Raymond d'Izarny, "Mariage et consécration virginale au IVe siècle," *La Vie spiri-tuelle*, supplement 25 (1953): 99; Philip Lyndon Reynolds, *Marriage in the Western Church: The Christianization of Marriage during Patristic and Early Medieval Periods* (Boston: Brill, 2001), pp. 25–35, 76.

97. The earliest liturgies for marriage are contained within nuptial masses, dating from the seventh and eight centuries (Reynolds, *Marriage in the Western Church*, pp. 323–24). This evidence was sufficiently late that the authors of the ninth-century False Decretals found it expedient to cite Popes Evaristus (ca. 99–108) and Callixtus I (ca. 217–22) as authorities for the nuptial blessing. The first known instance of such a blessing was over the marriage of Charles the Bald's daughter, Judith, and hence inseparable from her coronation as queen (Pierre Toubert, "La théorie du mariage chez moralistes carolingiens," in *Il Matrimonio nella società altomedievale*, Settimane di studio del Centro Italiano di studi sull'alto medioevo, 24 [Spoleto: Presso la sede del Centro, 1977], 1:273–4).

98. Ep. 19, *To Vigilium Trid.*, as cited in Vogel, "Les rites," 1:420. Also see d'Izarny, "Mariage et consécration virginale," pp. 94–95.

99. Vogel, "Les rites," 1:420; Reynolds, *Marriage in the Western Church*, pp. 93, 321.

100. Ambrose, *Exhortatio virginitatis* 7.42, *PL* 16:364.

101. D'Izarny, "Mariage et consécration virginale," pp. 109–11. Note, however, that the symbolism was significantly anticipated by the virgins of North Africa, where Tertullian first enforced the title *sponsa Christi*. These virgins assumed a *mitra*, essentially the headdress that marked a married woman. It is possible that Ambrose was familiar with this custom (ibid., pp. 111–13, 114). Cf. the description of the Eastern ritual in Pseudo-Athanasius's *On Virginity* c. 29, ed. Brakke, *Corpus Scriptorum Christianorum Orientalium*, vol. 592, trans. Brakke, *Corpus Scriptorum Christianorum Orientalium*, vol. 593, p. 11. This ceremony does not simulate marriage. Moreover, according to Brakke, it is more developed than any other rite extant in Athanasius's time (Pseudo-Athanasius, *On Virginity*, *Corpus Scriptorum Christianorum Orientalium*, vol. 592, introd., p. xi). According to Elm, Basil of Caesarea (d. 379), a contemporary of Ambrose, also used a public ceremony modeled on secular marriage in the consecration of virgins (*Virgins of God*, p. 121).

102. Ambrose, *De virginibus* 1.11.65, p. 206, trans. *LNPNFC*, 2nd ser., 10:373.

103. Pelagius, Ep. 130, *To Demetrias*, *PL* 23:1107–8, trans. *LNPNFC*, 2nd ser., 6:261. This letter, long attributed to Jerome (and included in his works), is now believed to have been written by Pelagius, whose teachings were deemed heretical by Ambrose, Jerome, and Augustine. See Johannes Quasten, *Patrology* (Westminster, Md: Newman Press, 1986), 4:469, 474. Pelagius's optimistic view of human nature was more sympathetic to the leanings of Jovinian and Helvidius.

104. Ambrose, *De virginibus* 1.8.52, pp. 186–88, trans. *LNPNFC*, 2nd ser., 10:371 (I

have altered to pronouns in the translation to make it more literal); cf. *Exhortatio virginitatis* 4.19, *PL* 16:357.

105. Ambrose, *De virginibus* 1.8.53, p. 188, trans. *LNPNFC*, 2nd ser., 10:371.

106. Among the different Latin fathers, Bugge sees Ambrose's reading of the Song of Songs as the most important (*Virginitas*, p. 62).

107. Matter, *Voice of My Beloved*, pp. 25, 36.

108. Ambrose, *De virginitate* 14.92, *PL* 16:289, trans. Daniel Callam, *On Virginity* (Saskatoon: Peregrina Translation Series, 1980), p. 31.

109. Ambrose, *De virginibus* 1.7.37, 38, pp. 162, 162–64, trans. *LNPNFC*, 2nd ser., 10:309.

110. Ambrose, *De virginitate* 15.93, *PL* 16:290, trans. p. 32.

111. Ambrose, *De virginibus* 1.11.57–60, pp. 196–98, trans. *LNPNFC*, 2nd ser., 10:372. He meets much of this resistance head-on in the treatise *De virginitate*, esp. 3.10, 5.25–26, 6.27–28, 7.36–39, *PL* 16:268–69, 272–73, 273, 275–76, trans. pp. 4–5, 9, 9–10, 13–14. See McLynn, *Ambrose of Milan*, pp. 65–66. McLynn assumes that ecclesiastical personnel friendly to Ambrose's ascetical program were responsible for sending virgins for consecration.

112. Athanasius, Ep. 1, *To Virgins* cc. 36–43, trans. Brakke, *Athanasius and Asceticism*, app. A, pp. 286–88.

113. See Ambrose, *De virginibus* 3.1.1–3.3.14, pp. 272–96, trans. *LNPNFC*, 2nd ser., 10:381–83.

114. Jerome, Ep. 117, *To a mother and daughter living in Gaul* c. 5, *PL* 22:956, trans. *LNPNFC*, 2nd ser., 6:217.

115. Cf. the later strategies that will be adopted in the male-authored rules for anchoresses in Sandi Hubnik, "(Re)Constructing the Medieval Recluse: Performative Acts of Virginity and the Writings of Julian of Norwich," *Historian* 67 (2005): 50–52.

116. Ambrose, *De virginibus* 1.2.9, p. 112, trans. *LNPNFC*, 2nd ser., 10:364. The erotics of such a scene are undeniable. Virginia Burrus describes Agnes as "surg[ing] toward an erotic consummation, joyfully impaling herself on the steely blade that may be exchanged for a heavenly husband" (*The Sex Lives of Saints: An Erotics of Ancient Hagiography* [Philadelphia: University of Pennsylvania, 2004], p. 53).

117. Ambrose, *De virginibus* 1.11.65, p. 206, trans. *LNPNFC*, 2nd ser., 10:373.

118. Ambrose, *De virginibus* 3.7.35, p. 332, trans. *LNPNFC*, 2nd ser., 10:387. Also see his account of the martyrdom of the cross-dressing virgin of Antioch (ibid. 2.4.22–33, pp, 236–56, trans. *LNPNFC*, 2nd ser., 10:377–79).

119. Ambrose, *De virginibus* 3.7.33, 34, pp. 326, 328, trans. *LNPNFC*, 2nd ser., 10:386, 387.

120. This principle is clearly articulated in the martyrdom of Polycarp (d. 155), bishop of Smyrna. The reason given is that a certain Quintus, who came forth voluntarily, attesting to his faith, apostatized out of fear of martyrdom. Hence, the author states, "Wherefore, brethren, we do not commend those who give themselves up [to suffering], seeing the Gospel does not teach to do so" (*Martyrium S. Polycarpi* c. 4, in *Patres Apostolici*, ed. F. X. Funk [Tübingen: Henricus Laupp, 1901], 1:318–19, trans. *ANF*, 1:40). This report circulated

as an encyclical letter from the Church of Smyrna. Cyprian himself was said to express the same sentiment when questioned at the trial preceding his martyrdom (*Acta proconsularia* c. 1, in *Cypriani opera*, 3, 3:CXI).

121. Ambrose, *De virginibus* 3.7.38, p. 334, trans. *LNPNFC*, 2nd ser., p. 387.

122. See Ambrose, Ep. 5 (49), *To Syagrius, PL* 16:929–37. The letter has been translated as Ep. 32 by Mary Beyenka, in Ambrose's *Letters, 1–91*, Fathers of the Church, 26 (Washington, D.C.: Catholic University Press, 2002), pp. 152–63. I will be using my own translation, however. On this case, see F. Martroye, "L'affaire Indicia: Une sentence de Saint Ambrose," *Mélanges Paul Fournier* (Paris: Recueil Sirey, 1929), pp. 503–10; and Vratislav Bušek, "Der Prozeß der Indicia," *Zeifschrift für Rechtsgeschichte, Kanonistische Abteilung* 29 (1940): 446–61. Kathleen Kelly also gives a brief account of the case, but wrongly assumes that Indicia did have to undergo the exam (*Performing Virginity and Testing Chastity in the Middle Ages* [London: Routledge, 2000], p. 34).

123. Ambrose, Ep. 5 (49), *To Syagrius* c. 17, *PL* 16:935.

124. Ibid. c. 18, *PL* 16:935; see Martroye, "L'affaire Indicia," p. 508.

125. Ambrose, Ep. 5 (49), *To Syagrius* c. 19, *PL* 16:935.

126. Ibid. c. 1, *PL* 16:930; c. 15, *PL* 16:934.

127. Ibid. c. 17, *PL* 16:935.

128. Martroye, "L'affaire Indicia," p. 508.

129. Ambrose, Ep. 5 (49), *To Syagrius* c. 1, *PL* 16:930.

130. Ibid. c. 20, *PL* 16:936.

131. Ibid. cc. 17–18, *PL* 16: 934–35.

132. Ibid. c. 4, *PL* 16:931.

133. Ibid. cc. 19–20, *PL* 16:935–36.

134. Ibid. c. 24, *PL* 16:936.

135. McLynn interprets this case as indicating possible strains between Italian bishops (*Ambrose of Milan*, pp. 286–87).

136. Martroye, "L'affaire Indicia," p. 507. The milder penalty of excommunication over exile is perhaps an early indication of the ecclesiastical courts' ongoing reputation for comparative clemency.

137. Ambrose, Ep. 5 (49), *To Syagrius* c. 2, *PL* 16:930.

138. Ibid. c. 4, *PL* 16:931.

139. Ibid. c. 4, *PL* 16:931; cf. c. 2, col. 930. According to McLynn's analysis, Syagrius was attempting to avoid the official hearing that Ambrose insisted upon (*Ambrose of Milan*, p. 287). This could account for some of the irregularities that Ambrose excoriates.

140. Ambrose, Ep 5(49), *To Syagrius* c. 7, *PL* 16:931–32.

141. Ibid. c. 21, *PL* 16:936.

142. Ibid. c. 5, *PL* 16:931.

143. Ibid. c. 6, *PL* 16:931.

144. Ibid. c. 8, *PL* 16:932.

145. Ibid. c. 9, *PL* 16:932.

146. Ibid. c. 10, *PL* 16:932.

147. Ibid. c. 12, *PL* 16:933.

148. Ibid. c. 14, *PL* 16:933–34.

149. Ibid. c. 14, *PL* 16:934.

150. Ambrose, *De viduis* 4.26, *PL* 16:242, trans. *LNPNFC*, 2nd ser., 10:395.

151. Chrysostom, *On the Necessity of Guarding Virginity* c. 2, p. 100, trans. Clark, *Jerome, Chrysostom, and Friends*, p. 213.

152. *The Protoevangelium of James* cc. 19–20, *ANF*, 8:365. Although Plumpe leads off his evidence for postpartum virginity with Irenaeus, the *Protoevangelium* is nevertheless his earliest witness and certainly the most explicit. He construes the graphic nature of the tale as a rebuttal to Gnostic denials of the incarnation ("Some Little-Known Early Witnesses," p. 572).

153. Cf. a parallel incident at the Virgin's funeral when the high priest of the Jews attempts to wrest the coffin from the apostles. His arms were desiccated to the elbows, while his hands, actually adhering to the coffin, were wrested off. When he accepts Mary and Christ, he is healed (*The Passing of Mary* cc. 11–13, *ANF*, 8:597).

154. See n47, above.

155. Sulpicius Severus, *Chronica* (or *Sacra historia*) 1.2, *PL* 20:96–97, trans. *LNPNFC*, 2nd ser., 11:71–72.

156. See Bugge, *Virginitas*, p. 15n27. Note that the Book of Enoch was deemed canonical until the fourth century. Hilary, Jerome, and especially Augustine denounced it (see *De civitate dei* 15.23.4, 18.38, *PL* 41:470, 598, trans. *LNPNFC*, 1st ser., 2:305, 383). But it continued to be read by Marcionites, Valentinians, Manicheans, and other encratite and dualist sects.

157. Ps.-Cyprian, *De singularitate clericorum* c. 27, p. 204.

158. Augustine, *Quaestionum in Heptateuchum libri VII* bk. 1, q. 3, *PL* 34:549. See Dyan Elliott, *Fallen Bodies: Pollution, Sexuality, and Demonology in the Middle Ages* (Philadelphia: University of Pennsylvania Press, 1999), pp. 9–10, 52–53.

159. John Cassian, *Conférences* 8.21, ed. E. Pichery, *SC* 54 (Paris: Editions du Cerf, 1958), 2:28, trans. Boniface Ramsey, *The Conferences, ACW*, 57 (New York: Paulist, 1997), p. 305; cf. the later *Biblia Latina cum glossa ordinaria: Facsimile Reprint of the Editio Princips of Strassburg 1480/81*, introd. Adolph Rusch, Karlfried Froehlich, and Margaret Gibson (Turnhout: Brepols, 1992), *Gen. 6.2 ad v. filii dei*, p. 35.

160. Kuefler overemphasizes this usage, however, presenting the *sponsa* as a primary point of clerical identification until authorities, like Ambrose, decided to share it with consecrated virgins. The evidence for such a reading is slim (*Manly Eunuch*, pp. 137–42). *Regula Sancti Benedicti* 58.24, ed. Timothy Fry (Collegeville, Minn.: Liturgical Press, 1981), p. 268; see the note on p. 270.

161. Ibid. 59.1, p. 270. On the practice of wrapping the hand, see the discussion in Chapter 3.

162. By the same token, his rationale for propelling the sexed body into the afterlife may have been lost, and yet by virtue of Augustine's defense of Edenesque sexuality, Tertullian's permanent division of the sexes ultimately prevailed. To establish the sexed body's claim on the paradisial past was to secure its share in future glory.

163. Ambrose, *Exhortatio virginitatis* 13.86, *PL* 16:377.

164. Fulgentius, Ep. 3, *To Proba* c. 10, 17, in *Sancti Fulgentii episcopi Ruspensis opera*, ed. J. Fraipont, *CCSL*, 91 (Turnhout: Brepols, 1968), pp. 216, 219 (hereafter cited as *Fulgentii . . . opera*), trans. Robert Eno, *Selected Works*, *FC*, 95 (Washington, D.C.: Catholic University Press, 1997), pp. 316–17, 321. Fulgentius wrote two letters to the consecrated virgin Proba. According to an anonymous contemporary life, Fulgentius was an erstwhile monk who was seized in his monastic cell and forcibly made bishop by the citizens of Ruspe (Ferrand, deacon of Carthage, *Vie de Saint Fulgence de Ruspe*, ed. G. G. Lapeyre [Paris: Lethielleux, 1929], p. 73, trans. Eno, *Life of Fulgentius* c. 14, in *Fulgentius: Selected Works*, *FC*, 95, p. 31).

165. Fulgentius, Ep. 3, *To Proba* c. 11, in *Fulgentii . . . opera*, ed. Fraipont, *CCSL*, 91, p. 217, trans. p. 317.

166. Ambrose, *Exhortatio virginitatis* 6.34, *PL* 16:361.

167. Michel Rouche, "Des mariages païen au mariage chrétien." Sacrè et sacrement, in *Segni e riti nella chiesa altomedievale occidentale*, Settimane di studio del Centro Italiano di studi sull'alto medioevo, 33 (Spoleto: Presso la sede del Centro, 1987), 2:843; Diana Moses, "Livy's Lucretia and the Validity of Coerced Consent in Roman Law," in *Consent and Coercion to Sex and Marriage in Ancient and Medieval Societies*, ed. Angeliki Laiou (Washington, D.C.: Dumbarton Oaks, 1993), pp. 45–49.

168. Livy, *Ab urbe condita* 1.4, 1:6–19. The Greek prototypes for the Roman gods were no better. See Mary Lefkowitz, "Seduction and Rape in Greek Myth," in *Consent and Coercion to Sex and Marriage in Ancient and Medieval Societies*, ed. Angeliki Laiou (Washington, D.C.: Dumbarton Oaks, 1993), pp. 17–38.

169. Livy, *Ab urbe condita* 1.58, 1:202–3. See Moses, "Livy's Lucretia," pp. 39–81, esp. 68–79. Also see Rouche, "Des mariages païen au mariage chrétien," p. 843.

170. Jerome, *Adversus Jovinianum* 1.43, *PL* 23:266, trans. *LNPNFC*, 2nd ser., 6:381. He is allegedly citing Dido's view on second marriage after the death of her husband. He needn't extrapolate on what a disaster it was for her when she broke her chaste resolve for Aeneas. Cf. Tertullian, *De exhortatione castitatis* 13.2–3, in *Tertulliani opera*, 2:1034–35, trans. *ANF*, 4:57, who deploys both Dido and Lucretia. Also note Burrus's view: "holy women—like virgin martyrs—only really become representable in the moment of their dying, the moment when they meet their Bridegroom" (*The Sex Lives of Saints*, p. 59).

171. Augustine, Ep. 111, *To Victorianus* c. 7, *PL* 33:426.

172. Ibid. c. 8, *PL* 33:426–27.

173. Augustine, *De civitate dei* 1.16, *PL* 41:30, trans. *LNPNFC*, 1st ser., 2:12.

174. Ibid. 1.19.3, *PL* 41:33, trans. *LNPNFC*, 1st ser., 2:13.

175. See Elliott, *Fallen Bodies*, pp. 47–48; Jane Schulenburg, *Forgetful of Their Sex: Female Sanctity and Society, ca. 500–1100* (Chicago: University of Chicago Press, 1998), pp. 130–33.

176. Augustine, *De civitate dei* 1.19–20, *PL* 41:32–35, trans. *LNPNFC*, 1st ser., 2:13–15.

177. Schulenburg, *Forgetful of Their Sex*, pp. 139–55.

178. Venantius Fortunatus, *Vita Sancti Hilarii* c. 6, ed. Bruno Krusch, *MGH, Auct. Ant.*, 4,2:3.

179. Fortunatus, *Vita Sancti Hilarii* c. 13, *MGH, Auct. Ant.*, 4,2:6. Barbara Newman

treats a parallel maternal tough love in " 'Crueel Corage': Child Sacrifice and the Maternal Martyr in Hagiography and Romance," in *From Virile Woman to WomanChrist: Studies in Medieval Religion and Literature* (Philadelphia: University of Pennsylvania Press, 1995), pp. 76–107.

180. Adhémar Esmein, *Le Mariage en droit canonique* (Paris, 1891; reprt., New York: Burt Franklin, 1968), 1:271–73.

181. Council of Tours (567) c. 21, in *Concilia Galliae A. 511–A. 695*, ed. C. de Clercq, *CSEL*, 148a (Turnhout: Brepols, 1963), p. 188; Council of Arles (538) c. 19, ibid. p. 121. There were even provisions made for emergency veilings of women who were pressured into marriage by a powerful suitor or her family, was in danger rape, or feared dying un-veiled, even if she was underage (Council of Tours [567] c. 21, ibid. p. 186). According to this particular council, twenty-five is the stipulated age, in keeping with the age of majority in Roman law.

182. Theod. 9.25.1. The punishment pertains even if the woman in question subse-quently consents to marriage; 9.25.2 extends this sentence to unsuccessful solicitors as well. This stern penalty is cited with approval in 567 by the Council of Tours, c. 21 (*Concilia Gal-liae*, ed. C. de Clercq, *CSEL*, 148a, p. 186). Note, however, that the Council of Paris in 614 allegedly was prepared to exact the death penalty for anyone who abducted or attempted to marry a consecrated virgin (ibid. c. 18, p. 285). See Réginald Grégoire, "Il matrimonio mis-tico," in *Il Matrimonio nella società altomedievale*, Settimane di studio del Centro Italiano di studi sull'alto medioevo, 24 (Spoleto: Presso la sede del Centro, 1977), 2:730.

183. *De lapsu virginis consecratae liber unicus* 4.13, *PL* 16:372. Cf. Basil the Great, Ep. 46, *Ad virginem lapsam*, *PG* 32:369–82, trans. *LNPNFC*, 2nd ser., 8:149–52.

184. *De lapsu* 5.20 *PL* 16:372. Cf. 8.34, col. 377.

185. Ibid. 5.21, *PL* 16:372.

186. Ibid. 6.26, *PL* 16:374.

187. Ibid. 8.32–38, *PL* 16:376–79. Susanna's situation provides a classic instance of blaming the victim in order to establish guilt: "But you will say: I did not wish this evil, I endured violence. That most strong [Old Testament] Susanna, whose name you fallaciously bear, will answer you: I was [trapped] between two priests, and between two judges of the people, all alone in the woods [Dan. 13.20ff.] I was not able to be conquered because I did not wish it. How were you able to be carried off by force by one most inept youth, in the middle of the city, unless you wantonly wished to be defiled? In short, who heard your cries? Who apprehended your struggles?" (ibid. 4.12, *PL* 16:370).

188. Siricius, Ep. 10, *To the Bishops of Gaul* 1.4, *PL* 13:1183; a similar elision is apparent at the Council of Tours (567), c. 21 (*Concilia Galliae*, ed. C. de Clercq, *CSEL*, 148a, pp. 185–86). On Frankish church councils, see Suzanne Wemple, *Women in Frankish Society: Mar-riage and the Cloister, 500 to 900* (Philadelphia: University of Pennsylvania, 1981), pp. 157–58.

189. Siricius, Ep. 10, *To the Bishops of Gaul* 1.4, *PL* 13:1183. His successor, Innocent I, would also assess the informal vow as binding (Ep. 2, *To Victricius of Rouen* 14.16, *PL* 20:479–80). This view would eventually be enshrined in Gratian (C. 27 q. 1 c. 9). Cf. Leo I's Ep. 167, *To Rusticus of Narbonne* q. 15, *PL* 54:1208. See Grégoire, "Il matrimonio mistico," pp. 730–31. Note that Basil's addressee, an anonymous lapsed virgin, denies that she made

any public pledge, though Basil is intent on refuting her on this point (Ep. 46, *Ad virginem lapsam* c. 2, *PG* 32:371, trans. *LNPNFC*, 2nd ser., 8:149).

190. Leo I, Ep. 12, *To the Bishops of Mauritania Caesariensis in Africa* cc. 8, 12, *PL* 54:653, 655.

191. Augustine, *De civitate dei* 1.28, *PL* 41:41–42, trans. *LNPNFC*, 1st ser., 2:19. Note that the bulk of Augustine's *Of Holy Virginity* addresses the question of humility at such great length that he anticipates objections: "Here some one will say, This is now not to write of virginity, but of humility" (*De sancta virginitate* c. 52, *PL* 40:426, trans. *LNPNFC*, 1st ser., 3:436).

CHAPTER 3

1. Livy, *Ab urbe condita* 8.15, 4:62–63.

2. *Lycurgus and Numa* 4.1–3, as cited by Cloke, '*This Female Man of God,*' p. 48. Also see Aline Rousselle, *Porneia: On Desire and the Body in Late Antiquity,* trans. Felicia Pheasant (Oxford: Basil Blackwell, 1988), pp. 32–33.

3. *Didascalia apostolorum* c. 17, trans. Margaret Gibson (London: C. J. Clay and Sons, 1903), p. 80; see Vogel, "Les rites," 1:413.

4. Pio Fedele, "Vedovanza e seconde nozze," in *Il Matrimonio nella società altomedievale,* Centro Italiano di studi sull'alto medioevo, 24 (Spoleto: Presso la sede del Centro, 1977), 2:828.

5. Tertullian, *De exhortatione castitatis* 13.1, in *Tertulliani opera,* 2:1034, trans. *ANF,* 4:57.

6. Fedele, "Vedovanza e seconde nozze," 2:830–31; Vogel, "Les rites," 1:422–23.

7. Esmein, *Le Mariage en droit canonique,* 2:101; Vogel, "Les rites," 1:424–25.

8. Wemple, *Women in Frankish Society,* pp. 157–58. This would basically be treating these unions as any other instances of Germanic abduction, which the parents ratified after the fact. See Suzanne Wemple, "Consent and Dissent to Sexual Intercourse in Germanic Societies," in *Consent and Coercion to Sex and Marriage in Ancient and Medieval Societies,* ed. Angeliki Laiou (Washington, D.C.: Dumbarton Oaks, 1993), pp. 229–34.

9. Hincmar of Reims, *Communi episcoporum nomine ad regem, De coercendo et exstirpando raptu viduarum, puellarum ac sanctimonialium* c. 4, *PL* 125:1020–21 (hereafter cited as *De coercendo*). Though Hincmar ultimately backs away from this stern sentence, he does suggest that the abductor of an unwilling holy woman be enslaved to her parents (col. 1027). This is similar to the penalties imposed by early Salic law (Wemple, "Consent and Dissent," p. 229).

10. Hincmar, *De coercendo* c. 12, *PL* 125:1026–27.

11. Caesarius of Arles, *Regula virginum* c. 2 [I], *Oeuvres monastiques,* ed. Albert de Vogüé and Joël Courreau, *SC,* 345 (Paris: Editions du Cerf, 1988), 1:180. On possible precedents for claustration, see ibid., editors' introduction, pp. 70–84. On Caesarius's rule and its adoption by various Merovingian communities, see Jo Ann McNamara, "The Ordeal of Community: Hagiography and Discipline in Merovingian Convents," *Vox Benedictina* 3 (1986): 297–98.

12. Tacitus, *Germania* c. 19, in *Agricola, Germania, Dialogus*, trans. W. Hutton, Loeb Classical Library, 35 (Cambridge, Mass.: Harvard University Press, 1920), 1:158–61.

13. Rouche, "Des mariages païen au mariage chrétien,"2:842.

14. Gregory of Tours, *Libri historiarum X* 9.27, ed. Bruno Krusch and Wilhelm Arndt, rev. ed., *MGH, Scrip. Rer. Merov.*, 1, 1 (Hannover: Hahn, 1951), p. 446; trans. Lewis Thorpe, *History of the Franks* (Harmondsworth, Middlesex: Penguin, 1974), p. 514 (hereafter cited as *LHX*).

15. The very first liturgical collection to provide detailed directions, however, anticipated the Romano-Germanic pontifical by perhaps as much as fifty years. See René Metz, "L'ordo de la consécration des vierges dans le pontifical dit de Saint-Aubin d'Angers (IXe/Xe siècle)," in *Mélanges en l'honneur de Monseigneur Michel Andrieu* (Strasbourg: Palais Universitaire, 1956), pp. 327–37. On the collections anticipating the Romano-Germanic pontifical, see Metz, *La Consécration des vierges*, pp. 138–61. On the Romano-Germanic pontifical and the manuscript tradition, see ibid., pp. 163–82.

16. *Le Pontifical romano-germanique du dixième siècle* no. 20, c. 1, 4, ed. Cyrille Vogel and Reinhard Elze (Vatican City: Biblioteca Apostolica Vaticana, 1963–71), *Studi e Testi*, 226, 1:39 (hereafter cited as *PRG*). Cf. M. Andrieu, ed., *Le Pontifical romain du 12e siècle*, vol. 1 of *Le Pontifical romain au moyen-âge*, Studi e Testi, 86 (Vatican City: Biblioteca Apostolica Vaticana, 1938), no. 12, 1:155. On the wrapping of the hand, see Metz, *La Consécration des vierges*, pp. 188–89. In secular marriage rites we also see the reverse, so that the widow's hand is covered and the virgin's is naked (Jean-Baptiste Molin and Protais Mutembe, *Le Rituel du marriage en France du XIIe au XVIe siècle* [Paris: Beauchesne, 1974], pp. 89–90; cf. 81–82). The *PRG* has two ceremonies for consecrating virgins—one for those entering religious communities and a simpler one for virgins living out their vocation in the world. I will be using the former. Translations are mine when not specified otherwise.

17. *PRG*, no. 20, cc. 6–9, pp. 39–41.

18. Metz, *La Consécration des vierges*, pp. 198–200.

19. Ibid., no. 20, c. 13, p. 42.

20. Ibid., no. 20, c. 15, pp. 42–43.

21. Ibid., no. 20, c. 16, p. 44.

22. Ibid., no. 20, cc. 23–24, p. 45.

23. Ibid., no. 20, c. 28, p. 46.

24. Ibid., no. 20, c. 15, pp. 42–43.

25. *Sacramentarium Veronese*, ed. L. C. Mohlberg (Rome: n.p., 1956); *Rerum ecclesiasticarum documenta: Series maior: Fontes I*, as cited by Grégoire, "Il matrimonio mistico," 2:721.

26. *PRG*, no. 20, c. 9, p. 40.

27. Ibid., no. 23, cc. 13, 16, p. 53.

28. See Grégoire, "Il matrimonio mistico," pp. 722–23; Reynolds, *Marriage in the Western Church*, p. 374.

29. For a survey of recent scholarship, see Gary Macy, *The Hidden History of Female Ordination: Female Clergy in the Medieval West* (Oxford: Oxford University Press, 2008), pp. 3–22. The evidence for female ordination to the diaconate is especially strong in the

Eastern Church. See Kyriarki Karidoyanes Fitzgerald, *Women Deacons in the Orthodox Church: Called to Holiness and Ministry*, rev. ed. (Brookline, Mass.: Holy Cross Orthodox Press, 1999).

30. Already at the Council of Chalcedon (451) it was stipulated that the deaconess should be at least forty years of age and a celibate (c. 15, *Decrees of the Ecumenical Council*, 1:94). This would encourage the conflation of the two offices—especially considering the age stipulation for the church's inscribed widows, which the pastoral epistles placed at sixty (1 Tim. 5.9).

31. The exception here is the English rite attributed to Egbert, the earliest extant ritual in the West. One episcopal blessing, in particular, associates the deaconess with the virgin state. See *The Pontifical of Egbert, Archbishop of York, A.D. 732–766*, ed. W. Greenwall, Surtee Society 27 (London: T. and W. Boone, 1853), B, p. 94; Macy, *Hidden History*, pp. 70–71. Macy has reprinted the rites of ordination for deaconesses and abbesses in two appendices. He does not, however, analyze the language of the rituals and hence does not discuss the penitential tone usually associated with the making of a deaconess.

32. "Quia etiam sanctus Siricius de benedictione sponsarum in decretis suis quaedam ponere studuit. De quibus, quod notum est, sacri canones decernunt, et nos exinde aliqua diximus, et plura alia diceremus si his nuptiis, de quibus loquimur benedictionem sacerdotalem datam fuisse ex more ecclesiastico audiremus. Sed quibus debita fides defuit, locum benedictio sacerdotalis non habuit," Hincmar of Reims, Ep. 22, *Ad Rodulfum Bituricensem et Frotarium Burdigalensem, Metropolitanos Aquitaniae: De nuptiis Stephani, et filiae Regimundi comitis*, *PL* 126:152 ; Esmein, *Le Mariage en droit canonique*, 1:107n5; also see 2:99–104.

33. Fedele, "Vedovanza e seconde nozze," 2:824.

34. *PRG*, no. 24, *Ad diaconam faciendam* c. 14, p. 57; cf. c. 19, p. 58.

35. Ibid., no. 25, *Consecratio viduae* c. 8, p. 60.

36. Ibid., no. 24, *Ad diaconam faciendam* c. 8, p. 56; cf. ibid., no. 25, *Consecratio viduae* cc. 14, 8, pp. 61, 60. This widespread patristic allocation of merit on the basis of degrees of chastity is based on an exegesis of Matthew 13.8. See, for example, Jerome's indignant appeal to this standard when Jovinian attempted to assert that marriage and virginity were equal in *Adversus Jovinianum* 1.3, *PL* 23:222–24, trans. *LNPNFC*, 6:347–48.

37. William Durandus, *Rationale divinorum officiorum* 2.1.48, ed. A. d'Avril and T. Thimbodeau, *CCCM*, 140 (Turnhout: Brepols, 1995), p. 143.

38. *PRG*, no. 24, c. 3, p. 59; though see no. 20, p. 39, which seems to contradict this point.

39. Durandus, *Rationale divinorum officiorum* 2.1.43, p. 140.

40. See *Tituli et decretorum Papae Gelasii* c. 13, *PL* 59:52. These canons were probably not written by Gelasius but produced sometime in the sixth century—in either Italy or Gaul. The canon in question was widely repeated. See, for example, Regino of Prüm, *De ecclesiastica disciplina* 2.41, 49, *PL* 132:379, 381; Burchard of Worms, *Decretum* 8.36, *PL* 140:797.

41. *PRG*, no. 24, *Ad diaconam faciendam* c. 10, 1:56; cf. no. 25, *Consecratio viduae* c. 2, 1:59.

42. Ibid., no. 25, *Consecratio viduae* c. 3, 1:59.

43. Council of Tours (567) c. 21, *Concilia Galliae, CSEL* 148a, p. 187. On the consecration of a virgin, see ibid. 2.1.39–45, pp. 137–41; for widows, see 2.1.46–47, pp. 142–43.

44. Hucbald, *Vita S. Rictrudis viduae* 1.14, *AA SS*, May, 3:84 (hereafter cited as *VRV*), trans. Jo Ann McNamara, John Halborg, and E. Gordon Whatley, *Sainted Women of the Dark Ages* (Durham, N.C,: Duke University Press, 1992), p. 206 (hereafter cited as *SW*). Cf. the incident described by Ambrose of a woman sticking her head under the altar as a mode of consecration in Chapter 2, p. 47, above.

45. Grégoire, "Il matrimonio mistico," pp. 724–25. Needless to say that there was no such requirement for a man to enjoy full privileges as a monk. See Giles Constable, "The Ceremonies and Symbolism Entering Religious Life and Taking the Monastic Habit, From the Fourth to the Twelfth Century," in *Il Matrimonio nella società altomedievale*, Settimane di studio del Centro Italiano di studi sull'alto medioevo, 24 (Spoleto: Presso la sede del Centro, 1977), 2:771–834. Constable notes that most of the materials he examines on the entry to the religious life presuppose a single male candidate. Some ceremonies for different orders have interlinear additions in the manuscripts to accommodate the plural or the female subject (p. 784). He concludes that the rituals were essentially the same for both sexes. This does not, however, accommodate the veiling, which, for the choir nun, is more salient than profession into a particular order.

46. Aldhelm, *De virginitate (prosa)*, ed. Rudolf Ehwald, *MGH, Auct. Ant.*, 15, 1:226–323 (hereafter cited as *DVP*), trans. Michael Lapidge and Michael Herren, *Aldhelm: The Prose Works* (Ipswich: D. S. Brewer, 1979); Aldhelm *De virginitate (carmen)*, ed. Rudolf Ehwald, *MGH, Auct. Ant.*, 15, 2:350–471 (hereafter *DVC*), trans. Michael Lapidge and James Rosier (Ipswich: D. S. Brewer, 1985). We know little of Aldhelm apart from what Bede tells us in his *Ecclesiastical History of the English People* 5.18, trans. and ed. Bertram Colgrave and R. A. B. Mynors (Oxford: Oxford University Press, 1969), pp. 512–15. See Lapidge and Herren's discussion of his life and works in *Aldhelm: The Prose Works*, pp. 5–19. On Ambrose's possible influence, see the editors' introduction to *DVP*, p. 56. Aldhelm also honors Ambrose by including him in the ranks of the virgins (*DVP* c. 26, p. 260, trans. pp. 84–85).

47. See Janemarie Luecke, "The Unique Experience of Anglo-Saxon Nuns," in *Peaceweavers*, vol. 2 of *Medieval Religious Women*, ed. Lillian Shank and John Nichols (Kalamazoo, Mich.: Cistercian Publications, 1987), pp. 55–66. On Hildelith, Barking, and Aldhelm, see ibid., pp. 61–63; Schulenburg, *Forgetful of Their Sex*, pp. 98–99, 330–31.

48. See Felice Lifshitz's discussion in "Priestly Women, Virginal Men: Litanies and Their Discontents," in *Gender and Christianity in Medieval Europe*, ed. Lisa Bitel and Felice Lifshitz (Philadelphia: University of Pennsylvania Press, 2008), pp. 97–101.

49. This is true of a number of works circulating under the name of Clement of Rome. See, for example, the *Second Epistle of Clement on Virginity*, in *Patres Apostolici*, ed. F. Diekamp (Tübingen: Henricus Laupp, 1913), 2:29–49, trans. *ANF*, 8:61–66.

50. For Tertullian, see Chapter 1, n60, above; Augustine, Serm. 132, c. 2, *PL* 38:736.

51. Aldhelm, *DVP* c. 2, p. 230, trans. pp. 59–60.

52. Ibid. cc. 20–21, pp. 249–51, trans. pp. 76–78; cf. *DVC*, pp. 363–67, trans. pp. 108–10.

53. Aldhelm, *DVP* c. 21, p. 262, trans. p. 78.

54. Ibid. c. 23, p. 254, trans. p. 80.

55. Ibid. c. 23, p. 255, trans. pp. 80–81. John's deathless sleep is omitted in *DVC*, pp. 369–71, trans. pp. 111–13.

56. Aldhelm, *DVP* c. 24, p. 256, trans. p. 81.

57. Ibid. c. 31, p. 270, trans. p. 91. According to Jerome's account, however, Malchus fled his home before his parents could marry him. Nor was he martyred. Malchus was simply married against his will by Saracen masters. (Moreover, the marriage's legality would have been questionable because the woman's husband, who was led off somewhere else as a captive, was presumably still alive, as Malchus attempted to argue.) He would have taken his own life had his wife not suggested a spiritual marriage (Jerome, *Vita Malchi monachi captivi* cc. 3–6, *PL* 23:56–59, trans. *LNPNFC*, 6:315–18. Also see Elliott, *Spiritual Marriage*, pp. 65–66 n7).

58. On this phenomenon, see Elliott, *Spiritual Marriage*, esp. pp. 55–73.

59. See ibid., app. 1.

60. For Cecilia's *passio*, see *Historia passionis B. Caeciliae*, in *Sanctuarium seu Vitae sanctorum*, ed. Bonino Mombrizio (Paris: Albert Fontemoing, 1901), 1:332–41; Elliott, *Spiritual Marriage*, pp. 64–67, 69.

61. Aldhelm, *DVP* c. 40, p. 292, trans. p. 107. The conditional note is presumably over whether the person who stands in the position of brother-in-law merits the title if the marriage remains unconsummated.

62. Other virgins in the column are Victoria, Constantina, Eustochium, and Demetrias. The virgin Victoria bests a dragon, thereby saving the people of Tribula from mass slaughter. Her executioner's arm was immediately blighted (Aldhelm, *DVP* c. 42, pp. 308–9, trans. pp. 120–21). But the others are largely distinguished by their relations to eminent men. Constantina was said to have inspired many patrician women to embrace chastity, but her main claim to fame was as Constantine's daughter. By the same token, the longevity of the reputation of both Eustochium and Demetrias were a function of Jerome's notice (*DPV* cc. 48–49, pp. 302–4, trans. pp. 115–16. See Jerome, Ep. 22, *To Eustochium*, *PL* 22:394–425, trans. *LNPNFC*, 6:22–41; Pelagius, Ep. 130, *To Demetrias*, *PL* 22:1107–24, trans. *LNPNFC*, 6:260–372). In fact, the epistle to Demetrias is now believed to be the work of Pelagius. See Chapter 2, n103, above.

63. Some patristic reflections on modest dress (Cyprian) and chastity as a state of mind (Augustine) follow. He concludes by asking the "soldiers of Christ" for prayers.

64. See Jo Ann McNamara and Suzanne Wemple, "Marriage and Divorce in the Frankish Kingdom," in *Women in Medieval Society*, ed. Susan Stuard (Philadelphia: University of Pennsylvania Press, 1976), pp. 38–41. On Merovingian marriages, see Ruth Mazo Karras, "The History of Marriage and the Myth of Friedelehe," *Early Medieval Europe* 14 (2006): 145–46. Also see Elliott, *Spiritual Marriage*, pp. 74–83.

65. See Hincmar's efforts to hold Lothar to his marriage in *De divortio Lotharii regis et Theutbergae reginae*, L. Böhringer, ed., *MGH*, Concilia IV, suppl. 1 (Hannover: Hahnsche Buchhandlung, 1992). See Jane Bishop, "Bishops as Marital Advisors in the Ninth Century," in *Women in the Medieval World: Essays in Honor of John Mundy*, ed. Julius Kirshner

and Suzanne Wemple (Oxford: Basil Blackwell, 1985), pp. 53–84; S. Airlie, "Private Bodies and the Body Politic," *Past and Present* 161 (1998): 3–38; Karras, "Myth of Friedelehe," pp. 147–48.

66. Herren and Lapidge, introd., in Aldhelm, *DVP*, pp. 51–57; Luecke, "Unique Experience of Anglo-Saxon Nuns," p. 61.

67. Aldhelm, *DVP* cc. 8–9, pp. 235–38, trans. pp. 64–66.

68. Ibid. c. 9, pp. 237–38, trans. p. 66.

69. Ambrose, *De virginibus (Über die Jungfrauen)* 1.6.24–29, pp. 140–50, trans. *LNPNFC*, 2nd ser., 10:367–68; Augustine, *De sancta virginitate* c. 1, *PL* 40:397, trans. *LNPNFC*, 1st ser., 3:417. See Chapter 2, n93, above.

70. Aldhelm, *DVP* c. 19, pp. 248–49, trans. p. 75.

71. Ibid. c. 14, p. 243, trans. p. 71.

72. Ibid. c. 13, p. 242, trans. p. 70.

73. Ibid. c. 37, p. 285, trans. pp. 102–3; Elliott, *Spiritual Marriage*, p. 62.

74. Aldhelm, *DVP* cc. 35, 36, pp. 278, 281, trans. pp. 98, 100; Elliott, *Spiritual Marriage*, pp. 62n50, 64n57, 69.

75. Aldhelm, *DVP* c. 35, p. 280, trans. p. 99. See Elliott, *Spiritual Marriage*, p. 70.

76. Aldhelm, *DVP* c. 10, p. 238, trans. p. 66.

77. Ibid. c. 10, p. 238, trans. p. 67.

78. Katherine Jansen, *The Making of Magdalen: Preaching and Popular Devotion in the Later Middle Ages* (Princeton, N.J.: Princeton University Press, 2000), pp. 32–35.

79. Aldhelm, *DVP* c. 53, p. 310, trans. pp. 121–22.

80. Ibid. c. 53, pp. 311–12, trans. pp. 122–23.

81. Judith is preceded by a brief discussion of other prefigurations of Christ (virginity constituting a prefiguration) and a condemnation of finery in dress that brings women back into the picture. In keeping with the inversion of male virginity over female, however, Aldhelm leads off the discussion with the soldier Achar, who stole a cloak and gold from the doomed city of Jericho, also ensuring his own destruction (Jos. 7.11, *DVP* c. 55, pp. 113–14, trans. p. 124). This is followed by an eclectic series of biblical citations, church fathers (including a healthy dose of Cyprian), and even Vergil (*DVP* cc. 55–56, pp. 314–16, trans. pp. 125–27).

82. Aldhelm, *DVP* c. 57, p. 317, trans. pp. 126–27. Aldhelm's ambivalence about dress is such that he cannot resist likening Judith's positive gesture to the nameless woman from Proverbs (allegedly prefiguring Synagogue) who destroys her husband by posing as a harlot (Prov. 7.23, *DVP* c. 57, p. 317, trans. p. 127).

83. Ambrose's paradigm of good widowhood is the prophetess Anna (*De viduis* 4.21–22, *PL* 16:241, trans. *LNPNFC*, 2nd ser., 10:394–95). Augustine, while less explicit as to regime, also encourages cautious living in order to avoid scandal (*De bono viduitatis* 22.27, *PL* 40:448–49, trans. *LNPNFC*, 1st ser., 3:453).

84. Aldhelm, *DVP* cc. 23, 48, 49, pp. 253, 302, 304, trans. pp. 79, 115, 116.

85. Ibid. c. 18, p. 247, trans. p. 74. Also see ibid. cc. 7, 17, pp. 234, 246, trans. pp. 63, 73.

86. Ibid. c. 15, p. 244, trans. p. 71 (italics mine).

87. For Aldhelm's original promise, see ibid. c. 40, p. 321, trans. pp. 130–31. In the

DVC, however, he only says "let these promised songs be composed in new verse," going on to describe the various poetic tropes he will attempt (p. 355, trans. 104).

88. Lapidge and Rosier make this point, noting the frequent use of the verb *calcare* (to trample). See introd., Aldhelm, *DVC*, pp. 98–99.

89. Aldhelm, *DVC*, p. 361, trans. p. 107.

90. Ibid., p. 358, trans. p. 105. And yet the surly Malchus, who did unilaterally repudiate his wife, was omitted. Interestingly, Jerome, the author to whom we are indebted for the legend of Malchus, is inserted at the end of the male virgins (ibid., pp. 420–33, trans. pp. 138–39).

91. Ibid., pp. 424, 428, 433, 442–43, 446–47, 450, trans. pp. 141, 143, 146, 151, 153, 155.

92. Aldhelm, *DVP* c. 49, p. 303, trans. p. 115. Jerome was Blaesilla's spiritual director. See his justification of the austerities that led to her death, addressed to the patrician widow Marcella and the letter of consolation to Blaesilla's mother, Paula (Eps. 38, 39, *PL* 22:463–65, 465–75, trans. *LNPNFC*, 6:47–49, 49–54).

93. Aldhelm, *DVC*, pp. 440–41, trans. p. 150.

94. Posterity did not share Aldhelm's enthusiasm for the male virgin, and hence female virgins were restored to the limelight. But Aldhelm's vision may have been influential in other ways. His columns of virgins anticipated the Carolingian reformers' creation of a distinct category of virgins in the litanies of saints. And, as Felice Lifshitz has argued, this nomenclature tended to dissociate women from the prestigious categories of apostle and martyr—titles that would have sustained the argument for female office holding and an active female ministry in the church (Felice Lifshitz, "Gender Trouble in Paradise: The Case of the Liturgical Virgin," in *Images of Medieval Sanctity: Essays in Honour of Gary Dickson*, ed. Debra Strickland [Leiden: Brill, 2007], pp. 25–39). There is also evidence that female sanctity tended to remain frozen in the past, as the number of contemporary women regarded as saints was seriously in decline. Joseph-Claude Poulin notes that it was only men who merited a vita in Carolingian Aquitaine. Holy abbots were especially favored (*L'Idéal de sainteté dans l'Aquitaine Carolingienne d'après les sources hagiographiques, 750–950* [Quebec City: Les presses du l'Université Laval, 1975], pp. 34, 37).

95. *DVP* c. 19, p. 248, trans. p. 75. Note that because this section was part of the lengthy prologue, it was deleted from the poetic version.

96. Cf. the lives of the noble Eustadiola of Bourges (d. 684) who may or may not have existed (*Vita Eustadiolae abb. Bituricensis*, AA SS, June, 2:131–33, trans. *SW*, pp. 107–12; see *SW*, p. 106n4) and Balthild, queen of Neustria (*Vita sanctae Balthildis*, MGH, Scrip. Rer. Merov., 2:482–508, trans. *SW*, pp. 268–79). Also see the discussions of Radegund and Rictrude, below.

97. See Bede, *Ecclesiastical History of the English People* 4.19, pp. 390–97; Elliott, *Spiritual Marriage*, pp. 74–75, 79–80. The Anglo-Saxon saints Cuthburga, Cyneburga, Cyneswitha, and Osyth seemed to have followed Æthelthryth's lead (ibid., pp. 75, 76, 172n126, 206). For other early instances of virginal royal unions, see app. 3. On Æthelthryth's cult and her importance as a prototype for Anglo-Saxon royal women, see Virginia Blanton, *Signs of Devotion: The Cult of St. Æthelthryth in Medieval England* (University Park, Pa.: Pennsylvania State University Press, 2007); Susan Ridyard, *The Royal Saints of*

Anglo-Saxon England (Cambridge: Cambridge University Press, 1988), pp. 82–86; Robert Folz, *Les Saintes reines du Moyen Age en Occident (VIe–XIIIe siècles)* (Brussels: Société des Bollandistes, 1992), pp. 24–32.

98. Jean Gaudemet, "Le legs du droit romain en matière matrimoniale," in *Il Matrimonio nella società altomedievale*, Settimane di studio del Centro Italiano di studi sull'alto medioevo, 24 (Spoleto: Presso la sede del Centro, 1977), 1:144–45; Gaudemet, "Originalité et destin du mariage romain," in *Sociétés et mariage* (Strasbourg: Cerdic-Publications, 1980), pp. 154–55; Gaudemet, "Le mariage en droit romain: *Justum matrimonium*," in *Sociétés et mariage*, pp. 56–57. On efforts to ensure the free consent of the woman, see ibid., pp. 76–81.

99. See Wemple, *Women in Frankish Society*, pp. 33–34. But Germanic and Roman custom were not as polarized as this might suggest. See Karras, "Myth of Friedelehe," pp. 139, 140.

100. "Quae nuptiae, licet inter ingenuos et inter aequales, paterno arbitrio desponsationem atque dotationem praecedente, fuerunt celebratae, etiamsi jam sexuum commistio eas subsequeretur, legitimam conjugii copulam obtinere non possent" (Hincmar of Reims, Ep. 22, *Ad Rodulfum Bituricensem et Frotarium Burdigalensem*, PL 126:139). See Reynolds, *Marriage in the Western Church*, pp. 337, 339; James Brundage, *Law, Sex, and Christian Society in Medieval Europe* (Chicago: University of Chicago Press, 1987), pp. 136–37. In the twelfth century, the canonist Gratian would continue to distinguish between a marriage initiated by consent and ratified by consummation (C. 27 q. 2 c. 34 dpc; c. 37; c. 39 dpc; c. 45 dpc). Gratian also cites Hincmar permitting the dissolution of an unconsummated marriage of a bewitched couple (C. 33 q. 1 c. 4). Reynolds points out Gratian's indebtedness to Hincmar (Reynolds, *Marriage in the Western Church*, p. 315).

101. 1 Cor. 7.13–14. Also see Augustine's stern chastisement of the widow Ecdicia, who acted unilaterally (Ep. 262, *To Ecdicia*, PL 33:1078–82). On Radegund, see Etienne Delaruelle, "Sainte Radegonde et la Chrétienté de son temps," in *Etudes Mérovingiennes: Actes des journées de Poitiers, 1–3 mai 1952* (Paris: Picard, 1953), pp. 65–74; Georges Marié, "Sainte Radegonde et le milieu monastique contemporain," in *Etudes Mérovingiennes*, pp. 219–25; and Folz, *Les Saintes reines*, pp. 13–21. On the different points of emphases of her hagiographers, see Sabina Gäbe, "Radegundis: Sancta, Regina, Ancilla. Zum Heiligkeitsideal der Radegundisviten von Fortunat und Baudonivia," *Francia* 16 (1989): 1–30. Michel Rouche notes, however, that both authors participate in a politic silence over certain questions of church and state ("Fortunat et Baudonivie: Deux biographies pour une seule sainte," in *La Vie de Sainte Radegonde par Fortunat, Poitiers, Bibliothèque municipale, manuscript 250 [136]*, ed. Jean Favier [Poitiers: Seuil, 1995], p. 244).

102. *LHX* 9.42, pp. 470–71, trans. pp. 535–38; *De excidio Thoringiae*, MGH, Auct. Ant.. 4, 1:271–75, trans. *SW*, pp. 65–70.

103. At the very least, the poem seems collaborative. There is a flavor reminiscent of the *ubi est* of Anglo-Saxon poems, such as *The Wanderer* or the Finn episode in *Beowulf*. The poem in question is one of three written for, and to some extent with, Radegund, intended to garner help from her powerful relatives in attaining the relic of the holy cross. See Judith George, *Venantius Fortunatus: A Latin Poet in Merovingian Gaul* (Oxford: Clarendon, 1992), pp. 163–67. On Fortunatus's life and works, see ibid., pp. 18–34.

104. Baudonivia, *De vita Sanctae Radegundis libri duo*, MGH, *Scrip. Rer. Merov.*, 2:364–95. The books are treated as one life with two books. Fortunatus's vita is book 1 (cited hereafter as *VSRF*, pp. 364–77, trans. *SW*, pp. 70–86); Baudonivia's vita is book 2 (cited hereafter as *VSRB*, 2:377–95, trans. *SW*, pp. 86–105). On Baudonivia and female authors of hagiography, see Louise Coudanne, "Baudonivie, moniale de Sainte-Croix et la biographie de sainte Radegonde," in *Etudes Mérovingiennes*, pp. 45–51; Suzanne Wemple, "Female Spirituality and Mysticism in Frankish Monasticism: Radegund, Balthild and Aldegund," in *Peaceweavers*, ed. Shank and Nichols, 2:42–45.

105. For an examination of the challenges monasticism presented to women in general, see McNamara, "Ordeal of Community," pp. 293–326.

106. Jo Ann McNamara argues, however, that Gregory did not have much time for celibate women and was not particularly fulsome in his praise of Radegund either ("Chastity as a Third Gender in the History and Hagiography of Gregory of Tours," in *The World of Gregory of Tours*, ed. Kathleen Mitchell and Ian Wood [Leiden: Brill, 2002], pp. 205–6).

107. Tacitus mentions that members of the nobility were polygamous (*Germania* c. 18, pp. 156–57). The most notorious of the Franks in this respect was probably Chilperic. See, for example, *LHX* 4.28, pp. 160–61, trans. 22–23. In fact, the bishops did complain when Clothar began sleeping with Vuldetrada, the widow of Theudebald, his half-brother's son. This seduction was doubtless a way of consolidating his takeover of Theudebald's kingdom. It is unclear whether the bishops were objecting to incest, promiscuity, or both. But their criticisms got results as Clothar did stop sleeping with Vuldetrada (*LHX* 4.9, pp. 140–41, trans. p. 203).

108. Gregory clumps together the marriages that produced children. (*LHX* 4.3, pp. 142–43, trans. pp. 196–97). Gunthuec and Radegund are treated separately (*LHX* 3.6, pp. 136–37, trans. p. 167).

109. Such as Vuldetrada; see n107, above.

110. Gunthuec disappears from the narrative, but Clothar seems to have been married to Ingund, Aregund, and Chunsina simultaneously. The latter was the mother of Clothar's son Chramn, who was probably born right around the time that Clothar's marriage with Radegund was solemnized. On Clothar's marriages, see McNamara and Wemple, "Marriage and Divorce in the Frankish Kingdom," pp. 98–99; Wemple, *Women in Frankish Society*, pp. 38–39.

111. Jerome, *Commentaria in Epistolam ad Ephesios* bk. 3, ad c. 5, vv. 22–23, *PL* 26:530–31. This was a view that resonated with posterity. See Ivo of Chartres, *Decretum* 8.22, *PL* 161:645; Gratian, C. 32 q. 2, c. 3.

112. *LHX* 3.7, p. 105, trans. p. 168.

113. Ibid. 9.42, p. 474, trans. p. 535.

114. Ibid. 9.40, p. 464, trans. pp. 530–31.

115. Rouche, "Deux biographes," pp. 244–45.

116. See Raymond Van Dam's discussion in *Saints and Their Miracles in Late Antique Gaul* (Princeton, N.J.: Princeton University Press, 1993), pp. 28–36; Folz, *Les Saintes reines*, pp. 16–18; and Barbara Rosenwein, "Inaccessible Cloisters: Gregory of Tours and Episcopal Exemption," in *The World of Gregory of Tours*, ed. Mitchell and Wood, pp. 188–94.

117. *VSRB* 2.16, p. 389, trans. *SW*, p. 98.

118. *LHX* 9.42, p. 471, trans. p. 536. See Rosenwein, "Inaccessible Cloisters," pp. 191–92.

119. *LHX* 9.40, 42, pp. 464–65, 470, trans. pp. 530, 535.

120. Van Dam, *Saints and Their Miracles*, p. 33. Van Dam makes reference to Gregory's tacit incredulity over the community's chief relic in Gregory of Tours, *Liber in gloria martyrum* c. 5, ed. B. Krusch, *MGH, Scrip. Rer. Merov.*, 1, 2:490, trans. Raymond Van Dam, *The Glory of the Martyrs* (Liverpool: Liverpool University Press, 1988), p. 23 (hereafter cited as *GM*).

121. Gregory of Tours, *Libri de virtutibus sancti Martini episcopi* 2.44, ed. Bruno Krusch, *MGH, Scrip. Rer. Merov.*, 2, 1:625. As Gäbe notes, Fortunatus wisely ignores the topic of Maroveus altogether ("Radegundis," pp. 17–18).

122. Gaudemet, "Le legs du droit romain," pp. 152–53.

123. Karras, "Myth of Friedelehe," p. 148.

124. Fredegar, *Chronicarum quae dicuntur Fredegarii Scholastici, libri IV cum continuationibus* 4.36, ed. Bruno Krusch, *MGH, Scrip. Rer. Merov.*, 2 (Hannover: Hahn, 1888), p. 135, trans. J. M. Wallace-Hadrill, *The Fourth Book of the Chronicle of Fredegar* (London: Thomas Nelson and Sons, 1960), p. 24. Brunhild might be regarded as having God on her side, for when Columbanus left the court, there was a resounding thunderclap as he crossed the threshold. "But it did not quench the fury of the wretched woman," who from that time plotted against Columbanus.

125. Rigunth asserted she was the real mistress and that "her mother ought to revert to her original rank of serving-woman." Fredegund eventually retaliated by trying to break her daughter's neck as she was looking into a chest (*LHX* 9.34, pp. 454–55, trans. p. 521). Gregory first mentions Fredegund in the context of Chilperic's marriage to the Visigothic princess Galswinth. We are told that Chilperic already previously had (*habuerat*) Fredegund, the implication being that she was a concubine. Galswinth was soon murdered, and Chilperic married Fredegund within a few days (*LHX* 4.28, pp. 160–61, trans. p. 221. Note that Thorpe's translation is misleading in this context, as it claims that Chilperic was already married to Fredegund when Galswinth arrived on the scene.) In marrying Galswinth, Chilperic was following the example of his brother, Sigibert's, royal marriage to Brunhild, prompted by Sigibert's observation that "his bothers were taking wives who were completely unworthy of them and were so far degrading themselves as to marry their own servant" (*LHX* 4.27, p. 160, trans. p. 221). This is doubtless an allusion to Fredegund.

126. See, for example, the many abuses of Fredegund that Gregory puts in the mouth of the bishop of Reims, whom she murders for his efforts (*LHX* 8.31, pp. 387–88, trans. pp. 462–63).

127. This is suggested in a miracle related by Baudonivia when a housemaid dared to seat herself on the recently deceased Radegund's throne (*cathedra*) (*VSRB* 2.12, 385–86, trans. c. 12, p. 94).

128. Gregory of Tours, *Liber in gloria confessorum* c. 33, ed. B. Krusch, *MGH, Scrip. Rer. Merov.*, 1:768, trans. Raymond Van Dam, *The Glory of the Confessors* (Liverpool: Liverpool University Press, 1988), p. 46 (hereafter cited as *GC*).

129. Augustine makes reference to this more austere standard when he is attempting

to quell excessive virginal pride (*De sancta virginitate* cc. 45–46, *PL* 40:422–23, trans. *LNPNFC*, 1st ser., 3:434).

130. *GM* c. 5, pp. 489–90, trans. p. 22.

131. *LHX* 9.39, p. 460, trans. p. 526.

132. *GC* c. 104, p. 814, trans. p. 105.

133. Ibid. c. 104, p. 815, trans. pp. 105–6.

134. Ibid. c. 104, p. 816, trans. p. 107; *VSRB* 2.25, p. 103.

135. *GC* c. 104, p. 816, trans. p. 107.

136. *LHX* 9.2, p. 415, trans. p. 481.

137. *VSRB* 2.23, p. 393, trans. p. 103.

138. *GM* c. 62, p. 530, trans. p. 86; Gregory of Tours, *Liber vitae patrum* 12.3, ed. Bruno Krusch, *MGH, Scrip. Rer. Merov.*, 1, 2: (Hanover: Hahn, 1885), p. 715, trans. Edward James, *The Lives of the Fathers*, p. 85 (hereafter cited as *VP*); *GC* c. 83, p. 802, trans. p. 90.

139. *VP* 7.4, p. 690, trans. p. 47.

140. *GC* c. 102, p. 813, trans. p. 103.

141. Gregory uses this term when discussing Bishop Valerius's state of preservation (ibid. c. 83, p. 802, trans. p. 90).

142. Ibid. c. 34, p. 769, trans. p. 48.

143. Ibid. c. 104, p. 815, trans. p. 106.

144. Ibid. c. 104, p. 815, trans. p. 107; cf. *VSRB* 2.24, p. 393, trans. p. 103.

145. Ibid. c. 104, p. 816, trans. p. 108.

146. *LHX* 5.39, p. 232, trans. pp. 38–39.

147. Ibid. 6.34, p. 305, trans. p. 356. I have adjusted the translation slightly to make it more literal.

148. Ibid. 6.45, 7.9, pp. 318, 331, trans. pp. 378–79, 393–94.

149. *VSRB* 2.4, p. 88, trans. *SW*, p. 88.

150. *LHX* 4.26, p. 159, trans. p. 220.

151. Felix, bishop of Nantes, made his niece don the habit to thwart her marriage plans. She, however, was one of the lucky ones who engineered a rescue by her fiancé. (*LHX* 6.16, pp. 285–86, trans. p. 347). On other instances of female monasteries as jails, see McNamara, "Ordeal of Community," pp. 302–4.

152. Stephanus, Presbyter Africanus, *Vita de S. Sancto Amatore* c. 4, *AA SS*, May, 1:54.

153. *Vita Wandregiseli* c. 4, *MGH, Scrip. Rer. Merov.*, 5:15.

154. Gäbe draws attention to the difference in tone between the poet, who shows considerable familiarity with the community, and the hagiographer, whose intimacy with Radegund is largely suppressed ("Radegundis," p. 5).

155. Fortunatus, *De virginitate* ll. 5, 25–26, bk. 8, carm. 3, *MGH, Auct. Ant.* 4, 1:182. While Lifshitz makes an argument that association with the Virgin Mary was potentially empowering for women in saints' litanies, I find this reading overoptimistic ("Priestly Women, Virginal Men," pp. 95, 102).

156. Fortunatus, *De virginitate* ll. 85–89, 95–6, 105–6, bk. 8, carm. 3, *MGH, Auct. Ant.* 4, 1:183, 183, 184; cf. Fortunatus, *Ad virgines* ll. 33–36, bk. 8, carm. 4, *MGH, Auct. Ant.* 4, 1:193; Fortunatus, *Ad abbatissam* l. 6, bk. 11, carm. 6, *MGH, Auct. Ant.* 4, 1:260.

157. Fortunatus, *De virginitate* ll. 127–28, bk. 8, carm. 3, *MGH, Auct. Ant.* 4, 1:184; cf. *Ad abbatissam* app. 23, ll. 15–18, in ibid., p. 287.

158. Fortunatus, *De virginitate* ll. 99–102, bk. 8, carm. 3, *MGH, Auct. Ant.* 4, 1:183.

159. Ibid. ll. 325–34, bk. 8, carm. 3, *MGH, Auct. Ant.* 4, 1:189–90.

160. Ibid. l. 345, bk. 8, carm. 3, *MGH, Auct. Ant.* 4, 1:190.

161. Ibid. ll. 374–80, 384, bk. 8, carm. 3, *MGH, Auct. Ant.* 4, 1:191.

162. Fortunatus, "concipiente fide Christi Radegundis amore / Caesarii lambit regula quidquid habet," *De virginitate* ll. 47–48, bk. 8, carm. 3, *MGH, Auct. Ant.* 4, 1:182.

163. Fortunatus, *De virginitate* ll. 55–56, bk. 8, carm. 3, *MGH, Auct. Ant.* 4, 1:182.

164. Fortunatus, *(Ad Radegundem) Item aliud ad eadem de natalico abbatissae* 11.3, bk. 11, carm. 3, *MGH, Auct. Ant.* 4, 1:259; on his writings to Radegund and Agnes, see George, *Venantius Fortunatus*, pp. 161–77.

165. Fortunatus, *Ad abbatissam* l. 12, bk. 11, carm. 6, *MGH, Auct. Ant.* 4, 1:260.

166. This is not the strategy appropriate to the *Thuringian Wars*, however, in which he sustains Radegund's bid for royal support by casting her as a tragic heroine. This meant sidelining her many secular successes. See George, *Venantius Fortunatus*, p. 165.

167. *VSRF* 1.2, p. 366, trans. pp. 71–72.

168. Ibid. 1.3, p. 366, trans. p. 72.

169. Ibid. 1.3, 8, 4, 6, 9, pp. 366, 367, 366, 367, 368, trans. pp. 72, 74, 72–73, 73, 74.

170. Ibid., 1.5, pp. 366–67, trans. p. 73.

171. Jerome, Ep. 39, To Paula, c. 4, *PL* 22:471.

172. Tacitus describes a woman as "priscae sanctimoniae virgo" in *Annales* 3.69, in *The Histories: Books IV–V; The Annals: Books 1–3*, trans. John Jackson, Loeb Classical Library, 249 (Cambridge, Mass.: Harvard University Press, 1931), 3:632; and marriage with "feminam nobilitate puerperiis sanctimonia insignem" in ibid. 12.6, Loeb, 312, 4:322; and of a Vestal virgin who "septem et quinquaginta per annos summa sanctimonia Vestalibus sacris praesederat" in ibid. 2.86, 3:516. See the entry for *sanctimonalis* in Charleton Lewis, *A Latin Dictionary* (Oxford: Clarendon, 1879; reprt., 1980), p. 1625. This also seems to be Abelard's assumption: "But the consecration of virgins, being more precious and so rarer [than of monks], has reserved for itself the exultation of chief festivals." He goes on to say that the profession of nuns (*sanctimoniales*) draws its name from the word holy (*sanctimonia*) (J. T. Muckle, ed., "The Letter of Heloise on Religious Life and Abelard's First Reply," *Mediaeval Studies* 18 [1956]: 268, trans. C. K. Scott Moncrieff, *The Letters of Abelard and Heloise* [New York: Alfred A. Knopf, 1942], p. 155). He stipulates that *monacha*, conversely, is from *one* or *solitary*, and it accommodates nonvirgins ("monachas quae viros noverant," in Muckle, "Letter of Heloise," p. 276; trans. Moncrieff, p. 168).

173. "Ibique paucas collegens monachas, cum fide integra et oratione degebat," *VP* 19.2, p. 738, trans. p. 121.

174. For the greater austerity of married saints and the distinction between their inner and outer lives, see Elliott, *Spiritual Marriage*, pp. 231–45.

175. On Elisabeth's life and ascetic practices, see Dyan Elliott, *Proving Woman: Female Spirituality and Inquisitional Culture* (Princeton, N.J.: Princeton University Press, 2004), ch. 2. Elisabeth, of course, was a Thuringian princess by marriage rather than birth.

176. *VSRF* 1.12, p. 368, trans. p. 75.

177. Ibid. See McNamara, *Sisters in Arms*, p. 98.

178. The first condemnation against "the ministry of women" occurred at the Synod of Nimes in 396 (*Concilia Galliae, CSEL* 148, c. 2, p. 50). Cf. the first Synod of Orange in 441 (ibid. c. 2, p. 91). The Synod of Epaon (517) condemns "the consecration of widows, called deaconesses" (ibid., *CSEL*, 148a, c. 21, p. 29). The second Synod of Tours (567) cites Epaon (ibid. c. 21, p. 187).

179. *VSRF* 1.15, p. 369, trans. p. 76. Wemple argues that Fortunatus chooses his words carefully to imply that she was basically consecrated a widow, which would mean that she was not actually veiled by the bishop but imposed the veil herself (*Women in Frankish Society*, p. 140).

180. Fortunatus, (*Ad Radegundem*) *Ad eandem cum se reclauderet* ll. 15–16, in *Opera poetica*, bk. 8, carm. 9, p. 195; (*Ad Radegundem*) *Ad eandem cum rediit* l. 4, in ibid. bk. 8, carm. 10, p. 195.

181. *VSRB* 2.3–4, pp. 380–81, trans. pp. 87–88; *SRVB* 2.6–7, p. 382, trans. pp. 89–90.

182. See *VSRB* 2.4, 7, pp. 380–81, 382, trans. pp. 88, 90. Wemple, *Women in Frankish Society*, p. 132.

183. *VSRF* 1.13, p. 369, trans. pp. 75–76.

184. Ibid. 1.14, p. 369, trans. p. 76.

185. Ibid. 1.15–20, pp. 369–71, trans. pp. 76–79.

186. Ibid. 1.21, p. 371, trans. p. 79.

187. Ibid. 1.21, p. 371, trans. p. 79.

188. Elliott, *Proving Woman*, pp. 63–64.

189. In fact, there is even some scholarly contention as to whether Radegund actually took monastic vows and remained at Poitiers. According to Delaruelle, her status of deaconess would exempt her from such claustration ("Sainte Radegonde," p. 67). As McNamara points out, however, the text clearly implies stability within the community after her enclosure (*SW*, p. 75n53). See *VSRF* 1.24, p.372, trans. p. 81, where she is described as having accepted the rule of St. Caesarius. Moreover in the letter of foundation she says explicitly, "I submitted myself in regular obedience to her [Agnes's] authority (*LHX* 9.42, pp. 470–71, trans. p. 535). In the *Thuringian Wars* she writes to her kinsmen that she would seek him out personally "if the monastery's sacred cloister did not keep me back" (*De excidio Thoringiae*, l. 105, *MGH, Auct. Ant.*, 4, 1:273, trans. *SW*, p. 68).

190. *VSRF* 1.23, p. 372, trans. p. 80.

191. Ibid. 1.21–22, pp. 371–72, trans. pp. 79–80.

192. Ibid. 1.25, pp. 372–73, trans. p. 81.

193. Ibid. 1.26, p. 373, trans. p. 81. See John Kitchen's discussion of Radegund as *tortrix* in *Saints' Lives and the Rhetoric of Gender: Male and Female in Merovingian Hagiography* (New York: Oxford University Press, 1998), pp. 117–22.

194. Cf. Gäbe, who contrasts Fortunatus's depiction of an accretion in Radegund's holiness with Baudonivia's portrait of the queen's steady piety throughout her life ("Rade-gundis," p. 4).

195. *VSRB* 2.8, p. 382, trans. p. 90.

196. Ibid. 2.7, p. 382, trans. p. 90. Kitchen notes the diminished austerities in Baudonivia's life, but nevertheless argues that "despite Baudonivia's recasting of Radegund's ascetic profile, she still insists on interpreting the saint's life as a martyrdom" (*Saints' Lives and the Rhetoric of Gender*, p. 144).

197. Ibid. 2.7, p. 383, trans. pp. 90–91. See Caesarius of Arles, *Regula virginum* cc. 15 [13], 67, 68, 69, 19 [17], 9 [7], in *Oeuvres monastiques*, 1:190, 258, 259, 192, 266, 186–88; cf. *SW*, p. 90n94.

198. *VSRB* 2.4, p. 381, trans. p. 88; ibid. 2.16, p. 389, trans. p. 98; ibid. 2.10, pp. 384–35, trans. p. 93.

199. Ibid. 2.5, p. 381, trans. p. 89.

200. Ibid. 2.1, p. 380, trans. p. 87.

201. Ibid. 2.5, p. 381, trans. p. 89.

202. Ibid. 2.4, p. 381, trans. p. 88.

203. Ibid. 2.3, p. 380, trans. p. 88.

204. Ibid. 2.20, p. 391, trans. p. 101.

205. Ibid. 2.4, p. 381, trans. p. 88. The apparatus in *MGH* indicates that the manuscript tradition has both *conjugium* (marriage) and *coniunx* (spouse) as possible variants. I have followed the lead of the Latin edition; *SW* translates the variant.

206. *VSRB* 2.6, p. 388, trans. pp. 97–98.

207. Ibid. 2.23, p. 393, trans. p. 103.

208. *Vita sanctae Balthildis* c. 18, *MGH, Scrip. Rer. Merov.*, 2:506, trans. *SW*, p. 277.

209. And in fact, Grégoire sees Radegund's life as the first biography of a saint that emphasizes the role of *sponsa Christi* ("Il matrimonio mistico," p. 731; cf. 767).

210. On the Carolingian and post-Carolingian efforts to promote widows and sometimes married women as saints, see Anne-Marie Helvétius, "*Virgo* et *Virago:* Réflexions sur le pouvoir du voile consacré d'après les sources hagiographiques de la Gaule du Nord," in *Femmes et pouvoirs des femmes à Byzance et en Occident (VIe–XIe siècles)*, ed. Stéphane Lebecq et al. (Lille: Centre de Recherche sur l'histoire de l'Europe du Nord-Ouest, 1999), pp. 194–95. The same pattern is apparent with the revival of the empire in Ottonian Saxony. See Patrick Corbet, *Les Saints Ottoniens: Sainteté dynastique, sainteté royale et sainteté feminine autour de l'an Mil* (Sigmaringen: Thorbecke, 1986).

211. *VRV* 1.9–10, p. 83, trans. pp. 203–4.

212. Ibid. 1.9, p. 83, trans. p. 203.

213. Ibid. 1.6, p. 82, trans. pp. 200–201.

214. Ibid. 1.11, p. 83, trans. p. 204.

215. Ibid. 2.14, 2.17, pp. 84, 85, trans. pp. 206, 208.

216. Ibid. 2.17, p. 85, trans. p. 208.

217. Ibid. 2.19, p. 85, trans. p. 209.

218. Ibid. preface and 1.1, p. 81, trans. pp. 197–98.

219. Ibid. 3.25, p. 87, trans. p. 214; also see ibid. 1.9, p. 83, trans. p. 202.

220. Ibid. 3.26, p. 87, trans. pp. 214–15; cf. Bridget of Sweden's aggressive treatment of her virginal daughter, Catherine (see the near contemporary life of the Briggitine monk

Ulphonsus [d. 1433], *Vita S. Catharinae Suecicae, AA SS*, March, 3:506); also see Elliott, *Spiritual Marriage*, pp. 278–81.

221. *VRV* 3.27, p. 87, trans. p. 215.

222. Ibid. 3.28, p. 88, trans. p. 215.

223. Ibid. 3.32, p. 88, trans. p. 218. This is in spite of the fact that Gertrude was abbess at Hamay. This prejudice against married women as abbesses could reflect the progressive effect of the reforms of St. Columbanus (d. 615).

CHAPTER 4

1. Jerome, Ep. 22, *To Eustochium* c. 5, *PL* 22:397, trans. *LNPNFC*, 2nd ser., 6:24.

2. Thus Goscelin recounts how when he first came to England "as a very young man— you were only a baby" (*Liber confortatorius* bk. 4, ed. C. H. Talbot, in *Studia Anselmiana*, fasc. 37, *Analecta Monastica*, 3rd ser. [Rome: Herder, 1955], p. 102, trans. W. R. Barnes and Rebecca Hayward in *Writing the Wilton Women: Goscelin's Legend of Edith and Liber confortatorius*, ed. Stephanie Hollis [Turnhout: Brepols, 2004], p. 188). On Goscelin, see André Wilmart, "Eve et Goscelin," pt. 1, *Revue Bénédictine* 46 (1934): 414–38; pt. 2, 50 (1938): 42–83.

3. Goscelin of Saint-Bertin, *The Hagiography of the Female Saints of Ely*, ed. and trans. Rosalind Love (Oxford: Clarendon, 2004), p. 127. On his age, see Wilmart, "Eve et Goscelin," pt. 2, p. 51.

4. Goscelin, *Vita Sancte Wihtbvrge* c. 18, in *Hagiography*, pp. 76–77. Cf. St. Waerburgh, daughter of the sixth-century Æthelbert of Kent, who "for love of perpetual virginity … flew to the bridegroom of eternal integrity, and with angelic modesty … repelled royal suitors and lovers." Her holy intransigence was enacted through her body, which remained perfectly intact for nine years after her death: "her face was radiant, her cheeks rosy, like in the first flower of youth." This condition endured until the Viking invasions (Goscelin, *Vita Sanctae Werbvrge* cc. 2, 11–12, in *Hagiography*, pp. 34–35, 48–51). For a discussion of the reinvention of virgin donors in the wake of the Norman Conquest, see Joscelyn Wogan-Browne, *Saints' Lives and Women's Literary Culture: Virginity and Its Authorizations* (Oxford: Oxford University Press, 2001), pp. 57–90.

5. Goscelin, *Vita Sancte Wihtbvrge* c. 20, in *Hagiography*, pp. 78–79.

6. This is a point to which he often returns (Goscelin, *Vita Sancte Wihtbvrge* proem, cc. 8, 15, 24, in *Hagiography*, pp. 54–55, 66–67, 74–75, 82–83).

7. Goscelin, *In festivitate Sancte Sexbvrge, In natale Sancte Eormenhilde*, in *Hagiography*, pp. 8–9, 20–21. But Goscelin's other writings also made it clear that chastity was not just the prerogative of women: his biography of Edward the Confessor emphasizes that the king's marriage was unconsummated. See his *The Life of King Edward Who Rests at Westminster*, ed. and trans. Frank Barlow (London: Nelson, 1962), p. 60; cf. pp. 42, 76; Elliott, *Spiritual Marriage*, pp. 120–23. Karen Winstead demonstrates how the ongoing fascination with virginity remains a constant in late medieval England, and yet the discourse can still be

adapted to different readers and cultural contexts, in *Virgin Martyrs: Legends of Sainthood in Late Medieval England* (Ithaca, N.Y.: Cornell University Press, 1997).

8. See Barbara Newman's analysis of gender differences in twelfth-century literature on the spiritual vocation, in which the emphasis on virginity renders the portrayal of the female vocation as less dynamic (*From Virile Woman to WomanChrist*, pp. 19–45, esp. 29–34, 40–45; also see her app. A, which lists this material). Cf. the more apologetic reading of Elisabeth Bos, in "The Literature of Spiritual Formation for Women in France and England, 1080–1180," in *Listen Daughter: The Speculum Virginum and the Formation of Religious Women in the Middle Ages*, ed. Constant Mews (New York: Palgrave, 2001), pp. 201–20. Also see Clarissa Atkinson's "'Precious Balsam in a Fragile Glass': The Ideology of Virginity in the Later Middle Ages," *Journal of Family History* 8 (1983): 131–43.

9. *Speculum virginum* bk. 5, ed. Jutta Seyfarth, *CCCM*, 5 (Turnhout: Brepols, 1990), p. 117.

10. Ælred of Rievaulx, *De institutione inclusarum* 2.14, in *La Vie de recluse: La Prière pastorale*, *SC*, 76, ed. Charles Dumont (Paris: Editions du Cerf, 1961), pp. 80, 82. Following Goscelin's lead, Ælred also wrote another life of Edward the Confessor, one that particularly emphasized the king's chaste marriage as a claim to sanctity. See Ælred of Rievaulx, *Vita S, Edwardi regis, PL* 195:737–90.

11. Ivo of Chartres, *Decretum* 7.128, *PL* 161:574. Some eight chapters later, however, he also includes Ambrose's rejection of the gynecological solution in his letter to Syagrius (ibid., 7.136, *PL* 161:578).

12. See Anders Winroth, *The Making of Gratian's Decretum* (Cambridge: Cambridge University Press, 2000), which demonstrates that this work was not the work of one man, but something of a collective effort that evolved over time.

13. C. 32 q. 5 c. 4; C. 32 q. 5 dpc 13.

14. C. 32 q. 5 c. 14 and dpc.

15. Thus he argues that the church can only assess outer things and therefore is not privy to whatever inner delectation a violated virgin might have experienced. Thomas Aquinas, *Commentum in quatuor libros sententiarum* bk. 4, dist. 38, q. 1, art. 5 ad 4, in *Opera omnia* (Parma: Petrus Fiaccadori, 1858; rprt., New York: Musurgia, 1948), 7, 2:1013.

16. Although he is prepared to grant that a virgin who had consented to coitus could potentially recoup her mental integrity, if the physical dimension is compromised the prospects are much bleaker (Aquinas, *Commentum in quatuor libros sententiarum* bk. 4, dist. 33, q. 3, art. 1, resp. ad 4, 7, in *Opera omnia*, 7, 2:977; quodlib. 5, q. 2, art. 3, resp., in ibid., 9:529). Cf. the doctor-theologian Guerric of Saint-Quentin (d. 1245), who seems less optimistic about the regaining of mental integrity (*Quaestiones de quolibet* quodlib. 5, 2a, resp., ed. Walter Principe, *Texts and Studies* 143 [Toronto: Pontifical Institute, 2002], p. 265).

17. On Christina, see the recent collection of articles edited by Samuel Fanous and Henrietta Leyser, *Christina of Markyate: A Twelfth-Century Holy Woman* (London: Routledge, 2005).

18. There is Ralph, bishop of Durham, whose frustration led him to encourage the suit of Burthred, the man Christina was constrained to marry; Robert, bishop of Lincoln, who

reversed his original judgment in favor of Christina's vocation to later support the marriage after having received bribes from Christina's parents and who continued to persecute Christina for years; and the anonymous cleric to whom Christina was entrusted by Archbishop Thurstan (*The Life of Christina of Markyate* c. 6, 22, 43, 43–44, ed. and trans. C. H. Talbot [Oxford: Clarendon Press, 1959], pp. 42–45, 70–71, 112–19; hereafter cited as *CM*). Abbot Geoffrey also presents a tacit threat to Christina's chastity, as will be seen below.

19. *CM* c. 7, pp. 44–47; c. 10, pp. 50–55.

20. *CM* c. 23, pp. 74–75.

21. *CM* c. 10, 12, pp. 50–51, 52–54. On Christina's psalter, see Christopher Holdsworth, "Christina of Markyate," in *Medieval Women*, ed. Derek Baker, Studies in Church History, Subsidia, 1 (Oxford: Basil Blackwell, 1978), pp. 189–92; Tony Hunt, "The Life of St. Alexis, 475–1125," in *Christina of Markyate*, ed. Fanous and Leyser, pp. 217–28. Christina also received prophetic dreams that helped to guide her virgocentric vocation, reminiscent of early martyrs like Perpetua. After the aborted wedding night when her mother's rage had reached a boiling point, she dreamt that she was comforted by a priest about to perform Mass who gave her a flowering branch to offer an enthroned lady. The lady returned a twig, entrusting it to Christina's care, and promised her protection. As Christina withdrew from her presence, she encountered Burthred, prostrate on the ground. "And as soon as he saw her passing by her stretched out his hand to seize her and hold her fast. But she, gathering her garments about her and clasping them to her side, for they were white and flowing, passed him untouched." The dream ends when she again apprehends a lofty upper chamber to which she is anxious to ascend but fearful over the difficulty of the steps. The lady again assisted her and promised that she would eventually bring both Christina and the Old Testament Judith to her chamber (*CM* cc. 24–25, pp. 75–77; also see c. 26, pp. 78–79). This is reminiscent of the dream in which Perpetua mounted a series of threatening stairs to arrive at a comforting garden in which she is fed curd by a white-haired man (*Passion of SS. Perpetua and Felicity* c. 4, pp. 6–7, 26). At a later juncture, Christina saw herself surrounded by menacing bulls who were immobilized by a swamp. "Whilst she gazed on this sight in astonishment, a voice was heard saying: 'If you take a firm stand in the place where you are, you will have no cause to fear the ferocity of those beasts. But if you retreat one step, at that same moment you will fall into their power'" (*CM* c. 37, pp. 98–99). The wild bulls could be considered a latter-day correlative to the experiences of Perpetua and Thecla, both pitted against wild animals in the gladiatorial ring—in particular a wild cow (*Passion of SS. Perpetua and Felicity* c. 20, pp. 18–19, 39–40). Also see Samuel Fanous's discussion of Christina as ascetical virgin martyr ("Christina of Markyate and the Double Crown," in *Christina of Markyate*, ed. Fanous and Leyser, pp. 53–78).

22. See Winstead, *Virgin Martyrs*, pp. 64–111; Wogan-Browne, *Saints' Lives and Women's Literary Culture*, pp. 106–17.

23. *CM* cc. 16, 17, pp. 62–63. When Fredebert, impressed with Christina's wit, tells her to stop joking, she offers to take the ordeal of hot iron, obliquely reminiscent of the many queens in the early Middle Ages accused of adultery only to reveal that they have all along been participants in a spiritual marriage. See Elliott, *Spiritual Marriage*, pp. 76–77, 129–31; cf. p. 90.

24. *CM* c. 22, pp. 72–73. This argument did not seem to impress Burthred, however, who immediately tried to grab her by her mantle. But Christina "like another Joseph" eluded Burthred (now demeaned and feminized as Potiphar's wife) and escaped by leaving the garment in his hands.

25. See Thomas Head's important discussion of Christina's justification of her commitment to Christ not simply in terms of nuptial metaphor but in terms of the twelfth-century consensual view of marriage ("The Marriages of Christina of Markyate," *Viator* 21 [1990]: 71–95; rev. in *Christina of Markyate*, ed. Fanous and Leyser, pp. 116–37). Although Head is undoubtedly right about Christina's line of defense, I would argue that this had been standard fare in ecclesiastical circles. I argue that consensuality had spread from marriage to Christ to secular marriage, rather than the reverse. It is significant, however, that we find an essentially unschooled laywoman making the argument for the indissoluble marriage to Christ through the prism of ecclesiastical changes on secular marriage.

26. Herriman, *Liber de restauratione S. Martini Tornacensis* c. 62, MGH, SS, 4:304.

27. Eremburg was not designated as *abbatissa*, however, but *magistra*—which signified the community's dependence on the male house. The other part of the community was under a different *magistra* (Herriman, *Liber de restauratione* c. 69, p. 307). *Conversus/a*, although a notoriously ambiguous term, generally refers to pious laypeople who were at one time married—either associated with a monastery or actually living within its precincts. Thus the urban house probably contained women recently converted from the world who were either widowed or separated from their husbands, as was Maisend. On the complexities of this term, see Duane Osheim, "Conversion, *Conversi*, and the Christian Life in Late Medieval Tuscany," *Speculum* 58 (1983): 368–90.

28. The priest who attended the community happened to be someone with whom Maisend was familiar during her time in the world. No doubt anticipating possible complaints, Eremburg ordered Maisend not to utter a word to the priest, apart from confessing her sins. On his departure, however, Maisend requested that the priest pray for her, a request that the *magistra* interpreted as rank disobedience deserving of excommunication—which in monastic terms signifies ostracism from the life of the community.

29. Her happiness was complete when a visiting monk discovered her ignominious position and compared her to St. Alexis, who returned from the east to live as an unknown pilgrim under his father's stairs for seven years (Herriman, *Liber de restauratione* c. 69, p. 307). The monk carried back a report of this treatment to his abbot, who interceded on Maisend's behalf.

30. See Jacques Dalarun, *Robert of Arbrissel: Sex, Sin, and Salvation in the Middle Ages*, trans. Bruce Venarde (Washington, D.C.: Catholic University of America Press, 2006), pp. 65–67. Dalarun notes that in all probability Petronilla was still married. Later translations into French give her the less ambiguous title of widow. The consecration of an abbess had, as we have seen, become progressively associated with the rite for veiling virgins. Hence, the prospective abbess was assimilated with the virginal choir of wise virgins who were always on the lookout for their bridegroom. See, for example, no. 22, *Ordinatio abbatissae* c. 5, in *PRG*. Also see Grégoire, "Il matrimonio mistico," pp. 724–25. Hence Robert's privileging of a woman who had once been sexually active (Petronilla had been married four times)

is very much out of sync with this tradition and could even be construed as correspond-ing to his early promotion of Mary Magdalene. On a practical level, the appointment was contentious because it subjected not only virgins to matrons but also men to women. This latter hierarchical inversion was included in the founding charter as a precaution (*Diplo-mata* c. 5, *PL* 162, cols. 1083–84, trans. Bruce Venarde, *Robert of Arbrissel: A Medieval Religious Life* [Washington, D.C.: Catholic University Press, 2003], p. 86; Andrea of Fontevrault, *Vita altera B. Roberti de Arbrissello* 2.7–9, *PL* 162:1061–62, trans. in *Robert of Arbrissel: A Medieval Religious Life*, pp. 29–31). There is also an Old French version of Andrea's life, written ca. 1500, that is more complete than the Latin version, which ends in the midst of c. 42. See *La Vie venerable pere maistre Robert de Arbrinsel*, ed. Jacques Dalarun, in *L'Impossible sainteté: La vie retrouvée de Robert d'Arbrissel (v. 1045–1116) fondateur de Fontevraud* (Paris: Editions du Cerf, 1985). Venarde's translation uses the Old French for the latter part of the life. On Robert's pio-neering efforts in pastoral care, see Fiona Griffith, "The Cross and the *Cura monialum*: Robert of Arbrissel, John the Evangelist, and the Pastoral Care of Women in the Age of Reform," *Speculum* 83 (2008): 303–30.

31. Baldric of Dol, *Vita* c. 4, 20, *PL* 162:1054, trans. pp. 17–18; Andrea of Fontevrault, *Vita altera* 3.11, 1062–63, trans. pp. 31–32; *La Vie venerable pere maistre Robert de Arbrin-sel* c. 66, ed. Dalarun, *L'Impossible*, p. 295, trans. pp. 62–63; cf. Dalarun's introduction, *L'Impossible*, p. 185.

32. Fortunately, Ælred, that champion of virginity par excellence, came to the fledg-ling order's rescue. He provided adroit damage control by arguing that the love of chastity that motivated this act of violence was deserving of admiration, if not the act itself. For Ælred's defense, see *De santimoniali de Wattun, PL* 195:789–96. It is translated in the appen-dix of John Boswell's *Kindness of Strangers: The Abandonment of Children in Western Europe from Late Antiquity to the Renaissance* (Chicago: University of Chicago, 1998), pp. 452–58. See Giles Constable, "Ælred of Rievaulx and the Nun of Watton: An Episode in the Early History of the Gilbertine Order," in *Medieval Women*, ed. Derek Baker, Studies in Church History, Subsidia 1 (Oxford: Basil Blackwell, 1978), pp. 205–26; Brian Golding, *Gilbert of Sempringham and the Gilbertine Order, c. 1130–c. 1300* (Oxford: Clarendon, 1995), pp. 33–38. This distinction between admiring the virtue inherent in a pious excess versus imitating the act itself anticipated the apologist note that would be struck by hagiographers of medieval mystics when attempting to justify their excessive acts of penance. Jacques de Vitry relied heavily on this distinction in his life of Mary of Oignies. On this, see Richard Kieckhefer, *Unquiet Souls: Fourteenth-Century Saints and Their Religious Milieu* (Chicago: University of Chicago, 1984), pp. 12–14. The Gilbertine story takes a miraculous turn when the woman, who is chained up one night, is discovered to be no longer pregnant—a happy ending that smacks of infanticide. John Boswell sees parallels between this episode and the popular exemplum of the pregnant abbess who is saved from exposure by a miracle of the Virgin (*Kindness of Strangers*, pp. 372–74), translated in app., pp. 459–60. Also see Nancy Warren's discussion of this exemplum in *Spiritual Economies: Female Monasticism in Later Medieval England* (Philadelphia: University of Pennsylvania Press, 2001), pp. 73–76.

33. See Metz, *La Consécration des vierges*, p. 246.

34. Ibid., pp. 265–67. See Andrieu, *Le Pontifical Romain au Moyen-Age*, vol. 1, *Le*

Pontifical Romain du XIIe siècle, Studi e Testi 86 (Vatican: Biblioteca Apostolica Vaticana, 1938), no. 12, pp. 154–59 (hereafter cited as *PR*); Andrieu, *Le Pontifical Romain au Moyen-Age*, vol. 2, *Le Pontifical Romain de la Curie Romaine au XIIIe siècle, Studi e Testi* 87 (Vatican: Biblioteca Apostolica Vaticana, 1940), no. 18, pp. 414–18 (hereafter cited as *PRC*).

35. This is especially true of the heretics discovered at Monforte (ca. 1028), who prized virginity above all else and believed that the human race could perpetuate itself like bees, which were believed to reproduce without sexual activity (Landulf the Senior, *Mediolanensis historiae libri quatuor* 2.27, ed. Alessandro Cutulo, *Rerum Italicarum Scriptores*, vol. 4, 2, rev. ed. [Bologna: N. Zanichelli, 1942], p. 68, trans. Walter Wakefield and Austin Evans, *Heresies of the High Middle Ages* [New York: Columbia University Press, 1969], pp. 87–88). Cf. the heretics discovered at Arras-Cambrai, who "despised lawful marriage." Paul Fredericq, ed., *Corpus documentorum inquisitionis haereticae pravitatis Neerlandicae* (Ghent: J. Vuylsteke; The Hague: Martinus Nijhoff, 1889), 1:5, trans. Wakefield and Evans, *Heresies of the High Middle Ages*, p. 83. See Hugette Tavani, "Le mariage dans l'hérésie de l'an mil," *Annales, ESC* 32 (1977): 1074–84.

36. Eberwin of Steinfeld was one of the first to describe Cathar beliefs. See his appeal to Bernard of Clairvaux (ca. 1143–44) in Ep. 472, To Bernard, *PL* 182:676–80, trans. Wakefield and Evans, *Heresies of the High Middle Ages*, pp. 127–32. On the Cathar aversion to procreation (and, by implication, marriage), see Peter Biller, "Cathars and the Material Woman," in *Medieval Theology and the Natural Woman*, ed. Peter Biller and Alaistair Minnis (Woodbridge, Suffolk: Boydell and Brewer, 1997), esp. pp. 81–102. For a general overview, see Malcolm Lambert, *The Cathars* (Oxford: Basil Blackwell, 1998).

37. Serm. 66, 2.3, in *Sermons sur le Cantique*, ed. J. Leclercq and Raffaele Fasetta, *SC*, 472 (Paris: Editions du Cerf, 2004), 4:342, trans. Kilian Walsh and Irene Edmonds, *Bernard of Clairvaux: On the Song of Songs III*, Cistercian Father Series, no. 31 (Kalamazoo, Mich.: Cistercian Publications, 1979), 3:193.

38. Pierre des Vaux-de-Cernay, *Petri Vallium Sarnaii monachi Hystoria albigensis* cc. 38–39, ed. Pascal Guébin and Ernst Lyon (Paris: Librairie Honoré Champion, 1926), 1:35–37. When one of the wives asked to enter religion, preferring first the Cistercians and then Robert of Arbrissel's foundation at Fontevrault, Raymond insisted that she become a Cathar perfect—in which case he would support her financially.

39. I have discussed the interrelations between the Gregorian reform, the disparagement of marriage, the growth of popular piety, and the rise of Mariology in *Spiritual Marriage*, pp. 95–113, and *Fallen Bodies*, ch. 4. For a more devotion-centered approach to the rise of Mariology, see Rachel Fulton, *From Judgement to Passion: Devotion to Christ and the Virgin Mary, 800–1200* (New York: Columbia University Press, 2002), pt. 2.

40. There is a definite correlation between misogamy and misogyny. A number of key texts have been collected in Blamires, *Woman Defamed and Woman Defended*. Also see Wilson and Makowski, *Wykked Wyves and the Woes of Marriage*.

41. See Bloch, *Medieval Misogyny and the Invention of Western Romantic Love*.

42. On this process, see Elliott, *Spiritual Marriage*, pp. 134–42.

43. Augustine, *De nuptiis et concupiscentia* 1.11.12–1.12.13, *PL* 44:420–23, trans. *LNPNFC*, 1st ser., 5:268–69. See Elliott, *Spiritual Marriage*, pp. 47–48.

44. See Hugh of St. Victor, *De sacramentis* 2.11.3–5, *PL* 176:482–88, trans. Roy Deferrari, *On the Sacraments of the Christian Faith* (Cambridge, Mass.: Medieval Academy, 1951), pp. 324–33; Peter Lombard, *Sententiae in IV libris distinctae* 4.26.6.3, ed. Fathers of the College of St. Bonaventure (Grottaferrata, Rome: College of St. Bonaventure at Claras Aquas, 1971), 2:421. See Penny Gold, "The Marriage of Mary and Joseph in the Twelfth-Century Ideology of Marriage," in *Sexual Practices and the Medieval Church*, ed. Vern Bullough and James Brundage (New York: Pantheon, 1982), pp. 102–17, 249–51. This consensual view was ratified by Alexander III. See Charles Donahue, "The Policy of Alexander III's Consent Theory of Marriage," in *Proceedings of the Fourth International Congress of Canon Law*, ed. Stephan Kuttner, Monumenta Iuris Canonici, Ser. C, Subsidia 5 (Vatican City: Biblioteca Apostolica Vaticana, 1976), pp. 251–81.

45. The more pragmatic canonists had a harder time coming to terms with a theory of marriage devoid of consummation. See Brundage's discussion of Gratian in *Law, Sex, and Christian Society in Medieval Europe*, pp. 235–42.

46. See John Noonan, "Power to Choose," *Viator* 4 (1973): 419–34; also see Noonan, "Marital Affection in the Canonists," *Studia Gratiana* 12 (1967): 481–509.

47. It is not always clear that the bishop would be involved, however. Various authorities inveighed against abbesses who usurped the right to impose the veil. Burchard of Worms cites a decree of Pope Eutychus (d. 283; c. 13) to that effect (*Decretum* 8.17, *PL* 140:795).

48. Denis Bethel, "The Lives of St. Osyth of Essex and St. Osyth of Aylesbury," *Analecta Bollandiana* 88 (1970): 87, 99.

49. On Ermengard, see J. de Petigny, ed., "Une lettre inédite de Robert d'Arbrissel à la Comtesse Ermengarde," *Bibliothèque de l'Ecole de Chartes* ser. 3, 5 (1854): 213–16, trans. Venarde, *Robert of Arbrissel*, pp. 73–79; Therese Latzke, "Robert von Arbrissel, Ermengard und Eva," *Mittellateinisches Jahrbuch* 19 (1984): 122–25; Dalarun, *L'Impossible sainteté*, pp. 93–101.

50. Geoffrey of Vendôme, Ep. 258 (bk. 5, 23), *To Robert, PL* 157:205.

51. See R. W. Southern's account of Anselm's attempted interventions in *Saint Anselm: A Portrait in a Landscape* (Cambridge: Cambridge University Press, 1990), pp. 260–64. Also see Stephanie Hollis, "Wilton as a Centre of Learning," in *Writing the Wilton Women: Goscelin's Legend of Edith and Liber confortatorius*, ed. Stephanie Hollis (Turnhout: Brepols, 2004), pp. 321–22; and Walter Frölich's introduction, *Letters of Saint Anselm of Canterbury* (Kalamazoo, Mich.: Cistercian Publications, 1990): 1:43–44. For possible political motivations behind these proposed matches, see Frank Barlow, *William Rufus* (Berkeley: University of California, 1983), pp. 312ff. Also see Eleanor Searle, "Women and the Legitimization of Succession at the Norman Conquest," *Proceedings of the Battle Conference on Anglo-Norman Studies*, III, 1980, ed. R. Allen Brown (Woodbridge: Boydell, 1981), pp. 159–70, esp. 166–69. Clearly, apostasy from monasticism would remain an ongoing problem. See F. Donald Logan, *Runaway Religious in Medieval England, c. 1240–1540* (Cambridge: Cambridge University Press, 1996). On the motives peculiar to female religious, such as abduction, see pp. 83–89; Mathilda and Gunhilda are briefly discussed on pp. 6–7.

52. Anselm, Ep. 168, *To the nun Gunhilda, daughter of King Harold*, in *Epistolae*, in

S. Anselmi Cantuariensis archiepiscopi opera omnia, ed. Francis Schmitt (Edinborough: T. Nelson, 1951), 4:44–45, trans. Frölich, 2:66. On Gunhilda, also see D. A. Wilmart, ed., "Une lettre inédite de S. Anselme à une moniale inconstante," *Revue Bénédictine* 40 (1928): 319–32. According to William of Malmesbury, Wulfstan II, bishop of Worcester (d. 1087), cured Gunhilda of a tumor in her eye. Reginald Darlington, *The Vita Wulfstani of William of Malmesbury* 2.11 (London: Royal Historical Society, 1928), p. 34. William's account is based on a lost life by Coleman, a chaplain of Wulfstan.

53. Anselm, Ep. 168, *To the nun Gunhilda,* in *Epistolae,* 4:46, trans. Frölich, 2:67.

54. Anselm, Ep. 169, *To the nun Gunhilda,* in *Epistolae,* 4:47–48, trans. Frölich, 2:70. Anselm also rebukes Gunhilda for an extenuating circumstance that he had heard: that Gunhilda only assumed the habit in the first place because she was promised the position of abbess, a promise that never materialized. But Anselm, in turn, characterized Christ's response as follows: " 'Render to me, handmaid of mine … what you have promised me and have already begun….' If they lied to you, how have I sinned that you should lie to me? Rather I am prepared to lead you as my chosen and beloved spouse into the bridal chamber of my glory and set you over all my possessions," ibid., 4:49, trans. Frölich, 2:72.

55. Scholars speculate that Gunhilda did, in fact, return, as she seems to have been regarded with honor at Wilton. See Frölich's introduction, *Letters of Saint Anselm,* 1:43; Darlington, ed., *Vita Wulfstani of William of Malmesbury,* p. 34n3. Searle, in contrast, thinks Gunhilda's fate remains a mystery: she left no legitimate heir, because the ancestral land went to another family ("Women and the Succession," p. 168).

56. Both Ivo of Chartres and Anselm make the point that early monks and nuns required no public profession or blessing and that these were later innovations. See Constable, "Ceremonies and Symbolism Entering Religious Life," 2:803; Timothy Fry's discussion in *Regula Sancti Benedicti,* app. 5, pp. 449, 456.

57. *The Monastic Constitutions of Lanfranc,* ed. David Knowles, rev. Christopher Brooke (New York: Oxford University Press, 2002), pp. 162–65; Hollis, "Wilton as a Centre of Learning," p. 320.

58. See, for example, the Council of Paris (615) in *Sacrorum conciliorum nova, et amplissima collectio,* ed. G. D. Mansi (Paris, 1901; reprt., Graz: Akademische Druck, 1961), c. 13, 10:542; C. 27 q. 1 c. 7. Gratian attributes this ruling to the Fourth Council of Toledo, however. Cf. Hincmar of Reims, who cites a similar canon, in this case attributed to the Tenth Council of Toledo, which argues that once monastic dress is assumed there is no escape, "although they may wish to hide behind various and diverse arguments of falsity" (*De coercendo et exstirpando raptu viduarum, puellarum ac sanctimonialium, PL* 125:1035; see Toledo X [657], c. 5, in *Sacrorum conciliorum … collectio,* ed. Mansi, 11:36). This canon is among the list of authorities that Hincmar appended to his treatise. In fact, c. 5 of the Tenth Council of Toledo is not this exacting. It maintains that all women entering religion should cover their heads and confirm their profession in writing. They will not be permitted to leave after this document has been drawn up (C. 27 q. 1 c. 36).

59. Anselm, Ep. 177, *To Osmond, bishop of Salisbury,* in *Epistolae,* 4:60, trans. 2:91. See Frölich's discussion of why these letters were left out of the usual collections of Anselm's letters (introd., *Letters of St. Anselm of Canterbury,* 1:43–44).

60. Eadmer, *Historia novorum* bk. 3, *PL* 159:426, trans. Geoffrey Bosanquet, *History of Recent Events in England* (London: Cresset Press, 1964), pp. 127–28.

61. Ibid. bk. 3, *PL* 159:426–27, trans. pp. 128–29.

62. Ibid. bk. 3, *PL* 159:427, trans. p. 131. Lanfranc expresses this policy in Ep. 53, *To the Bishop of Rochester*, in *Letters of Lanfranc*, ed. and trans. Helen Clover and Margaret Gibson (Oxford: Clarendon Press, 1979), pp. 166, 167.

63. Mathilda refers to Anselm's blessing at their marriage in Ep. 242 (in *Epistolae,*, 4:150, trans. 2:221), as does Anselm in his reply (Ep. 243, in *Epistolae*, 4:153, trans. 2:226).

64. Augustine, *De bono viduitatis* 10.13–11.14, *PL* 40:438–39, trans. *LNPNFC*, 3:446.

65. Gratian cites a series of gloomy texts to this effect: the Council of Carthage (398) excommunicates widows who marry after consecration and says they are guilty of adultery (C. 27 q. 1 c. 1); according to Innocent I, they cannot be admitted to penance (c. 10); Gratian himself thinks that someone guilty of this offense can only be admitted to penance after the death of the other spouse (C. 27 q. 1 dpc 43). There is, however, no consensus, as Gratian is well aware (c. 40 dpc). For instance, Innocent II as recently as 1139 had required the couple to separate (c. 40), yet Gratian also includes the Augustinian view that these marriages should not be dissolved (c. 41).

66. Elliott, *Spiritual Marriage*, pp. 161, 162.

67. Ep. 242, *To Mathilda*, in *Epistolae*, 4:150, trans. 2:221.

68. Ep. 243, *To Mathilda*, in ibid., 4:153, trans. 2:226.

69. On Mathilda's political utility, see especially the following letters from Anselm to Mathilda: Ep. 246, in *Epistolae*, 4:156, trans. 2:229; Ep. 288, in *Epistolae*, 4:207–8, trans. 2:301; Ep. 296, 4:216, trans. 2:313–14; Ep. 321, in *Epistolae*, 4:250–51, trans. 3:30; Ep. 329, in *Epistolae*, 4:261–62, trans. 3:46; and from Mathilda to Anselm: Ep. 317, in *Epistolae*, 5:244–46, trans. 3:23; Ep. 320, in *Epistolae*, 5:248–49, trans. 3:29; Ep. 395, in *Epistolae*, 5:395, trans. 3:155. Mathilda also intervenes with Pope Paschal II. See Ep. 323, in *Epistolae*, 5:253–54, trans. 3:35. See his letters to Mathilda: Ep. 352, in *Epistolae*, 5:292, trans. 3:87; Ep. 397, in *Epistolae*, 5:340–42, trans. 3:157. See Eadmer's account of Anselm's travails with Henry I over lay investiture in *Historia novorum* bk. 3. pp. 138–39 [131–32 Latin], 144–49 [137–41], 153–57 [144–49], 160–68 [152–58]; bk. 4, 173–82 [162–70], 194–96 [181–84], 199 [186], 200 [186–87]; Eadmer, *The Life of St. Anselm: Archbishop of Canterbury* 2.50–52, 54, ed. R. W. Southern (Oxford: Clarendon, 1962), pp. 127–30, 134. Also see Southern, *Saint Anselm*, pp. 289–307. Anselm's role as Mathilda's spiritual director is discussed below.

70. *CM* cc. 15–18, pp. 58–65.

71. Ibid. c. 21, pp. 70–71.

72. Ibid. c. 29, pp. 82–83.

73. *Vita S. Alexii confessoris, AA SS*, July, 4:252. The gifts are a later introduction. In earlier versions, however, Alexis flees his wife immediately (Elliott, *Spiritual Marriage*, p. 105n46).

74. *CM* c. 42, pp. 108–9. The three priests were Burthred's witnesses; the five hermits were Roger's. Burthred had initially arrived with two witnesses that were deemed by Roger to have "little public standing," so he had to obtain others.

75. Ibid. c. 4, pp. 40–41.

76. Ibid. c. 13, pp. 54–55.

77. Ibid. c. 17, pp. 60–63. In fact, this is not strictly speaking correct. Christina made a private vow in a public place. There were plenty of witnesses to attest to her presence, but none to the vow. The closest thing she had to a witness was Canon Sueno, whom she subsequently informed of her vow.

78. Ibid. c. 19, pp. 64–65.

79. Ibid. c. 35, pp. 94–97.

80. Abelard, Ep. 7, ed. J. T. Muckle, "The Letter of Heloise on Religious Life and Abelard's First Reply," *Mediaeval Studies* 17 (1985): 281, trans. C. K. Moncrieff, *The Letters of Abelard and Heloise* (New York: Alfred A. Knopf, 1942), p. 175. Ep. 7 is the only letter not translated in its entirety by M. T. Clanchy in his revised edition of Betty Radice's translation of *The Letters of Abelard and Heloise* (Middlesex: Penguin Books, 2003), which I will be using for the other letters. I have adopted the traditional numbering of the letters, beginning with *Historia calamitatum* as Ep. 1. For detailed analyses, see Mary McLaughlin, "Peter Abelard and the Dignity of Women: Twelfth Century 'Feminism' in Theory and Practice," in *Pierre Abélard: Pierre le Vénérable; Les courants philosophiques, littéraires et artistiques en Occident au milieu du XIIe siècle, Abbaye de Cluny 2 au 9 juillet 1972* (Paris: Editions du Centre national de la recherche scientifique, 1975), pp. 287–333; and Alcuin Blamires, "*Caput a femina, membra a viris* : Gender Polemic in Abelard's Letter 'On the Authority and Dignity of the Nun's Profession,'" in *The Tongue of the Fathers: Gender and Ideology in Twelfth-Century Latin*, ed. David Townsend and Andrew Taylor (Philadelphia: University of Pennsylvania Press, 1998), pp. 55–79.

81. X.3.32.2; X.3.32.7; see Elliott, *Spiritual Marriage*, pp. 142–44.

82. Atkinson, "'Precious Balsam,'" pp. 138–39.

83. Literary scholars such as Wogan-Browne go much further, arguing that virginity was always a rhetorical and turbulent category whose meaning was never stabilized (*Saints' Lives and Women's Literary Culture*, pp. 40–56).

84. See David Brakke, "The Problematization of Nocturnal Emissions in Early Christian Syria, Egypt, and Gaul," *Journal of Early Christian Studies* 3 (1995): 419–60; Conrad Leyser, "Masculinity in Flux: Nocturnal Emission and the Limits of Celibacy in the Early Middle Ages," in *Masculinity in Medieval Europe*, ed. D. Hadley (London: Longmans, 1998), pp. 103–19; Elliott, *Fallen Bodies*, pp. 14–34. Female ascetics of the East were, however, occasionally tormented by the spirit of fornication. See Brakke, *Demons and the Making of the Monk*, pp. 184–85.

85. Ælred of Rievaulx, *De institutione inclusarum* 2.14, pp. 80, 82. Ælred is also aware of the possibility of same-sex intimacies (ibid., 2.15, pp. 84–85).

86. *CM* c. 51, pp. 126–29. Apparently the crown had three long, white fillets down the back, which Christina likened to a bishop's miter. This could be her unconscious way of resolving the problem should the bishop choose to reject her as a candidate for consecration.

87. Augustine, *De civitate Dei* 1.19.1, *PL* 41:32, trans. *LNPNFC*, ser. 1, 2:13. See the discussion in Chapter 2, pp. 58–59, above.

88. Elliott, *Spiritual Marriage*, pp. 48–49, 59–60, 66, 192.

89. On her life in the context of the anchoritic lifestyle, which was pioneering for

the continent, see Anneke Mulder-Bakker, *Lives of the Anchoresses*, trans. Myra Heerspink Scholz (Philadelphia: University of Pennsylvania Press, 2005), pp. 24–50.

90. Guibert is rather contradictory on this point, as the first time he mentions the enchantment he says it lasted only three years (Guibert of Nogent, *Autobiographie* 1.12, ed. Edmond-René Labande [Paris: Belles Lettres, 1981], p. 76, trans. John Benton, *Self and Society in Medieval France* [Toronto: University of Toronto Press, 1984], p. 64). But the number seven is subsequently given several times (ibid. 1.12, pp. 78, 82, 84, trans. pp. 65, 66, 67). Benton thinks the number seven is a reference to Jacob's service for Rachel (*Self and Society*, p. 65n4); Labande thinks it is an error and resolves the difference in favor of seven years (*Autobiographie*, pp. 78–79, n3).

91. Guibert, *Autobiographie* 1.12, p. 76, trans. p. 64.

92. This is generally understood as the impossibility of penetration, either due to the size of the man's genitalia or the narrowness of the vagina. See X.4.15.3, and Raymond of Peñafort, *Summa de poenitentia et matrimonio* bk. 4, tit. 16 c. 2 (Rome: Joannes Tallini, 1603), pp. 559–60.

93. Guibert, *Autobiographie* 1.18, p. 150, trans. p. 94.

94. Ibid. 1.12, p. 84. I have supplied my own literal translation.

95. Ibid. 1.18, 13, pp. 146, 90, trans. pp. 92, 70.

96. A number of authorities thought that the smothering variety of incubi were actually due to either mental or physical illness. See Thorndike, *History of Magic and Experimental Science*, 1:574, 2:299.

97. See, for example, Ælred's evocation of the incubus as a metaphor for sin: "Sed pilosus qui incubo dicitur, animal petulcum et hispidum, et semper ad coitum aestuans, libidinum significat incentive" (*Sermones de oneribus* no. 14, *PL* 195:415).

98. Guibert, *Autobiographie* 3.19, p. 456, trans. p. 223.

99. Ibid. 1.13, p. 90, trans. p. 70. Nancy Partner likewise sees this as an allusion to the sex act. "The Textual Unconscious: What Does Psychoanalysis Do for Historians?" a lecture in Northwestern University's Medieval Studies Colloquium, Evanston, Ill., October 16, 2008. In contrast, Mulder-Bakker sees this incident simply as a measure of anxiety with no particular sexual overtones (*Lives of the Anchoresses*, pp. 25–26).

100. Guibert, *Autobiographie* 1.14, p. 98, trans. p. 73.

101. Ibid. 1.14, p. 102, trans. p. 75. Since this was a male community, the status of the old woman is unclear. But probably the term *sanctimonialis* implies that she was not just a nun, but one who had been veiled bride of Christ.

102. Ibid. 2.4, p. 244, trans. p. 133.

103. Mulder-Bakker, *Lives of the Anchoresses*, pp. 29–31.

104. *PRG*, no. 24, cc. 3, 9, 10, pp. 54, 56.

105. Cf. Warren, *Spiritual Economies*, pp. 26–27.

106. Freud also maintains that "unpleasurable dreams are wish-fulfillments no less than the rest" (*The Interpretation of Dreams*, *SE*, 5:557). If the visitation of the incubus was construed as a bad dream, and the incubus is understood as a surrogate for the husband, perhaps the wish resided not so much in the desirability of sex with a demon as it was in the demon/husband being routed by a good spirit.

107. Guibert, *Autobiographie* 1.14, p. 98, trans. p. 73.

108. Ibid. 2.4, pp. 244–46. The article in question is a *peplum*. Benton translates this as a "costly robe" (p. 133), its original meaning, but by the time Guibert was writing it had also come to mean "wimple or veil." Later on in the same chapter it becomes clear that the object is indeed a veil. See R. E. Latham's *Revised Medieval Latin Word-List from British and Irish Sources* (London: Oxford University Press for the British Academy, 1965), p. 340.

109. *PRG*, no. 20, c. 9, p. 40.

110. *PRG*, no. 20, c. 16, p. 44. Cf. *PRG*, no. 24, c. 10, p. 56; no. 25, c.10, p. 61, each of which use the term *velamen* without an adjective.

111. Guibert, *Autobiographie* 2.4, p. 246, trans. p. 134.

112. For background, see M. T. Clanchy, *Abelard: A Medieval Life* (Oxford: Basil Blackwell, 1997); Constant Mews, *Abelard and Heloise* (Oxford: Oxford University Press, 2005); Mews, "Heloise," in *MHW*, pp. 267–89.

113. Heloise, Ep. 2, *Héloïse-Abélard: Correspondance, Lettres I–VI*, ed. François d'Amboise (Paris: Editions Hermann, 2007), p. 97, trans. p. 47. For many years the authenticity of the so-called personal letters between Abelard and Heloise were in doubt. The two works that did most to establish their authenticity were Peter Dronke, *Women Writers of the Middle Ages : A Critical Study of Texts from Perpetua (d. 203) to Marguerite Porete (d. 1310)* (Cambridge: Cambridge University Press, 1984), pp. 107–43; and Barbara Newman, "Authority, Authenticity, and the Repression of Heloise," *Journal of Medieval and Renaissance Studies* 22 (1992): 121–57, reprt. in *From Virile Woman to WomanChrist*, pp. 19–45. Recently Constant Mews has argued that the collection of love letters known as *Epistolae duorum amantium*, transcribed by a fifteenth-century Cistercian, represents the early romantic correspondence between Abelard and Heloise. I am still skeptical and have not included these letters in this study. See Mews's lengthy discussion preceding the edition and translation of the letters in, *The Lost Love Letters of Abelard and Heloise: Perceptions of Dialogue in Twelfth-Century France*, ed. Ewald Konsgen, trans. Constant Mews and Neville Chiavaroli (New York: St. Martin's Press, 1999). The letters have initiated some lively debate. See C. Stephen Jaeger's "*Epistolae duorum amantium* and the Ascription to Abelard and Heloise," in *Voices in Dialogue: Reading Women in the Middle Ages*, ed. Linda Olson and Kathryn Kerby-Fulton (Notre Dame, Ind.: University of Notre Dame Press, 2005), pp. 125–66; Giles Constable, "The Authorship of *Epistolae duorum amantium*: A Reconsideration," ibid., pp. 167–78; Jaeger, "A Reply to Giles Constable," pp. 179–86.

114. Heloise, Ep. 2, *Héloïse-Abélard*, p. 106, trans. Radice, p. 53. Cf. Abelard's related point that all we do against conscience is a sin (Ep. 8, ed. T. P. McLaughlin, "Abelard's Rule for Religious Women," *Mediaeval Studies* 18 [1956]: 268, trans. Betty Radice, *The Letters of Abelard and Heloise*, rev. M. T. Clanchy [Middlesex: Penguin Books, 2003], p. 171). By the same token, you can eat anything that does not go against conscience (Ep. 8, ed. McLaughlin, "Abelard's Rule," pp. 268–69, trans. Radice, p. 172).

115. Christopher Brooke makes the argument that Heloise's negative views on marriage are not so surprising for someone who grew up in the cathedral close—rife with clerical intellectuals as well as their concubines (*The Medieval Idea of Marriage* [Oxford: Oxford

University Press, 1989], pp. 91–92, 104, 105–7, 111, 259–64). On Abelard's misogamy, see McLaughlin, "Peter Abelard and the Dignity of Women," pp. 310–11.

116. Abelard, Ep. 1, in *Correspondance*, ed. d'Amboise, pp. 47–51, trans. pp. 13–16; Heloise, Ep. 2, *Correspondance*, ed. d'Amboise, pp. 103–4, trans. pp. 51–52.

117. Heloise, Ep. 2, in *Correspondance*, ed. d'Amboise, p. 104, trans. p. 51.

118. Abelard, Ep. 1, *Correspondance*, ed. d'Amboise, pp. 46, 47, 51–52, trans. pp. 13 (bis), 16.

119. Ibid., p. 52, trans. p. 17.

120. Ibid., p. 55, trans. p. 18. See W. G. East's discussion of the religious trope of the monastic life as death and its special salience in Abelard and Heloise's cases in "Abelard, Heloise and the Religious Life," in *Medieval Theology and the Natural Body*, ed. Biller and Minnis, pp. 43–60. Note particularly the analysis of Abelard's subtle allusions, which compare Heloise to Jeptha's virginal daughter whom the father sacrificed in fulfillment of a vow (pp. 54–59).

121. Heloise, Ep. 2, in *Correspondance*, ed. d'Amboise, p. 103, trans. p. 51. See Barbara Newman's analysis of Heloise's excessive devotion to Abelard, likening her to a mystic manqué (*From Virile Woman to WomanChrist*, pp. 70–74).

122. Heloise, Ep. 2, in *Correspondance*, ed. d'Amboise, p. 108, trans. p. 54; cf. Heloise, Ep. 4, in *Correspondance*, ed. d'Amboise, p. 130, trans. p. 69, where she claims that her sole concern was to avoid offending Abelard rather than God.

123. Heloise, Ep. 4, in *Correspondance*, ed. d'Amboise, p. 130, trans. p. 69. I have altered the translation for Heloise's allusion to Psalm 7.10 in order to correspond to the translation from *Ethics* employed above.

124. Heloise, Ep. 6, *Correspondance*, ed. d'Amboise, p. 186, trans. p. 108.

125. Cf. Clanchy, *Abelard*, pp. 278–79.

126. Abelard, Ep. 1, *Correspondance*, ed. d'Amboise, pp. 52–53, trans. p. 17.

127. Lateran II, c. 6, in *Decrees of the Ecumenical Councils*, ed. Tanner, 1:198.

128. Abelard, Ep. 1, in *Correspondance*, ed. d'Amboise, pp. 52–53, trans. *Letters*, p. 17; Cf. Clanchy, who argues that by dressing Heloise in this way he was "signaling that he was divorcing her" (*Abelard*, p. 254n40).

129. Abelard, Ep. 5, *Correspondance*, ed. d'Amboise, p. 148, trans. pp. 80–81 (italics mine).

130. Abelard, *Sic et non: A Critical Edition,* ed. Blanche B. Boyer and Richard McKeon (Chicago: University of Chicago Press, 1976), pp. 446–48; Abelard, Ep. 5, *Correspondance*, ed. d'Amboise, p. 152, trans. p. 83.

131. Abelard, *Sic et non*, pp. 449–52. Heloise articulates her complaint in Ep. 4, *Correspondance*, ed. d'Amboise, pp. 123–25, trans. pp. 65–66. See Abelard's response in Ep. 5, *Correspondance*, ed. d'Amboise, p. 145, trans. p. 79.

132. Heloise, Ep. 4, *Correspondance*, ed. d'Amboise, p. 124, trans. pp. 65–66; Abelard, Ep. 5, *Correspondance*, ed. d'Amboise, pp. 142–43, trans. p. 79.

133. Abelard, *Sic et non*, pp. 453–54.

134. Ibid., pp. 454–56.

135. Ibid., pp. 456–57.

136. Ibid., p. 457.

137. Ibid., pp. 458–62.

138. *Publii Syri Sententiae* Prov. 19, 20, 21, 22, cited in Abelard, *Sic et non*, p. 494.

139. *Publii Syri Sententiae* Prov. 36, cited in Abelard, *Sic et non*, p. 494.

140. Augustine, *De fide et operibus* 7.10; Augustine *De civitate dei* 1.19.1–3, cited in Abelard, *Sic et non*, pp. 494, 494–95.

141. Augustine, *De bono coniugali* 21.25, cited in Abelard, *Sic et non*, p. 495.

142. On Abelard's writings for Heloise and the nuns of the Paraclete, see John Marenbon, *The Philosophy of Peter Abelard* (Cambridge: Cambridge University Press, 1997), pp. 72–81; Mews, *Abelard and Heloise*, pp. 156–173.

143. Abelard, *Peter Abelard's Ethics*, ed. and trans. D. E. Luscombe (Oxford: Clarendon, 1971), pp. 4–5. Unfortunately, of the two proposed books, only the first book and the opening to the second were completed. Book 1 addresses vice, sin, and penitence; Book 2 was to address merit (Marenbon, *Philosophy*, pp. 67–69). Some aspects of Abelard's theory of sin and culpability appear in his *Commentaria in epistolam Pauli ad Romanos*, which appeared ca. 1137. See, for example, bk. 1, ad 4.8; bk. 4, ad 14.23, in *Opera theologica*, *CCCM*, 11, ed. E. M. Buytaert (Turnhout: Brepols, 1969), 1:126, 306–7. Although the *Commentaria* appeared slightly before his *Ethics*, Abelard nevertheless maintains that some of the same questions would be addressed in *Ethics*, already planning to explore certain matters in greater depth (ibid. bk. 4, ad 13.10, 1:292–93). On his concept of sin, see William Mann, "*Ethics*," in *The Cambridge Companion to Abelard*, ed. Jeffrey Brower and Kevin Guilfoy (Cambridge: Cambridge University Press, 2004), pp. 279–304. For the relation between outer action, intention, and consent in the larger context of patristic and other twelfth-century writers, see Marenbon, *Philosophy*, pp. 51–55; on Abelard's contribution to this discourse, see ibid., pp. 255–56; Robert Blomme, *La Doctrine du péché dans les écoles théologiques de la première moitié du XIIe siècle* (Louvain: Publications Universitaires de Louvain; Gembloux: J. Duculot, 1958), pp. 133–217.

144. Abelard, *Ethics*, pp. 38–41, 42–43. I have altered the translation of the biblical quotation to correspond with the wording used in Radice's translation of Heloise's letters.

145. Ibid., pp. 18, 19.

146. Ibid., pp. 20, 21.

147. Ibid., pp. 22, 23.

148. Ibid., pp. 16, 17.

149. Charles Burnett and David Luscombe, ed., "A New Student for Peter Abelard: The Marginalia in British Library MS Cotton Faustina A.X," in *Itinéraires de la raison: Etudes de philosophie médiévale offertes à Maria Cândida Pacheco*, ed. J. F. Meirinhos, Textes et Etudes du Moyen Age, 32 (Louvain-la-Neuve: Fédération Internationale des Instituts d'Etudes Médiévales, 2005), pp. 169–70; for dating, see p. 165. Cf. Abelard, *Ethics*, pp. 16, 17. The excursus on chastity recorded in the marginalia develops out of the question of whether Adam or Eve were guiltier of sin—a question Abelard determines is impossible to answer. Marenbon cites this document as evidence that Abelard tried out his arguments orally before incorporating them into *Ethics* (*Philosophy*, pp. 68–69). I am indebted to Robert Lerner for drawing this question to my attention.

150. Abelard, Ep. 5, *Correspondance*, ed. d'Amboise, pp. 145–46, trans. p. 79.

151. Newman, *From Virile Woman to WomanChrist*, p. 70.

152. Heloise, Ep. 2, *Correspondance*, ed. d'Amboise, p. 104, trans. p. 51.

153. Abelard, Ep. 3, *Correspondance*, ed. d'Amboise, pp. 113–16, 117, trans. pp. 58–60, 61.

154. Abelard, Ep. 3, *Correspondance*, ed. d'Amboise, p. 114, trans. p. 61.

155. Abelard, Ep. 3, *Correspondance*, ed. d'Amboise, pp. 118–19, trans. pp. 61–62; cf. Abelard, Ep. 5, *Correspondance*, ed. d'Amboise, p. 156, trans. pp. 85–86, where he asserts that this should be Heloise's lot as well: wailing for the death of the bridegroom, since she was, after all, his bride.

156. Abelard, Ep. 5, *Correspondance*, ed. d'Amboise, p. 135, trans. p. 73 (italics mine).

157. Ep. 22, *To Eustochium* c. 1, *PL*, 22:395; trans. *LNPNFC*, 2d ser., 6:23; Abelard, Ep. 5, *Correspondance*, ed. d'Amboise, p. 136, trans. p. 73.

158. Abelard, Ep. 5, *Correspondance*, ed. d'Amboise, pp. 136, 137, 138, trans. pp. 73, 74 (bis). For a discussion of Abelard's use of the bride's blackness in terms of bodily abjection, see Peggy McCracken, "The Curse of Eve: Female Bodies and Christian Bodies in Heloise's Third Letter," in *Listening to Heloise: The Voice of a Twelfth-Century Woman*, ed. Bonnie Wheeler (New York: St. Martin's Press, 2000), pp. 218–19.

159. Abelard, Ep. 5, *Correspondance*, ed. d'Amboise, p. 139, trans. p. 75.

160. Ibid., p. 150, trans. p. 82. Note that in the ascetical tradition there is an association between the Ethiopian body with heightened sexuality. See Brakke, *Demons and the Making of the Monk*, pp. 166–67.

161. "Nihil vmquam (Deus scit) in te nisi te requisiui; te pure, non tua concupiscens" (Heloise, Ep. 2, *Correspondance*, ed. d'Amboise, p. 103, trans. p. 50).

162. "Quid in te quaerit nisi teipsam? Verus est amicus, qui te ipsam, non tua desiderat" (Abelard, Ep. 5, *Correspondance*, ed. d'Amboise, pp. 156–57, trans. p. 86).

163. Ibid., p. 157, trans. p. 86.

164. See Linda Georgianna, " 'In Any Corner of Heaven': Heloise's Critique of Monastic Life," in *Listening to Heloise: The Voice of a Twelfth-Century Woman*, ed. Bonnie Wheeler (New York: St. Martin's Press, 2000), pp. 187–216, esp. 195ff.; and Dronke, *Women Writers*, pp. 130–34.

165. Heloise, Ep. 6, *Correspondance*, ed. d'Amboise, p. 173, trans. pp. 99–100.

166. Cf. Peggy McCracken's statement: "She reclaims the material body that Abelard had effaced through metaphor" ("Curse of Eve," p. 225). See Karma Lochrie's discussion of fissured flesh and ascetical efforts to shore it up in the sealed body in *Margery Kempe and Translations of the Flesh* (Philadelphia: University of Pennsylvania, 1991), pp. 23–27.

167. Cf. Blamires, "*Caput a femina*," p. 55.

168. Abelard, Ep. 7, ed. Muckle, "Letter of Heloise on Religious Life and Abelard's First Reply," p. 253, trans. p. 131.

169. Ibid., p. 260, trans. p. 143.

170. Ibid., p. 261, trans. p. 143.

171. Ibid., p. 263, trans. p. 148.

172. Ibid., p. 253, trans. p. 131; cf. ibid., p. 258, trans. p. 140.

173. Ibid., p. 270, trans. p. 160; ibid., p. 280, trans. p. 175.

174. Ibid., p. 271, trans. p.160.

175. Ibid., p. 271, trans. p. 160; also see ibid., pp. 254–58, trans. pp. 132–40.

176. Ibid., p. 275, trans. p. 166.

177. John 4.25; Abelard, Ep. 7, ed. Muckle, "Letter of Heloise on Religious Life and Abelard's First Reply," pp. 272–73, trans. pp. 162–63.

178. Luke 2.36ff.; Abelard, Ep. 7, ed. Muckle, "Letter of Heloise on Religious Life and Abelard's First Reply," p. 263, trans. p. 147.

179. Abelard, Ep. 7, ed. Muckle, "Letter of Heloise on Religious Life and Abelard's First Reply," p. 271, trans. p.160.

180. *PR*, no. 14, c. 6, p. 168.

181. On this work, see Clanchy, *Abelard*, pp. 279–81.

182. For example, this is what the ninth-century chronicler Agnellus tells us occurred upon the consecration of Sergius, bishop of Ravenna (Elliott, *Fallen Bodies*, p. 87). Also see Macy, *Hidden History*, pp. 74–77; McNamara, *Sisters in Arms*, pp. 58–59.

183. *PRG*, no. 24, c. 8, p. 56. Also see n196, below.

184. The Carthusian nun is only permitted to wear these tokens again at her monastic jubilee and at her death. She is, however, authorized to sing the epistle (without a maniple) and to read the gospel at matins when there is no priest, in which case she dons a stole. See Herbert Thurston, "Deaconesses," *Catholic Encyclopaedia*, http://www.newadvent.org/cathen/04651a.htm; D. R. Webster, "The Carthusian Order," *Catholic Encyclopaedia*, http://www.newadvent.org/cathen/03388a.htm. For another instance of the deaconess being associated with the virgin state, see Chapter 3, n31, above.

185. *PR*, no. 14, c. 6, p. 168.

186. Durandus, *Rationale divinorum officiorum* 2.1.48, p. 143; Durandus, *Le Pontifical de Guillaume Durand* no. 22, ed. Michel Andrieu, in *Le Pontifical romain au Moyen-Age*, *Studi e Testi*, 88 (Vatican: Biblioteca Apostolica Vaticana, 1940), 3:411.

187. Macy, *Hidden History*, pp. 93–95. Cf. McLaughlin, "Peter Abelard and the Dignity of Women," pp. 298–301. In a similar vein, Kitchen tentatively links the miracles attributed to Radegund by Fortunatus to her quasi-clerical status as deaconess (*Saints' Lives and the Rhetoric of Gender*, p. 122).

188. On Abelard as a protofeminist, see McLaughlin, "Peter Abelard and the Dignity of Women," esp. pp. 296ff.; Alcuin Blamires, *The Case for Women in Medieval Culture* (Oxford: Clarendon Press, 1997), pp. 200–207; Newman, *From Virile Woman to WomanChrist*, pp. 19–20; Fiona Griffiths, "'Men's Duty to Provide for Women's Needs': Abelard, Heloise, and Their Negotiation of the *Cura monialium*," *Journal of Medieval History* 30 (2004): 1–24. For Abelard's positive influence on the female vocation beyond the community of the Paraclete, see Fiona Griffiths, "Brides and *Dominae*: Abelard's *Cura monialium* at the Augustinian Monastery of Marbuch," *Viator* 34(2003): 57–88; Macy, *Hidden History*, pp. 95–96. Scholars are nevertheless prepared to acknowledge his ambivalence about women. See McLaughlin, "Peter Abelard and the Dignity of Women," pp. 293, 305–10.

189. Abelard, Ep. 8, ed. McLaughlin, "Abelard's Rule," pp. 244–46, trans. pp. 133–37.

190. Ibid., pp. 258–60, trans. pp. 155–58. The complaint about the presumption of

abbesses is an old one. See, for example, the Capitularies of Aachen of 789, c. 74, *Sacrorum conciliorum ... collectio*, ed. Mansi, 17b:238; Council of Paris VI (829), c. 43, in ibid., 14:564. This latter council claims the custom is widespread and to be found in every monastery. Moreover, female communites preferred this mode of veiling since it allowed them to turn a blind eye at various forms of corruption.

191. See, for example, Heloise, Ep. 2, *Correspondance*, ed. d'Amboise, p. 102, trans. p. 50. Also see Clanchy, *Abelard*, pp. 165–66.

192. Abelard, Ep. 1, *Correspondance*, ed. d'Amboise, p. 55, trans. p. 18.

193. Abelard, Ep. 7, ed. Muckle, "Letter of Heloise on Religious Life and Abelard's First Reply," p. 265, trans. p. 150.

194. Ep. 4, *Correspondance*, p. 120, trans. p. 63.

195. Heloise, Ep. 6, *Correspondance*, ed. d'Amboise, p. 172, trans. p. 99. This decree is included in Gratian (C. 27 q. 1 c. 23). Its ultimate source is the Council of Chalcedon, c. 15 (451), in *Decrees of the Ecumenical Councils*, ed. Tanner, 1:94; cf. 1 Nicaea, c. 19, in ibid., 1:15. The latter reference to deaconess has particular historical salience. For if Heloise was, in fact, a deaconess around 1132, which is about the time she wrote this letter, it would mean she was at least forty years of age, corroborating Michael Clanchy's contention that Heloise was born sometime around 1090, hence probably about eleven years older than has been traditionally assumed (see Clanchy's introduction to *The Letters of Abelard and Heloise*, ed. Radice, p. lxxiv).

196. *PR*, no. 14, cc. 14–15, p. 169. Prior to the twelfth century, the deaconess also said, "I am married to him" at the moment she imposed the veil on herself—paralleling the veiling of virgins (*PRG*, no. 24, c. 10, p. 56; cf. no. 20, c. 19, p. 44). Interestingly, these words are also omitted in the less elaborate veiling of a virgin who wishes to pursue her vocation in the world (see *PRG*, no. 23, p. 52). The older rite also describes the deaconess's proposition as "not inconsistent with one of perfect virginity" (ibid. c. 8, p. 56). The twelfth-century rite, however, substitutes "perfect widowhood" (*PR*, no. 14, c. 6, p. 168). Abelard shows his sensitivity to the power of liturgy in his description of the veiling of a virgin, discussed below.

197. *PR*, no. 14, c. 6, pp. 168–69; cf. *PRG*, no. 24, c. 8, p. 56.

198. Abelard, Ep. 7, ed. Muckle, "Letter of Heloise on Religious Life and Abelard's First Reply," p. 263, trans. p. 148.

199. Ibid., p. 263, trans. p. 149.

200. Ibid., p. 264, trans. p. 149.

201. See, for example, no. 22, *Ordinatio abbatissae* c. 5, *PRG*, p. 49. Also see Grégoire, "Il matrimonio mistico," pp. 724–25.

202. Abelard, Ep. 7, ed. Muckle, "Letter of Heloise on Religious Life and Abelard's First Reply," p. 267, trans. p. 153.

203. Ibid., pp. 266–67, trans. pp. 152–53.

204. Ibid., pp. 267–68, trans. pp. 154–55. See Chapter 3, n172, above.

205. Ibid., p. 275, trans. pp. 166–67.

206. Abelard, Ep. 8, ed. McLaughlin, "Abelard's Rule," p. 281, trans. p. 192. Hildegard was critiqued for distinguishing virgins on high holidays by allowing them to wear white veils topped with crowns bearing pictures of a lamb and four angels (Barbara Newman,

Sister of Wisdom: St. Hildegard's Theology of the Feminine [Berkeley: University of California, 1987], pp. 221–22).

207. Abelard, *Theologia Christiana* 2.93, in *Opera theologica*, ed. E. M. Buytaert, *CCCM*, 12 (Turnhout: Brepols, 1969), p. 173. *Theologia Christiana* was published ca. 1123. It was an expanded version of *Theologia*, his work on the trinity that had been condemned at the Council of Soissons (1121).

208. Abelard, Ep. 8, ed. McLaughlin, "Abelard's Rule," p. 252, trans. p. 145, and passim.

209. Ibid., p. 252, trans. pp. 145–46.

210. Clanchy, *Abelard*, pp. 238, 253, 256. On the parallels between Abelard and other twelfth-century founders/reformers, especially Robert, see McLaughlin, "Peter Abelard and the Dignity of Women," pp. 313–16.

211. Abelard, Ep. 7, ed. Muckle, "Letter of Heloise on Religious Life and Abelard's First Reply," p. 267, trans. p. 153.

212. Jerome, Ep. 22.2, cited by Abelard, ed. Muckle, "Letter of Heloise on Religious Life and Abelard's First Reply," p. 267, trans. p. 153.

213. Ep. 7, ed. Muckle, "Letter of Heloise on Religious Life and Abelard's First Reply," p. 267, trans. p. 154.

214. Jerome, Ep. 22.16, cited by Abelard, Ep. 7, ed. Muckle, "Letter of Heloise on Religious Life and Abelard's First Reply," p. 267, trans. p. 154.

215. Cf. his analogy likening the abbot's relationship to the abbess of the community that he presides over with a king's steward: "who does not oppress the queen by his powers but treats her wisely ... and performs all his services outside the bedchamber without ever penetrating into its privacy" (Abelard, ed. Muckle, "Abelard's Rule," p. 259, trans. p. 157).

216. Heloise, Ep. 2, *Correspondance*, ed. d'Amboise, p. 108, trans. p. 54.

217. Abelard, Ep. 8, ed. McLaughlin, "Abelard's Rule," p. 254 (bis), trans. pp. 148, 149.

218. Heloise, Ep. 2, *Correspondance*, ed. d'Amboise, p. 54, trans. p. 54.

219. Abelard, Ep. 8, ed. McLaughlin, "Abelard's Rule," p. 276, trans. p. 184.

220. Abelard, Ep. 8, ed. McLaughlin, "Abelard's Rule," p. 278, trans. p. 187 (italics mine). Note that, although Abelard's introduction of the subject of sex may seem unnecessary in a rule for celibates, the two topics are linked by 1 Timothy 4 in the discussion of heretics who will forbid marriage and meat. See also Ivo of Chartres' *Decretum*, perhaps the most authoritative collection of canon law when Abelard was writing, and the discussion of how God's servants abstain from flesh and wine, not because these items are impure, but for the sake of celibacy. Those not vowed to chastity, however, are free to marry more than once (7.142, *PL* 161:77).

221. Abelard, *Problemata Heloissae* q. 14, *PL* 178:701.

222. Abelard, *Sententie* c. 231, ed. David Luscombe, *CCCM*, 14 (Turnhout: Brepols, 2006), pp. 122–23. This work was written ca. 1134 either by Abelard himself or by students recording the master's views.

223. "Utrum aliquis in eo quod facit a Domino sibi concessum, vel etiam jussum, peccare posit quaerimus"? (Abelard, *Problemata Heloissae* q. 42, *PL* 178:723; see Mews, *Abelard and Heloise*, pp. 200–202). Cf. "Quo modo etiam in eo quod est concessum dici potest committi peccatum?" Abelard, *Ethics*, pp. 18, 19.

224. Abelard, *Problemata Heloissae* q. 42, *PL* 178:723.

225. Ibid., cols. 723–24.

226. Ibid., cols. 725–27.

227. Ibid., col. 730.

228. See Clanchy, *Abelard*, pp. 96–99.

CHAPTER 5

1. John Boswell, *Christianity, Social Tolerance, and Homosexuality: Gay People in Western Europe from the Beginning of the Christian Era to the Fourteenth Century* (Chicago: University of Chicago Press, 1980), pp. 207ff.; Ruth Karras, "Friendship and Love in the Lives of Two Twelfth-Century English Saints," *Journal of Medieval History* 14 (1988): 305–20; Brian McGuire, *Friendship and Community: The Monastic Experience* (Kalamazoo, Mich.: Cistercian Publications, 1988), pp. 194ff.; C. Stephen Jaeger, *Ennobling Love: In Search of a Lost Sensibility* (Philadelphia: University of Pennsylvania Press, 1999), pp. 110–14; and Fulton, *From Judgment to Passion*. Also note the increasingly variegated discussions of love in twelfth-century letters (Barbara Newman, *God and the Goddesses: Vision, Poetry, and Belief in the Middle Ages* [Philadelphia: University of Pennsylvania Press, 2003], pp. 138–51).

2. McNamer, *Affective Meditation*. Cf. Thomas Williams's analysis of the pivotal role Abelard gives to compassion for Christ's passion in our redemption ("Sin, Grace, and Redemption," in *The Cambridge Companion to Abelard*, ed. Jeffrey Brower and Kevin Guilfoy [Cambridge: Cambridge University Press, 2004], pp. 258–78).

3. For an overview of Jerome's female ascetical circle, see Rader, *Breaking Boundaries*, see pp. 99–109; on Jerome and Paula, see pp. 100–103.

4. See Elliott, *Fallen Bodies*, pp. 104, 110, 115, 119. See also Lester Little, "The Personal Development of Peter Damian," in *Order and Innovation in the Middle Ages: Essays in Honor of Joseph R. Strayer*, ed. William Jordan, Bruce McNab, and Teofilo Ruiz (Princeton, N.J.: Princeton University Press, 1976), pp. 330–32; Fulton, *From Judgment to Passion*, pp. 89–106, 224–25.

5. On Peter and his friendship with men, see McGuire, *Friendship and Community*, pp. 205–8. McGuire sees Damian as a transitional figure with respect to monastic friendship.

6. Peter Damian, Ep. 149, *To Agnes*, in Die *Briefe des Petrus Damiani*, ed. K. Reindel, *MGH, Die Briefe der deutschen Kaiserzeit* (Munich: MGH, 1983–93), 3:547. For similar laments to Agnes, see Ep. 130, 3:435; Ep. 144, 3:526. For the chronology of Agnes's comings and goings, see Little, "Personal Development," p. 324.

7. Damian, Ep. 124, *To Agnes*, in *Die Briefe*, 3:410. Cf. his admonishment that she would soon be exchanging her purple robes for a tomb, where she would be food for worms (Ep. 130, *To Agnes*, ibid. 3:436).

8. Ep. 123, *To Damianus*, ibid., 3:400–401. Peter corresponded with other women as well. See, for example, his letter to Countess Beatrice of Tuscany commending her recent transition to a spiritual marriage with her husband, Godfrey, and urging her to greater acts

of hospitality and bequests to the church (Ep. 51, *To Beatrice*, ibid., 2:132–37). Cf. the correspondence of Pope Gregory VII, who was especially close to Beatrice and her daughter Mathilda (Jo Ann McNamara, "The *Herrenfrage*: The Restructuring of the Gender System, 1050–1150," in *Medieval Masculinities: Regarding Men in the Middle Ages*, ed. Clare Lees [Minneapolis: University of Minnesota Press, 1994], p. 11).

9. Thus Goscelin recounts how when he first came to England "as a very young man, when you were only a little girl" (*Liber confortatorius* bk. 4, p. 102, trans. p. 188). On their relationship, see Wilmart, "Eve et Goscelin," pt. 1, 46 (1934): 414–38; pt. 2, 50 (1938): 42–83. On Goscelin's age, see ibid., pt. 2, p. 51.

10. Hilarius, *Versus et Ludi, Epistolae, Ludus Danielis Belouacensis*, ed. Walther Bulst and M. L. Bulst-Thiele (Leiden: Brill, 1989), p. 23.

11. Goscelin, *Liber confortatorius* bk. 1, p. 35, trans. p. 110.

12. Sharon Elkins, *Holy Women of Twelfth-Century England* (Chapel Hill: University of North Carolina Press, 1988), pp. 24–27. On Hervey's association with Robert, see Latzke, "Robert von Arbrissel," 141.

13. Geoffrey of Vendôme, Ep. 27, *To Hervey*, in *Oeuvres*, ed. and trans. Geneviève Giordanengo (Turnhout: Brepols, 1996), p. 47; see Wilmart, "Eve et Goscelin," pt. 1, pp. 417–19; Latzke, "Robert von Arbrissel," pp. 143ff.

14. Hilarius, *Versus*, p. 23. Hervey was also criticized on an unrelated matter after Eve's death. See Geoffrey of Vendôme, Ep. 45, *To Hervey*, in *Oeuvres*, p. 80.

15. Hilarius, *Versus*, p. 24.

16. For other examples, see Elkins, *Holy Women of Twelfth-Century England*, pp. 38–46.

17. Anselm of Bec, Ep. 414, *To Robert and his nuns*, in *Epistolae*, 5:359–60; cf. an earlier letter in which only Seit and Edit are mentioned (Ep. 230, *To Robert, Seith, and Edith*, in *Epistolae*, 4:134–35). See Elkins, *Holy Women of Twelfth-Century England*, p. 40; Ann Warren, *Anchorites and Their Patrons in Medieval England* (Berkeley and Los Angeles: University of California Press, 1985), p. 105.

18. Anselm, Ep. 414, *To Robert and his nuns*, in *Epistolae*, 5:360–61, trans. 3:185. Anselm basically says that an individual should not struggle with such thoughts but rout them with useful ones. Cf. Cassian's discussion on concupiscence of the flesh and spirit (no. 4) and on chastity (no. 12) in *Conférences*, ed. E. Pichery, *SC* 42, 1:166–87; *SC* 54, 2:120–46, trans. pp. 155–80, 435–58.

19. Anselm, Ep. 414, *To Robert and his nuns*, in *Epistolae*, 5:361–62, trans. 3:186.

20. Marbod of Rennes, Ep. 6, *To Robert of Arbrissel*, *PL* 171:1481–82, trans. Bruce Venarde in *Robert of Arbrissel: A Medieval Religious Life* (Washington, D.C.: Catholic University Press, 2003), pp. 93–94. For the early church, see Pseudo-Cyprian, *De singularitate clericorum*, pp. 173–220.

21. Marbod of Rennes, Ep. 6, *To Robert of Arbrissel*, *PL* 171:1482–83, pp. 94–95.

22. See the Ps.-Cyprian's third-century *De singularitate clericorum* cc. 3–6, app., esp. pp. 176–79.

23. Marbod of Rennes, Ep. 6, *To Robert of Arbrissel*, *PL* 171:1486, trans. p. 100.

24. Geoffrey of Vendôme, Ep. 79, *To Robert of Arbrissel*, in *Oeuvres*, pp. 148, 150.

25. Marbod of Rennes, Ep. 6, *To Robert of Arbrissel*, *PL* 171:1481, trans. p. 93.

26. Abelard, *Ethics*, pp. 20, 21.

27. See particularly McNamara, "*Herrenfrage*," pp. 3–29.

28. John Chrysostom, *Against Those Men Cohabiting with Virgins* c. 10, trans. Elizabeth Clark, in *Jerome, Chrysostom, and Friends: Essays and Translations* (New York: Edwin Mellen, 1982), p. 195. Also see Elizabeth Clark, "John Chrysostom and the *Subintroductae*," *Church History* 46 (1977): 181–82.

29. One of the most famous exponents of this view is C. S. Lewis in *The Allegory of Love: A Study in Medieval Tradition* (Oxford: Oxford University Press, 1985).

30. Blossom Stefaniw resists the idea that the focus on monastic love was indebted to the secular realm. See "Spiritual Friendship and Bridal Mysticism in an Age of Affectivity," *Cistercian Studies Quarterly* 41.1 (2006): 65–78. The relationship between later mystical discourse and *fin amor* is discussed in Chapter 6.

31. See Chapter 2, pp. 49–50, above.

32. Jerome, Ep. 45, *To Asella*, c. 3, *PL* 22: 480, trans. *LNPNFC*, 2nd ser., 6:59. On Jerome's circle of female friends, see Clark, "Friendship between the Sexes: Classical Theory and Christian Practice," in *Jerome, Chrysostom, and Friends*, pp. 35–106. Also see McNamara's discussion of male friendship with women in *Sisters in Arms*, pp. 61–68. For parallels between these early ascetical circles and those appearing in the late eleventh century, see ibid., pp. 236–39.

33. Abelard, Ep. 1, *Correspondance*, ed. d'Amboise, p. 85, trans. p. 36.

34. *CM*, pp. 174–75; cf. 144–45, 172–73.

35. On spiritual marriage and martyrdom, see Elliott, *Spiritual Marriage*, pp. 67, 69–70. For the practice of spiritual marriage among the higher clergy, see ibid., pp. 89–91. On church trepidation over the actual practice, see ibid., pp. 41, 167–70. Also see two ideologically different retellings of the fraught marriage of Bishop Severus of Ravenna, in Elliott, *Fallen Bodies*, pp. 85–100.

36. One of the most vocal representatives of this group was the Norman Anonymous. See *Die Texte des Normannischen Anonymous*, ed. Karl Pellens (Wiesbaden: Steiner, 1966). See Anne Llewellyn Barstow's discussion in *Married Priests and the Reforming Papacy: The Eleventh-Century Debates* (New York: Edwin Mellen, 1982), pp. 157–73.

37. McLaughlin, "Bishop as Bridegroom," p. 220; Matter, *Voice of My Beloved*, pp. 106–11; Fulton, *From Judgment to Passion*, pt. 2.

38. Petigny cites the poem in full in, "Une lettre," p. 216. It is translated by Regine Pernoud in *Women in the Days of the Cathedrals*, trans. Anne Côté-Harriss (San Francisco: Ignatius Press, 1998), pp. 124–25. On Marbod's bifurcated view of women, see Jaeger, *Ennobling Love*, pp. 91–94.

39. Petigny, "Une lettre," pp. 213–14; Latzke, "Robert von Arbrissel," pp. 122–25.

40. Petigny, "Une lettre," p. 226, trans., p. 74.

41. Ibid., p. 227, trans., p. 74.

42. Ibid., pp. 233–34, trans., p. 78. Venarde argues that Robert was probably more concerned about the alleged brutality of Count Baldwin VII of Flanders than the fact that the couple was related in the sixth degree (*Robert of Arbrissel*, pp. 141–42, n21).

43. Petigny, "Une lettre," pp. 220–21; Pernoud, *Women*, p. 126.

44. Pernoud, *Women*, p. 125. Petigny says that the marriage was dissolved as consanguineous and probably never consummated ("Une lettre," p. 214).

45. The construction was not without its problems. According to her son, Ermengard was persuaded to stop construction by some malcontents. When the site was visited by Bernard, she was reprimanded and recommitted to the project. See Bruno James's introductory comments to Ep. 110 (= 116) in *The Letters of St. Bernard of Clairvaux* (Chicago: Henry Regnery, 1953), p. 181.

46. On this exchange, see Jean Leclercq, *Women and Saint Bernard of Clairvaux* (Kalamazoo, Mich.: Cistercian Publications, 1989), pp. 45–52. Leclercq mentions modern scholars' discomfort with Bernard's exuberance (p. 45).

47. Ep. 116, *To Ermengard*, in *Sancti Bernardi Opera*, ed. J. Leclercq and H. Rochais (Rome: Editiones Cistercienses, 1974), 7:296, trans. James, *The Letters of St. Bernard of Clairvaux*, p. 181 (numbered as Ep. 119).

48. Petigny, "Une lettre," p. 222; Pernoud, *Women*, pp. 124–26.

49. Ep. 117, *To Ermengard*, in *Bernardi Opera*, 7:297, trans. p. 182 (numbered as Ep. 120).

50. Petigny, "Une lettre," p. 223; Latzke, "Robert von Arbrissel," pp. 135–36.

51. Goscelin, *Liber confortatorius* bk. 1, p. 40, trans. p. 116.

52. Both holy women had parallel brushes with marriage. We have seen that the betrothed Thecla heard Paul's preaching and, hence, on the eve of her marriage, rejected her future spouse and won the eternal enmity of her family. Both heroines receive parallel tests: Paul keeps rejecting Thecla, refusing to credit her conversion and dismissing her as a seductive and shallow woman. Not only did he refuse to baptize her but on one occasion he even abandoned Thecla to a besotted Syrian ruler, resulting in her arrest and condemnation to wild animals in the Circus Maximus. She took this opportunity to baptize herself in the tank for wild seals (*The Acts of Paul* cc. 26–34, trans. James, *Apocryphal New Testament*, pp. 277–79). Christina, too, is constantly tested by the disaffection of her supporters. Sueno disinvests in his holy client upon the news of her marriage: "Thinking she had changed her mind about the vow of virginity, he accused her of feminine inconstancy, saying: 'She in whom I put all my trust has deceived me'" (*CM*, pp. 54–55). This pattern recurs in miniature when Roger, her later spiritual director, first learns that Christina is married (*CM*, pp. 82–83, 94–95). For the initial parallels between Christina and the desert fathers, see Dyan Elliott, "Alternative Intimacies: Men, Women, and Spiritual Direction in the Twelfth Century," in *Christina of Markyate: A Twelfth-Century Holy Woman*, ed. Samuel Fanous and Henrietta Leyser (London: Routledge, 2004), pp. 161–63.

53. *CM*, pp. 98–99.

54. Ibid. c. 39, pp. 102–5. On the impact of the desert tradition, see Warren, *Anchorites and Their Patrons*, pp. 7–14; Henrietta Leyser, *Hermits and the New Monasticism: A Study of Religious Communities in Western Europe, 1000–1500* (New York: St. Martin's Press, 1984), pp. 7–17.

55. *CM*, pp. 114–17.

56. Ibid., pp. 118–19.

57. Jaeger, *Ennobling Love*, pp. 181–83.

58. *CM*, pp. 144–45, 148–49.

59. Ibid., pp. 144–45.

60. Ibid., pp. 140–41.

61. Ibid., pp. 144–45.

62. Ibid., pp. 148–49.

63. Ibid., pp. 192–93.

64. See Lisa Bitel, *Women in Early Medieval Europe, 400–1100* (Cambridge: Cambridge University Press, 2002), pp. 114–25.

65. Dhuoda, *Manuel pour mon fils* 8.14, 10.5, ed. Pierre Riché, *SC*, 225 (Paris: Editions du Cerf, 1975), pp. 318–21, 354, trans. Carol Neel, *A Handbook for William: A Carolingian Woman's Counsel for Her Son* (Washington, D.C.: Catholic University Press, 1991), pp. 87–88, 100.

66. See Sharon Farmer, "Persuasive Voices: Clerical Images of Medieval Wives," *Speculum* 61 (1986): 517–43. For the clergy's subordination of the wife's physical and spiritual health to that of the husband, see Elliott, *Spiritual Marriage*, pp. 146ff.

67. *CM*, pp. 152–53.

68. Ibid., pp. 126–27. This absorption of female into male communities is a common pattern in this period. See Elkins, *Holy Women of Twelfth-Century England*, pp. 46–50.

69. *CM*, pp. 146–47.

70. Judith Bennett, *Women in the Medieval Countryside: Gender and Household in Brigstock before the Plague* (Oxford: Oxford University Press, 1989).

71. See Dalarun, *Robert d'Arbrissel*, pp. 67–71; Dalarun, "Robert d'Arbrissel et les femmes," *Annales, ESC* 39 (1984): 1146–51; also see Dalarun, *L'Impossible sainteté: La vie retrouvée de Robert d'Arbrissel* (Paris: Editions du Cerf, 1985), pp. 183ff.

72. Golding, clearly uncomfortable with this anomaly, makes the rather sophistical argument that Gilbert's vita "does not state that Gilbert did not intend to establish a community for women, but that he wished to use his *resources* for the support of a male community" (*Gilbert of Sempringham*, p. 18).

73. Abelard, Ep. 1, *Correspondance*, ed. d'Amboise, p. 83, trans. p. 35. For another view, see Griffiths, " 'Men's Duty to Provide,' " pp. 7–10.

74. See, for example, Goscelin, *Liber confortatorius* bk. 1, p. 36 (bis), trans. pp. 111, 112.

75. Ibid. bk. 1, p. 31, trans. p. 106.

76. Ibid. bk. 1, p. 34, trans. p. 110.

77. Ibid. bk. 1, p. 27; bk. 4, p. 117, trans. pp. 101, 206.

78. Ibid. bk. 1, p. 33; bk. 4, p. 117, trans. pp. 108, 207 and passim.

79. Abelard, Ep. 5, *Correspondance*, ed. d'Amboise, p. 162, trans. p. 89. See Clanchy, *Abelard*, p. 153.

80. Peter the Venerable, Ep. 116, *To Heloise,* in *The Letters of Peter the Venerable*, ed. Giles Constable (Cambridge, Mass.: Harvard University Press, 1967), 1:308, trans. Radice, *Letters of Abelard and Heloise*, p. 284. See Clanchy's discussion of Peter the Venerable's vision of love (*Abelard*, pp. 158–61).

81. On the popular projection of the marriage bond beyond the grave, see Elliott, *Spiritual Marriage*, pp. 69–73.

82. "Quasi reparato matrimonio, ei redderet in coelis, qui castitatis amore a carnali commercio se subtraxerat in terris" (James of Vitry, *Vita B. Mariae Oigniacensis* 1.1.14, *AA SS*, June, 5:550).

83. Thomas of Cantimpré, *Vita Margarete de Ypris* c. 28, ed. G. Meersseman, in "Les Frères Prêcheurs et le movement dévot en Flandre au XIIIe siècle," *Archivum Fratrum Praedicatorum* 18 (1948): 120, trans. King and Newman, p. 189. This becomes a central image for Mechtild of Hackeborn (*Liber specialias gratiae* 2.19, 27; 3.1, 17, ed. Louis Paquelin et al., in *Revelationes Gertrudianae ac Mechtildianae II: Sanctae Mechtildis virginis ordinis Sancti Benedicti Liber specialis gratiae; Accedit sororis Mechtildis ejusdem ordinis Lux divinitatis* [Poitiers: Oudin, 1877], pp. 154, 172, 195, 217–18, and passim); cf. the description of Christ's heart as a marriage bed (ibid. 2.20, p. 158). See the visualization of this motif in the art of German communities of nuns in the later Middle Ages, in Jeffrey Hamburger, *Nuns as Artists: The Visual Culture of a Medieval Convent* (Berkeley: University of California Press, 1997), pp. 137–75.

84. Goscelin, *Liber confortatorius* bk. 1, p. 27, trans. p. 101.

85. Goscelin, *Life of King Edward*, p. 60; cf. pp. 42, 76. See Elliott, *Spiritual Marriage*, pp. 120–23.

86. Goscelin, *Liber confortatorius* bk. 4, p. 104, trans. p. 190.

87. Ibid., pp. 104–5, trans. p.192.

88. Ibid., p. 105, trans. p. 192.

89. Ibid., p. 107, trans. p. 194.

90. Abelard, Ep. 5, *Correspondance*, ed. d'Amboise, p. 148, trans. pp. 80–81.

91. Donna Alfano Bussell, "Heloise Redressed: Rhetorical Engagement and the Benedictine Rite of Initiation in Heloise's Third Letter," in *Listening to Heloise*, ed. Wheeler, p. 243.

92. Stephen of Bourbon, *Anecdotes historiques, légendes et apologues tirés du recueil inédit d'Etienne de Bourbon* c. 347, ed. A. Lecoy de la Marche (Paris: Librairie Renouard, 1877), p. 304. Apparently Francis was being goaded by a heretic to denounce the priest for his sinfulness. Stephen clearly thinks this point is worth repeating since it appears in his collection twice with only a few changes (ibid. c. 316, p. 265).

93. See Elliott, *Proving Woman*, ch. 1.

94. In Freud's words, "The patient is not satisfied with regarding the analyst in the light of reality as a helper and adviser who, moreover, is remunerated for the trouble he takes and who would himself be content with some such role as that of a guide on a difficult mountain climb. On the contrary, the patient sees in him the return, the reincarnation, of some important figure out of his childhood or past, and consequently transfers on to him feelings and reactions which undoubtedly applied to this prototype. This fact of transference soon proves to be a factor of undreamt-of importance, on the one hand an instrument of irreplaceable value and on the other hand a source of serious dangers. This transference is *ambivalent*: it comprises positive (affectionate) as well as negative (hostile) attitudes towards the analyst, who as a rule is put in the place of one or other of the patient's parents, his father or mother" (*An Outline of Psychoanalysis*, in *SE*, 23:174–75).

95. *CM*, pp. 160–61.

96. See Michel Foucault's *History of Sexuality: An Introduction*, trans. Robert Hurley (New York: Vintage, 1990), 1:61–63.

97. Geoffrey of Vendôme, Ep. 79, *To Robert of Arbrissel*, in *Oeuvres*, p. 150, trans. p. 105.

98. Dalarun, "Robert d'Arbrissel et les femmes," pp. 1143–45. If there were prostitutes in their midst, this could be the beginning of the long tradition of religious houses founded for their reformation (Jansen, *Making of the Magdalen*, pp. 177–84).

99. Cf. the situation of the two-part female community described by Herrimann in Chapter 4.

100. Jansen, *Making of the Magdalen*, pp. 37–39, 124ff.

101. Thais remained in a penitential mode for three years until it was divinely revealed that her sins had been forgiven. She died within a fortnight. See Ruth Karras, "Holy Harlots: Prostitute Saints in Medieval Legend," *Journal of the History of Sexuality* 1 (1990): 3–32; Wogan-Browne, *Saints' Lives and Women's Literary Culture*, pp. 132–42. For Paphnutius, see Cassian, *Conférences* 3, ed. Pichery, 1:138–65, trans. pp. 119–47.

102. Marbod of Rennes, *Thais poenitens in Aegypto. Vita metrica alter, AA SS*, October, 4:226–8. The conditions endured by Christina of Markyate in the course of her enclosure in Roger's cell are strikingly similar to those visited upon the legendary harlot (*CM*, pp. 102–5). If Roger was deliberately imitating Paphnutius in his treatment of Christina it may have been due to the fact that she was once married, which initially caused Roger to refuse Christina assistance (see *CM*, pp. 82–83). For a discussion of the relationship between anchoritic enclosure and the life of Thais, see Wogan-Browne, *Saints' Lives and Women's Literary Culture*, pp. 132–37.

103. Geoffrey of Vendôme, Ep. 79, *To Robert of Arbrissel*, in *Oeuvres*, p. 148, trans. p. 104. In fact, Geoffrey is wrong in his assumption that this practice was unprecedented. See Roger Reynolds, "*Virgines subintroductae* in Celtic Christianity," *Harvard Theological Review* 61 (1968): 559–60.

104. See Chapter 4, n206, above.

105. Fulton, *From Judgment to Passion*, pp. 289–91.

106. Abelard, Ep. 8, ed. McLaughlin, "Abelard's Rule for Religious Women," p. 243, trans. p. 131.

107. For an overview, see McGinn, *Growth of Mysticism*, pp. 158–224; Matter, *Voice of My Beloved*, pp. 123–32.

108. Bernard of Clairvaux, Serm. 69, 1.1, *Sermons, SC*, 511, 5:38, trans. 4:26–27; Serm. 78, 1.1, *Sermons, SC*, 511, 5:242, trans. 4:129. The association between the Virgin Mary as bride is muted in Bernard. See Serm. 78, 3.8, *Sermons, SC*, 511, 5:254, trans. 4:135; Fulton, *From Judgment to Passion*, pp. 303–5.

109. On Bernard's use of maternal imagery in the sermons, see Caroline Walker Bynum, *Jesus as Mother: Studies in the Spirituality of the High Middle Ages* (Berkeley and Los Angeles: University of California Press, 1982), pp. 117–20; and on Bernard's use of the bridal metaphor, see Jean Leclercq, *Monks and Love in Twelfth-Century France: Psycho-Historical Essays* (Oxford: Clarendon, 1979), pp. 121–29. Recently, however, Shawn Krahmer has argued against associating the bride with female frailty, instead associating her with the virago

of the early Christian tradition in "The Virile Bride of Bernard of Clairvaux," *Church History* 69 (2000): 304–27.

110. Bernard of Clairvaux, Serm. 7, 2.2, *Sermons, SC*, 414, 1:156, trans. 1:39.

111. Ibid. 41, 3.3, *Sermons, SC*, 452, 3:192–94, trans. 2:206–7.

112. Ibid. 85, 4.13, *Sermons, SC*, 511, 5:306–8, trans. 4:209; Serm. 52, 2.4, *Sermons, SC*, 472, 4:66–68, trans. 3:52–54; Serm. 49, 1.4, *Sermons, SC*, 452, 3:334, trans. 3:24; Serm. 62, 3.4, *Sermons, SC*, 472, 4:270, trans. 3:155; Serm. 52, 1.2, *Sermons, SC*, 472, 4:62–64, trans. 3:50–51; Serm. 84, 1.1, *Sermons, SC*, 511, trans. 3:155.

113. Ibid. 46, 1.1., *Sermons, SC*, 452, 5:356–58, trans. 4:188–89.

114. But it is also expressed by other dramatic images such of being eaten by God. See ibid. 71, 3.5, *Sermons, SC*, 511, 5:86, trans. 4:52.

115. Ibid. 74, 2.6–7, *Sermons, SC*, 511, 5:168–70, trans. 4:91–92; cf. Serm. 23, 6.15, 16, *Sermons, SC*, 431, 2:230, 234, trans. 2:38, 40; Serm. 57, 3.5, *Sermons, SC*, 472, 4:162, trans. 3:100.

116. Ibid. 43, 3.5, *Sermons, SC*, 452, 3:336, trans. 2:223–24.

117. Ibid. 43, 2.3, *Sermons, SC*, 452, 3:352–53, trans. 2:222; Serm. 61, 3.7, *Sermons, SC*, 472, 4:254–56, trans. 3:146–47.

118. Ibid. 67, 1.1, 2.3, *Sermons, SC*, 472, 4:368–70, 372, trans. 4:4, 6; Serm. 82, 1.1, *Sermons, SC*, 511, 5:320–22, trans. 4:171.

119. This tradition evolved after his death as a function of Bernard's own Marian devotion in conjunction with his (and other Cistercians') emphasis on lactation as a metaphor for spiritual nurture and grace. See Léon Dewez and Albert van Iterson, "La lactation de saint Bernard: Legende et iconographie," *Cîteaux in de Nederlanden* 7 (1956): 165–66; Brian McGuire, *The Difficult Saint: Bernard of Clairvaux and His Tradition* (Kalamazoo, Mich.: Cistercian Publications, 1991), pp. 189–226.

120. Is. 24.16; Bernard of Clairvaux, Serm. 23, 4.9, *Sermons, SC*, 431, 2:218, trans. 2:34.

121. "[E]ven one soul, if it loves God clearly, wisely, and ardently, is the Bride," Bernard of Clairvaux, Serm. 73, 3.10, *Sermons, SC*, 511, 5:152, trans. 4:83.

CHAPTER 6

1. Thomas of Cantimpré, *Bonum universale de apibus* 2.30.19 (Douai: B. Belleri, 1627), p. 329 (hereafter cited as *De apibus*).

2. On the education of young clerics, see Ruth Mazo Karras, *From Boys to Men: Formations of Masculinity in Late Medieval Europe* (Philadelphia: University of Pennsylvania, 2003), pp. 67ff. On Andrew the Chaplain as a transmitter of the Ovidian tradition, see John Baldwin, *The Language of Sex: Five Voices from Northern France around 1200* (Chicago: University of Chicago Press, 1994), pp. 16–20, 51–53, 58–60.

3. Alan de Lille, *De planctu Naturae, PL* 120:449–50, trans. James Sheridan, *The Plaint of Nature* (Toronto: Pontifical Institute of Mediaeval Studies, 1980), pp. 133–35. Mark Jordan brings out the many "unnatural" anomalies in Alan's presentation of Nature—that she

was probably a hermaphrodite born of incest who seems incapable of defending hetero-normal sex, her alleged purpose. See *The Invention of Sodomy in Christian Theology* (Chicago: University of Chicago Press, 1997), pp. 70–91; cf. Newman's analysis of the cipher presented by Alan's Nature in *God and the Goddesses*, pp. 66–72. Newman sees a gradual secularization in the depiction of the goddess Nature over the course of the twelfth and thirteenth centuries, allowing for the possibility of discussing sex separately from religion (in ibid., pp. 90–137).

4. Andrew the Chaplain, *De amore, libri tres* 1.6, g; 1.7, ed. E. Trojel, 2nd ed. (Munich: Eidos, 1964), pp. 188–89, 219–21, trans. John Jay Parry, *The Art of Courtly Love* (New York: Columbia University Press, 1960), pp. 125, 141–42. Note, however, that there is no consensus about whether or not Andrew was, in fact, being ironical. See Don Monson's more sober reading in *Andreas Capellanus, Scholasticism, and the Courtly Tradition* (Washington, D.C.: Catholic University Press, 2005), pp. 143–66. According to Georges Duby, Andrew worked in the chancery of Philip Augustus (*The Knight, the Lady, and the Priest: The Making of Modern Marriage in Medieval France*, trans. Barbara Bray [Chicago: University of Chicago Press, 1983], pp. 216–17). For a comparison of some of these different discourses, see Baldwin, *Language of Sex*.

5. See Joan Cadden, *The Meanings of Sex Difference in the Middle Ages* (Cambridge: Cambridge University Press, 1993), pp. 94–97, 117–30; Monica Green, *Making Women's Medicine Masculine: The Rise of Male Authority in Pre-Modern Gynaecology* (Oxford: Oxford University Press, 2008), pp. 45–69; Ruth Mazo Karras, *Common Women: Prostitution and Sexuality in Medieval England* (New York: Oxford University Press, 1996).

6. See, for example, Abelard's contention that if a woman was sexually defiled in a church, the perpetrator would have sinned more in his offense against the woman—"a true temple of God"—than through his sacrilegious use of the building (*Ethics*, p. 43). For Ælred, see Chapter 4.

7. Albert the Great, *De animalibus libri XXVI* 26.1.3, ed. Hermann Stadler, *Beiträge zur Geschichte der Philosophie des Mittlelalters: Texte und Untersuchungen*, vol. 2, 16 (1920): 1350.

8. Aquinas, *Summa Theologia* 1a 2ae, art. 1, resp.; see Sigmund Freud, *Instincts and Their Viccisitudes*, SE, 14: 126–28.

9. See Walter Stephens, *Demon Lovers: Witchcraft, Sex, and the Crisis of Belief* (Chicago: University of Chicago Press, 2002), pp. 63–65, 69–71.

10. This change was first broached in Gratian, C. 33 q. 4 dpc. 11. See Brundage, *Law, Sex, and Christian Society in Medieval Europe*, p. 242.

11. Jean-Louis Flandrin, *Un Temps pour embrasser: Aux origines de la morale sexuelle occidentale (Ve–XIe siècle)* (Paris: Editions du Seuil, 1983).

12. See Chapter 4, pp. 117, 121–23, 147–48, above.

13. Jacqueline Murray, "On the Origins and Role of 'Wise Women' in Causes for Annulment on the Grounds of Male Impotence," *Journal of Medieval History* 16 (1990): 235–49.

14. Michael Sheehan, "The Formation and Stability of Marriage in Fourteenth-Century England: Evidence of an Ely Register," *Mediaeval Studies* 33 (1971): 228–63.

15. See William of Rennes's gloss to Raymond of Peñafort's *Summa de poenitentia et matrimonio* 4.2.11 (Rome: Joannes Tallini, 1603), gloss p ad v. *debet reddere*, pp. 517–18.

16. For the one exception to this, see Chapter 4, p. 120, above.

17. See Pierre Payer, *Sex and the New Literature of Confession, 1150–1300* (Toronto: Pontifical Institute, 2009).

18. This is a common image in confessors' manuals. See William of Auvergne (d. 1249), *Tractatus novus de poenitentia* c. 2, in *Opera omnia* (Paris: A. Pralard, 1674; reprt., Frankfurt am Main: Minverva, 1963), 1:465, 487.

19. See, for example, the seven different degrees of culpability for nocturnal emissions listed by Thomas of Chobham, *Summa confessorum* (ca. 1216), 7.2.1.1.1, *Analecta Mediaevalia Namurensia*, 25, ed. F. Broomfield (Louvain: Nauwelaerts, 1968), pp. 330–33.

20. I examine the origins of the relatively common exemplum regarding the unfortunate sex partners who get stuck together when having sex in a church in *Fallen Bodies*, ch. 3.

21. See Dyan Elliott, "Women and Confession: From Empowerment to Pathology," in *Gendering the Master Narrative: Women and Power in the Middle Ages*, ed. Maryanne Kowaleski and Mary Erler (Ithaca, N.Y.: Cornell University Press), p. 44; Alexander Murray, "Counseling in Medieval Confession," in *Handling Sin: Confession in the Middle Ages*, ed. Peter Biller and Alastair Minnis (York: York Medieval Press in association with Boydell and Brewer, 1998), pp. 72–73.

22. Robert le Bougre is discussed later in this chapter. On the sex scandals associated with the confessional in the early modern period, see Stephen Haliczer, *Sexuality in the Confessional: A Sacrament Profaned* (New York: Oxford University Press, 1996).

23. See Elliott, *Proving Woman*, pp. 32–33.

24. The classic work on the Beguines is Ernest McDonnell, *The Beguines and Beghards in Medieval Culture with Special Emphasis on the Belgian Scene* (New Brunswick, N.J.: Rutgers University Press, 1954). For an excellent recent study that stresses how the Beguines actually lived and supported themselves, see Walter Simons, *Cities of Ladies: Beguine Communities in the Medieval Low Countries, 1200–1565* (Philadelphia: University of Pennsylvania Press, 2001).

25. See Caroline Bynum, *Holy Feast and Holy Fast: The Religious Significance of Food to Medieval Women* (Berkeley: University of California Press, 1987). On eucharistic culture generally, see Miri Rubin, *Corpus Christi: The Eucharist in Late Medieval Culture* (Cambridge: Cambridge University Press, 1992).

26. For a list of the early Beguines and their sources, see Walter Simons, "The Beguines," in *MHW*, pp. 647–62.

27. For an overview of the Beguine mystics, see Bernard McGinn, *The Flowering of Mysticism: Men and Women in the New Mysticism, 1200–1350*, vol. 3 of *The Presence of God: A History of Western Mysticism* (New York: Crossroad, 1998), pp. 199–265. See Barbara Newman's discussion of "la mystique courtoise," in *From Virile Woman to WomanChrist*, pp. 137–67.

28. This is a dominant idiom in her Poems in Stanza. See "Knight Errant" (no. 10), in *Hadewijch: The Complete Works*, trans. Columba Hart (New York: Paulist Press, 1980), pp. 152–53. See Saskia Murk-Jansen, "Hadewijch," *MHW*, pp. 663–85.

29. Mechtild of Magdeburg, *Das fliessende Licht der Gottheit: Nach der Einsiedler Hanschrift in kritischen Vergleich mit gesamten Überlieferung* 3.2, ed. Margot Schmidt (Munich: Artemis, 1990), pp. 84–85, trans. Frank Tobin, *The Flowing Light of the Godhead* (New York: Paulist Press, 1998), pp. 107–8. On Mechtild, see Amy Hollywood and Patricia Beckman, "Mechtild of Magdeburg," *MHW*, pp. 411–25; Amy Hollywood, *The Soul as Virgin Wife: Mechtild of Magdeburg, Marguerite Porete, and Meister Eckhart* (Notre Dame, Ind.: University of Notre Dame Press, 1995), pp. 87–119; McGinn, *Flowering of Mysticism*, 3:222–44.

30. For a discussion of the community of mystics at Helfta, see McGinn, *Flowering of Mysticism*, 3:267–82; Bynum, *Jesus as Mother*, pp. 170–262, esp. 186–95.

31. This is true of books 2–4. See Gertrude the Great, *Les Exercices*, ed. Jacques Hourlier and Albert Schmitt, *Oeuvres spirituelles*, SC, 127 (Paris: Editions du Cerf, 1967), 1:80–154, trans. Gertrud Lewis and Jack Lewis, *Spiritual Exercises* (Kalamazoo, Mich.: Cistercian Publications, 1989), pp. 34–72.

32. Gertrude the Great, *Les Exercises* bk. 4, SC, 127, 1:130, trans. p. 60. On this imagery in hagiography, see pp. 180, 187, 188, 221, below.

33. Ibid. bk. 3, SC, 127, 1:122, trans. p. 56. Cf. ibid. bk. 6, 1:248, trans. p. 116.

34. A voice rings out announcing the virgin's entry and the entire heavenly court rejoices. God can see himself in the eyes of the virgin like a mirror, as they gaze at one another with mutual satisfaction (Mechtild of Hackeborn, *Liber specialias gratiae* 2.37, ed. Paquelin et al., in *Revelationes Gertrudianae ac Mechtildianae II: Sanctae Mechtildis virginis ordinis Sancti Benedicti Liber specialis gratiae; Accedit sororis Mechtildis ejusdem ordinis Lux divinitatis* [Poitiers: Oudin, 1877], pp. 184–85; hereafter *LSG*). See Rosalynn Voaden, "Mechtild of Hackeborn," *MHW*, pp. 431–51. Mechtild's visions, which began when she was five, were only revealed to the other nuns in the last eight years of her life when she was an invalid. They were recorded by two other nuns, one of whom was almost certainly Gertrude (ibid., pp. 432–33). I am very grateful to Rosalynn Voaden for supplying me with an edition of *LSG*.

35. *LSG* 1.11, p. 36. Elsewhere, however, Christ acknowledges that all the souls united to him in love are his queens (ibid. 1.20, p. 74).

36. Sentences like "Virginum sponsus, visus est ad altare accedere" are probably purposefully vague (ibid. 5.5, pp. 22–23). Cf. instances in which the Virgin was similarly seen to present ailing nuns to their future groom (ibid. 5.6, p. 326).

37. Ibid. 1.1, pp. 9–10.

38. Ibid. 2.29, p. 186. The concept of the *arrha* had spiritual currency outside the Beguine movement. See, for example, Hugh of St. Victor's *Soliloquium de arrha animae PL* 176: 951–70.

39. *LSG* 1.23, pp. 82–83. In secular marriage ceremonies the bride and groom actually were wrapped in a mantle in certain areas of Europe (Molin and Mutembe, *Le Rituel du mariage en France du XIIe au XVIe siècle*, pp. 228–33).

40. *LSG* 2.18, p. 153; cf. 3.38, p. 242. Also note Mechtild's pique over the fact, because she had been married to God in a religious habit since childhood, she could not love Christ as much as the equally youthful Agnes—the prototype for consecrated virgins (1.11, p. 35).

This is to some extent redressed when she achieves Agnes's singular gift of being simultane-ously virgin and mother, discussed later in this chapter.

41. *LSG* 3.3, pp. 196–97. In a letter, Mechtild also anticipates a mystical union for a friend, in which the bride's eager, languid body anticipates being embraced by an equally ardent groom. But the bed on which the union was to be consummated was the cross (Voaden, "Mechtild of Hackeborn," *MHW*, p. 439n38). Another of Mechtild's matrimonial "complaints" leads to the reception of a different ring whose seven gems are seven ways of understanding Christ in the Mass (*LSG* 3.19, p. 220).

42. *LSG* 3.29, p. 233.

43. *LSG* 4.15, pp. 271–72.

44. Mechtild of Magdeburg, *Das fliessende Licht der Gottheit* 1.44, ed. Schmidt, pp. 29–34, trans. pp. 58–63. Cf. Mecthild of Hackeborn's experience of heaven, where her soul led the entire heavenly family (dressed in livery) in a dance (*LSG* 1.19, p. 69).

45. *LSG* 2.32, p. 177.

46. Augustine had distinguished between corporeal, spiritual (i.e., containing images), and intellectual vision (*De Genesi ad litteram libri duodecimo* 12.25, *PL* 34:475–76, trans. John Hammond Taylor, *The Literal Meaning of Genesis*, *ACW*, 42 [New York: Newman Press, 1982], 2:215–16). See Barbara Newman, "What Did It Mean to Say 'I Saw'? The Clash between Theory and Practice in Medieval Visionary Culture," *Speculum* 80 (2005): 1–43.

47. See Bynum, *Holy Feast*, pp. 153–61.

48. See Gordon Rudy, *The Mystical Language of Sensation in the Later Middle Ages* (New York: Routledge, 2002), pp. 67–100. Note, however, that Rudy warns against the temptation to interpret Hadewijch's expressions as in any way autobiographical or experi-ential. Such an interpretation necessarily undermines the theological content of her work (pp. 72–75).

49. Mechtild of Magdeburg, *Das fliessende Licht der Gottheit* 1.44, ed. Schmidt, p. 61, trans. pp. 58–59. See Hollywood and Beckman, "Mechtild of Magdeburg," pp. 420–21.

50. *LSG* 2.34, 4.21, pp. 179, 278. Mary also adds her voice to the dangers of the senses (*LSG* 3.52, pp. 254–55). Mechtild does commend a focus on the image of the cross to both the inner and outer senses, however. Note that Christ also praises Mechtild for seeking God with her five carnal senses (*LSG* 3.18, 3.44, pp. 218, 246–47).

51. *LSG* 1.23, pp. 82, 83.

52. *LSG* 2.17, p. 152; Voaden, "Mechtild of Hackeborn," *MHW*, p. 439.

53. On Gertrude's use of erotic language, see Alexandra Barratt, "'The Woman Who Shares the King's Bed': The Innocent Eroticism of Gertrude the Great of Helfta," in *Inter-sections of Sexuality and the Divine in Medieval Culture: The Word Made Flesh*, ed. Susannah Mary Chewning (Aldershot: Ashgate, 2005), pp. 107–20.

54. Gertrude the Great, *Le Héraut memorial des largesses de l'amour divin* 2.1.2, 2.2.1, in *Oeuvres spirituelles*, ed. Pierre Doyère, *SC*, 143 (Paris: Editions du Cerf, 1986), 2:230, 232, trans. Margaret Winkworth, *The Herald of Divine Love* (New York: Paulist Press, 1993), pp. 95, 96. See Alexandra Barratt and Debra Stoudt, "Gertrude the Great of Helfta," *MHW*, pp. 453–73.

55. Gertrude the Great, *Le Héraut* 2.4.3, *SC*, 143, 2:244, trans. p. 100; Barratt and Stoudt, "Gertrude the Great of Helfta," p. 457.

56. Gertrude the Great, *Le Héraut* 2.21.3, *SC*, 143, 2:324, trans. p. 126.

57. Ibid. 1.1.6, *SC*, 127, 2:124, trans. p. 55. This was placed in the biographical section preceding the revelations proper. Gertrude only wrote *The Spiritual Exercises* and book 2 of *The Herald* (Barratt and Stoudt, "Gertrude the Great of Helfta," p. 456). Book 3 treats the subject of Gertrude's illness and particularly engages the body: "It happened one night that whilst [Gertrude] was occupied in meditating devoutly on the Lord's passion, she was thrown into a state of agitation by the vehemence of her emotions. She felt her liver much inflamed within her by the exceedingly great thirst of her desires, and said to the Lord: 'My sweetest lover, if anyone knew what I now feel, that person would say that I should abstain from such fervor in order to recover my bodily health. . . . I am powerless to resist the emotion caused by your sweetness, penetrating and thrilling every fiber of my being.' To which the Lord replied: 'Who, unless he were altogether devoid of feeling could be unaware of how ineffably the stirring of the sweetness of my divinity exceeds by far all human and carnal pleasures?'" (*Le Héraut* 3.44.1, *SC*, 143, 3:198, trans. p. 213). I have restored the word "*liver*," for which the translator had substituted "*heart*."

58. Amy Hollywood in particular has argued that women's somatic spirituality was by and large imposed by male hagiographers. Hollywood supports her argument by comparing the anonymous author's rendition of the life of Beatrice of Nazareth with Beatrice's own work (*Soul as Virgin Wife*, pp. 25–36; Hollywood, "Inside Out: Beatrice of Nazareth and Her Hagiographer," in *Gendered Voices: Medieval Saints and Their Interpreters*, ed. Catherine Mooney [Philadelphia: University of Pennsylvania Press, 1999], pp. 78–98). A similar point is made by Else Marie Wiberg Pedersen, "The In-carnation of Beatrice of Nazareth's Theology," in *New Trends in Feminine Spirituality: The Holy Women of Liège and Their Impact*, ed. Juliette Dor, Lesley Johnson, and Jocelyn Wogan-Browne (Brussels: Brepols, 1999), pp. 61–80. There is undoubtedly some truth to this argument. But the nuns who wrote book 3 of Gertrude of Helfta's *The Herald* describe her spirituality in terms that bear much in common with the intense physicality in male-authored hagiographical texts. Cf. n57, above.

59. Elisabeth of Spalbeek, for example, enacted painstaking re-creations of the Crucifixion and received the stigmata. See Philip of Clairvaux's account, "Vita Elizabeth sanctimonialis in Erkenrode, Ordinis Cisterciensis," in *Catalogus codicum hagiographicorum bibliothecae regiae bruxellensis*, ed. Bollandists (Brussels: Polleunsis, Ceuterick et de Smet, 1886), 1:362–78. On Elisabeth, see Jesse Njus, "The Politics of Mysticism: Elisabeth of Spalbeek in Context," *Church History* 77 (2008): 285–318; Elliott, *Proving Woman*, pp. 186–89. On the performative aspects of Beguine visions, see Walter Simons, "Reading a Saint's Body: Rapture and Bodily Movement in the *Vitae* of Thirteenth-Century Beguines," in *Framing Medieval Bodies,* ed. Sarah Kay and Miri Rubin (Manchester: Manchester University Press, 1994), pp. 10–23; Joanna Ziegler, "On the Artistic Nature of Elisabeth of Spalbeek's Ecstasy: The Southern Low Countries Do Matter," in *The Texture of Society: Medieval Women in the Southern Low Countries*, ed. Ellen Kittell and Mary Suydam (New York: Palgrave, 2004), pp. 181–202; and Mary Suydam, "Bringing Heaven Down to Earth: Beguine Constructions of Heaven," in *Envisaging Heaven in the Middle Ages*, ed. Carolyn Muessig and Ad Putter (London: Routledge, 2007), pp. 93–97. Penny Galloway reminds us that such women are, by definition, exceptional and attempts to give a more balanced

perspective on communal worship in "Neither Miraculous nor Astonishing: The Devotional Practice of Beguine Communities in French Flanders," in *New Trends in Feminine Spirituality: The Holy Women of Liège and Their Impact*, ed. Juliette Dor, Lesley Johnson, and Jocelyn Wogan-Browne (Turnhout: Brepols, 1999), pp. 107–27. The lives discussed in the following section is determined by the canon of thirteenth-century Beguine lives established by Barbara Newman in the preface to the lives of Goswin of Villers, translated by Martinus Cawley in *Send Me God: The Lives of Ida the Compassionate of Nivelles, Nun of la Ramé, Arnulf, Lay Brother of Villers, and Abundus, Monk of Villers* (University Park: Pennsylvania State University Press, 2006), pp. xlviii–xlix. Goswin was a monk and cantor at the Cistercian abbey of Villers (Newman, *Send Me God*, Preface, p. xxxiii). He wrote the lives of Ida of Nivelles and Abundus of Huy, discussed below.

60. This pattern is established in James of Vitry's life of Mary of Oignies. See *Vita B. Mariae Oigniacensis* 8.5.75, *AA SS*, June, 5:563–64, trans. pp. 101–2. On female saints and illness, see Caroline Bynum, "The Female Body and Religious Practice in the Later Middle Ages," in *Fragmentation and Redemption: Essays on Gender and the Human Body in Medieval Religion* (New York: Zone Books, 1991), pp. 181–238.

61. Dyan Elliott, "The Physiology of Rapture and Female Spirituality," in *Medieval Theology and the Natural Body*, ed. Peter Biller and Alastair Minnis (Woodbridge, Suffolk: York Medieval Press in association with Boydell and Brewer, 1997), pp. 162–63.

62. *Vita Venerabilis Idae Lovaniensis* 1.3.13–14, 19, *AA SS*, April, 2:162–63, 163; also see 2.3.13, p. 174. Ida unsuccessfully attempted to hide the stigmata. She then prayed to God to make them invisible. She nevertheless retained the pain (ibid., 1.3.15–16, p. 163). Ida's anonymous vita was probably based on notes left by her confessor. See Simons, "Beguines," *MHW*, pp. 641–42 and n56.

63. For instance, oil flowed from the breasts of Christina Mirabilis, and she used it to smear on her bread and wounds (Thomas of Cantimpré, *Vita S. Christinae Mirabilis virginis* 2.19, *AA SS*, July, 5:654, trans. Margot King and Barbara Newman, *Thomas of Cantimpré: The Collected Saints' Lives* [Turnhout: Brepols, 2008], p. 138). On miraculous lactations, see Bynum, *Holy Feast*, pp. 273–75.

64. Bynum, *Holy Feast*, esp. pp. 245–76. See the summary of supernatural affects that were especially characteristic of women in Bynum, "Female Body," in *Fragmentation and Redemption*, p. 194.

65. On the relationship between Beguine spirituality and Cistercian spirituality, see Simone Roisin, "L'efflorescence cistercienne et le courant féminin de piété au XIIIe siècle," *Revue d'histoire ecclésiastique* 39 (1943): 342–78; Roisin, *L'hagiographie cistercienne dans la diocèse de Liège au XIIIe siècle* (Louvain: Bibliothèque de l'Université, 1947). For James of Vitry's conflation of Cistercian and Beguine values, see Herbert Grundmann, *Religious Movements in the Middle Ages*, trans. Steven Rowan (Notre Dame, Ind.: University of Notre Dame Press, 1995), pp. 82–83; McDonnell, *Beguines and Beghards in Medieval Culture*, pp. 320–40. Ida of Louvain lived in a Beguine milieu both before and after becoming a Cistercian nun (Hugh of Louvain, *Vita Venerabilis Idae Lovaniensis* 1.5.27, 1.7.39, 2.2.6, *AA SS*, April, 2:165, 169, 172). The traditional historiographic view is that the Cistercians soon vigorously attempted to distance themselves from women, refusing female branches in the

early thirteenth century. See, for example, Grundmann, *Religious Movements*, pp. 91–92; Sally Thompson, "The Problem of Cistercian Nuns in the Twelfth and Early Thirteenth Centuries," in *Medieval Women*, ed. Derek Baker (Oxford: Basil Blackwell, 1978), pp. 227–52. For a revision of this view, see Constance Berman, *The Cistercian Evolution: The Reinvention of the Order in Twelfth-Century Europe* (Philadelphia: University of Pennsylvania Press, 2000), pp. 39–45.

66. James of Vitry, *Vita B. Mariae Oigniacensis* 2.8.90, *AA SS*, June, 5:567, trans. p. 113. Cf. the devotion of Juliana of Mont-Cornillon in *Vita de B. Juliana virgine priorissa Montis-Cornelii apud Leodium* 1.6, *AA SS*, April, 1:444, trans. Barbara Newman, *The Life of Juliana Mont-Cornillon* (Toronto: Peregrina, 1991), pp. 33–34; and Mechtild of Hackeborn, in *LSG* 1.28, pp. 97–98. Book 1 of Gertrude the Great's *The Herald*, which contextualizes Gertrude and her revelations and was probably written by another nun at Helfta, takes particular pains to align Gertrude's life and revelations with the authority of Bernard (*Le Héraut* 1.5.1, 1.6.1, 1.9.1, 1.11.5, in *Oeuvres spirituelles*, *SC*, 127, 2:146, 150, 160, 174, trans. pp. 61–62, 63, 66, 72).

67. See Caroline Bynum, "'...And Woman His Humanity': Female Imagery in the Religious Writing of the Later Middle Ages," in *Fragmentation and Redemption*, pp. 151–79; Matter, *Voice of My Beloved*, pp. 137–38.

68. On nuptial imagery, see Roisin, *L'hagiographie cistercienne*, pp. 111–12, 115–17.

69. Bernard of Clairvaux, *Liber de diligendo Deo* 10.28, in *L'Amour de Dieu: La Grâce et le libre arbitre*, ed. Jean Leclercq et al., *SC*, 393 (Paris: Editions du Cerf, 1993), p. 132, trans. Robert Walton with an analytical commentary by Emergo Stiegman, *On Loving God* (Kalamazoo, Mich.: Cistercian Publications, 1995), p. 30.

70. Thomas of Cantimpré, *Vita S. Lutgardis virginis Cisterciensis* 2.43, *AA SS*, June, 4:204, trans. Newman and King, in *Thomas of Cantimpré*, p. 272; *Vita B. Idae Lewensis* 5.48, *AA SS*, October, 13:121. Ida was from a noble family that held the village of Gorsleeuw. Her vita was written by an anonymous Cistercian who, not knowing her personally, relied on interviews with her friends (Simons, "Beguines," *MHW*, p. 641 and n54). In the life of Beatrice of Nazareth, her anonymous hagiographer uses a parallel image of a drop of water uniting with the sea in his translation of her work (*Seven Manieren van Minne*, in *The Life of Beatrice of Nazareth*, ed. and trans. Roger De Ganck [Kalamazoo, Mich.: Cistercian Publications, 1991], pp. 304–5, left columns). Also see Mechtild of Habeborn's usage in *LSG*, 2.17, p. 152.

71. See Robert Lerner, "The Image of Mixed Liquid in Late Medieval Mystical Thought," *Church History* 40 (1971): 397–411.

72. Martha Newman, "Crucified by Virtues: Monks, Lay Brothers, and Women in Thirteenth-Century Cistercian Saints' Lives," in *Gender and Difference in the Middle Ages*, ed. Sharon Farmer and Carol Braun Pasternack (Minneapolis: University of Minnesota Press, 2003), pp. 182–209. Occasionally, this was also a point of identification for male mystics. See Carolyn Muir's discussion of Henry Suso in "Bride or Bridegroom? Masculine Identity in Mystic Marriages," in *Holiness and Masculinity in the Middle Ages*, ed. P. H. Cullum and Katherine Lewis (Cardiff: University of Wales, 2004), pp. 58–78.

73. See John Coakley's formulation of the clergy trading sacerdotal power for saintly

charisma in "Friars as Confidants of Holy Women in Medieval Dominican Hagiography," *Images of Sainthood in the Later Middle Ages*, ed. Renate Blumenfeld-Kosinski and Timea Szell (Ithaca, N.Y.: Cornell University Press, 1991), pp. 222–46.

74. The potential dangers of this scenario are compounded by what Claire Waters describes as the necessary "doubleness" of the clergy whereby the priest is personally fallible as a man but vocationally God-like (*Angels and Earthly Creatures: Preaching, Performance, and Gender in the Later Middle Ages* [Philadelphia: University of Pennsylvania Press, 2004], pp. 31–56).

75. James appeals to Mary as a mother when he finds himself in a tight place while traveling with his baggage train at risk. See Ep. 1, in *Lettres de Jacques de Vitry*, ed. R. B. C. Huygens (Leiden: E. J. Brill, 1960), p. 72. See John Coakley's discussion of the relationship between Mary and James in *Women, Men, and Spiritual Power: Female Saints and Their Male Collaborators* (New York: Columbia University Press, 2006), pp. 68–88.

76. *Vita B. Mariae Oigniacensis* prol., c. 3, *AA SS*, June, 5:547, trans. pp. 42–43.

77. Despite their implication in more worldly marriages, James nevertheless goes on to commend "holy matrons serving the Lord devoutly in marriage ... keeping honourable nuptials and 'an undefiled wedding bed'" (*Vita B. Mariae Oigniacensis* prol., c. 3, *AA SS*, June, 5:547–48, trans. p. 43).

78. James of Vitry, *Vita B. Mariae Oigniacensis* prol., c. 6, 7, 8, *AA SS*, June, 5:548, trans. pp. 45, 46 (bis), 48.

79. Ibid. 2.2.48, *AA SS*, June, 5:558, trans. pp. 83–84.

80. Ibid. 2.6.77, *AA SS*, June, 5:264, trans. p. 103.

81. Ibid. 2.8.87, *AA SS*, June, 5:566, trans. p. 110.

82. Ibid. 2.10.95, *AA SS*, June, 5:568–69, trans. p. 117.

83. Ibid. 2.13.107, 2.11.98, *AA SS*, June, 5:571, 569, trans. pp. 125, 119. On the song as a reclamation of female speech in the church, see Carolyn Muessig, "Prophecy and Song: Teaching and Preaching by Medieval Women," in *Women Preachers and Prophets through Two Millennia of Christianity*, ed. Beverly Kienzle and Pamela Walker (Berkeley: University of California Press, 1998), pp. 146–59. Also see Bruce Holsinger's discussion of the song as James's theological instantiation of the new somatic spirituality he was attempting to promote in *Music, Body, and Desire in Medieval Cultur : Hildegard of Bingen to Chaucer* (Stanford, Calif.: Stanford University Press, 2001), pp. 216–19. On James's tendency to downplay Mary's "magisterial" revelations, see Coakley's discussion of Mary's song in *Women, Men, and Spiritual Power*, pp. 74–75. For other bridal imagery, see James of Vitry, *Vita B. Mariae Oigniacensis* 1.4.15, 2.3.52, 2.4.57, *AA SS*, June, 5:550, 559 (mislabeled in the edition as 557), 560, trans. pp. 56, 88, 91.

84. For glimpses of Lutgard's role as spiritual director, see Thomas of Cantimpré, *Vita S. Lutgardis virginis Cisterciensis* 2.2.32, 2.3.38, *AA SS*, June, 4:202, 202–3, trans. pp. 262, 266. Also see Jean-Baptiste Lefevre, "Sainte Lutgarde en son temps (1182–1246)," *Collectanea Cisterciensa* 58 (1996): 277–35, esp. pp. 288–91.

85. Thomas of Cantimpré, *Vita S. Lutgardis virginis Cisterciensis* 2.3.42, 43, *AA SS*, June, 4:203, 203–4, trans. pp. 269, 270 (bis); also ibid. 3.2.9, p. 206, trans. pp. 282–83. Barbara Newman notes that Lutgard's spirituality is more passion-oriented than nuptial, which

could explain Thomas's less than stellar performance with this image. See her introduction to *Thomas of Cantimpré: The Collected Saints Lives*, p. 48.

86. *Vita B. Idae Lewensis* 2.13, *AA SS*, October, 13:112.

87. *Vita de B. Juliana virgine priorissa Montis-Cornelii apud Leodium* 5.26, *AA SS*, April, 1:451, trans. p. 59. Juliana's religious status is impossible to pinpoint because external circumstances interrupted her vocation at every turn. At different times she was a Beguine, a nun of a couple of different persuasions, and a recluse. See Barbara Newman's introduction to her vita, pp. 14–16. Also see Mulder-Bakker's discussion of her life and her efforts to institute the feast of Corpus Christi in *Lives of the Anchoresses*, pp. 78–117.

88. See Sarah Salih's astute discussion of some of the difficulty inherent in interpreting erotic discourse in "When Is a Bosom Not a Bosom? Problems with 'Erotic Mysticism,'" in *Medieval Virginities*, ed. Anke Bernau, Ruth Evans, and Sarah Salih (Toronto: University of Toronto Press, 2003), pp. 14–32.

89. Alaistair Minnis, *Medieval Theory of Authorship*, 2nd ed. (Philadelphia: University of Pennsylvania Press, 1988), p. 5.

90. Hugh of Louvain, *Vita Venerabilis Idae Lovaniensis* 1.5.28, 1.4.23, *AA SS*, April, 2:166, 164–65.

91. Goswin of Villers, *Vita beatae Idae de Niuelle sanctimonialis in monasterio de Rameya* cc. 20, 22, ed. Chrysostom Henriquez, pp. 248, 254–55, trans. pp. 61, 65.

92. Hugh of Louvain, *Vita Venerabilis Idae Lovaniensis* 2.3.11, *AA SS*, April, 2:174.

93. Thomas of Cantimpré, *Vita S. Lutgardis virginis Cisterciensis* 1.1.13, *AA SS*, June, 4:193, trans. pp. 228–29.

94. Thomas of Cantimpré, *De apibus* 2.49.2, p. 442.

95. See Elliott, *Proving Woman*, pp. 54–57.

96. Thomas of Cantimpré, *Vita S. Lutgardis virginis Cisterciensis* 1.1.2, *AA SS*, June, 4:192, trans. p. 218. On Lutgard's relations with Christ, see Lefevre, "Sainte Lutgarde," pp. 298–301. This story (or one very much like this) will be retold in Thomas's later *De apibus*. See pp. 211–12, below.

97. Thomas of Cantimpré, *Vita Margarete de Ypris* c. 25, 119, trans. p. 186.

98. *The Life of Beatrice of Nazareth* 1.76, ed. De Ganck , pp. 98–101. For other instances of spousal imagery and evocations of the Canticles, see 1.73, 74, 76; 2.196, 197; 3.203, 204, 205, 207; pp. 92–93, 94–95, 96–99, 228–29 (bis), 234–35, 236–37 (bis), 240–41 and the following note. The testimony of Beatrice's life is especially valuable because it is based on an autobiography that has since been lost. De Ganck speculates that the autobiography may have been destroyed lest some of the more arcane aspects of Beatrice's mysticism arouse the suspicions of the authorities (*Life of Beatrice of Nazareth*, introduction, pp. xxvii–xxxii). The anonymous author describes his method of interweaving his own work with the original autobiography (ibid. 3.275–76, pp. 342–45). At certain junctures Beatrice's original work can be discerned, however. Of particular significance is the short mystical text that Beatrice wrote titled *The Love of God and Its Seven Degrees*, which was incorporated into the third book of the vita. In the freestanding vernacular version of the original treatise, which is still extant, the spousal imagery is reserved only for the most elevated stages of love. (De Ganck edits the two versions side by side. See the Latinized translation of the Flemish vernacular

version in the right column in *Seven Manieren van Minne*, in *Life of Beatrice of Nazareth*, pp. 312–15, 327, 331.) Some spousal imagery is also introduced to the treatise in the version given in the vita (*Life of Beatrice of Nazareth* 3.249, 256, pp. 295, 311). On the possible superimposition of somatic spirituality on Beatrice, see n58, above.

99. Goswin of Villers, *Vita beatae Idae de Niuelle* c. 8, in *Quinque prudentes virgines*, ed. Henriquez, p. 221, trans. p. 43; cf. c. 28, p. 271, trans. p. 77. Ida is represented as experiencing the kind of eucharistic devotion frequently associated with Beguine spirituality. See Bynum, *Holy Feast*, pp. 115–29.

100. Goswin of Villers, *Vita beatae Idae de Niuelle* c. 26, in *Quinque prudentes virgines*, ed. Henriquez, p. 265, trans. pp. 72–73.

101. Ibid. c. 27, in *Quinque prudentes virgines*, ed. Henriquez, p. 267, trans. pp. 74–75.

102. Hugh of Louvain, *Vita Venerabilis Idae Lovaniensis* 1.7.42–43, *AA SS*, April, 2:169–70.

103. James of Vitry, *Vita B. Mariae Oigniacensis* 1.2.20, *AA SS*, June, 5:551, trans. p. 59.

104. Ibid. 2.8.75, *AA SS*, June, 5:564, trans. p. 102.

105. James of Vitry, Serm. 29, To White and Grey Nuns," *Sermones vulgares*, in *Analecta Novissima Spicilegii Solesmensis: Altera continuatio, Tusculana*, vol. 2, ed. J. B. Pitra (Paris: Roger and Chernowitz, 1888), p. 385.

106. See the exemplum concerning the pious matron who frequented the church where she spoke to a certain monk about God, at least initially (James of Vitry, *Exempla or Illustrative Stories from the Sermones Vulgares of Jacques de Vitry*, ed. Thomas Frederick Crane, Folk-Lore Society Publications, 26 [London: Folklore Society, 1878], no. 282, pp. 117–19).

107. On Thomas's life, see Barbara Newman's biographical essay for the introduction of *Thomas of Cantimpré: The Collected Saints' Lives* (pp. 4–11) as well as the chronological time chart for his life (pp. 1–2). Also see R. Godding, "Vie apostolique et société urbaine à l'aube du XIIIe siècle: Une oeuvre inéditee de Thomas de Cantimpré," *Nouvelle Revue Théologie* 104 (1982): 692–95. For Thomas as a hagiographer of holy women, see John Coakley, "Thomas of Cantimpré and Female Sanctity," in *History in the Comic Mode: Medieval Communities and the Matter of Person*, ed. Rachel Fulton and Bruce Holsinger (New York: Columbia University Press, 2007), pp. 44–55; and Simone Roisin, "La méthode hagiographique de Thomas de Cantimpré," in *Miscellanea Historica in Honorem Albert de Meyer* (Louvain: Bibliothèque de l'Université, 1946), 1:546–57.

108. On John's ministry, see Godding, "Vie apostolique et société urbaine à l'aube du XIIIe siècle," pp. 705–18. Thomas mentions his age in the prologue, which was added later (Thomas of Cantimpré, *Vita Ioannis Cantipratensis*, in "Une Oeuvre inédite de Thomas de Cantimpré: La '"Vita Ioannis Cantipratensis,'" *Revue d'histoire ecclésiastique* 76 [1981]:257, trans. Newman, *Thomas of Cantimpré*, p. 57).

109. Thomas of Cantimpré, *Vita Ioannis Cantipratensis* 1.12, p. 266, trans. p. 67.

110. Ibid.

111. Ibid. 2.3, p. 280, trans. p. 82.

112. Ibid. 3.2, pp. 309–10, trans. 114–15.

113. Ibid. 3.3,4, pp. 312, 312–13, trans. pp. 116–17, 118. Also see the time when he

encouraged her to obey the summons of her husband, Baldwin, who had just been crowned emperor over the conquered Byzantine Empire during the fourth crusade. Unfortunately, he died before she reached him (ibid. 3.5, p. 314, trans. pp. 119–20).

114. Ibid. 2.6, 2.21, 2.18, pp. 221–22, 304, 301, trans. pp. 84–85, 106–7, 103–4.

115. Ibid. 3.8 (bis), p. 291, trans. p. 93.

116. Thomas of Cantimpré, *Supplementum ad vitam S. Mariae Oigniacensis* prol., *AA SS*, June, 5:572, trans. Hugh Feiss, *Mary of Oignies: Mother of Salvation*, ed. Anneke Mulder-Bakker (Turnhout: Brepols, 2007), p. 137.

117. Thomas of Cantimpré, *Supplementum* 1.2, *AA SS*, June, 5:573, trans. p. 141. See James of Vitry, *Vita B. Mariae Oigniacensis* 2.6.69, 2.12.101, *AA SS*, June, 5:562–63, 570, trans. pp. 99, 121. According to James, Mary also revealed all the preacher's temptations and sins on her deathbed, so that the prior later said, "Have you told lady Mary your sins? While she was singing she told your sins as if she had seen them written plainly in a book." Clearly prophetic insight was not constrained by anything like a seal of confession. Coakley perceives the position of James as Mary's preacher in terms of a role reversal (*Women, Men, and Spiritual Power*, pp. 80, 83–85, 86).

118. Thomas of Cantimpré, *Supplementum* 1.3, *AA SS*, June, 5:573–74, trans. pp.141–42.

119. Ibid. 4.20, *AA SS*, June, 5:578–59, trans. p. 158.

120. Ibid. 4.21, *AA SS*, June, 5:579, trans. pp. 158–59. James also appealed to Mary when he was at risk of losing his baggage train. See n75, above.

121. Thomas of Cantimpré, *Supplementum* 4.22–23, *AA SS*, June, 5:579, trans. pp. 160–61. The terms in which James rejects Mary's warnings are both dismissive and intimate. When the prior tells James that he had a vision of Mary in which she stated her opposition, James laughed and said, " 'Lady Mary said the same thing to me. I am not moved by such things.' "

122. Ibid. 3.15–17, *AA SS*, June, 5:577–78, trans. pp. 153–56.

123. Ibid. 4.24–27, *AA SS*, June, 5:579–81, trans. pp. 161–65.

124. Ibid. 4.27, *AA SS*, June, 5:851, trans. p. 164.

125. Thomas of Cantimpré, *Vita S. Christinae* 1.5, 5.52–53, *AA SS*, June, 5:651, 659, trans. pp. 130, 153–54. Note that Christina does have raptures, however (ibid. 3.35–36, *AA SS*, 5:656, trans. pp. 145–46). See Margot King's astute discussion of Christina's profoundly literal and embodied spirituality as a kind of "living sermon" in "The Sacramental Witness of Christina Mirabilis: The Mystic Growth of a Fool for Christ's Sake," in *Peaceweavers*, vol. 2 of *Medieval Religious Women*, ed. Lillian Shank and John Nichols (Kalamazoo, Mich.: Cistercian Publications, 1987), pp. 145–64. For the different ways a medieval and modern audience might interpret Christina, see Barbara Newman, "Possessed by the Spirit: Devout Women, Demoniacs, and the Apostolic Life in the Thirteenth Century," *Speculum* 73 (1998): 733–70.

126. Thomas of Cantimpré, *Vita S. Christinae* 4.41–45, *AA SS*, July, 5:657–58, trans. pp. 148–50. Christina's mission on behalf of souls in purgatory is the main thing she has in common with other Beguine lives. See Newman, *From Virile Woman to WomanChrist*, pp. 109ff.; Elliott *Proving Woman*, pp. 74–84, esp. 74–75.

127. *Vita S. Christinae* 1.11, 1.12, 2.15, 2.16, 1.9, 2.19, July, 5:652 (bis), 653 (bis), 653–54,

652, trans. pp. 133–34, 134, 136 (bis), 132, 138. Who could doubt but that such a bizarre life was destined to be immensely popular? Apparently twelve manuscripts of Thomas's Latin vita are extant, as well as translations into Middle English and Middle Dutch. See Newman's introduction to *Thomas of Cantimpré: The Collected Saints' Lives*, p. 8.

128. See Michèle Mulchahey, *"First the Bow Is Bent in Study . . .": Dominican Education before 1350* (Toronto: Pontifical Institute of Mediaeval Studies, 1998), esp. ch. 4. Mulchahey sees Thomas's *On the Nature of Things* as one of the first of the encyclopedias of the period. She also notes not only how this genre complemented preaching but also that Thomas wrote with a lay audience in mind. There were translations in the vernacular in his lifetime (p. 466).

129. *Vita Margarete* prol., p. 106, trans. p. 163.

130. This insecurity is still apparent toward the end of his life. In his introductory letter to the life of John of Cantimpré, which he had more or less written when he was twenty-three but only put the finishing touches on sometime between 1263 and his death in 1270, Thomas makes the appeal that upon his death that they offer the same commemorative rites appropriate to a member of their order : "for even though I am now a friar of a different order, yet I lived among you as your brother without scandal or hatred, as I trust, for fifteen years or more" (*Vita Ioannis Cantipratensis* prol., p. 258, trans. p. 58).

131. Thomas of Cantimpré, *Vita Margarete* prol., p. 106, trans. p. 163.

132. See Margot King's introduction to her original translation of Thomas's *Life of Margaret of Ypres* (Toronto: Peregrina, 1990), pp. 16–17; Alexandra Barratt, "Undutiful Daughters and Metaphorical Mothers among the Beguines," in *New Trends in Feminine Spirituality*, pp. 83–86; and Barbara Newman's introduction in *Thomas of Cantimpré: The Collected Saints' Lives*, pp. 37–39.

133. Thomas of Cantimpé, *Vita Margarete* prol., p. 107 (bis), trans. pp. 163, 164.

134. Ibid. cc. 6, 7, pp. 109, 109–10, trans. p. 169 (bis).

135. Ibid. c. 8, p. 110, trans. p. 170.

136. Ibid. c. 9, p. 110, trans. p. 171.

137. Ibid. c. 27, pp. 119–20, trans. pp. 187–88.

138. Ibid. c. 9, p. 110, trans. p. 171; cf. ibid. c. 8, p. 110, trans. p. 170.

139. Ibid. c. 10, pp. 110–11, trans. pp. 171–72.

140. Ibid. c. 12, p. 112, trans. p. 174.

141. Ibid. c. 24, p. 119, trans. p. 186.

142. Ibid. c. 25, p. 119, trans. pp. 186–87.

143. Ibid. c. 34, pp. 122–23, trans. pp. 193–94.

144. On the basilisk, see Albert the Great, *De animalibus* 25.2.13, 2:1561–62. Even younger women had considerable power to do damage. Albert the Great compares the basilisk's lethal gaze to a menstruating woman, whose glance can discolor a mirror (ibid. 7.2.5, 1:553). See Elliott, *Fallen Bodies*, pp. 155, 264n156. Also note, however, that women who retain more seed when menstruating also have more of a desire for sex. Thus menopause could also make a woman sexually voracious (Albert the Great, *De animalibus* 18.2.4, 2:1228).

145. Thomas's excursus into optics demonstrates that science and sanctity were not

necessarily discreet categories and that science could be used to clarify the boundaries between the natural and the supernatural. He was hardly alone in this endeavor. Over the course of the thirteenth century, the papacy was progressively applying a parallel scientific rigor to miraculous cures (Francis Antonelli, *De inquisitione medico-legali super miraculis in causis beatificationis et canonizationis* [Rome: Pontificium Athenaeum Antonianum, 1961], pp. 22–30). Also see the later inquiry into the miracles of St. Thomas of Cantilupe (d. 1282) edited in Appendix 1 of André Vauchez, *Sainthood in the Later Middle Ages*, trans. Jean Birrell (Cambridge: Cambridge University Press, 1997), pp. 540–58.

146. Thomas of Cantimpé, *Vita Margarete* cc. 40–50, pp. 124–28, trans. pp. 197–203; note that she had also been ill earlier, though the nature of the affliction is not mentioned (ibid. c. 14, p. 113, trans. pp. 175–76).

147. Ibid. c. 9, p. 110, trans. p. 171.

148. Furthermore, if the retention of seed made an older woman's gaze similar to the basilisk, who is to say that in a younger woman such a condition might not make her eyes function like a lynx?

149. Thomas of Cantimpré, *Liber de natura rerum* 2.13 (Berlin: W. de Gruyter, 1973), 1:92–93.

150. William Durandus, *De benedictione et consecratione virginum* c. 51, in *Le Pontifical de Guillaume Durand*, ed. Andrieu, 3:421; *Passio Agnetis*, AA SS, January, 2:714–18. See Chapter 2, p. 50, and Chapter 4, p. 145, above. Cf. Lefevre, "Sainte Lutgarde," pp. 303–4.

151. Thomas of Cantimpé, *Vita Margarete* c. 55, p. 129, trans. p. 205. Cf. the monk who came back from the dead and described the soul as "a glassy spherical vessel … [with] eyes both before and behind" (Caesarius of Heisterbach, *Dialogus miraculorum* 1.32, ed. Joseph Strange [Cologne: J. M. Heberle, 1851], 1:39, trans. H. Von E. Scott and C. C. Swinton Bland, *The Dialogue on Miracles* [London: Routledge, 1929], 1:42; hereafter cited as Caesarius).

152. As cited by McGinn, *Flowering of Mysticism*, p. 221. This reference appears in Hadewijch's "list of the perfect" that follows her visions in the manuscript. On Hadewijch, see ibid., pp. 200–222. It is unclear whether Hadewijch was arrested by the inquisition. See Columba Hart's introduction in *Hadewijch: The Complete Works*, p. 22. Newman discusses the strange anomaly that the anonymous knight errant in one of Hadewijch's visions may well be Abelard, and the possible affinity she felt for his persecutions in *From Virile Woman to WomanChrist*, pp. 168–71. See *Hadewijch: The Complete Works* vis. 8, ll. 109–12, p. 284.

153. On Robert's career, see Charles Homer Haskins, "Robert le Bougre and the Beginnings of the Inquisition in Northern France," in *Studies in Mediaeval Culture* (Oxford: Clarendon Press, 1929), pp. 193–244; Henry Charles Lea, *A History of the Inquisition of the Middle Ages* (New York: Macmillan, 1906), 2:113–17. I discuss this incident in *Proving Woman*, p. 229.

154. Thomas of Cantimpré, *Vita Margarete* c. 6, p. 109, trans. p. 168.

155. Thomas of Cantimpré, *De apibus* 2.30.48, p. 354.

156. For Thomas's account of the purge in Cambrai, see ibid. 2.57.68, pp. 592–93.

157. Roisin, "La méthode hagiographique," p. 549; cf. Coakley, "Thomas of Cantimpré and Female Sanctity," p. 50.

158. Both spurned carnal marriage in favor of its spiritual counterpart, and Lutgard, like Margaret before her, is compared to Agnes (Thomas of Cantimpré, *Vita S. Lutgardis virginis Cisterciensis* 1.1.3, *AA SS*, June, 4:192, trans. p. 219). Both Margaret and Lutgard also suffer from spontaneous issues of blood. When Lutgard was actually wishing that she could experience martyrdom like Agnes, a sudden hemorrhage in her breast covers her with blood. The visionary Christ explains that this signified the fulfillment of her wish for martyrdom. Moreover, this experience coincides with Lutgard's early menopause (ibid. 2.2.21, *AA SS*, June, 4:200, trans. p. 255). As discussed above, it is possible that Margaret would represent something of a martyr in the eyes of Thomas if he believed that there was a connection between her virginity and her illness. On Beguines as living martyrs, see Elliott, *Proving Woman*, pp. 58–74.

159. Coakley, "Thomas of Cantimpré and Female Sanctity," pp. 47, 49, 50, 51.

160. On the reserved sin, see Mary Mansfield, *The Humiliation of Sinners: Public Penance in Thirteenth-Century France* (Ithaca, N.Y.: Cornell University Press, 1995), pp. 81–84.

161. He does admit, however, that he has "often been unbearably tempted at other times" (Thomas of Cantimpré, *Vita S. Lutgardis virginis Cisterciensis* 2.3.38, *AA SS*, June, 4:202–3, trans. pp. 266–67).

162. Thomas of Cantimpré, *Vita S. Lutgardis virginis Cisterciensis* 2.1.3, 3.1.5, *AA SS*, June, 4:196–97, 205, trans. pp. 241, 277. This is also the same amount of time that Mary sang her mysterious song on her deathbed. One wonders if there is any connection.

163. Thomas of Cantimpré, *Vita S. Lutgardis virginis Cisterciensis* 1.2.21, *AA SS*, June, 4:195, trans. pp. 235–36. Cf. the parallel advice of how an anchoress should respond to an importunate cleric desiring to see her face in *Ancrene Wisse* c. 2, *Anchoritic Spirituality: Ancrene Wisse and Associated Works* (New York: Paulist, 1991), pp. 82–84.

164. Note, however, that book 2 of Gregory the Great's *Dialogues* is a sustained account of Benedict's life.

165. Thomas of Cantimpré, *De apibus* 2.32.5, 2.33.4, pp. 369, 372. The latter anecdote could either refer to Mary of Oignies (Thomas of Cantimpré, *Supplementum* 3.18, *AA SS*, June, 5:578, trans. p. 156) or Christina Mirabilis (Thomas of Cantimpré, *Vita S. Christinae* 2.35, *AA SS*, July, 5:656, trans. pp. 145–46). On Thomas's depiction of Christina's quasi-musical spirituality, see Holsinger, *Music, Body, and Desire*, pp. 222–25. Also see the example above concerning the French woman who expired when she heard a preacher speaking about union with God.

166. Thomas of Cantimpré, *De apibus* 1.9.8, 2.52.4, 2.54.18, 2.57.14, pp. 40, 482–83, 529–30, 546.

167. *Book of Beasts: A Facsimile of MS. Bodley 764*, introduction by Christopher de Hamel (Oxford: Bodleian Library, 2009), fol. 89, trans. T. H. White, *A Book of Beasts* (New York: G. P. Putnam's Sons, 1954), pp. 153–59.

168. See Mulchahey, "*First the Bow Is Bent in Study*," p. 256.

169. Brenda Bolton, "*Mulieres sanctae*," in *Medieval Women*, ed. Susan Stuard (Philadelphia: University of Pennsylvania Press, 1976), pp. 151–52.

170. Humbert of Romans, *Epistola de tribus votis substantialibus religionis* 1.22, in *Opera de vita regulari*, ed. Joachim Joseph Berthier (Rome: A Befani, 1888), 1:15.

171. Ibid. 1.23, 1:15.

172. Ibid. 1.30, 1:19. Tanya Miller discusses this kind of clerical ambivalence to female spirituality in "What's in a Name? Clerical Representations of Parisian Beguines (1200–1328)," *Journal of Medieval History* 33 (2007): 60–86.

173. Humbert, *Epistola* 2.89, 1:279–83.

174. Ibid. 1:283.

175. Ibid. 1:285.

176. Thomas of Cantimpré, *De apibus* 2.30.19, p. 329.

177. Ibid. 2.30.20, p. 330. After pausing to speculate whether this was a miracle or if it could happen naturally, Thomas decides that it could be both (ibid. 2.30.21, p. 331).

178. Although a number from the series of exempla that follow are drawn from instances in the secular world, the commentary itself is especially concerned with relations between holy men and women (ibid. 2.30.23, p. 332). Humbert's signs are less sexually explicit, consisting of sight, touch, kisses and embraces, frequent speech, and laughter (*Epistola* 1.23, 1:15).

179. Thomas of Cantimpré, *Vita S. Lutgardis virginis Cisterciensis* 1.5, *AA SS*, June, 4:192, trans. p. 220.

180. Thomas's exoneration of the youth is unnerving—especially since *deflorare* might suggest rape, while *renuit stuprum* could also mean that the youth in question "turned away from" or "denied" the violation (*De apibus* 2.30.27, pp. 334–35). Cf. two instances, both bearing on the culpability of the eyes. A beautiful woman who successfully prays to become ugly so she will no longer be a source of temptation is reviled by her Dominican confessor for not taking her husband into account. He addresses her as "most wretched and stupid of women" (*miserrima et stultissima mulierum*). She prays to be returned to her usual appearance out of obedience to "my spiritual father, to whom I have committed myself with total devotion." But later on Thomas gives the puzzling example, attributed to Ambrose, of a young man of incredible beauty who, commendably, mutilates his face so he would not tempt women (ibid. 2.30.29, 35, pp. 336–37, 340–41). This apparent bias is in keeping with Dominican pastoral counsel, which requires the wife to remain sexually attractive to their husbands for the purpose of rendering the debt, lest the men be tempted to commit adultery. See Dyan Elliott, "Bernardino of Siena versus the Marriage Debt," in *Desire and Discipline: Sex and Sexuality in Premodern Europe*, ed. Jacqueline Murray and Konrad Eisenbichler (Toronto: University of Toronto Press, 1996), pp. 168–200.

181. Thomas of Cantimpré, *De apibus* 2.30.44, pp. 348–49. Cf. Humbert's similar evocation of this part of Augustine's rule in *Epistola* 2.89, 1:77. I discuss some of the following instances in "Women and Confession," pp. 42–44.

182. Thomas of Cantimpré, *De apibus* 2.30.45, pp. 349–51. Cf. Humbert of Romans, *Epistola* 2.89, 1:281–82.

183. Thomas of Cantimpré, *De apibus* 2.30.46, p. 351.

184. Ibid. 2.30.46, p. 352. Note that when he claims to speak as a bishop he means as someone who hears confessions on behalf of the bishop.

185. Ibid. 2.30.47, p. 353.

186. Ibid. 2.30.49, p. 394.

187. Ibid. 2.30.50, p. 354.

188. Ibid. 2.30.50, pp. 354–55. Cf. his commendation of the female penitent who does, in fact, punch a cleric and bloodies his nose (ibid. 2.30.51, p. 356).

189. Ibid. 2.30.54, p. 358.

190. Ibid. 2.30.42, pp. 346–47.

191. Ibid. 2.30.49, p. 394.

192. Ibid. 2.30.22, p. 332.

193. The group is called the "New Spirit" as opposed to the later "Free Spirit." A list of their errors remains that is attributed to Albert. See Wilhelm Preger, *Geschichte der deutschen Mystik im Mittelalter* (Leipzig: Dörffling und Franke, 1874), pp. 461–71; also printed in Joseph Hansen, ed., *Quellen und Untersuchungen zur Geschichte des Hexenwahns und der Hexenverfolgung im Mittelalter* (Bonn, 1901; reprt., Hildesheim: Georg Olms, 1963), 2:395–402. See esp. nos. 53, 54, pp. 465–66. The democratization of virginity is apparent in the claim that the mother of five remains a virgin (no. 97, p. 469). There is also a later anonymous compilation that seems to pertain to the same heresy with even more extreme claims. It is edited in C. Schmidt, "Actenstücke besonders zur Geschichte der Waldenser," *Zeitschrift für die historische Theologie* 22 (1852): 248–50. See Robert Lerner, *The Heresy of the Free Spirit in the Later Middle Ages* (Notre Dame, Ind.: University of Notre Dame Press, 1972), pp. 14–18.

194. Lerner, *Heresy of the Free Spirit*, p. 21.

195. The examiner was a former doctor who had since entered the order (Hugh of Louvain, *Vita Venerabilis Idae Lovaniensis* 2.4.16–17, *AA SS* April, 2:175). Ida at first refused to open her eyes until she was warned by Christ what conclusions would be drawn (ibid. 2.4.18, pp. 175–76). The life of Ida of Nivelles also draws attention to the slippage between carnal and spiritual love on multiple occasions (Goswin of Villers, *Vita beatae Idae de Ni-uelle* c. 6, 12, in *Quinque prudentes virgines*, ed. Henriquez, pp. 214–15, 230–31, trans. pp. 39–40, 48–49; also see Goswin's life of laybrother Abundus of Villers, ed. A. M. Frenken in "De Vita van Abundus van Hoei," c. 17, *Cîteaux* 10 [1959]: 29, trans. Cawley, *Send Me God*, p. 239).

196. *Vita B. Odiliae viduae Leodiensis* 1.15–18, *Analecta Bollandiana* 13 (1894): 221–25. Her life was written between 1241 and 1247.

197. For an analysis of Yvette's life stressing the development of her spirituality, see Mulder-Bakker, *Lives of the Anchoresses*, pp. 51–77. See Jennifer Carpenter's discussion of Yvette's conflicted experience of family life and how it continues to haunt her after she has left the world in "Juette of Huy, Recluse and Mother (1158–1228): Children and Mothering in the Saintly Life," in *Power of the Weak: Studies on Medieval Women*, ed. Jennifer Carpenter and Sally-Beth MacLean (Champagne: University of Illinois Press, 1995), pp. 57–93.

198. Hugh of Floreffe, *B. Juetta sive Jutta, vidua, recluse, Hui in Belgio* 22.62, *AA SS*, January, 2:158, trans. Jo McNamara, *The Life of Yvette* (Toronto: Peregrina, 1999), p. 84.

199. His masterstroke of seduction was to pretend a revelation from the Holy Spirit to the effect that she could only be saved if she removed to another place. Otherwise her reputation for virtue would lead to damnable pride. He convinced her to leave town with him (ibid. 24.73, 75, *AA SS*, January, 2:159, 159–60, trans. pp. 91, 92). Fortunately, she returned

safe and sound with her virginity intact because of the prayers of Yvette (ibid. 25.80, *AA SS*, January, 2:160, trans. p. 95). On the perils of female travel, see Katrien Heene, "Gender and Mobility in the Low Countries: Travelling Women in Thirteenth-Century Exempla and Saints' Lives," in *The Texture of Society*, pp. 31–49. Yvette was miraculously apprised when the local sacristan consummated his seduction of a woman in the church itself. She promptly summoned him to do penance (Hugh of Floreffe, *De B. Juetta* 26.81–82, *AA SS*, January, 2:160–61, trans. pp. 96–97).

200. When she was suddenly taken ill, the priest sent a mediatrix who convinced her not to make a valid confession to a third party, assuring her she would recover. Hence she died in mortal sin (Hugh of Floreffe, *De B. Juetta* 32.91, 92, *AA SS*, January, 2:162, trans. pp. 102, 103). This was revealed to Yvette, who called him to account (ibid. 32.93–94, trans. pp. 103–4). Only once do we find a woman taking any sexual initiative, and her efforts are rather oblique. A newly made monk was "ambushed by a certain young woman, hiding like a lion in her cave who had plotted familiar speech in secret." As a parting gift, she gave him a rich piece of cloth for making a monk's headdress—something worn under the cowl. He could not stop thinking about her until Yvette prophetically gleaned the presence of the headdress and told him to get rid of it (ibid. 35.97–98, *AA SS*, January, 2:163, trans. p. 107).

201. Cf. Barratt, "Undutiful Daughters and Metaphorical Mothers," pp. 82–83, 87. Katrien Heene mentions several of Thomas of Cantimpré's disparaging remarks, but ultimately exonerates him: "Thomas's attitude towards women has a very positive ring because he does not refer to women as men's inferiors but seems to approach and appreciate them as equal human beings," in "Hagiography and Gender: A Tentative Case-Study on Thomas of Cantimpré," in *"Scribere sanctorum gesta": Recueil d'études d'hagiographie médiévale offert à Guy Philippart*, ed. Etienne Renard et al. (Turnhout: Brepols, 2005), pp. 113–15, 121.

202. Thomas of Cantimpré, *Vita Ioannis Cantipratensis* 2.3, 3.2, pp. 280, 310, trans. pp. 82, 115.

203. *Vita Margarete* c. 27, 32, pp. 119–20, 121, trans. pp. 188, 191. Newman observes *Ancrene Wisse* also enlists the image about the clucking hen (*Thomas of Cantimpré: The Collected Saints' Lives*, p. 188n97).

204. Thomas of Cantimpré, *Vita S. Lutgardis virginis Cisterciensis* 2.2.21, *AA SS*, June, 4:200, trans. p. 256. Albert the Great also notes that asceticism can affect a woman's menstrual cycle. There are certain women who engage in fasts, vigils, and self-mortification who stop menstruating for many months at a time. In other words, even if this is not a supernatural gift, it is still a symbol of merit because it is rooted in ascetical practices (*De animalibus* 9.1.2, 1:682).

205. Thomas of Cantimpré, *Vita S. Lutgardis virginis Cisterciensis* 3.3.19, *AA SS*, June, 4:208, trans. p. 290.

206. Ibid. 1.1.2, *AA SS*, June, 4:192, trans. pp. 217–18.

207. Thomas of Cantimpré, *De apibus* 2.57.25, p. 556.

208. Thomas of Cantimpré, *Vita S. Lutgardis virginis Cisterciensis* 1.2.22, 2.2.1, *AA SS*, June, 4:195, 196, trans. pp. 236–8, 239.

209. See Newman's chronological time charts in *Thomas of Cantimpré: The Collected Saints' Lives*, pp. 1–2, 209–10.

210. On the Council of Vienne and the events leading up to it, see Lerner, *Heresy of the Free Spirit*, pp. 61–84. On the difficulties of discerning the origin of the anti-Beguine decrees and subsequent glosses, see Elizabeth Makowski, *"A Pernicious Sort of Woman": Quasi-Religious Women and Canon Lawyers in the Later Middle Ages* (Washington, D.C: Catholic University Press, 2005), pp. 23–50.

211. See, for example, James of Vitry's treatment of the "sacerdotissa" in *Exempla* no. 242, p. 101; see Elliott, *Fallen Bodies*, pp. 121–22; also see his attack on the Dominicans who revealed the temptations of religious women, hence breaking the seal of confession in *Exempla* no. 80, p. 36; Elliott, *Proving Woman*, p. 33.

212. James of Vitry, *Vita B. Mariae Oigniacensis* prol., c. 4, *AA SS*, June, 5:548, trans. p. 43; Thomas of Cantimpré, *Vita S. Lutgardis virginis Cisterciensis* 3.1.5, *AA SS*, June, 4:205, trans. p. 278. James's sermons also address the difficulty of the Beguine vocation. In addition to their detractors, he cites the pressures placed upon young women to marry, thus discouraging the pursuit of a religious vocation in the parental home (Brenda Bolton, "Thirteenth-Century Religious Women: Further Reflections on the Low Countries' 'Special Case,'" in *New Trends in Feminine Spirituality*, ed. Dor et al., pp. 141–42). On some of the Beguines' early detractors, see ibid., p. 143, and Renate Blumenfeld-Kosinski, "Satirical Views of the Beguines in Northern French Literature," in *New Trends in Feminine Spirituality*, ed. Dor et al., pp. 237–49.

213. On Nider's choice of title, see Werner Tschacher, *Der Formicarius des Johannes Nider von 1437/38: Studien zu den Anfängen der Europäischen Hexenverfolgungen im Spätmittelalter* (Aachen: Shaker, 2000), pp. 51–70, pp. 139–46. Nider's work is discussed in Chapter 7.

214. *Vita B. Idae Lewensis* 5.50, *AA SS*, October, 13:122.

215. For an overview, see E. Ann Matter, "Italian Holy Women: A Survey," *MHW*, pp. 529–55.

216. Although Clare of Assisi was not herself the recipient of the kind of mystical revelations described above, nevertheless she often employs nuptial imagery to describe the soul's relationship with Christ. But Clare's usage is more in the tradition of twelfth-century monastic authors like the Victorines than the heightened eroticism of the Beguines (see McGinn, *Flowering of Mysticism*, 3:66–69).

217. Gerardesca of Pisa did not even put up a good fight for her virginity. Although she was reluctant to marry, her parents insisted. An obedient daughter, "she did not deny her assent; rather was mute like a sheep being shorn" (*Vita S. Gerardeschae Pisanae* 1.1, *AA SS*, May, 7:162). The one feint toward mystical marriage in Humility's life was when a relative of Frederick II's sought her in marriage, and she answered that "she wanted Christ and no other." The youth graciously left her undisturbed. This did not stop the parents from marrying her off soon after to a nobleman from Faenza (*Vita S. Humilitatis Abbatissae* 1.3–4, *AA SS*, May, 5:208; cf. *Le Vite di Umilità da Faenza* cc. 8–9, ed. Adele Simonetti [Florence: Sismel, Edizioni del Galluzzo, 1997], p. 5). The Latin life was written between 1311 and 1322, probably by a Vallambrosan monk, while the Italian life was written ca. 1345 by yet another Vallambrosan monk, Silvestro Ardenti. The two lives are sufficiently similar that scholars postulate that both are based on a lost exemplar. See Catherine Mooney, "Authority and

Inspiration in the *Vitae* and Sermons of Humility of Faenza," in *Medieval Monastic Preaching*, ed. Carolyn Muessig (Leiden: Brill, 1998), pp. 124–25.

218. Giunta Bevignati, *Legenda de vita et miraculis beate Margarite de Cortona* 2.23, 33, 4.56, 69, 5.82,100, *AA SS*, February, 3:308, 310, 314, 317, 319, 324, and passim. Bevignati was Margaret's confessor.

219. *Umiltà da Faenza: Sermones; Le lezioni di una monacha*, ed. Adele Simonetti (Florence: Sismel, Edizione del Galluzzo, 2005). See Mooney, "Authority and Inspiration," pp. 133–41.

220. For references to the generic soul marriage (incidentally addressing an audience of "fratres"), see serm. 2.58, 2.65; 9.27, in *Umiltà da Faenza*, ed. Simonetti, pp. 40, 44, 226; the virginal nun as *sponsa Christi*, serm. 6.19–22, ibid., p. 126; John as the spouse of ecclesia, serm. 13.1, ibid., p. 290.

221. For Mary, see serm. 1.32; 2.67; 3.10, 17; 9.31, 36, 40, 42, 50, 55, 122, 127, 12.2, ibid., pp. 18, 44, 48, 52, 194 (bis), 196 (bis), 200, 202, 224, 226, 272.

222. Guy of Cortona, *Vita B. Humilianae de Cerchis* 1.6, *AA SS*, May, 4:387.

223. Ibid. 2.12, p. 389. Humiliana also felt the wound in Christ's side in her heart, which is compared to the bundle of myrrh between the breasts of the beloved (Sg 1.12).

224. Ibid. 4.30, May, 4:395. Humiliana never actually met this monk; she only knew of his reputation for holiness.

225. Ibid. 6.60, p. 400. She is also given a second crown for preserving the "faith of chastity" inviolate.

226. Conrad Castillerio, *Vita de B. Benevenuta Bojanis* 2.13–19, *AA SS*, October, 13:152–85.

227. Clare's profound identification with the passion, and repeated statement that she bore the crucifixion in her heart, ultimately led the sisters to perform an informal autopsy on her body, wherein resided physical vindication of her claim. See the life by the procurator for her canonization, Berengar of Saint Affrique, *La vita di S. Chiara da Montefalco scritta da Berengario di S. Africano* cc. 131–32, 141–50, ed. Michele Faloci-Pulignani, in *Archivio storico per le Marche e per l'Umbria* 2 (1885): 224–25, 232–37. During Clare's lifetime, it was repeatedly revealed to a certain Margaret that Clare bore the passion on her heart. Margaret, however, thought that this was metaphoric and did not bother to tell anyone until the revelation of the marvel had already occurred (ibid. c. 118, p. 216). Perhaps the best testimony to her spirituality is in her process, however. Regarding the revelation of the instruments of the passion in Clare's heart, see Enrico Menestò, ed., *Il processo di canonizzazione di Chiara da Montefalco* (Regione dell'Umbria: La Nuova Italia, 1984), esp. the responses to article 159 by Sister Johanna, witness 1, pp. 85–87; Sister Marina, witness 38, pp. 153–54; Sister Francescha, witness 67, p. 339. On Clare's spirituality, see Chiara Frugoni, "'Domine, in conspectu tuo omne desiderium meum': Visioni e immagini in Chiara da Montefalco," in *S. Chiara da Montefalco e il suo tempo*, ed. Claudio Leonardi and Enrico Menestò (Perugia: La Nuova Italia, 1985), pp. 154–74. On the possible impact of Beguine spirituality on Italian mystics such as Clare, see Romana Guarnieri, "La 'Vita' di Chiara da Montefalco e la pieta Brabantina del '200. Prime indagini su un'ipotesi di lavoro," in *S. Chiara da Montefalco e il suo tempo*, ed. Leonardi and Menestò, pp. 305–67. Also see

Katharine Park's discussion of the implications of the opening of Clare's body as precedential in medical terms in *The Secrets of Women: Gender, Generation, and the Origins of Human Dissection* (New York: Zone Books, 2006), pp. 39–76.

228. *La Legenda di Vanna da Orvieto* 3.8, 10.20, 11–13, ed. Emore Paoli and Luigi Ricci (Spoleto: Centro Italiano di Studi sull'Alto Medioevo, 1996), pp. 141, 157, 156–57, trans. Maiju Lehmijoki-Gardner, *Dominican Penitent Women*, ed. Maiju Lehmijoki-Gardner (New York: Paulist Press, 2005), pp. 65, 76, 75–76. This is in spite of the fact that imagistic opportunities abounded. There is an allusion to the holy drunkenness she suffered longing for her Christ. She was even cured of a bout of vomiting by a dram of celestial wine. Although extremely abstemious, Vanna nevertheless was round in figure because of the spiritually caloric celestial food, which tasted of honey. Yet none of this is ever woven into the familiar skein of the celestial wedding feast (ibid. 5.32, 6.2, 5.3, 6.16, pp. 147, 148, 143, 148–49, trans. pp. 68, 69, 66, 70). Vanna's vita was traditionally attributed to Giacomo Scalza de' Predicatori Scalza, who died around 1343. Recently, his authorship has been challenged, rendering the dating of Vanna's vita uncertain.

229. Ibid. 1.7, 4.8, pp. 140, 143, trans. pp. 63, 65–66.

230. Angela of Foligno, *Memoriale* c. 1, 8th step; c. 6, 4th supplementary step, in *Il Libro della Beata Angela da Foligno*, ed. Ludger Thier and Abele Calufetti (Grottaferrata, Rome: College of St. Bonaventure, 1985), pp. 136, 276, trans. Paul Lachance, *Angela of Foligno: Complete Works* (New York: Paulist Press, 1993), pp. 126, 175–76. Angela's revelations were coauthored with her confessor. See Catherine Mooney, "The Authorial Role of Brother A. in the Composition of Angela of Foligno's Revelations," in *Creative Women in Medieval and Early Modern Italy: A Religious and Artistic Renaissance*, ed. E. Ann Matter and John Coakley (Philadelphia: University of Pennsylvania Press, 1994), pp. 34–63.

231. Angela of Foligno, *Memoriale* c. 3, 1st supplementary step, p. 188, trans. p. 142.

232. See Guarnieri's discussion of the importation of Beguine spirituality into the life of Clare of Montefalco via James of Vitry's life of Mary of Oignies, in "La 'Vita' di Chiara da Montefalco e la pieta Brabantina del '200." In this instance, it was clearly the somatic spirituality and focus on Christ's passion that was formative, not the nuptial spirituality. Dante's *Divine Comedy* possibly provides further evidence of the impact of the Beguines. A certain Matelda, who appears in his *Purgatory* (canto 28), has frequently been identified with Mechtild of Hackeborn. This is entirely plausible. Soon after her death, Mechtild's work was translated into Italian as *La Laude di donna Matelda*. It was popular in Florence just around the time that Dante was finishing *Purgatory* (between 1314 and 1318 or 1319). See Gertrude Casanova's entry "St. Mechtilde," in the *Catholic Encyclopaedia* at http://www.newadvent.org/cathen/10105b.htm. I am grateful to Robert Lerner for pointing out the possible link between Mechtild and Dante's *Purgatory*.

233. On Catherine's life and spirituality, with a particular emphasis on her food asceticism, see Bynum, *Holy Feast*, pp. 165–80; Rudolph Bell, *Holy Anorexia* (Chicago: University of Chicago Press, 1985), ch. 1.

234. See F. Thomas Luongo, *The Saintly Politics of Catherine of Siena* (Ithaca, N.Y.: Cornell, 2006).

235. Raymond of Capua, *Vita S. Catharinae Senensis* 1.7.114–16, *AA SS*, April, 3:890–91,

trans. Conleth Kearns, *The Life of Catherine of Siena* (Wilmington, Del.: Michael Glazier, 1980), pp. 107–8. See Bynum, "'And Woman His Humanity': Female Imagery in the Religious Writing of the Later Middle Ages," in *Fragmentation and Redemption*, pp. 172–73. On the various influences on Catherine's mystical marriage and its representations, see Zarri, *Recinti*, pp. 288–311.

236. See Karen Scott, "Mystical Death, Bodily Death: Catherine of Siena and Raymond of Capua on the Mystic's Encounter with God," *Gendered Voices*, ed. Mooney, pp. 139, 152–53, 162; Coakley, *Women, Men, and Spiritual Power*, p. 178.

237. Catherine alludes to her ring in Ep. 39, *To Joanna, Queen of Naples*, in *Epistolario di Santa Caterina da Siena*, ed. Eugenio Dupré Theseider (Rome: R. Istituto storico italianio per il Medio Evo, 1940), 1:158, trans. Suzanne Noffke, *Letters of Catherine of Siena* (Binghamton, N.Y.: Medieval and Renaissance Texts and Studies, 1988), 1:128. On the significance of Catherine's devotion to the holy foreskin, see Bynum, *Holy Feast*, pp. 175, 176, 178.

238. Ep. 31, *To Raymond of Capua*, in *Epistolario di Santa Caterina*, 1:130–31, trans. 1:108–11. Daniel Bornstein analyzes this incident in terms of the burgeoning of spiritual kinship that was occurring in the wake of the Black Death in "Spiritual Kinship and Domestic Devotions," in *Gender and Society in Renaissance Italy*, ed. Judith Brown and Robert Davis (New York: Longman, 1998), p. 178. Cf. Luongo's reading in terms of Sienese politics in *Saintly Politics of Catherine of Siena*, pp. 98–102. On the nuptial implications of the wound in Christ's side, see ibid., pp. 103–16. Also see Scott, "Mystical Death, Bodily Death," p. 149; Coakley, *Women, Men, and Spiritual Power*, pp. 183–84.

239. Cf. the celebrated instance where Raymond of Capua reports that Catherine's face became that of a bearded man, merging with Christ (*Vita S. Catharinae Senensis* 1.9.90, *AA SS*, April, 3:884, trans. p. 82). Coakley also comments on Catherine's tendency to collapse the roles of priest and holy woman (*Women, Men, and Spiritual Power*, pp. 186, 183).

240. See G. Marcianese, *Narratione della nascita, vita, e morte della B. Lucia da Narni* cc. 4, 6 (Ferrara: V. Buldini, 1616), pp. 24–25, 32–34; cf. Luigi Jacobilli, *Vite de' santi e beati dell' Vmbria* (Foligno, 1647–61; reprt., Bologna: Forni, 1971), 3:33; Serafino Razzi, *Vite dei santi e beati così del sacro Ordine de' frati predicatori* (Florence: Bartolomeo Sermartelli, 1577), p. 180. Also note that Christ and Lucia address one another as spouse throughout her revelations, with the exception of the last one, which is a visionary dialogue between Lucia and her brother-in-law. See Chapter 7, n184, below. These revelations, written in Lucia's own hand in her last year of life, were only recently discovered. See the edition by E. Ann Matter, Armano Maggi, and Maiju Lehmijoki-Gardner, "'Le Rivelazioni' of Lucia Brocadelli da Narni," *Archivum Fratrum Praedicatorum* 71 (2001): 311–44, trans. E. Ann Matter, *Dominican Penitent Women*, ed. Maiju Lehmijoki-Gardner (New York: Paulist Press, 2005), pp. 212–43.

241. Judith Brown, *Immodest Acts: The Life of a Lesbian Nun in Renaissance Italy* (New York: Oxford University Press, 1986), pp. 67–72.

242. This does not hold true for Central Europe, however. Gábor Klaniczay posits that this was because that area had not been influenced by either mysticism or courtly

love. See *Holy Rulers and Blessed Princesses: Dynastic Cults in Central Europe* (Cambridge: Cambridge University Press, 2002), p. 272. One possible exception would be Elisabeth of Hungary (d. 1231), who grew up in Thuringia and so could possibly have been influenced by literary and spiritual currents. One of her ladies in waiting testified that after the death of her husband, when Elisabeth was indigent and living in a humble hostel, she had a vision in which the sky opened and Christ spoke to her. She answered, "So Lord: you want to be with me and I want to be with you and never separate from you" (*Der sog. Libellus de dictis quatuor ancillarum S. Elisabeth confectus*, ed. Albert Huyskens [Kempten: Jos. Kösel'schen, 1911], Ysentrud, pp. 122–23). Klaniczay is inclined to see this incident as part of the *sponsa Christi* tradition, but, if this is the case, the allusion is extremely subtle—so much so that Caesarius of Heisterbach does not take the opportunity to develop it in his official vita. See "Des Cäsarius von Heisterbach Schriften über die hl. Elisabeth von Thüringen," ed. Albert Huyskens, *Annalen des historischen Vereins für den Niederrhein* 86 (1908): 36. Any efforts to identify Elisabeth as Christ's bride comes from Gregory IX's bull of canonization. See Klaniczay, *Holy Rulers*, pp. 271–72. On Elisabeth and her holy lineage, see ibid., pp. 209–43; on her spirituality and her relationship with her confessor, see Elliott, *Proving Woman*, ch. 2.

243. On her life and revelations, see Claire Sahlin, *Birgitta of Sweden and the Voice of Prophecy* (Woodbridge, Suffolk: Boydell, 2001).

244. Luongo, *Saintly Politics of Catherine of Siena*, pp. 56–58. Luongo also suggests that Catherine may have deliberately looked to Bridget as a role model (p. 73).

245. *Vita b. Brigide prioris Petri et magistri*, in *Acta et processus canonizacionis Beate Birgitte*, ed. Isak Collijn (Uppsala: Almqvist and Wiksells, 1924–31), pp. 80–81; Bridget of Sweden, *Revelaciones Extravagantes* 47, ed. Lennart Hollman (Uppsala: Almqvist and Wiksells, 1956), pp. 62–63.

246. Bridget of Sweden, *Revelaciones* 4.20.12, ed. Hans Aili, pp. 117–18; Elliott, *Spiritual Marriage*, pp. 240–41.

247. See, for example, Bridget of Sweden, *Revelaciones* 1.7; 1.20.5, ed. Carl-Gustaf Undhagen, pp. 257–59, 294; ibid. 2.26, ed. Undhagen and Bergh, pp. 109–12. Certain distinctions were nevertheless observed. It is significant that when the visionary Christ apprised Bridget of her impending consecration as a nun in Rome, the term he used was *monacha*, not *sanctimonialis* (*Vita b. Brigide prioris Petri et magistri*, in *Acta et processus canonizacionis Beate Birgitte*, ed. Collijn, p. 101).

248. For an introduction to Margery's life, see Clarissa Atkinson, *Mystic and Pilgrim: The Book and the World of Margery Kempe* (Ithaca, N.Y.: Cornell University Press, 1983). Also see Anthony Goodman, "Margery Kempe," *MHW*, pp. 217–38.

249. That this abbreviation was not standard is suggested by the fact that when it first occurs, someone wrote "Brigytts" in the margin of the manuscript (*The Book of Margery Kempe* 1.17, ed. Barry Windeatt [Harlow, England: Longman, 2000], p. 115).

250. Ibid. 1.20, p. 129.

251. Ibid. 1.1, pp. 55–56.

252. Collijn, ed. *Acta et processus canonizacionis Beate Birgitte*, art. 23, pp. 20, 305, 505; *Vita b. Brigide prioris Petri et Magistri*, in ibid., pp. 79–80; Bridget of Sweden, *Revelaciones*

1, prol., cc. 14–15, p. 233 (by her first confessor, Master Matthias). See Elliott, *Spiritual Marriage*, pp. 245–46.

253. *Book of Margery Kempe* 1.11, pp. 186–90.

254. Margery did initially object that people would think she was a hypocrite, however (ibid. 1.15, pp. 102–3). As predicted, people did respond badly to Margery's garb. See, for example, the time when the mayor of Leicester accused her of attempting to separate wives from their husbands (ibid. 1.48, pp. 236–37).

255. Ibid. 1.31, p. 178. A nameless virgin in John Nider's *The Anthill* prayed to Christ for a ring and eventually found one in her garden (*Formicarium* 1.2 [Douai: Balthazaris Belleri, 1602], p. 17). Note that according to both the manuscript tradition and incunabula, the proper spelling of this title is *Formicarius*. I will, however, keep the spelling of the edition I am using in the notes.

256. Bridget of Sweden, *Revelaciones* 1.7.5, p. 258; cf. 1.10.1, p. 263.

257. Ibid. 1.2.5, p. 245.

258. Margery would have preferred to marry Christ, but things did not turn out as she expected (*Book of Margery Kempe* 1.35, pp. 190–91).

259. Ibid. 1.21, pp. 131–32.

260. Ibid. 1.36, p. 196.

261. Margery had at one point accompanied her widowed daughter-in-law back to her home in Danzig, where she spent five or six weeks (*Book of Margery Kempe* 2.4, pp. 398–99; Atkinson, *Mystic and Pilgrim*, pp. 179–81).

262. On Dorothea's life, see Kieckhefer, *Unquiet Souls*, pp. 22–33; Dyan Elliott, "Authorizing a Life: The Collaboration of Dorothea of Montau and John Marienwerder," in *Gendered Voices: Medieval Saints and Their Interpreters*, ed. Catherine Mooney (University of Pennsylvania Press, 1999), pp. 168–91; Coakley, *Women, Men, and Spiritual Power*, pp. 193–210; Ute Stargardt, "Dorothy of Montau," *MHW*, pp. 475–96.

263. John of Marienwerder, *Vita Dorotheae Montoviensis Magistri Johannis Marienwerder* 3.13, ed. Hans Westpfahl, *Forschungen und Quellen zur Kirchen- und Kulturgeschichte Ostdeutschlands* (Cologne: Böhlau, 1964), 1:129–31 (hereafter cited as *VL*). *VL* is the longest of several lives that John wrote for Dorothea. It incorporates most of the earlier *Vita Lindana* (named for its eighteenth-century editor) printed in *AA SS*, October 13: 499–560 (hereafter cited as *Ld*). On John's various writings regarding Dorothea, see Elliott, "Authorizing a Life," pp. 246–47, n9. On Dorothea's marriage, see Elliott, *Spiritual Marriage*, pp. 229–31, 259–61.

264. *VL* 2.32, pp. 94–95. Note that John Marienwerder enters these under her wounds of sin in the index (*tabula*) that he contrived for the *VL* (p. 407).

265. *VL* 2.32.c–d, pp. 94–95. See the testimony of John Mönch, bishop of Pomerania, at Dorothea's process of canonization in *Die Akten des Kanonisationsprozesses Dorotheas von Montau von 1394 bis 1521*, ed. Richard Stachnik (Cologne: Böhlau, 1978), ad 6, p. 413. Also see John Marienwerder, *Libellus de vita* c. 14, in ibid., p. 306. This was a short treatise on Dorothea's virtues that John included in the process of canonization.

266. On Dorothea's relationship with John and the production of Dorothea's revelations, see Coakley, *Women, Men, and Spiritual Power*, pp. 193–210; Elliott, "Authorizing a Life."

267. *VL* 1.6.k–l, pp. 43–44.

268. *VL* 3.26.c, p. 147; *Ld* c. 55, p. 529.

269. *VL* 3.27.e, p. 149; this is almost verbatim from *Ld* c. 56, p. 530.

270. On this image, see pp. 178, 180, 187, 188, above. Cf. *Vita Abundi* c. 10, ed. Frenken, p. 21, trans. Cawley, *Send Me God*, p. 225.

271. *VL* 3.28.h, p. 151; *Ld* c. 56, p. 530. There is considerable consensus on the necessity for Dorothea's stabilization from surprisingly different quarters. Christ glossed his desire to stabilize Dorothea in one fixed location, asserting that she was too often in a state of flux ("qui interdum fluctuabat"). Christ's rationale actually evokes the devil's ridicule of Dorothea, who often accused her of crazily running around from church to church in search of indulgences—thus tempting her to the sin of diffidence (*VL* 2.34.n, p. 98; *Ld* c. 20, p. 509). The devil's charge is echoed by Adalbert, who, interestingly, chained Dorothea up for several days in an effort to prevent her from running around and neglecting her domestic duties (*VL* 2.41.b, p. 107; *Ld* c. 28, p. 514). Note that the depth of Dorothea's feelings for John was apparently reciprocal, as the tenth of the twenty-four proofs of authenticity of her visions was that she miraculously intuited that John loved her more than any of his other spiritual daughters or even his own brother—as did John Reyman (*VL* 1.6.l, pp. 43–44). In *Ld*, where only three proofs are given, John's love for Dorothea still figures as the third (c. 56, p. 531). John Marienwerder's love for Dorothea is also an aspect of article III, 18 in her process (*Akten des Kanonisationsprozesses*, ed. Stachnik, pp. 21–22).

272. *VL* 3.28.i, p. 151; *Ld* c. 56, p. 530.

273. On Dorothea's wounds of sin, see *VL* 3.19.d–e, p. 138; and John's *tabula* in ibid., p. 407; *Ld* ch. 51, p. 527. On one occasion she was also wounded for an exegetical error (*VL*, 1.6.u, pp. 46–47).

274. Thomas of Cantimpré, *De apibus* 1.23.2, p. 92.

275. Gertrude of Helfta, *Le Héraut* 2.5.1–2, in *Oeuvres spirituelles*, SC, 127, 2:248, 250, trans. p. 102.

276. *VL* 2.21.d, p. 82.

277. *VL* 2.24.a–d, pp. 86–87; cf. *Ld* ch. 17, pp. 507–8; also see *VL* 2.21.c, e, p. 82 where Christ reminds her how the wounds pained her from childhood, and he describes her as a cripple. On Dorothea's wounds, see Kieckhefer, *Unquiet Souls*, p. 27.

278. *VL* 2.24.d–h, p. 87.

279. *Akten des Kanonisationsprozesses Dorotheas*, ed. Stachnik, p. 285 ad 5.

280. *VL* 4.13.a, p. 170; cf. 2.24.a, p. 86; 2.24.i, p. 87.

281. *VL* 2.24.i, p. 87; 4.23.b, p. 185. Not only were the wounds known to have bled on Easter, but they had five different modes of causing pain, presumably corresponding to Christ's five wounds. John alluded to these different varieties of pain as Dorothea's five passions. The visionary Christ further likened the way Dorothea's wounds throbbed on the approach of a feast day with the way in which the average devout person's heart would fill with joy (*VL* 2.26.e, p. 89; 2.25.a, p. 88; 2.26.g, p. 90).

282. *VL* 7.16.a, p. 350. The mystical extraction of her heart occurred in 1385, which inaugurated a more intense phase in Dorothea's spirituality, coincided with more frequent wounding, greater pain, and more frequent raptures (*VL* 3.2.n, p. 115).

283. *VL* 2.22–23, pp. 84–85.

284. The self-wounding, and other aspects of Dorothea's spirituality, were stimulated by an accident with scalding water (*VL* 2.22.f–g, pp. 84–85); for Christ's prohibition, see 7.5, p. 334; cf. 4.14.b, p. 171.

285. *VL* 4.14.a, p. 171.

286. Christ's emphasis on his role as wounder undercuts the distinction delineated by Elaine Scarry's influential *The Body in Pain*, wherein she contends that, in contrast to Hebrew Scripture where God is depicted as rewarding through fertility and punishing by wounding, God's rapport with humanity is altered by his assumption of the burden of sentience in Christian Scripture. Thereafter, he is no longer constituted as tormentor (*The Body in Pain: The Making and Unmaking of the World* [New York: Oxford University Press, 1985], esp. pp. 197–219).

287. *VL* 4.15.a, p. 172.

288. *VL* 6.25.g, p. 326.

289. *VL* 6.24.a–f, pp. 323–24; cf. *Septililium B. Dorotheae* 1.11, ed. Franz Hipler, *AB* (1883): pp. 125–27. The *Septililium* is a series of Dorothea's revelations recorded by John of Marienwerder (hereafter cited as *Sept.*).

290. On the conflation of heart and womb, see Caroline Bynum, *Wonderful Blood: Theology and Practice in Late Medieval Northern Germany and Beyond* (Philadelphia: University of Pennsylvania Press, 2006), pp. 158–61. It is also common in devotional objects that appear in religious communities. As Jacqueline Jung argues, "The conceptual conflation of hearts and wombs meant that conventual people, though vowed to celibacy, were not prevented from experiencing in their bodies the fullness of new life, " in "Chrystalline Wombs and Pregnant Hearts: The Exuberant Bodies of the Katharinenthal Visitation Group," in *History in the Comic Mode*, ed. Fulton and Holsinger, p. 227.

291. *VL* 6.25.a, p. 325.

292. *VL* 6.25.d, pp. 325–26.

293. *VL* 2.32.c, p. 294.

294. *VL* 3.13, p. 131.

295. Elliott, "Physiology of Rapture and Female Spirituality," pp. 141–43.

296. *VL* 3.2.n, p. 115.

297. *VL* 6.14.a, c, e, f, i, pp. 308–9.

298. *VL* 6.14.a–b, p. 310.

299. *VL* 6.16.c–d, p. 311.

300. *VL* 6.17.b–c, pp. 312–13.

301. *VL* 6.17.e, p. 313; cf. 6.22.e, p. 321. Cf. the discussion on the swelling of Dorothea's uterus in *Sept.* 1.25, *AB* (1883): 452–54.

302. On mystical pregnancies, see Clarissa Atkinson, *The Oldest Vocation: Christian Motherhood in the Middle Ages* (Ithaca, N.Y.: Cornell University Press, 1991), pp. 181, 185–86; Bynum, *Holy Feast*, pp. 203–4, 256–57.

303. *Hadewijch: The Complete Works*, trans. Hart, Poems in Couplets, no. 14, p. 346.

304. *LSG* 1.11, 7.7, pp. 35, 399.

305. *Vita Venerabilis Idae Lovaniensis* 1.31, *AA SS*, April, 2:166; *Vita B. Idae Lewensis* 4.35, *AA SS*, October, 13:117.

306. See Barbara Koch, "Margaret Ebner," *MHW*, pp. 393–410; Coakley, *Women, Men, and Spiritual Power*, pp. 149–69. Some of Margaret's revelations seem to have been written herself, while others were recorded by the community. Margaret was greatly influenced by Mecthild of Magdeburg, and this is apparent in her devotion to Mary. See Margot Schmidt and Leonard Hindsley's introduction to *Margaret Ebner: Major Works* (New York: Paulist Press, 1993), pp. 53–54.

307. Margaret Ebner, *Die Offenbarungen*, in *Margaretha Ebner und Heinrich von Nördlingen: Ein Beitrag zur Geschichte der deustchen Mystik*, ed. Philipp Strauch (Freiburg: Akademische Verlagsbuchhandlung von J. C. B. Mohr, 1882), pp. 119–20, trans. Hindsley, p. 150. Interestingly, there is no analogy with Mary or the incarnation in the course of this experience, though it was followed by a great feeling of delight (p. 151).

308. Schmidt and Hindsley, *Margaret Ebner*, introd., p. 58. For some of Henry's other exuberant expressions on Margaret's nuptiality and spiritual fecundity, see Coakley, *Women, Men, and Spiritual Power*, pp. 158, 161, 164.

309. Bridget of Sweden, *Revelaciones* 6.88, ed. Birger Bergh, pp. 247–48. Cf. Caesarius's account of a priest whose heart was likewise afflicted with violent feelings so that his breast felt ready to burst whenever he celebrated communion. Even though Caesarius opens with the analogy of "his belly ... like new wine that has no vent ... is ready to burst new bottles," the physical feelings do not extend below his heart (Job 32.19; Caesarius, 9.32, 2:189, trans. 2:135). See Sahlin's discussion of Mary's mentorship of Bridget, culminating in the mystical pregnancy, as authorization for her vocation, in *Birgitta of Sweden*, pp. 78–107. Cf. Laura Saetveit Miles's reading of the power implicit in Bridget's identification with Mary's maternity in comparison with modern associations, in "Looking in the Past for a Discourse of Motherhood: Birgitta of Sweden and Julia Kristeva," *Medievalist Feminist Forum* 47 (2012).

310. According to Cistercian prior Peter Olaf, one of her several confessors, these movements were apprehended by the theologian Mathias, Bridget's earliest confessor, who was deceased at the time of the process for canonization (Collijn, *Acta et processus canonizacionis Beate Birgitte*, p. 500).

311. William of Auvergne, *De universo* 3a 2ae, c. 25, in *Opera*, 1:1072; cf. the experience of a woman who believed that she was known from within by a devil (ibid. c. 13, 1:1041).

312. Bridget of Sweden, *Revelaciones* 6.80, ed. Bergh, pp. 241–42. Because of her mortal sins, the woman had been skipping communion. Once the woman confessed and communicated, the demonic effects vanished.

313. Mechtild of Hackeborn periodically draws the distinction between Mary's blessed delivery and the average woman's experience (*LSG* 1.36, 41, pp. 118, 125). Cf. Fortunatus's horrific description of birth in Chapter 3.

314. *Sept.* 1.17, p. 437.

315. Nor was Dorothea's pregnancy a singular event: the experience would be repeated at each reception of the Eucharist. See *VL* 7.20.c, p. 357.

316. As it happens, Dorothea was not canonized until 1978, but this was due to larger shifts in local ecclesiastical politics versus her extreme mystical claims. See Ute Stargardt,

"The Political and Social Backgrounds of the Canonization of Dorothea von Montau," *Mystics Quarterly* 11 (1985): 107–222.

317. Schmidt, "Actenstücke besonders zur Geschichte der Waldenser," no. 28, p. 250. Because sexual congress was seen as literally merging the blood of two individuals, this belief substantiated the extreme claim of sharing Christ's blood (ibid., no. 32). See Lerner's comparison of the spirituality of Mechtild of Magdeburg, in *Heresy of the Free Spirit*, p. 18.

318. *Vita B. Odiliae* 1.7, p. 211.

319. Ibid.

320. Ibid. 1.1, p. 214.

321. Ibid. 1.12, p. 215.

322. Ibid. 1.15, p. 221.

323. Ibid. 1.17, p. 222.

324. Ibid. 1.18, p. 225. The other demon was called Carisium.

325. Ibid. 1.15, p. 220. Cf. the instance in which she tells one of her seducers that she would rather be burned than suffer "divorce" from God (ibid. 1.16, p. 221).

326. See Renate Blumenfeld-Kosinski, "The Strange Case of Ermine of Reims (1347–1396): A Medieval Woman between Demons and Saints," *Speculum* 85 (2010): 321–56. For a comparison of Ermine with contemporary models of female sanctity, see pp. 322–26.

327. John Le Graveur, *Entre Dieu et Satan: Les visions d'Ermine de Reims (+ 1396)*, ed. and trans. into modern French by Claude Arnaud-Gillet (Florence: Sismel, Edizioni del Galluzzo, 1997), p. 50, trans. p. 185 (hereafter cited as *VER*).

328. Enjoined by her confessor to observe matins, she would get up in the middle of the night and face the window, through which she could hear the service being celebrated in the priory (*VER*, pp. 50–51, trans. pp. 185–86).

329. *VER*, pp. 48, 54, 63, trans. pp. 184, 188, 195.

330. For instance, Margery's glorious visions of Christ as a handsome man were later juxtaposed with a demonically simulated kick-line of priests, both Christian and pagan, showing Margery their genitals and inspiring salacious thoughts (*Book of Margery Kempe* 1.59, p. 282).

331. *VER*, p. 62, trans. p. 194. This is not the only time she saw her husband. Also see pp. 55, 99, trans. pp. 190, 221.

332. Ibid., p. 58, trans. p. 191.

333. Ibid., pp. 88–89, trans. p. 213. On Ermine's sexual trials, see Blumenfeld-Kosinski, "Strange Case of Ermine," pp. 350–55. Often, however, demons would just show up in her bed, presenting a panoply of hideous forms (*VER*, pp. 61 [bis], 63, trans. pp. 193, 194, 195).

334. See Elliott, *Proving Woman*, ch. 6; Nancy Caciola, *Discerning Spirits: Divine and Demonic Possession in the Middle Ages* (Ithaca, N.Y.: Cornell University Press, 2003). For Ermine and discernment, see Blumenfeld-Kosinski, "Strange Case of Ermine," pp. 338–42.

335. They would also appear as the most beautiful angels with golden wings, filling the room with lovely scent, sometimes holding candles or playing musical instruments (*VER*, pp. 64, 73, 76, 77–78, 81, 83, 97–98, trans. pp. 196, 202, 204–5, 205–6, 208, 209, 220). Some of the saintly personae adopted by the demons are Leger, who attempted to affirm

his identity by reminiscing on how Ermine was baptized in his church and was a former member of his confraternity (p. 58, trans. p. 191); Andrew (p. 59, trans. p. 192); John the Baptist (p. 60, trans. p. 193); Mary Magdalene (pp. 66, 78–79, trans. pp. 197, 206–7), who is at one point accompanied by Catherine and Agnes—all dressed like fine ladies (p. 107, trans. pp. 226–27); Peter (pp. 70–71, 77, trans. pp. 200, 205); Remi (p. 91, trans. p. 215); deceased friends and people from her hometown (p. 61, trans. p. 193; cf. pp. 63, 68, trans. pp. 195, 199); her confessor (pp. 62, 65, trans. pp. 194, 196); Elisabeth, the mother of John the Baptist, accompanied by Gertrude (p. 98, trans. p. 220); Augustine, performing Mass and ingesting a host transformed into a small baby crying (p. 103, trans. p. 224; also see p. 105, trans. p. 225). Also when Ermine was pondering her salvation and suddenly became so fearful that she could not think about God, a lady dressed in white appeared holding a fleur-de-lis. When Ermine asked who she was, the lady responded that she was a saint in paradise not known in this world (p. 104, trans. p. 225).

336. *VER*, p. 73, trans. p. 202.

337. *VER*, p. 65, trans. p. 196.

338. *VER*, p. 80, trans. p. 207.

339. *VER*, p. 80, trans. p. 207.

340. *VER*, pp. 146–47, trans. pp. 256–57. Because the confessor is writing this account, it is unclear whether Ermine correctly discerned this particular demonic masquerade at the time or whether he is labeling the imposter as such retrospectively. Cf. the instance in which the voice of Satan predicted that her confessor and all his brethren were destined for hell (ibid., p. 157, trans. p. 262). Blumenfeld-Kosinski rightly points out that Paul the Simple is one of Ermine's more complicated visitors—sometimes a type of guardian angel and sometimes a deceptive demon ("Strange Case of Ermine," p. 341).

341. Guy of Cortona, *Vita B. Humilianae de Cerchis* 2.12, *AA SS*, May, 4:387, p. 389. She was also shown images of her daughters, who were still alive and being cared for by her husband's family, in their grave (ibid. 2.12, p. 388).

342. Ibid. 2.21, pp. 390–91.

343. Conrad Castillerio, *Vita de B. Benevenuta Bojanis* c. 2.13–19, *AA SS*, October, 13:154–55. As she matured, the demon's virtuosity was expressed in various ways: as a wandering friar, a dog, several cats with human voices, or, more true to form, a serpent that provocatively stretched itself across her body. When he appeared as a wandering friar, moreover, he attempted to undermine her faith by alleging that her confessor had left the order and run off with a woman (c. 2.15, p. 155).

344. *La Legenda di Vanna da Orvieto* 9.3–7, pp. 154–55, trans. pp. 74–75. Perhaps the apex of this kind of torment occurs in the life of Frances of Rome. See her confessor, John Matteotti's, account, *Acta S. Franciscae Romana* 3.1–4, *AA SS*, March, 2:155–64. Also see Guy Boanas and Lyndal Roper, "Feminine Piety in Fifteenth-Century Rome: Santa Francesca Romana," in *Disciplines of Faith: Studies in Religion, Politics and Patriarchy*, ed. Jim Obelkevich, Lyndal Roper, and Raphael Sameul (London: Routledge and Kegan Paul, 1987), pp. 185–90. She also saw demons tormenting others in her visions of hell. Frances has special places assigned to fallen brides of Christ. They stood in a fire within bins of pitch and sulfur. Demons with forks periodically pitched them into bins of ice. Women who

were virgins in mind only were flagellated by fiery chains, lacerated and placed on pieces of fiery iron, while demons did improper things to them (Matteotti, *Acta S. Franciscae Romana* 3.6.67, 71, *AA SS*, March, 2:169, 170).

345. Castillerio, *Vita de B. Benevenuta Bojanis* cc. 2, 20–23, p. 155. Once she got the better of him, however, and, with God-given strength, wrestled him to the ground and sat on him. She eventually let him go, however, as he made so much noise (cc. 2, 23, p. 155).

346. *Vita S. Gerardeschae Pisanae* 5.49, *AA SS*, May, 7:161.

347. On Christine's demonic torments, see Aviad Kleinberg, *Prophets in Their Own Country: Living Saints and the Making of Sainthood in the Later Middle Ages* (Chicago: University of Chicago Press, 1991), pp. 87–92; John Coakley, "A Marriage and Its Observer: Christine of Stommeln, the Heavenly Bridegroom, and Friar Peter of Dacia," in *Gendered Voices*, ed. Mooney, pp. 111–15.

348. As cited by Kleinberg, *Prophets in Their Own Country*, p. 90.

349. Castillerio, *Vita de B. Benevenuta Bojanis* cc. 2, 24, *AA SS*, October, 13:156. Vanna's mystical raptures were so intense that she was occasionally lifted off the ground (*La Legenda di Vanna da Orvieto* c. 5, pp. 17–18), trans. p. 68.

350. Peter of Dacia, Christine's clerical confidant, stresses that her spiritual consolations took a nuptial form, while Christine's own writings focus on her demonic torments. Coakley argues convincingly, however, that the two accounts are complementary and that Christine's nuptial spirituality is implicit in her own account ("A Marriage and Its Observers," pp. 110–11). Kleinberg, in contrast, seems more skeptical about the accuracy of Peter's nuptial embroidering (*Prophets in Their Own Country*, p. 87).

CHAPTER 7

1. Origen, *In Canticum* prol., *PL* 13:67, trans. p. 30.

2. See Renate Blumenfeld-Kosinski's discussion of how aspects of Ermine of Reim's visions, particularly sexualized demons and night flights, anticipate the rise of witchcraft ("Strange Case of Ermine of Reims," 348–49, 354).

3. See Elliott, *Fallen Bodies*, pp. 144–45.

4. In *The Vision of Isaiah*, a Bogomil work that reached the West in the early thirteenth century, the visionary sees souls stripped of their robes of flesh. Eventually, he too has to reassume his robe, which had been cast aside for travel (4.7–9, 6.35, trans. Walter Wakefield and Austin Evans, *Heresies of the High Middle Ages* [New York: Columbia University Press, 1969], pp. 453, 456). According to Moneta of Cremona, the Cathars likewise compared the body to earthenware vessels destined for destruction, based on their exegesis of Romans 9.21 (*Adversus Catharos et Valdenses libri quinque* 1.4.1, ed. T. A. Ricchini [Rome: Palladis, 1743; reprt., Ridgewood, N.J.: Gregg, 1964], p. 52). See Peter Biller's discussion of Moneta in "Cathars and the Material Woman," pp. 81–88.

5. Moneta of Cremona, *Adversus Catharos et Valdenses* 2.1.2, p. 321, trans. Wakefield and Evans, *Heresies*, p. 321; cf. *De heresi catharorum in Lombardia*, ed. Antoine Dondaine, "La Hiérarchie cathare d'Italie I," *Archivum Fratrum Praedicatorum* 19 (1949): 310–11, trans.

Wakefield and Evans, *Heresies*, pp. 165–66; and *Le Livre secret des cathares: 'Interrogatio Io-hannis,'* ed. Edina Bozóky (Paris: Beauchesne, 1980), p. 60. The anonymous *De heresi* was written ca. 1200–1214 by a Lombard.

6. *Disputatio inter catholicum et paterinum haereticum*, in *Thesaurus novus anecdoto-rum*, ed. Edmund Martène and Ursinus Durand (Paris: Lutetia, 1717; reprt., New York: Burt Franklin, 1968), 5:1710, trans. Wakefield and Evans, *Heresies*, p. 295. The anonymous *Disputatio* was written in the mid-thirteenth century and was widely circulated. The *Liber antiheresis*, a work of Waldensian provenance intended for refuting the Cathar heresy, al-leges that Satan made the angels fornicate in heaven. This was the reason they rose up and revolted against God (C. Thouzellier, ed., "Controverses vaudoises-cathares à la fin du XIIe siècle [d'après le livre II du *Liber antiheresis*, MS Madrid 114 et les sections correspondantes du MS BN lat. 13446]," *Archives d'histoire doctrinale et littéraire du moyen âge* 35 [1960], 2.2, p. 216).

7. Bonacursus, *Vita haereticorum*, PL 204:775–76, trans. Wakefield and Evans, *Her-esies*, pp. 171–72; cf. *Disputatio*, 5:1711, trans. Wakefield and Evans, *Heresies*, p. 295. Also see Moneta of Cremona, *Adversus Catharos et Valdenses* 2.1.2, p. 111, trans. Wakefield and Evans, *Heresies*, p. 321.

8. Raoul Manselli, ed., *De confessione hereticorum et de fide eorum* c. 3, in "Per la storia dell'eresia nel secolo XII: Studi minori," *Bullettino dell'Istituto storico italiano per il medio evo e Archivio Muratoriano* 47 (1955): 206.

9. The exegesis of the gloss borrows from Cassian, who, as we saw, interprets the sons of God as the "religious sons of Seth" (*filii seth religiosi*), and the daughters of men as the lineage of Cain (*de stripe cayn*), in *Biblia Latina cum glossa ordinaria*, p. 35. See the discus-sion in Chapter 2.

10. Hincmar of Reims, *De divortio Lotharii regis and Theutbergae reginae* q. 15, resp., ed. L. Böhringer, *MGH, Concilia IV*, suppl. 1 (Hannover: Hahnsche Buchhandlung, 1992), p. 208. For an analysis of this treatise, see Bishop, "Bishops as Marital Advisors in the Ninth Century," pp. 53–84.

11. Hincmar of Reims, *De divortio* q. 15, resp., p. 205. See Catherine Rider's discussion of Hincmar's interventions in the attempted divorce of Emperor Lothar from his wife, Theutberga, as well as in the unconsummated union of the Aquitainian count Stephen in *Magic and Impotence in the Middle Ages* (Oxford: Oxford University Press, 2006), pp. 31–42. Rider argues that Hincmar does not distinguish between magical aphrodisiacs and magic effecting impotence (p. 33). On the political climate in which Hincmar formed these posi-tions, see Janet Nelson, *Charles the Bald* (London: Longman, 1992), pp. 196–200.

12. Hincmar of Reims, *De divortio* q. 15, resp., pp. 209–12. Of course he had to sign a contract selling his soul, which led to certain legal complications.

13. Ibid., pp. 205–6.

14. Ibid., p. 208. Hincmar is alluding to Martin of Dumio's rather circumlocutious rulings at the second Council of Braga (572, c. 75) against Christian women who perform vain works when working wool. Instead they should be invoking God's aid because he is responsible for their gift of weaving (*Sacrorum conciliorum . . . collectio*, ed. Mansi, 9:578). Canon 69, pp. 71–74, also addresses superstitious and magical practices (ibid., 9:857–58).

Cf. Burchard of Worms, "Quod non liceat mulierculas Christianas vanitates in suis lanificiis observare," in *Libri decretorum* 10.19, 19.5, *PL* 140:836, 961. On love potions, see Richard Kieckhefer, "Erotic Magic in Medieval Europe," in *Sex in the Middle Ages: A Book of Essays*, ed. Joyce Salisbury (New York: Garland, 1991), pp. 30–55.

15. Hincmar, *De divortio* q. 15, resp., p. 213. Demons could also pose as lovers in order to attack the saintly. The reputation of Empress Cunegund (d. 1033), whose marriage to Henry II allegedly remained unconsummated for reasons of piety, was assailed by a crafty demon who was seen repeatedly entering and exiting her chamber in the shape of a handsome knight. This episode is a later addition to Henry's life. See Adalbert of Bamberg, *Vita Henrici II, Addimentum* c. 3, *MGH, Scrip.*, 4:819; Elliott, *Spiritual Marriage*, pp. 129–30.

16. The *Canon Episcopi* is from Regino of Prüm (*De ecclesiasticis disciplinis et religione Christiana* 2.364, *PL* 132:352–53). Burchard of Worms incorporated the *Canon Episcopi* into book 19 of his *Decretum*, which was known as the *Corrector* or *Medicus in Libri decretorum* 19.5, *PL* 140:963–64. See Burchard's introduction to the book for the rationale for the name (ibid., *PL* 140:949). The *Corrector* was written as a penitential and often circulated separately. See Martha Rampton, "Burchard of Worms and Female Magical Ritual," in *Medieval and Early Modern Ritual: Formalized Behavior in Europe, China and Japan*, ed. Joëlle Rollo-Koster (Leiden: Brill, 2002), pp. 7–34.

17. Burchard of Worms, *Libri decretorum* 19.5, *PL* 140:971.

18. Geoffrey of Monmouth, *History of the Kings of Britain* 6.107, ed. Michael Reeve (Woodbridge, Suffolk: Boydell, 2007), p. 139 (translation mine). In order for a tower that Vortigern was attempting to erect to remain standing, the king had been counseled to find a child without a father, kill him, and sprinkle his blood on its foundation (6.106, p. 137).

19. In *Yonec*, the knight first metamorphoses from a bird to a knight, then takes the form of the lady. In this latter instance, his intent was to feign illness and receive last rites in order to reassure the lady that he is not a demon (ll. 145–90). The lady's form in *Lanval* is much more stable, except that she can appear at the knight's command and was usually invisible to others (see esp. ll. 153–88), trans. Glyn Burgess and Keith Busby, *The Lais of Marie de France*, 2nd ed. (Harmondsworth, Middlesex: Penguin Books, 1986), pp. 88, 75.

20. For Map's various supernatural brides, see *De nugis curialium: Courtier's Trifles* dist. 2, cc. 11–13; dist. 4, cc. 9–11, ed. and trans. M. R. James, rev. C. N. L. Brooke and R. A. B. Mynors (Oxford: Clarendon, 1983), pp. 148–51, 154–61, 344–61.

21. Ibid. dist. 4, c. 11, pp. 352–53. See Bernard's discussion of the noontide demon and its masquerade as the angel of light and how it convinces one to commit evil under the guise of good (Serm. 33, 5.9, in *Sermons, SC*, 452, 3:54–56, trans. 2:152–53).

22. Map, *De nugis curialium* dist. 4, c. 10, pp. 346–49.

23. Ibid. dist. 4, c. 11, pp. 360–61.

24. He was cured by a visit to St. Ethelbert's tomb in Hereford (ibid. dist. 2, c. 12, pp. 158–59).

25. Melusine was made famous by John of Arras (d. 1394). The children that resulted from her very fecund union with Count Raymond Lusignan were all defective in some way, and most of them had an evil turn. The sixth child, Geoffrey, had one tooth that protruded from his mouth like an animal's fang. He burned down a monastery and its monks,

one of whom was his brother. The eighth child, Eudes (nicknamed Horrible), had three eyes and was reputedly so cruel (he allegedly killed two nurses at the age of four by biting their breasts) that he was consigned to death by his own mother (*Mélusine, roman du XIVe siècle par Jean d'Arras: Publié pour la première fois, d'après le manuscrit de la Bibliothèque de l'Arsenal avec les variantes des manuscrits de la Bibliothèque nationale*, ed. Louis Stouff [Dijon: Bernigaud et Privat, 1932], pp. 80, 251–53, 258). Gabrielle Spiegel sees Melusine and her monstrous offspring as an expression of categorical confusion, mutability, and crisis of legitimacy during the Hundred Years' War ("Maternity and Monstrosity: Reproductive Biology in the *Roman de Mélusine*," in *Melusine of Lusignan: Founding Fiction in Late Medieval Literature*, ed. Donald Maddox and Sara Sturm-Maddox [Athens: University of Georgia Press, 1996], pp. 100–124).

26. Map, *De nugis* dist. 2, c. 12, p. 159.

27. Ibid. dist. 4, c. 11, p. 355.

28. Ibid. dist. 4, c. 11, pp. 356–57, 360–61.

29. A number of scholars have demonstrated how scholasticism definitively forced figures of folklore, supernatural entities that were more or less morally neutral, into the realm of the demonic. See n182, below.

30. See Chapter 4, pp. 122–23, above.

31. Ernaldus, Abbot of Bona-Vallis, *S. Bernardi vita et res gestae* 2.6.34, *PL* 185, col. 287 (Ernaldus is only responsible for book 2 of this multiauthored contemporary life). Note that this entire passage is from a different codex than the one primarily used (see the editor's note, cols. 223–24). Caesarius of Heisterbach makes reference to this episode in *Dialogus miraculorum* 3.7, ed. Joseph Strange (Cologne: J. M. Heberle, 1851), 1:120, trans. H. Von E. Scott and C. C. Swinton Bland, 1:134–35. *The Dialogue on Miracles* (London: Routledge, 1929), 1:134 (hereafter Caesarius).

32. Moreover, James of Vitry had fashioned his life of Mary of Oignies as riposte to the Cathar threat, and much of the somatic and eucharistic spirituality of the Beguines was presented (and possibly invented) with the Cathar threat in mind. See Elliott, *Proving Woman*, ch. 2. For an important aspect of James of Vitry's anti-Cathar initiative in his preaching, see Carolyn Muessig, "Heaven, Earth, and the Angels: Preaching Paradise in the Sermons of Jacques de Vitry," in *Envisaging Heaven in the Middle Ages*, ed. Carolyn Muessig and Ad Putter (London: Routledge, 2007), pp. 57–72.

33. William of Auvergne, *De universo* 2.3.25, in *Opera omnia*, 1:1070.

34. Ibid., col. 1071. This legend concerning the Huns is from Jordanes, *De origine actibusque Getarum (sive: Getica)* 24.122, ed. Theodor Mommsen. *MGH, Auct. Ant.*, 5:1 (Berlin: Weidmann, 1882), p. 89.

35. Aquinas *De potentia* q. 6, art. 8, resp. ad obj. 7, in *Opera omnia* (Parma: Petrus Fiaccadori, 1852–73; reprt., New York: Musurgia, 1948–50), 8:141–42, trans. English Dominican Fathers, *On the Power of God* (Westminster, Md.: Newman Press, 1952), p. 212; and *Summa theologiae* 1a, q. 51, art. 3, resp. ad obj. 6, 9:43; Aquinas, *Commentum in quatuor libros sententiarum* bk. 2, dist. 8, art. 4, quaestinuncula 2, in *Opera omnia*, 6:456. Stephens, *Demon Lovers*, pp. 58–86.

36. On the wide range of demons and demonic activity in both Caesarius of

Heisterbach and Thomas of Cantimpré, see Alexander Murray, "Demons as Psychological Abstractions," in *Angels in Medieval Philosophical Inquiry: Their Function and Significance*, ed. Isabel Iribarren and Martin Lenz (Aldershot, England: Ashgate, 2008), pp. 171–84.

37. Caesarius, 5.5, 1:281–85, trans. 1:321–25.

38. Ibid. 13.12, 1:24, trans. 1:139.

39. Ibid. 3.6, 1:16, trans. 1:130.

40. Ibid. 3.13, 1:125, trans. 1:140–41.

41. Ibid. 5.44, 1:328–29, trans. 1:377; also see 5.45, 1:331, trans. 1:380; 5.46, 1:331, trans. 1:380–81; 5.47, 1:332, trans. 1: 381–82.

42. Geoffrey of Monmouth, *History* 6.106, p. 139.

43. Caesarius, 3.12, 1:124, trans. p. 139.

44. Ibid. 3.8, 1:121, trans. 1:136.

45. Alvar Pelayo, *De planctu ecclesiae* bk. 2, art. 6, in Henry Charles Lea, *Materials toward a History of Witchcraft*, ed. Arthur Howland (New York: Thomas Yoseloff, 1957), 1:159; cf. Alfonso of Spina, who claims that nuns frequently are dragged out of bed by demons or accosted when praying. The demons then put the nuns to bed gently, and the nuns later awaken to find themselves polluted as if they had been with men (*Fortalicium fidei*, ca. 1464 or 1467, in Lea, *Materials*, 1:289).

46. Caesarius of Heisterbach, "Des Cäsarius von Heisterbach Schriften über die hl. Elisabeth von Thüringen," ed. Albert Huyskens, *Annalen des historischen Vereins für den Niederrhein* 86 (1908): 1–59.

47. He was traveling to see a Cistercian nun who had already obtained this gift for a monk of Villers when his hostess offered to introduce him to a good woman, whose prayers fulfilled his desire (Caesarius, 2.20, 1:89–90, trans. 1:99–100; cf. 2.19, 1:88–89, trans. 1:98–99). On Mary's gift of tears, see James of Vitry, *Vita B. Mariae Oigniacensis*, 2.5.16–18, *AA SS*, June, 5:550–51, trans. pp. 56–58.

48. Rachel Maines, *The Technology of the Orgasm: "Hysteria," the Vibrator and Women's Sexual Satisfaction* (Baltimore: Johns Hopkins University Press, 1999), p. 58.

49. Caesarius, 3.6, 1:116, trans. 1:130.

50. Aquinas maintained that divination through demons necessarily involved a pact "whether expressed through invoking them, or tacit, by seeking knowledge out of human reach" (*Summa theologiae* 2a2ae, q. 95, art. 6, resp., 40:58–59). Euan Cameron, however, argues that Aquinas's abstract positions were not "preachable" and stresses the importance of subsequent pastoral theologians in the development of concepts like the pact (*Enchanted Europe: Superstition, Reason, and Religion, 1250–1750* [Oxford: Oxford University Press, 2010], p. 102).

51. For instance, a man and woman who were persistently guilty of fornication with one another could be warned by the ecclesiastical court that further intercourse would render them ipso facto married (Michael Sheehan, *Marriage, Family, and Law in Medieval Europe: Collected Studies* [Toronto: University of Toronto Press, 1996], pp. 66–68). By the same token, a couple who has exchanged future consent to marry and subsequently has sex is automatically married (Brundage, *Law, Sex, and Christian Society in Medieval Europe*, pp. 436–37). On the pact, see Jeffrey Russell, *Witchcraft in the Middle*

Ages (Ithaca, N.Y.: Cornell University Press, 1972), pp. 144–47; Cameron, *Enchanted Europe*, pp. 106–10.

52. *Vita S. Lutgardis virginis Cistercersiensis* 2.11, *AA SS*, June, 4:198, trans. p. 248.

53. Thomas of Cantimpré, *Bonum universale de apibus* 2.57.14, p. 546; Elliott, *Fallen Bodies*, p. 54; Newman, "Possessed by the Spirit," pp. 743–44.

54. Brakke, *Demons and the Making of the Monk*, pp. 200–206.

55. See Girolamo Visconti, *Lamiarum sive striarum opusculum* (ca. 1460), in *Quellen und Untersuchungen zur Geschichte des Hexenwahns und der Hexenverfolgung im Mittelalter*, ed. Joseph Hansen (Bonn, 1901; reprt., Hildesheim: Georg Olms, 1963), who attributes this view to Raynerius of Pisa (p. 205).

56. Elliott, *Fallen Bodies*, pp. 35–60; Caciola, *Discerning Spirits*, pp. 129–61.

57. Henricus Kramer Institoris and Jacobus Sprenger, *Malleus maleficarum* pt. 2, q.1, c. 4, ed. and trans. Christopher Mackay (Cambridge: Cambridge University Press, 2006), 1:411ff. trans. 2:254ff. See Stephens, *Demon Lovers*, pp. 32–57. Also see Hans Broedel's recent study, *The Malleus Maleficarum and the Construction of Witchcraft* (Manchester: Manchester University Press, 2003), in which he argues that *The Hammer* managed to connect witchcraft, femininity, and a rampant but hostile sexuality in a new and powerful way (pp. 176–79). There are aspects of Broedel's argument that are disturbing, however. The authors of *The Hammer* allege that their insistence that most witches are women is not based on prejudice but on their own experience—a rationale that Broedel seems prepared to take at face value (p. 175). Most scholars now believe that Kramer was responsible for the entire work and used Sprenger's name for legitimation. For the religious justification of inquisitorial zeal, see Christine Caldwell Ames, *Righteous Persecution: Inquisition, Dominicans, and Christianity in the Middle Ages* (Philadelphia: University of Pennsylvania Press, 2009).

58. Bernard of Clairvaux, Serm. 7, 3.4, *Sermons, SC*, 414 1:160, trans. 1:40. He also has the common belief that humans will restore the ranks of the fallen angels (Serm. 62, 1.1, *Sermons, SC*, 472, 4:260, trans. 3:150).

59. Ibid. Serm. 5 speaks extensively about the bodies of angels (*Sermons, SC*, 414, 1:122–37, trans. 1:25–31). McGinn claims that Bernard gave more emphasis to angels than most Latin mystics, but I doubt that is the case if you take into account the experience of women, in *The Growth of Mysticism*, vol. 2 of *The Presence of God: A History of Western Christian Mysticism; Gregory the Great through the Twelfth Century* (New York: Crossroad, 1996), 2:209. Also see Elliott, "Physiology of Rapture and Female Spirituality," pp. 49–51.

60. Bernard of Clairvaux, Serm. 54, 1.1–2.2, *Sermons, SC*, 472, 4:98–104, trans. 3:70–71.

61. James of Vitry, *Vita B. Mariae Oigniacensis* prol. 7. 2, 11.95, *AA SS*, June, 5:548, 568, trans. pp. 47, 117. Mary also saw a seraph standing beside her once when she mutilated herself (1.7.22, p. 552, trans. p. 60). Also see Thomas of Cantimpré, *Vita S. Lutgardis virginis Cisterciensis* 2.42, June, 4:203, trans. p. 169. Cf. the instance described by Caesarius of Heisterbach in which a woman is preserved from the gallows through the mediation of angels holding her up (1.40, 1:49, trans. 1:53).

62. Thomas of Cantimpré, *Vita Margarete de Ypris* c. 21, 117, trans. p. 183; Goswin of Villers, *Vita beatae Idae de Niuelle sanctimonialis in monasterio de Rameya* c. 7, 26, pp. 216, 264, trans. pp. 41, 72. Cawley notes that the original Latin is "per familiarem sibi

spiritum Domini," and translates accordingly. Henriquez's edition changes this and similar references to more innocuous phrases such as "spiritu divino," lest Ida's familiar spirit be mistaken for something diabolical (*Send Me God*, p. 41n35).

63. Hugh of Louvain, *Vita venerabilis Idae Lovaniensis* 1.4.20, *AA SS*, April, 2:164. Apparently Ida felt a great fervor for the host but had been too intimidated to ask her confessor.

64. Thomas of Cantimpré, *De apibus* 2.50.6, p. 461. On the presence of celestial beings in Cistercian-inflected hagiography, see Roisin, *L'hagiographie cistercienne*, pp. 165–77.

65. McGinn, *Growth of Mysticism*, vol. 2 of *The Presence of God*, 2:182.

66. Bernard of Clairvaux, Serm. 83, 1.2, *Sermons*, *SC*, 511, 5:342, trans. 4:181.

67. Thomas of Cantimpré, *De apibus* 2.27.25, pp. 555–57.

68. Stephen of Bourbon, *Anecdotes historiques, légendes et apologues tirés du recueil inédit d'Etienne de Bourbon*, pp. 198–99.

69. Thomas of Cantimpré, *De apibus* 2.57.24, p. 555.

70. See Dyan Elliott, "True Presence/False Christ: Antinomies of Embodiment in Late Medieval Spirituality," *Mediaeval Studies* 64 (2002): 241–65.

71. On this genre in the later Middle Ages, see Rosalynn Voaden, *God's Words, Women's Voices: The Discernment of Spirits in the Writing of Late-Medieval Women Visionaries* (Woodbridge, Suffolk: Boydell, 1999); Caciola, *Discerning Spirits*, esp. pp. 274ff.; Elliott, *Proving Woman*, pp. 257ff.

72. On Gerson's life, see Brian McGuire, *Jean Gerson and the Last Medieval Reformation* (University Park: Pennsylvania State University Press, 2005).

73. See Elliott, *Proving Woman*, pp. 277–84.

74. Gerson, *De probatione de spirituum*, in *Oeuvres complètes*, ed. Palémon Glorieux (Paris: Desclée, 1960–73), 9:177–85 (hereafter cited as GL). The other two treatises specifically dedicated to the subject of spiritual discernment were *De distinctione verarum revelationum a falsis*, GL, 3:36–56 (written in 1401) and *De examinatione doctrinarum*, GL, 9:458–75 (written in 1423). In addition to his apprehension of female mysticism generally, Gerson also blamed the papal schism on Bridget of Sweden and Catherine of Siena because he regarded them as instrumental in the pope's return to Rome (ibid. 9:471–72). On the efforts of Catherine and Bridget to this effect, see Renate Blumenfeld-Kosinski, *Poets, Saints, and Visionaries of the Great Schism, 1378–1417* (University Park: Pennsylvania State University Press, 2006), pp. 35–46.

75. Daniel Hobbins, *Authorship and Publicity before Print: Jean Gerson and the Transformation of Late Medieval Learning* (Philadelphia: University of Pennsylvania Press, 2009), p. 195. Hobbins examines Gerson in terms of the rising phenomenon of the public intellectual who is extremely assiduous in circulating his own works.

76. Gerson, *De mystica theologia practica* consideratio 2, GL, 8:22, trans. Brian McGuire, *Jean Gerson: Early Works* (New York: Paulist Press, 1998), p. 294.

77. Gerson, *De elucidatione scholastica mysticae theologiae*, GL, 8:154–55; cf. *De simplificatione cordis* c. 16, GL, 8:93.

78. Gerson, *De meditatione cordis* c. 16, GL, 8:81–82.

79. Gerson, *De simplificatione cordis* cc. 1–2, 7, GL, 8:85–86, 88. Gerson suggests that

the unlearned might be able to undertake this process as well. He uses the example of a child who is told that his far-away father loves him. The child develops affection and love without the use of images (ibid. cc. 13–14, 8:91–93).

80. Gerson, *De meditatione cordis* c. 18, GL, 8:83.

81. Gerson, *De simplificatione cordis* c. 18, GL, 8:94.

82. See D. Catherine Brown, *Pastor and Laity in the Theology of Jean Gerson* (Cambridge: Cambridge University Press, 1987), pp. 178–82. Also see Jeffrey Fisher, "Gerson's Mystical Theology," which argues that Gerson's writings on mysticism progressively demote affect in favor of intellect, in *A Companion to Jean Gerson*, ed. Brian McGuire (Leiden: Brill, 2006), pp. 205–48.

83. For example, Gerson raised the question at the end of *Contra curiositatem studentium*, promising to return to it (GL, 3:249), which he soon did at beginning of *De theologia mystica lectiones sex* (GL, 3:250).

84. On this movement, see John Van Engen, *Sisters and Brothers of the Common Life: The Devotio Moderna and the World of the Later Middle Ages* (Philadelphia: University of Pennsylvania Press, 2008). For Gerson's defense of lay religiosity, and critique of monasticism's supposed spiritual ascendancy at Constance, see ibid., pp. 216–17, 246–47. At the Council of Basel, theologians such as John Wenck and the Dominican Matthew Grabow would make an effort to have such lay religious groups suppressed altogether—be they Beguines, third order mendicants, or proponents of the so-called Common Life (Lerner, *Heresy of the Free Spirit*, pp. 169–70; Van Engen, *Sisters and Brothers of the Common Life*, pp. 212–16).

85. See Daniel Hobbins, "Gerson on Lay Devotion," in *A Companion to Jean Gerson*, ed. McGuire, pp. 70–74.

86. Gerson, *La Montagne de contemplation* cc. 4, 7, GL, 7, 1:18, trans. McGuire, *Jean Gerson: Early Works*, p. 78; cf. Ep. 13, *To Bartholomew Clantier* (first letter against Ruusbroec), GL, 1:60–61, trans. McGuire, *Jean Gerson: Early Works*, pp. 208–9. See Brown, *Pastor and Laity*, pp. 183–94; Hobbins, "Gerson on Lay Devotion," pp. 52–53, 67–68.

87. Gerson, Ep. 12, *To Nicolas*, GL, 2:54. In fact, these two aspects that he cites admiringly are from Giselbertus, the continuator of Bernard's sermon cycle (GL, 2:54n); also see Brian McGuire, "Gerson and Bernard: Languishing with Love," *Cîteaux* 46 (1995):133–34.

88. Gerson, *La Montagne de contemplation* c. 1, GL, 7, 1:16, trans. McGuire, p. 75. On Gerson's writing for his sisters, see McGuire, "Late Medieval Care and the Control of Women: Jean Gerson and his Sisters," *Revue d'histoire ecclésiastique* 92 (1997): 5–36, and McGuire, *Jean Gerson and the Last Medieval Reformation*, pp. 102–10, 115–20. In fact, Gerson's eldest sister, Marion, had been married but had lost her husband, so she was presumably not a virgin (ibid., p. 106).

89. Gerson, *La Montagne de contemplation* cc. 12, 30, 40, GL, 7, 1:23, 38, 50, trans. McGuire, pp. 84, 103, 118.

90. He does note, however, that other foci of Bernard's are useful for his sisters' contemplative practices, for instance meditation on the passion. At this juncture, Gerson briefly reviews some other authors, such as Gregory the Great, Augustine, Richard of St.

Victor, and Jerome. It is predictably Jerome's letter to Eustochium, however, that he most recommends (*La Montagne de contemplation* c. 37, GL, 7, 1:46–47, trans. McGuire, pp. 114–15). Note that in his introduction he acknowledges that there are already several excellent treatises on contemplation, and he lists Bernard's sermons on the Song of Songs as one of them. Here he describes these treatises as the domain of "clerics who know Latin" (ibid. c. 1, GL, 7, 1, 1:16, trans. McGuire, p. 75).

91. Gerson goes on to impugn the work of a certain Marie of Valenciennes, who claimed that divine love freed the individual from all law, thus falling into error (*De distinctione*, GL, 3:51–52, trans. McGuire, pp. 356–57; see ibid., 3:56, trans. McGuire, p. 363, for further disparagement of the Beguines). Robert Lerner was the first to recognize that Marie of Valenciennes was none other than Marguerite Porete (*Heresy of the Free Spirit*, p. 165). Gerson also describes a man in a close spiritual friendship with a nun, who almost slipped into carnal love—an incident that McGuire perceives as autobiographical (*De distinctione*, GL, 3:52, trans. McGuire, pp. 357–58; McGuire, "Jean Gerson and the End of Spiritual Friendship: Dilemmas of Conscience," in *Friendship in Medieval Europe*, ed. Julian Halsedine [Thrupp, UK: Sutton, 1999], pp. 230–50). Cf. his denunciation of the so-called Turlupins (see n260, below).

92. Gerson, *De meditatione cordis*, GL, 8:83–84.

93. Gerson, Ep. 26, *To Bartholomew Clantier* (second letter against Ruuesbroec), GL, 2:102, trans. McGuire, p. 255. He also objected to the extent of their alleged union with God, which, as we have seen, was often conveyed through the image of wine merging with the ocean (see *De theologia mystica lectiones sex* consideratio 41, 3:285–88). For Gerson's apprehension of spiritual excess, which he particularly associates with women, see Hobbins, "Gerson on Lay Devotion," pp. 62–67.

94. Gerson, *Super Cantica canticorum*, GL, 8:579, 566.

95. Gerson, *La Mendicité spirituelle*, GL, 7, 1:240; *Tractatus de oculo*, GL, 8:151; cf. *De elucidatione scholastica mysticae theologiae* c. 6, GL, 7, 1:157.

96. Gerson, *De nuptiis Christi et Ecclesiae*, GL, 6:196. This was written in 1417, toward the end of the Council of Constance. On Gerson's concern with magical practices among the laity, see Brown, *Pastor and Laity*, pp. 37–38, 159–60. On the theologians' growing concern with magically induced impotence in this period, see Rider, *Magic and Impotence*, pp. 190–205. Gerson's imagery may also have been influenced by the popular pope prophecies. See Blumenfeld-Kosinski, *Poets, Saints, and Visionaries*, pp. 31–33.

97. Gerson, *De auferibilitate sponsi ab ecclesia*, GL, 3:294–313. This treatise was originally written for the Council of Pisa (1410), an aborted attempt to end the papal schism, and reissued in 1415 for the Council of Constance (Hobbins, *Authorship and Publicity*, p. 195). Gerson used this metaphor in other ways to describe the crisis of the church. For instance, in a sermon on the feast of St. Anthony, preached at the Council of Constance in 1417, he likened the marriage of Cana, graced with Mary's blessed presence, to the council, which represented the marriage of Cana (= zeal) and Galilee (= transmigration). The transmigration is the council leading them to God and to building the city of Jerusalem out of Cana. He invokes Mary to be present at the council, even as she was present at Cana (*Sermo in festo S. Antonii*, GL, 5:376; cf. 382).

98. Gerson, *Collectorium super Magnificat*, GL, 8:216.

99. Gerson, *Josephina*, GL, 4:31–100. Written between 1414 and 1418, its purpose was to try and inject Joseph into the early years of Christ's life. On Gerson's promotion of Gerson's cult, see Palémon Glorieux, "Saint Joseph dans l'oeuvre de Gerson," *Cahiers de joséphologie* 19 (1971): 414–28; McGuire, *Jean Gerson and the Last Medieval Reformation*, pp. 235–39, 255–64, 237–39. On *Josephina*, see ibid., pp. 295–99; Hobbins, *Authorship and Publicity*, pp. 97–100.

100. Gerson, *Considérations sur Saint Joseph*, GL, 7, 1:63; *De nuptiis Christi et Ecclesiae*, GL, 6:197. Gerson vehemently denounces the blasphemers who imagine their marriage to be consummated (*Pour la fête de S. Joseph*, GL, 8:59; *Sur le culte de S. Joseph*, 8:62–63. Also see *Josephina* dist. 4, GL, 4:55–61).

101. Gerson, *Considérations sur Saint Joseph*, 7, 1:63. Joseph received his full due as husband except with respect to the conjugal debt—a prerogative that Gerson also stressed repeatedly that Joseph could have exercised had he so chosen (*Poenitemini: De la chasteté conjugale [collation]*, GL, 7, 2:843).

102. Gerson, *Considérations sur Saint Joseph*, GL, 7, 1:63, *Prosa super Epithalamium Joseph*, GL, 4:111–12; cf. *Pour la fête de la desponsation Notre Dame*, GL, 7, 1:14–15. See Newman, *God and the Goddesses*, pp. 286–87.

103. Gerson, *Discours sur l'excellence de la virginité*, in *Joannis Gersonii opera omnia*, ed. Louis Ellies du Pin (Antwerp, 1706; reprt., Hildesheim: Georg Olms, 1978), 3:829, 830. He goes on to describe the two paths available to women in terms of regular marriage—a path he describes as generous and wide—and the virgin's mystical marriage to Christ, "which is narrow and in our time little travelled" (ibid., 3:830). Carnal marriage begins by delighting and ends full of cares, while virginity is just the reverse, beginning with difficulty, but ending in delight (ibid., 3:380–81). The bulk of the treatise goes on to argue the *molestiae nuptiarum* from a woman's perspective. The image of the *sponsa Christi*, however, is hardly sustained throughout: toward the end of the treatise he praises "the excellence and security of life outside of marriage," presenting virginity as an alternative to marriage rather than an alternative marriage (ibid., 3:840). I am using this earlier edition, as the treatise printed in Glorieux (7, 1:416–41) is incomplete. Also see *Dialogue spirituel* (1407), GL, 7, 1:158.

104. Gerson, *La Montagne de contemplation* c. 40, GL, 7, 1:50, trans. McGuire, p. 118.

105. Gerson, *Pitieuse complainte*, GL, 7, 1:213. He says in *La Montagne de contemplation* that he wanted to expand the poem into a larger work. And, in fact, it was later incorporated into Gerson's *La Mendicité* (1401). See McGuire, *Jean Gerson and the Last Medieval Reformation*, p. 406n92.

106. Gerson, *De elucidatone scholastica mysticae theologiae* c. 4, GL, 8:157.

107. Gerson delivered the sermon in Paris on the feast of St. Bernard, August 20, 1402.

108. Gerson, *In festo S. Bernardi*, GL, 5:325, trans. McGuire, p. 128.

109. Ibid., GL, 5:325, trans. McGuire, p. 129.

110. According to McGuire, it is only in this one regard that Gerson disagrees with Bernard's reading ("Gerson and Bernard," p. 134).

111. Gerson, *In festo S. Bernardi*, GL, 5:325, 326 (bis), trans. McGuire, pp. 128, 129, 130.

112. Ibid., GL, 5:328, trans. McGuire, p. 132.

113. Ibid., GL, 5:329–36, trans. McGuire, pp. 133–44. This was not the only time that Gerson used the trope of a school. See, for example, Gerson's poems, *L'Ecole de la raison* and the attendant *Complainte de la conscience*, GL, 7, 1:103–8, 109–11.

114. McGuire, "Gerson and Bernard," p. 153.

115. Gerson, *In festo S. Bernardi*, GL, 5:331, trans. McGuire, p. 136.

116. Gerson, *La Montagne de contemplation* c. 11, GL, 7, 1:22–23, trans. McGuire, pp. 83–84.

117. See, for example, Ezekiel 16.22ff.; Ps. 72.27. Cf. the great harlot in Apoc. 2.20, 17.2.

118. Augustine, *In Joannis evangelium* 42.7, *PL* 35:1702; cf. Augustine, *De fide, spe et charitate* c. 45, *PL* 40:254. Others will follow suit. See, for example, Bede, *Explanatio Apocalypsis*, *PL* 93:138; Bede, *In evangelium S. Joannis*, *PL* 92:751.

119. Jerome, *Commentaria in Ezechielem*, *PL* 25:147.

120. X.4.19.12 (Alexander III, ca. 1172), X.4.19.7 (Innocent III, 1199). See Charles Reid, *Power over the Body, Equality in the Family: Rights and Domestic Relations in Medieval Canon Law* (Grand Rapids, MI: William B. Eerdman, 2004), p. 147. Theologians concurred. See Peter Lombard, *Sententiae in IV libris distinctae* 4.39.3, 2:487.

121. Waters, *Angels and Earthly Creatures*, p. 43.

122. Abelard, *Ethics*, pp. 32–35.

123. David d'Avray, *Medieval Marriage: Symbolism and Society* (Oxford: Oxford University Press, 2005), p. 58.

124. Jerome, Ep. 22, *To Eustochium* c. 6, *PL* 23:397, trans. *LNPNFC*, 6:24. Jerome's advice would be recycled by Abelard (Ep. 8, ed. McLaughlin, "Abelard's Rule," p. 269, trans. p. 173).

125. See Elliott, *Fallen Bodies*, ch. 4.

126. Hildegard of Bingen, *Sciuias* 3.11.25, ed. Adelgundis Führkötter and Angela Carlevaris, *CCCM*, 43A (Turnhout: Brepols, 1978), 2:589–90, trans. Columba Hart and Jane Bishop (New York: Paulist Press, 1990), pp. 502–3. Renate Blumenfeld-Kosinski, *Not of Woman Born: Representations of Caesarean Birth in Medieval and Renaissance Culture* (Ithaca, N.Y.: Cornell University Press, 1990), pp. 131–35.

127. This anxiety is reflected in the culture of prophecy in this period. See Robert Lerner, *The Powers of Prophecy: The Cedar of Lebanon Vision from the Mongol Onslaught to the Dawn of the Enlightenment* (Berkeley: University of California Press, 1983), esp. chs. 4–7; Blumenfeld-Kosinski, *Poets, Saints, and Visionaries*.

128. See, for example, *Ancrene Wisse* c. 4, p. 128; c. 7, pp. 190–92, 194–95. Also see *The Wooing of Our Lord*, in *Anchoritic Spirituality: Ancrene Wisse and Associated Works*, ed. and trans. Anne Savage and Nicholas Watson (New York: Paulist, 1991), pp. 247–57.

129. Phyllis Roberts has edited the single surviving copy of this sermon in the appendix to "Stephen Langton's *Sermo de virginibus*," in *Women of the Medieval World*, ed. Julius Kirshner and Suzanne Wemple (Oxford: Basil Blackwell, 1985), pp. 110–18. Because this sermon was found in a manuscript with three others concerning the religious life, it seems fair to assume that this was intended for nuns (ibid., p. 104).

130. Stephen Langton, *Sermo de virginibus* c. 1, in appendix to Roberts, "Stephen Langton's *Sermo de virginibus*," p. 110.

131. Ibid. c. 6, p. 112.

132. Ibid. c. 7, p. 113. Not surprisingly, Vashti is ultimately replaced by Esther.

133. Ibid. cc. 10–11, pp. 114–15. She does end up running mad through the streets, which inspires an allusion to the bride's running around in the Song of Songs (Sg 3.2).

134. Gerson, *Le profit de savoir quel est péché mortel et véniel*, GL, 7, 1:387–88.

135. R. C. Famiglietti argues that Isabel was, in fact, not only faithful but the perfect wife according to medieval standards, in *Tales from the Marriage Bed from Medieval France (1300–1500)* (Providence, R.I.: Picardy Press, 1992), pp. 188–95. Once the king was irretrievably mad, however, Isabel's enemies started rumors, probably groundless, that the queen and her brother-in-law, the duke of Orleans, were keeping the king in a condition of extreme squalor. If Gerson heard them, he did not seem to believe them, however, since in November 1405 he preached a sermon in the queen's residence that, while addressing the lamentable state of the kingdom, did not dwell on the king's physical health, instead attempting to make the monarchy a rallying point for France's flagging fortunes (*Pour la réforme du royaume [Vivat Rex]*, GL, 7, 2:1137–85; see McGuire's discussion, *Jean Gerson and the Last Medieval Reformation*, pp. 187–89). In fact, Gerson argued that the king had three lives—corporal, political, and spiritual—which anticipates the kind of political theory outlined in Ernst Kantorowicz's classic *The King's Two Bodies*. See Bernard Guenée, *La Folie de Charles VI: Roi Bien Aimé* (Paris: Perrin, 2004), pp. 244–49.

136. Gerson, *De signis bonis et malis*, GL, 9:164. Note that the title is somewhat misleading, as Gerson only gives signs of evil, not good.

137. Gerson, *Poenitemini: Contre la Luxure*, GL, 7, 2:819. This prejudice is sustained in his frequent revisitation of the question of why a wife cannot have two husbands, but a husband can (*Poenitemini: De la chasteté conjugale [collatio]*, GL, 7,2:866; *Regulae mandatorum*, GL, 9:130). Theologians and canonists alike are in agreement concerning women's greater moral responsibility when it came to sex, despite their physically determined moral limitations. See Brundage, *Law, Sex, and Christian Society*, pp. 350–51, 426–27. Gratian himself is aware of this problem (C. 32 q. 5 c. 22 dpc).

138. Gerson, *Poenitemini: Contre la luxure*, GL, 7, 2:821. Gerson links the sixth commandment, though shalt not steal, with the introduction of an illegitimate heir (*Le miroir de l'âme*, GL, 7, 1:195).

139. Gerson, *Poenitemini: De la chasteté conjugale (collation)*, GL, 7, 2:865.

140. Ibid., GL, 7, 2:868.

141. See Elliott, *Proving Woman*, pp. 277–78.

142. From this perspective, it is no accident that the women whose spirituality Gerson commends tend to be virgins. He credits the Holy Virgin with a life above reproach, who, somewhat inconsistently, presents herself to God with the humble demeanor of an adulterous wife before her husband (*De remediis contra pusillanimitatem*, GL, 10:375).

143. Gerson, *De simplificatione cordis*, GL, 8:95; Gerson, *De examinatione doctrinarum*, GL, 9:474. Gerson's original assessment of Ermine was solicited by Jean Morel, prior to the confessor who recorded Ermine's visions. See Ep. 25, *To Jean Morel* (ca. 1408), GL, 2:93–96, trans. McGuire, pp. 244–49.

144. Gerson, *De distinctione*, GL, 3:43, trans. McGuire, pp. 343–44.

145. Gerson, *De distinctione*, GL, 3:51, trans. McGuire, p. 356. The woman whom he censured was probably Marguerite Porete (see n91, above); the one he commended was probably Angela of Foligno (McGuire, *Jean Gerson: Early Works*, p. 459n53). We know from Angela's autobiographical *Memoriale*, which famously opens with her account of her prayers for the death of her husband and children, that Angela was no virgin. Although we have no information on Marguerite's marital status, her independent itinerant behavior suggests that she was not married. So it is possible that Gerson got it entirely wrong. On Gerson's hostility, not just to female mystical writers, but to female authorship generally, see Elliott, *Proving Woman*, pp. 269–70.

146. For Gerson's thwarted intervention in the debate over Joan, see Dyan Elliott, "Seeing Double: John Gerson, the Discernment of Spirits, and Joan of Arc," *American Historical Review* 107, no. 1 (2002): 26–54. Also see Daniel Hobbins, "Jean Gerson's Authentic Tract on Joan of Arc: *Super facto puellae et credulitate sibi praestanda* (13 May 1429)," *Mediaeval Studies* 67 (2005): 99–155. Hobbins provides definitive proof of which treatise was, in fact, written by Gerson, along with a new edition of the treatise.

147. Hobbins, *Authorship and Publicity*, pp. 203–11. Also see Caciola, *Discerning Spirits*, p. 315.

148. McGuire, *Jean Gerson and the Last Medieval Reformation*, pp. 240–83; Michael Bailey, *Battling Demons: Witchcraft, Heresy, and Reform in the Late Middle Ages* (University Park: Pennsylvania State University Press, 2003), pp. 22–28; Tschacher, *Der Formicarius des Johannes Nider von 1437/38*, pp. 51–70. There is a distinct link between the reform movement and the rise of witchcraft.

149. See, for example, Gerson's many vernacular treatises in *Oeuvres*, 7, 1, particularly his *Contre conscience trop scrupuleuse*, 7, 1:140–41; cf. Nider, *Consolatorium timorate conscientie* (Jehan Petit, [1502?]); and *De morali lepra* (Louvain: Johann von Paderborn, 1481); Brown, *Pastor and Laity*, esp. ch. 3; McGuire, *Jean Gerson and the Last Medieval Reformation*, pp. 172–96; Bailey, *Battling Demons*, pp. 101–6. Both Nider's *Consolatorium* and *De morali lepra* are indebted to Gerson's various pastoral works. Although the latter work repeatedly mentions the "Cancellarius" reverentially for some reason Nider never mentions Gerson by name in *The Anthill*. See Gábor Klaniczay, "The Process of Trance, Heavenly and Diabolic Apparitions, in Johannes Nider's *Formicarius*," Collegium Budapest, Institute for Advanced Study Discussion Paper Series 65 (June 2003): 1–81.

150. See Michael Bailey, "A Late-Medieval Crisis in Superstition?" *Speculum* 84 (2009): 633–61; Thorndike, *History of Magic and Experimental Science*, 4:274–307; Tschacher, *Der Formicarius*, pp. 269–91.

151. See, for example, the appeal made by Gerson concerning Ermine of Reims (Elliott, *Proving Woman*, pp. 279–80); cf. Nider's monitoring of Magdalena Beutler, n160, below.

152. Nider, *Formicarium* 2.1, pp. 101ff.

153. Gerson had demurred, saying he did not want to say anything against the religious life, but he had his reasons for not wanting his sisters to become nuns (*Discours sur l'excellence de la virginité*, ed. du Pin, 3:830). Certainly this could partly be so that they could care for their parents, as part of his plan was for them to remain at home as long as

they lived (3:840). McGuire thinks that part of this reluctance may have been financial, but that Gerson also had his apprehensions about contemporary religious communities for women ("Late Medieval Care and the Control of Women," p. 12).

154. Nider, *Formicarium* 1.7, p. 55; see Bailey, *Battling Demons*, p. 107.

155. As Jeffrey Hamburger has shown, the nuns' use of images in their spirituality was very much at issue (*The Visual and the Visionary: Art and Female Spirituality in Late Medieval Germany* [New York: Zone, 1998], pp. 427–67).

156. Nider, *Formicarium* 3.12, p. 195. The story of the reform is detailed on pp. 194–95. Apparently the nuns had already successfully resisted efforts at reform in 1398. See Tschacher, *Der Formicarius*, pp. 51–60. Bailey cites a study that suggests that the nuns were not, in fact, resistant to reform the second time around (*Battling Demons*, pp. 19–20). Apparently, one of the factors that caused the town council to intervene was when wealthy widows began immigrating to stricter houses elsewhere. See Regina Schiewer, "Sermons for Nuns of the Dominican Observance Movement," in *Medieval Monastic Preaching*, ed. Carolyn Muessig (Leiden: Brill, 1998), pp. 79–81

157. Nider, *Formicarium* 5.2, pp. 344–46. Nider said this disturbance occurred right around the time of the Council of Constance, which places the resistance to reform in the context of the larger resistance of the entire church.

158. Ibid. 1.10, pp. 70–75.

159. Hamburger, *Visual and the Visionary*, pp. 456–57; Klaniczay, "Process of Trance," p. 58.

160. Magdalena Beutler, a member of the Poor Clares in Freiburg, was celebrated for her extensive raptures, on which occasions she would literally disappear for several days at a time. But these idiosyncratic performances were soon eclipsed in 1431 when she dramatically prophesized the day of her death—an event that was elaborately staged and observed with expectation by many religious dignitaries, including a representative from Nider's community, in attendance (Nider, *Formicarium* 3.8, pp. 230–32; see Elliott, *Proving Woman*, pp. 218, 197–200; Klaniczay, "Process of Trance," pp. 13–14). Klaniczay notes the truncation of Nider's account compared to how other contemporary sources related this event, with the effect of rendering it more suspect. By the same token, a recluse of Radolfzell (Celle), who had garnered many devout and high-powered spiritual clients among the clergy, predicted her own reception of the stigmata—a moment that never arrived (Nider, *Formicarium* 3.11, p. 327; Klaniczay, "Process of Trance," pp. 37–38). One of the few positive examples of a cloistered nun is Sister Coleta of France, an effective reformer. The fact that she was also a Poor Clare to some extent offsets the example of Magdalena (Nider, *Formicarium* 4.9, p. 309).

161. In fact, Bailey argues that Nider's *The Anthill* repeatedly challenges the contemporary pessimism regarding the church (*Battling Demons*, p. 103).

162. Nider, *Formicarium* 1.12, pp. 92–94.

163. Adelheyd also had two virginal siblings, Catherine and John. The purity of this pious trio was foretold by the color of certain flowering trees that each had adopted as children. The two girls had white flowers; John's was red, which betokened his death by a lingering illness (Nider, *Formicarium* 2.1, pp. 99–100).

164. Ibid. 4.5, pp. 284–85. Despite her apparent sanctity, she was sufficiently naïve as to ask Nider if meditation on the Crucifixion was superstitious.

165. Ibid. 1.4, pp. 33–35.

166. Ibid. 2.9, p. 153.

167. Ibid. 1.4, p. 35.

168. He goes on to maintain that in adjacent cities, the lack of virgins is due to a dissolute clergy and temporal lords attempting to subject the women to marriage "unwilling and against natural law." As a result these areas suffer a lot of famines and a dearth of truly inspired men free from error (ibid. 1.4, p. 36).

169. Ibid. 1.5, pp. 38–45.

170. Ibid. 2.9, pp. 153–55. He also adds that the only daughter did not cease to fight for God "so that sometimes he thought she was possessed by a good angel."

171. Ibid. 4.5, p. 283.

172. This application is but a natural extension of Nider's monasticized view of married life. But this potentially bold deviation from tradition is not obvious because the title *bride of Christ* is used sparingly throughout *The Anthill.* There are two contemporary recastings of virginal *passiones* in which the respective women besought the help of their celestial "spouse" to preserve them from carnal marriage: in each case, the prayers were fulfilled by fatal disease (ibid. 4.4, pp. 278–80). A third reference is mere innuendo: when eulogizing the many marvels that occur among the humble—"especially humble women"—Nider gives the example of a poor, but beautiful, woman from Nuremburg who wanted to dedicate herself to Christ. For years, however, she was tested by the devil: her house would echo with screams and blows during her nighttime struggles. After many years of beseeching Christ for a ring as a token of his love, she eventually found one in her garden of an unknown metal, similar to silver, with two hands joined together (ibid. 1.2, p. 17).

173. Ibid. 3.2., pp. 207–9.

174. Ibid. 5.8, p. 383.

175. Ibid., p. 384.

176. Ibid.

177. Ibid., p. 385.

178. Ibid. 4.8, p. 386. Joan's story is framed by imposters and acolytes. The history of Claude, "the false Joan," precedes Nider's account of the real Joan, which is one of the author's deauthorizing strategies. See Elliott, "Seeing Double," pp. 26–54. As with Nider's treatment of Joan, the question of the discernment of spirits is foregrounded in each of these different recitations. Hence the fact that Claude ended her days as a clerical concubine demonstrates "by which spirit she was led" (Nider, *Formicarium* 3.8, p. 386). Subsequent to his account of Joan, Nider also reports on two women who arose up in the wake of Joan and preached in her support. They were seized by the inquisition "just as enchantresses or witches" ("velut magae, vel maleficae"). When examined by theologians, it was determined that they had been misled by evil spirits. One recanted and the other was burned (ibid., p. 387).

179. Ibid., pp. 386–87.

180. The rubrics for the enveloping chapters are "What it means to consume [i.e.,

destroy] in order to purge; How witches sometimes harm judges, how they see when absent, and how they sometimes say contradictory things" (ibid. 5.7, p. 378), and "There are three ways of correcting vices; and what are incubus and succubus demons, just as is proved through exempla and authorities" (ibid. 5.9, p. 391). Note that the haunting of the unfortunate community of St. Catherine's is also included in book 5.

181. Ibid. 5.10, p. 402.

182. The role of university-trained clerics in the rise of witchcraft has been addressed in other ways as well. Richard Kieckhefer attributes the rise of witchcraft to the imposition of learned notions on popular tradition in *European Witch Trials: Their Foundations in Popular and Learned Cultures, 1300–1500* (London: Routledge and Kegan Paul, 1976). Also see Russell, *Witchcraft in the Middle Ages*, pp. 142–47. Alain Boureau perceives the pontificate of John XXII (d. 1334), which assimilated witchcraft and heresy, as formative. See *Satan the Heretic: The Birth of Demonology in the Medieval West*, trans. Teresa Lavender Fagan (Chicago: University of Chicago Press, 2006).

183. Nider is clearly aware that a number of Dominican authorities were against a one-sided vow of chastity (i.e., not to exact the debt) on the basis that it would be onerous for the other spouse to always be initiating, and seems to agree. Elsewhere, however, he cites authorities that permit a one-sided vow, which is considered better for the health, provided that the person is prepared to render the debt (*De morali lepra* c. 16, fol. 82v). Nider manifests his liberal views in a number of other ways. For instance, he permits a husband who has difficulty getting or sustaining an erection to stimulate himself manually, with embraces that are otherwise considered illicit, as well as with foods that have aphrodisiac potential (ibid., fols. 80r–81v).

184. Nider, *Formicarium* 2.9, pp. 154–55. Margery Kempe also received divine assistance in this respect: she called upon Christ and her husband "had no power to towche hir at that tyme in that wyse, ne nevyr aftyr with no fleschly knowying" (*Book of Margery Kempe* 1.9, ed. Windeatt, p. 82). Cf. the parallel incident in Lucia Brocadelli of Narni's life where an angel intervened (Marcianese, *Narratione della nascita*, p. 61). One of Lucia's revelations also seems to allude to an unsuccessful attempt at rape by her brother-in-law (E. Ann Matter, Armano Maggi, and Maiju Lehmijoki-Gardner, eds., "'Le Rivelazioni' of Lucia Brocadelli da Narni," *Archivum Fratrum Praedicatorum* 71 [2001]: 339–40, trans. E. Ann Matter, *Dominican Penitent Women*, ed. Maiju Lehmijoki-Gardner [New York: Paulist Press, 2005], pp. 241–42).

185. See Marcello Craveri, *Sante e streghe: Biografie e documenti dal XIV al XVII secolo* (Milan: Feltrinelli economica, 1980); Peter Dinzelbacher, *Heilige oder Hexen? Schicksale auffälliger Frauen in Mittelalter und Frühneuzeit* (Zurich: Artemis and Winkler, 1995); Gabriella Zarri, *Le Sante vive: Cultura e religiosità femminile nella prima età moderna* (Turin: Rosenberg and Sellier, 1990); Elspeth Whitney, "International Trends: The Witch 'She'/The Historian 'He'; Gender and the Historiography of the European Witch-Hunts," *Journal of Women's History* 7 (1995): 91–92; Klaniczay, "Process of Trance," pp. 77–78; Klaniczay, "Miraculum and Maleficium: Reflections Concerning Late Medieval Female Sanctity," in *Problems in the Historical Anthropology of Early Modern Europe*, ed. R. Po-Chia Hsia and R. W. Scribner, Wolfenbütteler Forschungen, vol. 78 (Harrasowitz, Wiesenbaden:

Wolfenbüttel, 1997), pp. 49–73. For a critique of the view that medieval culture would in any way be inclined to confuse the saint and the witch, see Richard Kieckhefer, "The Holy and the Unholy: Sainthood, Witchcraft, and Magic in Late Medieval Europe," *Journal of Medieval and Renaissance Studies* 24 (1994): 335–85, esp. 360–72. On the witch's mark, see François Delpech, "La 'marque' des sorcières: Logique(s) de la stigmatization diabolique," in *Le Sabbat des sorciers: XVe-XVIIIe siècles*, ed. Nicole Jacques-Chaquin and Maxime Préaud (Grenoble: Jérôme Millon, 1993), pp. 347–68. According to Delpech, one of the first mentions occurred in a demonological treatise in 1458. It becomes more common in the sixteenth and seventeenth centuries (ibid., pp. 350–51).

186. See Tamar Herzig, "Witches, Saints, and Heretics: Heinrich Kramer's Ties with Italian Women Mystics," *Magic, Ritual, and Witchcraft* 1 (2006): 24–55.

187. See Stuart Clark's classic "Inversion, Misrule, and the Meaning of Witchcraft," *Past and Present* 87(1980): 98–127.

188. This is vividly brought home by the popularity of the casuist question that swept the universities in the fourteenth century concerning the culpability of a person who adored Satan masquerading as Christ (see Elliott, "True Presence/False Christ," pp. 241–65).

189. On the papal efforts to make belief in Francis of Assisi's stigmata compulsory, see André Vauchez, "Les stigmates de Saint François et leurs detracteurs" *Mélanges de l'Ecole Française de Rome: Temps modernes* 80 (1968): 595–625.

190. Nider, *Formicarium* 5.9, pp. 395ff. See especially the discussion of how an incubus impregnates a woman (5.10, p. 401).

191. The other formative texts, including the pertinent sections from Nider (*Formicarium* 2.4, and bk. 5, passim) have all been reedited in *L'Imaginaire du sabbat: Edition critique des texts les plus anciens (1430 c.–1440c.)*, ed. Martine Ostorero, Agostino P. Bagliani, and Kathrin Utz Tremp (Lausanne: Cahiers lausannois d'histoire médiévale, 1999) (hereafter cited as *Imaginaire*). With the exception of Nider, this is the edition I will be using in the ensuing discussion. On these authors, see Tschacher, *Der Formicarius*, pp. 293–340. On the characteristics of the witchcraft charges that developed in this area, see Richard Kieckhefer, "Mythologies of Witchcraft in the Fifteenth Century," *Magic, Ritual, and Witchcraft* 1 (2006): 84–87; also see Kieckhefer, *European Witch Trials*, pp. 22–26.

192. Recent work on the sabbath includes Michael Bailey, "The Medieval Concept of the Witches' Sabbath," *Exemplaria* 8 (1996): 419–39; Martine Ostorero, "The Concept of the Witches' Sabbath in the Alpine Region (1430–1440): Text and Context," in *Witchcraft Mythologies and Persecutions*, ed. Gábor Klaniczay and Éva Pócs (Budapest: Central European Press, 2008), pp. 15–34. Also see the collection of articles dedicated to this subject, *Le Sabbat des sorciers: XVe-XVIIIe siècles*, ed. Jacques-Chaquin and Préaud (Grenoble: Jérôme Millon, 1993); see esp. articles by Éva Pócs, "Le sabbat et les mythologies indo-européennes," pp. 23–32; Alain Boureau, "Le sabbat et la question scolastique de la personne," pp. 33–46; Jacques Vidal, "L'arbitraire des juges d'Eglise en matière de sorcellerie," pp. 75–99; Gábor Klaniczay, "Le sabbat raconté par les témoins des procès de sorcellerie en Hongrie," pp. 227–46. Both Carlo Ginzburg (*Ecstasies: Interpreting the Witches' Sabbath*, trans. Raymond Rosenthal [New York: Pantheon Books, 1991], esp. pt. 2) and Pócs stress the folkloric contribution. See also Gustav Henningsen, " 'The Ladies from Outside': An

Archaic Pattern of the Witches' Sabbath," *Early Modern European Witchcraft: Centres and Peripheries*, ed. Bengt Ankarloo and Gustav Henningsen (Oxford: Clarendon, 1990), pp. 191–215. One of the ironies of *The Hammer of Witches*, the most celebrated witch-hunting manual, is that it includes no discussion of the sabbath.

193. Nider, for example, thought that night flights were the fantasies of old women and left them out of his description of the sabbath altogether (Nider, *Formicarium* 2.4, pp. 123–24). The anonymous inquisitor who wrote the *Errors of the Gazari* makes reference to the devil bestowing sticks and unguents on his followers, presumably for flying to the assemblies (*Errores gazariorum seu illorum qui scopam vel baculum equitare probantur*, in *Imaginaire*, p. 298). There are two versions of this text. The original (MS V) was probably written before 1437. A second, longer version (MS B) to some extent depends on an inquisitional trial that occurred in July 1438, and thus is later. See the introduction to these editions by Kathrin Utz Tremp and Martine Ostorero (*Imaginaire*, pp. 273–74). Also see the composite edition, which compares the two versions (ibid., pp. 288–99). Note that *Gazar* literally means Cathar, which, at least in this context, is synonymous with the term *witch*. The poet Le Franc, discussed below, is equivocal: in his mock dialogue, the Adversary makes the charge that women fly to the sabbath on broomsticks. This is refuted by the Champion, who nevertheless grants that the devil has the capacity to make one believe that he or she is flying (*Le Champion des dames* ll. 17457–64, 17545–60, in *Imaginaire*, pp. 455–56, 458–59). Fründ's and Thoulan's versions of night flights are treated below. The night flight is first referred to in the ninth-century *Canon Episcopi* (discussed above), which dismisses it as fantasy. Gratian cites the *Canon Episcopi* in the same spirit of incredulity (C. 25 q. 5 c. 12). By Nider's time, such healthy skepticism has been eroded.

194. Hans Fründ, *Rapport sur la chase aux sorciers et aux sorcières menée dès 1428 dans le diocèse de Sion*, in *Imaginaire*, pp. 33, 35.

195. Elsewhere, however, he alleges that the devil can move his confederates from mountaintop to mountaintop. Equipped with diabolical ointment with which they anoint chairs, moreover, the sectarians are able to move from town to town, preferring the ones with the best wine, and having a general good time—perhaps in groups (Fründ, *Rapport*, in *Imaginaire*, p. 34). Fründ also describes "schools" (*schulen*) where the diabolical master preaches sermons against the Christian faith, especially forbidding them the sacrament of confession. They are required to confess to the devil, however, if they happened to attend church or performed any good deeds, for which they would receive due penance. Some of the witches are said to cook infants, which they share with the rest of their society (ibid., pp. 36–37).

196. Claude Tholosan, *Ut magorum et maleficiorum errores* cc. 2–4, in *Imaginaire*, pp. 362, 364.

197. Ibid. c. 6, p. 368.

198. Cf. Marc Bloch's description of the classic ritual: "Imagine two men face to face; one wishing to serve, the other willing or anxious to be served. The former puts his hands together and places them, thus joined, between the hand of the other man—a plain symbol of submission, the significance of which was sometimes further emphasized by a kneeling posture. At the same time, the person proffering his hands utters a few words—a very

short declaration—by which he acknowledges himself to be the 'man' of the person facing him. Then chief and subordinate kiss each other on the mouth, symbolizing accord and friendship. . . . The ceremony was called 'homage'" (*Feudal Society*, vol. 1, *The Growth of the Ties of Dependence*, trans. L. A. Manyon [Chicago: University of Chicago Press, 1961], 1:145–46). Bloch goes on to distinguish homage from fealty, the swearing of a solemn oath on a gospel or other relic, which he construes as a religious imposition on the original act of homage. Cf. Jacques Le Goff, "The Symbolic Ritual of Vassalage," in *Time, Work, and Culture in the Middle Ages*, trans. Arthur Goldhammer (Chicago: University of Chicago Press, 1980), pp. 239–48.

199. Nider, *Formicarium* 5.3, p. 352; also see a briefer account from the same source that involves trampling and spitting on the crucifix (ibid., p. 351).

200. Kieckhefer, *European Witch Trials*, pp. 6–7, 22–26. Lea also argues that the early secular trials are free of devil worship (*Materials*, 1:245).

201. See Kathrin Utz Tremp and Martine Ostorero's introduction to *Errores gazariorum*, in *Imaginaire*, p. 273.

202. *Errores gazariorum* c. 2, 3, in *Imaginaire*, pp. 288, 290.

203. Le Franc, *Champion* ll. 17445–500, in *Imaginaire*, pp. 455–57.

204. Ibid. ll. 17505–520, in *Imaginaire*, p. 457.

205. Ibid. ll. 17531–36, in *Imaginaire*, p. 458.

206. William of Auvergne, *De legibus* c. 26, in *Opera omnia*, 1:83. (Note William also maintains that the taboo against menstrual blood in part arose from the way in which it was manipulated by witches, in ibid. c. 6, p. 36). There is a gradual amplification of the feudal imagery—especially in the *Errors of the Gazari*, which explicitly aligns the induction into the sect with the bonds of vassalage. This initiative is to some extent sustained in *The Champion of Ladies*: the pact to the devil is referred to as "homage," even as the manner in which the devil metes out justice before the assembly resembles the curia of a feudal court. The more explicit feudal references might correspond to papal initiative: in 1437, Eugenius IV issued a letter to the inquisitors of heretical depravity that made reference to a new sect that did "homage" to demons (in *Quellen*, ed. Hansen, p. 17, trans. *Witchcraft in Europe, 1400–1700: A Documentary History*, ed. Alan Kors and Edward Peters, 2nd ed. [Philadelphia: University of Pennsylvania Press, 2001], p. 154).

207. Guibert of Nogent, *Autobiographie* 3.17, ed. Labande, p. 430, trans. p. 213.

208. See Charles Zika, *The Appearance of Witchcraft: Print and Visual Culture in Sixteenth-Century Europe* (London: Routledge, 2007), pp. 63–65.

209. Note, however, that promiscuity with demons also occurred in some of Tholosan's trials. In the 1437 trial of Iubert of Bavaria, conducted under Claude Tholosan, three demons flew out of a book on necromancy—Lust, Pride, and Greed. They asked Iubert to adore them and renounce God. Lust had assumed the form of a twelve-year-old virgin, and Iubert had sex with her, while the other demons looked on snickering (Hansen, *Quellen*, pp. 540–41).

210. This change will be famously articulated in Kramer and Sprenger. See the Conclusion, p. 285, below.

211. Freud would probably categorize the poem as an obscene joke that created an

opportunity for Le Franc to talk about "smut" and/or express hostility. Such jokes "make possible the satisfaction of an instinct (whether lustful or hostile) in the face of an obstacle that stands in its way" (*Jokes and Their Relation to the Unconscious, SE,* 8:101).

212. This area includes the Val d'Aoste, Bern and its environs, the diocese of Lausanne, and the regions surrounding the Valais and the Dauphiné. For a discussion of these earliest texts and the significance of the geography, see Ostorero, "Concept of the Witches' Sabbath," pp. 15–34.

213. Kieckhefer, "Mythologies of Witchcraft," pp. 84–86, 91, 100.

214. Even as the treatise *The Errors of the Gazari* associates the witch's cult with Cathars, the Vauderie is the French form of the Waldensian sect and would become associated with diabolical practices from the fourteenth century onward. See Gordon Andreas Singer, *La Vauderie d'Arras, 1459–1491: An Episode of Witchcraft in Later Medieval France* (PhD diss., University of Maryland, 1974), ch. 4. Neither the Cathars nor the Waldensians had any beliefs that resembled witchcraft accusations. The Vauderie received considerable attention at the time. The *Mémoires* of chronicler James Du Clercq are undoubtedly the best source. See *Mémoires J. Du Clercq sur le règne de Philippe le Bon, Duc de Bourgogne,* ed. F. de Reiffenberg (Brussels: J. M. Lacrosse, 1836) (hereafter cited as Du Clercq), esp. bk. 4 (vol. 3). The appropriate sections have also been excerpted in *Corpus documentorum inquisitionis haereticae pravitatis Neerlandicae,* ed. Paul Fredericq, 5 vols. (Ghent: J. Vuylsteke; The Hague: Martinus Nijhoff, 1896; hereafter cited as Fredericq). For in-depth studies, see Singer, *La Vauderie d'Arras*; Franck Mercier, *La Vauderie d'Arras: Une chasse aux sorcières à l'automne du Moyen Age* (Rennes: Presses Universitaires de Rennes, 2006). For brief accounts of this debacle, see Lea, *History of the Inquisition,* 3:519–28; Norman Cohn, *Europe's Inner Demons: The Demonization of Christians in Medieval Christendom,* rev. ed. (Chicago: University of Chicago Press, 1993), pp. 207–9. For the extension of the inquiry beyond Arras, see Du Clercq, 4.4, 3:20, 31–32. Also see the excerpt from the *Registre des prévôts et jurés* for Tournai and the accusation of a woman in Lille, in Fredericq, 2:264–66.

215. Du Clercq 4.3, 3:10–11.

216. Ibid. 4.4, 3:25–26.

217. In addition to Deniselle, at least another five prostitutes were executed (ibid. 4.8, 15, 3:36, 75). Cf. the parallel case of two prostitutes burned for sorcery discussed by Dyan Elliott, "Women in Love: Carnal and Spiritual Transgressions in Late Medieval France," in *Living Dangerously: On the Margins in Medieval and Early Modern Europe,* ed. Barbara Hanawalt and Anna Grotans (Notre Dame, Ind.: University of Notre Dame Press, 2007), pp. 55–86.

218. Jacquier, *Flagellum haereticorum fascinariorum* in *Quellen,* ed. Hansen, pp. 133, 136. On Jacquier, see Mercier, *La Vauderie,* pp. 64–66.

219. Du Clercq 4.16, 3:81–84. Du Clercq alleges that no one believed the allegations, perceiving the accusations as the natural consequence of torture (4.28, 3:135).

220. The final deliberation was only made in 1491 and is copied by Du Clercq (3:267–93). Also see the excerpt from the *Registres de Parlement,* excerpted by Du Clercq (3:251–66). The perpetrators were eventually ordered to make reparation (Fredericq, 3:117–18).

221. Du Clercq 4.3, 3:13.

222. They advocated the release of the prisoners, urging that the death penalty should only be applied for murder or host desecration (ibid. 4.4, 3:17). Du Bois's frightening degree of certainty was complemented by the perverse dedication of the bishop of Beirut, who assisted in these proceedings. A former papal penitentiary, and hence presumably acquainted with all manner of sin, this bishop claimed he could recognize a witch by sight. He also alleged that many of his fellow bishops were implicated in witchcraft (ibid. 4.4, 3:18). The two of them also were persistent in their efforts to extract a denunciation of the absentee bishop for his participation in witchcraft, but never succeeded (ibid. 4.37, 3:190).

223. Ibid. 4.26, 38, 3:128–29, 198.

224. Note that the title, *Recollectio casus, status, et condicionis Valdensium ydolatrarum*, is, in fact, the incipit. The treatise itself is untitled. It is printed in Hansen, *Quellen*, pp. 149–81. Hansen also prints the short disquisition on demons, which was appended to the manuscript, written in the same hand (pp. 181–83). Mercier summarizes its contents (*La Vauderie*, pp. 32–33). On the likelihood of du Bois's authorship, see Lea, *History of the Inquisition*, 3:521, 529; Mercier, *La Vauderie*, pp. 32, 58. The inquisitor, Nicolas Jacquier, is another possible contender for authorship of the *Recollectio*. See, however, Mercier's contentions against Jacquier on the basis of terminology used in the *Flagellum*, his treatise against witchcraft (*La Vauderie*, p. 65).

225. *Recollectio* art. 1, in Hansen, *Quellen*, pp. 150–53.

226. Ibid. art. 1, pp. 154–58. He returns to the subject of torture in art. 6, pp. 167–68.

227. Ibid. art. 1, p. 154.

228. Ibid. art. 7, p. 169. He eventually denounced many people, however (Du Clercq 4.4, 3:25).

229. The demon always appears in a male form, though he can appear as any number of different men or animals, or it may be a different demon altogether, for there are many options. If the postulant is lowborn, the demon, the father of pride, will make a fuss and require some special offering, like an important wicked deed (*Recollectio* art. 3, in Hansen, *Quellen*, p. 159). It may be the episcopal-like deference paid to the demon that led Russell to assert mistakenly that the representative was *the* devil himself (*Witchcraft in the Middle Ages*, p. 248).

230. She makes a singular promise not to frequent church, not to accept the sprinkling of holy water or confess (except in pretense), and especially not to betray the sect. If required to observe the elevation of the host at Mass, she should always spit on the ground in disrespect when no one is looking. After any pretense of piety, she must say under her breath to the devil, "Sir, may it not displease you" (*Recollectio* art. 3, in Hansen, *Quellen*, p. 159).

231. Then he instructs that an imperfect cross be made from the mud. He additionally orders a consecrated host to be carried to the congregation to be defiled and stamped on by the one being accepted, with the others assisting.

232. She swears most solemnly not to reveal this in court. And also those in the sect should only confess rarely and unwillingly. The demon never, as said above, negotiates or makes a pact, especially an expressed pact, unless the soul has already been given to him (*Recollectio* art. 3, in Hansen, *Quellen*, p. 159).

233. And in turn the demon compensates with some grace or special ability: either

the promise of money (for he knows where hidden treasure is with God's permission), or he gives her the faculty of enjoying women or men, or he gives her the grace of healing (through superstitious practices). There is a lengthy explanation of how demonic healing works and why God permits it. But these gifts are often fake, because the devil is the father of lies. This applies to abilities such as finding lost things or predicting weather. Sometimes the demon manufactures the weather in order to comply with his predictions. He can also help people obtain offices or ingratiate themselves with the great (sometimes enlisting simony or bribery). Sometimes the devil makes people compliant by tampering with their food or humors (ibid., pp. 160–61).

234. The rings are the first items mentioned. The devil's token could also be a piece of thread (*filum*) or a round piece of papyrus covered in unknown letters. Whatever the object may be, it activates the special power he has bestowed upon the witch (ibid., p. 161). Additionally the devil makes two promises: to give the supplicant every abundance and never be absent or away—especially when invoked in time of necessity. (The author adds that this is a fallacy: the devil is often unavailable when the witch needs him, but the devil is, after all, a liar. He does nothing to help his followers when they are caught, though sometimes he visits them in prison. The author then goes on a tangent about Waldensians who often evoke demons, at least when they are not imprisoned. The sectarians themselves deny it, of course.)

235. Ibid., p. 161.

236. The demon penetrates her first vaginally, ejaculating foul, yellow semen stolen from nocturnal emissions or some other place, and then anally, hence forcing her to commit the "sin against nature." The devil's entire body is cold, while the penis itself is described as cold and soft (ibid., p. 162).

237. Sometimes the food is conveyed earlier by demons and members of the congregation. Occasionally the devils pretend to eat as well.

238. After reprising his earlier precepts, the devil adds new ones in the following sequence: (1) not to confess or speak to a priest; (2) not to speak about the sect in the world; (3) to maintain that the sabbath is but a dream or illusion in order to fool the authorities; (4) to realize that if the judge learns about the reality of the sabbath, this does not mean clemency either in terms of acquittal or release from prison; (5) that if seized by justice to choose death rather than betray the others, though the devil will succor them so they will not die; (6) to instruct and seduce as many people as possible in order to be rewarded with a greater number of demons; (7) never to confess giving their souls to the demon; (8) to return frequently to the congregations; (9) to absent themselves from the executions of fellow sectarians; (10) to conceal their maleficia both in court and elsewhere. After stating the time and place of the next sabbath, the devil dismisses them (ibid., pp. 163–64).

239. Mercier, *La Vauderie*, p. 80.

240. The numbers in the text coincide with the chapters numbered in *De benedictione et consecratione virginum* of William Durandus's rite (in *Le Pontifical de Guillaume Durand*, 3:411–25). Note, however, that Durandus's version omits the participation of the parents, probably in keeping with the trend in matrimony to emphasize individual consent (Metz,

La Consécration, p. 278). In their place, an archpriest is introduced to prepare and present the postulants.

241. Other references to the ring occur in the *Recollectio* arts. 1, 3, in Hansen, *Quellen*, pp. 155, 161. For *arrhae*, see ibid., art 3, pp. 159, 160. Usually the *arrha* is given by the man to the woman, however. In the Barbarian successor states, the verb *subarrhare anulo* soon became interchangeable with contracting marriage. See Metz, *La Consécration*, pp. 211–12.

242. See, for example, Gen. 31.2; 1 King 10.5; 2 King 6.5; 1 Par. 13.8; Job 21.3, 12; Is. 5.12, 30.32; cf. Jude 15.15, in which the women and virgins rejoiced, while the youths played on organs and cithars and Ex. 15.20, in which Miriam, the sister of Aaron, led the women in a dance with a tambour in hand. Later Ambrose will present the Virgin Mary herself as playing the tambour while leading the column of virgins in the celestial kingdom (*De virginibus [Über die Jungfrauen]* 1.3.12, 2.2.17, ed. Dückers, pp. 118, 230, trans. *LNPNFC*, 10:365, 376). Both women are "Maria" in Latin.

243. On the mystical dances of the two Mechtilds, see Chapter 6, pp. 178, 179, above. For Gertrude the Great's allusions to the cithar, see *Les Exercices* bks. 5, 6, ed. Hourlier and Schmitt, *Oeuvres spirituelles*, SC, 127, 1: bk. 5, p. 176; bk. 6, pp. 220, 230, 234, trans. pp. 82, 103, 108, 110.

244. In the ensuing orgy, people switched partners at the command of the presiding demon. Nor did the participants limit themselves to heterosexual fornication: women went with women, men with men, men abused women against nature with ejaculation occurring outside the "vas debitum." The witches allegedly experience more delight and lust at these gatherings than at other times. This is partially drug induced (*Recollectio* art. 3, in Hansen, *Quellen*, pp. 162–63).

245. Russell alleges that they are arranged in a circle (*Witchcraft in the Middle Ages*, p. 248), but the text says very clearly that they were not arranged in a circle, but in rows (*non in circulum, sed in reugas extensas in longum*). Nevertheless they are still assembled with diabolical strangeness—either with their faces pressed up close to one another, or back to back (*Recollectio* art. 3, in Hansen, *Quellen*, p. 162).

246. Metz also notes that the same gesture of homage is present in the ordination of the priest, only the kiss on the mouth exchanged between men is replaced by the nun's more discreet gesture of kissing the bishop's hand (*La Consécration*, pp. 287–89). The rite of homage described in the witch's induction also requires a kiss on the hand or foot.

247. Ibid., pp. 274–75.

248. In his *Rationale divinorum officiorum*, Durandus explains the significance of the candles with the comment, "their [the virgins'] Spouse is Christ, whom the bishop—his vicar—represents" (2.1.40, p. 138). On Durandus's innovations, see Metz, *La Consécration*, pp. 294, 299–300, 303, 305; Zarri, *Recinti*, pp. 278–81.

249. See Le Goff, "Symbolic Ritual of Vassalage," pp. 256, 261, 275. Also see Fry's discussion of possible marriage imagery in the rule of St. Benedict in Chapter 2, p. 56, above. This indebtedness may to some extent explain the controversy surrounding the rituals uniting men that John Boswell has argued are, in fact, marriage. See his *Same-Sex Unions in Premodern Europe* (New York: Villard, 1994).

250. Mercier, *La Vauderie*, p. 80.

251. As Paul Hyams points out with regard to homage, "Full prostration was never part of the ritual. . . . When a man actually kneeled in homage, the fact seems to have been specifically noted as unusual. It was not even normal to kiss the lord's hand; the mouth-to-mouth kiss offered instead was . . . a quintessential symbol of mutuality," in "Homage and Feudalism: A Judicious Separation," in *Die Gegenwart des Feudalismus: Présence du féodalisme et présent de la féodalité; The Presence of Feudalism*, ed. Natalie Fryde, Pierre Monnet, and Otto G. Oexle (Göttingen: Vandenhoeck and Ruprecht, 2002), pp. 24–25.

252. Michael Bailey, "The Feminization of Magic and the Emerging Idea of the Female Witch in the Late Middle Ages," *Essays in Medieval Studies* 19 (2002): 121. Bailey also makes the argument that necromancy requires higher learning, while witchcraft was a more equal opportunity art, opening the door for female practitioners (pp. 126–28). Also see Stuart Clark's analysis of the feminization of witchcraft as a result of binary thinking in "The 'Gendering' of Witchcraft in French Demonology: Misogyny or Polarity?" in *New Perspectives on Witchcraft, Magic and Demonology*, vol. 4, *Gender and Witchcraft*, ed. Brian Levack (New York: Routledge, 2001), pp. 54–65. Robin Briggs, however, does his best to downplay any link between gender and witchcraft, despite the clear majority of women ("Women as Victims? Witches, Judges, and Community," in ibid., pp. 40–53). This position seems to exemplify the tendency characterized by Whitney of male historians to downplay the persecution of witches as an antiwoman phenomenon ("International Trends").

253. Kramer and Sprenger, *Malleus maleficarum* pt. 1 q. 6, 1:282–92, trans. 2:112–22. This association was soon solidified by graphic representations. See Zika, *Appearance of Witchcraft*, esp. ch. 3.

254. Kieckhefer estimates that about two-thirds of accused witches were female (*European Witch Trials*, p. 96).

255. Fredericq, 1:349. Like most of the accused, Deniselle's confession was only extracted after severe torture (Du Clercq 4.3, 3:11–12).

256. *Recollectio* art. 3, in Hansen, *Quellen*, pp. 162–63. There is plenty of human same-sex activity, however.

257. On the demonic revulsion to sodomy, see Elliott, *Fallen Bodies*, pp. 152–54. Stephens wrongly assumes that Kramer is rather singular in this respect (*Demon Lovers*, pp. 54–55). When the inquisitor Peter Le Broussart describes the rite in a sermon, ritual copulation is omitted. Moreover, in the orgy he notes that the devil has sex with his various followers, taking the form of a man when he is with a woman, and a woman when he is with a man. He goes on to say that the adherents even engage in sodomy and other sins against nature that he will refrain from mentioning. But as in the *Recollectio*, it seems to be the humans who are responsible for this particular set of outrages—not the demons (Du Clercq 4.4, 3:21–22). By the same token, when Broussart is relating the various confessions of the convicted, it is only a woman, Colette Lescrebée, who confesses to having had sex with the devil (Du Clercq 4.8, 3:37). In contrast, the knight, Sr. Beaufort, confessed to having sex with a woman at the orgy, but claimed that when the devil asked for his soul, he only gave him four hairs from his head (Du Clercq 4.14, 3:63). Beaufort was sentenced with three other men, none of whom confessed to sexual acts of any kind (Du Clercq 4.14, 3:64–68). This taboo against male sex with the devil begins to break down in the sixteenth

century. See Lyndal Roper's *Witch Craze: Terror and Fantasy in Baroque Germany* (New Haven, Conn.: Yale University Press, 2004), pp. 90–91. According to Roper, however, the description of such sex acts in the male defendants' narratives tends to become convoluted and confused. Moreover, the devil will frequently shapeshift into a woman or an animal. Likewise, in the sixteenth century certain Italian theologians will begin to grant that demons do engage in sodomy with male witches. See Tamar Herzig, "The Demons' Reaction to Sodomy: Witchcraft and Homosexuality in Gianfrancesco Pico della Mirandola's *Strix*," *Sixteenth-Century Journal* 34, no. 1 (2003): 53–72.

258. E. William Monter, *Witchcraft in France and Switzerland: The Borderlands during the Reformation* (Ithaca, N.Y.: Cornell University Press, 1976), pp. 21–22.

259. See Lerner, *Heresy of the Free Spirit*.

260. On this episode, see Paul Beuzart, *Les Hérésies pendant le Moyen Age et la Réforme jusqu'à la mort de Philippe II, 1598, dans la région de Douai, d'Arras, et au pays de l'Alleu* (Le Puy: Peyriller, Rouchon, et Gamon, 1912), pp. 39–49. Note, however, that this name only seems to have been applied by later writers. Beuzart thinks that Gerson is the best witness to this group because he attacked a group of antinomian seducers that he referred to as the Turlupins who were still active in his day (*De examinatione doctrinarum* GL, 9:472–73; Beuzart, *Les Hérésies*, pp. 51–52). Lerner establishes that Turlupin is a synonym for Beghard (Lerner, *Heresy of the Free Spirit*, pp. 52–53, 66–67).

261. Fredericq, 3:90.

262. Marguerite Porete, *Le Mirouer des simples âmes* c. 118, ed. Romana Guarnieri and Paul Verdeyen, *CCCM*, 69 (Turnhout: Brepols, 1986), pp. 316–34, trans. Ellen Babinsky, *The Mirror of Simple Souls* (New York: Paulist Press, 1993), pp. 189–94. Regarding the seven stages of the soul, see Hollywood, *Soul as Virgin Wife*, pp. 97–103. On Marguerite, see Michael Sargant, "Marguerite Porete," *MHW*, pp. 291–309. The documents for the trial of Marguerite and a cleric who attempted to defend her are edited by Paul Verdeyen in "Le Procès d'inquisition contre Marguerite Porete et Guiard de Cressonessart (1309–1310)," *Revue d'histoire ecclésiastique* 81 (1986): 47–94. Verdeyen also includes select chroniclers who discussed the trial.

263. Porete, *Le Mirouer des simples âmes* c. 9, ed. Guarnieri and Verdeyen, p. 32, trans. p. 87. See Robert Lerner's recent proof that the Middle English version of *The Mirror* is not only the closest surviving text to Marguerite's original but also more doctrinally bold than the later version ("New Light on *The Mirror of Simple Souls*," *Speculum* 85 [2010]: 91–116). One of the more flamboyant differences is the omission of the phrase appended to the above quotation: "but this nature is so well-ordered ... that it never demands anything forbidden." Scholars had hitherto argued that this clause should have been sufficient to clear Marguerite from any antinomian charges, but that the bigoted judges had chosen to ignore it (Lerner, "New Light," pp. 102–3).

264. Jan Van Ruusbroec, *De ornatu spiritalium nuptiarum (Die Geestelike Brulocht)*, ed. J. Alaerts, trans. Latin, L. Surius, trans. English, H. Rolfson, *CCCM*, 103 (Turnhout: Brepols, 1988), pp. 550–66.

265. Ruusbroec, *Vanden XII Beghinen* 1, 2a, ed. M. M. Kors; English trans., H. Rolfson; Latin trans., L. Surius, *CCCM*, 107a (Turnhout: Brepols, 2000), pp. 8, 9, 88ff. Also see

Van Engen, *Brothers and Sisters of the Common Life*, p. 23. On Ruusbroec and the Devotio Moderna, see n84, above.

266. Van Engen argues that the parallels between Ruusbroec's views and the female mystics who became linked with the Free Spirit led to Ruusbroec's own denunciation of these women's writings (*Sisters and Brothers of the Common Life*, pp. 33–37; also see Lerner, *Heresy of the Free Spirit*, pp. 192–93). Gerson acknowledges, however, that Ruusbroec did not actually use the notorious wine image. See Gerson, Ep. 13, *To Bartholomew Clantier* (first letter against Ruusbroec), GL, 2:57, trans. McGuire, p. 204. Gerson was rather scornful of the claims circulating that the work was written by an illiterate and hence was all the more marvelous (ibid., 2:56–57, trans. McGuire, pp. 203–4). In fact, Ruusbroec was not university educated (Van Engen, *Sisters and Brothers of the Common Life*, pp. 32–33). For an exhaustive analysis of Gerson's objections to Ruusbroec, see André Combes, *Essai sur la critique de Ruysbroeck par Gerson*, 2 vols. (Paris: Librairie Philosophique J. Vrin, 1945–48).

267. Denis the Carthusian, *Ennaratio canticum canticorum* ad c. 1, art. 2, in *D. Dionysii Cartusiani opera omnia* (Tournai: Typis Cartusiae S. M. de Pratis, 1898), 7:296. Denys Turner has translated excerpts of this work in his *Eros and Allegory*, pp. 411–44.

268. Denis the Carthusian, *De contemplatione libri tres*, in *Opera omnia*, 41; *Opera minora*, 9:135–289; *De reformatione monialium dialogus*, in ibid., vol. 38, 6:245–61; *De discretione et examinatione spirituum*, in ibid., vol. 4, 8:267–319. Denis's work on the discernment of spirits was dependent on Gerson. See Adam Wittmann's analysis in *De Discretione spirituum apud Dionysium Cartusianum*, (Ph.D. diss., Pontificia Universitas Gregoriana, Debrecen, 1938), pp. 42–44. There is a certain irony in this dependency since Gerson is believed not to have been a mystic, but had maintained that someone who was both learned and a true contemplative was best situated for discerning spirits—someone like Denis. As with Gerson, Denis also actively campaigned against superstition. See Thorndike, *History of Magic*, 4:291–94. He also wrote sermons for a secular audience. Denis was the object of an inquiry due to complaints launched against him to the general chapter, probably because the level of his productivity was out of keeping with the contemplative nature of the Carthusians. See Denys Turner, "Denys the Carthusian—*Sermones ad Saeculares*," in *Medieval Monastic Preaching*, ed. Carolyn Muessig (Leiden: Brill, 1998), pp. 22–23.

269. Mercier, *La Vauderie*, p. 29.

CONCLUSION

1. Regino of Prüm, *De ecclesiasticis disciplinis et religione Christiana* 2.364, *PL* 132:352, trans. p. 62.

2. Johan Huizinga, *The Autumn of the Middle Ages*, trans. Rodney Payton and Ulrich Mammitzsch (Chicago: University of Chicago Press, 1996), p. 178.

3. Kramer and Sprenger, *Malleus maleficarum* pt. 2, q. 1, c. 4, 1:416, trans. 2:259. Kramer sees the newly sexually active witch as having definitely emerged by 1400, though he does not dismiss the possibility that women voluntarily sought out such relations in earlier centuries as well (ibid.). For a discussion of this newly sexualized view of the witch,

see Lène Dresen-Coenders, "Witches as Devils' Concubines: On the Origin of Fear of Witches and Protection against Witchcraft," in *New Perspectives on Witchcraft, Magic and Demonology*, vol. 4, *Gender and Witchcraft*, ed. Brian Levack (New York: Routledge, 2001), pp. 413–36.

4. Hugh of Louvain, *Vita venerabilis Idae Lovaniensis* 1.4.23, *AA SS*, April, 2:164–65.

5. Alfonso of Jaén, *Epistola solitarii ad reges* c. 6, in *Alfonso of Jaén: His Life and Works*, ed. Arne Jönsson (Lund: Lund University Press, 1989), pp. 163–64. Others were more careful, however. In his prologue to her visions, Master Mathias, another confessor, stipulated that Bridget's visions were received with her intellectual vision (*Revelaciones*, bk. 1, pp. 234–35.) To his mind, however, this manner of seeing was even more spectacular than if she saw God in the flesh. See Barbara Newman, "What Did It Mean to Say 'I Saw'? The Clash between Theory and Practice in Medieval Visionary Culture," *Speculum* 80 (2005): 1–43.

6. Gerson, *De distinctione verarum revelationum a falsis*, GL, 3:51, trans. pp. 355–56.

7. Ibid., GL, 3:48, trans. pp. 351–52.

8. Jacquier, *Flagellum haereticorum fascinariorum*, in *Quellen*, ed. Hansen, pp. 134–35.

9. Ibid., pp. 136–41.

10. Du Clercq 4.11, 3:50.

11. Southern authorities seemed more inclined to question its reality. The Castilian theologian Alfono of Spina, writing in 1459, insisted that the sabbath was illusory, though diabolically wrought. The devil made an adherent believe that he or she had flown leagues when, in fact, the devil merely took a look into his or her imagination and created a dream that matched the adherent's expectations. All the while, the individual would lie insensible and invisible, concealed by the shadow of the devil. Alfonso even goes so far as to assert that belief in a real versus illusory sabbath was heretical (Alfonso of Spina, *Fortalicium Fidei*, in *Quellen*, ed. Hansen, pp. 147–48). He is clearly deferring to the determination of the *Canon Episcopi*. See the epigraph for this chapter, above. By the same token, the Dominican Jerome Visconti, also writing at the time of the Arras trials, reasons that the sabbath is an illusion, even though he grants that the devil would be capable of making such things happen in reality if he were so inclined (Visconti, *Lamiarum sive strirarum opusculum*, in *Quellen*, ed. Hansen, pp. 203–4); cf. Jordanes of Bergamo's *Quaestio de strigis* (1470–71) on the illusory nature of the sabbath, in *Quellen*, ed. Hansen, pp. 198–99.

12. Tinctor's treatise dwelt on the gravity of the demonic threat at Arras, ending with a passionate appeal to the secular authorities. It enjoyed a strange kind of cachet: a French version exists in several luxury editions made for the likes of the Duke of Burgundy. A single printed edition was even perceived as worthy of being bound and circulated with the works of an authority with the intellectual standing of Gerson. The original Latin *Sermo contra sectam vaudensium* exists in four manuscripts and one printed edition, bound with Gerson's works. Part has been edited by Hansen in *Quellen*, pp. 184–88; see Zika, *Appearance of Witchcraft*, pp. 59–61. Tinctor translated the treatise into French himself. See Jan Veenstra, "*Les fons d'aulcuns secrets de la théologie*: Jean Tinctor's *Contre la Vauderie*; Historical Facts and Literary Reflections of the Vauderie d'Arras," in *Literatur—Geschichte— Literaturgeschichte: Beiträge zur mediävistischen Literaturwissenschaft*, ed. Nine Miedema and Rudolf Suntrup (Frankfurt am Main: Peter Lang, 2003), p. 437. The French translation

has been newly edited as *Invectives contre la secte de Vauderie*, ed. Emile Van Balberthe and Frédéric Duval (Tournai: Archives du Chapitre cathedral; Louvain-la-Neuve: Université catholique de Louvain, 1999). On the wide dissemination of his text, see Emile Van Balbherghe and Jean-François Gilmont, "Les théologiens et la 'Vauderie' au XVe siècle: A propos des oeuvres de Jean Tinctor à la Bibliothèque de l'Abbaye de Parc," in *Miscellanea Codicologica F. Masai dedicata MXMLXXIX*, ed. Pierre Cockshaw, Monique-Cecile Garand, and Pierre Jodogne (Gand: E. Story-Scientia S.P.R.L., 1979), 2:393–411.

13. *Vauderye de Lyonois en brief*, in *Quellen*, ed. Hansen, pp. 189–90.

BIBLIOGRAPHY

PRIMARY SOURCES

Anonymous saints' lives and apocrypha will be alphabetized according to the name of the saint or biblical figure. Pseudonymous works are entered after the name of the alleged author.

Abelard, Peter. *Commentaria in epistolam Pauli ad Romanos*. In *Opera theologica*. Edited by E. M. Buytaert. *CCCM*, 11:41–340. Turnhout: Brepols, 1969.

———. *Peter Abelard's Ethics*. Edited and translated by D. E. Luscombe. Oxford: Clarendon, 1971.

———. *Problemata Heloissae*. *PL* 178: 677–730.

———. *Sententie*. Edited by David Luscombe. *CCCM*, 14. Turnhout: Brepols, 2006.

———. *Sic et non: A Critical Edition*. Edited by Blanche B. Boyer and Richard McKeon. Chicago: University of Chicago Press, 1976.

———. *Theologia Christiana*. In *Opera theologica*. Edited by E. M. Buytaert. *CCCM*, 12:71–372. Turnhout: Brepols, 1969.

Abelard, Peter. *Ep. 7*. Edited by J. T. Muckle. "The Letter of Heloise on Religious Life and Abelard's First Reply." *Mediaeval Studies* 17 (1985): 240–81. Translated by C. K. Moncrieff. In *The Letters of Abelard and Heloise*, 131–75. New York: Alfred A. Knopf, 1942.

———. *Ep. 8*. Edited by T. P. McLaughlin. "Abelard's Rule for Religious Women." *Mediaeval Studies* 18 (1956): 241–92. Translated by Betty Radice. *The Letters of Abelard and Heloise*. Revised by M. T. Clanchy, 130–210. Middlesex: Penguin Books, 2003.

Abelard and Heloise. *Héloïse-Abélard: Correspondance, Lettres I–VI*. Edited by François d'Amboise. Paris: Editions Hermann, 2007.Translated by Betty Radice. *The Letters of Abelard and Heloise*. Revised by M. T. Clanchy, 47–111. Middlesex: Penguin Books, 2003.

Abelard (and anonymous student of). "A New Student for Peter Abelard: The Marginalia in British Library MS Cotton Faustina A.X." Edited by Charles Burnett and David Luscombe. *Itinéraires de la raison: Etudes de philosophie médiévale offertes à Maria Cândida Pacheco*. Edited by J. F. Meirinhos, 163–86. Textes et Etudes du Moyen Age, 32. Louvain-la-Neuve: Fédération Internationale des Instituts d'Etudes Médiévales, 2005.

Adalbert of Bamberg. *Vita S. Henrici, Additamentum*. *MGH, Scrip.*, 4:816–20.

Ælred of Rievaulx. *De institutione inclusarum*. In *La Vie de recluse: La Prière pastorale*. Edited by Charles Dumont. *SC* 76. Paris: Editions du Cerf, 1961.

———. *De sanctimoniali de Wattun*. *PL* 195:789–96. Translated by John Boswell in the appendix of *Kindness of Strangers: The Abandonment of Children in Western Europe from Late Antiquity to the Renaissance*, 452–58. Chicago: University of Chicago, 1998.

———. *Sermones de oneribus*. *PL* 195:362–500.

———. *Vita S. Edwardi regis*. *PL* 195:737–90.

Agnes, St. *Passio Agnetis*. *AA SS*, January, 2:714–18.

Alan de Lille. *De planctu Naturae*. *PL* 210:279–482. Translated by James Sheridan. *The Plaint of Nature*. Toronto: Pontifical Institute of Mediaeval Studies, 1980.

Albert the Great. *De animalibus*. Edited by Hermann Stadler. *Beiträge zur Geschichte der Philosophie des Mittlelalters: Texte und Untersuchungen*. 2 vols. Munster: Asghendorff-sche Verlagsbuchhandlung, 1916, 1920.

Aldhelm. *De virginitate (prosa)*. In *Aldhelmi opera*. Edited by Rudolf Ehwald. *MGH, Auct. Ant.*, 15, 1:226–323. Translated by Michael Lapidge and Michael Herren. *Aldhelm: The Prose Works*. Ipswich: D. S. Brewer, 1979.

———. *De virginitate (carmen)*. In *Aldhelmi opera*. Edited by Rudolf Ehwald. *MGH, Auct. Ant.*, 15, 2: 350–471. Translated by Michael Lapidge and James Rosier. In *Aldhelm: The Poetic Works*. Ipswich: D. S. Brewer, 1985.

Alexis, St. *Vita S. Alexii confessoris*. *AA SS*, July, 4:251–54.

Alfonso of Jaén. *Epistola solitarii ad reges*. In *Alfonso of Jaén: His Life and Works*. Edited by Arne Jönsson. Lund: Lund University Press, 1989.

Ambrose. *De sancta Mariae virginitate perpetua* (also known as *Liber de institutione virginis*). *PL* 16:305–34.

———. *De viduis*. *PL* 16:233–62. Translation in *LNPNFC*, 2nd ser., 10:389–407.

———. *De virginibus (Über die Jungfrauen)*. Edited and introduced by Peter Dückers. Turnhout: Brepols, 2009. Translation in *LNPNFC*, 2nd scr., 10:361–87.

———. *De virginitate*. *PL* 16:187–302. Translated by Daniel Callam. *On Virginity*. Saskatoon: Peregrina Translation Series, 1980.

———. *Ep. 5* (49), *To Syagrius*. *PL* 16:929–37. Translated as Ep. 32 by Mary Beyenka. In Ambrose, *Letters, 1–91*, Fathers of the Church, 26:152–63. Washington, D.C.: Catholic University Press, 2002.

———. *Exhortatio virginitatis*. *PL* 16:351–80.

Ancrene Wisse. In *Anchoritic Spirituality: Ancrene Wisse and Associated Works*. Translated and edited by Anne Savage and Nicholas Watson, 47–207. New York: Paulist, 1991.

Andrea of Fontevrault. *Vita altera B. Roberti de Arbrissello*. *PL* 162:1057–78. Translated by Bruce Venarde. In *Robert of Arbrissel: A Medieval Religious Life*, 22–67. Washington, D.C.: Catholic University of America Press, 2003.

Andrew the Chaplain. *De amore, libri tres*. Translated by John Jay Parry. *The Art of Courtly Love*. New York: Columbia University Press, 1960.

Andrieu, M., ed. *Le Pontifical romain du 12e siècle*. 2 vols. *Le Pontifical romain au moyen-âge*. Studi e Testi, 86–87. Vatican City: Biblioteca Apostolica Vaticana, 1938–39.

Angela of Foligno. *Memoriale*. In *Il Libro della Beata Angela da Foligno*. Edited by Ludger

Thier and Abele Calufetti. Grottaferrata, Rome: College of St. Bonaventure, 1985. Translated by Paul Lachance. In *Angela of Foligno: Complete Works*, 123–218. New York: Paulist Press, 1993.

Anselm of Bec. *Epistolae*. In vols. 4–5 of *S. Anselmi Cantuariensis archiepiscopi opera omnia*. Edited by Francis Schmitt. 6 vols. Edinburgh: T. Nelson, 1951. Translated by Walter Frölich. *The Letters of St. Anselm of Canterbury.* 3 vols. Kalamazoo, Mich.: Cistercian Publications, 1990–94.

Aphrahat. *Les Exposés*. Translated by Marie-Joseph Pierre. *SC*, 359. Paris: Editions du Cerf, 1988.

The Apocryphal New Testament. Translated by M. R. James. Oxford: Clarendon, 1924.

Aquinas, Thomas. *Commentum in quatuor libros sententiarum Petri Lombardi*. In *Opera omnia*. Vols. 6–7. Parma: Petrus Fiaccadori, 1856–58. Reprint, New York: Musurgia, 1948.

———. *De potentia*. In *Opera omnia*, 8:1–218. Parma: Petrus Fiaccadori, 1852–73. Reprint, New York: Musurgia, 1948–50. Translated by the English Dominican Fathers. *On the Power of God*. Westminster, Md.: Newman Press, 1952.

———. *Summa Theologiae*. London: Blackfriars, in conjunction with Eyre and Spottiswoode; New York: McGraw-Hill, 1964–81.

Ardenti, Silestro. *Le Vite di Umilità da Faenza*. Edited by Adele Simonetti. Florence: Sismel, Edizioni del Galluzzo, 1997.

Athanasius. *(First) Letter to Virgins*. Translated by David Brakke. In *Athanasius and Asceticism*, Appendix A, 274–91. Oxford: Clarendon, 1995. Reprint, Baltimore: Johns Hopkins University Press, 1998.

———. *(Second) Letter to Virgins*. Translated by David Brakke. In *Athanasius and Asceticism*, Appendix B, 292–302. Oxford: Clarendon, 1995. Reprint, Baltimore: Johns Hopkins University Press, 1998.

———. *On Virginity*. Translated by David Brakke. In *Athanasius and Asceticism*, Appendix C, 303–9. Oxford: Clarendon, 1995. Reprint, Baltimore: Johns Hopkins University Press, 1998.

Pseudo-Athanasius. *Discourse on Salvation to a Virgin*. Translated by Teresa Shaw. In *Religions of Late Antiquity in Practice*. Edited by Richard Valantasis, 82–99. Princeton, N.J.: Princeton University Press, 2000.

———. *On Virginity*. Edited by David Brakke. *Corpus Scriptorum Christianorum Orientalium*, vol. 592, Scriptores Syri, vol. 232. Louvain: Peeters, 2002. Translated by David Brakke. *Corpus Scriptorum Christianorum Orientalium*, vol. 593, Scriptores Syri, vol. 233. Louvain: Peeters, 2002.

Augustine. *De bono coniugali*. *PL* 40::373–96.

———. *De bono viduitatis*. *PL* 40:431–50. Translation in *LNPNFC*, 1st ser., vol. 3:441–56.

———. *De civitate dei*. *PL* 41:13–804. Translation in *LNPNFC*, 1st ser., vol. 2.

———. *De fide, spe et charitate*. *PL* 40:231–90.

———. *De Genesi ad litteram libri duodecimo*. *PL* 34:246–486. Translated by John Hammond Taylor. *The Literal Meaning of Genesis*. 2 vols. *ACW* 41–42. New York: Newman Press, 1982.

———. *De nuptiis et concupiscentia. PL* 44:413–74. Translation in *LNPNFC,* 1st ser., vol. 5:257–308.

———. *De sancta virginitate. PL* 40:397–428. Translation in *LNPNFC,* 1st ser., vol. 3:417–38.

———. *Epistolae. PL* 33:61–1094.

———. *In Joannis evangelium. PL* 35:1379–1976.

———. *Quaestionum in Heptateuchum libri VII. PL* 34:547–824.

———. *Sermo 132. PL* 38:735–37.

Baldric of Dol. *Vita B. Roberti de Arbrissello. PL* 162:1043–58. Translated by Bruce Venarde. In *Robert of Arbrissel: A Medieval Religious Life,* 6–21. Washington, D.C.: Catholic University Press, 2003.

Balthild, St. *Vita sanctae Balthildis. MGH, Scrip. Rer. Merov.,* 2:482–508. Translated by Jo Ann McNamara, John Halborg, and E. Gordon Whatley. In *Sainted Women of the Dark Ages,* 268–79. Durham, N.C.: Duke University Press, 1992.

Basil the Great. *Ep. 46, Ad virginem lapsam. PG* 32:369–82. Translation in *LNPNFC,* 2nd ser., vol. 8:149–52.

Baudonivia. Book 2 of *De vita Sanctae Radegundis libri duo. MGH, Scrip. Rer. Merov.,* 2:377–95. Translated by Jo Ann McNamara, John Halborg, and E. Gordon Whatley. In *Sainted Women of the Dark Ages,* 86–105. Durham, N.C.: Duke University Press, 1992.

Beatrice of Nazareth. *Life of Beatrice of Nazareth.* Edited by Roger De Ganck. Kalamazoo, Mich.: Cistercian Publications, 1992.

Bede. *Ecclesiastical History of the English People.* Edited and translated by Bertram Colgrave and R. A. B. Mynors. Oxford: Oxford University Press, 1969.

———. *Explanatio Apocalypsis. PL* 93:129–206.

———. *In evangelium S. Joannis. PL* 92:633–938.

Benedict of Nursia. *Regula Sancti Benedicti.* Edited by Timothy Fry. Collegeville, Minn.: Liturgical Press, 1981.

Berengar of Saint Affrique. *La vita di S. Chiara da Montefalco scritta da Berengario di S. Africano.* Edited by Michele Faloci-Pulignani. In *Archivio storico per le Marche e per l'Umbria* 1 (1884): 583–625; 2 (1885): 193–266.

Bernard of Clairvaux. *Epistolae.* In *Sancti Bernardi opera.* Edited by J. Leclercq and H. Rochais. Vols. 7–8. Rome: Editiones Cistercienses, 1974. Select letters translated by Bruno James. *The Letters of St. Bernard of Clairvaux.* Chicago: Henry Regnery, 1953.

———. *Liber de diligendo Deo.* In *L'Amour de Dieu: La Grâce et le libre arbitre.* Edited by Jean Leclercq et al. *SC,* 393. Paris: Editions du Cerf, 1993. Translated by Robert Walton with commentary by Emergo Stiegman. *On Loving God.* Kalamazoo, Mich.: Cistercian Publications, 1995.

———. *Sermons sur le Cantique.* Edited by J. Leclercq, H. Rochais, and C. H. Talbot. *SC,* 414, 431, 452, 472, 511. Paris: Editions du Cerf, 1996–2007. Translated by Irene Edmonds and Kilian Walsh. *Song of Songs.* 4 vols. Kalamazoo, Mich.: Cistercian Publications, 1971–81.

Bevignati, Giunta. *Legenda de vita et miraculis beate Margarite de Cortona. AA SS,* February, 3:302–63.

Biblia Latina cum glossa ordinaria: Facsimile Reprint of the Editio Princips of Strassburg

1480/81. Introduced by Adolph Rusch, Karlfried Froehlich, and Margaret Gibson. Turnhout: Brepols, 1992.

Blamires, Alcuin, ed. *Woman Defamed, Woman Defended: An Anthology of Medieval Texts.* New York: Oxford University Press, 1992.

Böhringer, L., ed. *De divortio Lotharii regis and Theutbergae reginae. MGH,* Concilia IV, suppl. 1. Hannover: Hahnsche Buchhandlung, 1992.

Bonacursus. *Vita haereticorum. PL* 204:775–92. Translated in part by Walter Wakefield and Austin Evans. In *Heresies of the High Middle Ages,* 171–73. New York: Columbia University Press, 1969.

Book of Beasts: A Facsimile of MS. Bodley 764. Introduced by Christopher de Hamel. Oxford: Bodleian Library, 2009. Translated by T. H. White, *A Book of Beasts.* New York: G. P. Putnam's Sons, 1954.

Bridget of Sweden. *Revelaciones.* Vols. 1–8, and *Extravagantes.* Edited by Carl-Gustaf. Undhagen et al. Samlingar utgivna av Svenska Fornskriftsällskapet, ser. 2, Latinsk Skrifter. Uppsala, 1956–2002.

Brocadelli of Narni, Lucia. "'Le Rivelazioni' of Lucia Brocadelli da Narni." Edited by E. Ann Matter, Armano Maggi, and Maiju Lehmijoki-Gardner. *Archivum Fratrum Praedicatorum* 71 (2001): 311–44. Translated by E. Ann Matter. In *Dominican Penitent Women.* Edited by Maiju Lehmijoki-Gardner, 212–43. New York: Paulist Press, 2005.

Burchard of Worms. *Decretum (Libri decretorum). PL* 140:537–1057.

Caesarius of Arles. *Regula virginum.* In *Oeuvres monastiques.* Edited by Albert de Vogüé and Joël Courreau. *SC,* 345. Paris: Editions du Cerf, 1988.

Caesarius of Heisterbach. "Des Cäsarius von Heisterbach Schriften über die hl. Elisabeth von Thüringen." Edited by Albert Huyskens. *Annalen des historischen Vereins für den Niederrhein* 86 (1908): 1–59.

———. *Dialogus miraculorum.* Edited by Joseph Strange. 2 vols. Cologne: J. M. Heberle, 1851. Translated by H. Von E. Scott and C. C. Swinton Bland. *The Dialogue on Miracles.* London: Routledge, 1929.

Cassian, John.*Conférences.* Edited by E. Pichery. *SC,* 42, 54, 64. Paris: Editions du Cerf, 1955–59. Translated by Boniface Ramsey. *John Cassian: The Conferences. ACW, 57.* New York: Paulist Press, 1997.

Castillerio, Conrad. *Vita de B. Benevenuta Bojanis. AA SS,* October, 29:152–85.

Catherine of Siena. *Epistolario di Santa Caterina da Siena.* Edited by Eugenio Dupré Theseider. Vol. 1. Rome: R. Istituto storico italianio per il Medio Evo, 1940. Translated by Suzanne Noffke. *Letters of Catherine of Siena.* Binghamton, N.Y.: Medieval and Renaissance Texts and Studies, 1988.

Cecilia, St. *Historia passionis B. Caeciliae.* In *Sanctuarium seu Vitae sanctorum.* Edited by Bonino Mombrizio, 1:332–41. Paris: Albert Fontemoing, 1910.

Christina of Markyate. *The Life of Christina of Markyate.* Edited and translated by C. H. Talbot. Oxford: Clarendon Press, 1959.

Chrysostom, John. *Against Those Men Cohabiting with Virgins.* Translated by Elizabeth Clark. In *Jerome, Chrysostom, and Friends: Essays and Translations,* 164–208. New York: Edwin Mellen Press, 1979.

————. *De non iterando conjugio.* *PG* 48:609–20. Translated by Sally Shore. In *On Virginity: Against Remarriage*, 129–45. New York: Edwin Mellen, 1983.

————. *La Virginité.* Edited by Herbert Musurillo. *SC*, 125. Paris: Editions du Cerf, 1966. Translated by Sally Shore. *On Virginity: Against Remarriage.* New York: Edwin Mellen, 1983.

————. *On the Necessity of Guarding Virginity.* Edited by Jean Dumortier. In *Les Cohabitations suspectes: Comment observer la virginité.* Paris: Société Editions "Les Belles Lettres," 1955. Translated by Elizabeth Clark. In *Jerome, Chrysostom, and Friends: Essays and Translations*, 209–48. New York: Edwin Mellen Press, 1979.

Pseudo-Clement. *First Epistle of Clement on Virginity.* In *Patres Apostolici.* Edited by F. Diekamp, 2:1–28. Tübingen: Henricus Laupp, 1913. Translated in *ANF*, 8:55–60.

————. *Second Epistle of Clement on Virginity.* In *Patres Apostolici.* Edited by F. Diekamp, 2:29–49. Tübingen: Henricus Laupp, 1913. Translated in *ANF*, 8:61–66.

Collijn, Isak, ed. *Acta et processus canonizacionis Beate Birgitte.* Uppsala: Almquist and Wiksells, 1924–31.

Concilia Galliae A. 314–A. 506. 2 vols. Edited by C. Munier and C. de Clercq. *CSEL*, 148, 148a. Turnhout: Brepols, 1963.

Corpus documentorum inquisitionis haereticae pravitatis Neerlandicae. Edited by Paul Fredericq. 5 vols. Ghent: J. Vuylsteke; The Hague: Martinus Nijhoff, 1889–1903.

Cyprian. *De bono pudicitiae*, In *S. Thasci Caecili Cypriani opera omnia.* Edited by W. Hartel. *CSEL*, 3,3: 13–25.

————. *De habitu virginum.* In *S. Thasci Caecili Cypriani opera omnia.* Edited by W. Hartel. *CSEL*, 3,1:185–203. Translation in *ANF*, 5:430–36.

————. *Ep. 4, To Pomponius.* In *S. Thasci Caecili Cypriani opera omnia.* Edited by W. Hartel. *CSEL*, 3,2:472–78. Translated in *Library of the Fathers.* Oxford: Henry Parker, 1844.

Cyprian, St. (anonymous account concerning). *Acta proconsularia.* In *S. Thasci Caecili Cypriani opera omnia.* Edited by W. Hartel. *CSEL*, 3,3:cx–cxiv.

Pseudo-Cyprian. *De singularitate clericorum.* In *S. Thasci Caecili Cypriani opera omnia.* Edited by William Hartel. *CSEL*, 3,3:173–220. Vienna: C. Geroldi Filium Bibliopolam Academiae, 1881.

Damian, Peter. *Die Briefe des Petrus Damiani.* Edited by K. Reindel. 4 vols. *MGH*, Die Briefe der deutschen Kaiserzeit 4.1–4. Munich, 1983–93.

Decrees of the Ecumenical Councils. Edited by Norman Tanner. 2 vols. London: Sheed and Ward, 1990.

De heresi catharorum in Lombardia. Edited by Antoine Dondaine. "La Hiérarchie cathare d'Italie I." *Archivum Fratrum Praedicatorum* 19 (1949): 310–11. Translated by Walter Wakefield and Austin Evans. *Heresies of the High Middle Ages*, 165–66. New York: Columbia University Press, 1969.

De lapsu virginis consecratae liber unicus. PL 16:367–84.

Denis the Carthusian. *De contemplatione libri tres.* In *D. Dionysii Cartusiani opera omnia in unum corpus digesta*, vol. 41. *Opera minora*, 9:135–289. Tournai: Typis Carthusiae S. M. de Pratis, 1911.

———. *De discretione et examinatione spirituum*. In *D. Dionysii Cartusiani opera omnia in unum corpus digesta*, vol. 4. *Opera minora*, 8:267–319. Tournai: Typis Carthusiae S. M. de Pratis, 1911.

———. *De reformatione monialium dialogus*. In *D. Dionysii Cartusiani opera omnia in unum corpus digesta*, vol. 38. *Opera minora*, 6:245–61. Tournai: Typis Carthusiae S. M. de Pratis, 1911.

———. *Ennaratio canticum canticorum*. In *D. Dionysii Cartusiani opera omnia*, 7:291–477. Tournai: Typis Carthusiae S. M. de Pratis, 1898.

Dhuoda, *Manuel pour mons fils*. Edited by Pierre Riché. *SC*. 225, Paris: Editions du Cerf, 1975. Translated by Carol Neel. *A Handbook for William: A Carolingian Woman's Counsel for Her Son*. Washington, D.C.: Catholic University Press, 1991.

Didascalia apostolorum. Trans. Margaret Gibson. London: C. J. Clay and Sons, 1903.

Disputatio inter catholicum et paterinum haereticum. In *Thesaurus novum anecdotorum*. Edited by Edmond Martène and Ursin Durand, 5:1705–11. Paris, 1717. Translated by Walter Wakefield and Austin Evans. *Heresies of the High Middle Ages*, 289–95. New York: Columbia University Press, 1969.

Dorothea of Montau and John of Marienwerder. *Septililium B. Dorotheae*. Edited by Franz Hipler. *Analecta Bollandiana* 2 (1883): 381–472 (treatise 1); 3 (1884): 113–40, 408–48 (treatises 2–3); 4 (1885): 207–51 (treatises 4–7).

Du Clercq, James. *Mémoires J. Du Clercq sur le règne de Philippe le Bon, Duc de Bourgogne*. Edited by F. de Reiffenberg. 4 vols. Brussels: J. M. Lacrosse, 1835–36.

Durandus, William. *Le Pontifical de Guillaume Durand*. Edited by Michel Andrieu. Vol. 3 of *Le Pontifical Romain au Moyen-Age*. Studi e Testi, 88. Vatican City: Biblioteca Apostolica Vaticana, 1940.

———. *Rationale divinorum officiorum*. Edited by A. d'Avril and T. Thimbodeau. *CCCM*, 140, 140a. Turnhout: Brepols, 1995–98.

Eadmer. *Historia novorum*. *PL* 159:347–524. Translated by Geoffrey Bosanquet. *Eadmer's History of Recent Events in England*. London: Cresset Press, 1964.

———. *The Life of St. Anselm: Archbishop of Canterbury*. Edited by R. W. Southern. Oxford: Clarendon, 1962.

Eberwin of Steinfeld. Ep. 472, *To Bernard of Clairvaux*. *PL* 182:676–80. Translated in Walter Wakefield and Austin Evans. *Heresies of the High Middle Ages*, 127–32. New York: Columbia University Press, 1969.

Ebner, Margaret. *Die Offenbarungen*. In *Margareta Ebner und Heinrich von Nördlingen: Ein Beitrag zur Geschichte der deutschen Mystik*. Edited by Philipp Strauch, 1–161. Freiburg: Akademische Verlagsbuchhandlung von J. C. B. Mohr, 1882. Translated by Leonard Hindsley. *Margaret Ebner: Major Works*. Edited by Margot Schmidt and Leonard Hindsley, 83–182. New York: Paulist Press, 1993.

Elisabeth of Hungary. *Der sog. Libellus de dictis quatuor ancillarum S. Elisabeth confectus*. Edited by Albert Huyskens. Kempten: Jos. Kösel'schen, 1911.

Enoch. *The Book of Enoch*. Translated by M. A. Knibb. In *The Apocryphal Old Testament*. Edited by H. Sparks, 169–320. Oxford: Clarendon Press, 1984.

Ernaldus, Abbot of Bona-Vallis. *S. Bernardi vita et res gestae*. *PL* 185:267–302.

Errores gazariorum seu illorum qui scopam vel baculum equitare probantur. In *L'Imaginaire du sabbat: Edition critique des texts les plus anciens (1430 c.–1440 c.).* Edited by Martine Ostorero, Agostino P. Bagliani, and Kathrin Utz Tremp, 289–300. Lausanne: Cahiers lausannois d'histoire médiévale, 1999.

Eugenius IV. *Letter to inquisitors* (undated). In *Quellen und Untersuchungen zur Geschichte des Hexenwahns und der Hexenverfolgung im Mittelalter.* Edited by Joseph Hansen, 17–18. Bonn, 1901. Reprint, Hildesheim: Georg Olms, 1963. Translated in *Witchcraft in Europe, 1400–1700: A Documentary History,* 2nd ed. Edited by Alan Kors and Edward Peters, 154. Philadelphia: University of Pennsylvania, 2001.

Eusebius. *Historia ecclesiae. PG* 20:45–906. Translation in *LNPNFC,* 2nd ser., 1:73–403.

Eustadiola of Bourges. *Vita Eustadiolae abb. Bituricensis. AA SS,* June, 2:131–33. Translated by Jo Ann McNamara, John Halborg, and E. Gordon Whatley. In *Sainted Women of the Dark Ages,* 107–12. Durham, N.C.: Duke University Press, 1992.

Ferrand, deacon of Carthage. *Vie de Saint Fulgence de Ruspe.* Edited by G. G. Lapeyre. Paris: Lethielleux, 1929. Translated by Robert Eno. In *Fulgentius: Selected Works. FC,* 95:1–56. Washington, D.C.: Catholic University Press, 1997.

Fortunatus, Venantius. *Opera poetica. MGH, Auct. Ant.* 4,1.

———. *Vita Sancti Hilarii. MGH, Auct. Ant.,* 4,2:1–11.

———. Book 1 of *De vita Sanctae Radegundis libri duo. MGH, Scrip. Rer. Merov.,* 2:364–77. Translated by Jo Ann McNamara, John Halborg, and E. Gordon Whatley. In *Sainted Women of the Dark Ages,* 70–86. Durham, N.C.: Duke University Press, 1992.

Fredegar. *Chronicarum quae dicuntur Fredegarii Scholastici, libri IV cum continuationibus.* Edited by Bruno Krusch. *MGH, Scrip. Rer. Merov.,* 2. Hannover: Hahn, 1888. Translated by J. M. Wallace-Hadrill. *The Fourth Book of the Chronicle of Fredegar.* London: Thomas Nelson and Sons, 1960.

Fredericq, Paul, ed. *Corpus documentorum inquisitionis haereticae pravitatis Neerlandicae.* Ghent: J. Vuylsteke; The Hague: Martinus Nijhoff, 1889.

Fründ, Hans. *Rapport sur la chase aux sorciers et aux sorcières menée dès 1428 dans le diocèse de Sion.* In *L'Imaginaire du sabbat: Edition critique des texts les plus anciens (1430 c.–1440 c.).* Edited by Martine Ostorero, Agostino P. Bagliani, and Kathrin Utz Tremp, 30–52. Lausanne: Cahiers lausannois d'histoire médiévale, 1999.

Fulgentius. *Sancti Fulgentii episcopi Ruspensis opera.* Edited by J. Fraipont. 2 vols. *CCSL,* 91, 91a. Turnhout: Brepols, 1968. Translated by Robert Eno. In *Fulgentius: Selected Works, FC,* 95. Washington, D.C.: Catholic University Press, 1997.

Gelasius I, Pope. *Episotlae et Decreta. PL* 59:47–57.

Geoffrey of Monmouth. *History of the Kings of Britain.* Ed. Michael Reeve. Woodbridge, Suffolk: Boydell, 2007.

Geoffrey of Vendôme. *Oeuvres.* Edited and translated by Geneviève Giordanengo. Turnhout: Brepols, 1996.

Gerardesca of Pisa, St. *Vita S. Gerardeschae Pisanae. AA SS,* May, 7:161–76.

Gerson, John. *Collectorium super Magnificat.* In *Oeuvres complètes* (hereafter GL). Edited by Palémon Glorieux, 8:163–534. Paris: Desclée, 1960–73.

———. *Complainte de la conscience. GL,* 7,1:109–11.

————. *Considérations sur Saint Joseph.* GL, 7,1:63–99.

————. *Contra curiositatem studentium.* GL, 3:224–49.

————. *Contre conscience trop scrupuleuse.* GL, 7,1:140–42.

————. *De auferibilitate sponsi ab ecclesia.* GL, 3:294–313.

————. *De distinctione verarum revelationum a falsis.* GL, 3:36–56. Translated by Brian McGuire. In *Jean Gerson: Early Works,* 334–64. New York: Paulist Press, 1998.

————. *De elucidatione scholastica mysticae theologiae.* GL, 8:154–62.

————. *De examinatione doctrinarum.* GL, 9:458–75.

————. *De meditatione cordis.* GL, 8:77–84.

————. *De mystica theologia practica.* GL, 8:18–47. Translated by Brian McGuire. In *Jean Gerson: Early Works,* 288–333. New York: Paulist Press, 1998.

————. *De nuptiis Christi et Ecclesiae.* GL, 6:190–210.

————. *De probatione spirituum.* GL, 9:177–85.

————. *De remediis contra pusillanimitatem.* GL, 10:374–98.

————. *De signis bonis et malis.* GL, 9:162–66.

————. *De simplificatione cordis.* GL, 8:85–96.

————. *De theologia mystica lectiones sex.* GL, 3:250–92. Extracts translated by Brian McGuire. In *Jean Gerson: Early Works,* 262–87. New York: Paulist Press, 1998.

————. *Dialogue spirituel.* GL, 7,1:158–93.

————. *Discours sur l'excellence de la virginité.* In *Joannis Gersonii opera omnia.* Edited by Louis Ellies du Pin, 3:829–41. Antwerp, 1706. Reprint, Hildesheim: Georg Olms, 1978.

————. *L'Ecole de la raison.* GL, 7,1:103–8.

————. *Ep. 12, To Nicolas.* GL, 2:54–55. Translated by Brian McGuire. In *Jean Gerson: Early Works,* 200–202. New York: Paulist Press, 1998.

————. *Ep. 13, To Bartholomew Clantier (first letter against Ruusbroec).* GL, 1:55–62. Translated by Brian McGuire. In *Jean Gerson: Early Works,* 202–10. New York: Paulist Press, 1998.

————. *Ep. 25, To Jean Morel.* GL, 2:93–96. Translated by Brian McGuire. In *Jean Gerson: Early Works,* 244–49. New York: Paulist Press, 1998.

————. *Ep. 26, To Bartholomew Clantier (second letter against Ruusbroec).* GL, 2:97–102. Translated by Brian McGuire. In *Jean Gerson: Early Works,* 249–56. New York: Paulist Press, 1998.

————. *In festo S. Bernardi.* GL, 5:325–39. Translated by Brian McGuire. In *Jean Gerson: Early Works,* 128–48. New York: Paulist Press, 1998.

————. *Josephina.* GL, 4:31–100.

————. *La Mendicité spirituelle.* GL, 7,1:220–80.

————. *La Montagne de contemplation.* GL, 7,1:16–55. Translated by Brian McGuire. In *Jean Gerson: Early Works,* 75–127. New York: Paulist Press, 1998.

————. *Le miroir de l'âme.* GL, 7,1:193–206.

————. *Pitieuse complainte.* GL, 7,1:213–16.

————. *Poenitemini: Contre la luxure.* GL, 7,2:810–21.

————. *Poenitemini: De la chasteté conjugale (collation).* GL, 7,2:862–68.

————. *Pour la fête de la desponsation Notre Dame.* GL, 7,1:14–15.

————. *Pour la fête de S. Joseph.* GL, 8:55–61.

————. *Pour la réforme du royaume (Vivat Rex).* GL, 7,2:1137–85.

————. *Le Profit de savoir quell est péché mortel et véniel.* GL, 7,1:370–89.

————. *Prosa super Epithalamium Joseph.* GL, 4:111–12.

————. *Regulae mandatorum.* GL, 9:94–132.

————. *Sermo in festo S. Antonii.* GL, 5:376–98.

————. *Super Cantica canticorum.* GL, 8:565–639.

————. *Sur le culte de S. Joseph.* GL, 8:61–66.

————. *Tractatus de oculo.* GL, 8:149–54.

Gertrude of Helfta (the Great). *Les Exercises.* In *Oeuvres spirituelles.* Edited by Jacques Hourlier and Albert Schmitt. *SC*, 127. Paris: Editions du Cerf, 1967. Translated by Gertrud Lewis and Jack Lewis. *Spiritual Exercises.* Kalamazoo, Mich.: Cistercian Publications, 1989.

————. *Le Héraut memorial des largesses de l'amour divin.* In *Oeuvres spirituelles.* Edited by Jacques Hourlier and Albert Schmitt. *SC*, 139, 143, 255, 331. Paris: Editions du Cerf, 1967–. Translated by Margaret Winkworth. *The Herald of Divine Love.* New York: Paulist Press, 1993.

Goscelin of Saint-Bertin. *The Hagiography of the Female Saints of Ely.* Edited and translated by Rosalind Love. Oxford: Clarendon, 2004.

————. *Liber confortatorius.* Edited by C. H. Talbot. In *Studia Anselmiana,* fasc. 37, *Analecta Monastica,* 3rd ser. Rome: Herder, 1955. Translated by W. R. Barnes and Rebecca Hayward. In *Writing the Wilton Women: Goscelin's Legend of Edith and Liber confortatorius.* Edited by Stephanie Hollis, 99–207. Turnhout: Brepols, 2004.

————. *The Life of King Edward Who Rests at Westminster.* Edited and translated by Frank Barlow. London: Nelson, 1962.

Goswin of Villers (Goswin of Bossut). "The Life of Abundus of Villers" (*Vita Abundi*). Edited by A. M. Frenken. In "De Vita van Abundus van Hoei." *Cîteaux* 10 (1959): 5–33. Translated by Martinus Cawley. *Send Me God: The Lives of Ida the Compassionate of Nivelles, Nun of la Ramé, Arnulf, Lay Brother of Villers, and Abundus, Monk of Villers,* 209–46. Turnhout: Brepols, 2003. Reprint, University Park: Pennsylvania State University Press, 2006.

————. *Vita beatae Idae de Niuelle sanctimonialis in monasterio de Rameya.* In *Quinque prudentes virgines.* Edited by P. F. Chrysostom Henriquez, 199–297. Antwerp: Apud Ioannem Cnobbaert, 1630. Translated by Martinus Cawley. "The Life of Ida 'the Compassionate' of Nivelles." In *Send Me God: The Lives of Ida the Compassionate of Nivelles, Nun of la Ramé, Arnulf, Lay Brother of Villers, and Abundus, Monk of Villers,* 29–99. Turnhout: Brepols, 2003. Reprint, University Park: Pennsylvania State University Press, 2006.

Gregory of Nazianzus. *Epigrammata. PG* 38:81–130.

Gregory of Tours. *Liber in gloria confessorum.* Edited by Bruno Krusch. *MGH, Scrip. Rer. Merov.,* 1:474–820. Translated by Raymond Van Dam. *The Glory of the Confessors.* Liverpool: Liverpool University Press, 1989.

————. *Liber in gloria martyrum.* Edited by Bruno Krusch. *MGH, Scrip. Rer. Merov.*, 1, 2:484–561. Translated by Raymond Van Dam. *The Glory of the Martyrs.* Liverpool: Liverpool University Press, 1988.

————. *Liber vitae patrum.* Edited by Bruno Krusch. *MGH, Scrip. Rer. Merov.*, 1,2:661–744. Hanover: Hahn, 1885. Translated by Edward James. *The Life of the Fathers.* Liverpool: Liverpool University Press, 1985.

————. *Libri de virtutibus sancti Martini episcopi.* Edited by Bruno Krusch. *MGH, Scrip. Rer. Merov.*, 2,1:554–661.

————. *Libri historiarum X.* Edited by Bruno Krusch and Wilhelm Arndt. *MGH, Scrip. Rer. Merov.*, 1,1. Rev. ed. Hannover: Hahn, 1951. Translated by Lewis Thorpe. *History of the Franks.* Harmondsworth, Middlesex: Penguin, 1974.

Guerric of Saint-Quentin. *Quaestiones de quolibet.* Edited by Walter Principe. *Texts and Studies*, 143. Toronto: Pontifical Institute, 2002.

Guibert of Nogent. *Autobiographie.* Edited by Edmond-René Labande. Paris: Belles Lettres, 1981. Translated by John Benton. *Self and Society in Medieval France.* Toronto: University of Toronto Press, 1984.

Guy of Cortona. *Vita B. Humilianae de Cerchis. AA SS*, May, 4:385–400.

Hadewijch. *Hadewijch: The Complete Works.* Translated by Columba Hart. New York: Paulist Press, 1980.

Hansen, Joseph, ed. *Quellen und Untersuchungen zur Geschichte des Hexenwahns und der Hexenverfolgung im Mittelalter.* Bonn, 1901. Reprint, Hildesheim: Georg Olms, 1963.

Heloise. See Abelard and Heloise.

Herriman of Tournai. *Liber de restauratione Monasterii Sancti Martini Tornacensis.* In *MGH, Scrip.*, 14:274–317.

Hilarius. *Versus et Ludi, Epistolae, Ludus Danielis Belouacensis.* Edited by Walther Bulst and M. L. Bulst-Thiele. Leiden: Brill, 1989.

Hildegard of Bingen. *Sciuias.* Edited by Adelgundis Führkötter and Angela Carlevaris. *CCCM*, 43–43A. Turnhout: Brepols, 1978. Translated by Columba Hart and Jane Bishop. New York: Paulist Press, 1990.

Hincmar of Reims. *Communi episcoporum nomine ad regem, De coercendo et exstirpando raptu viduarum, puellarum ac sanctimonialium. PL* 125:1017–36.

————. *De divortio Lotharii regis and Theutbergae reginae.* Edited by L. Böhringer. *MGH, Concilia IV,* suppl. 1. Hannover: Hahnsche Buchhandlung, 1992. *PL* 126:619–772.

————. *Ep. 22, Ad Rodulfum Bituricensem et Frotarium Burdigalensem, Metropolitanos Aquitaniae: De nuptiis Stephani, et filiae Regimundi comitis. PL* 126:132–53.

Hucbald. *Vita S. Rictrudis viduae. AA SS*, May, 3:81–88. Translated by Jo Ann McNamara, John Halborg, and E. Gordon Whatley. In *Sainted Women of the Dark Ages*, 195–219. Durham, N.C.: Duke University Press, 1992.

Hugh of Floreffe. *B. Juetta sive Jutta, vidua, recluse, Hui in Belgio. AA SS*, January, 2:145–69. Translated by Jo McNamara. *The Life of Yvette.* Toronto: Peregrina, 1999.

Hugh of Louvain. *Vita Venerabilis Idae Lovaniensis. AA SS*, April, 2:158–89.

Hugh of St. Victor. *De sacramentis Christiani fidei. PL* 176:183–618. Translated by Roy

Deferrari. *On the Sacraments of the Christian Faith*. Cambridge, Mass.: Medieval Academy, 1951.

———. *Soliloquium de arrha animae. PL* 176: 951–70.

Humbert of Romans. *Epistola de tribus votis substantialibus religionis*. In *Opera de vita regu-lari*. Vol. 1. Edited by Joachim Joseph Berthier. Rome: A Befani, 1888.

Humility of Faenza. *Umiltà da Faenza: Sermones; Le lezioni di una monacha*. Edited by Adele Simonetti. Florence: Sismel, Edizioni del Galluzzo, 2005.

———. *Vita S. Humilitatis Abbatissae. AA SS*, May, 207–14.

Ida of Gorsleeuw, St. *Vita B. Idae Lewensis. AA SS*, October, 13:107–24.

Innocent I. *Ep. 2, To Vitricius of Rouen. PL* 20:469–81.

Institoris, Henricus [= Kramer] and Jacobus Sprenger. *Malleus maleficarum*. Edited and translated by Christopher Mackay. 2 vols. Cambridge: Cambridge University Press, 2006.

Isaiah. *The Vision of Isaiah*. Translated by Walter Wakefield and Austin Evans. In *Heresies of the High Middle Ages*, 449–58. New York: Columbia University Press, 1969.

Ivo of Chartres. *Decretum. PL* 161:47–1022.

Jacobilli, Luigi. *Vite de' santi e beati dell' Vmbria*. Foligno, 1647–61. Reprint, Bologna: Forni, 1971.

Jacquier, Nicolas. *Flagellum haereticorum fascinariorum*. In *Quellen und Untersuchungen zur Geschichte des Hexenwahns und der Hexenverfolgung im Mittelalter*. Edited by Joseph Hansen, 133–45. Bonn, 1901. Reprint, Hildesheim: Georg Olms, 1963.

James, apostle. *The Protoevangelium of James. ANF*, 8:361–67.

James of Vitry. *Exempla or Illustrative Stories from the Sermones Vulgares of Jacques de Vitry*. Edited by Thomas Frederick Crane. Folk-Lore Society Publications, 26. London: Folklore Society, 1878.

———. *Lettres de Jacques de Vitry*. Edited by R. B. C. Huygens. Leiden: E. J. Brill, 1960.

———. *Sermones vulgares*. In *Analecta Novissima Spicilegii Solesmensis: Altera continuatio 2, Tusculana*. Edited by J. B. Pitra. Paris: Roger and Chernowitz, 1888.

———. *Vita B. Mariae Oigniacensis. AA SS*, June, 5:547–72. Translated by Margot King. In *Mary of Oignies: Mother of Salvation*. Edited by Anneke Mulder-Bakker, 33–127. Turnhout: Brepols, 2006.

Jerome. *Adversus Jovinianum. PL* 23:206–338. Translation in *LNPNFC*, 2nd ser., 6:347–416.

———. *Commentaria in Epistolam ad Ephesios. PL* 26:439–554.

———. *Commentaria in Ezechielem. PL* 25:15–490.

———. *De perpetua virginitate B. Mariae. PL* 23:183–206. Translation in *LNPNFC*, 6:335–46.

———. *Epistolae. PL* 22. Translation of select letters in *LNPNFC*, 2nd ser., 6:1–295.

———. *Vita Malchi monachi captivi. PL* 23:56–59. Translation in *LNPNFC*, 2nd ser., 6:315–18.

John, apostle. *Le Livre secret des cathares: Interrogatio Iohannis*. Edited by Edina Bozóky. Paris: Beauchesne, 1980.

John Le Graveur. *Entre Dieu et Satan: Les visions d'Ermine de Reims (+ 1396)*. Edited and translated into modern French by Claude Arnaud-Gillet. Florence: Sismel, Edizioni del Galluzzo, 1997.

John of Arras. *Mélusine, roman du XIVe siècle par Jean d'Arras: Publié pour la première fois, d'après le manuscrit de la Bibliothèque de l'Arsenal avec les variantes des manuscrits de la Bibliothèque nationale.* Edited by Louis Stouff. Dijon: Bernigaud et Privat, 1932.

John of Marienwerder. *Vita Dorotheae Montoviensis Magistri Johannis Marienwerder.* Edited by Hans Westpfahl. *Forschungen und Quellen zur Kirchen- und Kulturgeschichte Ostdeutschlands,* vol. 1. Cologne: Böhlau, 1964.

———. *Vita Lindana. AA SS,* October, 13:499–560.

Jordanes of Bergamo. *Quaestio de strigis.* In *Quellen und Untersuchungen zur Geschichte des Hexenwahns und der Hexenverfolgung im Mittelalter.* Edited by Joseph Hansen, 195–200. Bonn, 1901. Reprint, Hildesheim: Georg Olms, 1963.

Jordanes. *De origine actibusque Getarum (sive: Getica).* Edited by Theodor Mommsen. *MGH, Auct. Ant.,* 5:1, 53–138. Berlin: Weidmann, 1882.

Juliana of Mont-Cornillon, St. *Vita de B. Juliana virgine priorissa Montis-Cornelii apud Leodium. AA SS,* April, 1:435–75. Translated by Barbara Newman. *The Life of Juliana Mont-Cornillon.* Toronto: Peregrina, 1991.

Justin Martyr. *Apologie pour les chrétiens.* Edited and translated by Charles Munier. SC, 507. Paris: Editions du Cerf, 2006.

Kempe, Margery. *The Book of Margery Kempe.* Edited by Barry Windeatt. Harlow, England: Longman, 2000.

Knowles, David, ed. *The Monastic Constitutions of Lanfranc.* Revised by Christopher Brooke. New York: Oxford University Press, 2002.

Landulf the Senior. *Mediolanensis historiae libri quatuor.* Edited by Alessandro Cutulo. *Rerum Italicarum Scriptores,* vol. 4,2. Rev. ed. Bologna: N. Zanichelli, 1942.

Lanfranc. *Letters of Lanfranc.* Edited and translated by Helen Clover and Margaret Gibson. Oxford: Clarendon Press, 1979.

———. *The Monastic Constitutions of Lanfranc.* Edited by David Knowles. Revised by Christopher Brooke. New York: Oxford University Press, 2002.

Langton, Stephen. *Sermo de virginibus.* In Appendix to Phyllis Roberts, "Stephen Langton's *Sermo de virginibus.*" In *Women of the Medieval World.* Edited by Julius Kirshner and Suzanne Wemple, 103–18. Oxford: Basil Blackwell, 1985.

Le Franc, Martin. *Le Champion des Dames.* In *L'Imaginaire du sabbat: Edition critique des texts les plus anciens (1430 c.–1440 c.).* Edited by Martine Ostorero, Agostino Paravicini Bagliani, and Kathrin Utz Tremp, 451–82. Lausanne: Cahiers lausannois d'histoire médiévale, 1999.

Leo I. *Ep. 12, To the bishops of Mauritania Caesariensis. PL* 54:645–56.

———. *Ep. 167, To Rusticus of Narbonne. PL* 54:1197–1209.

Liber antiheresis. Edited by C. Thouzellier. "Controverses vaudoises-cathares à la fin du XIIe siècle (d'après le livre II du *Liber antiheresis,* MS Madrid 114 et les sections correspondantes du MS BN lat. 13446)." *Archives d'histoire doctrinale et littéraire du moyen âge* 35 (1960): 137–227.

Livy. *Ab urbe condita*. Translated by B. O. Foster. Loeb Classical Library. 14 vols. Cambridge, Mass.: Harvard University Press, 1961–68.

Manselli, Raoul, ed. *De confessione hereticorum et de fide eorum*. In "Per la storia dell'eresia nell secolo XII: Studi minori." *Bullettino dell'Istituto storico italiano per il medio evo e Archivio Muratoriano* 47 (1955): 189–264.

Mansi, G. D., ed. *Sacrorum conciliorum nova, et amplissima collectio*. 53 vols. Paris, 1901–27. Reprint, Graz: Akademische Druck, 1961.

Map, Walter. *De nugis curialium: Courtier's Trifles*. Edited and translated by M. R. James. Revised by C. N. L. Brooke and R. A. B. Mynors. Oxford: Clarendon, 1983.

Marbod of Rennes. *Ep. 6, To Robert of Arbrissel*. PL 171:1481–86. Translated by Bruce Venarde. In *Robert of Arbrissel: A Medieval Religious Life*, 88–100. Washington, D.C.: Catholic University Press, 2003.

———. *Epithalamium* (On the occasion of Ermengard of Brittany's marriage to William of Aquitaine). Edited by J. de Petigny. In "Une lettre inédite de Robert d'Arbrissel à la Comtesse Ermengarde." *Bibliothèque de l'Ecole de Chartes*, ser. 3,5 (1854): 216. Translated by Regine Pernoud. In *Women in the Days of the Cathedrals*. Translated by Anne Côté-Harriss, 124–25. San Francisco: Ignatius Press, 1998.

———. *Thais poenitens in Aegypto. Vita metrica alter*. AA SS, October, 4:226–28.

Marcianese, G. *Narratione della nascita, vita, e morte della B. Lucia da Narni*. Ferrara: V. Buldini, 1616.

Mary, Virgin. *The Passing of Mary*. ANF, 8:592–98.

Matteotti, John. *Acta S. Franciscae Romana*. AA SS, March, 2:89–219.

Marguerite Porete. *Le Mirouer des simples âmes.*. Edited by Romana Guarnieri and Paul Verdeyen. *CCCM*, 69. Turnhout: Brepols, 1986. Translated by Ellen Babinsky. *The Mirror of Simple Souls*. New York: Paulist Press, 1993.

Marie de France. *The Lais of Marie de France*. Translated by Glyn Burgess and Keith Busby. 2nd ed. Harmondsworth, Middlesex: Penguin Books, 1986.

McNamara, Jo Ann, John Halborg, and E. Gordon Whatley, eds. *Sainted Women of the Dark Ages*. Durham, N.C.: Duke University Press, 1992.

Mechtild of Hackeborn. *Liber specialias gratiae*. In *Revelationes Gertrudianae ac Mechtildianae II: Sanctae Mechtildis virginis ordinis Sancti Benedicti Liber specialis gratiae; Accedit sororis Mechtildis ejusdem ordinis Lux divinitatis*. Vol. 2. Edited by Louis Paquelin et al. Poitiers: Oudin, 1877.

Mechtild of Magdeburg. *Das fliessende Licht der Gottheit: Nach der einsiedler Handschrift in kritischen Vergleich mit gesamten Überlieferung*. Edited by Margot Schmidt. Munich: Artemis, 1990. Translated by Frank Tobin. *The Flowing Light of the Godhead*. New York: Paulist Press, 1998.

Menestò, Enrico, ed. *Il processo di canonizzazione di Chiara da Montefalco*. Regione dell'Umbria: La Nuova Italia, 1984.

Methodius, *Le Banquet*. Edited by Herbert Musurillo. SC, 95. Paris: Editions du Cerf, 1963. Translated by Herbert Musurillo. *The Symposium: A Treatise on Chastity*. ACW, 27. London: Longman, 1958.

Moneta of Cremona. *Adversus Catharos et Valdenses libri quinque*. Edited by T. A. Ricchini.

Rome: Palladis, 1743. Reprint, Ridgewood, N.J.: Gregg, 1964. Excerpted and translated by Walter Wakefield and Austin Evans. *Heresies of the High Middle Ages*, 307–29. New York: Columbia University Press, 1969.

Muckle, J. T., ed. "The Letter of Heloise on Religious Life and Abelard's First Reply." *Mediaeval Studies* 17 (1955): 240–81. Translated by C. K. Scott Moncrieff. In *The Letters of Abelard and Heloise.* New York: Alfred A. Knopf, 1942.

Nider, John. *Consolatorium timorate conscientie.* Jehan Petit, [1502?].

———. *De morali lepra.* Louvain: Johann von Paderborn, 1481.

———. *Formicarium.* Douai: Balthazaris Belleri, 1602.

Novatian. *De bono pudicitiae.* In Cyprian, *S. Thasci Caecili Cypriani opera omnia.* Edited by W. Hartel, *CSEL*, 3:13–25.

Odilia of Liège, St. *Vita B. Odiliae viduae Leodiensis. Analecta Bollandiana* 13 (1894): 197–287.

Olivi, Peter John. *Quodlibeta quinque.* Edited by Stephan Defraia. Grottaferrata, Rome: College of St. Bonaventure at Claras Aquas, 2002.

Optatus. *De schismate Donatistarum. PL* 11:885–1104.

Origen. *Commentariorum in Epistolam B. Pauli ad Romanos. PG* 14:837–1292. Translated by Thomas Scheck. *Commentary on the Epistle to the Romans. FC*, 103–4. Washington, D.C.: Catholic University Press, 2001–2.

———. *Commentariorum in Evangelium secundum Joannem. PG* 14:21–832. Translated in *ANF*, 9:297–408.

———. *Commentarium in Matthaeum. PG* 13:829–1800. Translated in *ANF*, 9:409–512.

———. *De principiis. PG* 11:111–414. Translated in *ANF*, 4:237–384.

———. *Homilia in Cantica canticorum. PG* 13:35–58. Translated by R. P. Lawson. In *Commentary on the Canticle of Canticles.* In *Origen: The Song of Songs: Commentary and Homilies, 265–305. ACW*, 26. New York: Newman Press, 1956.

———. *In Canticum canticorum. PG* 13:37–218. Translated by R. P. Lawson. In *Origen: The Song of Songs: Commentary and Homilies, 21–263. ACW*, 26. New York: Newman Press, 1956.

———. *In Leviticum homiliae. PG* 12:405–572.

———. *In Lucam homilia. PG* 13:1801–1900.

Ostorero, Martine, Agostino P. Bagliani, and Kathrin Utz Tremp, eds. *L'Imaginaire du sabbat: Edition critique des texts les plus anciens (1430 c.–1440 c.).* Lausanne: Cahiers lausannois d'histoire médiévale, 1999.

Osyth, St. "The Lives of St. Osyth of Essex and St. Osyth of Aylesbury." Edited by David Bethel. *Analecta Bollandiana* 88 (1970): 75–127.

Paul, apostle. *Acts of Paul and Thecla.* Translated by M. R. James. *The Apocryphal New Testament*, 270–99. Oxford: Clarendon Press, 1924. Reprint, 1966.

Pelagius. *Ep. 130, To Demetrias.* (Formerly attributed to Jerome.) *PL* 22:1107–24. Translation in *LNPNFC*, 2nd ser. 6:260–372.

Pellens, Karl, ed. *Die Texte des Normannischen Anonymous.* Wiesbaden: Steiner, 1966.

Perpetua, St. *The Passion of SS. Perpetua and Felicity.* Translated and edited by W. H. Shewring. London: Sheed and Ward, 1931.

Peter Lombard. *Sententiae in IV libris distinctae.* Edited by the Fathers of the College of St. Bonaventure. 2 vols. Grottaferrata, Rome: College of St. Bonaventure at Claras Aquas, 1971–81.

Peter the Venerable. *The Letters of Peter the Venerable.* Edited by Giles Constable. 2 vols. Cambridge, Mass.: Harvard University Press, 1967.

Petigny, J. de, ed. "Une lettre inédite de Robert d'Arbrissel à la Comtesse Ermengarde." *Bibliothèque de l'Ecole de Chartes*, ser. 3, 5 (1854): 209–35.

Philip, apostle. *Gospel of Philip.* In *The Nag Hammadi Library.* Edited by James Robinson, 141–60. Revised ed. San Francisco: Harper and Row, 1990.

Philip of Clairvaux. "Vita Elizabeth sanctimonialis in Erkenrode, Ordinis Cisterciensis." In *Catalogus codicum hagiographicorum bibliothecae regiae bruxellensis.* Edited by the Bollandists, 1:362–78. Brussels: Polleunsis, Ceuterick et de Smet, 1886.

Pierre des Vaux-de-Cernay (Peter of Vaux Cernai). *Petri Vallium Sarnaii monachi Hystoria albigensis.* Edited by Pascal Guébin and Ernst Lyon. 3 vols. Paris: Librairie Honoré Champion, 1926–39.

Polycarp, St. *Martyrium S. Polycarpi.* In *Patres Apostolici.* Edited by F. X. Funk, 314–45. Tübingen: Henricus Laupp, 1901. Translation in *ANF*, 1:39–44.

The Pontifical of Egbert, Archbishop of York, A.D. 732–766. Edited by W. Greenwall. Surtee Society 27. London: T. and W. Boone, 1853.

Le Pontifical Romain de la Curie Romaine au XIIIe siècle. Vol. 2 of *Le Pontifical Romain au Moyen-Age.* Edited by Michel Andrieu. Studi e Testi 87. Vatican: Biblioteca Apostolica Vaticana, 1940.

Le Pontifical Romain du XIIe siècle. Vol. 1 of *Le Pontifical Romain au Moyen-Age.* Edited by Michel Andrieu. Studi e Testi 86. Vatican: Biblioteca Apostolica Vaticana, 1938.

Le Pontifical romano-germanique du dixième siècle. Edited by Cyrille Vogel and Reinhard Elze. 3 vols. Studi e Testi 226, 227, 269. Vatican City: Biblioteca Apostolica Vaticana, 1963–71.

Radegund. *De excidio Thoringiae. MGH, Auct. Ant.* 4, 2:271–75.

Raymond of Capua. *Vita S. Catherinae Senensis. AA SS*, April, 3:862–967. Translated by Conleth Kearns. *The Life of Catherine of Siena by Raymond of Capua.* Wilmington, Del.: Michael Glazier, 1980.

Raymond of Peñafort. *Summa de poenitentia et matrimonio.* Rome: Joannes Tallini, 1603.

Razzi, Serafino. *Vite dei santi e beati così del sacro Ordine de' frati predicatori.* Florence: Bartolomeo Sermartelli, 1577.

Recollectio casus, status, et condicionis Valdensium ydolatrarum. In *Quellen und Untersuchungen zur Geschichte des Hexenwahns und der Hexenverfolgung im Mittelalter.* Edited by Joseph Hansen, 149–81. Bonn, 1901. Reprint, Hildesheim: Georg Olms, 1963.

Regino of Prüm. *De ecclesiasticis disciplinis et religione Christiana. PL* 132:185–400.

Robert of Arbrissel. *Diplomata. PL* 162:1083–88. Excerpted and translated by Bruce Venarde. In *Robert of Arbrissel: A Medieval Religious Life*, 68–87. Washington, D.C.: Catholic University Press, 2003.

Robert of Arbrissel, (anonymous life of). *La Vie venerable pere maistre Robert de Arbrinsel.* Edited by Jacques Dalarun. In *L'Impossible sainteté: La vie retrouvée de Robert d'Arbrissel (v. 1045–1116) fondateur de Fontevraud.* Paris: Editions du Cerf, 1985.

Ruusbroec, Jan Van. *De ornatu spiritalium nuptiarum (Die Geestelike Brulocht)*. Edited by J. Alaerts. Latin translation by L. Surius. Translated into English by H. Rolfson. *CCCM*, 103: 550–66. Turnhout: Brepols, 1988.

———. *Vanden XII Beghinen*. Edited by M. M. Kors. English translation by H. Rolfson. Latin translation by L. Surius. *CCCM*, 107a. Turnhout: Brepols, 2000.

Schmidt, C., ed. "Actenstücke besonders zur Geschichte der Waldenser." *Zeitschrift für die historische Theologie* 22 (1852): 238–62.

Severus, Sulpicius. *Chronica (Sacra historia)*. *PL* 20:95–160. Translation in *LNPNFC*, 2nd ser., 11:71–122.

Siricius, Pope. *Epistolae et decreta*. *PL* 13:1131–96.

Speculum virginum. Edited by Jutta Seyfarth. *CCCM*, 5. Turnhout: Brepols, 1990.

Stachnik, Richard, ed. *Die Akten des Kanonisationsprozesses Dorotheas von Montau von 1394 bis 1521. Forschungen und Quellen zur Kirchen- und Kulturgeschichte Ostdeutschlands*, vol. 12. Cologne: Böhlau, 1978.

Stephanus, Presbyter Africanus. *Vita de S. Sancto Amatore*. *AA SS*, May, 1:53–61.

Stephen of Bourbon. *Anecdotes historiques, légendes et apologues tirés du recueil inédit d'Etienne de Bourbon*. Edited by A. Lecoy de la Marche. Paris: Librairie Renouard, 1877.

Tacitus, Cornelius. *Annales*. In *The Histories: Books IV–V; The Annals: Books 1–3*. Translated by John Jackson. Loeb Classical Library, 249. Cambridge, Mass.: Harvard University Press, 1931.

———. *Germania*. In *Agricola, Germania, Dialogus*. Translated by W. Hutton. Loeb Classical Library, 35, 1:119–218. Cambridge, Mass.: Harvard University Press, 1920.

Tertullian. *Ad uxorem*. In *Quinti Septimi Florentis Tertulliani opera*. *CCSL*, 1: 371–94. Turnhout: Brepols, 1954. Translation in *ANF*, 4:39–49.

———. *Adversus Iudaeos*. In *Quinti Septimi Florentis Tertulliani opera*. *CCSL*, 2:1339–96. Translation in *ANF*, 3:151–74.

———. *Adversus Marcionem*. In *Quinti Septimi Florentis Tertulliani opera*, 1:441–726. Translation in *ANF*, 3:269–474.

———. *Adversus Praxean*. In *Quinti Septimi Florentis Tertulliani opera*, 2:1159–1205. Translation in *ANF*, 3:597–627.

———. *Adversus Valentinianos*. In *Quinti Septimi Florentis Tertulliani opera*, 2:753–78. Translation in *ANF*, 3:503–20.

———. *Apologeticum*. In *Quinti Septimi Florentis Tertulliani opera*, 1:85–171. Translation in *ANF*, 3:17–55.

———. *De anima*. In *Quinti Septimi Florentis Tertulliani opera*, 2:781–869. Translation in *ANF*, 3:181–235.

———. *De baptismo*. In *Quinti Septimi Florentis Tertulliani opera*, 1:277–95. Translation in *ANF*, 3:669–79.

———. *De carne Christi*. In *Quinti Septimi Florentis Tertulliani opera*, 2:873–917. Translation in *ANF*, 3:521–42.

———. *De cultu feminarum*. In *Quinti Septimi Florentis Tertulliani opera*, 1:343–70. Translation in *ANF*, 4:14–26.

———. *De exhortatione castitatis.* In *Quinti Septimi Florentis Tertulliani opera*, 2:1015–35. Translation in *ANF*, 4:50–58.

———. *De idololatria.* In *Quinti Septimi Florentis Tertulliani opera*, 2:1101–24. Translation in *ANF*, 3:61–76.

———. *De monogamia.* In *Quinti Septimi Florentis Tertulliani opera*, 2:1229–53. Translation in *ANF*, 4:59–72.

———. *De oratione.* In *Quinti Septimi Florentis Tertulliani opera*, 1:257–74. Translation in *ANF*, 3:681–91.

———. *De praescriptione haereticorum.* In *Quinti Septimi Florentis Tertulliani opera*, 1:187–224. Translation in *ANF*, 3:243–65.

———. *De pudicitia.* In *Quinti Septimi Florentis Tertulliani opera*, 2:1281–1330. Translation in *ANF*, 4:73–101.

———. *De resurrectione mortuorum.* In *Quinti Septimi Florentis Tertulliani opera*, 2, 1:921–1012. Translation in *ANF*, 3:545–94.

———. *De testimonia animae.* In *Quinti Septimi Florentis Tertulliani opera*, 1:175–83. Translation in *ANF*, 3:175–79.

———. *De virginibus velandis.* In *Quinti Septimi Florentis Tertulliani opera*, 2:1209–26. Translation in *ANF*, 4:27–37.

Thecla, St. *Acts of Paul and Thecla.* Translated by M. R. James. *The Apocryphal New Testament*, 270–99. Oxford, 1924. Reprint, 1966.

Tholosan, Claude. *Ut magorum et maleficiorum errores.* In *L'Imaginaire du sabbat: Edition critique des texts les plus anciens (1430 c.–1440 c.).* Edited by Martine Ostorero, Agostino Paravicini Bagliani, and Kathrin Utz Tremp, 361–415. Lausanne: Cahiers lausannois d'histoire médiévale, 1999.

Thomas, apostle. *Gospel of Thomas.* In *The Nag Hammadi Library.* Edited by James Robinson, 126–38. Leiden: Brill, 1978. Revised, San Francisco: Harper and Row, 1988.

Thomas of Cantilupe. *The Life and Miracles of St. Thomas Cantilupe.* Edited by André Vauchez in Appendix 1 to *Sainthood in the Later Middle Ages.* Translated by Jean Birell, 540–58. Cambridge: Cambridge University Press, 1997.

Thomas of Cantimpré. *Bonum universale de apibus.* Douai: B. Belleri, 1627.

———. *Liber de natura rerum.* Berlin: W. de Gruyter, 1973.

———. *Supplementum ad Vitam S. Mariae Oigniacensis. AA SS*, June, 5:572–83. Translated by Hugh Feiss. In *Mary of Oignies: Mother of Salvation.* Edited by Anneke Mulder-Bakker, 129–65. Turnhout: Brepols, 2007.

———. *Vita Ioannis Cantipratensis.* In "Une Oeuvre inédite de Thomas de Cantimpré: La 'Vita Ioannis Cantipratensis.'" *Revue d'histoire ecclésiastique* 76 (1981): 241–316. Translated by Barbara Newman. In *Thomas of Cantimpré: The Collected Saints' Lives*, 57–121. Turnhout: Brepols, 2008.

———. *Vita Margarete de Ypris.* Edited by G. Meersseman. "Les Frères Prêcheurs et le movement dévot en Flandre au XIIIe siècle." *Archivum Fratrum Praedicatorum* 18 (1948): 106–30. Translated by Margot King and Barbara Newman. In *Thomas of Cantimpré: The Collected Saints' Lives*, 163–213. Turnhout: Brepols, 2008.

———. *Vita S. Christinae Mirabilis virginis. AA SS*, July, 5:650–60. Translated by Margot

King and Barbara Newman. In *Thomas of Cantimpré: The Collected Saints' Lives*, 127–57. Turnhout: Brepols, 2008.

———. *Vita S. Lutgardis virginis Cisterciensis*. *AA SS*, June, 4:189–210. Translated by Margot King and Barbara Newman. In *Thomas of Cantimpré: The Collected Saints' Lives*, 211–96. Turnhout: Brepols, 2008.

Thomas of Chobham. *Summa confessorum*. Edited by F. Broomfield. *Analecta Mediaevalia Namurensia*, 25. Louvain: Nauwelaerts, 1968.

Tinctor, John. *Invectives contre la secte de Vauderie*. Edited by Emile Van Balberthe and Frédéric Duval. Tournai: Archives du Chapitre cathedral; Louvain-la-Neuve: Université catholique de Louvain, 1999.

Vauderye de Lyonois en brief (anonymous). In *Quellen und Untersuchungen zur Geschichte des Hexenwahns und der Hexenverfolgung im Mittelalter*. Edited by Joseph Hansen, 188–95. Bonn, 1901. Reprint, Hildesheim: Georg Olms, 1963.

Ulphonsus. *Vita S. Catharinae Suecicae*. *AA SS*, March 3:509–29.

Vanna of Orvieto, St. *La Legenda di Vanna da Orvieto*. Edited by Emore Paoli and Luigi G. G. Ricci, 137–76. Spoleto: Centro Italiano di Studi sull'Alto Medioevo, 1996. Translated by Maiju Lehmijoki-Gardner. In *Dominican Penitent Women*. Edited by Lehmijoki-Gardner, 61–86. New York: Paulist Press, 2005.

Verdeyen, Paul, ed. "Le Procès d'inquisition contre Marguerite Porete et Guiard de Cressonessart (1309–1310)." *Revue d'histoire ecclésiastique* 81 (1986): 47–94.

Visconti, Girolamo. *Lamiarum sive striarum opusculum*. In *Quellen und Untersuchungen zur Geschichte des Hexenwahns und der Hexenverfolgung im Mittelalter*. Edited by Joseph Hansen, 200–207. Bonn, 1901. Reprint, Hildesheim: Georg Olms, 1963.

Wandrille, St. *Vita Wandregiseli*. *MGH, Scrip. Rer. Merov.*, 5:1–24.

Wakefield, Walter and Austin Evans, eds. *Heresies of the High Middle Ages*. New York: Columbia University Press, 1969.

William of Auvergne. *Opera omnia*. Paris: A. Pralard, 1674. Reprint, Frankfurt am Main: Minerva, 1963.

William of Malmesbury. *The Vita Wulfstani of William of Malmesbury*. Edited by Reginald Darlington. London: Royal Historical Society, 1928.

William of Rennes. Glosses to Raymond of Peñafort's *Summa de poenitentia et matrimonio*. Rome: Joannes Tallini, 1603.

The Wooing of Our Lord. In *Anchoritic Spirituality: Ancrene Wisse and Associated Works*. Edited and translated by Anne Savage and Nicholas Watson, 247–57. New York: Paulist, 1991.

SECONDARY SOURCES

Adnès, Pierre. "Le mariage spiritual." In *Dictionnaire de la spiritualité*. Edited by Marcel Viller, F. Cavallera, and J. de Guibert, 10:388–407. Paris: Beauchesne, 1932–95.

Agius, Ambrose. "The Blessed Virgin in Origen and St. Ambrose." *Downside Review* 50 (1932): 126–37.

Airlie, Stuart. "Private Bodies and the Body Politic." *Past and Present* 161 (1998): 3–38.

Alexandre, Jérôme. *Une Chair pour la gloire: L'anthropologie réaliste et mystique de Tertullien.* Paris: Beauchesne, 2001.

Ames, Christine Caldwell. *Righteous Persecution: Inquisition, Dominicans, and Christianity in the Middle Ages.* Philadelphia: University of Pennsylvania Press, 2009.

Antonelli, Francis. *De inquisitione medico-legali super miraculis in causis beatificationis et canonizationis.* Rome: Pontificium Athenaeum Antonianum, 1961.

Atkinson, Clarissa. *Mystic and Pilgrim: The Book and the World of Margery Kempe.* Ithaca, N.Y.: Cornell University Press, 1983.

———. *The Oldest Vocation: Christian Motherhood in the Middle Ages.* Ithaca, N.Y.: Cornell University Press, 1991.

———. " 'Precious Balsam in a Fragile Glass': The Ideology of Virginity in the Later Middle Ages." *Journal of Family History* 8 (1983): 131–43.

Bailey, Michael. *Battling Demons: Witchcraft, Heresy, and Reform in the Late Middle Ages.* University Park: Pennsylvania State University Press, 2003.

———. "The Feminization of Magic and the Emerging Idea of the Female Witch in the Late Middle Ages." *Essays in Medieval Studies* 19 (2002): 120–34.

———. "A Late-Medieval Crisis in Superstition?" *Speculum* 84 (2009): 633–61.

———. "The Medieval Concept of the Witches' Sabbath." *Exemplaria* 8 (1996): 419–39.

Baldwin, John. *The Language of Sex: Five Voices from Northern France around 1200.* Chicago: University of Chicago Press, 1994.

Barlow, Frank. *William Rufus.* Berkeley: University of California, 1983.

Barratt, Alexandra. "Undutiful Daughters and Metaphorical Mothers among the Beguines." In *New Trends in Feminine Spirituality: The Holy Women of Liège and Their Impact.* Edited by Juliette Dor, Lesley Johnson, and Jocelyn Wogan-Browne, 81–104. Turnhout: Brepols, 1999.

———. " 'The Woman Who Shares the King's Bed': The Innocent Eroticism of Gertrude the Great of Helfta." In *Intersections of Sexuality and the Divine in Medieval Culture: The Word Made Flesh.* Edited by Susannah Mary Chewning, 107–20. Aldershot: Ashgate, 2005.

Barratt, Alexandra, and Debra Stoudt. "Gertrude the Great of Helfta." *MHW*, 435–73.

Barstow, Anne Llewellyn. *Married Priests and the Reforming Papacy: The Eleventh-Century Debates.* New York: Edwin Mellen, 1982.

Bell, Rudolph. *Holy Anorexia.* Chicago: University of Chicago Press, 1985.

Bennett, Judith. *Women in the Medieval Countryside: Gender and Household in Brigstock before the Plague.* Oxford: Oxford University Press, 1989.

Berman, Constance. *The Cistercian Evolution: The Reinvention of the Order in Twelfth-Century Europe.* Philadelphia: University of Pennsylvania Press, 2000.

Beuzart, Paul. *Les Hérésies pendant le Moyen Age et la Réforme jusqu'à la mort de Philippe II, 1598, dans la région de Douai, d'Arras, et au pays de l'Alleu.* Le Puy: Peyriller, Rouchon, et Gamon, 1912.

Biller, Peter. "Cathars and the Material Woman." In *Medieval Theology and the Natural Woman.* Edited by Peter Biller and Alastair Minnis, 61–107. Woodbridge, Suffolk: Boydell and Brewer, 1997.

Bishop, Jane. "Bishops as Marital Advisors in the Ninth Century." In *Women in the Medieval World: Essays in Honor of John Mundy*. Edited by Julius Kirshner and Suzanne Wemple, 53–84. Oxford: Basil Blackwell, 1985.

Bitel, Lisa. *Women in Early Medieval Europe, 400–1100*. Cambridge: Cambridge University Press, 2002.

Blamires, Alcuin. "*Caput a femina, membra a viris*: Gender Polemic in Abelard's Letter 'On the Authority and Dignity of the Nun's Profession.'" In *The Tongue of the Fathers: Gender and Ideology in Twelfth-Century Latin*. Edited by David Townsend and Andrew Taylor, 55–79. Philadelphia: University of Pennsylvania Press, 1998.

———. Alcuin Blamires, *The Case for Women in Medieval Culture*. Oxford: Clarendon Press, 1997.

Blanton, Virginia. *Signs of Devotion: The Cult of St. Æthelthryth in Medieval England*. University Park: Pennsylvania State University Press, 2007.

Bloch, Marc. *Feudal Society*. Vol. 1, *The Growth of the Ties of Dependence*. Translated by L. A. Manyon. Chicago: University of Chicago Press, 1961.

Bloch, R. Howard. *Medieval Misogyny and the Invention of Western Romantic Love*. Chicago: University of Chicago Press, 1991.

Blomme, Robert. *La Doctrine du péché dans les écoles théologiques de la première moitié du XIIe siècle*. Louvain: Publications Universitaires de Louvain, 1958.

Blumenfeld-Kosinski, Renate. *Not of Woman Born: Representations of Caesarean Birth in Medieval and Renaissance Culture*. Ithaca, N.Y.: Cornell University Press, 1990.

———. *Poets, Saints, and Visionaries of the Great Schism, 1378–1417*. University Park: Pennsylvania State University Press, 2006.

———. "Satirical Views of the Beguines in Northern French Literature." In *New Trends in Feminine Spirituality: The Holy Women of Liège and Their Impact*. Edited by Juliette Dor, Lesley Johnson, and Jocelyn Wogan-Browne, 237–49. Turnhout: Brepols, 1999.

———. "The Strange Case of Ermine of Reims (1347–1396): A Medieval Woman between Demons and Saints." *Speculum* 85 (2010): 321–56.

Boanas, Guy, and Lyndal Roper. "Feminine Piety in Fifteenth-Century Rome: Santa Francesca Romana." In *Disciplines of Faith: Studies in Religion, Politics and Patriarchy*. Edited by Jim Obelkevich, Lyndal Roper, and Raphael Samuel, 177–93. London: Routledge and Kegan Paul, 1987.

Bolton, Brenda M. "Mulieres sanctae." In *Medieval Women*. Edited by Susan Stuard, 141–58. Philadelphia: University of Pennsylvania Press, 1976.

———. "Thirteenth-Century Religious Women: Further Reflections on the Low Countries' 'Special Case.'" In *New Trends in Feminine Spirituality: The Holy Women of Liège and Their Impact*. Edited by Juliette Dor, Lesley Johnson, and Jocelyn Wogan-Browne, 129–58. Turnhout: Brepolis, 1999.

Bornstein, Daniel. "Spiritual Kinship and Domestic Devotions." In *Gender and Society in Renaissance Italy*. Edited by Judith Brown and Robert Davis, 173–92. New York: Longman, 1998.

Bos, Elisabeth. "The Literature of Spiritual Formation for Women in France and England, 1080–1180." In *Listen Daughter: The Speculum Virginum and the Formation of Religious*

Women in the Middle Ages. Edited by Constant Mews, 201–20. New York: Palgrave, 2001.

Boswell, John. *Christianity, Social Tolerance, and Homosexuality: Gay People in Western Europe from the Beginning of the Christian Era to the Fourteenth Century*. Chicago: University of Chicago Press, 1980.

———. *Kindness of Strangers: The Abandonment of Children in Western Europe from Late Antiquity to the Renaissance*. Chicago: University of Chicago, 1998.

———. *Same-Sex Unions in Premodern Europe*. New York: Villard, 1994.

Boureau, Alain. "Le sabbat et la question scolastique de la personne." In *Le Sabbat des sorciers: XVe-XVIIIe siècles*. Edited by Nicole Jacques-Chaquin and Maxime Préaud, 33–46. Grenoble: Jérôme Millon, 1993.

———. *Satan the Heretic: The Birth of Demonology in the Medieval West*. Translated by Teresa Lavender Fagan. Chicago: University of Chicago Press, 2006.

Brakke, David. *Athanasius and Asceticism*. Oxford: Clarendon, 1995. Reprint, Baltimore: Johns Hopkins University Press, 1998.

———. *Demons and the Making of the Monk: Spiritual Combat in Early Christianity*. Cambridge, Mass.: Harvard University Press, 2006.

———. *Gnostics: Myth, Ritual, and Diversity in Early Christianity*. Cambridge, Mass.: Harvard University Press, 2010.

———. "The Problematization of Nocturnal Emissions in Early Christian Syria, Egypt, and Gaul." *Journal of Early Christian Studies* 3 (1995): 419–60.

———. "Self-Differentiation among Christian Groups: The Gnostics and Their Opponents." In *The Cambridge History of Christianity*. Vol. 1, *Origins to Constantine*. Edited by Margaret Mitchell and Frances Young, 245–60. Cambridge: Cambridge University Press, 2006.

Briggs, Robin. "Women as Victims? Witches, Judges, and Community." In *Gender and Witchcraft*. Vol. 4 of *New Perspectives on Witchcraft, Magic and Demonology*. Edited by Brian Levack, 40–53. New York: Routledge, 2001.

Broedel, Hans. *The Malleus Maleficarum and the Construction of Witchcraft*. Manchester: Manchester University Press, 2003.

Brooke, Christopher. *The Medieval Idea of Marriage*. Oxford: Oxford University Press, 1989.

Brown, D. Catherine. *Pastor and Laity in the Theology of Jean Gerson*. Cambridge: Cambridge University Press, 1987.

Brown, Judith. *Immodest Acts: The Life of a Lesbian Nun in Renaissance Italy*. New York: Oxford University Press, 1986.

Brown, Peter. *The Body and Society: Men, Women, and Sexual Renunciation in Early Christianity*. New York: Columbia University Press, 1988.

Brundage, James. *Law, Sex, and Christian Society in Medieval Europe*. Chicago: University of Chicago Press, 1987.

Buckley, Jorunn Jacobsen. *Female Fault and Fulfillment in Gnosticism*. Chapel Hill: University of North Carolina, 1986.

Bugge, John. *Virginitas: An Essay in the History of a Medieval Idea*. The Hague: Martinus Nijhoff, 1975.

Burrus, Virginia. *The Sex Lives of Saints: An Erotics of Ancient Hagiography*. Philadelphia: University of Pennsylvania, 2004.

Bušek, Vratislav. "Der Prozeß der Indicia." *Zeifschrift für Rechtsgeschichte, Kanonistische Abteilung* 29 (1940): 446–61.

Bussell, Donna Alfano. "Heloise Redressed: Rhetorical Engagement and the Benedictine Rite of Initiation in Heloise's Third Letter." In *Listening to Heloise: The Voice of a Twelfth-Century Woman*. Edited by Bonnie Wheeler, 233–54. New York: St. Martin's Press, 2000.

Butler, Rex. *New Prophecy and "New Visions": Evidence of Montanism in the Passion of Perpetua and Felicitas*. Washington, D.C.: Catholic University Press, 2006.

Bynum, Caroline Walker. *Fragmentation and Redemption: Essays on Gender and the Human Body in Medieval Religion*. New York: Zone Books, 1992.

———. *Holy Feast and Holy Fast: The Religious Significance of Food to Medieval Women*. Berkeley: University of California Press, 1987.

———. *Jesus as Mother: Studies in the Spirituality of the High Middle Ages*. Berkeley and Los Angeles: University of California Press, 1982.

———. *The Resurrection of the Body in Western Christianity, 200–1336*. New York: Columbia University Press, 1995.

———. *Wonderful Blood: Theology and Practice in Late Medieval Northern Germany and Beyond*. Philadelphia: University of Pennsylvania Press, 2006.

Caciola, Nancy. *Discerning Spirits: Divine and Demonic Possession in the Middle Ages*. Ithaca, N.Y.: Cornell University Press, 2003.

Cadden, Joan. *The Meanings of Sex Difference in the Middle Ages*. Cambridge: Cambridge University Press, 1993.

Camelot, Thomas. "Les traités 'De virginitate' au IVe siècle." In *Mystique et continence: Travaux scientifiques du VIIe congrès international d'Avon*, 273–92. Paris: Les Etudes Carmélitaines chez Desclée de Brouwer, 1952.

Cameron, Euan. *Enchanted Europe: Superstition, Reason, and Religion, 1250–1750*. Oxford: Oxford University Press, 2010.

Carpenter, Jennifer. "Juette of Huy, Recluse and Mother (1158–1228): Children and Mothering in the Saintly Life." In *Power of the Weak: Studies on Medieval Women*. Edited by Jennifer Carpenter and Sally-Beth MacLean, 57–93. Champagne: University of Illinois Press, 1995.

Casanova, Gertrude. "Matilda von Hackeborn." http://en.wikisource.org/wiki/Catholic_Encyclopedia_(1913)/St._Mechtilde.

Church, F. Forrester. "Sex and Salvation in Tertullian." *Harvard Theological Review* 68 (1975): 85–101.

Clanchy, M. T. *Abelard: A Medieval Life*. Oxford: Basil Blackwell, 1997.

Clark, Elizabeth. "Ascetic Renunciation and Feminine Advancement: A Paradox of Late Ancient Christianity." In *Ascetic Piety and Women's Faith: Essays on Late Ancient Christianity*, 175–208. Lewiston: Edwin Mellen, 1986.

———. "The Celibate Bridegroom and His Virginal Brides: Metaphor and the Marriage of Jesus in Early Christian Ascetic Exegesis." *Church History* 77 (2008): 1–25.

———. "Friendship between the Sexes: Classical Theory and Christian Practice." In *Jerome, Chrysostom, and Friends: Essays and Translations*, 35–106. New York: Edwin Mellen Press, 1982.

———. "John Chrysostom and the *Subintroductae*." *Church History* 46 (1977): 171–85.

———. *The Origenist Controversy: The Cultural Construction of an Early Christian Debate.* Princeton, N.J.: Princeton University Press, 1992.

Clark, Stuart. "The 'Gendering' of Witchcraft in French Demonology: Misogyny or Polarity?" In *Gender and Witchcraft.* Vol. 4 of *New Perspectives on Witchcraft, Magic and Demonology.* Edited by Brian Levack, 54–65. New York: Routledge, 2001. Also in *French History* 5 (1991): 426–37.

———. "Inversion, Misrule, and the Meaning of Witchcraft." *Past and Present* 87 (1980): 98–127.

Cloke, Gillian. *"This Female Man of God": Women and Spiritual Power in the Patristic Age, AD 350–450.* London: Routledge, 1995.

Coakley, John. "Friars as Confidants of Holy Women in Medieval Dominican Hagiography." In *Images of Sainthood in the Later Middle Ages.* Edited by Renate Blumenfeld-Kosinski and Timea Szell, 222–46. Ithaca, N.Y.: Cornell University Press, 1991.

———. "A Marriage and Its Observer: Christine of Stommeln, the Heavenly Bridegroom, and Friar Peter of Dacia." In *Gendered Voices: Medieval Saints and Their Interpreters.* Edited by Catherine Mooney, 99–117. Philadelphia: University of Pennsylvania Press, 1999.

———. "Thomas of Cantimpré and Female Sanctity." In *History in the Comic Mode: Medieval Communities and the Matter of Person.* Edited by Rachel Fulton and Bruce Holsinger, 44–55. New York: Columbia University Press, 2007.

———. *Women, Men, and Spiritual Power: Female Saints and Their Male Collaborators.* New York: Columbia University Press, 2006.

Cohn, Norman. *Europe's Inner Demons: The Demonization of Christians in Medieval Christendom.* Rev. ed. Chicago: University of Chicago Press, 1993.

Colish, Marcia. "Ambrose of Milan on Chastity." In *Chastity: A Study in Perception, Ideals, and Opposition.* Edited by Nancy van Deusen, 37–60. Leiden: Brill, 2008.

Combes, André. *Essai sur la critique de Ruysbroeck par Gerson.* 2 vols. Paris: Librairie Philosophique J. Vrin, 1945–48.

Constable, Giles. "Ælred of Rievaulx and the Nun of Watton: An Episode in the Early History of the Gilbertine Order." In *Medieval Women.* Edited by Derek Baker. Studies in Church History, Subsidia 1, 205–26. Oxford: Basil Blackwell, 1978.

———. "The Authorship of the *Epistolae duorum amantium: A Reconsideration*." In *Voices in Dialogue: Reading Women in the Middle Ages.* Edited by Linda Olson and Kathryn Kerby-Fulton, 167–78. Notre Dame: University of Notre Dame Press, 2005.

———. "The Ceremonies and Symbolism Entering Religious Life and Taking the Monastic Habit, From the Fourth to the Twelfth Century." In *Il Matrimonio nella società altomedievale.* Settimane di studio del Centro Italiano di studi sull'alto medioevo, 24, 2:771–834. Spoleto: Presso la sede del Centro, 1977.

Corbet, Patrick. *Les Saints Ottoniens: Sainteté dynastique, sainteté royale et sainteté feminine autour de l'an Mil.* Sigmaringen: Thorbecke, 1986.

Coudanne, Louise. "Baudonivie, moniale de Sainte-Croix et la biographie de sainte Radegonde." In *Etudes Mérovingiennes: Actes des journées de Poitiers, 1–3 mai 1952*, 45–51. Paris: Picard, 1953.

Craveri, Marcello. *Sante e streghe: Biografie e documenti dal XIV al XVII secolo*. Milan: Feltrinelli economica, 1980.

Crouzel, Henri. *Virginité et mariage selon Origène*. Paris: Desclée de Brouwer, 1962.

Dalarun, Jacques. *L'Impossible sainteté: La vie retrouvée de Robert d'Arbrissel*. Paris: Editions du Cerf, 1985.

———. "Robert d'Arbrissel et les femmes." *Annales, ESC* 39 (1984): 1146–51.

———. *Robert of Arbrissel: Sex, Sin, and Salvation in the Middle Ages*. Translated by Bruce Venarde. Washington, D.C.: Catholic University of America Press, 2006.

D'Avray, David. *Medieval Marriage: Symbolism and Society*. Oxford: Oxford University Press, 2005.

Delaruelle, Etienne. "Sainte Radegonde et la Chrétienité de son temps." In *Etudes Mérovingiennes: Actes des journées de Poitiers, 1–3 mai 1952*, 65–74. Paris: Picard, 1953.

Delpech, François. "La 'marque' des sorcières: Logique(s) de la stigmatization diabolique." In *Le Sabbat des sorciers: XVe–XVIIIe siècles*. Edited by Nicole Jacques-Chaquin and Maxime Préaud, 347–68. Grenoble: Jérôme Millon, 1993.

Dewez, Léon, and Albert van Iterson. "La lactation de saint Bernard: Legende et iconographie." *Cîteaux in de Nederlanden* 7 (1956): 165–89.

Dinzelbacher, Peter. *Heilige oder Hexen? Schicksale auffälliger Frauen in Mittelalter und Frühneuzeit*. Zurich: Artemis and Winkler, 1995.

D'Izarny, Raymond. "Mariage et consécration virginale au IVe siècle." In *La Vie spirituelle*, supplement 25 (1953): 92–118.

Donahue, Charles. "The Policy of Alexander III's Consent Theory of Marriage." In *Proceedings of the Fourth International Congress of Canon Law*. Edited by Stephan Kuttner. Monumenta Iuris Canonici, Ser. C, Subsidia 5, 251–81. Vatican City: Biblioteca Apostolica Vaticana, 1976.

Dooley, William. *Marriage according to St. Ambrose*. Washington, D.C.: Catholic University Press, 1948.

Dresen-Coenders, Lène. "Witches as Devils' Concubines: On the Origin of Fear of Witches and Protection against Witchcraft." In *Gender and Witchcraft*. Vol. 4 of *New Perspectives on Witchcraft, Magic and Demonology*. Edited by Brian Levack, 413–36. New York: Routledge, 2001.

Dronke, Peter. *Women Writers of the Middle Ages: A Critical Study of Texts from Perpetua (d. 203) to Marguerite Porete (d. 1310)*. Cambridge: Cambridge University Press, 1984.

Duby, Georges. *The Knight, the Lady, and the Priest: The Making of Modern Marriage in Medieval France*. Translated by Barbara Bray. Chicago: University of Chicago Press, 1983.

East, W. G. "Abelard, Heloise and the Religious Life." In *Medieval Theology and the Natural Body*. Edited by Peter Biller and Alastair Minnis, 43–60. Woodbridge, Suffolk: Boydell and Brewer, 1997.

Elkins, Sharon. *Holy Women of Twelfth-Century England*. Chapel Hill: University of North Carolina Press, 1988.

Elliott, Dyan. "Alternative Intimacies: Men, Women, and Spiritual Direction in the Twelfth Century." In *Christina of Markyate: A Twelfth-Century Holy Woman*. Edited by Samuel Fanous and Henrietta Leyser, 160–83. London: Routledge, 2004.

———. "Authorizing a Life: The Collaboration of Dorothea of Montau and John Marienwerder." In *Gendered Voices: Medieval Saints and Their Interpreters*. Edited by Catherine Mooney, 168–91. Philadelphia: University of Pennsylvania Press, 1999.

———. "Bernardino of Siena versus the Marriage Debt." In *Desire and Discipline: Sex and Sexuality in Premodern Europe*. Edited by Jacqueline Murray and Konrad Eisenbichler, 168–200. Toronto: University of Toronto Press, 1996.

———. *Fallen Bodies: Pollution, Sexuality, and Demonology in the Middle Ages*. Philadelphia: University of Pennsylvania Press, 1999.

———. "Flesh and Spirit: Women and the Body." *MHW*, 13–46.

———. "The Physiology of Rapture and Female Spirituality." In *Medieval Theology and the Natural Body*. Edited by Peter Biller and Alastair Minnis, 141–73. Woodbridge, Suffolk: York Medieval Press in association with Boydell and Brewer, 1997.

———. *Proving Woman: Female Spirituality and Inquisitional Culture*. Princeton, N.J.: Princeton University Press, 2004.

———. "Seeing Double: John Gerson, the Discernment of Spirits, and Joan of Arc." *American Historical Review* 107, no. 1 (2002): 26–54.

———. *Spiritual Marriage: Sexual Abstinence in Medieval Wedlock*. Princeton, N.J.: Princeton University Press, 1993.

———. "True Presence/False Christ: Antinomies of Embodiment in Late Medieval Spirituality." *Mediaeval Studies* 64 (2002): 241–65.

———. "Women and Confession: From Empowerment to Pathology." In *Gendering the Master Narrative: Women and Power in the Middle Ages*. Edited by Maryanne Kowaleski and Mary Erler, 31–51. Ithaca, N.Y.: Cornell University Press, 2003.

———. "Women in Love: Carnal and Spiritual Transgressions in Late Medieval France." In *Living Dangerously: On the Margins in Medieval and Early Modern Europe*. Edited by Barbara Hanawalt and Anna Grotans, 55–86. Notre Dame, Ind.: University of Notre Dame Press, 2007.

Elm, Susanna. *Virgins of God: The Making of Asceticism in Late Antiquity*. Oxford: Oxford University Press, 1994.

Esmein, Adhémar. *Le Mariage en droit canonique*. Paris, 1891. Reprint, New York: Burt Franklin, 1968.

Famiglietti, R. C. *Tales from the Marriage Bed from Medieval France (1300–1500)*. Providence, R. I.: Picardy Press, 1992.

Fanous, Samuel. "Christina of Markyate and the Double Crown." In *Christina of Markyate*. Edited by Samuel Fanous and Henrietta Leyser, 53–78. London: Routledge, 2005.

Fanous, Samuel, and Henrietta Leyser, eds. *Christina of Markyate: A Twelfth-Century Holy Woman*. London: Routledge, 2005.

Farmer, Sharon. "Persuasive Voices: Clerical Images of Medieval Wives." *Speculum* 61 (1986): 517–43.

Fedele, Pio. "Vedovanza e seconde nozze." In *Il Matrimonio nella società altomedievale*. 2

vols. Settimane di studio del Centro Italiano di studi sull'alto medioevo, 24, 2:819–44. Spoleto: Presso la sede del Centro, 1977.

Fisher, Jeffrey. "Gerson's Mystical Theology." In *A Companion to Jean Gerson*. Edited by Brian McGuire, 205–48. Leiden: Brill, 2006.

Fitzgerald, Kyriaki Karidoyanes. *Women Deacons in the Orthodox Church: Called to Holiness and Ministry*. 1998. Revised, Brookline, Mass.: Holy Cross Orthodox Press, 1999.

Flandrin, Jean-Louis. *Un Temps pour embrasser: Aux origines de la morale sexuelle occidentale (Ve–XIe siècle)*. Paris: Editions du Seuil, 1983.

Folz, Robert. *Les Saintes reines du Moyen Age en Occident (VIe–XIIIe siècles)*. Brussels: Société des Bollandistes, 1992.

Foucault, Michel. *The Care of the Self*. Vol. 3 of *The History of Sexuality*. Translated by Robert Hurley. New York: Vintage, 1988.

———. *History of Sexuality*. Vol. 1, *An Introduction*. Translated by Robert Hurley. New York: Vintage, 1990.

Freud, Sigmund. *Instincts and Their Vicissitudes*. SE, 14:111–40.

———. *The Interpretation of Dreams*. SE. Vols. 4–5.

———. *Jokes and Their Relation to the Unconscious*. SE. Vol. 8.

———. *An Outline of Psychoanalysis*. SE, 23:141–296.

Frugoni, Chiara. " 'Domine, in conspectu tuo omne desiderium meum': Visioni e immagini in Chiara da Montefalco." In *S. Chiara da Montefalco e il suo tempo*. Edited by Claudio Leonardi and Enrico Menestò, 154–74. Perugia: La Nuova Italia, 1985.

Fulton, Rachel. *From Judgement to Passion: Devotion to Christ and the Virgin Mary, 800–1200*. New York: Columbia University Press, 2002.

Gäbe, Sabina. "Radegundis: Sancta, Regina, Ancilla. Zum Heiligkeitsideal der Radegundisviten von Fortunat und Baudonivia." *Francia* 16 (1989): 1–30.

Galloway, Penny. "Neither Miraculous nor Astonishing: The Devotional Practice of Beguine Communities in French Flanders." In *New Trends in Feminine Spirituality: The Holy Women of Liège and Their Impact*. Edited by Juliette Dor, Lesley Johnson, and Jocelyn Wogan-Browne, 107–27. Turnhout: Brepols, 1999.

Gaudemet, Jean. "Le legs du droit romain en matière matrimoniale." In *Il Matrimonio nella società altomedievale*. Settimane di studio del Centro italiano di studi sull'alto medioevo, 24, 1:139–89. Spoleto: Presso la sede del Centro, 1977.

———. "Le mariage en droit romain: *Justum matrimonium*." In *Sociétés et mariage*, 46–103. Strasbourg: Cerdic-Publications, 1980.

———. "Note sur le symbolisme médiévale: Le marriage de l'evêque." *L'Année canonique* 22 (1978): 71–80.

———. "Originalité et destin du mariage romain." In *Sociétés et mariage*, 140–84. Strasbourg: Cerdic-Publications, 1980.

George, Judith. *Venantius Fortunatus: A Latin Poet in Merovingian Gaul*. Oxford: Clarendon, 1992.

Georgianna, Linda. " 'In Any Corner of Heaven': Heloise's Critique of Monastic Life." In *Listening to Heloise: The Voice of a Twelfth-Century Woman*. Edited by Bonnie Wheeler, 187–216. New York: St. Martin's Press, 2000.

Ginzburg, Carlo. *Ecstasies: Interpreting the Witches' Sabbath*. Translated by Raymond Rosenthal. New York: Pantheon Books, 1991.

Glorieux, Palémon. "Saint Joseph dans l'oeuvre de Gerson." *Cahiers de joséphologie* 19 (1971): 414–28.

Godding, R. "Vie apostolique et société urbaine à l'aube du XIIIe siècle: Une oeuvre inedi-tée de Thomas de Cantimpré." *Nouvelle Revue Théologie* 104 (1982): 692–721.

Gold, Penny. "The Marriage of Mary and Joseph in the Twelfth-Century Ideology of Mar-riage." In *Sexual Practices and the Medieval Church*. Edited by Vern Bullough and James Brundage, 102–17. New York: Pantheon, 1982.

Golding, Brian. *Gilbert of Sempringham and the Gilbertine Order, c. 1130–c. 1300*. Oxford: Clarendon, 1995.

Goodman, Anthony. "Margery Kempe." *MHW*, 217–38.

Green, Monica. *Making Women's Medicine Masculine: The Rise of Male Authority in Pre-Modern Gynaecology*. Oxford: Oxford University Press, 2008.

Grégoire, Réginald. "Il matrimonio mistico." In *Il Matrimonio nella società altomedievale*. Settimane di studio del Centro Italiano di studi sull'alto medioevo, 24, 2:721–30. Spo-leto: Presso la sede del Centro, 1977.

Griffiths, Fiona. "Brides and *Dominae*: Abelard's *Cura monialium* at the Augustinian Mon-astery of Marbuch." *Viator* 34 (2003): 57–88.

———. "The Cross and the *Cura monialum*: Robert of Arbrissel, John the Evangelist, and the Pastoral Care of Women in the Age of Reform." *Speculum* 83 (2008): 303–30.

———. "'Men's Duty to Provide for Women's Needs': Abelard, Heloise, and Their Negotia-tion of the *Cura monialium*." *Journal of Medieval History* 30 (2004): 1–24.

Grundmann, Herbert. *Religious Movements in the Middle Ages*. Translated by Steven Rowan. Notre Dame, Ind.: University of Notre Dame Press, 1995.

Guarnieri, Romana. "La 'Vita' di Chiara da Montefalco e la pieta Brabantina del '200. Prime indagini su un'ipotesi di lavoro." In *S. Chiara da Montefalco e il suo tempo*. Ed-ited by Claudio Leonardi and Enrico Menestò, 305–67. Perugia: La Nuova Italia, 1985.

Guenée, Bernard. *La Folie de Charles VI: Roi Bien Aimé*. Paris: Perrin, 2004.

Haliczer, Stephen. *Sexuality in the Confessional: A Sacrament Profaned*. New York: Oxford University Press, 1996.

Hamburger, Jeffrey. *Nuns as Artists: The Visual Culture of a Medieval Convent*. Berkeley: University of California Press, 1997.

———. *The Visual and the Visionary: Art and Female Spirituality in Late Medieval Germany*. New York: Zone, 1998.

Haskins, Charles Homer. "Robert le Bougre and the Beginnings of the Inquisition in Northern France." In *Studies in Mediaeval Culture*, 193–244. Oxford: Clarendon Press, 1929.

Head, Thomas. "The Marriages of Christina of Markyate." *Viator* 21 (1990): 71–95. Revised in *Christina of Markyate*. Edited by Samuel Fanous and Henrietta Leyser, 116–37. London: Routledge, 2005.

Heene, Katrien. "Gender and Mobility in the Low Countries: Travelling Women in Thirteenth-Century Exempla and Saints' Lives." In *The Texture of Society: Medieval*

Women in the Southern Low Countries. Edited by Ellen Kittell and Mary Suydam, 31–49. New York: Palgrave, 2004.

———. "Hagiography and Gender: A Tentative Case-Study on Thomas of Cantimpré." In *"Scribere sanctorum gesta": Recueil d'études d'hagiographie médiévale offert à Guy Philippart.* Edited by Etienne Renard, Michel Trigalet, Xavier Hermand, and Paul Bertrand, 109–23. Turnhout: Brepols, 2005.

Heffernan, Thomas. *Sacred Biography: Saints and Their Biographers in the Middle Ages.* Oxford: Oxford University Press, 1988.

Helvétius, Anne-Marie. "*Virgo* et *Virago:* Réflexions sur le pouvoir du voile consacré d'après les sources hagiographiques de la Gaule du Nord." In *Femmes et pouvoirs des femmes à Byzance et en Occident (VIe–XIe siècles).* Edited by Stéphane Lebecq, A. Dierkens, R. Le Jan, and J. M. Sansterre, 189–204. Lille: Centre de Recherche sur l'histoire de l'Europe du Nord-Ouest, 1999.

Henningsen, Gustav. "'The Ladies from Outside': An Archaic Pattern of the Witches' Sabbath." In *Early Modern European Witchcraft: Centres and Peripheries.* Edited by Bengt Ankarloo and Gustav Henningsen, 191–215. Oxford: Clarendon, 1990.

Herzig, Tamar. "The Demons' Reaction to Sodomy: Witchcraft and Homosexuality in Gianfrancesco Pico della Mirandola's *Strix.*" *Sixteenth Century Journal* 34, no. 1 (2003): 53–72.

———. "Witches, Saints, and Heretics: Heinrich Kramer's Ties with Italian Women Mystics." *Magic, Ritual, and Witchcraft* 1 (2006): 24–55.

Hobbins, Daniel. *Authorship and Publicity before Print: Jean Gerson and the Transformation of Late Medieval Learning.* Philadelphia: University of Pennsylvania Press, 2009.

———. "Gerson on Lay Devotion." In *A Companion to Jean Gerson.* Edited by Brian McGuire, 41–78. Leiden: Brill, 2006.

———. "Jean Gerson's Authentic Tract on Joan of Arc: *Super facto puellae et credulitate sibi praestanda* (13 May 1429)." *Mediaeval Studies* 67 (2005): 99–155.

Hoch-Smith, Judith, and Anita Spring, eds. *Women in Ritual and Symbolic Roles.* New York: Plenum Press, 1978.

Holdsworth, Christopher. "Christina of Markyate." In *Medieval Women.* Edited by Derek Baker, Studies in Church History, Subsidia, 1, 185–204. Oxford: Basil Blackwell, 1978.

Hollis, Stephanie. "Wilton as a Centre of Learning." In *Writing the Wilton Women: Goscelin's Legend of Edith and Liber confortatorius.* Edited by Stephanie Hollis, 307–38. Turnhout: Brepols, 2004.

Holsinger, Bruce. *Music, Body, and Desire in Medieval Culture: Hildegard of Bingen to Chaucer.* Stanford, Calif.: Stanford University Press, 2001.

Hollywood, Amy. "Inside Out: Beatrice of Nazareth and Her Hagiographer." In *Gendered Voices: Medieval Saints and their Interpreters.* Edited by Catherine Mooney, 78–98. Philadelphia: University of Pennsylvania Press, 1999.

———. *The Soul as Virgin Wife: Mechtild of Magdeburg, Marguerite Porete, and Meister Eckhart.* Notre Dame, Ind.: University of Notre Dame Press, 1995.

Hollywood, Amy, and Patricia Beckman. "Mechtild of Magdeburg." *MHW,* 411–25.

Hubnik, Sandi. "(Re)Constructing the Medieval Recluse: Performative Acts of Virginity and the Writings of Julian of Norwich." *Historian* 67 (2005): 43–61.

Huizinga, Johan. *The Autumn of the Middle Ages.* Translated by Rodney Payton and Ulrich Mammitzsch. Chicago: University of Chicago Press, 1996.

Hunt, Tony. "The Life of St. Alexis, 475–1125." In *Christina of Markyate.* Edited by Samuel Fanous and Henrietta Leyser, 217–28. London: Routledge, 2005.

Hunter, David. *Marriage, Celibacy, and Heresy in Ancient Christianity: The Jovinianist Controversy.* Oxford: Oxford University Press, 2007.

Hyams, Paul. "Homage and Feudalism: A Judicious Separation." In *Die Gegenwart des Feudalismus: Présence du féodalisme et present de la féodalité; The Presence of Feudalism.* Edited by Natalie Fryde, Pierre Monnet, and Otto G. Oexle, 13–49. Göttingen: Vandenhoeck and Ruprecht, 2002.

Jacquart, Danielle and Claude Thomasset. *Sexuality and Medicine in the Middle Ages.* Translated by Matthew Adamson. Princeton, N.J.: Princeton University Press, 1988.

Jaeger, C. Stephen. *Ennobling Love: In Search of a Lost Sensibility.* Philadelphia: University of Pennsylvania Press, 1999.

———. "*Epistolae duorum amantium* and the Ascription to Abelard and Heloise." In *Voices in Dialogue: Reading Women in the Middle Ages.* Edited by Linda Olson and Kathryn Kerby-Fulton, 125–66. Notre Dame: University of Notre Dame Press, 2005.

———. "A Reply to Giles Constable." In *Voices in Dialogue: Reading Women in the Middle Ages.* Edited by Linda Olson and Kathryn Kerby-Fulton, 179–86. Notre Dame: University of Notre Dame Press, 2005.

Jansen, Katherine. *The Making of Magdalen: Preaching and Popular Devotion in the Later Middle Ages.* Princeton, N.J.: Princeton University Press, 2000.

Jantzen, Grace. *Power, Gender, and Christian Mysticism.* Cambridge: Cambridge University Press, 1995.

Jordan, Mark. *The Invention of Sodomy in Christian Theology.* Chicago: University of Chicago Press, 1997.

Jung, Jacqueline. "Crystalline Wombs and Pregnant Hearts: The Exuberant Bodies of the Katharinenthal Visitation Group." In *History in the Comic Mode.* Edited by Rachel Fulton and Bruce Holsinger, 223–37. New York: Columbia University Press, 2007.

Karras, Ruth Mazo. *Common Women: Prostitution and Sexuality in Medieval England.* New York: Oxford University Press, 1996.

———. "Friendship and Love in the Lives of Two Twelfth-Century English Saints." *Journal of Medieval History* 14 (1988): 305–20.

———. *From Boys to Men: Formations of Masculinity in Late Medieval Europe.* Philadelphia: University of Pennsylvania, 2003.

———. "The History of Marriage and the Myth of Friedelehe." *Early Medieval Europe* 14 (2006): 119–51.

———. "Holy Harlots: Prostitute Saints in Medieval Legend." *Journal of the History of Sexuality* 1 (1990): 3–32.

Kelly, Kathleen. *Performing Virginity and Testing Chastity in the Middle Ages.* London: Routledge, 2000.

Kieckhefer, Richard. "Erotic Magic in Medieval Europe." In *Sex in the Middle Ages: A Book of Essays.* Edited by Joyce Salisbury, 30–55. New York: Garland, 1991.

————. *European Witch Trials: Their Foundations in Popular and Learned Cultures, 1300–1500.* London: Routledge and Kegan Paul, 1976.

————. "The Holy and the Unholy: Sainthood, Witchcraft, and Magic in Late Medieval Europe." *Journal of Medieval and Renaissance Studies* 24 (1994): 335–85.

————. "Mythologies of Witchcraft in the Fifteenth Century." *Magic, Ritual, and Witchcraft* 1 (2006): 79–108.

————. *Unquiet Souls: Fourteenth-Century Saints and Their Religious Milieu.* Chicago: University of Chicago, 1984.

King, Margot. "Introduction." In Thomas of Cantimpré. *Life of Margaret of Ypres.* Translated by Margot King, 9–13. Toronto: Peregrina, 1990.,

————. "The Sacramental Witness of Christina Mirabilis: The Mystic Growth of a Fool for Christ's Sake." In *Peaceweavers.* Vol. 2 of *Medieval Religious Women.* Edited by Lillian Shank and John Nichols, 145–64. Kalamazoo, Mich.: Cistercian Publications, 1987.

Kitchen, John. *Saints' Lives and the Rhetoric of Gender: Male and Female in Merovingian Hagiography.* New York: Oxford University Press, 1998.

Klaniczay, Gábor. *Holy Rulers and Blessed Princesses: Dynastic Cults in Central Europe.* Cambridge: Cambridge University Press, 2002.

————. "Miraculum and Maleficium: Reflections Concerning Late Medieval Female Sanctity." In *Problems in the Historical Anthropology of Early Modern Europe.* Edited by R. Po-Chia Hsia and R. W. Scribner. Wolfenbütteler Forschungen, vol. 78, 49–73. Harrasowitz, Wiesenbaden: Wolfenbüttel, 1997.

————. "The Process of Trance, Heavenly and Diabolic Apparitions, in Johannes Nider's *Formicarius.*" Collegium Budapest, Institute for Advanced Study Discussion Paper Series 65 (June 2003): 1–81.

————. "Le sabbat raconté par les témoins des proces de sorcellerie en Hongrie." In *Le Sabbat des sorciers: XVe–XVIIIe siècles.* Edited by Nicole Jacques-Chaquin and Maxime Préaud, 227–46. Grenoble: Jérôme Millon, 1993.

Kleinberg, Aviad. *Flesh Made Word: Saints' Stories and the Western Imagination.* Cambridge, Mass.: Belknap Press of Harvard University Press, 2008.

————. *Prophets in Their Own Country: Living Saints and the Making of Sainthood in the Later Middle Ages.* Chicago: University of Chicago Press, 1991.

Koch, Barbara. "Margaret Ebner." *MHW*, 393–410.

Kraemer, Ross. "The Conversion of Women to Ascetic Forms of Christianity." *Signs* 6 (1980): 298–307.

Krahmer, Shawn. "The Virile Bride of Bernard of Clairvaux." *Church History* 69 (2000): 304–27.

Kuefler, Matthew. *The Manly Eunuch: Masculinity, Gender Ambiguity, and Christian Ideology in Late Antiquity.* Chicago: University of Chicago Press, 2001.

Lambert, Malcolm. *The Cathars.* Oxford: Basil Blackwell, 1998.

Latham, R. E. *Revised Medieval Latin Word-List from British and Irish Sources.* London: Oxford University Press for the British Academy, 1965.

Latzke, Therese. "Robert von Arbrissel, Ermengard und Eva." *Mittellateinisches Jahrbuch* 19 (1984): 115–54.

Lea, Henry Charles. *History of the Inquisition of the Middle Ages*. 3 vols. New York: Macmillan, 1906.

———. *Materials toward a History of Witchcraft*. Arthur Howland. 3 vols. New York: Thomas Yoseloff, 1957.

Leclercq, Jean. *Monks and Love in Twelfth-Century France: Psycho-Historical Essays*. Oxford: Clarendon, 1979.

———. *Women and Saint Bernard of Clairvaux*. Kalamazoo, Mich.: Cistercian Publications, 1989.

Lefevre, Jean-Baptiste. "Sainte Lutgarde en son temps (1182–1246)." *Collectanea Cisterciensa* 58 (1996): 277–335.

Lefkowitz, Mary. "Seduction and Rape in Greek Myth." In *Consent and Coercion to Sex and Marriage in Ancient and Medieval Societies*. Edited by Angeliki Laiou, 17–38. Washington, D.C.: Dumbarton Oaks, 1993.

Le Goff, Jacques. "The Symbolic Ritual of Vassalage." In *Time, Work, and Culture in the Middle Ages*. Translated by Arthur Goldhammer, 239–48. Chicago: University of Chicago Press, 1980.

Lerner, Robert. *The Heresy of the New Spirit in the Later Middle Ages*. Notre Dame, Ind.: University of Notre Dame Press, 1972.

———. "The Image of Mixed Liquid in Late Medieval Mystical Thought." *Church History* 40 (1971): 397–411.

———. "New Light on *The Mirror of Simple Souls*." *Speculum* 85 (2010): 91–116.

———. *The Powers of Prophecy: The Cedar of Lebanon Vision from the Mongol Onslaught to the Dawn of the Enlightenment*. Berkeley: University of California Press, 1983.

Lewis, C. S. *The Allegory of Love: A Study in Medieval Tradition*. Oxford: Oxford University Press, 1985.

Leyser, Conrad. "Masculinity in Flux: Nocturnal Emission and the Limits of Celibacy in the Early Middle Ages." In *Masculinity in Medieval Europe*. Edited by D. Hadley. London: Longmans, 1998.

Leyser, Henrietta. *Hermits and the New Monasticism: A Study of Religious Communities in Western Europe, 1000–1500*. New York: St. Martin's Press, 1984.

Lifshitz, Felice. "Gender Trouble in Paradise: The Case of the Liturgical Virgin." In *Images of Medieval Sanctity: Essays in Honour of Gary Dickson*. Edited by Debra Strickland, 25–39. Leiden: Brill, 2007.

———. "Priestly Women, Virginal Men: Litanies and Their Discontents." In *Gender and Christianity in Medieval Europe*. Edited by Lisa Bitel and Felice Lifshitz, 87–102. Philadelphia: University of Pennsylvania Press, 2008.

Little, Lester. "The Personal Development of Peter Damian." In *Order and Innovation in the Middle Ages: Essays in Honor of Joseph R. Strayer*. Edited by William Jordan, Bruce McNab, and Teofilo Ruiz, 317–41. Princeton, N.J.: Princeton University Press, 1976.

Llewellyn-Jones, Lloyd. *Aphrodite's Tortoise: The Veiled Women of Ancient Greece*. Swansea, Wales: Classical Press of Wales, 2002.

Lochrie, Karma. *Margery Kempe and Translations of the Flesh*. Philadelphia: University of Pennsylvania, 1991.

Logan, F. Donald. *Runaway Religious in Medieval England, c. 1240–1540*. Cambridge: Cambridge University Press, 1996.

Luecke, Janemarie. "The Unique Experience of Anglo-Saxon Nuns." In *Peaceweavers*. Vol. 2 of *Medieval Religious Women*. Edited by Lillian Shank and John Nichols, 55–66. Kalamazoo, Mich.: Cistercian Publications, 1987.

Luongo, F. Thomas. *The Saintly Politics of Catherine of Siena*. Ithaca, N.Y.: Cornell, 2006.

Macy, Gary. *The Hidden History of Female Ordination: Female Clergy in the Medieval West*. Oxford: Oxford University Press, 2008.

Maines, Rachel. *The Technology of the Orgasm: "Hysteria," the Vibrator, and Women's Sexual Satisfaction*. Baltimore, Md.: Johns Hopkins University Press, 1999.

Makowski, Elizabeth. *"A Pernicious Sort of Woman": Quasi-Religious Women and Canon Lawyers in the Later Middle Ages*. Washington, D.C.: Catholic University Press, 2005.

Mann, William. "Ethics." In *The Cambridge Companion to Abelard*. Edited by Jeffrey Brower and Kevin Guilfoy, 279–304. Cambridge: Cambridge University Press, 2004.

Mansfield, Mary. *The Humiliation of Sinners: Public Penance in Thirteenth-Century France*. Ithaca, N.Y.: Cornell University Press, 1995.

Marenbon, John. *The Philosophy of Peter Abelard*. Cambridge: Cambridge University Press, 1997.

Marié, Georges. "Sainte Radegonde et le milieu monastique contemporain." In *Etudes Mérovingiennes: Actes des journées de Poitiers, 1–3 mai 1952*, 219–25. Paris: Picard, 1953.

Marmion, Dom. *Sponsa Verbi: La Vierge consacrée au Christ*. Namur: Editions Maredsous, 1948.

Martin, Dale. *The Corinthian Body*. New Haven, Conn.: Yale University Press, 1996.

Martroye, F. "L'affaire Indicia: Une sentence de Saint Ambrose." In *Mélanges Paul Fournier*, 503–10. Paris: Recueil Sirey, 1929.

Matter, E. Ann. "Italian Holy Women: A Survey." *MHW*, 529–55.

———. *The Voice of My Beloved: The Song of Songs in Western Medieval Christianity*. Philadelphia: University of Pennsylvania Press, 1990.

McCracken, Peggy. "The Curse of Eve: Female Bodies and Christian Bodies in Heloise's Third Letter." In *Listening to Heloise: The Voice of a Twelfth-Century Woman*. Edited by Bonnie Wheeler, 217–32. New York: St. Martin's Press, 2000.

McDonnell, Ernest. *The Beguines and Beghards in Medieval Culture with Special Emphasis on the Belgian Scene*. New Brunswick, N.J.: Rutgers University Press, 1954.

McGinn, Bernard. *The Flowering of Mysticism: Men and Women in the New Mysticism, 1200–1350*. Vol. 3 of *The Presence of God: A History of Western Mysticism*. New York: Crossroad, 1998.

———. *Foundations of Mysticism: Origins to the Fifth Century*. Vol. 1 of *The Presence of God: A History of Western Christian Mysticism*. New York: Crossroad, 1997.

———. *The Growth of Mysticism*. Vol. 2 of *The Presence of God: A History of Western Christian Mysticism; Gregory the Great through the Twelfth Century*. New York: Crossroad, 1996.

McGinn, Sheila. "The Acts of Thecla." In *Searching the Scriptures: A Feminist Commentary*. Edited by Elisabeth Schüsler Fiorenza, 2:800–828. New York: Crossroad, 1994.

McGuire, Brian. *The Difficult Saint: Bernard of Clairvaux and His Tradition.* Kalamazoo, Mich.: Cistercian Publications, 1991.

———. *Friendship and Community: The Monastic Experience.* Kalamazoo, Mich.: Cistercian Publications, 1988.

———. "Gerson and Bernard: Languishing with Love." *Cîteaux* 46 (1995): 127–57.

———. "Jean Gerson and the End of Spiritual Friendship: Dilemmas of Conscience." In *Friendship in Medieval Europe.* Edited by Julian Halsedine, 230–50. Thrupp, UK: Sutton, 1999.

———. *Jean Gerson and the Last Medieval Reformation.* University Park: Pennsylvania State University Press, 2005.

———. "Late Medieval Care and the Control of Women: Jean Gerson and His Sisters." *Revue d'histoire ecclésiastique* 92 (1997): 5–36.

McLaughlin, Mary. "Peter Abelard and the Dignity of Women: Twelfth Century 'Feminism' in Theory and Practice." In *Pierre Abélard: Pierre le Vénérable; Les courants philosophiques, littéraires et artistiques en Occident au milieu du XIIe siècle, Abbaye de Cluny 2 au 9 juillet 1972*, 287–333. Paris: Editions du Centre national de la recherche scientifique, 1975.

McLaughlin, Megan. "The Bishop as Bridegroom: Marital Imagery and Clerical Celibacy in the Eleventh and Twelfth Centuries." In *Medieval Purity and Piety: Essays on Medieval Clerical Celibacy and Religious Reform.* Edited by Michael Frassetto, 210–37. New York: Garland, 1998.

McLynn, Neil. *Ambrose of Milan: Church and Court in a Christian Capital.* Berkeley: University of California Press, 1994.

McNamara, Jo Ann. "Chastity as a Third Gender in the History and Hagiography of Gregory of Tours." In *The World of Gregory of Tours.* Edited by Kathleen Mitchell and Ian Wood, 199–210. Leiden: Brill, 2002.

———. "The *Herrenfrage*: The Restructuring of the Gender System, 1050–1150." In *Medieval Masculinities: Regarding Men in the Middle Ages.* Edited by Clare Lees, 3–29. Minneapolis: University of Minnesota Press, 1994.

———. *A New Song: Celibate Women in the First Three Christian Centuries.* Binghamton, New York: Harrington Park Press, 1983.

———. "The Ordeal of Community: Hagiography and Discipline in Merovingian Convents." *Vox Benedictina* 3 (1986): 293–326.

———. *Sisters in Arms: Catholic Nuns through Two Millennia.* Cambridge, Mass.: Harvard University Press, 1996.

McNamara, Jo Ann, and Suzanne Wemple. "Marriage and Divorce in the Frankish Kingdom." In *Women in Medieval Society.* Edited by Susan Stuard, 95–124. Philadelphia: University of Pennsylvania Press, 1976.

McNamer, Sarah. *Affective Meditation and the Invention of Medieval Compassion.* Philadelphia: University of Pennsylvania Press, 2010.

Meeks, Wayne. "The Image of the Androgyne: Some Uses of a Symbol in Earliest Christianity." *History of Religions* 13 (1974): 165–208.

Mercier, Franck. *La Vauderie d'Arras: Une chasse sorcière à l'Automne du Moyen Ages*. Rennes: Presses Universitaires de Rennes, 2006.

Metz, René. *La Consécration des vierges dans l'église romaine*. Paris: Presses universitaires de France, 1954.

———. "L'ordo de la consécration des vierges dans le pontifical dit de Saint-Aubin d'Angers (IXe/Xe siècle)." In *Mélanges en l'honneur de Monseigneur Michel Andrieu*, 327–37. Strasbourg: Palais Universitaire, 1956.

Mews, Constant. *Abelard and Heloise*. Oxford: Oxford University Press, 2005.

———. "Heloise." *MHW*, 267–89.

———. *The Lost Love Letters of Abelard and Heloise: Perceptions of Dialogue in Twelfth-Century France*. Edited by Ewald Konsgen. Translated by Constant Mews and Neville Chiavaroli. New York: St. Martin's Press, 1999.

Miles, Laura Saetveit. "Looking in the Past for a Discourse of Motherhood: Birgitta of Sweden and Julia Kristeva." *Medievalist Feminist Forum* 47 (2012).

Miller, Tanya. "What's in a Name? Clerical Representations of Parisian Beguines (1200–1328)." *Journal of Medieval History* 33 (2007): 60–86.

Minnis, Alaistair. *Medieval Theory of Authorship*. 2nd ed. Philadelphia: University of Pennsylvania Press, 1988.

Molin, Jean-Baptiste and Protais Mutembe. *Le Rituel du marriage en France du XIIe au XVIe siècle*. Paris: Beauchesne, 1974.

Monson, Don. *Andreas Capellanus, Scholasticism, and the Courtly Tradition*. Washington, D.C.: Catholic University Press, 2005.

Monter, E. William. *Witchcraft in France and Switzerland: The Borderlands during the Reformation*. Ithaca, N.Y.: Cornell University Press, 1976.

Mooney, Catherine. "The Authorial Role of Brother A. in the Composition of Angela of Foligno's Revelations." In *Creative Women in Medieval and Early Modern Italy: A Religious and Artistic Renaissance*. Edited by E. Ann Matter and John Coakley, 34–63. Philadelphia: University of Pennsylvania Press, 1994.

———. "Authority and Inspiration in the *Vitae* and Sermons of Humility of Faenza." In *Medieval Monastic Preaching*. Edited by Carolyn Muessig, 123–44. Leiden: Brill, 1998.

Moore, Stephen. "The Song of Songs in the History of Sexuality." *Church History* 69 (2000): 328–49.

Moses, Diana. "Livy's Lucretia and the Validity of Coerced Consent in Roman Law." In *Consent and Coercion to Sex and Marriage in Ancient and Medieval Societies*. Edited by Angeliki Laiou, 39–81. Washington, D.C.: Dumbarton Oaks, 1993.

Muessig, Carolyn. "Heaven, Earth, and the Angels: Preaching Paradise in the Sermons of Jacques de Vitry." In *Envisaging Heaven in the Middle Ages*. Edited by Carolyn Muessig and Ad Putter, 57–72. London: Routledge, 2007.

———. "Prophecy and Song: Teaching and Preaching by Medieval Women." In *Women Preachers and Prophets through Two Millennia of Christianity*. Edited by Beverly Kienzle and Pamela Walker, 146–59. Berkeley: University of California Press, 1998.

Muir, Carolyn. "Bride or Bridegroom? Masculine Identity in Mystic Marriages." In *Holi-*

ness and Masculinity in the Middle Ages. Edited by P. H. Cullum and Katherine Lewis, 58–78. Cardiff: University of Wales, 2004.

Mulchahey, Michèle. *"First the Bow Is Bent in Study . . .": Dominican Education before 1350.* Toronto: Pontifical Institute of Mediaeval Studies, 1998.

Mulder-Bakker, Anneke. *Lives of the Anchoresses.* Translated by Myra Heerspink Scholz. Philadelphia: University of Pennsylvania Press, 2005.

Murk-Jansen, Saskia. "Hadewijch." *MHW,* 663–85.

Murray, Alexander. "Counseling in Medieval Confession." In *Handling Sin: Confession in the Middle Ages.* Edited by Peter Biller and Alastair Minnis, 63–77. York: York Medieval Press in association with Boydell and Brewer, 1998.

———. "Demons as Psychological Abstractions." In *Angels in Medieval Philosophical Inquiry: Their Function and Significance.* Edited by Isabel Iribarren and Martin Lenz, 171–84. Aldershot, England: Ashgate, 2008.

Murray, Jacqueline. "On the Origins of the Role of 'Wise Women' in Causes for Annulment on the Grounds of Male Impotence." *Journal of Medieval History* 16 (1990): 235–49.

Nelson, Janet. *Charles the Bald.* London: Longman, 1992.

Newman, Barbara. *From Virile Woman to WomanChrist: Studies in Medieval Religion and Literature.* Philadelphia: University of Pennsylvania Press, 1995.

———. *God and the Goddesses: Vision, Poetry, and Belief in the Middle Ages.* Philadelphia: University of Pennsylvania Press, 2003.

———. "Introduction." In *Thomas of Cantimpré: The Collected Saints' Lives.* Edited by Barbara Newman, 3–54. Turnhout: Brepols, 2008.

———. "Possessed by the Spirit: Devout Women, Demoniacs, and the Apostolic Life in the Thirteenth Century." *Speculum* 73 (1998): 733–70.

———. *Sister of Wisdom: St. Hildegard's Theology of the Feminine.* Berkeley: University of California, 1987.

———. "What Did It Mean to Say 'I Saw'? The Clash between Theory and Practice in Medieval Visionary Culture." *Speculum* 80 (2005): 1–43.

Newman, Charles. *The Virgin Mary in the Work of St. Ambrose.* Fribourg: University Press of Fribourg, 1962.

Newman, Martha. "Crucified by Virtues: Monks, Lay Brothers, and Women in Thirteenth-Century Cistercian Saints' Lives." In *Gender and Difference in the Middle Ages.* Edited by Sharon Farmer and Carol Braun Pasternack, 182–209. Minneapolis: University of Minnesota Press, 2003.

Njus, Jesse. "The Politics of Mysticism: Elisabeth of Spalbeek in Context." *Church History* 77 (2008): 285–318.

Noonan, John. "Marital Affection in the Canonists." *Studia Gratiana* 12 (1967): 481–509.

———. "Power to Choose." *Viator* 4 (1973): 419–34.

Osborn, Eric. *Tertullian: First Theologian of the West.* Cambridge: Cambridge University Press, 1997.

Osheim, Duane. "Conversion, *Conversi,* and the Christian Life in Late Medieval Tuscany." *Speculum* 58 (1983): 368–90.

Ostorero, Martine. "The Concept of the Witches' Sabbath in the Alpine Region (1430–1440): Text and Context." In *Witchcraft Mythologies and Persecutions*. Edited by Gábor Klaniczay and Éva Pócs, 15–34. Budapest: Central European Press, 2008.

Otten, Willemien. "Christ's Birth of a Virgin Who Became a Wife: Flesh and Speech in Tertullian's *De carne Christi*." *Vigiliae Christianae* 51 (1997): 247–60.

Pagels, Elaine. *The Gnostic Gospels*. New York: Random House, 1979.

———. *The Gnostic Paul: Gnostic Exegesis of the Pauline Letters*. Philadelphia: Fortress Press, 1975.

Park, Katharine. *The Secrets of Women: Gender, Generation, and the Origins of Human Dissection*. New York: Zone Books, 2006.

Partner, Nancy. "The Textual Unconscious: What Does Psychoanalysis Do for Historians?" A lecture in Northwestern University's Medieval Studies Colloquium, Evanston, Ill., October 16, 2008.

Patlagean, Evelyne. "L'histoire de la femme déguisé en moine et l'evolution de la sainteté feminine à Byzance." *Studi medievali*, 3rd ser., 17, no. 2 (1976): 597–623.

Payer, Pierre. *Sex and the New Literature of Confession, 1150–1300*. Toronto: Pontifical Institute, 2009.

Pedersen, Else Marie Wiberg. "The In-carnation of Beatrice of Nazareth's Theology." In *New Trends in Feminine Spirituality: The Holy Women of Liège and Their Impact*. Edited by Juliette Dor, Lesley Johnson, and Jocelyn Wogan-Browne, 61–30. Brussels: Brepols, 1999.

Pernoud, Regine. *Women in the Days of the Cathedrals*. Translated by Anne Côté-Harriss. San Francisco: Ignatius Press, 1998.

Plumpe, J. C. "Some Little-Known Early Witnesses to Mary's *virginitas in partu*." *Theological Studies* 9 (1948): 567–77.

Pócs, Éva. "Le sabbat et les mythologies indo-européennes." In *Le Sabbat des sorciers: XVe-XVIIIe siècles*. Edited by Nicole Jacques-Chaquin and Maxime Préaud, 23–32. Grenoble: Jérôme Millon, 1993.

Poulin, Joseph-Claude. *L'Idéal de sainteté dans l'Aquitaine Carolingienne d'après les sources hagiographiques, 750–950*. Quebec City: Les presses du l'Université Laval, 1975.

Preger, Wilhelm. *Geschichte der deutschen Mystik im Mittelalter*. Leipzig: Dörffling und Franke, 1874.

Quasten, Johannes. *Patrology*. 4 Vols. Westminster, Md.: Newman Press, 1950–86.

Rader, Rosemary. *Breaking Boundaries: Male/Female Friendship in Early Christian Communities*. New York: Paulist Press, 1983.

Rambaux, Claude. *Tertullien face aux morales des trois premiers siècles*. Paris: Société d'Edition "Les Belles Lettres," 1979.

Rampton, Martha. "Buchard of Worms and Female Magical Ritual." In *Medieval and Early Modern Ritual: Formalized Behavior in Europe, China and Japan*. Edited by Joëlle Rollo-Koster, 7–34. Leiden: Brill, 2002.

Reid, Charles. *Power over the Body, Equality in the Family: Rights and Domestic Relations in Medieval Canon Law*. Grand Rapids, Mich.: William B. Eerdman, 2004.

Reynolds, Philip Lyndon. *Marriage in the Western Church: The Christianization of Marriage during Patristic and Early Medieval Periods*. Boston: Brill, 2001.

Reynolds, Roger. "*Virgines subintroductae* in Celtic Christianity." *Harvard Theological Review* 61 (1968): 547–66.

Rider, Catherine. *Magic and Impotence in the Middle Ages*. Oxford: Oxford University Press, 2006.

Ridyard, Susan. *The Royal Saints of Anglo-Saxon England*. Cambridge: Cambridge University Press, 1988.

Ringrose, Kathryn. *The Perfect Servant: Eunuchs and the Social Construction of Gender in Byzantium*. Chicago: University of Chicago Press, 2005.

Roberts, Phyllis. "Stephen Langton's *Sermo de virginibus*." In *Women of the Medieval World*. Edited by Julius Kirshner and Suzanne Wemple, 103–18. Oxford: Basil Blackwell, 1985.

Roisin, Simone. "L'efflorescence cistercienne et le courant féminin de piété au XIIIe siècle." *Revue d'histoire ecclésiastique* 39 (1943): 342–78.

———. *L'hagiographie cistercienne dans la diocèse de Liège au XIIIe siècle*. Louvain: Bibliothèque de l'Université, 1947.

———. "La méthode hagiographique de Thomas de Cantimpré." In *Miscellanea Historica in Honorem Albert de Meyer*, 1:546–57. Louvain: Bibliothèque de l'Université, 1946.

Roper, Lyndal. *Witch Craze: Terror and Fantasy in Baroque Germany*. New Haven, Conn.: Yale University Press, 2004.

Rosenwein, Barbara. "Inaccessible Cloisters: Gregory of Tours and Episcopal Exemption." In *The World of Gregory of Tours*. Edited by Kathleen Mitchell and Ian Wood, 181–98. Leiden: Brill, 2002.

Rouche, Michel. "Des mariages des païen au mariage chrétien. Sacrè et sacrament." In *Segni e riti nella chiesa altomedievale occidentale*. Settimane di studio del Centro Italiano di studi sull'alto medioevo, 33, 2:835–73. Spoleto: Presso la sede del Centro, 1987.

———. "Fortunat et Baudonivie: Deux biographies pour une seule sainte." In *La Vie de Sainte Radegonde par Fortunat, Poitiers, Bibliothèque municipale, manuscript 250 (136)*. Edited by Jean Favier, 239–47. Poitiers: Seuit, 1995.

Rousselle, Aline. *Porneia: On Desire and the Body in Late Antiquity*. Translated by Felicia Pheasant. Oxford: Basil Blackwell, 1988.

Rubin, Miri. *Corpus Christi: The Eucharist in Late Medieval Culture*. Cambridge: Cambridge University Press, 1992.

———. *Mother of God: A History of the Virgin Mary*. New Haven, Conn.: Yale University Press, 2009.

Rudy, Gordon. *Mystical Language of Sensation in the Later Middle Ages*. New York: Routledge, 2002.

Ruether, Rosemary. "Misogynism and Virginal Feminism in the Fathers of the Church." In *Religion and Sexism: Images of Woman in the Jewish and Christian Traditions*. Edited by Rosemary Ruether, 150–83. New York: Simon and Schuster, 1974.

Russell, Jeffrey Burton. *Witchcraft in the Middle Ages*. Ithaca, N.Y.: Cornell University Press, 1972.

Salih, Sarah. "When Is a Bosom Not a Bosom? Problems with 'Erotic Mysticism.'" In *Medieval Virginities*. Edited by Anke Bernau, Ruth Evans, and Sarah Salih, 14–32. Toronto: University of Toronto Press, 2003.

Sahlin, Claire. *Birgitta of Sweden and the Voice of Prophecy.* Woodbridge, Suffolk: Boydell, 2001.

Sargant, Michael. "Marguerite Porete." *MHW*, 291–309.

Scarry, Elaine. *The Body in Pain: The Making and Unmaking of the World.* New York: Oxford University Press, 1985.

Schiewer, Regina. "Sermons for Nuns of the Dominican Observance Movement." In *Medieval Monastic Preaching.* Ed. Carolyn Muessig, 75–92. Leiden: Brill, 1998.

Schirrmacher, Thomas. *Paul in Conflict with the Veil.* Nürnberg: Verlag für Theologie und Religionswissenschaft, 2002.

Schulenburg, Jane. *Forgetful of Their Sex: Female Sanctity and Society, ca. 500–1100.* Chicago: University of Chicago Press, 1998.

Scott, Karen "Mystical Death, Bodily Death: Catherine of Siena and Raymond of Capua on the Mystic's Encounter with God." In *Gendered Voices: Medieval Saints and Their Interpreters.* Edited by Catherine Mooney, pp. 136–67. Philadelphia: University of Pennsylvania Press, 1999.

Searle, Eleanor. "Women and the Legitimization of Succession at the Norman Conquest." In *Proceedings of the Battle Conference on Anglo-Norman Studies*, III, 1980. Edited by R. Allen Brown, 159–70. Woodbridge: Boydell, 1981.

Sheehan, Michael. "The Formation and Stability of Marriage in Fourteenth-Century England: Evidence of an Ely Register." *Mediaeval Studies* 33 (1971): 228–63.

———. *Marriage, Family, and Law in Medieval Europe: Collected Studies.* Toronto: University of Toronto Press, 1996.

Simons, Walter. "The Beguines." *MHW*, 625–62.

———. *Cities of Ladies: Beguine Communities in the Medieval Low Countries, 1200–1565.* Philadelphia: University of Pennsylvania Press, 2001.

———. "Reading a Saint's Body: Rapture and Bodily Movement in the *vitae* of Thirteenth-Century Beguines." In *Framing Medieval Bodies.* Ed. Sarah Kay and Miri Rubin, 10–23. Manchester: Manchester University Press, 1994.

Singer, Gordon Andreas. *La Vauderie d'Arras, 1459–1491: An Episode of Witchcraft in Later Medieval France.* Ph.D. diss., University of Maryland, 1974.

Southern, R. W. *Saint Anselm: A Portrait in a Landscape.* Cambridge: Cambridge University Press, 1990.

Spiegel, Gabrielle. "Maternity and Monstrosity: Reproductive Biology in the *Roman de Mélusine.*" In *Melusine of Lusignan: Founding Fiction in Late Medieval Literature.* Edited by Donald Maddox and Sara Sturm-Maddox, 100–124. Athens: University of Georgia Press, 1996.

Stargardt, Ute. "Dorothy of Montau." *MHW*, 475–96.

———. "The Political and Social Backgrounds of the Canonization of Dorothea von Montau." *Mystics Quarterly* 11 (1985): 107–222.

Stefaniw, Blossom. "Spiritual Friendship and Bridal Mysticism in an Age of Affectivity." *Cistercian Studies Quarterly* 41, no. 1 (2006): 65–78.

Stephens, Walter. *Demon Lovers: Witchcraft, Sex, and the Crisis of Belief.* Chicago: University of Chicago Press, 2002.

Suydam, Mary. "Bringing Heaven Down to Earth: Beguine Constructions of Heaven." In *Envisaging Heaven in the Middle Ages*. Edited by Carolyn Muessig and Ad Putter, 91–107. London: Routledge, 2007.

Tabbernee, William. "Perpetua, Montanism, and Christian Ministry in Carthage." *Perspectives in Religious Studies* 32 (2005): 421–41.

———. *Prophets and Gravestones: An Imaginative History of Montanists and Other Early Christians*. Peabody, Mass.: Hendrickson, 2009.

Tavani, Hugette. "Le mariage dans l'hérésie de l'an mil." *Annales, ESC* 32 (1977): 1074–84.

Thompson, Sally. "The Problem of Cistercian Nuns in the Twelfth and Early Thirteenth Centuries." In *Medieval Women*. Edited by Derek Baker, 227–52. Oxford: Basil Blackwell, 1978.

Thorndike, Lynn. *History of Magic and Experimental Science*. 8 vols. New York: Columbia University, 1929–58.

Tilly, Maureen. "The Passion of Perpetua and Felicity." In *Searching the Scriptures*. Edited by Elisabeth Schüssler Fiorenza, 2:829–58. New York: Crossroad, 1995.

Toubert, Pierre. "La théorie du mariage chez moralistes carolingiens." In *Il Matrimonio nella società altomedievale*. Settimane di studio del Centro Italiano di studi sull'alto medioevo, 24, 1:233–82. Spoleto: Presso la sede del Centro, 1977.

Tschacher, Werner. *Der Formicarius des Johannes Nider von 1437/38: Studien zu den Anfängen der Europäischen Hexenverfolgungen im Spätmittelalter*. Aachen: Shaker, 2000.

Turner, Denys. "Denys the Carthusian—*Sermones ad Saeculares*." In *Medieval Monastic Preaching*. Ed. Carolyn Muessig, 19–35. Leiden: Brill, 1998.

———. *Eros and Allegory: Medieval Exegesis of the Song of Songs*. Kalamazoo, Mich.: Cistercian Publications, 1995.

Van Balbherghe, Emile, and Jean-François Gilmont. "Les théologiens et la 'Vauderie' au XVe siècle: A propos des oeuvres de Jean Tinctor à la Bibliothèque de l'Abbaye de Parc." In *Miscellanea Codicologica F. Masai dedicata MXMLXXIX*. Edited by Pierre Cockshaw, Monique-Cecile Garand, and Pierre Jodogne, 2:393–411. Gand: E. Story-Scientia S.P.R.L., 1979.

Van Dam, Raymond. *Saints and Their Miracles in Late Antique Gaul*. Princeton, N.J.: Princeton University Press, 1993.

Van Eijk, Ton H. C. "Marriage and Virginity, Death and Immorality." In *Epektasis: Mélanges patristiques offerts au Cardinal Jean Daniélou*. Edited by Jacques Fontaine and Charles Kannengiesser, 209–35. Paris: Beauchesne, 1972.

Van Engen, John. *Sisters and Brothers of the Common Life: The Devotio Moderna and the World of the Later Middle Ages*. Philadelphia: University of Pennsylvania Press, 2008.

Vauchez, André. *Sainthood in the Later Middle Ages*. Translated by Jean Birrell. Cambridge: Cambridge University Press, 1997.

———. "Les stigmates de Saint François et leurs detracteurs." *Mélanges de l'Ecole Francaise de Rome: Temps modernes* 80 (1968): 595–625.

Veenstra, Jan. "*Les fons d'aulcuns secrets de la théologie*: Jean Tinctor's *Contre la Vauderie*; Historical Facts and Literary Reflections of the Vauderie d'Arras." In *Literatur—Geschichte—Literaturgeschichte: Beiträge zur mediävistischen Literaturwissenschaft*.

Edited by Nine Miedema and Rudolf Suntrup, 429–54. Frankfurt am Main: Peter Lang, 2003.

Vidal, Jacques. "L'arbitraire des juges d'Eglise en matière de sorcellerie." In *Le Sabbat des sorciers: XVe-XVIIIe siècles*. Edited by Nicole Jacques-Chaquin and Maxime Préaud, 75–99. Grenoble: Jérôme Millon, 1993.

Voaden, Rosalynn. *God's Words, Women's Voices: The Discernment of Spirits in the Writing of Late-Medieval Women Visionaries*. Woodbridge, Suffolk: Boydell, 1999.

———. "Mechtild of Hackeborn." *MHW*, 431–51.

Vogel, Cyrille. "Les rites de la celebration du mariage: Leur signification dans la formation du lien durant le haut moyen âge." In *Il Matrimonio nella società altomedievale*. Settimane di studio del Centro Italiano di studi sull'alto medioevo, 24, 1:397–472. Spoleto: Presso la sede del Centro, 1977.

Warren, Ann. *Anchorites and Their Patrons in Medieval England*. Berkeley and Los Angeles: University of California Press, 1985.

Warren, Nancy. *Spiritual Economies: Female Monasticism in Later Medieval England*. Philadelphia: University of Pennsylvania Press, 2001.

Waters, Claire. *Angels and Earthly Creatures: Preaching, Performance, and Gender in the Later Middle Ages*. Philadelphia: University of Pennsylvania Press, 2004.

Wemple, Suzanne. "Consent and Dissent to Sexual Intercourse in Germanic Societies." In *Consent and Coercion to Sex and Marriage in Ancient and Medieval Societies*. Edited by Angeliki Laiou, 227–43. Washington, D.C.: Dumbarton Oaks, 1993.

———. "Female Spirituality and Mysticism in Frankish Monasticism: Radegund, Balthild and Aldegund." In *Peaceweavers*. Vol. 2 of *Medieval Religious Women*. Edited by Lillian Thomas Shank and John Nichols, 2:39–54. Kalamazoo, Mich.: Cistercian Publications, 1987.

———. *Women in Frankish Society: Marriage and the Cloister, 500 to 900*. Philadelphia: University of Pennsylvania, 1981.

Whitney, Elspeth. "International Trends: The Witch 'She'/The Historian 'He'; Gender and the Historiography of the European Witch-Hunts." *Journal of Women's History* 7 (1995): 77–101.

Wildfang, Robin Lorsch. *Rome's Vestal Virgins*. London: Routledge, 2006.

Williams, Norman Powell. *The Ideas of the Fall and of Original Sin*. London: Longman's, Green, and Company, 1927.

Williams, Thomas. "Sin, Grace, and Redemption." In *The Cambridge Companion to Abelard*. Edited by Jeffrey Brower and Kevin Guilfoy, 258–78. Cambridge: Cambridge University Press, 2004.

Wilmart, André. "Eve et Goscelin." Pt. 1, *Revue Bénédictine* 46 (1934): 414–38. Pt. 2, *Revue Bénédictine* 50 (1938): 42–83.

———, ed. "Une lettre inédite de S. Anselme à une moniale inconstante." *Revue Bénédictine* 40 (1928): 319–32.

Wilson, Katharina, and Elizabeth Makowski. *Wykked Wyves and the Woes of Marriage: Misogamous Literature from Juvenal to Chaucer*. Albany: State University of New York Press, 1990.

Winroth, Anders. *The Making of Gratian's Decretum*. Cambridge: Cambridge University Press, 2000.

Winstead, Karen. *Virgin Martyrs: Legends of Sainthood in Late Medieval England*. Ithaca, N.Y.: Cornell University Press, 1997.

Wittmann, Adam. *De discretione spirituum apud Dionysium Cartusianum*. Ph.D. diss., Pontificia Universitas Gregoriana, Debrecen, 1938.

Wogan-Browne, Joscelyn. *Saints' Lives and Women's Literary Culture: Virginity and Its Authorizations*. Oxford: Oxford University Press, 2001.

Zarri, Gabriella. *Recinti: Donne, clausura e matrimonio nella prima età moderna*. Bologna: Il Mulino, 2000.

———. *Le Sante vive: Cultura e religiosità femminile nella prima età moderna*. Turin: Rosenberg and Sellier, 1990.

Ziegler, Joanna. "On the Artistic Nature of Elisabeth of Spalbeek's Ecstasy: The Southern Low Countries Do Matter." In *The Texture of Society: Medieval Women in the Southern Low Countries*. Edited by Ellen Kittell and Mary Suydam, 181–202. New York: Palgrave, 2004.

Zika, Charles. *The Appearance of Witchcraft: Print and Visual Culture in Sixteenth-Century Europe*. London: Routledge, 2007.

ACKNOWLEDGMENTS

Acknowledgments are the hardest part of a book. When I resolve at the outset not to sound like one of those dopes at the Academy Awards, weeping tears of joy and dispensing sugary platitudes from the stage, I seem to end up sounding much worse. Certain perfunctory acknowledgments don't present a problem. For instance, I can state in a steady voice that an earlier version of Chapter 1 first appeared as "Tertullian, the Angelic Life, and the Bride of Christ," in *Gender and Christianity in Medieval Europe: New Perspectives*, ed. Lisa Bitel and Felice Lifshitz (Philadelphia: University of Pennsylvania Press, 2008), pp. 15–33, without any shameful wash of sentiment. But my Stoic apatheia abandons me entirely when it comes to people, certain places, and even the occasional animal. This exercise in ritual humiliation must begin with heartfelt effusions for my friends at the University of Pennsylvania Press. Ruth Karras, medieval series editor, was always encouraging and especially full of sage advice about what words would get me into trouble (like *Germanic*—there! Now I have said it). Jerry Singerman fully lived up to his title as humanities editor. He was patient and, yes, humane—even after he realized that he was getting an entirely different book from the one he had signed on for and when it took at least three more years than promised. I am abjectly grateful to Anne Koenig for her help with the bibliography.

And then there are those wonderfully serendipitous people and places that helped me turn important corners in my research. I am thinking particularly of the conference that George Ferzoco organized in the fall of 2006 on the premodern penis [*sic*] in beautiful Massa Marittima—home of the celebrated "Penis Tree" [*sic*] fresco. The proceedings were fascinating, but the conference itself provided the pretext for reexamining diabolical members from a different angle. A second piece of serendipity was a fellowship at the Liguria Study Center in Bogliasco (spring 2009). There I enjoyed good food, engaging company, and uninterrupted time to write in the most exquisite surroundings imaginable. Third time lucky, they say, and my third piece of serendipitous luck was having Gábor Klaniczay as a reader for the press—a scholar whose work I have admired for years. Not only did I benefit enormously from his learned comments, but I still marvel at his forbearance over the many imaginative ways in which I managed to garble his name in my notes.

I am deeply appreciative of the warm welcome, collegiality, and support that I have experienced since my arrival at Northwestern University in 2006. I must necessarily single out the medieval contingent in this respect—especially that erudite trinity of Richard Kieckhefer, Robert Lerner, and Barbara Newman. They are a fiercely learned bunch and, collectively, seem to know more about saints, witches, and heretics than any mortals could possibly know—at least through natural means. Let's hope some of it has rubbed off. I am also grateful to the Department of History and the Weinberg College of Arts and Science for their research support.

I would also like to remember my colleagues from Indiana University (I can't bear to use the word *former*). In particular, there is my generous "Ever-Colleague," David Brakke, who has read parts of this manuscript in draft, providing (I hope) a kind of safety net against potential late antique pitfalls. I am additionally grateful to Mary Favret, Don Gray, Andrew Miller, and Mary Jo Weaver for listening on those many occasions when I was dreaming this book out loud, and just for being them.

I owe a rather idiosyncratic conjugal debt to Rick Valicenti for his many kindnesses, unwavering patience, and charming bemusement over my research proclivities. His energy and creativity continue to be contagious, and I look forward to a future of loving collaboration. It would seem remiss if I didn't also mention our furry retainers—Dydo, queen of Carthage, and Roo the Irascible, who ensure that we never walk alone. May their beards grow long!

I conclude with sincere homage to a series of incomparable women—all muses in their own right. The first is the late Jo Ann McNamara. I will never forget her riveting, fearless example and her kind mentoring of so many of us in the profession. She will be greatly missed.

However unconventional it may seem, I would also like to thank my historical muses, the dear dead women whom I have stalked for many years now. If I tend to construe their lives rather grimly, the proverbial glass half-empty, it is my dearest hope that they once had a share in draining this glass—and that they drank with pleasure.

But my final debt is to a living muse, Susan Gubar—my Indiana "Über-Ever-Colleague." Thank you, Susan, for making me think about my relationship with my medieval subjects, for your interest in this project from its inception, for your general exuberance and unfailing sense of hilarity. But most of all, thank you for the incomparable gift of your friendship. This book is for you.